Like Wolves on the Fold

Dedication

To my boys
The privilege was mine

While it's Tommy this, an' Tommy that, an' 'Tommy, fall be'ind,'
But it's 'Please to walk in front, sir,' when there's trouble in the wind,
There's trouble in the wind, my boys, there's trouble in the wind,
O it's 'Please to walk in front, sir,' when there's trouble in the wind.

'Tommy', Rudyard Kipling

Like Wolves on the Fold

The Defence of Rorke's Drift

Lieutenant Colonel Mike Snook

Foreword by

Lieutenant Colonel Huw Lloyd-Jones

Greenhill Books,
London

Like Wolves on the Fold:
The Defence of Rorke's Drift

First published in 2006 by
Greenhill Books, Lionel Leventhal Limited, Park House,
1 Russell Gardens, London NW11 9NN
www.greenhillbooks.com

British Library Cataloguing-in-Publication Data
Snook, Mike
Like wolves on the fold: the defence of Rorke's Drift
Great Britain. Army. Regiment of Foot, 24th (2nd Warwickshire)
Rorke's Drift, Battle of, South Africa, 1879
Zulu War, 1897 – Campaigns
I. Title 968 045

ISBN-13 978-85367-659-8
ISBN-10 1-85367-659-4

Maps drawn by John Richards

Printed and Bound by the MPG Books Group Ltd.

Contents

Illustrations

Maps

Foreword

The Defence of Rorke's Drift is one of the most famous and enduring tales of British arms. Yet the fate of the nation did not hang on the outcome of the battle, as in 1940, nor did victory herald the final defeat of a sworn enemy, as was the case in 1815. The battle saw no great technological leap forward, nor did it entail any brilliant military innovations. Instead, our fascination with the Rorke's Drift episode has much more in common with the esteem in which we hold Henry V's band of brothers – a plucky few, far from home, outnumbered and with their backs to the wall, who pull off a seemingly impossible victory – for this too is a 'boy's own' story.

Just as Shakespeare's pen guaranteed Agincourt's place as an iconic moment in the history of these islands, so did Sir Stanley Baker's cinematic epic *Zulu* serve to immortalise the story of Rorke's Drift. It can be both a boon and a curse to the historian when the arts and the past collide. On the one hand great artistic portrayals can engender immense public interest in a subject, but on the other they tend to entrench distortion and myth. In this, the second of his Anglo-Zulu War books, my old friend and one-time company commander strips away the numerous misconceptions that surround Rorke's Drift. In doing so he succeeds in demonstrating why the true story is fit to be considered as one of the great tales of human fortitude and tenacity. Rightly, he draws no distinction between Briton and Zulu.

I was commissioned into The Royal Regiment of Wales, the modern-day descendant of the old 24th, in the 1980s. Now, twenty years on, it has fallen to me to be the last commanding officer of the last RRW battalion. I have served alongside the author throughout that time. As a subaltern I served under his command in the Far East. It falls to company commanders to bring up their young officers in the ways of the regiment, and to instil in them pride in the heroic deeds of their forbears. I could not have wished for a better education.

Inevitably the most gripping of Mike's stories were those of Isandlwana and Rorke's Drift; even then he seemed to know every detail of these hard-fought actions. Sitting in the officers' mess in Stanley Fort, Hong Kong, surrounded by the regiment's memorabilia, he could bring our paintings and artefacts to life like no other. In the years that followed he enthralled successive generations of our officers and soldiers, inspiring great regimental pride in them. At one point in his career he was posted to live and work in South Africa; as a consequence he brings to the party a highly developed understanding of the land and its people; not least he is a great admirer of the Zulu. He combines the historian's grasp of primary source material, a professional soldier's eye for ground, and a raconteur's turn of phrase. Here in these pages he unfolds the splendid tales he once told me, for the benefit of a much wider audience.

Through a series of name changes from the 24th Regiment of Foot, to The South Wales Borderers, to The Royal Regiment of Wales, the events of 1879 have remained pre-eminent in the regiment's folklore. Down the years, in all great moments of peril, from Flanders to Normandy, from Malaya to Aden, and from Belfast to Basra, the fight at Rorke's Drift has been an inspiration to our officers and soldiers. Inevitably the current round of reforms to the regimental system will once again require us to adjust our identity. On 1 March 2006 The Royal Regiment of Wales will merge with The Royal Welch Fusiliers to become a two-battalion regiment known as The Royal Welsh.

Needless to say the events of January 1879 will continue to be preserved prominently under the new arrangements. We are fortunate to have Mike's books as a historical handrail at such an important time. Our proudest traditions will march inexorably on. The Queen's Colour will continue to be adorned with a silver 'Wreath of Immortelles'; the battle honour 'South Africa 1877–8–9' will still be borne on the Regimental Colour; Nevill Coghill's sword will continue to hang in pride of place between the colours and, when on parade, be worn by the Queen's Colour ensign. We will commemorate Rorke's Drift Day each year, and will march-past to that most rousing of battle-songs, 'Men of

Harlech'. The second company of the 2nd Battalion will be known as 'B (Rorke's Drift) Company'.

In his first book, *How Can Man Die Better*, Mike analysed the disastrous sequence of events that culminated in the crushing Zulu victory at Isandlwana. That book has established him in the public eye as one of the foremost experts in the field. In my view no other author has been able to master the details of the fight, whilst at the same time recounting the episode with such clarity. He now brings these same skills to bear on those remarkable few hours at Rorke's Drift. *Like Wolves on the Fold* provides the most comprehensive assessment of the battle I have yet read and then goes on to address, and I would say resolve, the controversies that still surround Isandlwana. It is without doubt a work of the very highest quality.

Colonel Huw Lloyd-Jones
Commanding Officer, 1st Battalion,
The Royal Regiment of Wales (24th/41st Foot)

Preface

The Assyrian came down like the wolf on the fold
And his cohorts were gleaming in purple and gold;
And the sheen of their spears was like stars on the sea,
When the blue wave rolls nightly on deep Galilee.

Like the leaves of the forest when Summer is green,
That host with their banners at sunset were seen:
Like the leaves of the forest when Autumn hath blown,
That host on the morrow lay withered and strown.

'The Destruction of Sennacherib', Lord Byron.

By breakfast time the great chain of events was already in motion. Wednesday 22 January 1879 was set to become one of the most calamitous days in the long history of the British Empire, one of the most renowned in the august history of Britain's standing army, and one of the most momentous in the timeless history of Southern Africa. *Like Wolves on the Fold* picks up the story of that most remarkable of days from my first book, *How Can Man Die Better*. We left Lieutenant General Lord Chelmsford, Colonel Richard Glyn and the remnants of No. 3 Column bivouacked in a state of shocked and stunned disbelief amongst the grisly remains of their slaughtered comrades: men they had soldiered with, men they had admired, men they had great affection for; all of them reduced now to mere butchered carcasses, silent, still and strewn grotesquely through all that was left of their sacked encampment.

In Parts 1 and 2 of this second volume we examine the equally dramatic events which took place on the other bank of the Buffalo River, the famous episode centred upon the mission station at Rorke's Drift. The first two parts of this second book stand alone and can be read and enjoyed without reference to *How Can Man Die Better*. But additionally, in Part 3, we examine the subsequent course of the war, revisit Isandlwana to discuss the issue of culpability and blame, and reflect on the fates and destinies of many of the war's most notable participants, some of whom are central only to the first volume. To derive maximum enjoyment from Part 3 of this book it will have been beneficial to have read *How Can Man Die Better*, not as part of some cunning marketing ploy, but simply because of the way so rich and complex a story plays itself out across two more readily affordable volumes.

In these two books I have been moved to dissect the Battles of Isandlwana and Rorke's Drift specifically from a soldier's perspective, in the hope that the insights of a military professional might contribute usefully to our modern-day understanding of the events of 1879; I have done so partly out of concern that some recent contributions in the field seem to have led down a number of false trails. I hope then to straighten the tiller.

I am most grateful to Her Majesty the Queen for her gracious permission to reproduce works of art and photographs from the Royal Collection. I am also particularly grateful to Mr Jason Askew for his kind permission to use a number of his dramatic Anglo-Zulu War paintings as illustrations, and similarly to Mr David Cartwright for his equally generous permission to make use of *The Formidable 24th* and *Incident at Isandlwana*. The splendid tributes by both these artists to the men who fought in the AZW will I am sure be greatly appreciated by the reader. My thanks too to Dr Adrian Greaves, the owner of the two Askew paintings. John Richards drew the excellent maps and plans, which will be of great assistance in following the compelling tale of Rorke's Drift. Fieldwork in South Africa was as ever an immensely enjoyable experience, due largely to the kind hospitality of Ms Pat Stubbs at Isandlwana Lodge, of David and Nicky Rattray at Fugitives' Drift Lodge, and of Lourens and Nan Roos at the Battlefields Country Lodge, Dundee, all of whom looked after this particular thirsty, hungry traveller superbly well. I have provided a travel guide to visiting the battlefields as Appendix 7 which includes the contact details for all three establishments.

I am duty bound to acknowledge the inspiring work in the AZW field of such eminent figures as Ian Knight, David Jackson, and John Laband, whilst the published research of Julian Whybra and the late Norman Holme was essential, in particular, to the production of the nominal rolls in the appendices. Any errors in the acute detail will be of my own making. Colonel Mike McCabe RE was a mine of information on the part played by his corps in the Anglo-Zulu War, and a more than worthy devil's advocate on behalf of Colonel Anthony Durnford. I am most grateful to Major Martin Everett, Mrs Celia Green and the rest of the staff at the Brecon Museum of the Royal Regiment of Wales, who have invariably made me feel very much at home during my visits there. Mr Ron Sheeley has been particularly helpful and generous in making his private collection of photographs and other memorabilia available for publication.

Rorke's Drift, we all know, was the ultimate triumph against the odds – an impossible victory. How could a mere 150 men, of whom almost a quarter were hospital patients, standing behind an improvised barricade of mealie-bags, hold off some four and a half thousand assailants? We struggle to comprehend how this could happen. Often we mistakenly, but perhaps understandably, attribute it to being a victory of men armed with rifles, over men armed with spears. We put it down, inevitably, to British 'pluck', the same determination in adversity that got 338,000 men off the beaches at Dunkirk, when by rights this should not have been so. Perhaps, we reason, there is some magical quality in the British national temperament that leaps to the fore when things are going badly awry. The worse the situation, it seems, the brighter this quality shines forth. Never was there a better example than the defence of Rorke's Drift. But perhaps we British are just a little self-satisfied about this idiosyncratic national trait. The truth is that, just as there were sound military reasons why the Wehrmacht and Luftwaffe were unable to overwhelm the BEF in 1940, so too were there military factors which account for the inability of the Zulu to overrun a determined band of redcoats on the Buffalo River. That is not to say that British 'pluck' did not play an extensive role – it did. It may well be true that only the British infantry, that most steadfast caste of fighting men, could have done it.

If forced to put one's finger on the exact nature of this mysterious

British trait, it is perhaps best characterised as a stubborn refusal to panic. It was precisely this attribute which allowed the 1st Battalion of the 24th Regiment to make so brave a stand at Isandlwana. I hope that *How Can Man Die Better* conveyed this effectively. Panic is a killer, a destroyer of armies. It was the panic that seized Durnford's native horse that precluded any possibility of a strong enough stand being made in the saddle to hold back the Zulu left horn and so allow the 24th to fall back to a new line of defence. So panic had reared its virulently contagious head already that day. Unsurprisingly the terrified native infantry and the non-combatants had also been infected by it, then 'the fugitives' in their turn. Even at Rorke's Drift the contagion did not immediately come to a halt. Kipling famously characterised one of the essential qualities of manliness as the ability to keep one's head when all around are losing theirs. That is precisely what John Chard, Gonville Bromhead and the other 150 men who stood their ground at Rorke's Drift did; they kept their nerve, stopped the rot and did what their training told them was militarily prudent.

Famously neither of these officers was a cutting-edge thruster. But neither were they, as some modern historians would suggest, mere low-calibre plodders. Much of this cynicism is based on the back-biting correspondence of officers like Major Francis Clery, men who had themselves played a part in botching the Isandlwana campaign, and who were hugely jealous of the two subalterns' great achievement. Furthermore they were writing of the victors of Rorke's Drift, whom they had barely known beforehand, at a time when the two officers were recovering from an extremely traumatic experience. In 1879 there was nothing that would pass for the trauma counselling of today. It is hardly surprising that both men were withdrawn and little inclined to be patronised by those who were not there. Bromhead tended to move away whenever the subject came up. To his colleagues and the wider empire it was a glorious deed, but for Bromhead himself it had been a vicious, harrowing dogfight. In many ways there is an element of the miraculous about his survival, for he was fearlessly brave and terribly exposed throughout the fight. It must have seemed for a long while, minute by agonising minute, that it was only a matter of time before he was killed or maimed.

The uncharitable comments on Chard and Bromhead were penned at a time when they were in a psychological state for which today they would receive formal medical treatment, but which in the Victorian era went unheeded, unrecognised and untreated. In fact both Chard and Bromhead were typical of their kind; they were experienced professionals and knew their business well. Both were modest, mild-mannered men by temperament. Most men at Rorke's Drift were. And yet they fought like lions. Perhaps one of the most significant messages of this famous battle is that the most ordinary of men can move mountains when they are put to it. Maybe that is what we like best about the tale.

The cataclysmic events at Isandlwana were surely drama enough for one day. But, extraordinarily, as if to herald the portentous news to the rest of Southern Africa, its final stages were played out under a partial eclipse of the sun. When the last British soldier died beneath the sphinx, Wednesday 22 January had all but run its course. Sunset was only four hours away. The day may have been on its last legs, but the drama was far from over.

In this second book I hope to explain how it was that the apparently miraculous victory at Rorke's Drift was actually achieved. In doing so we will see that there was no miracle, but rather some soldiering of the very highest order. It was not confined to one man or a few men; every man present played his part. With only a few exceptions – Chard, Bromhead, Dalton and the half dozen soldiers fighting in defence of the hospital patients – the defenders of Rorke's Drift were not required to think or make decisions. This was war at its simplest – nose-to-nose, face-to-face, hand-to-hand. Each man had charge of his own little stretch of barricade and had nowhere else to go. His duty was to defend his sector, at the cost of his life if necessary and, where possible, help out the mates left and right of him with a well timed snap-shot or a lightning-quick thrust of the bayonet. It was the simplest of military propositions and to fail in it meant certain death.

Perhaps it is easier to fight for one's life at close quarters when there is no other option, than to skirmish forward into an extremely heavy fire, when alternatives abound. And yet this is precisely what the Zulu participants in the battle did. They took extremely heavy punishment for an hour, for two hours, for three – and still they fought on. They came on heroically, and then they came again. They kept coming – endlessly. They came until the corpses of the slain were piled high around the barricades and hundreds of men were lying maimed and bloodied in the shadows of the night. To sustain their attack for as long as they did was an extraordinary feat of endurance and determination, and one which has received but scant tribute.

Above all else, I hope in writing this book that we are able in our national consciousness to elevate the mighty Zulu above the role of mere extras in Sir Stanley Baker's movie, compelling entertainment as it undoubtedly was. For the Zulus of 1879 were real men: they had wives and they had children; they liked nothing better than to look proudly upon their cattle; they liked to gossip and they liked to laugh. And they were warriors too – surely to be numbered amongst the most formidable warrior societies in the history of mankind. Let us recognise, then, not only the remarkable achievement of the British soldiers who held Rorke's Drift, but also the quite extraordinary courage of the men who gave their lives, in the words borne on the war monument at Ulundi, 'in defence of the old Zulu order'.

These days we can but reflect upon the passing of the old ways, but let us not forget that the children of the men of 1879 had children in their turn, and they in theirs, and three more generations since. And should you be moved by this remarkable tale to visit modern Zululand, the chances are you will be struck immediately by its beauty and by the warmth of its people. But go deeper and you will learn something of its poverty, of the social ills consequent upon it, and of the devastating impact of pandemic disease. If you are a rich man or a wise man, please come home resolved to do whatever you can to help. Remarkably, for all their tribulations, the Zulus are smiling yet.

MIKE SNOOK

Like Wolves
on the Fold

Prologue

From the bluff high above Sothondose's Drift, Captain Alan Gardner looked down at the scenes of chaos and bloody carnage being played out beneath him. The river was full of bodies, live and dead, black and white, man and beast. The hillside opposite was swarming with the enemy. They were exultant, triumphant, victorious, and still they were mad for blood. Here and there a number of frenzied life or death chases through the rocks were in progress. Every so often handfuls of frantic horsemen would come clattering down Mpethe Hill at breakneck speed, to enter the maelstrom around the drift, some of them separated and riding alone, others clustered in groups of three or four. Some men did indeed break their necks, or might as well have done, for a fall of any kind meant virtually instantaneous death at the hands of their merciless pursuers. Other men zigged and zagged desperately, trying hard to avoid the nimble-footed warriors scrambling over the rocks towards them. Many men, too shocked to think, some too stupefied even to care, trusted instinctively to providence alone, and spurred their horses straight at the enemy, hoping somehow to break through at the gallop. Most of the terrified fugitives had long since emptied their revolvers. The pursuit had been relentless; there had been no question of pausing and hence no time to reload, so that now horsemanship was their only defence.

The lucky ones survived the frantic descent of Mpethe Hill and plunged over the river bank with a terrific splash. There were treacherous sub-surface boulders strewn in great quantities along both sides of the river, so that it was largely a matter of luck whether the riders kept their seats or not. Mounted or unhorsed, now they were just a target. Bullets threw up plumes of water around them. Throwing assegais came raining down about them. No. 3 Column was no longer fighting – it was running, hell for leather, every man for himself, the devil take the hindmost. The scenes being played out around Sothondose's Drift, soon to become better known as Fugitives' Drift, were more to do with bloody murder than with death in battle.

Gardner's mind raced with vividly dramatic and unpleasant memories of the past two and a half hours. He was glad to be alive; he was lucky to be alive; but he was shocked and he was frightened. Already his conscience was uneasy. Cavalryman and staff officer he may have been, but as a holder of the Queen's Commission his proper place was with the embattled infantrymen of the 24th Regiment. He had last seen them falling back slowly in the face of an overpowering enemy assault and, in common with many others, had lacked the inner strength to stand by them. Surely now, he reasoned, they were all dead. Henry Pulleine, William Degacher, Charlie Pope, George Wardell – all of them – dead and no doubt butchered. Gardner pulled himself together as best he could and tried to behave as an officer should behave in so grave a crisis. He tried to think of the wider military situation and what the enemy might do in the wake of so crushing a victory. Lord Chelmsford and his flying column were still at Mangeni, on the wrong side of the Zulu main *impi*. They were the largest force in the field and would have to shift for themselves. In the meantime there were two outposts on the lines of communication to worry about.

The garrisons of Rorke's Drift and Helpmekaar were in the gravest danger: isolated, lightly held and completely unfortified. The Rorke's Drift mission station was closest to the looming menace – just a few miles upstream – and there seemed to be nothing to prevent the Zulus descending upon it within the hour. Major Henry Spalding, as far as Gardner knew, was in charge there. Under his command was a company of the 2nd/24th, amounting to less than a hundred redcoats, a numerically much stronger body of black levies, the handful of men who constituted No. 3 Column's logistic staff, and around three dozen hospital patients. Helpmekaar was about twelve miles away. Gardner knew that there was at least one company of the 1st/24th there, and that by now it was distinctly possible that it had been joined by a second company of the same battalion.

The great majority of Isandlwana survivors, Alan Gardner included, deemed discretion to be the better part of valour. To go to Rorke's Drift would be to put their heads in the noose once more, all but tantamount to an act of suicide. Mostly they decided to head for distant Helpmekaar and struck out across country. The 'lucky five' regular officers were caught on the horns of a dilemma. They knew they could not go to Rorke's Drift without running the twin risks of being killed en route, or of being ordered by Major Spalding to stay there. When it came down to it, Spalding would not actually need to say anything; it would be their bounden duty to stay. This was all well and good if the garrison had a sporting chance, but it seemed to have no chance at all.

Gardner had made his decision: he was bound for Helpmekaar with everybody else. But his sense of duty obliged him at least to alert the garrison at Rorke's Drift to its peril. He collared one of Durnford's mounted natives, almost certainly a member of the Edendale Troop, and asked if he would ride via the mission station with a warning for the troops there. The man agreed to go and Gardner quickly scribbled a pencil note to the post commander into his damp pocket book. Moments later this unknown but faithful trooper turned his exhausted pony away to the north-west, riding parallel to the line of the Buffalo. Gardner spurred on to the south-west behind everybody else bound for the Biggarsberg high ground.

Unaware that Gardner's man was already ahead of them, a number of other fugitives, some of whose identities are uncertain, would also cross the river and make the seemingly selfless decision to head for Rorke's Drift rather than Helpmekaar. In fact most were inspired by a combination of instinct and necessity – the ingrained need to find a route that they knew. It is perhaps indicative of their terrible ordeal up to this point and the fear still coursing through their veins, that none of them stayed on at the mission to make a fresh stand; all would ride on after delivering a brief and doom-laden warning. In some cases they cantered past without stopping, shouting a few words of pessimistic advice to the enlisted men. Thus they evaded the time-consuming duty of making a full report to an officer and avoided any possibility of being ordered to stay.

Away to the north, still on the Zulu bank of the river, Lieutenant Gert Adendorff of 2nd/3rd Natal Native Contingent (NNC) had fallen in with a trooper of the Natal Carbineers.* Undoubtedly they got away from Isandlwana on the wagon road, some minutes before the Zulu right horn emerged from the hills to complete the 'horns of the buffalo' encirclement of the camp. It follows that both of them had given up the fight well before it was lost beyond redemption. But in their own minds at least, as they had looked down from the encampment at the great host manoeuvring impressively across the plain, there had been absolutely no doubt as to the outcome. Adendorff was a non-swimmer and, with the Buffalo in spate, was determined to avoid a risky river crossing if at all possible. Hence he had settled on the ponts at Rorke's Drift as his immediate destination, a journey of around 7½ miles. The two riders scanned the ground ahead for signs of the enemy, and from time to time looked back over their shoulders for any indication of a pursuit. They may have clapped eyes on harassed parties of Basuto or amaNgwane riders some way behind them, and would certainly have overtaken scattered bands of NNC levies on the road, but reassuringly, for the time being at least, there were no Zulus in sight. They skirted the north bank of the Buffalo, crossed the Batshe Stream, and rode on, until at length they came to the low ridge immediately above the ponts and began the long downhill gallop to the river.

Lieutenant John Chard of the Royal Engineers was taking his responsibilities as the temporary post commander none too seriously. Major Spalding would be back in a few hours and in the meantime Gonny Bromhead would have all the routine administration of the post well in hand. Chard had come up to Rorke's Drift only three days earlier, on Sunday 19 January. He had arrived just in time to watch No. 3 Column depart for Isandlwana early on Monday morning. Later that same day Colonel Durnford and his native troops had arrived at the river. They had crossed the Buffalo in the late afternoon and established their bivouac on the site only recently vacated by Colonel Glyn's men. After two nights on the river Durnford had also moved forward to Isandlwana, at 8.00 a.m. that very morning. It was now Wednesday 22 January 1879, a date destined to be immortalised by British historians and Zulu storytellers alike.

* Tentatively identified as Trooper Sibthorpe.

Chard had passed Durnford on the old wagon road, on his way back from an early morning excursion to Isandlwana, and had been used by the colonel to pass on instructions to the rearmost elements of his column. Now he was back at the river with nothing much to do for the rest of the day. Despite being Chard's junior in the Army List, Lieutenant Gonville Bromhead had been at the post from the outset, was an experienced regimental officer with recent combat experience, was two years older than Chard, and was the commander of the only formed body of regular troops in the vicinity. In such circumstances it would have been presumptuous of Chard to throw his weight around and, in any case, he was a quiet, modest man and that was not at all his way. Instead he was now sitting quietly beside his tent on the river bank, half a mile from the mission buildings, writing a few lines home. It was not surprising that the events of the day had moved him to put pen to paper. He had never been in action before, but only that morning had had sight of a substantial Zulu force as it manoeuvred on the high ground above the camp at Isandlwana. Nearby Driver Charles Robson was pottering about the little campsite, unloading the last of his master's kit from their mule-wagon, following the largely nugatory trip up country.

Somewhere close at hand was a young sergeant of the 2nd/3rd Regiment (The Buffs) called Fred Millne, and a civilian called Mr Daniels, who between them had charge of the crossing. The best asset at their disposal was a prefabricated pontoon, capable of taking a single ox-wagon or a half-company of troops. In August 1878, Colonel Durnford had surveyed all the border river crossings in preparation for the coming war, and had recommended that two ponts be installed at Rorke's Drift. In the event only one came up from Durban and in lieu of the second, Lieutenant Francis MacDowel, Colonel Glyn's engineer adviser, had constructed a substantial cask ferry of standard RE design, from timber and barrels. In addition to the pont and the ferry, both of which were hawser operated, there was a whaler, capable of taking something around fifteen rowers and passengers. Most contemporaneous orders and correspondence drew no distinction between the pont and the ferry, and referred to 'the ponts' in the plural – a convention which for convenience's sake will be followed from this point on. Standing guard over Millne, Daniels, and their handful of black employees, were a sergeant and half a dozen red-coated privates of B Company.

It was probably one of the sentries who drew Chard's attention to the two horsemen racing down the ridge on the other side of the river. Chard put down his pen and looked up. The riders were moving fast – too fast – nobody galloped at that sort of speed over the treacherous rocky terrain in this part of the country. It was hot – too hot – nobody rode at such a lick in such extremes of temperature. The men were waving and shouting. Something was wrong – something was badly wrong.

Part One

Race against Time

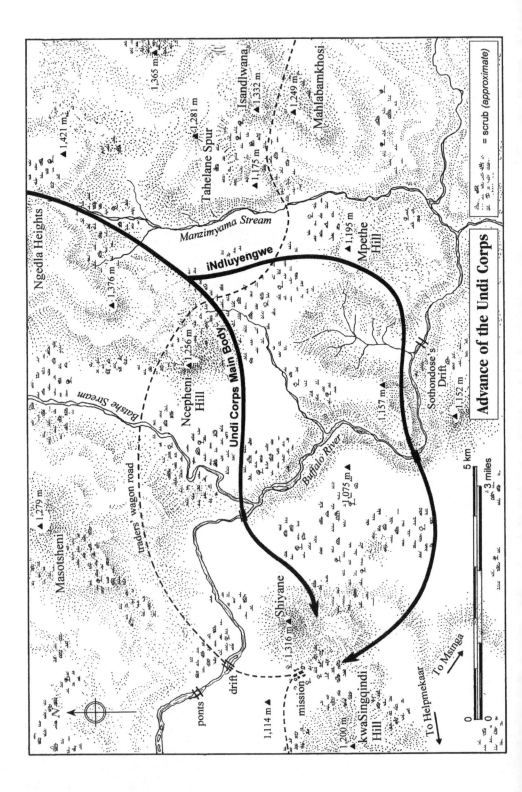

Advance of the Undi Corps

= scrub (approximate)

1,365 m ▲

Isandlwana ▲ 1,332 m

▲ 1,249 m

Mahlabamkhosi

1,421 m ▲

▲ 1,281 m

Tahelane Spur

▲ 1,175 m

Manzimyama Stream

iNdluyengwe

▲ 1,195 m

Mpethe Hill

Ngedla Heights

1,376 m ▲

Undi Corps Main Body

▲ 1,256 m

Ncepheni Hill

Baishe Stream

Sothondose's Drift

▲ 1,152 m

1,157 m ▲

traders wagon road

1,279 m ▲

Masotsheni

Buffalo River

1,075 m ▲

Shiyane

1,316 m ▲

drift

ponts

mission

1,114 m ▲

▲ 1,200 m

kwaSingqindi Hill

N

5 km

3 miles

0

0

To Helpmekaar

To Msinga

Chapter 1

Nothing Will Happen

A Quiet Day in the Offing

Rorke's Drift had been a bustling place for the past three weeks, but by the morning of 22 January the mood at the post had become distinctly downbeat. The campaign had moved on upcountry and the men at the mission had been left behind. B Company of the 2nd/24th had been detailed to garrison duty at the drift in Lieutenant Colonel Henry Degacher's battalion orders, as late as the evening before the invasion. There was profound disappointment at the news, even though it was expected to be only a temporary assignment pending the arrival of other troops. Thus it was, on Saturday 11 January, that No. 3 Column crossed the river-frontier, with Bromhead's company in the role of mere spectators. There had been some minor excitement the following morning, when the main body of the troops marched to attack kwaSokhexe, the homestead of the most prominent local chieftain, Sihayo, after which a few NNC casualties were brought back to the mission for treatment. After that nothing much happened. For the ensuing seven days the column remained encamped just across the river, whilst an advanced party improved the old traders' wagon-road ahead. The river was uncommonly high – swollen by the recent heavy summer rains into a powerful, surging torrent. The whites in Natal knew it as the Buffalo, but to their black workers and to the people of the proud nation-state on its far bank, it was the Mzinyathi.

Each morning the men of B Company paraded and drilled on their side of the river under Colour-Sergeant Bourne and the sergeant section-commanders, for that was the army way, but otherwise there was next to nothing for them to do. Meal times served to break up the monotony. Occasionally some heavily laden ox-wagons would come plodding down from Helpmekaar with a consignment of foodstuffs or other military materiel. This would bring Assistant Commissaries Walter Dunne and James Dalton and the storekeeper Mr Louis Byrne, bustling from their tents to supervise the cross-loading of the cargo to the one-time chapel, now a storehouse. Then the wagons would go plodding back again. From time to time one of the staff officers at the post would gallop off on some unknown errand. Then, two days ago, the main column had moved off to establish a new camp at the foot of Isandlwana, to be replaced later in the day by Colonel Durnford's native troops, ordered up from Vermaak's Farm on the Helpmekaar road.

The two thatched mission buildings were nestled beneath the steep western slopes of a commanding hill known in Zulu as Shiyane, or 'the eyebrow'. The resident Swedish missionary, Mr Otto Witt, had attempted arbitrarily to rename the feature 'the Oscarberg' in honour of his king, but nobody was much interested in a foreigner's views on the subject and mostly insisted on referring to it by its old African name. Witt's missionary society had acquired the property a little over three years earlier. It was purchased from the Surtees family,* who had lived there for only a short while, following the death of the first and most notable resident of the plot, who some said had died by his own hand.

It is thought that Jim Rorke was the son of an Irish soldier and that he had himself seen service in the 1846 'War of the Axe', the seventh of the Cape Frontier Wars with the Xhosa. Unlike his father, young Jim had never been a regular soldier and with the cessation of hostilities was free to go wherever the mood took him. The new frontier was to be found in Natal and so it was that he headed north in search of opportunity and adventure. Soon he was looking over a remote thousand-acre plot on the west bank of the Buffalo River. It was a pretty enough spot and he stayed. He lived by the usual frontier combination of hunting, trading and farming. When he built his house in 1849 the district was rich with big game, but it was not long before it had been shot out, a process in which Jim Rorke himself played a

---

* The short-lived residence of the Surtees family at Rorke's Drift, in between the widow Rorke and the Witts has only recently been uncovered by the eminent AZW historian Ian Knight, whose research into their occupancy is still ongoing. I am grateful to Ian for his kind permission to expose his discovery in advance of his own publication of his findings.

significant part. In due course he took a wife, had a son, and enlisted in a local part-time volunteer unit called the Buffalo Border Guard. On a good day the BBG might muster thirty men. Eventually Rorke rose to be its lieutenant, largely because by the 1870s he had been in the area much longer than most, rather than for any innate military talent he had.

The best river crossing for miles was on Rorke's spread, and with traders plying back and forth into Zululand he and his wife seldom went too long without receiving visitors. The Zulu came to refer to Rorke's place as 'kwaJim'. The traders were quick to fuel an apparently insatiable cross-border demand for firearms, compelling the colonial authorities in Pietermaritzburg to embargo the trade. In due course it was driven underground, but a good many weapons continued to find their way into Zululand via Rorke's Drift. Whether Rorke himself played a role in gun-running is not known, though as a member of what was in effect a part-time constabulary, this would seem improbable. By the middle of 1875, Rorke was engaged in negotiations to sell up, but in October that year he died. He was buried at the foot of Shiyane where his grave may still be seen to this day. Not long after her husband's death, Mrs Rorke vacated the property to make way for Mr and Mrs Robert Surtees, and their daughter and son-in-law.

Three years on, with the property having in the interim changed hands for a second time, Otto Witt had taken the requisitioning of his mission buildings by the military with reasonably good grace, encouraged in his co-operation by the prospect of receiving a substantial rent in recompense. At first he tried to exact an unreasonable price for the lease of a few rooms, but was soon put straight by irritated staff officers. When it was made plain to him that his entire property would be required, at a rent to be decided by the government, he sent his family away to stay near the magistracy at Msinga and acquired himself a tent from which to keep a watchful eye on things. Occasionally he made himself useful as an interpreter. Inevitably he befriended the Reverend George Smith, the Vicar of Estcourt, who had come up to the mission to serve as a temporary chaplain to the forces. Smith was born in Norfolk in 1845, went to college in Canterbury and later emigrated to South Africa to become a lay missionary. He had been ordained by the Bishop of Natal in 1872. The previous Sunday, Smith had conducted a drumhead service on the other side of the river at the request of Colonel Richard Glyn, in advance of the departure of the troops for Isandlwana the following morning. Since then Smith had devoted himself to one of the traditional roles of an army padre, that of fussing around the sick. Witt's house had been turned into a base hospital facility, a temporary home to between thirty and forty recuperating soldiers.

The precise number of patients cannot now be definitively established, but Surgeon Reynolds, who ought to have known, thought that there were thirty-five. The highest possibility is thirty-nine but any number in between is just as likely. Sergeant Robert Maxfield, a twenty-one-year-old section commander in G Company, 2nd/24th, from Newport,* Monmouthshire, was suffering from a raging typhoid fever and was in the most serious condition by far. Not unnaturally this had earned him preferential treatment from the doctor, who had bedded him down in the comfort of Mr and Mrs Witt's requisitioned bed. Everybody else was sleeping on mattresses resting on pallets, raised only a few inches off the floor. A few of the patients, such as Lieutenant Thomas Purvis and Corporal Jesse Mayer of 1st/3rd NNC, had been wounded a week earlier in the action at Sihayo's kraal. The only black patient was one of Commandant 'Maori' Browne's isiGqoza levies, wounded in the same action.† Others had been injured in one of the unfortunate accidents which invariably take a toll of a large military force deployed in the field. The majority were in various stages of typhoid fever, brought on by rough living in the field, though nobody else was in nearly so bad a state as young Maxfield.

Thirty-five-year-old James Henry Reynolds was an Irish-born army surgeon. He was raised at Dalyston House, Granard, County Longford, and went on to study medicine at Trinity College, Dublin, graduating in 1867. His first tour as a medical officer had been with the 36th Regiment in India, where he was commended by the Commander-in-Chief for his

---

* All subsequent references in the text to a Newport refer to Newport, Monmouthshire.

† Other black levies had been wounded at kwaSokhexe but must have been evacuated back to Helpmekaar or beyond.

devotion to duty during a cholera epidemic. He was now the regimental medical officer of the 1st/24th, to which he had been attached for the past four years. He had participated in the Diamond Fields Expedition of 1875 and in the Ninth Cape Frontier War.* Ordinarily he would have been with his battalion at Isandlwana. Instead, Surgeon-Major Peter Shepherd, the Principal Medical Officer, was taking care of all the units up with the column and had detached Reynolds to run the base hospital. The doctor was accompanied everywhere he went by a little terrier† which, so the story goes, belonged to Lieutenant Fred Godwin-Austen, until recently an officer in Bromhead's B Company, but now upcountry with Charlie Pope's G Company. To assist him in his work Reynolds had two misemployed privates of the 24th, plus Corporal Miller, Second Corporal McMahon and Private Luddington of the Army Hospital Corps. The twenty-eight-year-old Private Harry Hook, a decent and clean-living teetotaller from Monmouth‡ (a man whose memory was badly failed by his cinema portrayal), had been excused his routine duties with B Company in order to act as the hospital cook. Similarly, Private John Waters of the 1st/24th had been detached from his battalion to act as an additional hospital orderly.

The dirt road down to the drift ran north of the mission station for half a mile, with the Shiyane high ground on its right hand side, but on the opposite side of the river it swung eastwards in the direction of Isandlwana. This meant that it was quite impossible to see anything of the sphinx-like hill from the immediate area of the mission. In order to gain such a view it was necessary either to walk down to the river bank and look hard right, where Isandlwana was visible in a gap in the hills, or to climb to the summit of Shiyane, from where a much better view

* Interestingly it appears to have been the practice in British South Africa to forget or discard the various Dutch wars against the Xhosa. Hence General Sir Arthur Cunynghame's book on his time as GOC South Africa (he was Chelmsford's immediate predecessor) refers to the war of 1877–8 as the 'Sixth (Kafir) [sic] War, though today we refer to it as the Ninth Cape Frontier War.

† The name of the dog is unknown – notwithstanding Donald Morris's assertion that he was called 'Pip' – a claim which cannot be substantiated on the basis of source evidence.

‡ Born Churcham, Gloucestershire.

was to be had, incorporating the rear or western slopes of Isandlwana, the saddle immediately to its south, much of the Manzimyama Valley, and a good deal of the high ground to the north of Colonel Glyn's new camp. Even from here it was not possible to see anything of the camp itself, which was located on the far side of the sphinx, or anything very much of the great eastern plain beyond. Shiyane also blocked any view of the river gorge to the south-east, and hence of the old native crossing downstream, known after a local chief as Sothondose's Drift. Whilst there was no view downstream, the mission commanded a good view out across the Buffalo River valley in the upstream direction to the west, and in the direction of Helpmekaar and the Biggarsberg high ground. A thousand yards to the south-west was kwaSingqindi Hill, like Shiyane a dominating piece of high ground which restricted the wider view, but too far away from the mission to be of any real tactical significance.

Two junior officers of the transport staff, Lieutenant Horace Smith-Dorrien of the 95th and Sub-Lieutenant Thomas Griffith of the 24th, had departed for Isandlwana the previous afternoon. They had been due to bring a convoy of wagons down from the camp to replenish their loads from the commissariat store first thing that morning, but Smith-Dorrien had reappeared without them. He rode in to take breakfast with the rest of the officers not long after 7.00 a.m. As he ate he passed on all the news of the day: that the convoy had been indefinitely postponed; that he had met John Chard on the road on his way down from the camp; that he had just delivered a message for Colonel Durnford's troops to move up to Isandlwana; and that most of the 2nd/24th and the artillery had moved out with Lord Chelmsford at 4.00 a.m., to support the colonial and native troops on the far side of the great expanse of plain east of Isandlwana. There appeared to be, Smith-Dorrien continued, a strong likelihood of a fight. When Major Spalding was out of earshot, he confided to Gonny Bromhead that he intended going back upcountry to see if he could get involved in all the excitement. He was short of cartridges for his pistol and asked Bromhead if he could spare any. Bromhead gave him all he could, eleven rounds in all, and not long afterwards Smith-Dorrien was back in the saddle, bound once again for Isandlwana.

Brevet Major Henry Spalding of the 104th Regiment of Foot was

Deputy Assistant Adjutant-General (DAAG) of No. 3 Column, an appointment which today would be labelled Deputy Chief of Staff (DCOS). As such he was responsible to Colonel Richard Glyn, the column commander, for personnel and logistic matters. His principal task was to keep the supplies necessary to sustain No. 3 Column moving forward from the main logistic depot at Helpmekaar, via the storehouse at Rorke's Drift, to the backs of Glyn's wagons. As well as his role as No. 3 Column's chief logistician, Spalding also had a command function on the lines of communication. The garrisons of Rorke's Drift and Helpmekaar were both in his charge.

In addition to Bromhead's B Company there was also a large body of unassigned NNC levies at Rorke's Drift. Although they are commonly referred to as Stevenson's 'company', this is not a strictly accurate designation. They were, in fact, the surplus of men above and beyond the 2,200 required to constitute the two battalions of Commandant Rupert Lonsdale's 3rd Regiment NNC. Lonsdale had left a Captain William Stevenson in charge of them. Little is known of Stevenson's background, but he seems to have been from the Cape rather than Natal, and may possibly have been one of a number of volunteers who, having commanded 'Fingoe' levies in the Ninth Cape Frontier War, then came up from King William's Town to officer the newly raised NNC. Stevenson had only three European corporals to assist him. There is no agreement in the sources as to the overall strength of his command but it was certainly recognised as being far larger than the hundred-man norm for a company. The highest estimate offered by the men who fought at Rorke's Drift is 400, but a distinctly authoritative figure is to be found in Lord Chelmsford's correspondence:

> Lonsdale's regiment has been reinforced and is now about 500 over its strength – Natives are still coming in by twos and threes. I am leaving however those in excess of 2200 at Rorke's Drift. They will be useful for defence and also for working parties on the roads.*

Like all the native infantry contingents, Stevenson's levies were

* Chelmsford to Frere, 16 January 1879.

dressed only in a loincloth and were armed with their traditional African weapons – cowhide shields, assegais and knobkerries. If they were armed in accordance with the general policy for the NNC, one man in ten would have been issued with a rifle and five rounds of ammunition. It is more likely, however, as they were surplus to establishment, that no such allowance was made for them. As late arrivals they would have been all but untrained in any formal military sense. Unsure quite what to do with them, Major Spalding left them encamped on the long slope above the river, out of sight and out of mind. As long as he fed them well, he reasoned, they would be content enough.

B Company of the 2nd/24th was ninety-four strong. Its original company commander, the elder of two Godwin-Austen brothers in the battalion, had been accidentally wounded by one of his own men during the recent frontier war against the Xhosa. The Martini-Henry had no safety catch and in the dense bush country of the Amatola Mountains, where a man had to be ready to fire at a split second's notice, the odd negligent discharge was to some extent inevitable. Alfred Godwin-Austen had been unlucky, but his misfortune was to have a silver lining for Bromhead, who was elevated to command B Company in his stead.

Bromhead was 5 feet 10 inches tall and powerfully built. Now thirty-three years of age, he had been born at Versailles on 29 August 1845, though the family home was at Thurlby Hall in Lincolnshire. His father was Major Edmund de Gonville Bromhead, who had fought at Waterloo as a subaltern. As Gonny was his father's third son, the family baronetcy was destined never to pass to him. He was educated at the Magnus Grammar School in Newark. In the dying years of purchase, his father acquired him an ensign's vacancy in the 24th. He was appointed on 20 April 1867 and was promoted to lieutenant four years later. During his early years in the regiment, which included time in India, Bromhead boxed and wrestled with some distinction. He now had over eleven years of military service behind him. Supposedly he had already suffered significant hearing loss, but most seasoned infantrymen were deaf to a greater or lesser extent, and there are no really convincing references to a serious disability in the pre-January 1879 sources;

it would seem distinctly possible that his much more pronounced and noticeable deafness actually originated with the cacophony of small arms fire at Rorke's Drift. Bromhead was popular with his brother officers at a social level, but for some unknown reason his commanding officer seems to have had a low opinion of his merits as a soldier.* Whatever the origin of Henry Degacher's doubts, and he may simply have been a poor judge of character, events were to prove his curious lack of confidence in Bromhead to be entirely unwarranted. Perhaps he would never set the world on fire, but he knew his business as an infantry officer, and was a decent, warm-hearted man, traits which earned him the affection and loyalty of his men.

Bromhead had no other subaltern officer under him† and so the next senior man in the company was its colour-sergeant, the twenty-four-year-old Frank Bourne. He had been born one of eight sons and, with next to no prospect of a worthwhile inheritance on the land, had run away from his father's farm to enlist the very moment he came of age. He stood only 5 feet 6 inches tall and was so uncommonly young for a man of his rank that the senior men in the company referred to him behind his back as 'the kid'. The four section commanders were Sergeants Joseph Windridge, Henry Gallagher and George Smith, and Lance Sergeant Thomas Williams. There were also 4 corporals, 2 lance corporals, 2 drummers and 80 privates. Now that the 24th had acquired a new regional identity under Cardwell's Localisation Act, something around forty per cent of the 2nd Battalion was made up of young Welshmen from the rural market towns of mid-Wales and Monmouth-shire, or from the increasingly industrialised eastern valleys. By temperament, they were a stolid, determined and unflappable breed of men, all good qualities in a crisis. Most corners of England were also represented within the ranks of B Company and, as with any element

---

* Major Francis Clery, Colonel Glyn's chief of staff, described in a letter home how Henry Degacher had confided his uncomplimentary view of Bromhead to him.

† En route to the front as the company was encamped at Greytown, Bromhead had been assigned the younger Godwin-Austen as his subaltern. When B Company was detailed in battalion orders to stay at Rorke's Drift, Fred Godwin-Austen was cross-posted again, this time to G Company under Lieutenant Charlie Pope, alongside whom he would be killed at Isandlwana.

of Queen Victoria's army, there was the inevitable smattering of saints and scholars from across the Irish Sea.

Helpmekaar, a tiny hamlet of two dwelling houses and a couple of corrugated sheds erected by the commissaries, was located high above the Buffalo River valley, on the Biggarsberg plateau, some twelve miles south-west of Rorke's Drift. Captain Thomas Rainforth and G Company of the 1st/24th were temporarily encamped there, pending a move up to Rorke's Drift where they were to construct and man a protective redoubt on the ridge above the ponts. Brevet Major Russell Upcher had marched in to Helpmekaar with his D Company, 1st/24th, as recently as 6.00 p.m. on Tuesday evening, following the usual protracted and exacting march up the lines of communication from Pietermaritzburg, and before that Durban. Whilst Major Spalding had expected Rainforth to come up to the drift on Monday, Rainforth himself appears to have been under the impression that he should wait for Upcher to relieve him at Helpmekaar first. They were a well proven pairing; less than a year earlier they had trounced a Xhosa army at the Battle of Centane.* Inevitably the poor condition of the Greytown road, and the flooded watercourses astride it, had imposed significant delays on Upcher – not least when one of his transport wagons turned over in the Mooi River.

In the event orders were given first thing on Wednesday morning†

---

* Rainforth was still in command of the company he led at Centane – G Company. Upcher, however, had a new command. He had handed F Company, his Centane veterans, over to Captain William Mostyn at the end of the war in the Transkei. Accompanying Upcher up from Durban was a small draft of recruits for the 2nd/24th.

† Diary entry for 22 January by Lieutenant Wilfred Heaton, a subaltern in Upcher's company. The origin of the order is unclear. As Spalding did not know of the move it cannot have come down from the column. If it did not come from the front, then it must have come from the rear. Colonel Fairfax Hassard RE, the senior sapper officer in Natal, is known to have breakfasted at Helpmekaar that morning and could have been responsible for the instruction to Upcher to move on, based on the imminence of Colonel Bray's arrival. It is not inconceivable that Upcher made the decision on his own initiative. He must have known that Bray was not far behind him on the road. Either way, there would certainly have been a short period of time in which the depot was devoid of a guard. With 4,500 men of No. 3 Column between Helpmekaar and the enemy, this was probably not considered to be unduly risky. The relative lateness in the day of Rainforth's departure, with Upcher staggered half an hour behind him, might indicate that they delayed setting out as long as they possibly could, perhaps in the hope that Colonel Bray would arrive in the interim, or otherwise to

that both companies should depart for the front after lunch; Rainforth would halt at the river to build the redoubt and protect the crossing, whilst Upcher would overnight at Rorke's Drift and then continue on to Isandlwana to marry up with the main body of the 1st Battalion. Spalding was as yet unaware, however, that their combined move was now imminent. It was intended that in due course all the 24th Regiment companies employed on the lines of communication would be relieved in place by the five companies of the 2nd/4th (The King's Own Royal) Regiment, under the command of Colonel E. W. Bray,* which were even now marching up from Durban and Pietermaritzburg. When Bray's men were up and he had established his battalion headquarters at Rorke's Drift, the three 24th Regiment companies still in Natal would move on upcountry to rejoin their respective battalions in the field. Colonel Bray himself was some way in advance of his main body, travelling north along the border road with a convoy of twenty-eight wagons. There were only twenty-two men of his regiment in the escort, notwithstanding the fact that fifteen of the wagons were loaded with significant quantities of small arms ammunition. By Wednesday morning the convoy was nearing the Msinga magistracy. As the resident magistrate, Mr Henry Fynn, had gone up to Isandlwana to join Lord Chelmsford's staff as his political adviser, his friend Mr William Beaumont, ordinarily the magistrate at the frontier town of Newcastle, had come down to cover Fynn's duties and take care of his wife, children and sister-in-law. Beaumont also had charge of a number of small detachments of native levies deployed at various lookouts and outposts along the Buffalo River stretch of the frontier between Natal and Zululand. Colonel Bray might reasonably expect his convoy to get to Helpmekaar early on Thursday, though he personally could always ride on ahead of the wagons, in which case he would be able to complete the journey that day. By the end of the week at the latest,

---

minimise the length of time Helpmekaar would be left without a significant garrison. By 2.30–3.00 p.m. they had no choice but to move off if they were to complete the descent from the Biggarsberg to the Buffalo River by nightfall.

* The GOC evidently had mixed feelings about Bray – he described him as an 'energetic officer', but also as 'not a thorough gentleman'. Chelmsford to Frere 13 January 1879.

Spalding's command function on the lines of communication would be passed across to Bray, leaving the DAAG free to concentrate on sustaining No. 3 Column logistically.

Also moving on the border road that morning, having set off from Sandspruit at dawn, were the 1,000 black levies and 100 white officers and NCOs of 2nd/1st NNC, under the command of Major Harcourt Bengough, a regular officer of the 77th Regiment. Bengough had originally been assigned to Durnford's No. 2 Column, charged with defence of the border against counter-invasion. Now he was acting quasi-independently of his colonel, under the personal direction of Lord Chelmsford himself. His current orders were to cross the Buffalo at Eland's Kraal and march on into the Mangeni area. Only that morning his lordship had changed his mind yet again – a character trait to which he was notoriously prone. He now wanted Bengough up at Rorke's Drift instead. The order had been issued too late, however, to prevent 2nd/1st NNC marching for Eland's Kraal as originally planned.* The battalion would arrive at Msinga mid-morning and was then guided down the valley to the Eland's Kraal crossing by Mr Beaumont. By early afternoon Bengough and his men were in Zululand; fortunately they were well hidden in difficult hill country and were quite oblivious to the high drama being played out only a few miles away.

Spalding Hands over Command

After passing Durnford's orders down the line of his already over-extended column, John Chard rode on towards the Batshe Valley. A little way down the road he met his mule-wagon, his five sappers, and the two native employees he had taken on in Durban, coming the other way. Chard was worried that the large body of Zulus he had seen on the high ground above Isandlwana could now be somewhere between

---

* The change was included as a postscript to the order written by Lieutenant Colonel John Crealock, Lord Chelmsford's chief of staff, instructing Durnford to move his command up to Isandlwana. This was the note carried by Lieutenant Smith-Dorrien, which he delivered to Durnford's camp on the Buffalo at around 7.00 a.m. Durnford himself had gone off to requisition wagons on the Biggarsberg and probably did not have sight of the order until around 7.40 a.m., by which time Bengough had already been on the road for a couple of hours.

the camp and the river, and that they might constitute a threat to the ponts. Some 1,500 warriors had swept across the top of the Tahelane Spur at around 9.30 a.m. and had subsequently been reported by the pickets as having moved away to the north-west, that is to say towards the western end of the Ngedla Heights, from where it would be a simple matter for them to cut or threaten the road to Rorke's Drift. Chard must have realised that he had undertaken his trip to Isandlwana in altogether too lackadaisical a fashion. As his enquiries at the column headquarters had revealed that he was not personally required at Isandlwana, he now instructed his driver to turn the wagon in the road. Chard, his batman Robson, his driver and his *voorlooper*, a Cape Coloured man and a black teenager respectively, would be making the return journey to Rorke's Drift. Corporal Gamble and Sappers MacLaren, Wheatley and Cuthbert were needed at the camp, however, and were instructed to jump down from the wagon, hurry along behind Colonel Durnford's column, and report as soon as they were able to Lieutenant MacDowel RE who for the moment was upcountry with Lord Chelmsford and Colonel Glyn. It was now something around 10.00 a.m.; Chard and his three remaining companions cannot have reached the river much before 11.30 and a nerve-wracking journey it must have been.

Once he had been ferried across the river, Chard was shown a written order sent down from the mission station by Major Spalding. It stipulated that, since Durnford's command had now moved on, Bromhead was to find a seven-man guard for the ponts, and that Stevenson should supplement it with a party of fifty levies. The duty could be discontinued once Rainforth's company had established itself on the ridge above the drift. The B Company detail under Lance Sergeant Williams was already down at the river. The NNC company, however, was suffering from one of the periodic breakdowns in military efficiency that bedevil bodies of irregular troops, much to the annoyance of their regular army counterparts. Whilst a first fifty-man detail had turned up earlier in the day, their NCO had marched them away at the end of their shift, without having been relieved, and no second watch had yet put in an appearance. Spalding's order went on to direct that the ponts be secured each night on the Natal bank of the river.

Chard instructed his party to unload the mule-wagon and re-erect their two tents on the river bank. Then he spurred on to the mission in search of Spalding, so that he could brief him on the latest developments at Isandlwana. He found him at his tent and proceeded to describe how the troops left at the camp had been under arms since breakfast time. He went on to report that he had himself seen a large body of Zulus moving in the hills, which might conceivably represent a threat to the ponts. Spalding listened carefully. Chard went on to say that the crossing could not possibly be defended by only seven men, and they agreed that in the circumstances Rainforth's absence had become problematic. Spalding was already committed to making a trip to Helpmekaar after lunch and said that he would make it his business to hurry Rainforth down to the drift by last light. As Chard was turning his horse to ride back to the ponts, Spalding called after him, 'Which of you is senior, you or Bromhead?' When Chard replied that he didn't know, Spalding went back into his tent to check their respective entries in the Army List. He would find that Chard's seniority as a lieutenant was dated 15 July 1868 and Bromhead's 28 October 1871. 'I see you are senior,' said Spalding, 'so you will be in charge, although, of course, nothing will happen, and I shall be back again this evening, early.' Never has a military commander's assessment been more wide of the mark. The rules of seniority, with their various provisions for antedates, can sometimes create anomalies. Bromhead had in fact been in the army slightly longer than Chard.

John Rouse Merriott Chard had been born at Boxhill near Plymouth on 21 December 1847. He was educated at Plymouth New Grammar School and Cheltenham College, and then went on to the Royal Military Academy at Woolwich. As was the norm in the Royal Engineers, Chard was immediately commissioned into the rank of lieutenant. He served at Chatham initially, then spent three years in Bermuda, and next was posted to Malta for a year. In 1875 he returned to England for three years until, with No. 5 Company, Royal Engineers, he was warned for South Africa late in 1878. After a month-long journey Chard disembarked in Durban on 4 January 1879. He was sent on ahead of the company main body with a small advance party. He had never seen a shot fired in anger and Africa was entirely new to him. Now he found himself on the edge of enemy territory in command of No. 3 Column's advanced logistic depot. Already it was something of a pinnacle in his career: never before had he had so many men under his command. He had no intention of becoming over-excited at his new responsibilities, however, and characteristically rode off to have a quiet lunch down on the river bank.

The Sound of Distant Battle

It must have been not long after this that the sound of distant guns first came reverberating through the hills. This was the two 7-pounders at Isandlwana, engaging Zulu skirmishers on the Nyoni escarpment at a range of 3,000 yards, the opening of the battle proper. The firing triggered much curiosity and speculation at Rorke's Drift, though there was absolutely no reason for alarm. Colour-Sergeant Bourne and the section commanders, intensely annoyed that they were missing out on all the excitement upcountry, decided to walk to the top of Shiyane, as they had done on 12 January during the skirmish at Sihayo's kraal, to see what they could see. Because Chard's campsite was nestled between the low ridges above the ponts, nobody down at the river heard the distant gunfire. Blissfully unaware that No. 3 Column was now in action, Chard waited patiently for his man Robson to produce some lunch.

Spalding had his lunch at the mission and rode away as he had always planned at about 2.00 p.m. The twelve-mile ride to Helpmekaar would take him around two hours. He took a spare horse with him, which he intended to leave at Vermaak's Farm for the return journey, in order presumably to give both of his mounts some exercise. At 2.30 p.m. Rainforth hit the road from the opposite end, to be followed half an hour later by Upcher, both of them at the head of their respective companies, each about eighty strong, and both with one or two ox-wagons plodding along in their train.

Alarm

Gonny Bromhead had lunch with Walter Dunne. Dunne was a twenty-five-year-old regular officer of the Army Commissariat and Transport Department, the senior officer of his branch of the service at Rorke's

Drift. He had played the leading role in launching No. 3 Column with fifteen days' supply aboard its wagons and was expecting to be called forward soon to join the column in the field. When the summons came he planned to leave the store at Rorke's Drift in the care of his number two, an ex-ranker called James Langley Dalton.

Acting Assistant Commissary Dalton was a regular soldier no longer, but for all that had lost none of his professional edge. Born in London, he joined the 85th Regiment in 1849, at the age of seventeen. His infantry service took him first to Ireland and, in 1853, to Mauritius. He had been promoted to sergeant by the time his regiment moved to South Africa, where he saw active service against the Xhosa in the Eighth Cape Frontier War. After twelve years' service with the 85th, Dalton transferred to the Commissariat Staff Corps, which in due course became part of the Army Service Corps. He gained the rank of staff sergeant and served out the final spell of his twenty-two-year engagement in Canada. Dalton had enjoyed his experience of South Africa and, when he retired in 1871, emigrated to the Cape in search of new opportunities. No doubt he imagined himself living out his days comfortably and peacefully on a pretty frontier farm but, as is so often the case with the retirement plans of old soldiers, things did not quite work out as planned. When the ninth war with the Xhosa broke out late in 1877, he was caught up in the drama with everybody else. He volunteered to serve with the colonial forces and not unnaturally gravitated towards the short-handed commissariat, where he soon acquired officer status as an acting assistant commissary, the departmental equivalent of a lieutenant. It is not widely appreciated that he fought at Rorke's Drift as a colonial volunteer, not as a regular army man.

Before long Colour-Sergeant Bourne and the section commanders were back from Shiyane, having observed artillery fall-of-shot on the high ground to the north of Isandlwana. No doubt Bourne reported what he had seen to his company commander. In the meantime Surgeon Reynolds and the two clergymen had wandered off to make their own trip up the hill. The afternoon was fiercely hot as usual; when they had finished eating, Bromhead and Dunne retired to the shade of a canvas awning to smoke their pipes and chew the fat. As they sat looking down towards the Buffalo, they saw two groups of distant figures on the other side of the river, which in one instance they took to be a crowd of fleeing women and children, droving a few oxen, and in the other, a disorderly crowd of Durnford's native horse. Since these groups were seemingly not visible to Chard in his lower-lying position beside the ponts, they must still have been some considerable distance back from the general line of the river. The native cavalry cannot have been the same group who would later report to the mission, as the time and space equation does not add up, so the chances are that they were amaNgwane horsemen routing from Isandlwana. Probably they were moving to the north-west, in order to find a crossing point further upstream. In this way they would avoid their British lords and masters at Rorke's Drift and be able to get clean away, deeper into Natal.

If Bromhead and Dunne were bemused by these strange sightings, the air of mystery did not last for long. They stood up with the intention of walking down to the river to investigate, but had not gone more than a few steps when a soldier ran up to report that a galloper had come in and was asking to speak to an officer. Their attention was drawn to a commotion in front of the hospital, where a bare-headed white man in his shirtsleeves was babbling excitedly to a cluster of B Company NCOs and soldiers. This was almost certainly Private Edward Evans of the Buffs mounted infantry detachment. He was specifically remembered in the accounts of a number of B Company men as the man who first gave the alarm, probably because he was a Welshman and was well known amongst his countrymen in the 24th Regiment. Catching sight of Bromhead and Dunne as they appeared from behind the storehouse, Evans cantered across the yard to meet them. Dunne remembered that his first words were, 'The camp is taken by Zulus!'

Other riders were not far behind Evans. From his vantage point on Shiyane, Surgeon Reynolds had seen four apparently frantic riders galloping towards Rorke's Drift from the south-east, the direction of Sothondose's Drift. He identified at least one man as a regular, clearly a mounted infantryman in a red tunic. The cannon fire indicated that a significant general action had been fought upcountry, and Reynolds was worried that they might be gallopers sent by Dr Peter Shepherd to fetch additional medical help. He parted company with Otto Witt and

George Smith and dashed downhill to the mission, where he quickly became caught up in all the excitement.

Not long after Evans arrived, Private Daniel Whelan of the 1st/13th mounted infantry also came in, evidently the man in the red coat. Inevitably, he too drew an awe-struck crowd anxious for news. Gardner's man was probably one of the other two riders spotted by Reynolds, because his note was delivered before Chard came up from the ponts, an interval of not more than about ten minutes. If this third man was indeed a member of the Christian Edendale Troop, the chances are that he would have spoken reasonable English. If on the other hand he was amaNgwane, his command of the language may have been questionable or non-existent.* Either way nobody seems to have paid him much attention – perhaps he handed the note over to the nearest soldier and rode on. It was a short note which indicated that a defeat had occurred, that the mission was now in grave danger, and that it should be fortified at once. Reynolds was alarmed to note that one of these early fugitives (there is no clue as to which one) was riding Peter Shepherd's horse. Shepherd had in fact been killed by a throwing assegai which hit him as he was in the act of remounting his horse, having stopped to help a badly wounded man. Clearly his riderless horse must have galloped on instinctively, alongside other badly frightened animals, and then been appropriated by somebody who had lost his own, either in a fall of which there must have been a great many on such treacherous ground, or in the act of swimming the river, where a good proportion of the fugitives are known to have been unseated.

---

* Gardner said in his statement that he sent his note in the care of 'a Basuto', but it was commonplace for people to refer to Durnford's Natal Native Mounted Contingent as his 'mounted Basutos'. In fact only No. 4 of the five troops was actually a Basuto one. It left the battlefield en masse along the Rorke's Drift road; hence its men cannot have been anywhere near Sothondose's Drift or Alan Gardner. The amaNgwane (Nos. 1–3 Troops) were rather more scattered, but also fled Isandlwana at an early stage and similarly, for the most part, got out along the wagon road. A few stragglers may have escaped via Sothondose's Drift. Since the Edendale Troop tarried in the camp for a few minutes, in which time the Zulu right horn cut the road, and is known to have given covering fire to the fugitives at the river, it is far more likely that it was one of them who took Gardner's note.

Bromhead and Dalton Confer

Bromhead, Reynolds and Dalton drew apart from the chattering crowd of soldiers in front of the hospital to consider what was to be done. Dalton was the man for a crisis. He had done a course on field fortification during his infantry days and knew that the contents of the storehouse would be ideal for barricading the post. Their course of action was obvious, he declared. Bromhead agreed. The two of them quickly turned their minds to laying out a defensive perimeter, an act for which John Chard is most often given the credit. But Chard was only now looking up from his letter, at the two horsemen racing frantically downhill towards the ponts. Bromhead quickly scribbled out a note to Chard asking him to return to the mission immediately, and sent one of his men doubling down to the river with it. He went on to write a second note, this time to the officer commanding the 1st/24th at Helpmekaar: 'Intelligence has just reached camp that the camp at Isandula Hill [sic] is taken by the enemy.' He entrusted this peremptory despatch to Evans and Whelan, who were no doubt happy to have a legitimate reason to ride on.

Next, Bromhead ordered that the double row of bell tents behind the storehouse be dropped, and that the company's reserve ammunition be broken open. A work-party was quickly formed to heave B Company's two ox-wagons from the back of the post into the yard between the buildings. The details are far from clear, but somebody seems to have had the idea of sending the most serious hospital cases to safety in them. Reynolds makes reference in one of his accounts of the battle to a number of his patients being brought outside at this point. Chaplain Smith also remarks that an evacuation of the sick was mooted at an early juncture, but cannot himself have been an eyewitness to what went on, as he was still on top of Shiyane. Hook also recounted such a story, but far too long after the event to be regarded as a wholly reliable corroborative source; he may simply have been repeating something he had read elsewhere. If it was ever seriously considered, Bromhead must have decided pretty quickly that it was an entirely unrealistic proposition. It may have been a matter either of countermanding somebody else's bright idea, or even perhaps of changing his own mind, possibly on the basis of advice from Dalton. It could also be the case that Reynolds misinterpreted the fast-moving sequence of events unfolding around him, and that no such evacuation was actually mooted. Whatever the truth of the matter, it was soon apparent that the sick would have to take their chances with everybody else. It is abundantly clear that, contrary to the mistaken interpretations of some historians, no wholesale evacuation of the garrison was ever contemplated.

Already the men were clustered around Colour-Sergeant Bourne and the reserve ammunition. By the time everybody had topped themselves up to the standard seventy rounds a man (the number of .450-inch Boxer cartridges a man could sensibly carry before their weight became an impediment to his agility), Bourne had thirty-four boxes each of 600 rounds left, a total of 20,400 rounds. Having drawn their first line ammunition, the men turned their attention to the rapid out-loading of the storehouse.

Chard Hears the News

Down on the river, Adendorff and his companion had been ferried across to the Natal bank. It was now about 3.15 p.m. Chard must have removed his tunic to sit in the sun writing his letter, because Adendorff had to ask if he was an officer. When he replied that he was, Adendorff dismounted, drew him to one side, and broke the devastating news from Isandlwana. Chard asked a number of supplementary questions but found Adendorff's answers so unconvincing that at first he refused to believe his story. This is perhaps unsurprising as, in order to get away along the wagon road and be ahead of Durnford's Basuto Troop, as he was, Adendorff must have been amongst the very first men to flee the camp.* He had not actually seen the full extent of the disaster; rather he had sensed its inevitability. Lieutenant Higginson, who was in

---

* It is suggested in some quarters that Adendorff and his companion escaped in the direction of Sothondose's Drift, but then followed the line of the river without crossing it, until they came to the ponts at Rorke's Drift. Such a journey is inherently improbable, however, due to the extremely rugged nature of the terrain. The wagon road parallels the line of the river but is some distance away from the gorge delineating its course between Rorke's Drift and Sothondose's Drift.

the same company as Adendorff, was even now trying to avoid drowning at Sothondose's Drift. Clearly then, Adendorff left the field the instant the levies of No. 6 Company broke. He may have been one of the NNC Europeans whom Captain Essex saw unsuccessfully attempting to rally fleeing levies, even before the bugles of the 24th sounded retire.

Bromhead's runner now put in an appearance with the note asking Chard to come up to the mission. His doubts dispelled, Chard told Driver Robson to saddle his horse immediately. The driver and *voorlooper* were to harness the mules and pack the tools, tents and other paraphernalia back into the wagon. Next, Chard called Lance Sergeant Williams over and told him to move his six B Company men onto the ridge above the ponts, take up fire-positions amongst the boulders, and cover the opposite bank. He added that he would be back for them soon, or would send for them, but that in the meantime Sergeant Millne* and Mr Daniels were to moor the ponts midstream. The carbineer accompanying Adendorff rode on in the direction of Helpmekaar at this point, probably with Chard's blessing.

As soon as his horse had been readied, Chard galloped the half-mile to the mission. Adendorff seems to have gone with him at this point. Dispute still lingers over whether he stayed to fight in the battle. Chard stated emphatically in his reports on the action that he did, but it remains something of a curiosity that no other account mentions him. It has been suggested that he was one of a number of NNC officers said to have been arrested by the military in the aftermath of Isandlwana, but there is no compelling evidence to support such a contention. Chard's passing reference describes him fighting from the inside of the storehouse, so that whilst it can be argued that he might not have seen him with his own eyes, and could possibly have been mistaken, it might just as readily explain why nobody else mentioned him. In that respect the case can be argued either way. It is clear, however, that Adendorff must have gone up to the mission in order to have been

---

* Millne ended up detached from his regiment and in charge of the ponts because he had done a pioneer course at Chatham earlier in his career. Following a trawl for suitably qualified personnel, he was given the job of transporting the requisite engineering stores up from Pietermaritzburg.

mentioned by Chard at all, and it is difficult to conceive how he could subsequently have left without it being recorded in the sources. When the evidence is fairly tallied, there seems no good reason to doubt that Adendorff was indeed one of the defenders of Rorke's Drift. It is perhaps overly generous to laud him as the only man who fought both at Isandlwana and at Rorke's Drift, as he may safely be regarded as amongst the first of the Europeans to flee the doomed encampment.

As he approached the mission buildings, Chard could see that the post was already bustling with activity and that Bromhead had clearly taken the decision to fortify for defence. After quickly conferring with Bromhead and Dalton, Chard strode around the proposed perimeter with them, to be briefed on their plan. As they walked, he listened to the even more dire news that had come in from the direction of Sothondose's Drift, pausing occasionally to suggest refinements and enhancements to the defensive layout as they occurred to him. In all the excitement none of the officers spared a thought for the fire risk posed by the thatched roofs; it simply did not occur to them. It took the trio only a few minutes to complete the circuit, at which point Chard remounted and set out for the river to bring in his party. When he got back to the ponts, he found that Millne and Daniels had moored them midstream as ordered, and were about to sink the ropes and hawsers into the river so as to immobilise the crossing temporarily.

The group of 'native women and children with a few decrepit old men',* spotted by Bromhead and Dunne earlier, had arrived on the river bank whilst Chard was away. They called to be brought across on the ponts, but in recalling the incident in 1905 for the *Manchester Evening Chronicle*, Millne did not say whether he brought them across or not. Either way they were long gone by the time Chard got back; he seems to have been entirely unaware of them. Quite who they were will never be known for sure but, speculatively, they may have been refugees from Chief Gamdana's kraal near Isandlwana. Gamdana had surrendered to Lord Chelmsford some days earlier and had been living in fear of reprisals ever since. Rumours of the imminent arrival of a big *impi* had been abroad for a couple of days. Perhaps Gamdana's people

* Sergeant Millne.

began moving to seek sanctuary in Natal at first light; 'decrepit old men' must assuredly have been much slower-moving than mounted fugitives like Adendorff and his companion

Sergeant Millne and Daniels now made an offer to fight from the decks of the ponts with Lance Sergeant Williams' detail, but Chard swiftly declined their brave but ultimately foolhardy idea. He told Millne to bring everybody back to the mission as soon as the work of disabling the ponts was complete.

On the Helpmekaar Road

At around 3.30 p.m., or about the same time that Adendorff was briefing Chard on the river bank, Major Spalding would have been about three miles from Helpmekaar (having been riding at about 6 miles an hour for 90 minutes). At this point he met Captain Thomas Rainforth and G Company on the road. (G Company left Helpmekaar at 2.30 p.m. and was moving at between 2.5 and 3 miles an hour – the speed of an ox-wagon). It is often erroneously stated that Spalding was at the head of the troops when passing fugitives broke the news of the disaster. In fact a close reading of Major Spalding's report indicates that he continued on to Helpmekaar after meeting Rainforth; no doubt there were a number of other pressing matters for him to attend to, not merely the forward move of G Company. Spalding would have outlined his concerns about the security of the river-crossing, and would have emphasised the need for Rainforth to move at best speed and encamp himself on the ridge above the ponts, not beside B Company up at the mission. Perhaps a mile further up the road, now only two miles from his destination, he must then have come upon Major Russell Upcher and D Company, moving half an hour behind Rainforth.

None of the fugitives travelling the long cross-country route from Fugitives' Drift had yet reached Helpmekaar, but James Brickhill, the interpreter, had set off from the river in an entirely different direction and had by now made it to the Msinga magistracy. He raised the alarm with Mr Beaumont and was able to reassure Mrs Fynn that, as far as he knew, her husband Henry was still alive. Beaumont and the civilian jailer at the post, Mr Elkington, broke out their rifles and bandoliers and prepared to defend the women and children. Two or three settler families came in during the course of the afternoon, and eventually, much to everybody's relief, Colonel Bray and his detachment arrived, having encountered distraught fugitives on the Greytown–Helpmekaar leg of the border road. Bray made all the prudent defensive preparations he could, but mercifully for all concerned the Battle of Msinga was never fought.

Not long after Rainforth and Spalding had parted company, the head of the little G Company column encountered the first of the fugitives travelling the Rorke's Drift–Helpmekaar road. Probably the first men they clapped eyes on were amaNgwane riders, who may well have given the redcoats a wide berth and left them feeling somewhat bemused. Probably the first men Rainforth got any sense out of were Privates Evans and Whelan of the mounted infantry, who galloped in with Bromhead's curt and alarming note. Before Rainforth had even unfolded it, the couriers were burbling about an appalling disaster, and the fact that the garrison at Rorke's Drift was preparing to defend the post. Aghast at their news and shocked at the apparently certain loss of many of his closest friends, Rainforth halted, formed line and waited for his old comrade Upcher to close up. By 4.00 p.m. the two companies had united on the road. Evans and Whelan were adamant that the 1st/24th had been annihilated. But Upcher and Rainforth had been in tight corners before; less than a year earlier they had trounced 6,000 Xhosa warriors with just two companies. If the rest of the regiment was in trouble, there could be only course of action: Upcher waved the column forward along the Rorke's Drift road.

Chapter 2

Trouble in the Wind

Preparing the Post for Defence

The defensive works around the mission buildings were well underway when everybody's attention was drawn to the sound of pounding hooves. Lieutenant Alfred Henderson rode into sight from the direction of the ponts at the head of around a hundred black troopers. A civilian meat contractor called Bob Hall was the only other European in the party. Henderson was the troop officer of No. 4 Troop, Natal Native Mounted Contingent (NNMC), or Hlubi's Basutos. They had fought under Durnford, alongside the Edendale Troop of the NNMC and Captain Robert Bradstreet's colonial volunteers, during the stand in the Nyogane Donga – the defence of the British right flank. But when Durnford ordered a withdrawal, he quickly lost control of his command, largely because he loitered at the rear and was one of the last away, probably due to some misplaced show of personal gallantry. The Basutos, amongst others, failed to keep their nerve. Durnford had not helped matters by sending the troop officers of Nos. 4 and 5 Troops back to the camp to fetch ammunition. Neither Harry Davies of the Edendale Troop nor Alfred Henderson were with their men when the withdrawal was ordered.

The black troopers had galloped up the long slope towards the tents at the foot of Isandlwana and then, perhaps unsurprisingly given that there was nobody in front to tell them what to do, kept going, thus triggering a general panic amongst the native contingents, the civilian wagon-workers, and some, but not all, of the European mounted troops. The Basutos rode through the tent-line in the gap between the 1st/24th encampment and that of the mounted troops, and then fled the scene altogether through the saddle. Having been deployed on the British left, most of the amaNgwane troopers of Zikhali's Horse, the men of Nos. 1–3 Troops, NNMC, were by now queuing for carbine cartridges in the NNC lines. Observing a general move to the rear as their compatriots came galloping up from the donga, these men too started to wobble. It is a moot point whether the men from the right triggered the rout, or whether they were spooked by the flight of the amaNgwane; either way round, the desertion of the native horse became wholesale. Harry Davies failed to get back to his troop, which from this point on was led by Sergeant Simeon Kambula, whose father Elijah had been killed beside Durnford in the Bushman's River Pass fiasco of 1873. Kambula led his men across to the 1st/24th wagons where he hoped to procure some more cartridges.

Somewhere amidst all the confusion, Bob Hall swung himself into the saddle and made a break for Natal. Alfred Henderson spurred after his Basuto troopers with the intention of rallying them. Only Henderson himself would ever know whether he had been at the head of his troop or, more honourably, was chasing his men along the road, when they galloped across the stony drift on the Manzimyama Stream, and then fled up the opposite side of the valley in the direction of Ncepheni Hill. Moments later the Zulu right horn broke into the Manzimyama Valley, to begin driving the later fugitives on a left oblique in the direction of Mpethe Hill and Sothondose's Drift beyond. Many amaNgwane riders were intermingled with the Basutos. By the time Henderson had succeeded in restoring some measure of control, he found that around a hundred men had rallied to him. Bob Hall was one of them. Around another eighty of the amaNgwane failed to rally at all and continued a disorderly rout in the direction of Rorke's Drift. These must have been the men that Bromhead and Dunne saw a little while later as they sat smoking their pipes under the awning.

Eventually Henderson and the rallied troopers appeared on the ridge above the ponts. They were some considerable distance behind Adendorff, and thus found the river bank deserted and the ponts moored in the middle of the deep-water pool. They swam their ponies across at the drift and after the requisite half-mile canter Henderson reported to Chard. Chard was delighted at this unexpected reinforcement: a hundred men armed with Swinburne-Henry carbines*

* References to NNMC armament are few and far between but a letter from Chelmsford to Wood dated 28 January 1879 confirms they were equipped with the Swinburne-Henry.

would make all the difference to the defence of the post. He could now count on having around 450 men to hold the perimeter. Henderson appears to have told Chard that the force with Lord Chelmsford had been broken up into small parties, which were now making their way back into Natal. It was a strange remark and it is difficult to conceive what possessed Henderson to make it. Perhaps it was a guess or a rumour. Chard quickly concocted a role for the mounted men. They were to ride back in the direction of the drift and deploy as an early warning screen along the line of the river. This would put most of them on the far side of Shiyane and leave them completely out of sight from the mission. It may not have been the shrewdest military decision John Chard ever made. Once the Basutos had made contact, they were to impose whatever delay they could, then fall back to the buildings, turn their horses loose and take post within the perimeter. Interestingly there is no reference in the sources to Henderson asking anyone for ammunition, even though his men are known to have been critically short of cartridges by this stage in the day. He may have done so and it went unrecorded. If he failed altogether to address the problem, then it was a serious lapse on his part and might go a long way to explaining the later conduct of his men. As Henderson and his troopers wheeled away in the direction of the drift, everybody else resumed work on the barricades.

The Perimeter

The storehouse was packed to the rafters with Dunne's stores, particularly stockpiled foodstuffs, such as 200-lb mealie-bags and 100-lb cases of hardtack and tinned bully beef. These would provide ideal improvised defence stores, and Dunne and Byrne quickly formed work parties to get them out into the yard. There were already two big piles of mealie-bags in front of the storehouse, protected from the elements by tarpaulins but, as it was necessary as a matter of priority to clear out the rooms inside the building for defence, for the time being at least, these were left where they were. It will be helpful now to refer to Maps 2 and 3 on pages 36 and 40.

The mission buildings stood about thirty-five yards apart, with the storehouse staggered slightly to the right rear of the hospital. At about

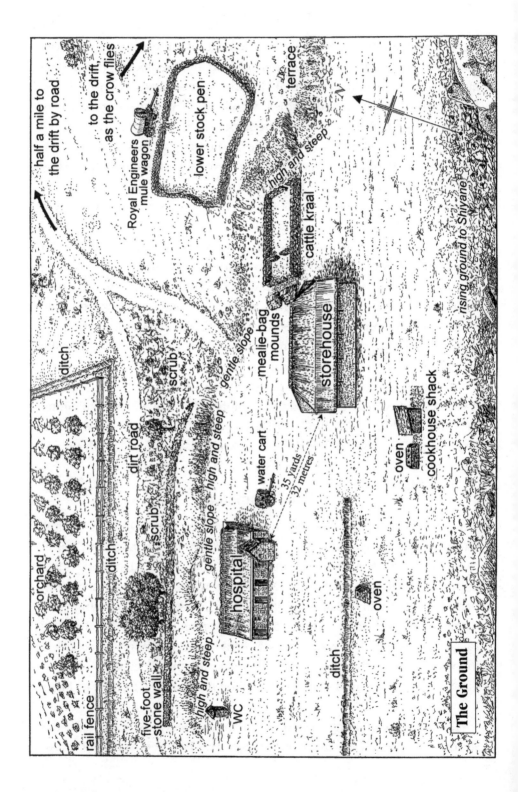

The Ground

ninety feet long by thirty feet wide, the hospital contained no fewer than eleven rooms, many of them small, dark and claustrophobic. The storehouse was slightly smaller but had only half as many rooms as the hospital. Both buildings were thatched and both had north-facing verandas enclosed at the ends; since these gave access to a number of rooms at the front, it was essential they be shielded by barricades. The mission stood on a raised shelf of ground some forty yards back from the lower-lying dirt road, but at the rear it was badly overlooked in its turn by the lower slopes of Shiyane, at a range of roughly 350 yards. The terrace just in front of the buildings was around three feet high in most places and was the obvious line along which to construct a north wall.* Immediately in front of the storehouse, however, where a short fork in the road ran up to his yard, Jim Rorke had raised a graded embankment to facilitate the passage of wagons. For a few yards at this point, the general line of the terrace would offer no significant advantage in terms of raising a defensive wall above general ground level. Conversely, immediately left and right of the graded embankment, the terrace was at its most pronounced; here there were rocky stretches, where there were large boulders embedded in its front face. Since some of the boulders were shoulder high to a tall man, the mealie-bag barricade atop them would be raised high above an attacker. Direct assault on this short stretch of the perimeter at least, might even prove impractical.

There was a second, much more significant weak point in front of the hospital, where there was a smooth-graded curve in the general line of the terrace, and where it was barely an obstacle at all. Just a few yards beyond the hospital, the terrace straightened, again became rockier, and developed a much steeper gradient. This stretch would lie outside the proposed perimeter, but since it was both sheer-sided and around four feet high, there would be a significant amount of dead ground at its base. This had the potential to pose a significant threat to defenders fighting in front of the hospital. Along this western side of the post, a short length of barricade would be required to close the gap

---

* The narrative conforms to Chard's reports and the compass directions on the sketch maps which accompanied them. In fact Chard actually plots direction slightly inaccurately.

between the gable-end of the hospital and the smooth-graded curve in the terrace. Right down at the opposite end of the post, a rectangular cattle kraal with good waist-high stone walls, would fulfil the same function and make an eastern mealie-bag wall unnecessary. All that was required here was to plug up the short gap between the corner of the kraal and the storehouse veranda. The buildings would be linked at the rear by a slightly oblique south wall, running from the front left corner of the storehouse to the right rear corner of the hospital. The necessity to protect the front of the hospital meant that the north wall would be considerably longer than the south wall.

It was fortunate that Jim Rorke had constructed the end-walls of his buildings from stone, as three of them would be exposed to direct attack as integral parts of the perimeter. The side-walls were made of conventional bricks and seemed robust enough; fortunately it was possible to drive loopholes through them with a bayonet. The interior partition walls between rooms were made from mud-clay bricks and were much less strong than the external walls. The internal doors were flimsy constructions at best, not that the outside doors were much better. Of the two buildings, the hospital was by far the more vulnerable, though Chard and the other officers probably had little time to take cognisance of the fact. At its rear and along its western end no fewer than four doors and two windows would be exposed to direct attack. To make matters worse, a small utility room at the south-east corner of the building protruded from the back wall at a right angle, just far enough to obscure the doors and windows from the south wall, and thus preclude any protective enfilading fire from the barricade, or from loopholes in the western end of the storehouse. This meant that, whilst attackers could be shot down in their approach to the doors and windows, once they had pressed themselves hard up against the wall, it was only the hospital defenders themselves who would have a chance of bringing fire to bear on them – and then only from the highly limited arcs offered by their loopholes.

By contrast there were no doors or windows at the back of the storehouse. There was a side door at the eastern gable-end of the building, but this was commanded at point-blank range from the walls of the cattle kraal and could be easily protected. At the western end there was a set of steps leading up to an attic door, but these were covered by the south wall, and for an attacker to climb them in plain view of thirty or more riflemen would be tantamount to suicide.

Having quickly made some impromptu medical arrangements for the reception and treatment of the wounded on the storehouse veranda, Surgeon Reynolds turned his attention to the protection of his existing patients. Some of them, such as the Swiss-born Corporal Schiess of 1st/3rd NNC, suffering from severe blisters, decided that they felt fit enough to take their place on the barricades. Schiess had been born in Berne, enlisted in the French Army at the age of fifteen, saw action in the Franco–Prussian War, and was now twenty-three years old. Other patients were too weak or immobile to emulate Schiess, but would be perfectly capable of using a rifle from a loophole or window. A few men, like Sergeant Maxfield, were completely helpless. Bromhead decided to supplement the eight or ten partially combatant patients with some fully fit members of his company. He and Colour-Sergeant Bourne detailed six privates to the task and quickly gave them their orders. They were Privates John Williams, Joseph Williams, Robert Jones, William Jones, Thomas Cole and Harry Hook. As the combatant officers were busy, and since in any case everybody was now a combatant in the face of a merciless foe, Doctor Reynolds supervised the loopholing of the walls and the barricading of the doors and windows. Because the six fighting men were to be sealed into the various wards, they were each given a haversack of additional cartridges with which to sustain the defence of the building.

Levies and regulars alike, every man at the mission was now working frantically to raise the perimeter walls. Captain Stevenson proved particularly energetic in supervising the work of his men. Commissary Dalton, too, showed the way, toiling personally at the same time as supervising the labours of others. The storehouse was emptied of mealie-bags first. Along the north wall where the terrace gave some added height above ground level, they were piled only three high, or not much more than groin level to a man of average height. Along the south wall, where the barricade itself would be the only obstacle to an attacker charging up to close quarters, a fourth layer of bags was added. In all cases the 200-lb bags were overlapped like

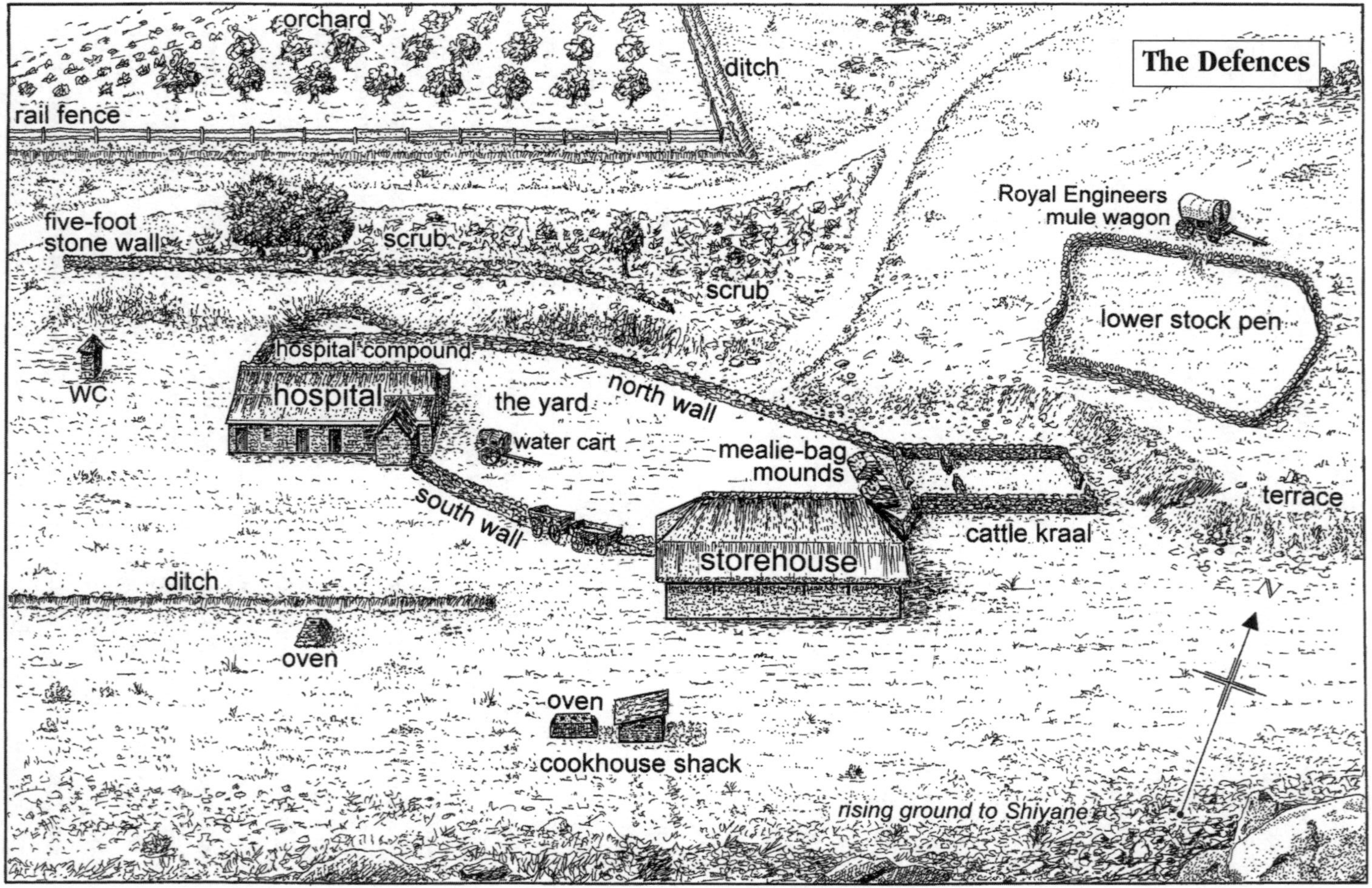

The Defences

orchard

ditch

rail fence

five-foot stone wall

scrub

scrub

WC

hospital compound

hospital

north wall

the yard

south wall

water cart

mealie-bag mounds

storehouse

cattle kraal

terrace

lower stock pen

Royal Engineers mule wagon

N

oven

ditch

oven

cookhouse shack

rising ground to Shiyane

bricks to give the barricades the requisite strength. The two ox-wagons were run into the line of the south wall near the storehouse. The gaps between the wheels were jammed up with biscuit boxes and mealie-bags. To give the wagons some additional height, a layer of mealie-bags was run across the top of them. There was some difficulty with the north wall in front of the hospital, where the curve in the terrace was drawing the line of the barricade a long way forward.

Realising that the enemy could appear at any moment, Bromhead turned his mind to the security of the post during its fortification. Calling Colour-Sergeant Bourne to his side, he instructed him to take out a few B Company skirmishers a short distance to the south-west. It is impossible now to state with certainty just how many men went out with Bourne, but the logical grouping would have been one of the four sections in the company: a sergeant, a junior NCO and about twenty men.

Chard meanwhile told Sergeant Windridge, a man with twenty years' service in the 2nd/24th behind him, to keep a close eye on the kegs of rum in the storehouse. This may not have been the best of choices, as unbeknown to Chard, a stranger to the men of the 24th Regiment, Windridge was by no means averse to drink.*

Fields of Fire

There was an abundance of good cover in the immediate vicinity of the mission, but Chard and Bromhead were unable to find either the time or the manpower to clear their fields of fire. Between the north wall and the road there was a belt of fairly dense scrub. Whilst this would offer only a limited amount of cover in daylight, it would doubtless be distinctly useful after dark, and sunset was now only just over three hours away. Of much greater concern was the stone wall running through the scrub, parallel to the road, and just beneath the rocky terrace. It was over fifty yards long, five feet high and solidly built. Day or night it was capable of sheltering anything up to 300–400 men from view and fire; importantly it was only twenty-five yards from the hospital, ran across the entire front

---

* Later in the year Windridge would be reduced to the ranks for an offence of drunkenness. His officers took good care of him, however, and got him back up to the rank of sergeant before his retirement in 1883.

of the building, and extended thirty yards beyond it to the west. Had anybody given any thought to the defence of Rorke's Drift in advance of 22 January, the wall would have been demolished. Now, when it really mattered, it was far too late to do so.

After a while one of the officers went to the front of the hospital and decided that barricading around the curve in the terrace would almost certainly render the sector untenable. There were three reasons for this. First, it would push the perimeter far too close to the stone wall for comfort. Second, a barricade raised on a forward slope would, in effect, be leaning downhill towards the enemy in such a way as to leave its defenders much more exposed to enemy fire. And third, curving a defensive perimeter creates a salient which can be attacked on three sides. Work was begun to raise an inner line of mealie bags, seven or eight yards further back. This ran in a straight line along the top of the gentle slope in front of the hospital, rather than around its outside edge. In the event time was so short that the defenders would be caught on the hop in this sector; work on the protruding outer wall was abandoned before it had been raised to full height, and the work on the straight inner wall had not yet been finished by the time the battle opened. This left a gap of perhaps two yards in width at one of the most vulnerable points on the perimeter. When time ran out, the gap was superficially closed up, merely by placing a plank of wood across it. At least the gap was partly shielded by the low arc of the aborted outer barricade.

Just behind the stone wall was a small grove of Cape poplars, and three tall gum trees that had often in the past acted as a landmark to travellers approaching the mission along the line of the Buffalo River valley. Beyond the wall, on the other side of the road, was an orchard of vines and fruit trees; Chaplain Smith wrote that it covered two or three acres. It was bounded by a ditch and a rail fence; whilst the fence would offer but little protection, the ditch was an altogether different matter. The orchard area looked certain to provide good cover in daylight and excellent cover after dark. The road itself was not a sunken road in the true sense of the expression, but it was slightly lower than general ground level and offered a certain amount of cover to men lying prone amongst the wagon ruts.

Neither was the rocky terrace an unmitigated blessing: whilst it would offer a very definite advantage to men defending the line of the north wall, it would, conversely, pose a serious threat at its extremities, where significant graze angles would allow crouched or crawling attackers to infiltrate to within a few yards of the hospital compound at one end of the line, or the cattle kraal at the other. Beyond the cattle kraal there was a second, much larger stock pen. This was lower-lying and was in large part screened from riflemen within the cattle kraal by virtue of the fact that it lay beyond a particularly steep-sided and rocky part of the terrace. It too had stone walls over three and a half feet high and would offer an ideal forming up area for hundreds of men, only a few yards from the eastern end of the perimeter. Chard's Cape Coloured driver parked the sapper wagon next to the gateway of the stock pen and turned his mules loose into the countryside. Then he decided to secrete himself in one of the small caves beneath a rocky shelf half way up Shiyane. It was a decision he would later come to regret. The black teenager employed as a *voorlooper*, waited until Chard had turned his back, stole one of his horses, and disappeared in the direction of the Helpmekaar plateau.*

There was less cover beyond the south or rear wall, but even so there were plenty of places where the Zulus could seek cover in darkness. Just behind the storehouse, there was a square native hut which served as a cookhouse, with a couple of large brick ovens beside it. Only a few yards away from the back of the hospital and the south wall, there was a shallow drainage ditch, perhaps two feet deep which, although it would be of little use in daylight, would again be particularly dangerous after dark. Just behind the drainage ditch, there was another stepped terrace of flat, open ground, only a foot or two higher than that on which the mission buildings stood. It sloped gently uphill until it merged into the lower slopes of Shiyane.

It is crucial in understanding the course of the battle to take note of the amount of good cover around the mission buildings, much of it only a few yards outside the perimeter. This was not by any stretch of

* The lad went on to bypass Helpmekaar, rode all the way to Pietermaritzburg where he handed Chard's horse over to the military, and then somehow made his way back to his home town, Durban, the place where Chard had first taken him on.

the imagination an inherently strong defensive position. The sectors where the British fields of fire were worst would be precisely the points at which the Zulus would come closest to achieving a break-in. As at Isandlwana the subtleties of the ground would play a critical role in shaping the course and conduct of the battle. Again it is necessary to remind ourselves, in the face of preconceptions that we may have acquired at the cinema, that the Zulu warrior was not a suicidal fanatic, but a courageous, crafty and dexterous light infantryman, who skirmished from cover to cover with consummate skill. He was fit, agile and athletic and could handle his traditional weapons with great expertise. Neither were his traditional weapons his only resort. As discussed in *How Can Man Die Better*, as many as one man in four carried a firearm of some kind, albeit, in many cases, that these were smoothbore black-powder muskets.

More Fugitives Come In

From time to time the odd fugitive appeared from the south-east, only to cause disruption to the barricade-building as the men clustered around them to hear their news. Invariably, after a moment or two, the officers barked out commands to get the men back to work and then took over to debrief the man or men concerned for any information which might prove useful. A Natal Carbineer rode past the post in a terribly bedraggled condition, without boots, tunic or a weapon. He looked across at the post and rode on without speaking to anyone, no doubt in a state of acute shock.

Privates Hector Grant and William Johnson were two of the four rocket battery survivors. Both were 24th men and had been amongst the first to make contact with the enemy. The battery had been shot to pieces in front of the conical koppie, Amatutshane, shortly before Durnford and his men fell back from the Qwabe Valley. The arrival of the Basutos and the Edendale Troop had brought a short breathing space, in which the Zulu skirmishers engaging the battery fell back to cover. This allowed the four hapless survivors to break clean in the direction of the camp. Poor Johnson had been abandoned on the open plain by Durnford, but somehow managed to scramble back to the Nyogane Donga on foot, where he found that the mounted troops were now making a stand. Here he managed to secure a horse, possibly the spare one being led by Durnford's orderly, earlier denied him, or possibly one belonging to a casualty. He and Grant, both of them badly traumatised by their near brush with death, fell back with Durnford's command and were amongst the crowd of frightened riders that immediately disappeared over the saddle. They must have been somewhere near Henderson at this time and probably rode back to the drift with the rallied elements of the native horse. Both said in their statements that they went via Rorke's Drift, but nobody at the mission remembered them, as undoubtedly they would have remembered fellow 24th men. Of course it was perfectly possible to go 'via Rorke's Drift' without going anywhere near the mission buildings, and this is clearly what they did, bearing away to the right once they had crossed the river. There was no need for them to give a warning to their regimental colleagues, as Henderson and his men were heading in that direction. Instead Grant and Johnson rode on down the Helpmekaar road, where in due course they would meet Captain Rainforth and G Company.

Next Corporal Doig and Trooper Shannon of the Natal Mounted Police came cantering through together, and were hailed by Trooper Harry Lugg,* a fellow policeman, and now a hospital patient. 'What, is it true?' Lugg asked. In reply he received the none too cheery answer, 'You will all be murdered.' The pair rode on. At some point in the proceedings, an unknown fugitive muttered an aside to Colour-Sergeant Bourne 'not a chance for you young feller'. There weren't many of them, but the string of arrivals and defections were undoubtedly having an unsettling effect on the native troops.

Next to go was Otto Witt, who came running down from the top of Shiyane with Chaplain Smith, to report that there was a large body of Zulus on the other side of the river. This was in fact the main body of the Undi Corps. The missionary was aghast at the damage already done to his house and furniture. Somebody calmed him down and explained the seriousness of the situation. When he had grasped the full extent of

---

* Born Oakhampton, 1859. A recent immigrant to South Africa, he had joined the NMP in Pietermaritzburg in May 1878.

the calamity, he declared that he had to go to Msinga immediately, in order to evacuate his family from the border area. Witt dashed off to saddle his horse. For some unknown reason he took Lieutenant Purvis with him, the NNC officer wounded at Sihayo's kraal, even though he was still in so serious a condition that he could barely stay in the saddle. Chaplain Smith decided that he ought to leave as well, but when he looked around for his horse was unable to find it. Perhaps unsurprisingly, he was unable to find his native groom either. With no other alternative left to him, Smith went off to fill a haversack with Boxer cartridges.

The Undi Corps

The Zulus now intent on ravaging the border district were the four regiments of the army reserve, known collectively as the Undi Corps. In all they may have amounted to 4,500–5,000 men. The 'horns of the buffalo' battle drill called for the younger, fitter regiments of the *impi*, those assigned to the left and right horns, to race rapidly around the enemy's flanks in a fast-moving double envelopment, and then crush him against the regiments of the chest. As ever, encirclement was the aim, annihilation the object. But, as any soldier knows, the maintenance of an unassigned reserve is essential in all phases of war; things can go wrong; attacks can stall; other enemy forces can unexpectedly appear. At such times the reserve will come into its own.

Traditionally, in a Zulu army of age-grouped regiments, it was the practice that the more mature *amabutho* would be assigned to the reserve. These were the veteran regiments, the men who had been through the mill on behalf of their monarch, and upon whom, in sign of his gratitude, the king had bestowed the right to marry. To betoken their married state, they wore the traditional *isicoco* head-ring. Shields of white boasted their elite standing. Amongst such men fearlessness was merely a norm. When a Zulu army attacked, it was commonly in a state of great excitement, bordering indeed on frenzy – whipped up by the spells of the witch doctors and the stimulus of the frequently narcotic local snuffs that most warriors carried in a small gourd around their neck. Often it could be extremely difficult for the senior indunas to control their *amabutho*; a Zulu attack was generally a one-shot option. In order for an army commander to have any influence at all over the course of a battle, it was crucial that the reserve regiments be kept under strict control. For this reason it was the practice to make the warriors of the reserve sit down with their backs to the action, until it was time to commit them. It was a sound and necessary control measure, for regardless of their age group all Zulu men sought glory in battle.

Isandlwana was out of the ordinary in that the British compromised the Zulu army as it lay concealed in the Ngwebeni Valley. Had this not been the case, the *impi* would have moved out early on Thursday morning, closed up to the camp as a pre-dawn preliminary move, and would then have launched the horns and chest in a fast moving first-light assault. As it turned out the attack had to be mounted at noon on Wednesday, across a lengthy approach of around five miles. In such a situation, it was not possible to leave the reserve sat with their backs to the enemy, for this would leave them well outside a practicable striking distance, and above all else the secret to committing a reserve decisively lies in timing the stroke well. Ntshingwayo kaMahole and Mavumengwana kaNdlela, the two co-commanders of the *impi*, understood this as well as Bonaparte understood it. Thus, whilst at first they held back the reserve in the approved fashion, this was merely to give the forward regiments time to clear the Ngwebeni Valley and shake out into battle formation. Once these regiments were formed and moving, it quickly became necessary to launch the reserve behind them. Only in this way could it be kept close enough to the action to play a meaningful role in the battle.

The four regiments concerned were the uThulwana, the uDloko, the iNdlondlo and the iNdluyengwe. In terms of status, rather than purely age, the uThulwana was the most senior regiment in the land. In western society it would have been branded a 'guard' regiment, for Cetshwayo himself had served in its ranks and it had spearheaded his uSuthu faction in the civil war that brought him to power. Inevitably some of the most powerful men in the kingdom were closely associated with the regiment. Since raising the much younger iNgobamakhosi regiment, 'the Humblers of Kings', Cetshwayo had plainly transferred some of his royal favour to his new *ibutho*. The two regiments had clashed with significant loss of life in January 1878, at the annual muster of the army for the so-called 'First Fruits' ceremony. Now the uThulwana and the iNgobamakhosi were mortal enemies and had to be kept apart. At least they had put their mutual antipathy into abeyance for the war against the British.

The men of the uThulwana were now fast approaching their mid-forties, and in most cases, due to the fondness of the Zulu male for his traditional sweet beer, were carrying a few pounds around their midriffs. But they were big, powerful men, and what they lacked in athleticism they made up for in experience and guile. Successful middle-aged married men they may have been, but they were still formidable warriors and bristled with the arrogance of a military elite. They may have numbered about 1,500 men. The iNdlondlo were a few years younger than the uThulwana, at roughly forty-one, and had been pretty much blistered on to the king's favourites in order to keep them up to strength. They still fought in their own companies, however, beside the men with whom they had grown up, so that to all intents and purposes they maintained a strong regimental identity of their own. They were around 900 strong.

The uDloko was the third senior regiment. These men were probably about thirty-nine or forty years of age. It too was a married regiment and like the uThulwana could also field about 1,500 men. The fourth and final regiment was a relatively junior one. The men of the iNdluyengwe were over a decade younger than those of the other regiments – probably something around twenty-nine to thirty-one. Certainly they were not yet married and carried predominantly black shields accordingly. Like all the younger *amabutho* they were in prime physical condition, lean, quick across the ground and strong in the fray. They seem to have been around 1,000 strong.

When they received permission from the army commanders to move, the regimental *izinduna* of the Undi Corps led their men off along the line of the Ngwebeni Stream, moving uphill to the plateau behind the Nyoni escarpment, via a wide re-entrant cut by the stream in the Mabaso Ridge. Once they were atop Mabaso they could see the impressive sight of the chest, 9,000 men or more, fanned out across the plateau and closing fast on the as yet invisible British camp at

Isandlwana. The leading regiment of the Undi Corps, almost certainly the iNdluyengwe, continued to trot uphill for the top of the Ngedla Heights and the Nqutu Plateau beyond. The others followed in their train. Soon the long regimental columns were moving west, behind the line of the Ngedla Heights, and quite invisible to anybody on the British side. After they had covered three or four miles, they swung to the south in order to re-cross the high ground and enter the battle area.

Now they could hear the unmistakeable tumult of a great fight. By the time they had swung down into the lower ground at the rear of Isandlwana, emerging from a valley within sight of Ncepheni Hill, the decisive phase of the battle had passed and the slaughter was in progress. Some 2½ miles back to the east, the 24th Regiment was now trapped in front of the mountain, under overpowering attack from the chest and horns. The native troops were scattered along the road to Rorke's Drift, whilst the European fugitives, a miscellany of police, gunners, mounted infantry, staff officers and volunteers, were scattered in flight along the line Isandlwana–Manzimyama Valley–Mpethe Hill–Sothondose's Drift. The warriors of the Undi Corps may have been wondering what had happened, but as they trotted back to the south-east, in the direction of the sounds of battle, it became clear that the British were running – that there had been a great victory. In the distance, elements of the right horn were harrying scattered bands of mounted men across the impossibly difficult terrain of Mpethe Hill. The iNdluyengwe swung the axis of advance in the direction of the Manzimyama Valley, and were then launched by their indunas towards Mpethe Hill, the rocky valley just to its west, and the Buffalo River beyond. By the time the uThulwana, the uDloko and the iNdlondlo regiments had descended from the hills, even the prospect of some peripheral excitement in pursuit of fleeing men had passed. They were too late.

Where was the battle? Where was the glory? How could they go home and brag to their fathers, their wives and their sons of their part in the great victory? What stories of daring did they have to tell? A terrible sense of frustration and disappointment settled over the warriors of the Undi Corps. They were simple men – by and large unable to appreciate the wider context of the war – unaware that the

British would be back, stronger than ever, and that there would be many more opportunities to exhibit their prowess in battle. The British had come and the British had been eaten up. The politically canny Cetshwayo knew better; that the Zulu nation was now locked in combat with a monolithic empire. But Cetshwayo was eighty miles away at Ulundi, in absolutely no position to control his military commanders. The reserve *amabutho* were angry, their warrior egos crushed. They may have blamed their leaders for steering them too wide, too slowly. And so it came about that Dabulamanzi kaMpande rallied the senior *izinduna* of the Undi Corps about him, to urge an attack on Natal. They were prominent and well known military men, yet so tenuous is our grasp on the Zulu side of this story, that with only two or three exceptions we know next to nothing of their identities.

Dabulamanzi was a royal prince, a son of King Mpande and half brother to Cetshwayo. Now about forty years of age, Dabulamanzi was not, as is often stated, in command of the Undi Corps, but of the uThulwana regiment only. Nonetheless, his royal status conveyed huge prestige and obliged the other regimental commanders to defer to him. Let us cross the river, he urged. Let us raid the farms and kraals in Natal. Dabulamanzi was not a local man; his own homestead was near Eshowe, over on the coastal strip. Even so, because it had been a major staging post for visiting European traders in the pre-war years, he had heard of Rorke's Drift. Let us attack and loot kwaJim, he urged. Doubtless the senior Zulu commanders had heard, via Sihayo's spies, that there was a small redcoat garrison at the drift. If anybody raised the king's prohibition against raiding the colony, the objection was swiftly brushed aside. The indunas began to nod their assent. What harm could come of it? And if the king was angered by such a raid, then his brother could shoulder the blame. Before long it had been agreed. The word was passed around the excited *amabutho*. Now they were men once more. One prominent figure we do know about was the regimental commander of the uDloko, Zibhebhu kaMapitha, a shrewd man with a great deal of political influence at the Zulu court. He was not prepared to jeopardise the king's favour. Pleading an injury, he excused himself from Prince Dabulamanzi's council of war and went quietly on his way.

The main body, the uThulwana, the uDloko and the iNdlondlo, wheeled to the west in their regimental columns and, keeping Ncepheni Hill on their right, began to jog-run the three miles down to the Buffalo River. They would hit it at a point mid-way between Sothondose's Drift and Rorke's Drift, roughly at its intersection with the Batshe Stream, where local knowledge told them the river would be fordable. The crossing point would bring them over the river only two miles east of Shiyane. For the garrison at the mission station, the clock was now ticking. The distances at issue were not great. The only time-consuming phase would be the river crossing; even so the *amabutho* had well tried drills with which to effect this, with only minimal delay.

The iNdluyengwe meanwhile had derived but little satisfaction from the slaughter of a few desperate and frightened riders. Had not the king told them they would know the soldiers by their red coats? There were no soldiers here. But again the local men spoke up. There were soldiers at kwaJim. Again, for proud and so far disappointed warriors, it was too tempting a target to resist. The regiment moved three-quarters of a mile upstream from Sothondose's Drift, to a point where the river rages through a narrow channel in the bedrock and, where local tradition would have it, the warriors crossed by means of long-jumping the gap. Having raced ahead of their elders to prosecute their pursuit of the fugitives, the men of the iNdluyengwe were down at their chosen crossing point rather more quickly than the senior regiments reached theirs.

The question of whether there were Martini-Henrys in use at Rorke's Drift, as Colour-Sergeant Bourne was to suggest some years later, is an interesting one. Bourne ought after all to have been able to recognise the sound. Only about fifty members of the 24th Regiment had been able to make it to the Manzimyama Valley. At the time several hundred warriors of the right horn were in hot pursuit, or were already some way down the Fugitives' Trail harassing the mounted men. The last handful of redcoats was cut down on the banks of the Manzimyama Stream, caught in a pincer between the warriors chasing them downhill and the warriors already ahead of them. Their rifles fell to the men who ran them to ground. Even so, these soldiers would have had barely a cartridge between them in these dying moments of the fight. There were then no 24th Regiment Martinis in the hands of the Undi Corps, three regiments of which were not at all concerned in the pursuit of the British.

The only regiment that had an opportunity to capture firearms was the faster-moving iNdluyengwe, and time and space considerations would suggest that even its men were late on the scene. They may have been able to acquire a few cavalry carbines, but literally a handful, and again would have been confronted with a great paucity of ammunition. There were different carbines in use with different units, but generally they tended to have the same breech design as the Martini-Henry rifle, and fired what was effectively the same cartridge loaded with a slightly smaller charge. It was perfectly possible to fire full-charge rifle cartridges through carbines of the same calibre, but only at the price of greatly increased recoil. In terms of both the noise at the point of discharge and the sound of a round flying overhead, carbines were all but indistinguishable from the rifle. Bourne may have heard a few of these weapons, but equally his remark about Martinis on Shiyane may simply be based on a flawed assumption. A handful of .450-inch cartridge cases have indeed been found over the years on Shiyane, but these can be accounted for by the presence of a few carbines as described above. Carbine variants of the Martini could certainly throw a round over the sort of distances at issue, but were much less accurate at such ranges due to their short barrels.

Down at the river the three senior *amabutho* used their customary technique for crossing fast-flowing water. This was much in the nature of a human bridge. First they fed man after man into the water, each anchored successively on his neighbour by means of linking arms. When there were two such strings of men across the river, perhaps six or seven yards apart, the regimental column then plunged into the water between them. Any men who lost their footing on the slippery sub-surface rocks, or were overpowered by the current, were washed against the human handrails and had the opportunity to recover themselves. One or two may have slipped through the safety net; they would have to rescue themselves at some point downstream or drown. The pause on the far bank was a good opportunity to take snuff and jeer at the companies still to cross. This was not an activity to be unduly rushed, since most Zulus were not strong swimmers, but given the scale of the undertaking – a river crossing by several thousand fighting men – the process was accomplished with impressive speed.

The first parties across dashed on ahead to harry the nearest settlements. Before long they had fired a number of kraals and put a deserted European farm to the torch. This was the Woodroffe farm,* located on the high ground above the Buffalo between Sothondose's Drift and Shiyane. Already there were scouting parties pushing up to the mission.

From the top of Shiyane, Chaplain George Smith and Otto Witt had been able to see the approach of the enemy clearly. Both recorded what they saw but, as Witt tends to be regarded as a generally questionable witness, it is Smith's account which is of greater relevance. He misuses the word 'company', for which 'regiment' has been substituted below to aid clarity. Some passages of poetic licence have been discarded:

> Three regiments of Zulus were formed upon the neck of land above the late camp, and marched towards Rorke's Drift: each regiment appeared to be from 1,000 to 1,500 strong. No. 1 Regiment (we will call it) marched on in advance in open order . . . They crossed the Buffalo River about four miles below Rorke's Drift [that is downriver of the ponts – not as the crow flies from the mission] just below where the river makes a bend, almost at right angles, between precipitous rocky sides, firing repeatedly into every cave, bush and crevice that might have afforded shelter for refugees. Being satisfied with the result, so far, they came on to a small green hill, sat down and took snuff all round.
>
> Regiments 2 and 3 then followed the example of Number 1, keeping some distance apart. They also advanced in open order – after going through various exercises, dividing off (apparently) into hundreds, then into tens, wheeling and quickly reforming; they crossed the river just above the bend, repeatedly firing amongst the bushes and rocks on both sides. They remained a long time in

---

* Mr Woodroffe was away commanding border levies. He is believed to have been at or in the vicinity of Msinga.

the river, forming a line across it . . . to assist one another in fording the stream.

By the time they had gained the rising ground upon this side, and sat down to take snuff, up started ten men of Number 1, and ran on in advance up the valley, which lies between the high ground at Helpmekaar and the hills at the back of Rorke's Drift. In the meantime another party of Zulus, who must have crossed the river some miles lower down [the iNdluyengwe], had set a European house and a kafir [sic] kraal on fire, about four or five miles away at the back of Rorke's Drift.

Number 1 Regiment followed their advanced guard at an easy pace. Number 2 Regiment started off, bearing away to their left, apparently to join and support Number 1. Number 3 Regiment started off two men straight for Rorke's Drift, who ran as hard as they could, followed by ten others who took it more easily; and then came on the rest, headed and led by two very corpulent chiefs on horseback.

By the time a number of small raiding parties had broken away from their regiments to harry points further afield, something in the region of 4,500 warriors remained with the main bodies for the attack on Rorke's Drift. For a long time the two clergymen thought that they were looking at bodies of NNC troops. Their naïveté almost defies belief, but only when they realised that the two horsemen they had earlier taken for European officers were in fact blacks, did it all finally fall into place. Then they fled for the mission as fast as the rocky hillside beneath their feet would allow.

Desertion of the Levies

At around 4.20 p.m. there was an outbreak of firing beyond Shiyane. Clearly Henderson was in contact on the river. Colour-Sergeant Bourne quickly contracted his skirmish line and brought his men in at the double. Only a minute or two later, the Basutos and amaNgwane came galloping back around Shiyane. All well and good thought Chard, expecting that they would now turn their ponies loose and join the rest of his troops behind the barricades. It very quickly became clear, however, that phase two of his plan for the native horse was never going to be enacted. All 100 horsemen disappeared in a cloud of dust and pounding hooves in the direction of the Helpmekaar plateau. Only two men reined in at the mission. As Bob Hall clattered to a halt on the road, he shouted, 'Here they come, black as hell and thick as grass!' Henderson called across the barricade to Chard that his men had refused orders. The pair of them then rode into the distance to reload their carbines, but did not immediately turn tail and follow the troopers.

This sudden and dramatic turn of events was altogether too much for Stevenson's NNC; in a trice they were over the barricades and streaming away into the countryside. Stevenson called out that he would ride after them to bring them back. He vaulted the barricade to recover his tethered horse and then galloped away behind them. Clearly he had kept a saddled horse close at hand all this time. Who can tell just how much this insurance policy may in itself have unsettled his men. Corporal Bill Anderson, one of Stevenson's three NCOs, also decided that it was time to go and jumped over the barricade behind his men. Little had been expected of the levies to begin with, for ultimately this was not their war. But at the sight of such arrant cowardice amongst the NNC Europeans, men who billed themselves as fellow Britons, the men of B Company erupted with disgust and resentment. A number of shots were fired. The officers bellowed commands of restraint, but it was already too late for Corporal Anderson who had been hit in the head and had fallen dead in the scrub beyond the north wall. Neither Chard, nor any of the other officers, ever formally reported this occurrence. Indeed, Chaplain Smith would even concoct a story describing how Anderson was killed early on by enemy fire. Private Fred Hitch of B Company was the only person to admit directly in one of his later accounts of the battle to having been one of the men who opened fire at this point. Whilst there was little sympathy for Anderson, there could be no denying that murder had been committed. But his offence was a capital one and his guilt plain for all to see. This was soldiers' justice at the rough end; B Company had tried and convicted Anderson in the time it took to raise a rifle to the shoulder. For the moment there was absolutely no time and precious little inclination to deal in recriminations.

Fred Hitch Opens the Battle

Bromhead shouted the order to stand to, whilst Chard paused to contemplate the dramatically different situation now confronting him. Where he had once counted on having something around 650 men to hold the mission, he now had only 154, of whom more than twenty were *hors de combat* in the hospital. The perimeter was perhaps 300 yards in circumference, a man every two yards at best. With the troops stood to at the barricades, Chard could see only too clearly that his line of defence was now far too extended for a force of such size. There was a particular problem on the eastern side of the perimeter, where he had intended that the cattle kraal would be held by Stevenson's levies. He quickly redeployed a handful of men to close the gap. Next he gathered a few more men in front of the storehouse and told them to begin out-loading biscuit boxes from the building. Then, calling Commissary Dunne and Mr Byrne to his side, he quickly explained what he wanted done. They were to throw up a new wall, bisecting the perimeter between the front corner of the storehouse and the north wall. This would create a three-sided compound in front of the storehouse which would serve as the garrison's inner keep, an area to which it could fall back if the pressure on the full length perimeter became too intense. It was quick and incisive thinking for which Chard deserves a great deal of credit. Without it the post might well have fallen. Leaving the work party to labour on what he called in his formal report his 'retrenchment' barricade, Chard dashed across to join Bromhead and Dalton in the yard between the buildings, from where they were peering anxiously over the south wall.

In the meantime Bromhead had sent Private Fred Hitch up onto the roof of the hospital to report what he could see. The final act of preparation for the onset of the enemy occurred when the order to 'fix bayonets' rang out. It was now half past four in the afternoon; there were two and a half hours of broad daylight remaining, and perhaps twenty-five minutes of twilight. Certainly by 7.45 p.m. it would be fully dark. Rorke's Drift had been successfully fortified in a little under an hour and a half. The defenders had needed every available minute, but even so there was still a two-yard gap in the north wall, just in front of the hospital. It was now that somebody placed the plank across it.

From his perch on the roof of the hospital, Private Hitch shouted down to Bromhead that the enemy were in sight. For a few minutes he was the only man at the post who could see the stalking *impi*. The first hostile acts of the battle, a series of pot-shots at long range, were directed at the twenty-two-year-old Londoner:

> I could see that [the] Zulus had got as near to us as they could without us seeing them. I told Mr Bromhead that they were at the other side of the rise and was [*sic*] extending for attack. Mr Bromhead asked me how many I thought there were. I told him that I thought [they] numbered from 4–6,000 [he was mistaken – the main body of the *impi* was not yet up]. A voice from below [said,] 'Is that all? We can manage that lot very well – for a few seconds!'* ... I stayed on the roof of the house watching the black mass extending into their fighting line [whilst at] the same time a number of them [were] creeping along under the rocks and took up cover in the caves, and keep [*sic* – kept] trying to dismount me from the top of the house. Their direction was good but their elevation bad. A few minutes later one appeared on the top of the mountain. From the other side he could see us in the laager plain enough to count us. I put myself in a laying position but my shot fell short of him. He then moved steadily to the right and signalled with his arm. The main body at once began to advance. I told Mr Bromhead that they would be all round us in a very short time.

Hitch fired three shots from the rooftop in all, before lowering himself down into the compound. He clicked his lunger bayonet onto the barrel of his Martini as he ran, and took post in front of the hospital. For a minute or two Lieutenant Henderson and Bob Hall fired on the enemy from the cover of some nearby scrub. When at last the Zulus began to move out of the dead ground to begin an assault on the south wall, the pair turned their horses and galloped away to safety.

---

* Hitch later identified this man as a Private Morris. There were two Private Morrises in B Company.

Spalding Catches On

Major Spalding did not tarry for long at Helpmekaar, and having attended to his business there turned again for Rorke's Drift. He soon caught up with Upcher and Rainforth. It was Russell Upcher who broke the news of the disaster to him. Now, at last, he was abreast of the crisis that had so suddenly descended upon the lines of communication. The column pushed on to Vermaak's Farm, where Spalding announced his intention to ride on ahead to scout the road and the wider situation. He took a mysterious 'Mr Dickson of the Buffalo Border Guard' with him, whom he must have picked up at Helpmekaar. Perhaps Dickson had come down as a messenger from No. 3 Column the previous day, or perhaps he had yet to muster with the rest of the BBG. Spalding also ordered the two mounted infantrymen riding with D and G Companies to accompany him who, although they are not named in his report, can only have been Privates Evans and Whelan. A little way down the road, perhaps understandably given their traumatised state, they slipped away when the major's back was turned.

Part Two

Thin Red Line of Heroes

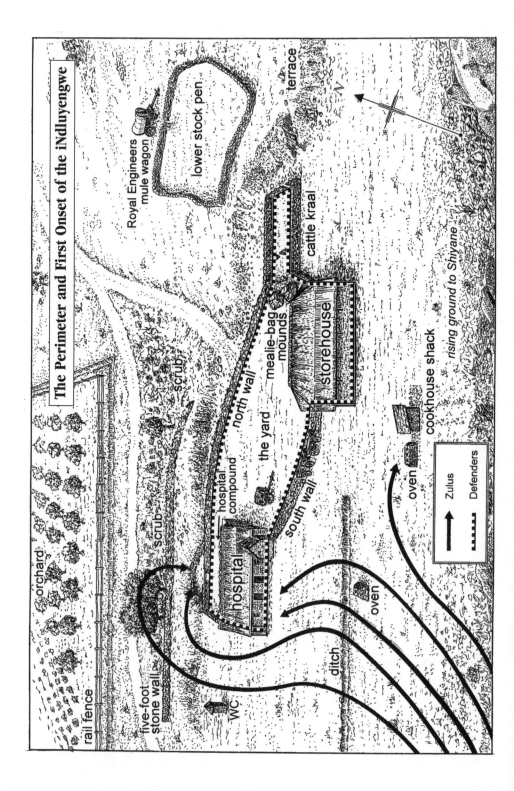

The Perimeter and First Onset of the iNdluyengwe

orchard

rail fence

five-foot stone wall

scrub

scrub

WC

ditch

oven

oven

cookhouse shack

rising ground to Shiyane

hospital

hospital compound

the yard

north wall

south wall

mealie-bag mounds

storehouse

cattle kraal

Royal Engineers mule wagon

lower stock pen

terrace

N

Zulus

Defenders

Chapter 3

At the Point of the Bayonet

Fighting by Daylight

The first wave of assault consisted of around 500–600 black-shielded warriors of the iNdluyengwe regiment. They broke from cover at around 700 yards, and began racing in on a forty-five-degree oblique for the hospital and the south wall. It quickly became obvious that the right wing of the assault would fall on the wagon and mealie-bag barricade, whilst the left wing would hit the western gable-end of the hospital, and lap around it to the strike the short western wall linking the front of the building to the terrace. Contrary to popular misapprehension, Rorke's Drift was not defended by synchronised volley firing: independent fire was permitted throughout; it was that sort of fight. The first shots rippled along the south wall at about 600 yards, far too great a range to be really telling. There cannot have been more than about thirty men along this stretch of barricade, including officers and NCOs, and for the time being they were the only men who could bring their weapons to bear. The iNdluyengwe dashed on, paying little or no heed to the shots falling amongst them. Here and there one of their number was hit a stunning kinetic blow and went reeling to the ground. At 400 yards the British fire started to exact a heavier toll. In response the warriors began to dart from cover to cover, but continued to close the distance. It is possible to load and fire the Martini-Henry every seven or eight seconds or so; hence the men on the south wall may have got off eight or nine rounds each, as the enemy came skirmishing towards them. Even this high rate of fire amounts to less than 300 rounds in all. It was nothing like enough to drive the iNdluyengwe to ground at long to medium range.

Private William Dunbar, a member of B Company, was a young soldier from Newport. He had been in the 24th for less than two years and had already undergone a meteoric rise and a dramatic fall. He was promoted to lance-corporal within seven months of enlisting and to full corporal only a month later. He must have caught the eye of his officers as an outstanding young soldier. After four months as a corporal, a period which coincided with the 2nd/24th's campaign service in the Amatolas, he committed some unknown offence for which he was court-martialled, sentenced to twenty-eight days' detention and reduced to the ranks. Famously, Dunbar is reputed to have shot eight or nine Zulus in as many successive shots. He is also known to have dropped an induna mounted on a grey mare. It is not entirely clear from the sources at which point in the fighting his long sequence of hits occurred, but Dunbar seems to have been shooting over the south wall at the time, and this first assault would seem to be the obvious moment for such excellent shooting to have caught the eye. Certainly it was in this first rush that he shot the induna from his horse. Dabulamanzi, who liked to ride, was almost certainly one of the two mounted indunas seen by the clergymen from the top of Shiyane, but on this occasion it was not the king's brother who fell to Dunbar's marksmanship.

As the Zulus closed to 200 yards the defenders were able to bring a few more weapons to bear. First the men in the hospital loopholes came into action, then a couple of riflemen defending the barricaded attic door in the gable-end of the storehouse, then the eight or nine men on the short western wall between the front of the hospital and the rocky terrace. Now, at last, the attackers were taking some heavy punishment. Corporal Attwood of the Army Service Corps was one of the men firing from the attic of the storehouse:

> I must tell you that I made an awful mess of one fellow. He was running towards the house in a slightly stooping position, when I let fly at him and struck him in the crown of the head, the effect of which was to blow the entire side of his face away. I must tell you that I was at an upper window, the only one in the barn [storehouse].

Fifty yards ... the men on the south wall and at the hospital loopholes, raced to eject their spent cases, thumbed a new round into the breech, and then loosed a last devastating salvo at point-blank range. It crashed into the iNdluyengwe like a hammer-stroke, all but sweeping away the leading wave of assault; probably something between twenty and thirty casualties fell as one, causing the shocked and stupefied survivors to hurl themselves headlong into the nearest cover. Thus was the right wing of the first Zulu assault shattered and defeated.

Some of the uninjured warriors sought shelter by crouching in the lee of the cookhouse outbuilding and its kilns, where they soon attracted the scorn of Commissary Dalton, already fighting mad with the heat of the moment. He is said to have clambered onto one of the wagons built into the south wall, to have taunted the enemy around the cookhouse to come on, and then, having no cartridges left in his pocket, to have hurled his foreign service helmet at them in disgust.* But the great majority of the Zulus on the right veered away from the south wall to the western side of the post, where they dodged around the hospital and joined up with the men of their left wing. This manoeuvre largely neutralised the fire of the men on the south wall; for the next hour they would have to content themselves with sniping at the warriors driven to ground at the back of the post, or with returning fire at the tell-tale puffs of smoke on the lower slopes of Shiyane, which indicated that Zulu riflemen had already ensconced themselves on the high ground.

The weight of fire brought to bear on the left flank of the iNdluyengwe assault was nothing like as heavy as the fire which defeated the right. Along the gable-end of the hospital, there were three rooms. Only the one in the centre had an external door opening onto the western side of the building, the side now under direct attack. None had a west-facing window. Probably the two corner rooms each had a single loophole in the gable-wall. At the south-western corner of the building, Harry Hook and Tom Cole also had a south-facing door and a second loophole to worry about. Clearly only one of them could fire through the gable to the west: to leave the other loophole undefended was to run the risk of a Zulu shoving the barrel of his musket through

---

* Reported by Captain Penn Symons, 2nd/24th, in an account he compiled by talking to the B Company men during the long wait at Rorke's Drift in the months after the battle.

the aperture and shooting one of them in the back. For the time being
it was Hook who was at the south-facing loophole, from where he was
engaging the warriors who had taken cover at the rear of the post. He
identified a rifleman firing from behind a termite mound as his next
target. He fired one shot and missed. Then he fired a second and
missed again. Eventually Hook got a third chance, after which the Zulu
appeared no more.

In the centre room of the row of three, two young B Company
privates, John Williams and Joseph Williams, both of them
Monmouthshire men, and the ambulatory patient Private William
Horrigan,* were also firing from gable-end loopholes. They may have
had one each, but certainly would have had at least two between them.
Probably then, only four or five rifles could be brought to bear from
the gable-end of the building. The western barricade was only about
six or seven yards in length and can only have had eight or nine men
manning it at most. In addition to the dearth of defensive fire on this
side, the rocky terrace and the general lie of the land enabled the
attackers to install themselves in good cover, very close to the barricade
in front of the hospital. In swinging their attack against this north-west
corner of the perimeter, the Zulus gave an immediate demonstration of
the instinctive nature of their fieldcraft.

The Fighting in Front of the Hospital

In all the tiny hospital compound, seven yards wide by twenty in
length, may have been manned by about twenty-five defenders.
Bromhead, Dalton and Bourne immediately dashed across from the
south wall to the front of the hospital, to meet the rush and direct the
close defence of the perimeter. As the men on the short western
barricade poured forth as rapid a rate of fire as they could manage, the
iNdluyengwe hurled themselves under the rocky terrace, or threw
themselves into the cover of the stone wall and the surrounding scrub.
Only a moment or two later, a couple of hundred warriors attacked the
corner of the hospital compound. Their assault was launched over a

---

* Horrigan was a twenty-nine year old from the 1st/24th. He had been in the army for over
fifteen years, having enlisted as a boy-soldier at the age of fourteen.

terribly short distance, less than twenty yards in many places, so that there was barely enough time for the defenders to get off a single well-aimed shot, before the enemy were up to the barricade flailing and jabbing with their assegais. The men of the 24th instinctively took half a pace backwards, just far enough to put themselves out of reach, and waited breathlessly for the first of their assailants to try and clamber over the barricade. Inevitably the warriors of the iNdluyengwe would become extremely vulnerable as they did so. Their principal defence would be sheer weight of numbers.

It was now that the Martini-Henry came into its own; never was there a better weapon for close-quarter fighting. The rifle itself was over four feet long, whilst the 'lunger' bayonet added a further twenty-two inches to the overall reach of the weapon. This outclassed the iNdluyengwe's short-shafted stabbing assegai, known in Zulu as the *iklwa*, by a length. It took only a one-second respite in the close combat to drop the lever, thus ejecting the spent round and exposing the empty breech. Then, when a man next had two or three seconds to spare, he could reach for a cartridge and thumb it home. Another spare second and he could snap the lever back up, thus closing the breech and cocking the weapon ready to fire. At no point in this process was it necessary to drop the point of the bayonet from a braced 'on guard' fighting position; the motions of the load could be carried out with the right hand only, leaving the left hand free to keep the weapon steady and levelled in front.

Still at their freshest, confident in the inevitability of their victory, and crazed with adrenalin, few of the Zulus thought twice about attempting to scale the barricade. Then the terrible bayonet points came jabbing forward. Where a warrior was caught off balance, or was lunged at from an unexpected direction, the blade went on to skewer flesh and bone. Even lunges that missed their mark could send a man tumbling backwards as he took hasty evasive action. The one advantage the Zulus had was their shields. If they kept their balance and covered up well, they might be able to clamber into the compound and so begin the slaughter of their enemies. But, whilst a cowhide shield might readily deflect all but the straightest, hardest, and most brutal of bayonet thrusts, it provided absolutely no defence against a heavy calibre bullet, and behind the line of jabbing, lunging enlisted men were Mr Dalton, a dead-eyed shot with a Martini, Mr Bromhead, no slouch as a marksman either, and young Frank Bourne, as good a shot as the two officers. There were other marksmen too. Although it was stretched to the limit, this fragile double line of defence somehow held its ground. The iNdluyengwe fell back a few yards. In a trice the men of the 24th had slipped a cartridge into the breech, had stepped back up to the barricade and were scanning for targets once more. A few more warriors fell to their fire. In a few places hands reached up from the foot of the barricade to grab at the rifle barrels above. Although the odd tussle took place for control of a weapon, it was the only the work of a second or two for a near neighbour to thumb a cartridge home and blast the writhing, grappling Zulu to eternity.

With scarcely a pause the Zulus came on again, more determined and more frenzied than before, fresh warriors taking the place of the fallen and the winded. Again a last moment fusillade was discharged at point-blank range, exacting a heavy toll. Then the cutting and slashing across the barricade began all over again. One of the Army Hospital Corps corporals (it is not clear whether it was Miller or McMahon) had acquired a rifle and joined in the defence of the north wall. As he was fighting to his front, a Zulu grabbed the barrel of his weapon, yanked him off balance and raised a stabbing assegai to finish him. Before he could strike his blow, Dalton shot the man dead. Both Bromhead and Dalton involved themselves in the very thick of the fray at this juncture and set an inspirational example. Any early hesitancy amongst the young soldiers, arising from the seriousness of their predicament, the enemy's overwhelming numbers, or the ferocity of their onset, had soon evaporated; already the red-coated soldiers were fighting like demons. The first and most crucial psychological battle had been won; B Company was not going to panic or fall apart in terror. Fred Hitch, a fearless and determined young man if ever there was one, positioned himself beside the gap in the barricade with only the plank to protect him.

In the room at the left rear corner of the hospital, Private Tom Cole suddenly declared that he was going outside to fight in the open. He pulled back the internal door and slipped out though the front rooms of the building to the veranda. Harry Hook cannot have been pleased at his departure as he now had two loopholes to worry about, and at any given moment one or the other would be left unguarded. The only patient in Hook's corner room was the isiGqoza Zulu of 1st/3rd NNC, but in the room next door there were nine patients, some of them immobile bed-cases, and some firing from loopholes.

Somehow the iNdluyengwe were again thrown back by the twenty-five stalwarts fighting in front of the hospital. By now a number of Zulu riflemen had wormed their way into fire positions close to the north wall. Every so often they would leap to their feet and fire over the edge of the terrace or the top of the stone wall. They were not the best of shots to begin with, and they were forced by the formidable nature of the return fire to snap-shoot virtually without aiming. Nonetheless, many of them succeeded in discharging a bullet or an improvised slug in the general direction of the barricade, often at about head height or slightly over. There was a good deal of lead in the air, which inevitably was deeply disconcerting to the heavily outnumbered men in the hospital compound. In response to the Zulu fire, the soldiers of the 24th tried to keep as low as they could, half-crouching behind the mealie-bags as they waited for the next available opportunity to get off a snap-shot of their own. There was no phalanx of black flesh to fire at and there were no sitting ducks, as perhaps is sometimes imagined; in between rushes the warriors dropped back into the scrub or the dead ground below the terrace, or sought cover behind the stone wall. At such times they presented only fleeting and testing targets. With the British popping their heads up only very briefly, many of the rounds they fired struck harmlessly into the ground, or sent slivers of rock flying from the stone wall.

Whilst these short but furious exchanges of fire were in progress, a new batch of warriors would come infiltrating in on their hands and knees, keeping low in good cover, until they were close enough to mount an assault. At the bellowed commands of their indunas, they would come surging out of cover, compelling the men in the hospital compound to brace themselves once more for a renewed bout of hand-to-hand fighting.

The Fate of 'Old King' Cole

One of Harry Hook's accounts of the battle can be taken to imply that Private Tom Cole was killed almost immediately after he left the building. This is the interpretation that historians have most commonly followed, but there is no way that Hook could have been an eyewitness to what happened to Cole. Fred Hitch, on the other hand, whose account clearly states that he was fighting near Cole and saw him killed, places the event much later in the fight. In support of this, Corporal Lyons's account records that he turned around for a moment and saw Cole killed to his rear; unfortunately this recounting of the incident lacks a definitive context with which to fix Lyons himself at that precise moment. For the first ninety minutes of the battle, however, Lyons was fighting on the south wall and could not have seen anything of the fight in front of the hospital. It seems clear then that Hook has been taken too literally and that Cole was not in fact killed immediately, but at some time after 6.00 p.m., of which more later. It has also been repeatedly suggested that Cole left the hospital out of a sense of claustrophobia or something similar. Again there is nothing in the sources to support such an interpretation – Hook does not say this – rather he recounts merely that Cole said he was going outside. It would seem much more likely that he did so in order to seek a more active role in the defence, as the enemy had not as yet made a serious attempt to force their way into the hospital. Nor would they, so long as the hospital compound was in British hands. Tom Cole was probably fighting mad and frustrated by the difficulty of engaging the enemy from the highly limited arcs of a loophole.

The Rest of the Impi Enters the Fray

For about twenty-five minutes the iNdluyengwe sustained the assault at the north-west corner alone. Then, at around 5.00 p.m., the great mass of the Undi Corps came into sight, attacked across the same ground as their vanguard regiment, and threw themselves into a sustained and terrifying assault on the north wall. Again we must not imagine that all the men that Dabulamanzi could field hurled themselves against the barricade simultaneously. Apart from anything else there were simply too many of them. They could fight only across the extent of the barricade, one man at a time for each yard of frontage, though each of them might have had three or four others echeloned behind him. In addition the warriors continued to avoid areas where there was little or no cover. For the time being the fighting raged around the line of the north wall, from the hospital compound on the left, to the point on the right at which Chard's new retrenchment barricade now bisected the yard. The melee was constrained between these identifiable left and right hand boundaries, because they roughly coincided with the belt of scrub in front of the north wall. Again, the stone wall running through the bushes allowed hundreds of men to shelter safely in its lee, and similarly played a crucial role in shaping the battle.

So it was that this phase of the fight was conducted over a frontage of sixty to seventy yards of barricade in all. The Zulus came on in rushes of three or four hundred men at a time, whilst around sixty of the defenders tried to keep them out of the post at the point of the bayonet. The Zulu reserves held themselves ready, crouched down in the brush and the orchard. The stretch of wall to the right of the retrenchment barricade commanded much more open fields of fire. Not unnaturally the Zulus avoided this area, enabling the defenders holding the north side of the cattle kraal and the length of the north wall in front of the storehouse to snipe across the road at the warriors infesting the orchard. Inevitably, as the fighting increased in intensity, the defenders fighting at close quarters around the hospital and in the yard occasionally left fleeting gaps in their line. In a trice a Zulu would be up and over the barricade at that point, only to be shot down by one of the officers or NCOs fighting in echelon behind the enlisted men. The noise now was tumultuous, as the uThulwana gave full vent to their famous 'uSuthu!' battle cry.

Somehow the assault was thrown back – but only across the few yards separating the north wall from the nearest cover. Then there would be another short-lived but furious exchange of close-range fire, only for more Zulus to come charging out of cover a few minutes later. Already there was a belt of corpses and wounded men in front of the barricade, which the attackers stepped on or over, in their attempts to slash at the defenders above. The rocky terrace proved critical: the stretch of barricade shielding the yard was raised a significant height above ground level and, whilst nobody could afford a lapse in concentration, here at least the perimeter was proving relatively secure.

Behind the fighting men, Chaplain George Smith had put his earlier faintheartedness behind him; he was now circling the perimeter with a haversack of cartridges, replenishing the firers where the opportunity presented itself, and sternly reproving any blasphemies which caught his ear. In his long black vestment and with his great chest-length beard, he looked for all the world like some Old Testament prophet, the very epitome of the church militant.

Sergeant George Mabin was a staff clerk who ordinarily worked for Major Spalding. Now he was wielding a Martini-Henry with everybody else. In common with many of the other men on the barricades, this was his first time in action:

> The first man I ever killed in my life was a big Zulu, carrying an assegai and shield, and as he advanced he took cover behind anything that presented itself. He dropped behind a rock prior to making another rush, when I covered the rock with my rifle, and as he rose to come on again I pulled the trigger, and he leaped at least five feet in the air and dropped dead.

The pressure continued to be worst in front of the hospital, where the grade of the terrace was gentle and offered the defenders none of the advantages enjoyed by the men fighting to their right. Here the British were so stretched that the Zulus were able to claw their way over the barricade in threes and fours at a time. Such groups were particularly dangerous. Killing them before they could run amok was both time-consuming and tiring, and physical exhaustion could be a deadly enemy in such circumstances. The braver a man was – the more he was to the forefront with his bayonet – the more tired he became. Whilst the worst of the day's heat had passed, the sun was still beating inexorably down upon the battlefield, so that everybody was sweating profusely. Here and there a few of the bravehearts had been compelled to take three or four paces back from the barricade to recover their breath momentarily. Then after a respite of only a few seconds, they would hurl themselves forward again. But men cannot keep up such a struggle indefinitely. Dehydration sets in quickly in so extreme a situation, magnifying the punishing effect of such physical exertion. For the time being it mattered not; there was no time for anything save wielding the bayonet, and adrenalin served to carry the men in front of the hospital through all the immediate physical barriers.

During this stage of the fighting Bromhead noticed one young induna in particular. He led and survived one unsuccessful charge against the hospital compound. Then he led another. Again he survived. But he was too determined for his own good; at the third attempt he was shot down and killed.

Fred Hitch was still fighting in defence of the hospital compound and soon became involved in a life-or-death tussle:

> They pushed on right up to us and not only got up to the laager but got in with us . . . during that struggle there was a fine big Zulu, see [sic] me shoot his mate down. He sprang forward dropping his rifle and assegais, seizing hold of the bayonet, thinking to disarm me. He pulled and tried hard to get the rifle from me but I had a firm hold of the small of the butt of my rifle with my left hand. My cartridges [were] on the top of the mealie-bags which enabled me to load my rifle and shoot the poor wretch whilst holding on to his grasp. For some minutes they dropped back into the garden which served [as] a great protection for them. Had it not been for the garden and dead wall they could not have prolonged the engagement for thirteen hours as they did.

The fighting in between rushes was much in the nature of a firefight, a shoot-out conducted at terrifyingly close range. The effect of such fighting on men's nerves is not to be underestimated; in such a scenario five minutes can feel like a lifetime. Each minute that one remains unharmed serves only to emphasise the apparent inevitability of eventual death or maiming. As had been the case at Isandlwana, British firepower was qualitatively but not quantitatively superior. The skill at arms of the 24th was of the highest order; they shot well and they handled their weapons quickly and slickly. The outmatched Zulu riflemen divided into the quick and the dead. The difficulty for the British was that there were altogether too many of them. Even shooting one of them dead did not preclude his weapon being picked up and used by somebody else.

In addition to the heavy short-range fire emanating from the brush in front of the north wall, there were also large numbers of Zulu riflemen on the lower slopes of Shiyane, who were firing down on the mission at a range of about 350 yards. By the standards of trained soldiers their fire was pitifully inaccurate, for few Zulus understood the sighting systems of their weapons or the principles of marksmanship. But, ultimately, a great number of loosely-directed rounds fired into a heavily populated confined space can pose just as great a threat as a smaller quantity of rounds fired by sharpshooters at point targets. The effect can be much the same. The men manning the north wall in the open yard between the two buildings may have enjoyed the twin advantages of the rocky terrace and the barricade in fighting to their front at close quarters, but their backs were completely exposed to the plunging fire from Shiyane. Already there were rounds thudding into the mealie-bags around them, or kicking up spurts of dust in the yard behind their legs. Undoubtedly some of the rounds fired from Shiyane would also have struck home amongst the Zulus in front of the north wall. Dabulamanzi could afford a few such casualties. The British could not.

In his 1880 report to the Queen, which is reproduced in full in Appendix 5, John Chard described the fighting along the north wall as follows:

> A series of desperate assaults was made on the hospital, and extending from the hospital, as far as the bush reached; but each was most splendidly met and repulsed by our men, with the bayonet. Each time as the attack was repulsed by us, the Zulus close to us, seemed to vanish in the bush, those some little distance off keeping up a fire all the time. Then as if moved by a single impulse, they rose up in the bush as thick as possible, rushing madly up to the wall, (some of them being already close to it), seizing where they could, the muzzles of our men's rifles, or their bayonets, and attempting to use their assegais, and to get over the wall. A rapid rattle of fire from our rifles, stabs with the

bayonet, and in a few moments the Zulus were driven back, disappearing in the bush as before, and keeping up their fire. A brief interval and the attack would be again made, and repulsed in the same manner. Over and over again this happened, our men behaving with the greatest coolness and gallantry.

Passing up and down the line, and generally to be found where the fighting was fiercest, Commissary Dalton continued to give distinguished service, both in terms of leadership and in terms of his personal skill at arms. Chard remarked that a Zulu seemed to fall each time he raised his rifle. But regardless of the apparently heavy Zulu losses, the sequence of charge, melee, repulse and firefight seemed to rotate endlessly round. Mercifully, for the time being at least, the pressure was restricted to the north wall. Chard very much doubted that he would be able to hold both walls against heavy simultaneous assault. Yet surely, sooner or later, the Zulu commanders would try to effect such a pincer. Chard's retrenchment barricade, constructed from biscuit boxes stacked two high, was now complete. He would dearly have loved to have occupied it, and to have been able to abandon the hospital compound and the yard, for such a step would reduce the over-extended perimeter significantly, but this would be to leave the men in the hospital in the lurch, and Chard was obliged to discount the proposal except as a measure of last resort. Ultimately it was the only trump card he had in his hand and for the time being he refrained from playing it.

In the meantime, the section on the south wall did their best to suppress the Zulu riflemen on Shiyane, under the direction of two of Bromhead's NCOs, Corporal John Lyons and Corporal William Allen, both of them good shots in their own right. Chard's wagon driver had been cowering at the back of one of the small caves on the hillside for some time. He was mortified when two or three Zulus took up position in the mouth of his hiding place and began firing down at the mission. All he could do was huddle himself into a ball in the shadows at the back of the cave and hope for the best. After a while one of the Zulus came reeling back into the gloom, dead, amply demonstrating the quality of the marksmanship from the south wall.

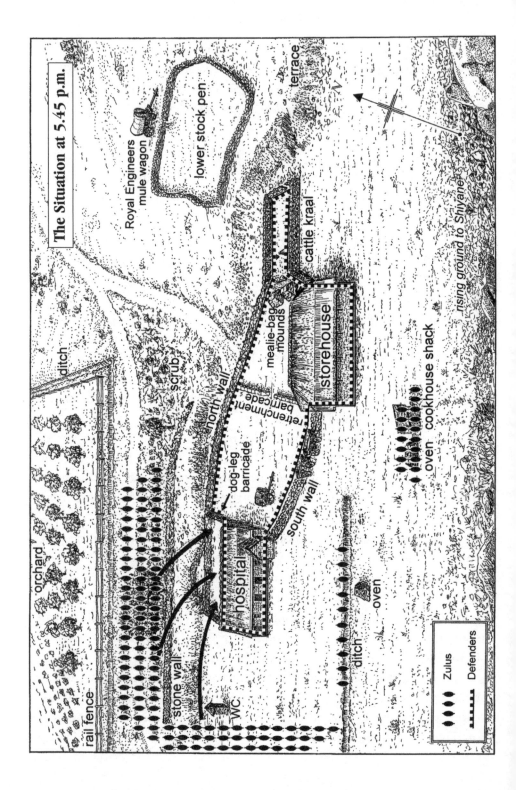

The Situation at 5.45 p.m.

orchard

rail fence

ditch

scrub

Royal Engineers mule wagon

lower stock pen

north wall

dog-leg barricade

retrenchment barricade

mealie-bag mounds

cattle kraal

terrace

stone wall

WC

hospital

south wall

storehouse

oven

ditch

oven

cookhouse shack

rising ground to Shiyane

Zulus

Defenders

Loss of the Hospital Compound

For a further thirty minutes or so after the main body of the *impi* had come up, Bromhead and Bourne continued to provide sterling leadership in front of the hospital. But by 5.30 p.m. it had become distinctly dangerous to lean over the barricade or even to show oneself above it, due to the heavy short-range fire from the terrace and the stone wall. A private soldier of the 24th was shot through the left shoulder, excused himself from the fighting and went in through the front door of the hospital to get somebody to look at his injury. He walked through the Witts' living area to the smaller rooms at the back, where he asked Harry Hook for help. Hook quickly dressed the wound as best he could and then returned to his loopholes. The wounded man went through into the room next door, the ward with nine patients, took up a place at one of the loopholes, and continued firing.

At the front of the building the defenders were slowly but surely losing control of the barricade. Chard found a few men and hastily threw up a short 'dog-leg' barricade across the gap between the north wall and the near corner of the hospital. Possibly because there was an insufficient quantity of defence stores close at hand, there was a gap in the barricade nearest the veranda. The new barricade enabled Bromhead and his men to fall back to its shelter, and to sweep the veranda and the hospital compound with fire. But the dog-leg also created a particularly dangerous corner at the point where it met the north wall. The Zulus were able to crawl along the line of the abandoned stretch of barricade and then leap up suddenly to attack the men manning the corner. It was far too dangerous for the defenders to lean over the mealie-bags to shoot at them, as they crept along the line of the terrace on their hands and knees.

Now that the hospital compound had effectively been abandoned and there was nobody holding the original line of defence in front of the veranda, the Zulus were able to come forward to the barricade and begin to break it down. Before long some of the topmost mealie-bags had been pushed to the ground, so that weak points were beginning to appear. A few Zulus leapt through the low gaps into the compound, only to find themselves cruelly exposed and quickly shot down. Soon a number of Zulu riflemen had occupied the lee-side of the north wall and busied themselves with snap-shooting at Bromhead and the men on the dog-leg barricade at impossibly close ranges. The abandonment of the hospital compound had served, however, to generate a small reserve of perhaps a dozen or fifteen men. Bromhead instructed them to load and prepare to charge. Then, with a roar of encouragement, he and Bourne led them through the gap in the new barricade, and charged fearlessly back into the hospital compound. They rushed up to the abandoned stretch of wall, delivered a short-range fusillade at the most troublesome warriors, and then on Bromhead's command quickly fell back to the dog-leg barricade. They repeated the exercise every few minutes to prevent the enemy getting too firm a hold on the lost ground. At length, a big rush came in and swamped the defences, perhaps two or three dozen warriors scaling the north wall together. Bromhead and his men loaded and fired as fast as they could and dropped a good many of them in the open area in front of the hospital, but a number got onto the veranda and rushed into the furthermost corner to take cover. The doors to the front rooms were well covered by fire from the dog-leg barricade, and so long as this remained the case it would be impossible for the Zulus to break into the front of the building.

At the now occupied end of the veranda, there was an open-sided utility room, literally just around the corner from the dog-leg barricade. This put the enemy party sheltering there less than six or seven yards from Bromhead's men. Doubtless two or three of them had firearms and took it in turns to risk a snapshot at point-blank range; probably only the muzzle of the weapon and a hand appeared around the side of the veranda. Such a fire, albeit largely unaimed, was completely intolerable and Bromhead immediately prepared for another charge. With a whoop and a yell, he and his men were off once again. Whilst some men broke to the right to cover the barricade, others charged around the corner and shot or stabbed all the Zulus skulking there. No doubt Bromhead led from the front as usual. It was blood-curdling stuff, but the defenders were desperate, were raging with adrenalin, and had little time to worry about the risks they were taking. By dint of his willingness to take aggressive offensive action, Bromhead had succeeded in restoring the situation around the hospital and in effecting a stalemate. And stalemate would do just fine; for the British it was akin to victory. His job done in this sector, Bromhead moved into the yard to encourage the other members of his company. At about this time, Corporal Carl Scammell of the NNC was shot in the shoulder and was helped to the storehouse veranda for treatment.

The Zulus Extend Their Attack Further East

Frustrated by the inability of their warriors to make a decisive breakthrough at the hospital compound, and the impossibly high barricade along the steep-sided central stretch of the terrace, the indunas swung a heavy thrust against the front of the storehouse compound. The blow fell on the point at which the fork in the road approached the mission, and the grade of the terrace was insignificant, a particularly vulnerable point much like the gentle slope in front of the hospital. This was the area that the Zulus had avoided earlier due to the absence of cover. Because of the pressure further along the line to their left, the defenders of this sector were stretched quite thinly. The sudden onslaught from the scrub and the orchard gave Chard a fright. For a moment or two it looked as if the Zulus were about to break in. He dashed across to the threatened stretch of barricade to participate in its defence. Two or three 24th men went with him, emptying their Martinis into the howling mob on the other side of the mealie bags, as they ran up to line the wall. In a trice Bromhead and two or three more men were alongside them, loosing a few more lethal shots into the crowd, and swinging their bayonets at the most ardent attackers. The assault intensified still further over the next few minutes, subjecting the defenders to the most severe pressure, but Bromhead's men aimed straight and true and again the line was held.

Withdrawal to the Retrenchment Barricade

The sudden assault on the storehouse compound had been such a close scrape that Chard finally felt obliged to order a withdrawal to the retrenchment barricade. It would be tough on the men defending the hospital, because the front of the building would be blind to the rest of the garrison and could be assaulted with relative impunity. But Chard felt that he now had no other option. Unless he contracted his over-extended perimeter and concentrated the defenders, he would run the risk of losing everything. The integrity of the storehouse compound, his keep, was crucial, and he had just come perilously close to losing control of it. He would sweep the abandoned yard with fire from the retrenchment barricade, and generally do the best that he could to support the hospital, but in essence it was now fated to become a British island in a Zulu sea.

Chard dashed around the principal leadership figures to advise them of his intent and then went into the yard with Bromhead to supervise as orderly a withdrawal as possible. The men on the dog-leg barricade were furthest away from sanctuary and would have been the first to fall back. They formed a line across the yard and walked slowly backwards to the retrenchment, peeling back the men on the barricades either side of them as they went. If the Zulus realised what was happening, they found themselves largely powerless to harass or disrupt the operation, which was conducted with the aid of plenty of suppressive fire. In not much more than a minute the last few men were filing back through the narrow gaps Walter Dunne had left in the biscuit box wall.

It was now 6.00 p.m. At least many of the defenders were now screened from the riflemen on Shiyane by the storehouse. Thus far the fighting had lasted ninety minutes; there was still another hour to go before sunset. Many men had been cut or grazed, but casualties up to this point had been remarkably light. In between treating one or two more badly injured men on the veranda of the storehouse, Doctor Reynolds made occasional forays to the barricade to assist and diagnose the newly wounded at the point of injury. In stark contrast to the relatively light British casualties, the Zulus had already taken some dreadful punishment. Nobody was quite sure what the extent of their loss might be. Certainly they had scores of dead, for there were a great many corpses in plain view. Even so, the ferocity of their so far largely fruitless waves of attack remained unabated. Unfortunately for the British, there was every danger that the worm might soon turn; more than thirty of their number were now stranded outside the new perimeter. Occasionally a face would appear in the head-high window in the eastern gable-end of the hospital; this looked out across the yard, now an empty no-man's-land, at the retrenchment barricade. Above the tumult and the firing, the defenders could hear a voice crying out for ammunition. It was an ominous sign.

At some point Chard realised he had erred badly in the course of the withdrawal. In a protracted fight for life a man needs only two military commodities – both are vital – one is ammunition and the other is water. There was still plenty of reserve ammunition on the storehouse veranda, but the water cart had been left outside the new perimeter. It was stranded in no-man's-land, on the far side of the yard, not far from the gable-end of the hospital.

Traditionally many of the British gunshot casualties are attributed to the plunging fire into the yard from the slopes of Shiyane. Often they are cited as the trigger for the abandonment of the yard. But Chard is emphatic in his more detailed account of 1880 that the cause was the heart-stopping assault on the north wall just in front of the storehouse. Close analysis of the sources will show that most of the more notable gunshot casualties occurred in the next ninety minutes and were therefore inflicted not by the plunging long-range fire, but by the short-range fire now poured into the storehouse compound from the cover of the abandoned outer barricades. Commissary Dalton, Corporal Lyons, Corporal Allen, and Privates Hitch, Fagan, Nicholas and Cole all seem to have been uninjured at the time Chard ordered the withdrawal to the retrenchment barricade. The plunging fire had been alarming and seemed to threaten significant losses, but ultimately its bark seems to have been a whole lot worse than its bite. Few casualties can be specifically attributed to it and the withdrawal to the retrenchment barricade largely neutralised it.

Not long after the withdrawal, Doctor James Henry Reynolds did a remarkable thing. In response to the cries for ammunition from the hospital, he filled his arms with packets of cartridges, slipped out through one of the narrow gaps in the biscuit box wall, and dashed across the abandoned yard to the high window in the gable-end. The fire from the retrenchment barricade meant that the Zulus had been unable to occupy the yard, but they were certainly crouched either side of it, in the lee of both the north and the south walls, and there would also have been a good many warriors on the veranda of the hospital, attacking the doors at the front. This placed them not more than twenty yards from Reynolds, as he was passing ammunition up to the Joneses. Fortunately the Zulus were blind-sided at the front of the building and were oblivious to his presence. At least one of the warriors crouched behind the south wall had the doctor in plain view however; a round struck Reynold's helmet without, miraculously, doing him any harm. He may have had a duty of care to his patients, but this heroic deed was a long way above and beyond its call. In a trice Reynolds was on his way back. One suspects that he would have received a cheer from the men on the barricade, but a damned good telling off from Chard and Bromhead who needed a doctor a whole lot more than they needed a hero. Heroic, though, it undoubtedly was.

Chard's batman, Driver Robson, had found himself a good vantage point on the north side of the cattle kraal. From there he could look down at the gateway of the stock pen, just beyond which was the sappers' wagon. As a good batman should, he was determined to keep an eye on his master's kit. A few Zulus had by now crossed the road, but if any of them had designs on looting Chard's possessions, then they had a challenge on their hands. Robson fired on any Zulu impertinent enough to go anywhere near the wagon.

Not long after the abandonment of the yard, the garrison suffered a bitter blow. Another Zulu rush had come charging out of the scrub and the orchard. As usual Dalton was in the thick of the fighting. Chard was just behind him. One of the warriors below them leapt at the north wall whilst Dalton was attempting to draw a bead on a second man. 'Pot that fellow!' snapped Dalton at one of the 24th men beside him. The Zulus were duly thrown back, but by now Dalton had turned away from the wall and had stumbled a yard to the rear. Chard could see there was something wrong and approached him. Dalton handed over his rifle, calmly waited for Chard to empty his pockets of cartridges, and was then helped away in the direction of the veranda; the round had struck him in the fleshy part of the shoulder and passed out through his back.

Chard was not wearing any ammunition pouches, and as the fight raged around him, struggled to keep himself supplied with Martini rounds. The wounded Corporal Scammell saw him casting about for cartridges and crawled to the north wall to hand over his own. The exertion exhausted Scammell, who now lay slumped against the barricade. Yet again the defence of the north wall was a touch-and-go affair, but after a few minutes of close-quarter fighting the Zulus once more fell back into cover. As ever their riflemen immediately resumed a close-range fire from the brush and the orchard. As Acting Storekeeper Louis Byrne was passing along the barricade, he saw Corporal Scammell pleading feebly for a drink of water. Byrne stopped and crouched down to give him a drink from his water bottle. As he stood up from his errand of mercy, Byrne was shot in the head and killed.

With the south wall in the hands of the enemy, there was now even more erratically aimed lead in the air. Corporal Lyons and Corporal Allen took it upon themselves to do something about it. From the rear corner of the storehouse compound, where the retrenchment barricade met the front of the building, the two corporals prosecuted a vigorous short-range firefight with evident disregard for their own safety. Lyons's account of the fight, as published in *The Cambrian* of 13 June 1879, is far from clearly expressed, but as a best guess Lyons is here describing an exchange of fire between the corner of the storehouse and the Zulu riflemen in and around the cookhouse shack and the ovens at the rear of the post.

> Corporal Allen and several men were with me, and we all consider we did good service. Lieutenant Bromhead was on the right face, firing over the mealies with a Martini-Henry. Mr Chard was also very busy. I only turned round once to see this, and in that brief interval I saw Private Cole shot, and he fell dead. Seeing this I kept myself more over the bags, knowing that the shot that had killed him had come over our heads, and I was determined to check this flank firing as much as possible. I became thus more exposed, and so did Corporal Allen. We fired many shots, and I said to my comrades 'They are falling fast over there,' and he [Allen] replied 'Yes we are giving it to them.'

Post of Danger

If it had become dangerous for Lyons, Allen and the men at the storehouse corner of the retrenchment barricade, it was doubly so at

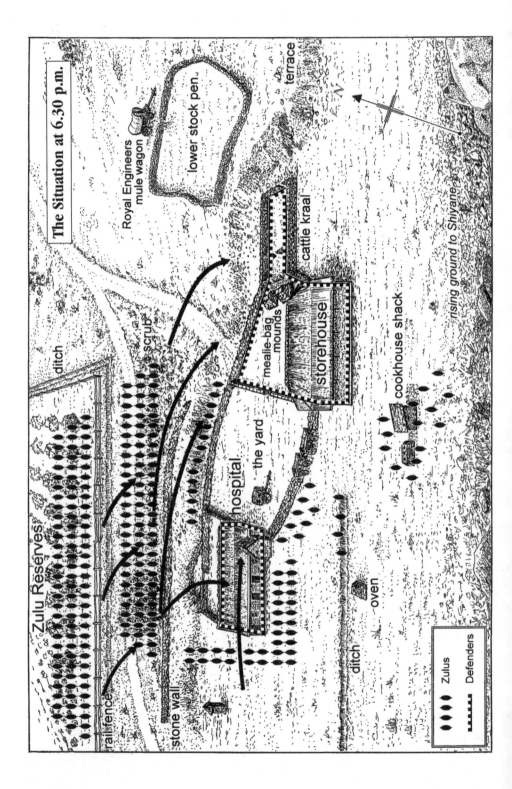

The Situation at 6.30 p.m.

Zulu Reserves

Royal Engineers mule wagon

lower stock pen

terrace

cattle kraal

storehouse

mealie-bag mounds

the yard

hospital

cookhouse shack

rising ground to Shiyane

scrub

ditch

rail fence

stone wall

oven

ditch

N

Zulus

Defenders

the far end of the line where the biscuit boxes met the north wall. The men fighting at this corner were exposed to fire across the widest possible arc; from the dog-leg barricade, from the south wall, even from the hospital veranda. It was also still possible to see them from parts of Shiyane along an oblique angle between the hospital and the storehouse. Worst of all they were only five or six yards from the thick scrub just below the north wall, and an even shorter distance from the tall, straight-sided boulders embedded in the front of the terrace. As described earlier these were shoulder high to a tall man, but with the mealie-bags of the abandoned stretch of the north wall piled three high on top of them, it was perfectly possible for parties of Zulus to stand upright in their shelter and still not be visible from the retrenchment barricade. The boulders protruded just far enough from the terrace to prevent a man right in the corner of the perimeter leaning over the wall to get a shot at them. Even had it been possible to do so, such an act would be tantamount to suicide, with the number of slugs and bullets thumping into the front of the mealie-bags.

Serious problems began when a number of Zulu riflemen sheltered themselves beneath the boulders and began a short-range firefight with the defenders. Sometimes they would gain a precarious toehold on the face of the terrace, suddenly raise their rifles above their heads and loose off a round in the general direction of the men at the exposed corner. At others, they would come dashing out a few yards to gain the requisite angle, hurriedly discharge their weapons, and then dash back into cover. On top of all this, this was precisely the point on the perimeter at which the ongoing Zulu rushes were falling most heavily. If the defenders here survived the close-range rifle fire, they still had to brawl hand-to-hand at regular intervals.

Unquestionably, it called for nerves of steel to fight on this part of the perimeter. It would have been perfectly reasonable and militarily sound, for Bromhead to have rotated men through this sector every ten minutes or so. Instead, in accordance with the traditional mantras of the British officer corps, he decided to play the leading role in the defence of this cruelly exposed corner in person. A number of other bravehearts stood by him. Private Edward Nicholas of the 1st/24th, a twenty-one-year-old Newport lad who had been one of Reynolds's hospital patients but had declared himself fit to fight on the barricades, was one of them. Corporal Schiess of the NNC was another. Also present were Lance Sergeant Thomas Williams and Privates Fred Hitch, Tom Cole, John Fagan and James Bushe of B Company. Commissary Dalton was the first to be shot in this corner. Most of the others would follow.

'Old King' Cole was probably next to go down. He was shot dead by one of the riflemen crouched in the nearby cover. The round that killed Cole passed through his head and, its velocity now largely spent, went on to hit Dublin-born Private James Bushe in the bridge of the nose. Bushe staggered away to seek medical attention and somebody else stepped forward to plug the gap; fortunately Bushe proved to be not too badly hurt.

Severely blistered feet or not, Corporal Schiess had distinguished himself during the fighting along the north wall. Now he found himself in the vital corner. One of the Zulu riflemen crouched beneath the big boulders finally got under Schiess's skin. Without any orders to do so, or even a word of warning to anybody else, he threw himself over the retrenchment barricade, dropped to his knees and crawled out along the line of the north wall. He had only four or five yards to cover before he had come up level with the Zulus below the terrace. As he leapt to his feet and clambered onto the mealie-bags to mount his one-man counter-attack, the troublesome rifleman saw him coming and loosed off a snap-shot which blew young Schiess's hat off. If anything his close shave served only to infuriate him further. The rifleman paid for his impudence with his life, as Schiess stabbed down hard with his bayonet. Quickly recovering the thrust, he raised his rifle to the shoulder and shot down a second Zulu. A third warrior rushed forward with his shield and assegai poised. Schiess penetrated his defences with a second lighting-quick lunge. Knowing that he had pushed his luck as far as he dare, Schiess hopped quickly back to safety.

A few moments later another assault wave came charging up to the barricades. Hitch was defending the north wall with Nicholas beside him:

> In one of these nasty rushes three Zulus were making for me; they seemed to have specially marked me out. The first fellow I shot; the second man I bayoneted; the third man got right into the

laager, but he declined to stand up against me. With a leap he jumped over the barricade and made off. A few yards from the barricade lay a wounded Zulu. We knew he was there, and that he had only been wounded, and so wanted watching. At the time we were far too busy with the more active members to find time to put him right out. Presently I saw him with rifle in hand, taking aim at one of my comrades. It was too late to stop him, and poor Nicholls [sic] fell dead, shot through the head.

Horrifically, as can sometimes be the case with a head-shot, Nicholas's brains were splattered over the men fighting near him. A short while later, as another bout of hand-to-hand fighting was raging along the front of the post, Bromhead was caught badly off guard. As he was leaning over the barricade to fire a few shots from his revolver, a Zulu who had scaled the wall further down, raised a throwing assegai behind his back. From four or five yards away Hitch caught sight of Bromhead's assailant. At the time he did not have a round in the breech of his rifle. Instead he saved Bromhead with ingenuity and low cunning alone; shouting loudly at the Zulu to attract his attention, Hitch ostentatiously raised his empty rifle to the present. The warrior took the hint and immediately threw himself back over the barricade with no harm done to either party.

If Bromhead owed his life to Hitch, then further down the barricade Chard owed his to Private David Jenkins of the 1st/24th.

> While I was intently watching to get a fair shot at a Zulu who appeared to be firing rather well, Private Jenkins, 24th, saying 'look out, Sir' gave my head a duck down just as a bullet whizzed over it. He had noticed a Zulu who was quite near in another direction, taking a deliberate aim at me.

At some point in the fray, Lance Sergeant Williams took a round through his left ribcage. The bullet passed through his body without lodging, but fractured a number of ribs en route. Williams was carried away to Surgeon Reynolds in a dangerously wounded condition. Amidst the mounting casualties even the fearless Schiess was forced to quit the barricades. As if his feet were not in bad enough condition at the start of the battle, he now took a round through his instep and was forced to retire to the storehouse veranda. Other men replaced those who fell at or near the exposed corner, but of its original defenders only Bromhead and Hitch now remained uninjured. In the hell that is a battlefield, it can take only minutes for men to forge the strongest of bonds. By now these two were the closest of friends.

And still the Zulus came.

Chapter 4

Like Rats in a Hole

The Evacuation of the Hospital

On the other side of the abandoned yard, a tense and dramatic struggle for life was now underway. Before the withdrawal to the retrenchment barricade, the men at the hospital loopholes were able to hold their own and inflict some heavy punishment on the enemy, but from about 6.15 p.m. the advantage began to tilt against them. Reynolds's courageous dash with a fresh supply of ammunition brought some succour to Robert Jones, William Jones and their charges in the two adjoining rooms at the right rear of the hospital, but on the far side of the building things were altogether more serious. First, there was very little ammunition left; second, all the potential escape routes were now controlled by the enemy; and third, there was no possibility of the men on the retrenchment barricade laying down any enfilading fire.

Many of the problems originated from the interior layout of the building and the failure of the hospital garrison to carry out an order Chard had given earlier – an instruction to interconnect the rooms by means of mouse-holing. This is the nickname that soldiers give to the act of knocking a hole in a partition wall at ground level, in order to create a crawl-way from one room to the next. No doubt this was not due to any wilful disobedience on their part, but to the multiplicity of higher priority tasks, such as barricading the doors and windows, and punching loopholes through the exterior walls. There had been two key deficiencies: tools with which to do the work and time. There seems only to have been one pick. This was used by Hook first, and then by the two Williamses, to loophole the stone gable-end. The men loopholing the much less robust side-walls had been forced to rely on their bayonets. Fortunately the 'lunger' proved equal to the task. Even more fortuitously, when the fighting started, for the room at issue opened only to the outside of the building, the pick was still leaning against the wall in the ward to which the Williamses had been assigned.

Whilst the fighting was raging along the line of the north wall, the veranda had been denied to the enemy. Even after Bromhead and his men ceded the hospital compound, it was covered by the close-range fire from the dog-leg barricade. Now, from the retrenchment wall, it was quite impossible to see the front door, which gave admittance to the two large rooms at the front of the building. This had been the Witts' main living area, which Reynolds had kept vacant within his hospital layout for casualty reception. As the rooms were empty and shielded at the outset by the north wall, nobody seems to have been specifically assigned to hold them. Thus, when the defenders were driven out of the hospital compound to the dog-leg barricade, it became necessary quickly to improvise some defensive arrangements. Two or three men may have dashed in through the front door at this point. It is also possible that some of the fitter patients from the ward next to Hook's corner room moved to the front of the building at this time. Certainly, when the withdrawal to the retrenchment barricade took place, there must have been something preventing the Zulus from breaking down the front door, though they would ultimately succeed in doing so. At this stage the door can only have been covered by rifle fire from men inside the building.

It is next to impossible due to the paucity of primary source material to pin every individual down to a specific room. Any reconstruction inevitably has elements of speculation based on mere snippets of information. With this caveat in place, it seems that the men defending the front of the building were Private William Roy, who had paired up with an unidentified 'old soldier' (which we may interpret as meaning one of the senior privates in B Company in his mid-thirties), and Gunner Arthur Howard, Colonel Harness's batman. Roy was a twenty-five-year-old patient who was suffering only with a sore throat and was to all practical intents and purposes fully fit to fight. We can assume therefore that he would have started the fight on the barricade, not in the hospital. Originally enlisted into the 32nd Regiment, Roy was born a Scotsman and would die an Australian. He had been compulsorily transferred into the 1st/24th at King William's Town in 1877, following a long spell of hospital treatment for primary syphilis.

We should try to locate these three men as best we can. Roy was fighting from a window in the Witts' living area (which it must by definition have had), having pulled back into the building from the fight in the hospital compound. The old soldier came in with him and was probably defending the front door in the adjacent room. Howard was on his own, either in the utility room to the right (looking out from the building) of the front door, having also fallen back there from the fight in the hospital compound, or in the even smaller utility room at the left end of the veranda. The front door itself was crucial in that it gave access via the Witts' living area, to the two small interconnected rooms at the left rear of the building – Hook's corner room where the isiGqoza Zulu was bedded down, and the small ward next door crowded with nine patients. Roy and the old soldier must have barricaded or wedged the front door in some way, perhaps with items of furniture.

As is the way in that part of the world, the late afternoon sun was sinking fast. The rooms in the hospital were gloomy to begin with, were made more so by the barricading of the windows, and now with the approaching sunset, were becoming distinctly dark. Short of ammunition as they were, and with the enemy enjoying the advantage of fading daylight, it was no longer possible for the men at the far end of the building to defend the outer doors effectively. A number of Zulus were laying in wait, crouched beneath the loopholes, to snatch suddenly at the muzzles of the defenders' rifles. Soon it had become all but impossible to get off an aimed shot. John and Joseph Williams were defending five patients in all: Private 'Billy' Horrigan, who was fighting alongside them, Privates Adams and Hayden, and two others, identities unknown, all of whom were non-combatant. When they saw that the door was beginning to give, the men within realised that it was now imperative that they find some other way out of the trap. Even though they had no view of what was going on outside, the occupants of the room seemed to know instinctively that they were outside the main defensive perimeter. Out of ammunition, short-handed, abandoned to their fate, surrounded on all sides by literally hundreds of the enemy, and pinned as Hook was later to put it, 'like rats in a hole', the situation could not possibly have been worse. Then the thatch began to smoulder. Somewhere above their heads, the roof was now on fire.

The men at the front of the building seem to have decided about now that the time had come to break out of the trap. No doubt the burning roof was the catalyst. Anxiously they waited for something that would pass for a lull in the fighting. Probably the first to go was Gunner Howard, who made the decision to fling himself over the abandoned north wall and seek cover in the deepening evening gloom. Gathering his breath, he threw open the door, dashed across the veranda, hurled himself across the mealie-bags and landed in a heap on the other side. Mercifully nobody had spotted him and he was able to crawl over to the corpses of four dead horses, killed by the Zulus earlier as they stood tethered near the stone wall. Howard slithered in amongst the dead animals and pulled leaves and branches over himself. His navy blue Royal Artillery tunic was just about ideal for night-time concealment, but he worried about the red stripes down the outside seams of his trousers.

Next to go were Roy and the old soldier. It seems that they were unlucky with the timing of their dash and acquired a tail. Roy described his fortuitous escape in a letter to his parents written not long after the battle:

> They took the hospital and set fire to it, while I and another old soldier were inside at the back* window, and we did not know they had taken it at the front. My rifle got disabled, so I fixed my bayonet and charged out of the house. While we were charging out the old soldier got wounded in the ear. There were about 30 Zulus chasing us [probably an exaggeration] but the men inside the fort shot them before they could harm us . . .

---

* The use of the word 'back' is of course subjective. What one man will call the back of a building, another will call the front. Some other explanation might be possible but Chaplain Smith refers to two or three men dashing to safety from what was actually the front of the building. It is hard to know who these men could have been if they were not Roy and his comrade. Roy might have referred to the window at the 'back' of the building because he had formerly been bedded down in a room which he had come to think of as the 'front' of his little world as a hospital patient, but which was actually at the 'rear' of the building in the wider sense.

The Waters Saga

Private John Waters has led historians a merry dance for the last thirty or forty years. He has been described as a hospital patient; has been placed as the lone defender of the utility room in the middle of the row of rooms at the back of the hospital; famously he hid in a wardrobe; and he has been described as breaking out over both the north wall, and out to the south from the back of the building.* It is time to pin him down.

First, Waters was not a patient. He was a 1st/24th soldier detached from his battalion as an additional hospital orderly. He was a fully fit infantryman. He was not, therefore, one of the original hospital defenders, as Bromhead posted only six such men whose identities are well known to us. How then did he come to be in the hospital? Back to the fight in the hospital compound: Waters was in fact fighting on the barricade, when he was shot in the shoulder. He was the man who had been patched up by Harry Hook, and then moved into the ward next door to continue the fight from the loopholes. Although Hook does not identify the man in his accounts beyond saying that he was a member of the 24th, a gunshot wound in the shoulder is a serious injury by any standard and must by definition have been recorded in the casualty return. It was: John Waters was the only 24th man so injured. Why did Harry Hook leave his loopholes to patch up a wounded man when others might have done so? Because Hook was the hospital cook and Waters the hospital orderly. They were a team.

When the roof began to burn, Waters decided to make his escape back the way he had come, that is to say out through the front door. He had no other option – the ward next to Hook had no outside door. By this stage the front door was undefended, and almost certainly ajar following the recent departure of Private Roy and the old soldier. They cannot have been gone long or the Zulus on the other side of the barricade would have spotted the open door and forced the front of the

---

* Another story has him blacking up his face and hiding himself by standing upright in the chimney or the fireplace of the cookhouse shack. It is a ludicrous story which I give no credence to, not only because of its inherent improbability, but also because the 'cookhouse' shack was actually a square African-built hut, and is highly unlikely to have had a substantial stone chimney.

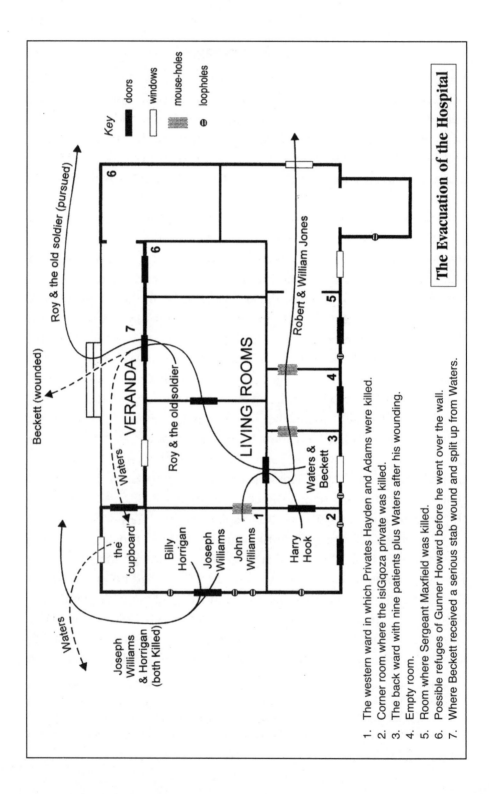

Key

doors

windows

mouse-holes

⊕ loopholes

Beckett (wounded)

Roy & the old soldier (pursued)

6

6

7

Waters

VERANDA

Roy & the old soldier

LIVING ROOMS

Robert & William Jones

5

4

3

1

2

Waters & Beckett

the 'cupboard'

Billy Horrigan

Joseph Williams

John Williams

Harry Hook

Waters

Joseph Williams & Horrigan (both Killed)

1. The western ward in which Privates Hayden and Adams were killed.
2. Corner room where the isiGqoza private was killed.
3. The back ward with nine patients plus Waters after his wounding.
4. Empty room.
5. Room where Sergeant Maxfield was killed.
6. Possible refuges of Gunner Howard before he went over the wall.
7. Where Beckett received a serious stab wound and split up from Waters.

The Evacuation of the Hospital

hospital in next to no time. Indeed it is possible that Roy or his companion called out to Waters and the rest of the men in the back ward that they were about to go. When Waters decided to make his own breakout attempt, the twenty-three-year-old Private Beckett, one of the nine patients trapped in the back ward, decided to go with him. It was literally a break for it, and was decided upon and executed at great speed.

Now to the business of the 'wardrobe'. Waters's account of his escape from the hospital, published in *The Cambrian* in June 1879, has been repeatedly misinterpreted. In most versions of the story of Rorke's Drift, we are presented with an image of Waters hiding in a 'wardrobe' inside the burning hospital, from which he shoots a number of Zulus in the back. Some historians even put Private Beckett in the wardrobe with Waters! It is quite an achievement to shoot accurately from a wardrobe with a rifle of over four feet in length. Indeed it all starts to sound somewhat comical, unbelievable even. It sounds unbelievable because it is unbelievable – it cannot have happened that way.

The word Waters actually used, or more accurately the word that his ghost-writer used, is 'cupboard'. It was John Chard who suggested in his report to the Queen that the cupboard was inside a room – the earliest beginnings of the wardrobe story. Since the word 'cupboard' occurs both when Waters told his story to Chard, and when he recounted it to a journalist five months later, it rather suggests that this is Waters's own chosen noun. Unlike Chard, however, Waters did not himself suggest that the cupboard was inside a room. It seems evident then that he meant that the room was the cupboard – a small utility room in other words. Many historians tell us that Waters delved into the bottom of the wardrobe and miraculously came up with Mr Witt's long black clergyman's cloak. Few clergymen will discard such fine and expensive garments in the bottom of a wardrobe. Nor did Mr Witt. The room at issue was the smallest one in the building – it faced onto the veranda just to the left of the front door. It was probably used as a cloakroom, and Mr Witt's cloak was no doubt hanging from a peg in plain view of Private Waters. Let us examine the account in *The Cambrian* in its original disjointed form:

I stopped there firing at the enemy through holes made by other men and others did the same, but we were not able to prevent the enemy coming right up to the hospital. Some of them came in and set fire to it. While I was there I took refuge in a cupboard, and Private Beckett came with me. As they were going out I killed many of them, and as I could not stay there long, the place being so suffocating, I put on a black cloak which I had found in the cupboard, and which must have belonged to Mr Witt, and ran out in the long grass and lay down. The Zulus must have thought I was one of their dead comrades, as they were all round me, and some trod on me. Beckett had gone out half an hour before me, and he, poor fellow, was assegaied right through his stomach … I saw Private Horrigan killed.

Let us now revisit Waters's story, with the substitution of the word 'cloakroom' for 'cupboard' and overlaid with some explanatory notes:

I stopped there [in the hospital – meaning that he was not there to begin with] firing at the enemy through holes made by other men [that is loopholes in one of the rooms on the outside of the perimeter – which means he can only have been in the room next to Hook, as it is the only such room that can be reached via the front of the building], and others did the same [that is to say they fired – not stopped there], but we were not able to prevent the enemy coming right up to the hospital. Some of them came in and set fire to it. While I was there I took refuge in a *cloakroom*, and Private Beckett came with me [this does but not necessarily mean that Beckett followed him into the cloakroom but that he came with him in the broader sense of making a break]. As they [the Zulus] were going out [of the front door of the hospital, to which the cloakroom was in defilade] I killed many of them [notice the apparent absence of Beckett – 'I killed' not 'we killed'], and as I could not stay there long, the place being so suffocating, I put on a black cloak which I had found in the *cloakroom*, and which must have belonged to Mr Witt, and ran out in the long grass and lay down. The Zulus must have thought I was one of their dead comrades, as they were all round me, and some trod on me.

Beckett had gone out half an hour before me [no such timing can
be regarded as reliable in the heat of battle], and he, poor fellow,
was assegaied right through his stomach . . . I saw Private Horrigan
killed [the death of Horrigan will be important later].

So what actually happened? When they realised that the roof was
smouldering, Waters and Beckett decided to make a break for it. Hook
was still in the corner room, with the isiGqoza patient, fighting from the
loopholes. Waters may have called through the door to encourage his
friend to join him in a breakout attempt, but Harry Hook was not the
man to leave the patients to their fate. At this stage the front door
appeared to be the only way out, whilst to stay where they were seemed
to bespeak certain death. We should not be hard or judgemental on
Waters and Beckett. Sometimes in war the disabled have to be left
behind. In civilised warfare it would be normal to treat with the enemy
for their safekeeping, but in 'savage' warfare no such option exists.
Waters was himself already seriously wounded. Young Beckett was not
fit to begin with. They held no rank and thus had no wider responsibility
for the safety of others. That they should adopt a policy of every man
for himself, in so dire a situation, is understandable.

If they were going to go, then speed was of the essence. They
moved from the back ward into the living rooms, and then charged out
through the front door, Beckett leading, much as Roy and the old
soldier had done. They were heading for the dog-leg barricade with the
aim of bearing to the right and sprinting across the yard to the
retrenchment. As it turned out, Beckett was particularly unlucky and
collided with a passing Zulu on the veranda. The warrior lashed out
with his assegai and succeeded in stabbing Beckett in the gut. His
wound did not bring him down, however, and he was able to evade
his assailant by changing direction and leaping over the north wall. Like
Gunner Howard, who cannot have been more than about twenty-five
yards away at the most, Beckett was able to crawl away into the
undergrowth and lie up, but he was very badly hurt and bleeding
profusely.

Just behind Beckett, Waters got the fright of his life at the
unexpected encounter with the Zulu (and there may have been more

than one); in a flash he side-stepped to the left, ran into the cloakroom at the end of the veranda and slammed the door shut behind him. He was not in there for anything like half an hour. It may have been five or ten minutes. Inside the hospital, somebody else from the back ward (who may at first have been trying to follow Waters and Beckett in their breakout attempt) must have barricaded the interconnecting door between the two living rooms. Some Zulus must have gone in through the front door at this juncture. Perhaps when they tried to force the interior door one of the patients fired through it. This may have been enough to deter the Zulus, or possibly there were too many of them inside the room – after all only a few warriors at a time could get at the doorway. Others may have turned about and gone to seek excitement elsewhere. Thus it was actually possible, 'as they were going out', for Waters to have 'killed many of them'. The sounds of his shots were indistinguishable above the hubbub of battle. 'Many', of course, probably amounted to three or four at best. Then Waters made his famous break wrapped in the missionary's cloak. It seems certain that he gave up any idea of getting away past the dog-leg barricade, turned hard left instead, jumped over the short western wall and ran out in the direction of the privy shack before flinging himself down in the grass. He may, indeed, have left the cloakroom via the window, which would have dropped him within a yard or two of the outer perimeter.

The Twelfth VC

Like the Williamses next door, Harry Hook had also lost confidence in a sagging outer door. Abandoned by 'Old King' Cole over an hour earlier, he had fought manfully in the interim to cover both loopholes. The floor of the room was littered with expended cartridge cases; Hook's ears were ringing, his head was pounding, and his shoulder and cheek were bruised. After bouts of prolonged firing, the recoil from a fouled Martini-Henry could become brutish. The isiGqoza man had a badly fractured femur and was quite unable to assist Hook in any way.

Whilst Joseph Williams and Billy Horrigan continued to fight from the loopholes in the western gable-wall, John Williams took up the pick and began to smash a hole in the back wall of the room. Fortuitously, as described earlier, the partition walls were made of mud-clay and were none too resistant to his frantic efforts. If he was successful his mouse-hole would give access to the Witts' living area. When the hole in the wall was big enough to look through, Williams realised that the front of the building was now under attack and quickly redoubled his efforts. Soon the hole was a foot wide.

As his corner room was now filling with thick, choking smoke, Hook decided that the time had come to evacuate it. The black patient was panicking, crying, and begging Hook to remove his bandages. Hook never really offered a convincing explanation for his inability to get the man out with him, but it can be safely assumed that he must have been under acute pressure at the time. With the outer door beginning to give, Hook dashed into the adjacent ward and slammed the interconnecting door shut behind him. Somehow he improvised a means of quickly barricading it. It necessarily follows that it must have opened inwards; he may have been able to wedge it shut with one of the wooden pallets serving as hospital beds. However he did it, the barricade was none too robust. Soon he could hear animated Zulu voices from the room next door. After some hostile questioning, the black patient was killed in his bed by his enraged kinsmen. Suddenly there were shoulders heaving at the interconnecting door. Hook fired a round through the woodwork to dissuade his pursuers at least temporarily. As the only other door in the room was the one which gave access to the front rooms and thence to the veranda, now in the hands of the enemy, there seemed to be no way out.

In attempting to comprehend the next set of events, the fall of the ward on the western side of the building, it is important to understand that the drama was played out in a matter of seconds not minutes. At first invisible to Hook because of the smoke inside the building, John Williams was now in the living room next door, having enlarged his mouse-hole to the point where it was just about passable. As he put his head back through the hole to begin assisting the patients through, he realised to his horror that the room had been forced and that Joseph Williams was fighting furiously in defence of the doorway. Joseph had fought like a lion all afternoon: the following morning fourteen dead Zulus would be found outside the door, with still more along his line of fire. He may have wounded as many more again. In a fight conducted at odds of thirty-to-one, Joseph Williams had already done more than enough. He had fired his last cartridge sometime earlier. Now he blocked the door with his body, to defend the helpless patients within. It was officially reported in despatches that, 'had he lived he would have been recommended for the Victoria Cross', exactly the same expression that was used of Melvill and Coghill. No retrospective award was ever made in Joseph Williams's case, however, but we should perhaps rightly extol his name as the twelfth VC winner of the battle. He did as much as Hook, John Williams or the Joneses – but the essential difference was that his courage was to cost him his life.

While Joseph and Horrigan fought in defence of the doorway with their bayonets, the patients inside the room were clustered at the mouse-hole in panic; John Williams was able quickly to heave one of them through. Then he put his head back into the room to reach for a second man. According to Hook, recollecting the events of that night many years later, John Williams came rushing into his room shortly afterwards and told him that Joseph had been 'dragged outside' and killed. He may have imagined this to be the case; perhaps he simply looked back into the room to see Joseph gone and leapt to that conclusion. On the balance of probability it would seem much more likely that Williams and Horrigan charged into the open, where they could swing their bayonets more freely, perhaps in order to defend the doorway better, or more probably to attempt a breakout around the side of the hospital. There are a number of references in the sources to men attempting to escape from the front of the building but being cut down in the process. Almost certainly this story would have had its origins in the positioning of some of the bodies when they were found the following morning, as there was only a very limited view of the front of the hospital from the retrenchment barricade. Lieutenant William Weallens of the 2nd/24th wrote a piece for the *Uppingham School Magazine* which appeared in October 1879. Weallens was not of course one of the defenders, but was stationed at the drift with the B Company survivors subsequently:

> One man, named Williams did a very plucky thing; he got into a
> small room by himself, and from the window fired off all the

ammunition he had. He then tried to make a bolt for it into the fort, but unfortunately fell in getting out of the window. He got up, however, and tried to join the fort, when he was wounded by an assegai. He was caught by the Zulus and literally cut to pieces, as they were so infuriated at the number of them he killed.

There are inconsistencies here: Joseph Williams was not on his own, there was no window in the western gable-end of the building, and there was nobody in a position to see him stumble in jumping out of a window. Yet Weallens is hardly likely to have made it all up. There is an outside possibility that, if Joseph was both quick off the mark and lucky, that he might have made it into the same cloakroom that Waters had vacated a few minutes earlier – this did have a window. But the broad message that we might reasonably deduce from Weallens is that there was a belief after the battle amongst his B Company comrades that Joseph Williams made a break for it and was cut down in the process.

It was now, as he crouched in the grass near the privy, that Waters saw Billy Horrigan die (or was it Joseph Williams – a misidentification is certainly possible in the circumstances). However the fate of Williams and Horrigan unfolded outside the building, suddenly there were Zulus in the room they had sallied forth from. With John Williams's help a second patient clawed his way through the mouse-hole to safety, but the other two men, Privates Robert Adams and Garret Hayden, both of D Company 2nd/24th, were quickly dragged outside and butchered. Hayden was stabbed sixteen times, slashed twice along the abdomen and had one of his cheeks sliced off. The loss of his friend Joseph would have hit John Williams hard. The two lads had done their Brecon training together, had ended up in the same company, and as new boys together must have become the best of friends.

Harry Hook and John Williams Pair Up

John Williams and the two surviving patients came stumbling into the rear ward from the Witts' living area and quickly improvised a barricade against the second door. Abergavenny-born Williams had only just turned twenty and had been in the army only a little over eighteen months. He had run away from his family home in Cwmbran to enlist and had adopted an assumed name to avoid being traced by his family; his real name was Fielding. Shouting at the patients to clear the way, he ran to the far side of the room with his pick and began to batter a second mouse-hole. Harry Hook defended the two doors, at times bracing them with his shoulder and at others firing through the splintering woodwork. The next room was a utility room which opened only to the outside of the building and had been left undefended.* The doorway was covered in defilade from the Joneses' ward where an extension to the corner room protruded from the back wall of the building at a right angle. This would certainly have been loopholed as part of any considered defence plan. Probably then, the door to the utility room was still intact, though it cannot have been barricaded. It is possible that Zulus had been into the room only to find that it was an empty cul-de-sac. For the next ten to fifteen minutes it would only take one Zulu to push the door open for the whole evacuation from the western end of the hospital to be compromised and no doubt overwhelmed.

Soon Williams was through the wall and enlarging. A few minutes later he was helping the first of the patients through his second mouse-hole. Behind them the door from the corner room was suddenly forced and Harry Hook had the fight of his life on his hands:

> The Zulus beat in the door and tried to enter. I stood at the side and shot and bayoneted several – I could not tell how many, but there were five or six lying at my feet. They threw assegais continually, but only one touched me, and that afflicted a scalp wound which I did not think worth while reporting. In fact I did not feel the wound at the time. One Zulu seized my rifle and tried to drag it away. Whilst we were tussling I slipped a cartridge in and pulled the trigger – the muzzle was against his breast, and he fell dead. Every now and then a Zulu would make a rush to enter – the door would only let in one man at a time – but I bayoneted or shot every one.

* This was the room in which many writers, following the lead of Donald Morris, have placed Waters and the wardrobe, erroneously, in my view, for the reasons described.

Hook's typically understated and modest account conveys little of the extreme difficulty of his task, or of the skill and determination that it takes repeatedly to outwit so many murderous attempts on one's life. He must have been a fine soldier. Certainly he had the heart of a lion and kept his nerve in a way that we can but admire. All the while the string of patients to his rear were clambering through the mouse-hole into the adjacent utility room. As they sat in the gloom recovering their breath, Williams was already picking at the far wall. Hook now glanced back to see that everybody was through, apart from Private John Connolly of G Company, 2nd/24th. Connolly was a twenty-two-year-old from the valley community of Trevethin near Pontypool, and was suffering from a badly dislocated knee incurred during a wagon accident. Looking back into the corner room to see that he would not immediately be pursued, Hook flew across the room, placed his rifle on the ground beside the mouse-hole, and reversed himself into the opening. He then seized Connolly by the shoulders and dragged him through after him. In recounting the story years later, Hook would say that Connolly had a broken leg and that he re-broke it in dragging him through the hole, but Connolly's service record would suggest that this was not so. Leaping to his feet, rifle in hand, Hook now stood poised over the mouse-hole to defend it. It was next to impossible for the Zulus to get through in such a situation, and relatively easy for Hook to repel all such attempts. Already Williams was almost through to the corner ward, where the two Joneses were still fighting furiously in defence of their patients.

By now the smouldering, smoking thatch had become a serious roof fire. The flames at the western end of the building, where the assegai-torches had first come thudding in, had now taken hold and were beginning to light up the night. It did not take long for the fire to spread over the length of the roof. Time was running out for the men still trapped inside the building. Ultimately, the fire would play an important role in shaping the course of the battle.

The Joneses

The Joneses were a very different pair. William was an old soldier. He had been born in Evesham and had been in the army for twenty years, including stints in Mauritius, Burma and India. A Natal newspaper report of June 1879 would indicate that he had recently been given leave of absence to return to Pietermaritzburg to tend his ailing wife, Elizabeth, to whom he had been married for three and a half years. He is said to have taken work repairing boots and shoes in order to obtain a few comforts for her.* Sadly, she died. It is said that William buried her the next day and then immediately set off to rejoin his battalion. He was now thirty-nine years of age. By contrast, Robert, another Monmouthshire man, from the rural community of Raglan, was only twenty-one years old and had been in the 24th for only three years. As recently as August he had been taught a severe lesson in the ways of his new profession. He was caught drunk on duty in Pietermaritzburg and was brought before a district court-martial. He was sentenced to 56 days' hard labour but was released from the city gaol after serving only eleven of them. He probably spent the rest of his sentence as a regimental defaulter, in itself far from being an easy ride. A chastened and a wiser man, young Robert was probably quite glad to march off to war. If a soldier has to make a new start with his commanding officer, winning the Victoria Cross is probably as good a way as any.

By now the Joneses were out of ammunition again, and the Zulus at the back of the hospital knew it. The outer door to the two-room ward was under heavy attack, as a party of Zulus attempted to shoulder-barge their way in. William and Robert dashed across to the door, braced it with their shoulders and prepared if necessary to defend it with the bayonet. In the far end-room, five of the patients incarcerated with them were anxiously gathering beneath the high window in the gable-end, contemplating an escape in the direction of the storehouse compound. Problematically a number of the men were completely immobile and stood little chance of making the dash unaided. Still on their beds were the delirious Sergeant Maxfield, and Corporal Jesse Mayer with his eleven-day-old leg wound. An attempt had already been made to dress young Maxfield, but he had a raging fever to begin with, and the smoke, flames and noise seem to have turned his troubled mind; he flailed about and resisted all attempts to help him. Clearly, in such a condition,

---

* This tends to corroborate the story, as his trade at enlistment is given as 'boot closer'.

he would be a terrible burden. For the time being he was left where he was, whilst priority was given to the survival of the sane.

John Williams was now through into the end ward. No doubt he gave the Joneses a fright at first, as he appeared through the wall behind their legs. Having identified himself through the hole, he worked quickly to enlarge it and then crawled through to join them. The string of ten patients began to clamber through behind him. Nine of them made it unaided, but at the rear Hook was again left with the problem of John Connolly. He successfully repeated the process of dashing for the mouse-hole and hauling Connolly through after him. Hook, John Williams and William Jones ushered and aided the sick down the length of the ward for the gable-end window. Robert Jones remained to guard the outside door. By now the first patients were dropping down into the yard.

Suddenly the outer door began to splinter. Robert Jones knew that in only a moment or two it would give and the Zulus would be upon them. He dashed to Jesse Mayer's bed, hauled him roughly to his feet, threw an arm around him, and dashed him down the ward shouting, 'They are on top of us.' Pushing Mayer into the sanctuary of the end room, Robert stood to one side of the interior doorway and awaited the onset of the enemy. William Jones came dashing back down the room to stand in the doorway alongside his young comrade. Hook and Williams, meanwhile, were down at the window, urging all possible speed on the patients and helping them where they could.

Now the Zulus were in the first room. Thrusting repeatedly with their bayonets from just inside the interconnecting doorway, the Joneses somehow managed to stand their ground. Robert Jones recalled the defence of the doorway for *The Strand Magazine* in 1891:

> There we crossed our bayonets, and as fast as they came up to the doorway we bayoneted them, until the doorway was nearly filled with dead and wounded Zulus. In the meanwhile, I had three assegai wounds, two in the right side and one in the left of my body. We did not know of anyone being in the hospital, only the Zulus, and then after a long time of fighting at the door, we made the enemy retire and then we made our escape out of the building.

The Dash

The situation confronting the patients as they dropped from the window was an acutely dangerous one. Twenty-five yards to their left was the abandoned stretch of the north wall, on the far side of which many hundreds, if not thousands, of Zulus were crouched in the brush. Almost immediately to the right hand side of the window, no more than four or five yards away, was the south wall, where scores more Zulus were crouched. Hook and Williams must have stood with their rifles poised, ready to snap-shoot at any enemy impertinent enough to pop his head over the barricade. Straight ahead, it was a thirty-five-yard dash to the retrenchment barricade. The yard of course was still being swept by fire from Shiyane.

One of the first men to drop down from the window, perhaps before anybody had taken post to cover the south wall, was a tall young trooper of the Natal Mounted Police called Sidney Hunter. He appeared to hesitate as if wondering which way to go. His hesitation was his downfall; in a trice a Zulu had vaulted the south wall and plunged a stabbing assegai into his back. As Hunter slumped to the ground dead, somebody behind the retrenchment barricade shot his assailant down. It was hardly an encouraging start to the evacuation, but with the building now burning fiercely around them, the rest of the patients had no option but to follow on regardless. One by one the ambulatory patients and their escorts dropped into the yard to make the dash. The necessity for the fighting fit to cover the south wall with their rifles raised at the present, meant that the able bodied were largely unable to assist the infirm. Three men were completely immobile and had to drag themselves across the yard. Chaplain George Smith described their escape:

> Corporal Mayer N. N. C. who had been wounded under the knee with an assegai at Sirayo's [sic] kraal. Bombardier Lewis, R. A., whose leg and thigh were much swollen from a wagon accident, and Trooper R. S. Green, N. M. P., also a patient, all got out of the little end window within the enclosure. The window being high up, and the Zulus already in the room behind them, each man had a fall in escaping, and then had to crawl (for none of them could

walk) through the enemy's fire, inside the retrenchment. Whilst
doing this, Green was struck in the thigh with a spent bullet.

At length it seemed to the Joneses that everybody behind them had
clambered outside to the yard. By now the ward was full of choking
smoke and lapping flame. Their deft bayonet work and the increasing
intensity of the fire seemed to have bought them a breathing space; no
more Zulus attempted to rush the doorway. This might be their one
remaining chance to make a dash for the gable window, before the
burning thatch and rafters above their heads came crashing down into
the room. William got through first. Robert clambered up behind him
and passed his rifle down to his comrade. At the last minute, he found
himself quite unable to leave the maddened Maxfield to his fate. Robert
turned back into the burning ward to make one more attempt to rescue
the sergeant, but quickly realised that it was far too late. Two or three
Zulus had pushed up behind the Joneses and were now busy hacking
the young sergeant to pieces. Mercifully he had been in no fit state to
sense the imminence or the savagery of his demise. Jones turned again,
dropped down into the yard, and dashed in the direction of the
retrenchment barricade. It is often stated that Hook was the last man to
leave the blazing hospital but this is not so: it was Robert Jones. As he
did so, the roof of the building began to collapse in on itself. Maxfield's
killers may have died in the inferno.

The evacuation of the hospital had been a truly remarkable
achievement. It was perhaps the ultimate example of a soldier's fight,
for the men who accomplished it did not have a NCO's chevron
between them. Neither, in the gloomy confines of the hospital, could
their actions be directed or even witnessed by anybody in authority. In
a scenario which could not have been more desperate or more
stressful, Hook and the Joneses never gave a moment's thought to
instincts of self-preservation; rather they stood in their doorways
wielding their bayonets, until they were satisfied that every man behind
them had clawed his way to safety. Truly this was 'Valour'.

By all rights nobody in the hospital should have been able to get
out; Hook's famous 'rats in a hole' metaphor was literally true. But, now
that it was all over, Waters, Beckett and Howard were still alive in their

respective hiding places; Roy and the old soldier had made it to safety; John Williams had brought out two of the five patients in the western ward; Hook had brought out eight of his ten (Beckett being the tenth man in the ward to begin with); and the Joneses had brought out five of their seven. Sergeant Robert Maxfield, Privates Joseph Williams, William Horrigan, Robert Adams and Garret Hayden, the isiGqoza private, and Trooper Sidney Hunter were the men who didn't make it. As near as can be determined, of the thirty-one men in the hospital when the withdrawal to the retrenchment barricade occurred, twenty-four made it to safety. Sadly, as he lay in the brush, doubled up and biting back the excruciating pain of his wound, young Bill Beckett was slowly but surely bleeding to death.

Chapter 5

The Night is Darkest before the Dawn

Defence of the Final Perimeter

Just before dusk somebody on the north wall said he could see redcoats on the Helpmekaar road. There was a spontaneous outbreak of cheering, the meaning of which quickly communicated itself to the enemy; for a few minutes there seemed to be a let-up in their attacks. Chard dashed across to the barricade to see what the excitement was about, but although several men told him they were sure of the sighting, he himself was unable to see anything. Nonetheless they were there; Walter Dunne could see them. A short while later it was said that the troops were turning. In one of his later accounts Fred Hitch said that Bromhead cried out, 'Don't lose heart. Our men will return as soon as they find we are holding out.'

Not long after they left Vermaak's Farm, Spalding and Dickson met the rocket battery survivors Privates Grant and Johnson. Unlike Evans and Whelan, these two men remained faithful to the major's orders and stayed by him. Further down the road, the four of them started to encounter the deserters from Rorke's Drift – principally Henderson's Basutos and the amaNgwane riding with them. Spalding reported that he met several white men on the road who all assured him that Rorke's Drift had fallen. There was villainy afoot here. Clearly Spalding was attempting to turn around everybody he encountered and was thereby inadvertently triggering a string of false reports and lies. Probably the men concerned included Stevenson, Henderson, Doig, Shannon and Hall, none of whom had any intention of going back to Rorke's Drift, and were no doubt prepared to say anything in order to avoid doing so.

Spalding and his three stalwart scouts descended from the Biggarsberg to the Buffalo River valley. Before long they encountered a party ostensibly of the enemy, formed across the road in open order. There was a donga to their rear which Spalding was concerned could be hiding a larger force. In fact these men might actually have been a group of Stevenson's levies, who in the half-light would have been indistinguishable from Zulus. Either way, believing them to pose a threat, Spalding turned his party away and galloped off to a flank to gain a nearby high point. From there he and his men could make out that the buildings at Rorke's Drift were on fire, from which we can deduce that it must now have been around 6.45 p.m. Two of the three men accompanying Spalding were badly shaken up, it was turning dark, and there were parties of the enemy abroad. There was no particular reason for Spalding to suspect that he had been lied to; indeed the distant flames served only to suggest that the reports of the fall of Rorke's Drift were true. Given the circumstances, it is impossible to criticise Spalding for his decision to turn back. To push on in the dark would have been nothing short of foolhardy. This did not stop one modern writer recently describing Spalding's conduct as 'craven', but this is nothing less than an outrageous and wholly unwarranted slur. Spalding had left Rorke's Drift some two and a half hours before anybody began building barricades, and his decision to turn back now for Helpmekaar was nothing more than a militarily prudent one. Nor was the decision his alone; he was no more senior in rank than was Russell Upcher. A little way back down the road, the scouting party encountered D and G Companies. Spalding, Upcher and Rainforth conferred briefly at the head of the column, and the two company commanders agreed that the only sensible course of action was to get back to Helpmekaar as soon as possible and fortify the post for defence. It is clear that, by the time this occurred, Upcher had brought his troops and wagons down the front face of the Biggarsberg into the Buffalo River valley. The eagle-eyed men on the north wall had indeed seen redcoats on the road.

Alerted in the late afternoon by the arrival of the first of the cross-country fugitives, Captain Edward Essex amongst them, Colonel F. C. Hassard RE had left Essex in charge at Helpmekaar and had ridden after

Upcher and Rainforth to recall them. He met them not long after they turned and immediately took command. It was to take the column the more than four hours of night-time marching to get back to Helpmekaar. It would arrive at around 11.00 p.m., much to the relief of Essex and the handful of fellow survivors who stood by him.

One of Upcher's subalterns, Lieutenant William Lloyd, recalled the events of the evening in a letter written from Helpmekaar only two days later:

> So we pushed on, got down into a deep valley with cliffs all around, and heard from a straggler that it was all over at the river – that all had been slaughtered, and that it was madness to go on. We were then about two miles from the river. The Kaffirs were swarming on the hills above us, and it was getting dark – so it was determined to fall back and try and save the stores here. So at eight o'clock [it must actually have been closer to seven] we turned back, tired out and sick with hunger, having had no dinner, and climbed the hill. How we got back without being attacked I don't know, as the sky was red with burning houses and kraals. I was on rearguard and the last wagon broke down in the dark. However, we got in here at 12 o'clock at night and found they had laagered the place.

With the infantry away, it had been an extremely tense evening at Helpmekaar. Essex had emplaced a number of ox-wagons around the corrugated storehouses, so as to form a rudimentary laager, but there were a number of desertions as the work of fortification was going on. The civilians and some of the NNC Europeans were the first to go, but it was not long before some of the volunteers became mutinous too. In fairness, they were now more concerned about the safety of their families than the faithful execution of a wider duty. Essex ordered that all the horses were to be turned loose, and that any which wandered back should be shot. Before his order could be enacted, there was a big row about it, and it proved only to be the catalyst for a few more desertions.

*****

While the men in the hospital were fighting from room to room, and the sun was setting in the west, the rest of the garrison was fighting hard to retain its grip on the storehouse compound. The perimeter now consisted, in the west, of the biscuit box wall (the retrenchment barricade); in the north, of a relatively short stretch of the original north wall; in the east, of the outside walls of the cattle kraal; and in the south, the back and gable-walls of the storehouse. In many respects the situation had improved markedly; not least because the new perimeter was of a much more manageable length and the heavy fire from Shiyane had been largely neutralised. Yet, since the withdrawal to the retrenchment, the casualty toll had risen dramatically. The reasons were twofold. First, the defenders were now clustered much more tightly together and, second, Chard had ceded a great deal of good cover within only a few yards of the new perimeter. At its simplest, the Zulus were firing on a much easier target over much shorter ranges.

One man who fell to the short-range Zulu fire was Private John Fagan, another B Company youngster. It is difficult to be certain at what time he was hit but since he was given a drink of water as he lay dying by twenty-one-year-old Private Edward Savage, a 2nd/24th hospital patient, it was obviously at some point after the evacuation of the hospital. Savage, another Newport man, had an injured knee, the condition of which had not been helped by the jump from the window in the gable-wall. After crawling over to comfort Fagan, he found himself a gap in the biscuit boxes and fought on lying on his side. Later on in the action he teamed up with Bromhead to open an ammunition box, but in doing so cut his hands badly; quite how this happened is unclear.

When another sustained assault came in against the north wall, Hitch and Bromhead were again amongst the men who met it at the point of the bayonet. This sunset attack seems to have been amongst the most fierce. Hitch wrote:

> They seemed to me as if they made up their minds to take Rorke's Drift with this rush. They rushed madly up notwithstanding the heavy loss they had already suffered. It was in this struggle that I

was shot. They pressed us hard, several of them mounting the
barricade. I knew this one had got his rifle presented at me but at
the same time I had got my hands full in front and I was at the
present when he shot me through the right shoulder blade and
passed through my shoulder which splintered the shoulder bone
very much ... I tried to keep my feet, but could not. He could
have assegaied me had not Bromhead shot him with his revolver.
Bromhead seemed sorry when he saw me down bleeding so
freely, saying, 'Mate I am sorry to see you down.'

Hitch slumped down inside the mealie-bags and somebody helped
him off with his tunic. His shoulder was shattered. Clearly it would now
be impossible for him to handle a Martini-Henry. But Hitch was not the
man to be so easily thwarted. He replaced his equipment, stuffed his
useless right arm down inside his waist-belt, and then pestered
Bromhead for his revolver. In a few moments Hitch was back on his
feet, firing the pistol left-handed into the gathering darkness at the foot
of the north wall. When the bayonet fighting subsided and everybody
ducked back down behind the barricades, Bromhead found the time to
reload for the determined young man beside him.

At the other end of the barricade, Corporal Lyons and Corporal Allen
were contending with the Zulus in the lee of the south wall. Like
Private Connolly, Lyons was from Trevethin. He was now thirty-four
years of age and had fourteen years' service behind him. The two
corporals had already taken a heavy toll of the enemy, but were
exposing themselves to short-range return fire in order to do so. In a
fight of this kind it was only a matter of time before their luck ran out,
as Lyons later recalled:

About half past seven, as near as I can tell, I received a shot
through the right side of the neck. The ball lodged in the back,
striking the spine ... I said, 'Give it to them, Allen. I am done; I am
dying,' and he replied, 'All right Jack,' and while I was speaking to
him I saw a hole in the right sleeve of his jacket, and I said, 'Allen,
you are shot,' and he replied, 'Yes; goodbye.' He walked away
with blood running from his arm.

Lyons had fallen to the ground in one of the narrow gaps in the biscuit box barricade. A few moments after he went down, John Chard appeared above him. Chard paid the badly wounded corporal no attention, as he had gained the impression that Lyons had been shot dead. He was surprised to hear a voice from below, 'Oh sir, you are not going to leave me here like a dog.' Chard and another man quickly pulled Lyons into the cover of the wall, propped him up against the biscuit boxes and bellowed for the surgeon. Reynolds dashed across from the storehouse veranda, now crowded not only with the freshly wounded, but also with the non-combatant refugees from the hospital. He treated Lyons where he lay. The unfortunate corporal would spend the rest of the night propped up against the barricade, perhaps because it was as good a place as any, but more probably because Reynolds was able to diagnose that the round had damaged his spine making it medically undesirable to move him. Harry Hook had taken a place on the retrenchment barricade and periodically responded to Lyons's agonised requests to move his head from one side to the other. Without the benefit of such modern pain suppressants as morphine, the extent of Lyons's agony is unimaginable.

Fred Hitch too must have been in terrible pain, but remained determined nonetheless to contribute usefully to the defence. When he had fired the last of Bromhead's revolver cartridges, he dashed away from the barricade to fetch ammunition for his comrades. Before long he and Corporal Allen had paired up as a team and, using their good arms, began to ferry ammunition around the perimeter.

The Zulus at last seemed to have made some progress. The hospital was burning fiercely and the British had been squeezed back into a tiny perimeter. Surely with only a few more rushes their defences would collapse and a final slaughter could be accomplished. The north wall had proved a desperately difficult proposition and casualties here had been extremely heavy. Every bush seemed to have a dead or dying man beneath it. There was little that could be done for the wounded, but in any case it was not the Zulu way to break off from a fight to aid the injured. Under the cover of darkness they switched their main offensive effort to the eastern side of the post. Now the attacks formed up behind the walls of the stock pen and surged in against the men holding the cattle kraal. The eastern extremity of the rocky terrace presented the defenders with the same problem that the men fighting in front of the hospital had encountered earlier: the Zulus were able to take cover within a few yards of the defences, which meant that when they launched themselves into an assault, there was time enough only for a single aimed shot. Worse still was the alarming close-range fire in between rushes.

The Redoubt

Fortunately John Chard's skills as a sapper were more than equal to the new crisis. Looking at the two great piles of mealie-bags just in front of the innermost wall of the cattle kraal, he quickly conceptualised a new strongpoint. Once more he called Assistant Commissary Walter Dunne to his side and, shouting over the deafening tumult of the battle, explained his new construction plan. By taking mealie-bags off the topmost layers and filling in the gap between the two piles, it should be possible to merge them into one big pile. Then, by hollowing bags out of the centre, and using them to raise a rim around the outside edge of the mound, they should be left with something that would pass for a redoubt. The aim was threefold. First, to reduce the graze angle beneath the rocky terrace, and thus expose some of the dead ground beyond the cattle kraal to fire. Second, to raise something in the region of fifteen or twenty riflemen above the heads of the men defending the barricades and so enhance the amount of firepower that could be brought to bear upon any threatened point. Last, to create a defence work which would provide one final bastion should the outer walls be overrun, or should the storehouse be fired like the hospital. A peripheral advantage was that some of the most badly wounded could be placed in the bottom of the redoubt, where they would be well protected from incoming fire and throwing assegais. Dunne gathered four or five men to his side and began the work at about 7.10 p.m. It would take an hour of hard physical toil to complete the task. For much of the time, Dunne himself, a tall man, stood in plain view on top of the redoubt, heaving mealie-bags around. Although it was soon dark, the flames of the burning hospital silhouetted him terribly. Chard wrote that 'the enemy's fire was very heavy at the time . . . from the usual Zulu

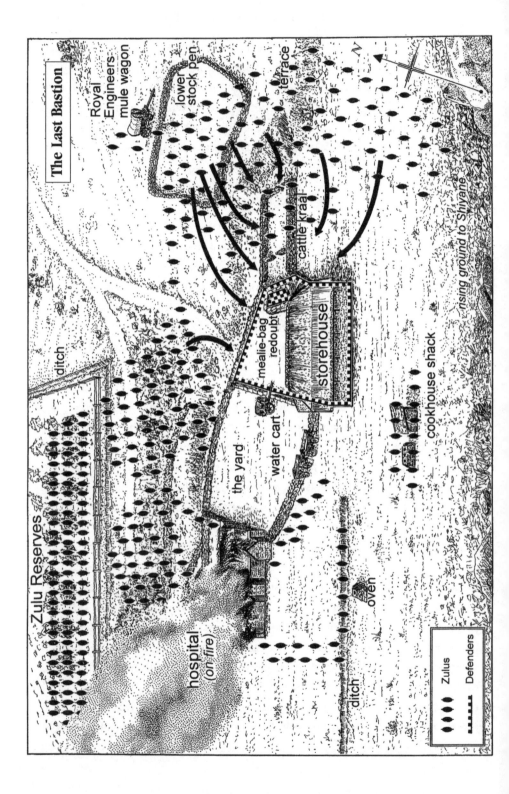

The Last Bastion

Royal Engineers mule wagon

lower stock pen

terrace

cattle kraal

mealie-bag redoubt

storehouse

water cart

the yard

hospital (on fire)

Zulu Reserves

ditch

oven

ditch

cookhouse shack

rising ground to Shiyane

N

Zulus

Defenders

fault of firing high, the place was one of particular exposure.' Dunne himself later recalled:

> Chard decided to form a sort of redoubt of mealie-bags, where a last stand could be made. We laboured at this till we dropped with exhaustion, but succeeded in building it up to about eight feet on the outside, and here the wounded were brought for protection. It was hard work, for the bags of mealies weighed 200lbs each. Overhead, the small birds disturbed from their nests by the turmoil and the smoke, flew hither and thither confusedly.

It is archetypal of the Victorian army that in writing of his own personal endeavours, Dunne chose to mention the frightened birds flying overhead, but to omit any mention of bullets and throwing assegais. Miraculously he remained uninjured.

The Night Fighting

All the while the stretch of the north wall in front of the storehouse, and the adjacent cattle kraal, were the focus of enemy attention. This owed a great deal to the inferno on the opposite side of the perimeter, which was serving to illuminate the yard and other fields of fire covered from the retrenchment barricade. After the severe punishment the four *amabutho* had already taken, good cover was becoming increasingly important to them. The warriors still on their feet and fighting were bemused. Notwithstanding the seemingly small numbers of red-soldiers opposing them, this was far from being the walkover they had been led to expect. Now they would have to box clever, and it was the dark side of the post that seemed to offer the best prospect of success. Having decided by some instinctive process that the eastern side of the perimeter was where they could achieve a break-in, the *amabutho* threw themselves into a fresh wave of assaults with seemingly unabated ardour. For a while the B Company soldiers holding the cattle kraal had to fight as hard as had the men in the hospital compound an hour and a half earlier.

Bromhead, meanwhile, was becoming increasingly concerned about ammunition. His men had been laying down an extremely heavy fire for a sustained period. It was crucial that the rate of expenditure be pegged back, in order to ensure that the ammunition would safely outlast the resolve of the enemy. Periodically he shouted instructions to make every round count or, in other words, that the men should remember their training, place accuracy ahead of rapidity, keep calm and shoot straight. It was good advice. Importantly it was good soldiering. There were many young soldiers in B Company, whose bodies and minds were coursing with a potent cocktail of adrenalin, determination, fear and anxiety. Hearing their company commander's voice did them a power of good. It exerted a steadying effect. B Company calmed itself, steeled itself and shot straighter.

As the ordeal wore on it became evident that the Martini-Henry was going to be subjected to stresses far in excess of anticipated battlefield norms. Nevertheless it is clear that it emerged from the ordeal with its reputation substantially intact. Strangely many modern historians have felt moved to exaggerate the rifle's failings, though the primary sources contain no great body of negative testimony. Military truisms dictate that all rifles have their failings and that battle conditions will always induce stoppages. It is important therefore that the failings of the Martini are kept in perspective.

When a Martini-Henry is fired continuously the barrel will become excessively hot. This is true of any firearm. The particular problem with the Martini was that the wood of the fore stock heated almost as badly. It had not taken long for old hands to devise a simple and effective countermeasure. The technique adopted in South Africa was to sew a cowhide hand-guard around the fore stock, soak and shrink it to fit, and then cut a hole for the leaf sight. By the mid-1880s improvised hand-guards were something thinking officers like Wolseley would expect to see in universal use when inspecting a battalion; but this was an expectation based on the battlefield experience gained in Zululand and Afghanistan at the turn of the decade. Prior to January 1879 the Martini had seen so little operational use that the necessity for hand-guards would not yet have been universally appreciated. That being so those members of B Company who had not taken the precaution of adding one would have been obliged, within half an hour of the battle commencing, to use dusters and rags beneath the fore stock in an attempt to prevent burns to their hands.

Over the years plenty of erroneous assertions about the Martini have been made. A good example is the apparent necessity to prise jammed cartridges out of the breech with a pocketknife. In truth the rim of the cartridge rests absolutely flush with the breech and is going nowhere by means of prising. The best means of clearing a jammed case, in fact, was to draw the steel cleaning rod and with a jerk of the wrist impel it hard down the barrel. The rod's momentum would be such that jammed cases would invariably be sent flying from the breech. The rod was recovered by simply upending the rifle. With the rod returned to its housing, the soldier could now proceed to reload. The drill could be completed in a mere ten seconds.

There is no question but that the Martini fouled relatively quickly – certainly the barrel became grimy after about 20 shots. This had two effects: first, it worsened recoil dramatically, (there being little recoil associated with the first few shots of the day), and second, it increased the incidence of stoppages. At Isandlwana where there would have been no time to scour the barrel and 70 rounds would have been fired without let up in little more than an hour's heavy fighting, the men of the 24th would have met their ends with bruised shoulders. At Rorke's Drift, however, the situation allowed individual soldiers to drop into cover to scour the barrel with cleaning rod, jag and flannel, a job of about 40 seconds. Even so it was probably the case that by sunset most defenders had a slightly bruised shoulder, but again this needs to be contextualised: in the midst of a battle for life, a tender shoulder is of no import.

With the garrison ensconced in the storehouse compound, a few jammed rifles were likewise of no real consequence. But it was vital that it never amounted to more than a few at any one time and thus imperative that the men worked rapidly to bring their weapons back into action. No doubt stoppages were the cause of a good deal of blaspheming, but fortunately Chaplain Smith was at hand to administer suitably stern admonishments and to bestow both forgiveness and cartridges.

Until the redoubt was finished Chard had no alternative but to hold the outside walls of the cattle kraal. For an hour between 7.00 p.m. and 8 p.m., the first hour of darkness, the attacks on this side of the post were extremely heavy. Given the significant number of gunshot casualties that occurred along the retrenchment barricade, it would be surprising if there were not also a number of casualties during the fight for the cattle kraal. Nobody on this side of the perimeter seems to have recorded their experiences in any detail, but if Sergeant George Smith, one of the B Company section commanders, was not on the retrenchment barricade, which he does not seem to have been, then he may have been in charge of the defence of the cattle kraal. Two days after the battle, he found time to write home to his wife. In his letter he wrote, 'One of our men was shot through the lungs, and he stuck to his post, and fired away for an hour, when he dropped down dead from loss of blood.' Two soldiers of the 24th died from gunshot wounds in otherwise unrecorded circumstances. One was Private John Scanlon of A Company, 2nd/24th, and the other was Private James Chick of D Company, 2nd/24th. Both had less than two years' service, both had originally been hospital patients, and both stood to on the barricades alongside everybody else. Logically Smith can only be referring to one of these two soldiers and there would seem to be a strong probability that the incident occurred in or near the cattle kraal. Whichever of them it was, he showed the most phenomenal courage and resolve; men have been awarded the Victoria Cross for less. It is a pity that Sergeant Smith was not more precise, but soldiers' letters to their families, dealing with situations their kith and kin can never hope to understand, are seldom too demonstrative. It is the soldier's way.

When Walter Dunne had finished his dangerous Herculean toil, no time was wasted in manning the redoubt with a score of riflemen. They were crammed shoulder to shoulder around the rim, for it was a tiny fortification only a few yards across, but when a rush came in, they were able to bring not less than six or seven additional rifles to bear on any threatened sector. It was not a one-way exchange by any means; from the eastern side of the post, the men inside the redoubt were silhouetted against the background of the blazing hospital and were plainly visible to Zulu riflemen crouching beneath the terrace. In between rushes though, the soldiers ducked down inside the mealie-bags to protect themselves from the shower of bullets and throwing assegais that invariably came raining in after a repulse.

Encouraged by the dramatic consequences of firing the hospital, the Zulus now made an attempt to ignite the storehouse. A number of throwing assegais wrapped in burning grass came thudding into the thatch, but none of them caused a serious fire. The recent rains had been a godsend after all. Then a warrior came running out of the shadows with some kind of flaming torch and raised it to the roof. Fortunately he was spotted by Corporal Attwood of the ASC from his attic loophole; he could just about bring his carbine to bear and was able to shoot the man before he could do any real harm. Other warriors tried to get in close, but it was difficult to find a blind spot to Sergeant Windridge's well-sited loopholes and the men inside the storehouse were able to bring them all down.

It is a sad but true fact of history that no worthwhile accounts of the Battle of Rorke's Drift have come down to us from the Zulu side. Apart from the fact that the iNdluyengwe spearheaded the first attack, little else is known of how the *amabutho* interacted or co-operated one with another. Certainly we have little idea what orders were given, when they were given, who gave them and who they gave them to. It is difficult to imagine how the regimental commanders could have managed their battle with any finesse, beyond keeping a number of companies in check in the brush or the orchard, and feeding them into the fray as they judged best. But there is absolutely no evidence to support even this basic notion. It is just as likely that the warriors got completely out of hand and that there was next to no command and control in play. There were only a limited number of manoeuvres which might potentially bear the hallmarks of premeditated command decisions. Only three of these were in any way noteworthy. The first was the decision at around 6.00 p.m. to swing an assault across the fork in the road to hit the north wall in front of the storehouse – the attack that triggered Chard's withdrawal to the retrenchment barricade. The second was the launching of a concerted, heavy and sustained attack at about sunset, or roughly between 7.20 and 7.40 p.m. The third was the decision to swing the main effort against the cattle kraal and the eastern side of the post after dark.

Even so there can be no certainty that these apparently significant moments were the product of conscious command decisions taken at regimental level. Certainly the decision to hit an apparently thinly defended stretch of barricade, as was the case with the 6.00 p.m. assault, might well be attributable to the local initiative of junior indunas operating at company level. The second and third instances might be attributable purely to the soldierly common sense of the Zulu fighting man; it does not take a military genius to know that a concerted effort at last light stands an infinitely greater chance of success than a series of fragmented and costly attacks conducted in broad daylight. Nor is it anything other than common sense to operate under the cover of darkness – hence the switch to the side of the cattle kraal – the point on the perimeter furthest from the illumination of the blazing hospital.

Certainly Dabulamanzi and the other senior indunas missed their best opportunity to break into the post by means of a carefully concerted battle plan. While the yard and the hospital compound were in British hands, the defenders were stretched thinly enough for the Undi Corps to have had a strong chance of achieving a break-in. If they could have thrown two *amabutho* at the north wall, at precisely the same time as a third regiment hit the south wall, with the fourth held in reserve to exploit a break-in quickly, then the chances are they would have swamped the defences. They had from about 4.45 p.m. to 6.00 p.m. to achieve a twin-pronged assault, but after that time the withdrawal to the retrenchment barricade changed the situation completely. No longer were the British thinly stretched around the perimeter; indeed, if anything, they were now a little too closely crowded together. The retrenchment covered a tiny surface area – in effect it was akin to a company 'receive cavalry' square, but with physical outer walls, not the more usual human ones. From 6.00 p.m. onwards the British perimeter was so small that it mattered not whether the indunas even had a plan. The only way in was by means of what today's British soldiers would term, 'B.F.I.' – 'brute force and ignorance'.

In essence then, the Zulu regimental commanders had only a limited window of opportunity in which to assert their overpowering superiority of numbers to marked advantage. Fortunately for Chard and Bromhead, Dabulamanzi and his colleagues were unable to sense the transient nature of their opportunity, and allowed it to pass them by. Probably they did so because it must have seemed for the first hour of the fight that they wouldn't have to try too hard – that ultimately victory was inevitable. By the time they realised that kwaJim was a much tougher nut to crack than they had at first thought, Chard had concentrated his force into a well entrenched company square. So it would seem that there was something sadly missing in the Zulus' higher management of the battle, and that it was in fact largely directed at a localised level by junior indunas.

Surgeon Reynolds had done what he could for the seriously wounded. A number were in need of an operation, generally to remove a bullet, but it was clearly impractical to attempt such sophisticated treatment in the current desperate situation. In the meantime he had done everything possible to staunch the flow of blood and to prevent severe shock setting in. Now it was largely a matter of individual resilience whether a gravely wounded man lived or died. Reynolds had a number of his most serious cases, including Dalton, lifted up to the men in the redoubt and lowered down inside.

By now Fred Hitch had utterly exhausted himself and was faint from loss of blood. He had a raging thirst and at last realised that he was completely played out. He sat himself down against the biscuit boxes to rest, only a few yards from the point at which he had been wounded. Somebody did their best to dress his shoulder with an improvised bandage – in fact it was the lining of Walter Dunne's tunic, temporarily discarded whilst he laboured on the redoubt. Still, after more than three hours, the fighting was relentless. Pessimism seems to have settled over a few of the defenders. Private George Deacon,* a young B Company private crouched down beside Hitch to speak to him. 'Fred, when it comes to the last, shall I shoot you?' he asked. 'No; they have very near done for me, and they can finish me right out, when it comes to the last,' replied Hitch. The last thing Hitch saw was his company commander still fighting in defence of the troublesome front corner. Then he lost consciousness. Perhaps it was Deacon who, with the help of others, lifted Hitch up to the outstretched arms of the

---

* Deacon was an enlistment alias; his real name was George Power.

men manning the redoubt. It had been a brave fight, but however it was destined to end, Fred Hitch was now well and truly out of it.

At around 8.00 p.m. there was a particularly heavy assault on the north-eastern corner of the perimeter. Large numbers of Zulus came boiling out of the shadows and came to close quarters. A good many were shot down, but it was all the men could do to stand their ground around the walls of the cattle kraal. The kraal protruded into enemy-held territory and the dark of the night. In an attempt to improve the situation and bring the men in the redoubt more fully into play, Chard gave orders that the men in the kraal should fall back to its inner partition wall. They quickly scrambled back the few yards to their new line of defence and, whilst two or three men plugged up the inner gateway with mealie bags and biscuit boxes, the rest waited for the enemy to show their heads above the outer wall. The warriors stood next to no chance of getting over, but for a while at least, it didn't seem to stop them trying. If they were not shot by somebody on the partition wall, they were soon picked off from the redoubt. Many tried crawling in beneath the rocky terrace to hit the north side of the kraal and the stretch of mealie-bag barricade just beyond, but there was no avoiding the fact that sooner or later they had to get their feet; invariably they were quickly shot down.

Although this side of the post was relatively secure, short-range fire from the shadows still made it an extremely dangerous place to be. To ease the pressure a little further, Chard gave orders at about 9.00 p.m. that the partition wall in the kraal should also be ceded. The men fell back to its nearside wall, directly beneath the redoubt. This meant that a Zulu attempting to get to close quarters now had to expose himself scaling the outer wall, dash to the cover of the partition wall, and would then face a second period of exposure to extremely short range fire when he tried to get over it. With never fewer than about fifteen to twenty rifles trained in this direction, it was a tall order. Nobody made it.

By now the Zulu assaults seemed to be lacking something of their earlier ardour. In between each onset, the voices of the indunas could be heard urging their men into a renewed attempt. There were outbreaks of chanting as the warriors formed up in the dark, intended no doubt to stiffen their resolve, but the practice served only to forewarn the defenders firstly that a new assault was imminent, and secondly on which sector of the perimeter it would fall. Each new rush was met with an unfaltering close-range fire which, combined with an ever-increasing sense of futility, was now driving the warriors to ground some way short of the barricades. A number of defenders said that not a single Zulu got inside the storehouse compound. It was not literally true, because Hitch for one fought hand-to-hand on the British side of the barricade, but it is a telling remark nonetheless. One would venture to suggest that the men who did get inside the barricade could be counted on the fingers of one hand. The last bastion had assumed an air of impregnability. It was the Zulus who sensed it first, but by now it had dawned on the British too.

Pause

Even if Chard and Bromhead dare not give utterance to the idea, it was beginning to look as if the enemy's momentum was spent. Exhausted as they were, the soldiers of the 24th began to realise that their ferocious defence of the perimeter had not merely been effective in maintaining its integrity, but that in the process it seemed to have ripped the heart out of the enemy. For the first time they dared to hope that they might live to see the dawn. Doubtless first light would be the cue for a massive, simultaneous attack on all sides, but for the time being at least, the defenders seemed to have the upper hand. As if to confirm their fears and expectations of the dawn, direct frontal assault on the perimeter petered out from about 9.30 p.m. Surely somewhere in the night the warriors were resting while the indunas planned the final push. The men took consolation from the fact that they had already held out for five hours. Nobody could say they had not tried. When the big dawn attack materialised, they would go down fighting. Perhaps they would be remembered. But some men are born optimists. Maybe, they said, the dawn attack could be broken too, or perhaps help would come. The cynics pointed out that everybody else in Natal would be forted up like them – that there was no help to be had.

Bromhead and his colour-sergeant were not interested in idle speculation. Direct assault might have abated temporarily, but the periodic outbreaks of firing on one side of the perimeter or the other, told them that the enemy were still lurking nearby. If the attack was renewed, then it could only be repelled with .450-inch Boxer cartridges. Bromhead ordered that a full replenishment of the men's pouches should take place. Then he and Bourne took stock. Of the 34 boxes of reserve ammunition with which they had started the fight, only 6 now remained, a mere 3,600 rounds, or an additional 30 per man. With the ammunition in the men's pouches, they had perhaps 12,000 rounds left in all, 100 rounds a man, with which to face the new day. Thus far they had fired some 25,000 rounds in five hours of heavy fighting. On average then, each man had already fired 210 rounds at a rate of 42 rounds an hour. With a rifle capable of firing 7–8 rounds a minute with ease, it is interesting to note that B Company had clearly exercised excellent fire control. If Bromhead did the mental arithmetic, he would have calculated that at the same rates of expenditure they could sustain the defence for 2½ hours more. No doubt he instructed his NCOs to keep tight control of the garrison's return fire during the hours of darkness.

Soon an hour had passed with nothing more dramatic than a few flurried exchanges of fire. The pause was welcome, and here and there a few of the men had dropped down with their backs to the barricade and were dozing gently. With each new fusillade they would wake with a start and leap to their feet, but no direct assault came in against the barricades. Before long it was midnight and the flames from the gutted hospital were beginning to die away. The men's water bottles had been dry for hours but there was no ready means of replenishing them. Everybody was desperately thirsty and there was particular concern that dehydration might kill some of the more dangerously wounded. Now that there was a lull, however, it might be possible to mount a sortie to recover the water cart. If it was dangerous work, then Bromhead was going to do it himself. He pulled half a dozen men together on the retrenchment barricade, including Harry Hook, quickly briefed them, and then led them over the wall into no-man's-land. They dashed the twenty-five yards to the water cart, secured it, and began heaving it back in the direction of the barricade. Bromhead and a couple of men stood with rifles poised, ready to deal with any attempt to interfere with the operation, but no resistance materialised and in a few moments the cart was nestled hard beside the retrenchment barricade. Fortunately it was equipped with long hose-pipes, which it was possible to drape over the biscuit boxes so that the men could fill their water bottles in relative safety.

As the night wore on into the early hours, Chard and Bromhead remained vigilant and stared anxiously into the gloom for any sign that the enemy might be infiltrating in against the barricades. From time to time they clambered onto the redoubt for a better view. But the only enemy activity now was intermittent sniping. The last shots were fired at around 4.00 a.m. Not much more than about half an hour later, the first hint of a new day was discernible in the eastern sky.

Chapter 6

Deliverance

The Relief of Rorke's Drift

Lord Chelmsford had prowled the outposts all night. He wished the darkness away a thousand times, but the more he wished it, the more the night seemed to drag endlessly on. Even before it was half-light, the general had shaken his staff officers awake and despatched them to rouse and form the troops. Not only was it his duty to march as quickly as possible to the relief of Rorke's Drift, but he was also extremely anxious to get the remnants of No. 3 Column on the road before the dawn revealed the full extent of the carnage around them. Whilst it was clear that there had been an overnight engagement at the foot of Shiyane, there was no news as yet of its outcome. But a gambling man could take no comfort from the glow in the sky the previous evening or in the stillness since midnight; neither were encouraging signs.

Everybody was tired, dirty, hungry and thirsty; grounds enough in their own right to bring on the mood of weary resignation that so typically settles over soldiers roused with the first hint of dawn. But this was no ordinary dawn. This was Isandlwana on the morning of Thursday 23 January 1879. In addition to the physical discomforts, there were overpowering sensations of despondency, bereavement and anxiety to contend with. Some men had to endure the awful burdens of guilt and shame also, not least the GOC himself. The stench of slaughter was fast taking hold, and for some reason the chemicals spilled in the looting of the hospital tents were giving off a particularly foul odour. Some of the men were covered in dried blood that was not their own. Huddles of company officers muttered darkly out of earshot; the pleas of the 2nd Battalion officers to be allowed to search the wreckage of the camp for their colours had gone unheeded. There was lots of ill-tempered shouting as the troops formed but, without any heavy transport to worry about, the column was ready to move soon enough.

Commandant Maori Browne of 1st/3rd NNC had quietly slipped away to search the camp for some of his personal belongings. He was one of the very few men to have traversed the full extent of the desolate encampment that morning. It would be many weeks before anybody dared return, by which time the Zulu dead had been carried away and the British dead were badly decomposed, so inevitably Browne's recollections are of particular interest. Even allowing for his colourful literary style, his memoirs offer a number of interesting insights into the scene. His tent was on the left of the camp. The majority of the 1st/24th fell in rallying squares in the saddle between Isandlwana and Mahlabamkhosi, whilst the men of the 2nd/24th were overwhelmed well to the front of the tent lines. The 24th bodies which Browne describes below are almost certainly those of A Company, 1st/24th, Captain William Degacher's men, who were cut off during the course of the retreat, amongst and behind the tents of the 2nd/24th – the camp next to Browne's:

> My God, in the grey dawn it was a sight! In their mad rush into the camp, the Zulus had killed everything. Horses had been stabbed at their picket lines. Splendid spans of oxen were lying dead in their yokes, mules lay dead in their harness and even dogs were lying stabbed among the tents. Ripped open sacks of rice, flour, meal and sugar lay everywhere. They had even in their savage rage thrust their assegais into tins of bully beef, butter and jam. Amongst all this debris singly and in heaps, or rather in groups of two or three, lay the ripped and mutilated bodies of the gallant 24th, showing how, when their formation was broken, they had stood it out, and fought back to back or in groups until they had been run over and destroyed. That they fought to the last gasp could be seen by the number of dead Zulus who lay everywhere in amongst them, the bayonet wounds on their bodies telling of the fierce, though short combat that had taken place after the right horn of the Zulus had swept round the hill. I had just time to get

to the door of my tent, inside of which I saw my old setter dog, dead with an assegai thrust through her. My two spare horses were also lying killed at their picket rope, with my Totty [Hottentot] groom dead between them ... I saw the bodies of two of my officers lying dead with heaps of empty cartridge shells by their sides. Both had been splendid shots and I bet they had done plenty of execution before they went under. As I reined up I glanced out to the left and left front of the camp, and saw heaps and heaps of Zulu dead. Where the volleys of the 24th had checked them, they lay in lines, and the donga I had ridden over on the morning of the 21st was chock full of them. Surely the 24th had died game, but bitter as I felt, a thrill of admiration passed through me when I thought of the splendid courage of the savages who could advance to the charge suffering the awful punishment they were getting.

I had not time to dismount as I heard the bugle sound the advance and I galloped back to my men as fast as I could without trampling on the bodies of my poor comrades. On my way I reined up my horse sharply, for there lay the body of my old friend Lieut-Col. Pulleine; I could no nothing for him, and it at once flashed through my mind our last words of chaff, so I saluted the poor remains and passed on as quickly as I could to my men.

The words of 'chaff' to which Browne refers were exchanged as he was marching out of camp on Tuesday morning. Pulleine had jokingly remarked as Browne rode past that a lot of the NNC leaders would be 'knocked over' during the course of the day. Browne's similarly light-hearted but supremely prophetic riposte was that he expected to find nobody alive at Isandlwana when he returned.

By now the 2nd/24th and 2nd/3rd NNC had already moved off, leaving the 1st/3rd NNC at the back of the solemn procession. Last of all came Major Wilsone Black of the 2nd/24th, who with characteristic grit had taken it upon himself to assume command of the rearguard, a section of the mounted infantry squadron. Browne and Black rode away from the dismal scene of destruction together.

Clearing Patrols

The pre-dawn stand to at Rorke's Drift was tense in the extreme. For a long time the garrison stared anxiously into the gloom for any sign of movement, but nothing stirred and the silence was broken only by the pitiful groaning of badly wounded men. With the gradual onset of daylight it became increasingly clear that the Zulus had withdrawn in the night, at least from the immediate environs of the mission. At length the surrounding hillsides became visible too, revealing that the wider landscape was also entirely deserted. For the first time the defenders dared to hope that their ordeal was over, that, miraculous as it seemed, they had somehow won a great victory. The mood at the post changed abruptly into one of light-hearted jubilation.

It would have been easy to sink into a bout of self-congratulation, or to slump down behind the barricades in a state of stunned disbelief, but Chard and Bromhead remained only too keenly aware of their isolation, and the consequent danger that the enemy might reappear at any moment. They detailed a number of clearing patrols to scour the immediate vicinity of the post, and set other men to gather up discarded enemy weapons. The top priorities were to de-thatch the roof of the storehouse, to repair and improve the barricades and to clear the fields of fire. One of the NCOs took a work party to pull down what was left of the hospital. The task was accomplished by heaving on ropes threaded from loophole to loophole. Other men dragged Zulu corpses clear of the mealie-bags. Hook went across to speak to a man who appeared to have fallen asleep over the barricade, only to realise that he had been shot in the head and was long since dead. Almost certainly this was Private Nicholas, the twenty-one-year-old Newport lad killed near Hitch as they were defending the exposed corner between the retrenchment barricade and the north wall.

As the work was getting under way, Gunner Arthur Howard came wandering in from the scrub, no doubt with shattered nerves and a very relieved smile on his face. The curiosity aroused by his sudden reappearance was suddenly dispelled when a Zulu leapt up from behind the walls of the cattle kraal and fired his musket into the yard. He was gone in a flash. Men ran after him and fired a few shots to hasten him on his way, but he was not hit and succeeded in rounding Shiyane at a run. Chard was secretly pleased that he made it to safety, for it was clear from the carnage all about him that his little force had inflicted more than enough damage on the Zulu nation for one day. The bodies were piled high along the line of the north wall, nowhere more so than in front of the hospital, where some of the most bitter close-quarter fighting had taken place. Suddenly Private Waters appeared from nowhere, still wrapped in Witt's cloak. Still nervous soldiers jerked rifles in his direction, but fortunately nobody fired. He was quickly ushered away to the doctor to have his wounded shoulder looked at.

In the meantime, somebody inspecting the Zulu dead in front of the hospital had stumbled upon young Private Beckett. Barely alive, he too was immediately rushed across to the surgeon for urgent medical attention. Reynolds probably did not even need to peel back his gore-covered tunic to know that this was a lost cause. His examination quickly revealed that the stab wound was every bit as bad as he feared. He did his best to make Beckett comfortable, but there was little else that could be done in such rough and ready conditions for a man who had lost quite so much blood. As he continued his never-ending round of the wounded, Reynolds could see in daylight that Lance Sergeant Williams's ribcage was very badly mangled.

Chard gave orders that a temporary mortuary for the British dead be established in the cattle kraal, where there was room to lay out the bodies decently. When Private Garret Hayden's body was found in the grass on the far side of the hospital, the numerous mutilations inflicted upon it caused a particular stir. Chard ordered that the corpses be covered up and had a sentry posted on the kraal to keep people away. The unpleasant task of recovering Sergeant Maxfield's badly charred remains from the ruins of the hospital was not undertaken immediately. It transpired that fifteen men had fallen in all, including the deserter Corporal Anderson. By the end of the day, the death toll would rise to seventeen; Beckett and Lance Sergeant Williams both succumbed to their injuries.

John Chard's description of some of the Zulu bodies strewn around the post conveys something of the horrific aftermath of battle:

One man's head was split open, exactly as if done with an axe. Another had been hit between the eyes, the bullet carrying away the whole of the back of his head, leaving his face perfect, as though it were a mask, only disfigured by the small hole made by the bullet passing through. One of the wretches we found, one hand grasping a bench that had been dragged from the hospital, and sustained thus in the position we found him in, while in the other hand, he still clutched the knife with which he had mutilated one of our poor fellows, over whom he was still leaning.

It is difficult to conclude positively which of the British bodies is at issue here. The implication is that the vignette was played out near the hospital. On the face of it Joseph Williams, Horrigan, Hayden and Adams would seem the most likely candidates, but they were killed on the far side of the hospital, in dead ground to the retrenchment barricade. It would be impossible for the Zulu to have been killed in the act of mutilating one of these bodies, but no immediately obvious alternative suggests itself, unless Reynolds was right when he wrote that Private James Jenkins was also killed in the hospital. Reynolds categorises Jenkins as being 'debilitated by fever' like Maxfield, yet the man at issue must have been fit enough to get out of the front of the hospital under his own steam. While the reference might conceivably tend to reinforce the notion that Joseph Williams made a break around the front of the hospital, probably his most likely course of action in the circumstances, ultimately it is impossible to state with any degree of certainty which of the British dead Chard is referring to.

At about 6.30 a.m. a lone black male came in to the post. He was probably lucky not to have been shot. Because he spoke no English, nobody was quite sure at first who he was. Chard sent for Daniels, the pont-man, whom he knew was a Zulu speaker. Daniels equipped himself with Major Spalding's sword for the impromptu interrogation, which he somewhat eccentrically flourished under the stranger's nose throughout the proceedings. It transpired that he was a NNC fugitive from Isandlwana. Notwithstanding Daniels having put the fear of God into him, he agreed to bear a note on Chard's behalf to the troops at Helpmekaar.

Hook was one of the men sent out to gather weapons. First he walked out to the termite mound behind the hospital, to see if he had in fact hit the man he had fired three successive shots at during the first onset of the iNdluyengwe. Sure enough, there he was, drilled through the head. Next, Hook wandered out beyond the cattle kraal, in the direction of the drift, his rifle at his side, curiously inspecting dead Zulus and gathering up assegais as he went:

> Suddenly I came across an unarmed Zulu lying on the ground apparently dead but bleeding from the leg. Thinking it strange that a dead man should bleed, I hesitated, and wondered whether I should go on, as other Zulus might be lurking about. But I resumed my task. Just as I was passing, the supposed dead man seized the butt of my rifle and tried to drag it away. The bunch of assegais rattled to earth. The Zulu suddenly released the grasp of the rifle with one hand, and with the other fiercely endeavoured to drag me down. The fight was short and sharp; but it ended by the Zulu being struck in the chest with the butt and knocked to the ground. The rest was quickly over. After this we were not allowed to go on with our task except in twos and threes.

Chaplain Smith recorded that over a hundred firearms and 400 assegais were recovered by the patrols. This is indicative of just how well provided with firearms the Zulu *amabutho* of 1879 were. It also shows just how much short-range fire was poured into the defences; these were the weapons of men who fell in assaults on the barricades. How many others were in action we can only guess at. It is wide of the mark to suggest, as many historians have done, that the bulk of the Zulu rifle fire came from Shiyane. Some of it did, certainly, but the fire from the close cover – the scrub, the lee side of the rocky terrace, the stone wall, the cookhouse and the orchard – had been the much more potent menace.

Enemy in Sight

By 7.00 a.m. it had been light for over two hours. The various work details were going about their business and the atmosphere amongst the troops was bordering on the euphoric. Typical post-traumatic symptoms, such as acute depression and an uneasy conscience, would descend upon the survivors at intervals varying between the next few hours and the ensuing four or five days. Suddenly somebody spotted a large body of Zulus moving into position on the forward slope of kwaSingqindi Hill. The alarm was raised, the patrols and work parties came rushing in, and everybody braced themselves at their stand-to positions for a renewed bout of fighting. The enemy's reappearance at this juncture can only have had a deeply distressing effect on men who had convinced themselves that their ordeal was over. Nonetheless, they were tough, motivated professionals and steeled themselves once more. They had beaten the Zulus back all night, still had plenty of ammunition in their pouches, and now that the sun was up, had a clear sense of the heavy punishment they had already inflicted upon the enemy. Let them come again if they want. The men of B Company rested their rifles on the mealie-bags and biscuit boxes and waited for the enemy to make the next move. By now the Zulus were formed across the hillside in their customary well ordered ranks. There they squatted down to watch the red-ant figures below.

Ships that Pass in the Night

Not long after they had crossed the Batshe valley, the mounted troops at the head of Colonel Glyn's column had a remarkable encounter. In the low ground down to their left, in the direction of the river, there was a large force of Zulus. They were only a few hundred yards away and well within small arms range. The senior officers and their staffs quickly cantered up to the head of the column for a look. Captain Henry Harford, a regular officer serving with the NNC, noticed more warriors further up the slope to the right of the road, and began to suspect a trap. In fact, each side seems to have been waiting for the other to initiate hostilities. Colonel Harness had already unlimbered his guns for action, but it soon became clear that there was next to no fight left in the enemy. Neither did Lord Chelmsford have any intention of bringing on an engagement. The 2nd/24th had marched from Isandlwana with the basic ammunition scale of seventy rounds per man. All the reserve ammunition had been lost with the camp, and it

was far from clear when or where the troops would next see an
ammunition box. This was not the time or the place to start a fight.

It seems clear that the retreating British column was in fact marching
through the middle of the Undi Corps, having cut across behind one
ibutho and ahead of another. The Zulus too were intent only on
withdrawal, and were in the process of re-crossing the river at the same
spot they had used the day before. Not all four *amabutho* were yet
clear of Rorke's Drift, for the British vanguard would not reach the river
until 7.00 a.m., at which point at least one regiment was still on
kwaSingqindi Hill. Although by now the Zulu regimental commanders
were probably acting independently of one another, it is possible that
one of them had taken it upon himself to loiter behind everybody else
as a rearguard. It was said later by the Lutheran missionaries who
settled at Eland's Kraal, that their local people spoke of a strong force
of Zulus which crossed the river there later that morning. It would seem
likely then that the rearguard regiment chose not to follow the other
amabutho over the crossing point behind Shiyane, but that it went
away downstream along a separate line of retreat to the south-east, thus
avoiding Lord Chelmsford's force altogether.

One brave Zulu with the main body of the Undi Corps ran back and
forth in front of his comrades demanding that they join him in an attack
on the remnants of No. 3 Column. His taunts were greeted with dumb
indifference. Suddenly he turned on his heel and came dashing uphill
alone. For a few moments the British looked on in the mistaken belief
that this was a mock-charge; that, like a nervous elephant, he would
eventually halt and turn away, having made his point. But then the lone
attacker started to get uncomfortably close. A few of the men in his
path raised their Martinis to the shoulder. Still he charged on. Then
came the inevitable ripple of shots which crumpled him into the grass,
the last member of the Zulu nation to fall in the Isandlwana campaign.

The British column moved on. The Zulus pinned against the river
waited for the enemy to clear their front and then likewise went on
their way. A story spread amongst the British in the ensuing weeks that,
believing all the red-soldiers upcountry to be dead, the Zulus who saw
them that morning took them for a ghost army. It is a nice story.

Salvation

Major John Dartnell and the Natal Carbineers were at the head of the column and were relieved to find, when they reached the drift, that the ponts were still intact. Some of the carbineers quickly swam their horses over in order to sort out the sunken ropes and hawsers. By now it was broad daylight. The officers of the staff were busily scanning the distant mission station with their binoculars, but by all accounts were unable to make a positive identification of the tiny figures in the distance. Certainly there was still some smoke drifting up from the ruins of the hospital. Lieutenant Colonel John Russell and part of the Imperial Mounted Infantry (IMI) detachment prepared to move on ahead of everybody else, to confirm the situation one way or the other. The carbineers dismounted and formed a skirmish line along the river bank, on which the IMI could fall back if anything went wrong at the top of the slope. Riding beside Russell was Lieutenant Henry Walsh, the officer who had twice crossed the plain between Isandlwana and Mangeni in the dark with despatches. The infantry and the artillery halted on the ridge above the river, in much the same positions they had occupied less than a fortnight earlier when they first entered Zululand.

Russell and Walsh led the IMI down to the river. They re-formed on the far bank and cantered off in the direction of Rorke's Drift, carbines at the ready, prepared for anything. Captain Penn Symons of the 24th went with them; he had spent many years in B Company, knew the men well, and was understandably anxious to discover their fate. 'Noggs' Norris-Newman, the newspaper correspondent, was also in the party. Soon the horsemen could make out that there were men in red coats dotted around the mission, but still a nagging doubt remained. The previous afternoon, Commandant Rupert Lonsdale, the regimental commander of 3rd NNC, had inadvertently ridden into the aftermath of the battle at the camp. He had described how many of the Zulus looting the camp had pulled on the red tunics of the British dead. The slaughtered white bodies that everybody had glimpsed that morning, as they were forming up in the half-light, had for the most part been naked to the waist or stripped to their grey flannel shirts. But it rapidly became clear as the party cantered on up the slope that this was no subterfuge. The men in red were waving, cheering and throwing their helmets into the air. There was a man on the roof waving a flag. The cheers of the defenders carried to the men down on the river, who raised a cheer of their own in response. Rorke's Drift had been held.

Walter Dunne remembered the first exchange with one of the officers at the head of the mounted infantry. It sounds from his reaction that it must have been Symons rather than a non-24th officer such as Russell or Walsh:

> Approaching cautiously at first, a mounted officer, when reassured, galloped up and anxiously enquired if any of the men from Isandlwana had escaped and joined us. Sadly we answered 'No!' Overcome by emotion at the terrible certainty conveyed by that short word, he bent down to his horse's neck trying in vain to stifle the sobs from his overcharged heart. No wonder his grief mastered him for he had passed during the night by that camp where hundreds of his brave comrades lay slaughtered, and the hope that some portion may have fought their way through was crushed forever.

Not long afterwards, the general, Colonel Glyn and the staff, came trotting up from the river. Lord Chelmsford thanked the men aloud for their gallant defence of the post and then ushered Chard and Bromhead to one side to hear their report. During all the excitement, the Zulu regiment on kwaSingqindi Hill moved quietly off downriver. This was the last element of the Undi Corps to re-cross the frontier. With their departure, Harry Hook excused himself from the barricades and headed over to the cookhouse shack where, having dragged some Zulu bodies out of his way, he got on with the essential business of brewing up some tea. Now that all the fuss was over, he was still the hospital cook; the expression, 'salt of the earth' might have been invented to describe Alfred Henry Hook. Not long after the arrival of the general and the mounted infantry, Chard's wagon driver came down from the hill babbling excitedly about his ordeal in the cave. Later in the day his mules were located safe and sound at their favourite piece of grazing down on the river bank. For all the concern about the strategically important ponts, and this says much about the often unsophisticated way in which warrior societies wage war, the *amabutho* had been nowhere near them.

Down on the river the carbineers soon had the ponts back in working order, so that the process of ferrying the infantry and the artillery across could get underway. Four 7-pounders, two ambulances and one wagon were all that remained of the wheeled transport, so that this crossing would be accomplished infinitely more quickly than the painstaking procedure of 11 January. Doctor Thrupp, the civilian surgeon attached to the 1st/24th but fortunately sent out of the camp with the 2nd/24th the previous morning, dashed across the river to help Reynolds with the wounded. Company by company, gun-crew by gun-crew, the troops came marching in to survey the scene of devastation around Rorke's Drift. When Major John Dartnell clapped eyes on Trooper Harry Lugg, he said, 'I never thought of seeing you alive again my boy. We saw the fire last night, and thought you were all murdered.' Lugg noticed that there were tears in the major's eyes.

All the evidence is that Bromhead had already formed a very clear impression of which of his men had particularly distinguished themselves in the fight. He wasted no time in strongly commending their behaviour to the GOC. A sergeant came over to Hook and told him to leave his kettles and pans and come at once to see Mr Bromhead. Like the good soldier he was, Hook wanted to go and fetch his tunic, but the sergeant insisted he should come at once. Still in his shirt-sleeves, with his braces dangling down behind him, Hook found himself ushered not just into the presence of his company commander, but of the general officer commanding himself. Hook was told to recount the story of the hospital fight to the general. One can imagine him standing bolt upright to attention and being told to relax by Chelmsford before beginning his tale. Afterwards, Bromhead took the general to speak to Fred Hitch, as he lay waiting for his shoulder to be probed by the surgeons. Chelmsford did not get the chance to speak to Commissary Dalton when he visited the wounded. Amazingly Dalton was already back on his feet and issuing rations to the troops in company with Walter Dunne. In a quiet moment Chard wandered down to his wagon to see how much of his kit had survived. He found a bottle of beer intact, which he shared with Bromhead a short while later.

At about noon Major Spalding and Lieutenant Horace Smith-Dorrien rode in from Helpmekaar. The major had received Chard's note from the hand of the NNC fugitive at about 9.00 a.m. On their way down the road they met Mr Henry Fynn, the resident magistrate from Msinga, who had been serving upcountry as the GOC's political adviser. No doubt he was on his way home to see if his family had survived the dramatic events of the past twenty-four hours. Before riding on, the anxious Fynn was able to confirm that the general was now back at Rorke's Drift. A little further down the road, Spalding and Smith-Dorrien encountered Russell and a few of his mounted infantrymen, who had been sent to check out the situation at Helpmekaar. Spalding was able to tell him that D and G Companies of the 1st/24th were intact and strongly entrenched around the base depot. If Russell hoped to hear that large numbers of men had escaped across country to Helpmekaar, he was to be disappointed. At Rorke's Drift, Major Spalding presented himself to the general and made his report. Over the next few weeks a spiteful rumour spread that he knew the Zulus were coming when he rode away to Helpmekaar, but this was manifestly untrue and he was never under any pressure from the official chain of command on this point. He had missed his date with destiny, but given the circumstances could not have done more than he did.

The last man to leave Zululand was the redoubtable Major Wilsone Black of the 2nd/24th. Commandant Maori Browne crossed just ahead of him and recalled the scene around the mission in his memoirs:

> The dead Zulus lay in piles, in some places as high as the top of the parapet. Some [were] killed by bullets and the wounds, at that short range, were ghastly but very many were killed by the bayonet. The attack must have been well pushed home and both sides deserve the greatest credit. The hospital was still smouldering and the stench from the burning flesh of the dead inside was very bad; it was much worse however when we came to clear the debris away two days afterwards. Some of our sick and wounded had been burned inside of the hospital and a number of Zulus had

been also killed inside of the building itself. In front of the hospital lay a large number of Zulus also a few of our men, who had been patients, and who when the hospital had been set on fire had, in trying to escape, rushed out among the enemy and been killed, their bodies being also ripped and much mutilated. [This can only be a reference to the bodies of Joseph Williams, Horrigan, Adams and Hayden.] A few dead horses lay about, either killed by the assegai or by the bullets of the defenders, and I wondered why they had not been driven away before the fighting began. One thing I noticed and that was the extraordinary way in which the majority of the Zulus lay. I had been over a good many battlefields and seen very many men who had been killed in action but I had never seen men lie in this position. They seemed to have dropped on their elbows and knees and remained like that with their knees drawn up to their chins. One huge fellow who must have been, in life, quite 7 feet high lay on his back with his heels on the top of the parapet and his head nearly touching the ground, the rest of his body supported by a heap of his dead comrades.

Browne went on to describe some of the events of the afternoon, including the despatch of a number of Zulu wounded found lying around the post. Just as the British wounded at Isandlwana could expect no mercy, neither could the Zulu casualties at Rorke's Drift. These were not lightly injured men; these were men in too weak a state even to get away from the immediate vicinity of the mission. Given their no doubt dreadful medical condition, these were as much acts of release as acts of retribution.

Well we went into the laager. No one seemed to know what to do and certainly no one tried to do anything. I spoke to several of the seniors and suggested that the thatch should be taken off the store* and more loopholes made, also that the stacks of forage be removed, but until I came to Colonel Harness RA, no one would pay the least attention. He at once saw things as I did and said,

---

* The defenders clearly had insufficient time to complete the task before the re-appearance of the Zulus.

'I will send my gunners to remove the thatch if you will get the forage away.' This we did and in a short time the place was secure from fire. No sooner had I seen my part of this work done than I began to feel as if I was rather hollow and I rejoined Lonsdale and Harford. Rations had been served out and we had bully beef, biscuit, tea and sugar in plenty but no cups, plates, knives, forks or spoons – not even a pot or kettle to boil water in. However we made shift to eat the bully beef and biscuits with our fingers, then boiled water in the empty bully tins, added tea and sugar and drank it with gusto. During the afternoon it was discovered that a large number of wounded and worn out Zulus had taken refuge in the mealie fields near the laager. My two companies of Zulus with some of my non-coms, and a few of the 24th quickly drew these fields and killed them with bayonet, butt and assegai. It was beastly but there was nothing else to do. War is war and savage war is the worst of the lot. Moreover our men were worked up to a pitch of fury by the sights they had seen in the morning and the mutilated bodies of the poor fellows lying in front of the burned hospital.

The main priority now was to re-fortify Rorke's Drift for the coming night. The barricades were improved and the 7-pounders emplaced. Other men dug a fire-pit for the disposal of the captured Zulu weapons, but many of the muskets were still loaded and discharged as they burnt. Fortunately nobody was hurt. Colonel Henry Degacher may have lost his brother William, over a quarter of his battalion and a large number of close regimental friends, but there was at least to be one consolation for him. After he had been a few hours at Rorke's Drift, his beloved Dalmatian 'Flip' came limping in to the mission in search of his master. The animal had a piece of rope around his neck and a stab wound above one of his forelegs. A great favourite with the men of the 2nd/24th, Flip's arrival drew a crowd and brought some short-lived cheer amidst all the bereavement. Sadly, Flip's play-mate 'Kreli', a mongrel acquired by the battalion in the Transkei, was never seen again.

The seventeen British dead were buried at the back of the post the following day. Chaplain Smith presided over their interment. In due course a stone wall was laid out around the cemetery. The whitewashed obelisk that stands over the graves today dates all the way back to 1879 and was carved over the ensuing few weeks by Bandsman Melsop of the 2nd/24th, who astonishingly, given the quality of the end result, did the work using bayonets for chisels.

The Zulu dead were buried in mass graves round about the post. The head count revealed that there were 351 of them, but that was only part of the story. Fifty bloodied shields were found on the river bank, which some people interpreted at the time as having been used to drag dead bodies down to the Buffalo to cast them into the water. Far more probably, however, these were used to carry badly wounded men down to the river bank, so that they could then be helped across by their able-bodied comrades. Over the ensuing few weeks several dozen more decomposing bodies were located in outlying areas, including the slopes of Shiyane. It seems likely that the fatal loss was more in the vicinity of 450. It is an almost irrefutable rule of military history that for every man killed in action, there are usually two wounded. Allowing that some proportion of the 450 were 'despatched' by the British, even if we reduce the directly fatal loss back to 350 it still seems unlikely that the Undi Corps could have suffered fewer than 1,000 casualties. Even if, as some would argue, the nature of the engagement would influence the traditional proportion of wounded to slain downwards, then on a one for one basis we are still left with a minimum loss of 700. But the rule of thumb stands the test of time across all types of engagement and all military eras. Thus we are faced with the inevitable conclusion that almost a quarter of the men who attacked Rorke's Drift became casualties. And so we can perhaps better appreciate the stubborn and indomitable courage of the warriors of the Undi Corps.

We might be able to draw some conclusions about the Zulu loss at Isandlwana from the outcome at Rorke's Drift. If we attribute one fifth of the total Zulu loss to bayonet wounds, then the defenders fired 25,000 rounds to cause 800 gunshot wounds. This means that an average of 31 rounds was fired to bring a skirmishing Zulu down. The 24th fielded in the region of 580 Martinis at Isandlwana. It can be presumed that by the time they were cut down most of these men had fired their basic issue of 70 rounds of ammunition. This means that they fired some 40,600 rounds, which ought, at the same ratio of hits to shots fired, to have caused 1,309 casualties, or 436 fatalities and 872 wounded. In addition something in the region of 300 mounted men fired off bandoliers of 50 rounds. This amounts to another 15,000 rounds, or another 483 casualties, of whom mathematically 161 were fatalities and 322 wounded. This is already a total of 1,792 casualties, without any allowance for the fire of the NNC and the artillery, the use of revolvers at short range or, crucially, the subsequent heavy losses in the close-quarter fighting. Consider also that the proportion of rounds fired to hits achieved at Rorke's Drift may be unduly high, because a good many shots were fired blindly into the night – whereas Isandlwana was fought to its bloody conclusion in broad daylight. Add the 1,792 gunshot casualties of Isandlwana to the 1,000 of Rorke's Drift and we are left with 930 fatalities and 1,861 wounded men. What percentage of the wounded would subsequently have died of their wounds through blood loss, shock or infection can only be guessed at; it would certainly have been a relatively high proportion as the Boxer cartridge fired a heavy slug, well known for inflicting the most terrible wounds. Let us imagine that the 24th and the volunteers, (principally carbineers and police), who stood at bay, say 650 men in all, inflicted casualties in the close-quarter fighting in roughly equal proportion to their own loss, and we can add another 216 Zulu dead and 433 wounded. Now we are up to 1,146 killed and 2,294 wounded in the day, still without allowance for artillery fire, any resistance offered by the NNC and the fugitives, a higher all-daylight ratio of hits to shots fired, or the superiority of the Martini-Henry and lunger over the *iklwa* in a close-quarter fight. Little wonder then that after the 'victory' of 22 January, Cetshwayo is said to have lamented, 'There are not enough tears to mourn for the dead.' It seems not unreasonable to conclude that there may have been something close to 4,500 Zulu casualties in all that day.

The Rorke's Drift wounded were evacuated to Helpmekaar on the morning of Sunday 26 January, but the conditions and facilities there were almost as bad as at the mission. Surgeon Blair Brown of the Army Medical Department did his best. Probably the most pressing case he

Private 24th Regiment. *(RRW Museum, Brecon)*

Lord Chelmsford. *(Ron Sheeley Collection)*

Incident at Isandlwana by David Cartwright. (*By kind permission of the Artist*)

Rorke's Drift: Defending the Storehouse by Jason Askew. *(By kind permission of the Artist)*

Alphonse de Neuville's *Defence of Rorke's Drift*. This is the artist's preliminary version or 'cartoon' which is still in the possession of the regiment. The full size oil is now in Australia. Erroneously, de Neuville shows the yard between the buildings still in the hands of the British as the hospital is being evacuated. Chard is fighting on the barricade on the right, Bromhead is in the centre pointing. Dr Reynolds is tending a casualty in the foreground and 'Ammunition Smith' is dispensing cartridges just behind him. (*1RRW*)

Rorke's Drift: Defending the Hospital by Jason Askew. Bromhead and Bourne confer in the foreground. Chard is in the centre, and Chaplain Smith on the extreme left.
(By kind permission of the Artist)

The Formidable 24th by David Cartwright. (By kind permission of the Artist)

The return of the recovered Queen's Colour to the remnant of the 1st/24th at Helpmekaar. *(Author's Collection)*

The Queen Empress decorates the Queen's Colour of the 1st/24th with a 'Wreath of Immortelles'. A photograph of the colour party appears on p. 172. (*Author's Collection*)

Officers of the 1st/24th in Malta at the beginning of the 1870s. Upcher standing at left with hand on hip; Porteous standing third from left; Wardell standing fifth from left; Harrison eighth from left; Melvill standing ninth from left; Paymaster White standing wearing civilian hat; Henry Degacher seated arms folded; Glyn seated on Degacher's left; Dunbar seated two down from Glyn; Mostyn third from the left on the ground. *(Ron Sheeley Collection)*

Lieutenant John Chard.
(RRW Museum, Brecon)

Lieutenant Gonville Bromhead.
(Ron Sheeley Collection)

Acting Asst Commissary J. L. Dalton. *(Royal Archives)*

Surgeon J. H. Reynolds. *(Royal Archives)*

Brevet Major Henry Spalding, DAAG No. 3 Column. *(MOD)*

Acting Storekeeper Louis Byrne. *(Author's Collection)*

The view towards Shiyane (*left*) and kwaSingqindi Hill from the Zulu bank of the Buffalo.
The mission is located in the v-shaped cleft between the two high features. *(Author)*

The drift proper viewed from the Natal bank. The ponts were some 500 yards upstream to the left of this point,
on a deep water pool. *(Author)*

The view towards Isandlwana (*right horizon*) from the area of Rorke's Drift. The drift is at the centre of the photograph; the mission is some way out of shot to the right. The slopes of Shiyane (*right*) make it impossible to see Isandlwana from the mission. *(Author)*

A newspaper illustration of the mission before the battle. It tends to exaggerate the steepness and the proximity of Shiyane.
(Author's Collection)

Rorke's Drift today. These modern buildings stand on the site of the original hospital (*right*) and the storehouse (*left*). The north wall followed the line of the terrace on which the buildings stand. The original barricade can be seen traced out on the ground in stones. A five-foot-high stone wall ran through the scrub in front of the north wall at this point. *(Author)*

A view of the rocky stretch of the terrace with the storehouse in the background. The cattle kraal can be seen between the building and the prominent tree. *(Author)*

The first Zulu attack came in from this direction – the hospital is on the left and the storehouse is on the right. The building in the centre should be disregarded. The prominent tree also post-dates 1879. The attack received heavy punishment at fifty yards and swung to the left around the hospital. *(Author)*

Having swung around the hospital the attackers found cover here, beneath the terrace, and behind the stone wall in front of the post, from where they proceeded to mount a series of heavy assaults on the hospital compound. *(Author)*

The hospital compound and the veranda. A number of Zulus got into the far corner of the veranda and were attacked and killed by Bromhead and a few of his men in a bayonet charge. The line of the initial barricade is marked in the foreground. *(Author)*

Mounting pressure forced Bromhead to fall back from the hospital compound to a short dog-leg barricade running from the corner of the hospital to the north wall. From here Bromhead led a number of bayonet charges to clear the front of the hospital. *(Author)*

Fighting for the north wall. *(Author's Collection)*

Just to the left of the boulders in the terrace was the dangerous corner where the biscuit boxes of the retrenchment barricade met the mealie bags of the north wall. It was this post of danger that Bromhead, Hitch and others occupied. It was here too that Corporal Schiess made his one-man sortie from the retrenchment to get at a number of Zulus crouched below the terrace. *(Author)*

The gable end of the hospital from which its defenders escaped. The line of the south wall is marked in stones. *(Author)*

After dark the attacks swung against the cattle kraal. The dead ground beneath the terrace again offered good cover to the attackers, as captured in this photograph. *(Author)*

The cattle kraal from inside the perimeter. The redoubt was constructed in the foreground and commanded the area of the cattle kraal, thus denying it to the enemy. *(1RRW)*

The relief of Rorke's Drift: Russell and the IMI arrive from the river. The original sketch on which this representation is based was drawn by Lieutenant Colonel Crealock. (*Author's Collection*)

One of the Zulu mass graves at Rorke's Drift. *(Author)*

The British cemetery at Rorke's Drift with Bandsman Melsop's obelisk at its centre. The men who fell in the battle and a small number who died subsequently of disease are buried here. *(Author)*

An iconic image of the era; return to Isandlwana. *(RRW Museum, Brecon)*

Another iconic image – Fort Bromhead. The storehouse, not long after the war, with its thatch removed, and surrounded by stone walls raised by the Royal Engineers in the wake of the battle. *(RRW Museum, Brecon)*

Major Wilsone Black returns the Queen's Colour to Colonel Richard Glyn at Rorke's Drift. *(Author's Collection)*

John Chard receiving his Victoria Cross from Sir Garnet Wolseley. *(Author's Collection)*

Bandsman Melsop's memorial. Remarkably it was carved in 1879 using bayonets for chisels. *(Author)*

Lieutenant Colonel J. M. G. Tongue (*left*) and the Colour Party which paraded the Colours of the 1st/24th before the Queen Empress at her Osborne House residence on the Isle of Wight. Victoria decorated the Queen's Colour with a 'Wreath of Immortelles' in recognition of the sacrifice of Melvill and Coghill and the 'Noble Defence of Rorke's Drift'. (*RRW Museum, Brecon*)

Lieutenant-General Richard Glyn in later life
(RRW Museum, Brecon)

Colonel John Chard VC in middle age.
(Ron Sheeley Collection)

Remembrance: the monument to the Zulu dead at Isandlwana with poppy wreaths laid by British diplomats and army officers, in the presence of H.M. King Goodwill at the 125th anniversary commemorative event. *(Author)*

Remembrance: keeping the old stories alive. The author recounts the story of Lieutenants Melvill and Coghill to a group of serving soldiers and veterans from the Royal Regiment of Wales. The high water mark is behind the visitors. *(1RRW)*

was confronted with was that of Corporal Lyons. It is easy in examining Rorke's Drift to dwell too much on its extraordinary outcome and not enough on its awful human consequences, which had both physical and mental dimensions. John Chard for example, a mature, intelligent officer, probably one of the most mentally robust men present, had terrible nightmares for days afterwards. How must the traumatised young privates have fared?

In terms of physical injury Corporal Lyons provides a horrific case study. It is worth reflecting on exactly what he went through, as it tells us much about the sheer grit of the Victorian infantryman. Let us not forget before proceeding further, that he was wounded not long after dark and spent most of the night of 22/23 January propped up against the biscuit box barricade. The only succour he received was when Harry Hook periodically ducked down from the fighting to help him move his head from one side to the other. In daylight on Thursday morning, Surgeon Reynolds and Doctor Thrupp made a no doubt excruciatingly painful attempt to remove the bullet from the entry wound in the side of his neck. Because it had lodged deep, hard against his spine, their extremely rudimentary probing was entirely unsuccessful. When he arrived at Helpmekaar on Sunday morning, and was examined by Surgeon Brown, Lyons had already been in agony for four days:

> He complained of great pain in the neck on the slightest movement ... he had lost almost all use of his arms and hands, especially the right one which he described as 'quite dead.' Painful 'twitchings' were experienced in the arms ... Next day I put him under chloroform; I made a prolonged attempt to find the bullet. The course I found it had taken was in a direct line with the spinal cord. I made a free opening in the middle line as far down the course as possible, and again attempted to reach the bullet. I found by digital examination now, that the processes of two adjacent vertebrae were smashed. I could also feel the spinal chord itself, and I felt a soft, smooth cord-like substance under my finger beyond. Pressure thereon instantly caused the patient to turn pale and the pulse to be almost imperceptible, and necessitated the

immediate withdrawal of the chloroform and adoption of artificial respiration. I took away several pieces of vertebrae which were very loose, but had to give up attempting to reach the bullet.

Lyons was next evacuated to the base hospital at Ladysmith, still in the same dangerous condition. On 27 February, Doctor Brown took over the hospital at Ladysmith and once again examined his former patient. This was over a month after he had been wounded. By now Lyons was experiencing such unimaginable pain in his arms that he pleaded with Brown to amputate them both:

> On examination I found a distinct hard substance on firm pressure beneath the ligamentum nuchae, which was not present on former occasions. On consultation with the Surgeon-General of the forces, who happened to be on an inspection tour at the time, I cut down upon it, and without much difficulty enucleated an ordinary round bullet, with a rather long rough projection extending from its smooth surface. This wound healed rapidly, but the original one continued to discharge slightly for a long time. In a few days the pain entirely disappeared from his arms, and their use nearly returned ... The gallant fellow bore the excruciating pain of the operation without making the slightest murmur, although he was not under the influence of chloroform or any other anaesthetic.

Clearly the bullet had moved in between examinations. Thankfully, having suffered so much, Lyons was able to make a prompt and full recovery. He wore the bullet on his watch chain for the rest of his life. Today it can be seen in the regimental museum at Brecon.

Part Three

The Leaves of Autumn

Chapter 7

Despise Not Your Enemy

The Subsequent Course of the War

News can travel fast and mysteriously in Africa. So it was with Isandlwana. It is said that the disaster was known about in the native settlements around Pietermaritzburg long before it was conveyed there by any recognisable means. The redcoats, it was said, lay as thick on the ground as the leaves of autumn. Europeans no doubt scoffed at their gossiping servants. In the event the metaphor proved to be painfully apt.

From vantage points around Rorke's Drift, flocks of vultures could be seen floating in the sky above the distant sphinx. Lord Chelmsford did not tarry long at the mission. Leaving Richard Glyn in charge, he departed post-haste for Pietermaritzburg where in the wake of the repulse there was much official business to be done. Before his departure, on the morning of Friday 24 January, the general gave orders for the disbandment of 3rd Regiment NNC. The Europeans would be kept on as an *ad hoc* unit of irregulars. The levies were sent off early one morning and according to Captain Henry Harford dispersed for their homes in great good humour. Nobody had advised the 1st/24th remnant at Helpmekaar what was going on and when a large swarm of blacks was seen in the distance, the order was given to stand to in the fortifications. In one last indignity at the hands of the British Army, the hapless former conscripts were fired on.

Glyn brooded on the awful fate of his beloved battalion, and in particular on the loss of the sixteen officers to whom he had been commander, father-figure, mentor and friend. He fortified the drift and the mission strongly and waited for orders. It was to prove a long wait. He became obsessed with security: the officers and men of the 2nd/24th were forbidden to wander far from the fortifications. With the central column's canvas burnt or looted from the grim battlefield over the river, there was little or no shelter to be had from the continued nightly downpours. The men of B Company were rewarded for their heroic endeavours, by being afforded the privilege of sleeping under a tarpaulin in the attic space of the de-thatched storehouse. Before long the crowded fortifications had been tramped into a muddy quagmire and the resultant filth was everywhere. There were few stores of any kind. For personal effects, officers and men alike had only a blanket and the clothes they stood up in. They slept on the sodden ground in misery. As soldiers usually do, people tried to put a brave face on things, but conditions were squalid in the extreme. A plague of flies settled over the post and sickness soon set in. The proximity of the mass graves to the defences was less than helpful. Soon typhoid and dysentery were abroad; a number of men died and there were regular funeral services at the new cemetery to darken the mood further. Amongst their number, sadly, was the other Private John Williams (934), not to be confused with his namesake John Williams (1395) VC, but a defender of Rorke's Drift all the same.

The Lost Colours

The unit of NNC irregulars were the only people that Glyn allowed to scout around the area. After a while they reported that the river was going down and speculation mounted that it might now be possible to locate the Queen's Colour of the 1st/24th. Henry Harford in particular, was keen to search the area of Sothondose's Drift. With the 24th still *in situ* at the mission station, he did not want to step on any toes by attempting to locate the colour uninvited. Yet Glyn's obsession with the strictest security measures seemed to preclude any regimental search parties.

Even in such dark times, the officers of the 24th did their best to keep up their reputation as a famously hospitable regiment. The homeless Harford had been warmly welcomed into their mess and soon made some firm friends:

> In the year of grace 1879, subaltern officers were of very small account, and in my position of Staff Officer to a Native Contingent

(with the honorary rank of Captain while so employed), and consequently an outsider, one did not expect very much from anyone, but the kindness and hospitality extended to me by the 24th Regiment very soon made me feel almost as one of them and many lasting friendships were the result. Major Black became an especially intimate friend of mine, and I could always go to him for advice and to talk over matters. Besides being a splendid soldier he was a most amusing companion and his fondness for bringing in lines of poetry to suit the occasion was a treat to listen to, with his Gaelic accent.

One evening in early February, Harford prevailed upon Black to seek Colonel Glyn's sanction for a search of Sothondose's Drift. The next morning he brought his patrol in early to find out how Black had got on. Glyn had given the go-ahead. The plan was that a strong party of the irregulars would go out the next day under Black's command. The major then decided that he and Harford should ride out to the drift to reconnoitre the area in preparation for the morrow. Looking down from the high bluff above the drift, they could see a good deal of debris from the flight of the fugitives lying along the high water mark. Black decided to push a little way down the old native path by which it was known that many of the fugitives had come up from the river. Before long the pair made a dramatic discovery:

> Both were clearly recognizable. Melvill was in red, and Coghill in blue uniform. Both were lying on their backs about a yard from each other, Melvill at right angles to the path and Coghill parallel to it, a little above Melvill and with his head uphill. Both had been assegaied, but otherwise their bodies had been left untouched. Major Black at once said, 'Now we shall see whether they have the Colours on them,' and proceeded to unbutton Melvill's serge, while I opened Coghill's patrol jacket, but there were no Colours. Presently Major Black said, 'I wonder if Melvill's watch is on him. He always carried it in the small waist-pocket of his breeches,' and on looking, there was his gold watch, which was subsequently sent to his widow. Nothing was found on Coghill, but his bad knee was still bandaged up. Undoubtedly, Melvill must have stuck to

him and helped him along, otherwise he never could have got so
far over such terrible ground.

For the time being Melvill's watch was left with his body. It was later
noted to have stopped at 2.10 p.m., potentially, but not necessarily,
fixing the time at which it was immersed in the river. Black and Harford
placed boulders and stones over the two bodies until a proper burial
service could be arranged with Chaplain Smith, and then returned to
Rorke's Drift where their news caused a stir. The next morning the main
search patrol set off not long after sunrise. On the bluff above the river,
the party quickly erected a sangar of rocks, which stands to this day.
The Isandlwana survivor Lieutenant Charlie Raw was detailed by Black
to command the covering party at the sangar, whilst Harford pushed on
down to the river bank in the company of two NNC officers, Captain
Harber and Lieutenant Wainwright. Almost immediately Harford found
the colour-case in which the Queen's Colour had been shrouded. A few
paces along the river bank he stopped dead in his tracks and remarked
to Harber, 'Do you see that straight bit of stick sticking up in the water
opposite you? It looks to me uncommonly like a colour pole.' Harber
waded into the river up to his waist and pulled the pole clear of the
water. To the great joy of the three officers, the precious silk was still
attached. As Harber handed the colour over to Harford, the gold-
embroidered regimental badge, at the centre of the red, white and blue
of the Union Flag, fell out, following its long and harmful immersion in
fast-flowing river water.* Black came racing down to the river in
response to the excited cheering, and joined in the celebrations with
unconfined joy, thanking the three officers profusely and shaking them
all warmly by the hand.

The 24th sentries atop Shiyane had been told to keep a weather eye
in the direction of Sothondose's Drift. The sound of clattering hooves
drew their attention to the return of the search party. At the head of the
little cavalcade of horsemen, they saw that Major Black was carrying

* By implication the colour must have been on dry land at this stage, so that the badge could
be picked up and sewn back into place later, as it was reported not long afterwards, in other
accounts, as being not too badly damaged by its immersion in the river, and still bears the
device at its centre to this day. Possibly the tailor sergeant of the 2nd/24th was called upon
to carry out some swift needle-work that very night.

something proudly upright. They strained their eyes to see if it could possibly be true. It was indeed true and they at once gave the pre-arranged signal to the fort at Rorke's Drift. Excited shouts around the camp alerted everyone to the fact that the search had been successful. Captain Penn Symons immediately turned out the guard and fixed bayonets. By the time Black came riding up to the mission, every man at Rorke's Drift was ready to greet his triumphant return. At Symons's word of command, the guard snapped briskly though the requisite three movements of the Present Arms. A huge cheer erupted from the men of the 2nd/24th and helmets were waved aloft or went flying up into the air. Richard Glyn stepped forward from the crowd. It is said that there were tears in his eyes as Wilsone Black lent forward in the saddle to hand the Colour down to him.

It was at Helpmekaar, in the care of the grieving Major Russell Upcher and D and G Companies of the 1st/24th, that the Regimental Colour awaited the return of its senior partner. A day or two after its recovery, Black, Harford and a sergeant of the 2nd/24th set out to return the Queen's Colour to Upcher. Glyn had gone on ahead. Customarily the colours are only ever handled by officers or sergeants who are fully-fledged members of the regiment. Harford was in the 99th Regiment of Foot. Part of the way down the road, Black relieved the sergeant of the Queen's Colour, and after saying a few kind words of appreciation for Harford's part in its recovery, handed it over to him to carry. It was a singular honour that Harford greatly appreciated; he recalled it in his memoirs as 'the proudest moment of my life'. On the final approach to Helpmekaar, Black took over the colour himself, for its final ceremonial return to its rightful home.

Upcher had formed up D and G Companies in line with bayonets fixed, officers to the front, sergeants to the rear. The Regimental Colour was on parade in the interval between the two companies. The senior subaltern stood at the front and centre of the parade, ready to accept back the Queen's Colour. Having done so he turned smartly about to face the parade, and Upcher ordered the present arms. As the rifles behind them cracked smartly through the movements of the present, Upcher and his officers lowered their swords in salute. At such moments it would be normal for the band to strike up with a few bars of a musical salute. For the decimated 1st/24th, this was tragically no longer possible. Thus it was in a sombre silence that the Queen's Colour ensign marched smartly back to the centre of the line. And so it was that the colours of the 1st/24th came to fly proudly side by side once more. It was a scene that seemed somehow to symbolise that in the British service men can be killed but regiments cannot. Colonel Glyn then addressed the parade in most 'touching and affectionate terms'.* Lieutenant Colonel Arthur Harness RA, who witnessed the proceedings, said that Glyn broke down as he spoke. We do not know exactly what he said, but he particularly thanked Major Black for his role in the recovery of the Queen's Colour. He also went on to recall its first presentation, at the Curragh in 1866, and remarked that it grieved him to think that, now, only a handful of the officers and men present that day were still alive.

When the colonel had finished speaking, somebody called for three cheers for Major Black. Black himself then stepped forward and made an address in response, which Harford was to describe in his memoirs as, 'a remarkably eloquent speech which must have stirred the feelings of every officer and man who had the privilege of listening to it.' Sadly we know very little of what was said, except that Charles Norris-Newman, who was not himself present at the parade but discussed it with Black subsequently, reported in his book that the major emphasised that he had not been alone, and that the grateful thanks of the 1st/24th should also be extended to the NNC officers who had been with him.

On the Defensive

As well as throwing Wood in the north and Pearson on the coast onto the defensive, the Isandlwana bombshell caused a flurry of barricade-building throughout the colony of Natal. Fortunately for the settlers, Cetshwayo still hoped to be able to negotiate a settlement with the British and no Zulu counter-invasion was ever launched. In public at least, Chelmsford was well supported by the Queen, by her government and by the War Office, which immediately despatched six

* Norris-Newman.

additional infantry battalions, two batteries of artillery and two regiments of cavalry: the King's Dragoon Guards and the 17th Lancers. Privately, Prime Minister Disraeli was furious with Frere and Chelmsford. The Commander-in-Chief, HRH The Duke of Cambridge, was much more sanguine. He was not going to bow to political pressure to dismiss one of his commanders in the field until he was entirely sure of his facts. For the time being he had only Chelmsford's own despatches as a source of information. The extent of the disaster was awkward for everybody; there had been nothing to compare with it since the retreat from Kabul. In the background Horse Guards began discreetly to probe the issue of Chelmsford's own culpability. And was bringing the war to a successful conclusion a job for 'our only general', as Sir Garnet Wolseley had been dubbed in the popular press? With his habitual conceit, Wolseley himself had no doubt that it was. But for the time being, with no other general officer in Southern Africa, and Natal in a state of panic-ridden hysteria, there could be no question of Chelmsford's dismissal.

It is often said that Pearson was besieged in the defensive position he adopted around Eshowe, but it would be more accurate to say that he was immobilised. Although no serious attack was ever mounted on his defences, a large swathe of his transport oxen was run off, so that he found himself quite unable to recover his column to Natal. On the Zulu side it was Dabulamanzi who led the harassment of the coastal column. Chelmsford made its extrication his immediate priority and, as his reinforcements began to arrive in South Africa, started to assemble a relief column on the lower Tugela. February and March were months of reconstitution.

Disaster at Ntombi Drift

Zulu resistance in the north was headed up by Prince Mbilini, an exiled Swazi royal who had settled in Zululand under Cetshwayo's protection and patronage. He proved to have a great talent for guerrilla-style raiding and soon had the border settlements on edge. In response a wing of the 80th Regiment was moved down to Luneberg to protect the district. On the night of 11/12 March, Mbilini struck at a company under Captain D. B. Moriarty, which for the previous five days had been attempting to get a convoy of supplies safely into Luneberg from the north. Heavy rains had caused the Ntombi River to rise as Moriarty was attempting to cross at the local drift; as a consequence he had ended up with his wagons split between both banks of the river. The escort pitched its tents with about seventy men under Moriarty himself on one bank, and just over thirty men under Lieutenant Harward on the other. Mbilini struck the slumbering encampment with about 800 warriors just before dawn on 12 March, the weight of the assault falling on Moriarty's main body. Surprise was total and the slaughter bloody, as the soldiers came stumbling out of their tents. On the opposite bank the smaller detachment rallied together to fight off the attack. Harward was the only man with a horse and rode away to get help from Luneberg, leaving Colour-Sergeant Booth in command. It was the wrong call. Harward was court-martialled for deserting his men, though ultimately he would be acquitted. Booth on the other hand was awarded the Victoria Cross for his leadership of a successful fighting withdrawal. Over eighty men had been killed on the British side, at a loss of only thirty to the Zulu. The general officer commanding was now in grave need of some good news.

Hlobane and Kambula

Evelyn Wood had occupied a strong hilltop position at Kambula, from where his mounted irregulars ravaged the surrounding countryside under the energetic leadership of Colonel Redvers Buller. On 28 March the cavalry mounted an operation against a huge mountain stronghold called Hlobane. They expected to encounter only Mbilini's local forces, and to be able to run off large numbers of cattle. By this stage in the war, Lieutenant Colonel John Russell and No. 1 Squadron of the IMI had been re-deployed to the north, as had two troops of Colonel Durnford's mounted natives, operating now under the command of William Cochrane, formerly a member of Durnford's staff, and one of the 'lucky five'. Much to everybody's surprise the Zulu main *impi* put in an appearance, and caught Buller and his men badly off guard. Russell continued his largely hopeless performance by retiring from the field at an inopportune moment. He claimed it was all the result of a misunderstanding, but it occurred at a time when Buller needed all the help he could get. Lieutenant Edward Browne, commanding the 1st/24th's detachment of the IMI, declined to retreat with Russell, and stayed on with a few of his men, including the Isandlwana survivor Private Power, to fight alongside Buller. The affair was to cause much ill-feeling. On the Zulu side, Ntshingwayo was again in command, and most of the veterans of Isandlwana and Rorke's Drift were with him, many of them now carrying Martini-Henry rifles. A wing of the *impi* harried Buller and his men across the mountain-top and drove them down a descent route that was all but impossible for mounted troops. They called it the 'Devil's Pass' and it cost the lives of fifteen officers and seventy-nine other ranks. Redvers Buller, as ever, was formidably brave and would be awarded the Victoria Cross for his conduct that day. Private Power also distinguished himself in the fighting and would receive the Distinguished Conduct Medal.

The next day Ntshingwayo moved on to attack the position at Kambula. Like Dabulamanzi before him, he did so in contravention of the king's prohibition against attacking fortified places. Wood was ready and primed in a series of mutually supporting defensive positions, based on a strongly held wagon laager, a redoubt and a defended cattle kraal. The mainstay of his defence was provided by seven companies of the 1st/13th Light Infantry, eight companies of the 90th Regiment and a battery of six guns. On the other side of the battlefield, the iNgobamakhosi had been assigned to the right horn and the umCijo to the left. In the centre were the uMbonambi, the iNdluyengwe, the iMbube, the uThulwana, the uDududu, the iNdlondlo and the iSangqu. Buller rode out with his surviving irregulars and some of the IMI to provoke the iNgobamakhosi on the Zulu right, and was successful in prompting an isolated regimental attack. When the warriors charged, one of the cavalry troopers was left behind, struggling to control and remount his horse. Lieutenant Edward Browne came flying back to his aid and tried to steady his mount for him. When the trooper was finally able to heave himself up for the saddle, his stirrup snapped suddenly under his weight. His panic-stricken horse immediately bolted along the front of the *impi*, by now a mere thirty yards away. Undeterred, Browne gave chase and brought the animal about, with the terrified trooper still clinging on to his saddle for grim death. Browne became the tenth member of the 24th Regiment to win the Victoria Cross in action against the Zulus. Interestingly, after their experiences at Isandlwana and Rorke's Drift, Hlubi's Basuto Troop declined to retire inside the redoubt with the rest of the cavalry and remained outside the main British position throughout the fight.

The first attack fell on the wagon laager. The iNgobamakhosi were in the forefront of the fighting and took still more heavy punishment at the hands of the Martini-Henry rifle. Even so, some of them had to be ejected at the point of the bayonet. When the rest of the *impi* came up, a much better co-ordinated attack went in. This time it fell upon the cattle kraal, compelling the company of the 1st/13th posted there to fall back to the redoubt. Wood initiated a counter attack from the laager by two companies of the 90th Regiment under the command of a Major Robert Hackett. Initially Hackett and his men drove the Zulus back, but in due course were compelled by mounting pressure to withdraw in their turn to the cover of the wagons. Hackett saw his men safely in but, just as he was about to regain the protection of the laager himself, he was hit in the head by a round that dislodged both of his eyeballs and blinded him instantly.

The attack was pressed hard for another three hours but to no avail. At length the Zulus appeared to be wavering and Wood launched another foray, this time by two companies of the 1st/13th. Deploying a firing line between the laager and the redoubt, the two companies swept the lower slopes clear of the enemy with a number of hard-hitting volleys. When the gun-smoke cleared from the laager and the redoubt, anything up to a thousand warriors lay dead in the grass. The ensuing mounted pursuit was pressed ruthlessly by Buller and the mounted troops. Allowing for men killed in the rout or who subsequently died of their wounds, the battle may have cost 2,000 Zulu lives in all. Wood lost only 18 men killed, and 8 officers and 57 men wounded. Kambula was another bitter lesson for the fighting men of the Zulu nation. It was also the turning point of the war. When the excitement had passed, Edward Browne approached Colonel Wood and handed him a personal letter in which he denounced Russell, his immediate superior, for cowardice over the Hlobane incident, and declared that he and his men would never serve under him again. The letter confirmed Wood's suspicions. At Ulundi, Browne was in command of the mounted infantry squadron.

All along the frontier British irregular forces were now laying waste to vulnerable Zulu communities. Kraals and crops were burnt and cattle run off in huge numbers. As the dark cloud of total war passed over the land, large tracts of the border zone became no-go areas for the Zulu people. Many were soon living rough in caves and other remote fastnesses.

Gingindlovu

On the same day as Kambula, Chelmsford crossed the Tugela with 5,000 men and set off to relieve Pearson at Eshowe. It may have come too late for the 1st/24th, but the GOC had absorbed the lessons of the Isandlwana campaign well. He moved slowly and deliberately and kept his force tightly concentrated throughout. Each afternoon he drew his wagons into a great square laager and dug a shelter trench around them. Four days after crossing the river, his advance was contested in open terrain at Gingindlovu. A mainly local force of around 11,000 warriors repeated the mistakes of Kambula by attacking the British in their laager. Amongst the leaders of the *impi* were Mavumengwana, who had been Ntshingwayo's co-commander at Isandlwana, and Dabulamanzi, who should have known better after his experiences at Rorke's Drift. It was a foolhardy attack, which when it was over had cost the Zulus more than a thousand dead. Dabulamanzi was shot in the thigh but lived to tell the tale and in due course made a full recovery. Chelmsford's loss to rifle fire amounted to 2 officers and 12 men killed, and 4 officers and 43 men wounded. Amongst the dead was the commanding officer of the 60th Rifles, Lieutenant Colonel Francis Northey, who was shot in the shoulder, retired to have his wound dressed, and then returned to the fight, before later collapsing and expiring. His grave may still be seen at the small British cemetery which stands on the site of the laager. If British casualties were light for once, the accumulated manpower losses of the Zulu nation were rapidly becoming unsustainable. In swift order Pearson and his men were successfully extricated from Eshowe. The British fell back on Natal to ready themselves for a new push on Ulundi.

Between Invasions: Reconstitution of the 1st/24th

The remainder of April and all of May were spent in preparing for the second invasion. Amidst all the bustle there was good news from home. On 2 May it was announced in the *London Gazette* that Chard, Bromhead, Allen, Hitch, Hook, Robert Jones, William Jones and John Williams had been awarded the Victoria Cross. In due course, following campaigns by lobbyists and their respective corps, Surgeon Reynolds (June 1879), Dalton (November 1879), and Corporal Schiess (New Year 1880), would also be gazetted as VCs. The Commissary General recommended Walter Dunne at the same time as Dalton, but the Duke of Cambridge declined to endorse both and preferred Dalton's candidacy ahead of Dunne's. Some modern writers cynically insinuate that the award of so many VCs was politically motivated and was designed to distract from the greater event at Isandlwana. In fact the six 24th Regiment enlisted men were specifically commended for their part in the action by Bromhead, and then immediately recommended for the Victoria Cross by Henry Degacher, their commanding officer, neither of whom had any vested interest in anything more devious than securing rightful recognition for the gallantry of their men. Chard and Bromhead were added to Degacher's list by the GOC, which likewise cannot be regarded as in any way improper, least of all in Bromhead's case, given his extremely courageous conduct. Reynolds, Schiess and Dalton were all added to the list subsequently, in response to strong public support for recognition of their actions. As shown by the dates cited above, two of these three additional awards were gazetted many months after the war had drawn to a close at Ulundi, by which time it was hardly necessary to distract attention from Isandlwana. As usual the facts in no way lend support to the ravings of the conspiracy theorists or the ramblings of the revisionists.

Lord Chelmsford's new concept of operations was not dissimilar from that enacted in January, but all of the columns were now formidably strong and would adhere to a *modus operandi* that paid all due cognisance to the formidable fighting qualities of the Zulu. There was to be a fresh push along the coast by a force known as the First Division. This would consist of the troops from Pearson's original command, plus those that had fought at Gingindlovu and gone on to relieve Eshowe. The main purpose of this column was to fix the attention of the coastal chiefs and their warriors. The army's main strike force was to concentrate around Dundee and launch into central Zululand across Landman's Drift on the Ncome River. This force would be known as the Second Division and was to be commanded by the newly arrived Major General Edward Newdigate. Richard Glyn was given command of the 1st Brigade. With Glyn's departure from Rorke's Drift, the post was left in the care of Henry Degacher who immediately expanded the crowded, unsanitary encampments outside the fortified walls into the surrounding countryside. The measure brought an immediate improvement in conditions. By now a new stone fort had been built on the ridge above the ponts, the ruins of which may still be seen to this day. The 24th had intended to name it 'Fort Revenge', but Chelmsford directed that it be called 'Fort Melvill' instead. Assigned to duty on Newdigate's lines of communication, the 2nd/24th was fated never to have an opportunity to revenge Charlie Pope and his men.

A British battalion cannot indeed be killed; by the end of February 520 volunteers from eighteen different regiments had been assembled at Aldershot to reconstitute the 1st/24th. On St David's Day the draft sailed for Africa on the troopship *Clyde*. Perhaps the volunteers began to suspect that they might have joined an unlucky regiment, when, on 4 April, a day after a coaling stop at Cape Town, the *Clyde* struck a reef and ran aground. The captain evacuated the troops safely to the shore, but when the tide came back in, his ship re-floated and then foundered with all her hold cargo including the battalion's baggage. Three days after the disaster the new draft set sail again, this time aboard the *Tamar*. They landed safely at Durban on 11 April and spent the rest of the month marching up to Dundee. Here they were joined by the D and G Company veterans, released at last from the tedium of garrison duty at dismal Helpmekaar. B Company under Captain Henry Harrison remained detached at its distant outpost at Port St John's, way down south on the coastline of Pondoland. William Dunbar, one of the 2nd Battalion majors, was elevated to lieutenant colonel and appointed as the new commanding officer. He re-designated Major Russell Upcher's D Company as A Company, Harrison's B Company as H Company, a change to which it must have been oblivious for some time, and formed the new draft into B to F Companies inclusive. Captain Thomas Rainforth's G Company remained unchanged.

On 13 May, Dunbar marched the new 1st/24th to Landman's Drift, where it was brigaded with the 58th and 94th Regiments for the second invasion. The 94th was under the command of Lieutenant Colonel P. R. Anstruther, who eighteen months later would lead his regiment to its own mini-disaster at Bronkhorstspruit in the Transvaal. In the action which initiated hostilities in the First Boer War, the 94th's battalion headquarters, its band, and two of its companies, were confronted on the line of march by a strong Boer commando. Amongst the 157 men shot down on the road was Anstruther himself; he was hit five times in the legs and thigh, had a leg amputated, and died of his wounds after six days of agonised suffering on Boxing Day 1880.

In the meantime the wagons necessary to sustain the second invasion were still in short supply, so on 21 May a strong expedition was mounted to the Isandlwana battlefield to recover any serviceable transport that could be found on the old wagon park. The opportunity was taken to give rough interment to the skeletons on the field, though those of 24th men were left undisturbed at the request of Colonel Glyn, who was anxious that the regiment should bury its own dead.

The Second Division was to operate in close concert with Wood's command, now re-designated as the 'Flying Column'. Both components would operate so as to be mutually supporting in the final advance on Ulundi. There were only so many ways of getting to the king's kraals, so that, whilst the new axis of advance initially bypassed the still grisly field of Isandlwana to the north, it then swung back onto the old traders' wagon road some fourteen miles further on.

The Second Invasion

On the last day of May the new invasion was launched. By the following evening, Chelmsford again had his head in his hands. During the course of the day the twenty-three-year-old heir to the exiled Napoleonic dynasty, the last of the Bonapartes, had been killed in an ambush on a nine-man mounted patrol, as it was at rest near a deserted kraal. With only four fatalities the incident was regrettable but militarily insignificant. Politically, and for Chelmsford personally, it was a disaster of the greatest magnitude. The Empress Eugenie enjoyed a very close relationship with Queen Victoria. The death of the Prince Imperial seemed certain to be the final nail in Chelmsford's coffin. For the past two months Prince Louis had been employed as an ADC to the general. The idea, as ever, when so important a personage came jollying into a war zone, was to keep him gainfully occupied, create an illusion of military adventure around him but, at all costs, never to allow him to be placed in any real danger. Even this simple proposition had gone horribly wrong.

On 16 June more depressing news reached Lord Chelmsford. He had been superseded by the dreadful upstart Wolseley, who even now was making haste for South Africa to assume supreme military and political authority in the north. Chelmsford resolved to try and press the campaign to a victorious conclusion before his removal could be effected. Over the ensuing weeks Cetshwayo's emissaries were consistently rebuffed. The day after the news of Wolseley's appointment broke, the anticipated junction took place between Wood and the Second Division. On 20 June a detachment of the 2nd/24th under Wilsone Black* finally made it to Isandlwana to begin burying the regimental dead. It would take Black two more return trips to complete the task. His atmospheric reports on his various expeditions, which include his personal interpretation of the battle, have not been that freely available in modern times and are incorporated for interest in Appendix 6.

Over the next fortnight the advance on Ulundi pressed ahead, but by 28 June Wolseley had landed in Durban, having sailed on rapidly from Cape Town. Much to Chelmsford's relief, he was still in command of the troops on 4 July when the Battle of Ulundi brought the war to a sad but victorious conclusion. The army advanced to contact in a huge square containing thirty-three companies of regular infantry, a dozen artillery pieces and two Gatling guns. Much to its disgust the reconstituted 1st/24th was amongst the troops left to guard the wagon laager on the banks of the White Umfolozi. In the centre of the square

---

* Black was by now a brevet lieutenant colonel. In fact his promotion had been gazetted in London in December 1878, but like everybody else in South Africa he was oblivious to the fact until February 1879.

were the 17th Lancers, Buller's volunteer cavalry and Wood's Irregulars, a body of mostly Swazi warriors. Richard Glyn was in command of his brigade and was accompanied on various pretexts by Lieutenant Colonel Dunbar and six other 1st/24th officers. No. 1 Squadron of the IMI was under the command of Edward Browne of course and contained twenty veterans of the old 1st/24th. In all there were around 5,000 men in the square. What followed was not so much a battle as a slaughter. For around forty minutes the Zulu *amabutho* tried their best, but at the end of that time over a thousand more men had been cut down and killed by British fire: remarkably some of them got to within thirty yards of the square. Many more warriors were staggering or crawling away through the bloodied grass. By contrast, Chelmsford's losses were three officers and ten men killed, and sixty-nine men wounded. Then, one wall of the square peeled open, and the 17th Lancers came thundering out, to ride down and spit the fleeing Zulu wounded in one last demonstration of the formidable military might of the British Empire. Everywhere the great royal kraals were soon in flames. In one of the king's huts the tinsel crown placed on Cetshwayo's head by Sir Theophilus Shepstone was found. There was a copy of his coronation photograph hung on the wall. Of the king himself there was no sign.

Twelve days after the battle Chelmsford turned over his command to Wolseley. Cetshwayo evaded capture for fifty-five days after the fall of his capital, but was eventually run to ground in the far north by Major Richard Marter. He was afforded all due deference to his royal rank by an army and a public which already felt nothing but respect for the courage of the Zulu.

'For Queen and Country Jesu Mercy'

On 14 April 1879 'Ammunition Smith' conducted the funeral service of Melvill and Coghill. Richard Glyn and Henry Degacher were both there. The bodies were exhumed from the piles of rocks that Black and Harford had placed over them and then decently interred on the hillside above Fugitives' Drift, side by side, only a yard or two from where they fell. Richard Glyn described the occasion in a letter to his daughter Bess:

Yesterday I went down to where poor Melvill and Coghill's remains were lying, to erect the cross Sir Bartle Frere and staff sent. I had two strong coffins made and exhumed the bodies, rolled them up in blankets, put them into the coffins and buried them just under the rock on which the cross is placed ... I got from Melvill's pockets a white silk pocket handkerchief, ten shillings and sixpence in silver, a little dog whistle and his gold watch and chain which I shall carefully keep until I hear from Mrs Melvill what she wishes done with them. The water when he was in the river has got into the watch and discoloured the face. It stopped at ten minutes past two which must have been about the time they crossed the Buffalo.

Sir Bartle Frere's cross still stands above the grave. The front bears the usual kind of engraved sentiment, but on the reverse side is carved the simple and moving inscription, 'For Queen and Country Jesu Mercy'. In 1907 King Edward VII was pleased to confer the award of the Victoria Cross on both officers. They were the first men to be posthumously honoured with their nation's supreme award 'For Valour'.

Chapter 8

How Did It Come to This?

The Blame Game

Where there is disaster, there must, it seems, be blame. Traditionally debate has focussed on whether Colonel Anthony Durnford was to blame for the catastrophic turn of events at Isandlwana, or whether the fault more properly lies with Lord Chelmsford. This has always been, and remains, by far the most controversial issue surrounding the events of 22 January 1879. Conventionally the debate has tended to focus on the essential notion that the villain of the piece must have made seriously flawed judgement calls on the day – the idea that whichever of them might legitimately be cast in that role was simply having a bad day, or perhaps even an 'unlucky' day. Thus attention has centred on their actions and decisions over a twenty-four-hour period, and their mutual interaction in that time, but not necessarily on their responsibilities, the kind of men they were, or their wider ability as professional soldiers. In *How Can Man Die Better* we touched from time to time on their respective roles and duties, their characters, their strengths and their failings. We now need to draw these threads towards a conclusion. The arguments for and against each of them are complex in their deliberation, but point, ultimately, towards a startlingly simple conclusion.

The blame debate goes all the way back to 1879 when an embarrassed Lord Chelmsford first pointed an accusing finger at the late Colonel Durnford. It is evident from his correspondence and conduct that the GOC saw Isandlwana purely as a defeat at the acute tactical level, and that he sincerely believed that no blame could or should be attached to him personally. If he was not there, how could he be in any way to blame? Yet as time wore on, the focus shifted to the operational level context of the defeat, and he found himself being blamed nonetheless. Because he perceived this to be unjust, and in this he was deluding himself, he made a number of fairly feeble attempts to spin the debate back in his favour. Unable as a matter of honour to make an all-out public attack on a man who had fallen in battle, Chelmsford resorted to only thinly disguised insinuations that the fault lay entirely with the sapper colonel.* In his confidential correspondence within the upper echelons of the military chain of command, he was much more direct.

Some modern writers now openly label Chelmsford's machinations as a 'cover-up', but in order for the expression to be used legitimately, it would be absolutely necessary for Chelmsford to have recognised his personal culpability, and then to have attempted to shift the blame onto somebody else by means of deliberate distortions of the truth. In fact it is quite apparent that Frederick Thesiger, the 2nd Baron Chelmsford, went to his grave quite genuinely believing that he was not in any way to blame for the Isandlwana disaster. Nor was the GOC the only man in the field that day to infer that the fault lay with Durnford. Many capable officers, with absolutely no vested interest in the attribution of blame, arrived at precisely the same conclusion.

In response to Lord Chelmsford's insinuations, not least a speech he made in his own defence in the House of Lords in August 1880, Durnford's outraged friends and family immediately sprang to the defence of their hero, offering in print a number of at best tenuous arguments to exonerate his alleged recklessness.† Those who were pre-disposed to believe in their case did so. Not least, Colonel Edward Durnford was extremely successful in defending his late brother's reputation within their own corps, aided in no small part by their father's exalted rank and reputation. The dashing hero myth was born. Sad to say, when fairly and impartially weighed in the balance, Anthony

---

* Though when he came under pressure on the absence of improvised fortifications at the camp, he also made an unworthy but quickly rebuffed attempt to shift that particular issue in the direction of Richard Glyn.

† The books at issue were *My Chief and I* and *The History of the Zulu War and its Origins* by Miss E. F. (Frances, or informally 'Nell') Colenso (daughter of Bishop John Colenso, one time Bishop of Natal), with whom Anthony Durnford was romantically linked, and Edward Durnford's *A Soldier's Life and Work in South Africa 1872–79: A Memoir of the Late Colonel A. W. Durnford, Royal Engineers.*

Durnford's flaws greatly outweighed his merits, so that the myth created around him in the early 1880s was removed by some considerable margin from historical reality.

Chelmsford and Durnford had entirely different fields of responsibility of course, and only rarely can military disaster be traced back to a single decision, omission or event, or to the actions of one particular individual. War, after all, is not conducted on only one level. Thus any interpretation of the evidence which concludes that one or the other of them was exclusively to blame is, by definition, unlikely to be sound.

Lord Chelmsford was responsible for the strategic and operational levels of command, or the planning of the war and the manoeuvring of the army to achieve Sir Bartle Frere's desired political and military outcome. But just what was the GOC's plan? Conventionally the history books offer us a rather too simplistic description of a strategy of converging columns, in which the British plan to advance directly to a central rendezvous just short of Ulundi and then contrive some form of final show-down with the Zulu royal house.

A letter written by Chelmsford to Frere on 16 January, when No. 3 Column was still encamped on the Zulu bank of the Buffalo River, throws some interesting light on the finer detail of the general's concept of operations, and shows that at this early stage in the war his plan was still evolving. If it had been allowed to run its course, the plan would have involved rather more lateral manoeuvre than we might customarily tend to think. It was written some four days before the grand advance from the river to Isandlwana, and two days after Chelmsford had reprimanded Durnford for not following orders.* For interest Chelmsford's original spelling of place-names has been retained:

> I consider that my original idea of driving, as far as possible all the Zulus forward towards the north-east part of their country, is still thoroughly sound. Without, therefore, attempting to push forward faster than our means will admit of [a reference to the cumbersome ox-drawn transport], I propose with Nos. 1, 2 and 3 Columns [led

* See *How Can Man Die Better*, pages 55–7.

by Pearson, Durnford and Glyn respectively], to thoroughly clear or subjugate the country between the Buffalo and Tugela Rivers and the Umhlatosi River, by means of expeditions made by these columns from certain fixed positions. No. 1 Column will, as already instructed, occupy Etshowi. Instead, however, of crossing the Umhlatosi River to Mr Samuelson's mission station (St Paul's), it will move a portion of its force to Entumeni, and occupy that position as well as Etshowi. Having established itself firmly in those two positions, the main object of this column will be to clear the Inkandhla bush and forest, or to induce the chiefs and headmen of the tribes residing or specially stationed in that part of the country to render their submission. No. 3 Column will first advance to a position near Insandwhlana hill, and from there, assisted by a portion of No. 2 Column will clear the Equideni [Quedeni] Forest, or induce the chiefs etc to submit. This work completed, the portion of No. 2 Column, under Lieutenant Colonel Durnford, will move towards the mission station near the Empand-leni Hill, while No. 3 Column advances to a fresh position near the Isipezi hill, detaching, if necessary, part of its force to support No. 2 Column. These combined movements will, I hope, have the effect of removing any dangerously large body from the Natal border. Colonel Wood, commanding No. 4 Column, has been informed of these intended movements, and has been instructed to act independently about the head waters of the White Umvoloosi River ...

We shall occupy a large extent of Zululand, and shall threaten the portion that remains to the King. We shall completely cover the Natal border, and shall to a considerable extent do the same for the Transvaal. We shall oblige Cetywayo to keep his army mobilized, and it is certain that his troops will have difficulty in finding sufficient food. If kept inactive, they will become dangerous to himself; if ordered to attack us, they will be playing our game.

In every way, therefore, so far as my judgement guides me, the modification of my original plan will be advantageous to us, and disadvantageous to our enemy.

A number of interesting themes can be detected in this despatch. One of them is Chelmsford's fixation with clearing areas of forest and other close country, a clear-cut pointer to his predisposition to fight the last war all over again. But, whilst the Xhosa did indeed operate guerrilla style from inaccessible forest strongholds, it was absolutely not the Zulu way. Neither had Chelmsford even begun to comprehend the sublime mobility of the Zulu *amabutho*. The idea that he could deny half the country to the Zulu field army with three or four ponderous infantry-heavy columns was naïve in the extreme; any one of them could have been bypassed with ease. So too was any notion that the Zulu army could ever go hungry within a livestock-rich nation state, half of which remained under the monarch's control. Also noteworthy are the implied references to the fragmenting of No. 3 Column's combat power, and the self-evident vulnerability of No. 2 Column within such a plan of campaign. Durnford's command simply did not have sufficient military clout to operate independently inside enemy territory.

At first glance the ideas outlined in the letter sound convincing enough, and they might well have satisfied Frere, who was fully conversant with the conduct and norms of Cape Frontier warfare. But this was manifestly not the Cape Frontier; a Zulu fighting force had little if anything in common with its Xhosa counterpart. Not only had Chelmsford failed to come to terms with the infinitely superior mobility of his enemy, but he had also failed to appreciate just how central to the Zulu military way was the spirit of the offensive. Zulu commanders liked to fight battles of decision; their kings expected it of them. There was seldom any room for complex campaign plans, delays of any kind, or other forms of tactical finesse. In this letter, and in other correspondence, Chelmsford seems almost to sneer at the very thought of the Zulu challenging him in the open field, an irresponsible mindset for any military commander to adopt, and way off course when it came to fighting this particular foe. Any intelligent reading of the document betrays his serious underestimation of the task confronting him. The enemy, it seems, is expected to wait politely and patiently in one corner of his country and do nothing too aggressive until his lordship is good and ready. So much for the operational level campaign plan. It is light on real substance and contains a number of badly flawed military assumptions – and it is on the quality of the assumptions underlying it that any plan will stand or fall.

By means of still more military malpractice, coupled with a dangerously inflated estimate of his own ability, Chelmsford also took upon himself the responsibility for the tactical level of operations on what we might term the central front. Without giving the matter so much as a second thought, he pushed Colonel Richard Glyn into the background and in the process caused a good deal of friction within the British command and staff system. Even having recognised that Chelmsford had appointed himself the *de facto* column commander, we must nonetheless remain mindful that he was not in command at Isandlwana on 22 January, and thus cannot in all fairness be held accountable for how the battle itself unfolded. Admittedly it was the general, operating at the tactical level, who allowed himself to be deceived – by circumstance rather than by any deliberate guile on the part of the his Zulu opposite numbers – but it was assuredly Durnford, the senior officer present at the camp, who must bear the lion's share of the blame for the ensuing disaster.

Chelmsford might have been an indifferent field commander, but Anthony Durnford was a fish out of water, both in terms of experience and, even more importantly, in the closely interlinked fields of judgement and temperament. He was a sapper plain and simple, a builder of roads and bridges, who had failed to add any more directly soldierly dimensions to his military CV, in stark contrast, for example, to his own father, a general officer, or to his direct contemporary and friend 'Chinese' Gordon, both of whom were Royal Engineers in a much more recognisably modern mould. Anthony Durnford was simply not qualified to hold a combat command. Sadly he deluded himself on this point and, for a while at least, fooled Lord Chelmsford, who by 22 January had uncovered some of his more obvious failings and had administered a dire warning threatening his removal. Inexcusably, Durnford was operating a selfish personal agenda at Isandlwana. From the moment he received the order calling him forward to the camp, he was interested only in contriving a set of circumstances in which he could demonstrate his competence as a dashing field commander. Not least was he anxious to impress the GOC following the 14 January reprimand. So strong were the inner demons that had preyed on his mind since the fiasco at Bushman's River Pass, however, that in effect his judgement was not to be trusted in the near presence of the enemy. That said there can be no question but that he fought bravely and died well. But neither can such a death serve as any form of exoneration for failures of judgement or character, for courage on a field of battle is no more than is customarily expected of a British officer.

If the greatest share of the blame for a tactical defeat must rest with the man in command at that level, then Durnford would at first glance appear to be squarely in the frame. But there has always been controversy over the command and control arrangements at Isandlwana; the events of the morning, prior to the Zulu onslaught, are not particularly clear-cut. Back then to the all-important conversation at Pulleine's tent, when Durnford first arrived at the camp.* Was Durnford the tactical level commander? What is Henry Pulleine's part in the equation?

The balance of the evidence would suggest that Pulleine was quite clear that somebody had to be in charge – as an infantry officer this was a stock-in-trade proposition for him. He knew that he could not himself be in overall command, as he was only a substantive major in the Army List to Durnford's lieutenant colonel. This much is clear: Pulleine attempted to hand over command, principally because he knew that he was bound by the conventions of the service to do so, but was unable to effect an unequivocal transfer of authority, because Durnford chose to shun the wider responsibilities unquestionably conferred upon him by his seniority. He did so with words to the effect that Pulleine should not worry about the overall command of their combined force, as he had no intention of interfering at the camp, or even of remaining there.[†] Yet there was nothing in either man's orders, or indeed Pulleine's more immediate understanding of the wider operational situation, to suggest that Durnford should be doing anything other than off-saddling his ponies, erecting his tents and awaiting the arrival of further orders. Indeed Durnford's last communication from the GOC had specifically

* As described by Lieutenant William Cochrane, who was present in person.

† Cochrane.

stated that he could expect to receive new orders, and the one before that had been the searing reprimand, which demanded that he should adhere strictly to the general's instructions and refrain from acting impulsively on his own initiative. In straight military terms Durnford had two simple options open to him: one, take command of the camp himself, or two, subordinate himself and his troops to the local commander, Pulleine, until such time as he received new orders calling No. 2 Column forward. In fact he was to contrive a third and militarily unsound option – two military forces operating in the same battlespace with no overall commander.

After the initial exchange with Pulleine, Durnford suggests that the troops at the camp should stand down. With nothing much happening at this juncture, the two colonels then adjourn their meeting in order to take a late breakfast at the officers' mess tent. When they reassemble at Pulleine's headquarters tent a short while later, they are confronted with vague reports which suggest that the enemy force beyond the Nyoni escarpment is retiring. Durnford now proceeds to take measures which lie outside the scope of his authority – as he himself has only just delimited it. Based on the messages from the outlying pickets, he decides to mount a foray from the camp, using his own troops.

Leaving aside the viability of Durnford's plan for a moment, and accepting that the continuing uncertainty over enemy movements make some form of further reconnaissance by mounted troops desirable, it can be argued that such a foray is sound enough military practice, provided that, as agreed, Pulleine's original guard force and the No. 2 Column assets continue to be regarded as separate commands engaged in distinctly separate tasks. In this way the spirit of the order to Pulleine to 'act strictly on the defensive' can be met, and further reconnaissance can be carried out without impinging upon the security of the camp. Durnford, however, then transgresses the only recently agreed demarcation line – a line drawn entirely at his own instigation – and drifts instead into an entirely illegitimate area, wherein he proceeds nonetheless to direct the activities of Pulleine's assets. Worse still, he demands that they act in an offensive role rather than remaining prudently on the defensive. In doing so he is inciting Pulleine specifically to disregard the orders of his higher headquarters. Whilst we know with the benefit of historical hindsight that Clery gave Pulleine his orders without personal reference to Richard Glyn or the GOC, this does not alter the fact that they were issued under a full colonel's authority, and in accordance with a lieutenant general's intent. Thus they carry more weight than any spur of the moment scheme dreamt up by a newly arrived lieutenant colonel.

At first it is just Captain Barry's picket company on Mkwene Hill which is at issue: Durnford declares that it should leave its position to act in support of Raw and Roberts on the plateau. This is a clear-cut transgression of the agreement he has only just concluded – 'I am not going to interfere with you' – and yet that is exactly what he is doing. Pulleine, after all, is particularly concerned about his northern flank; precisely the reason he has reinforced it with Cavaye's E Company shortly before Durnford's arrival. The last thing he now needs is a senior officer, a man who has already refused to assume any responsibility for the security of the camp, dabbling in his plan for the surveillance of the vulnerable sector around Mkwene Hill and the Tahelane Spur. Next, Durnford magnifies his initial transgression substantially, by at first requesting and then insisting, that Pulleine should give him two companies of the 24th to accompany his foray.

Now we need to return to the viability of Durnford's plan – two troops of irregular cavalry and a company of the NNC are to scour the plateau, east from Mkwene Hill, in order to drive the enemy into the arms of Durnford's two troops, the rocket battery and a second NNC company in the low ground beyond Amatutshane. It is only feasible if the force to be driven off the plateau is sufficiently small to get some rough handling at the hands of a hundred troopers of the NNMC, and there is no other significant enemy force in a position to menace the other elements of his command.

As was established in *How Can Man Die Better*, Durnford and Pulleine were not in fact oblivious to the presence of a very large Zulu force beyond the escarpment, as has traditionally been portrayed. Rather, they were fully aware that the cavalry vedettes had brought in a report of several thousand Zulus moving in the hills – this was the preparatory move of the uNodwengu Corps, the right horn, to take up its own position of concealment behind the Ngedla Heights (though the manoeuvre would not have been reported by the pickets in such clearly defined terms). Somebody had estimated that there were 7,000 warriors in the hills.* Launching three or four reconnaissance patrols, each of around half a dozen horsemen, would have been the correct military response – but Durnford was quite clearly looking for a fight. A force of several thousand warriors was far too large for him to engage with a total of 400 poorly trained native troops, with or without the addition of 160 slow-moving regular infantry. So even given the apparent situation (and the true situation was infinitely more menacing), Durnford's foray was not just a bad idea – it was nothing short of foolhardy.

So much for Durnford's plan – but to what extent was his battlefield performance shaped by his character and experience? Military men are of course as prone to human failings as men from any other walk of life, but almost all commissioned officers in a professional army will exude self-confidence, for this particular attribute is essential to leadership. Invariably it will be instilled in them at the outset of their careers. However, only a proportion of an officer corps will enjoy the sort of instinctive military skills which, given a level playing field, tend to bring success in battle. Experience of the right kind can in some measure compensate for a lack of military intuition. The very best tacticians draw on instinct and experience in perfect combination. At the other end of the spectrum, individually woeful combat commanders can be found in any army. An impulsive, inexperienced but self-confident officer is particularly ill-equipped for the sort of intuitive decision-making required on campaign and can prove to be a very dangerous creature indeed. Decisions in the field have to be rational and they have to be timely, but this is seldom as straightforward a proposition as it sounds.

Military history demonstrates only too well that any army will have its fair share of officers who are unable to maintain a coherent line of thought in a pressure situation – men who cannot make the requisite mental leaps in a fast-moving scenario. These are the people who will come up with a tactically unsound solution to a battlefield problem. If

* Lieutenant Charlie Pope's diary entry for 22 January cites this estimate.

the man at issue is a subordinate commander, then he will have peers to help him and a superior to tell him what to do – all may yet be well. If he has no superior, but is himself the senior officer in the field, then there is huge potential for things to go badly wrong. There is every danger that he will fall apart when confronted with the uncertainty engendered by a live enemy – an enemy manoeuvring in imprecise numbers, in unknown locations, to an uncertain end. This greatest of all military failings – the inability of a senior commander to make consistently sound and timely military decisions in the presence of the enemy – most commonly occurs as a function of inexperience in active field command at the junior and intermediate levels, or when officers are operating outside their particular comfort-zone.

Durnford was an experienced sapper but there is no avoiding the fact that for an officer of his age and seniority he was distinctly short of campaign service. Nonetheless he seems to have brimmed with a confidence in his own tactical ability, to which nothing in his service record particularly entitled him. Possessed of an unshakeable belief in his personal powers of judgment, he had adopted an overly dogmatic tactical mantra for tackling the Zulu: 'my idea is that wherever Zulus appear we ought to attack'. It should have been abundantly clear to all the British commanders of 1879 that a small, ponderous, imperial army, whilst it could campaign on the strategic offensive, had no choice but to confront significant bodies of Zulus on the tactical defensive – from positions of all-round defence with secure flanks and rear.

Teignmouth Melvill did particularly well to bring Durnford back under control, when Pulleine advised his adjutant that two companies of their battalion had been ordered out of camp to participate in a foray. The adjutant stood up to Durnford and effectively insisted that he think again. Although one senses that voices were not raised in this exchange, it seems clear that it must have been a very strained five minutes. The outcome confirms just how high was Melvill's standing in Lord Chelmsford's army. It was Durnford who backed down.

The proceedings at Pulleine's command post are brought to a close by Durnford bustling away impatiently, with a demand delivered as he turned on his heel, that Pulleine should support him if he was pressed. Quite how he imagines Pulleine can do this and still comply with his orders to act strictly on the defensive is a mystery: Durnford, after all, intends sallying several miles from the camp. Militarily it is an entirely nonsensical injunction. Durnford then leaves the conversation hanging in mid-air. In effect there is now a situation where the separation of the two parts of the force has been set in concrete and there is very little prospect of unified action, or even co-operation, between them. In the situation that will unfold over the ensuing hour, that is to say one in which both elements of the British force will make contact with a massive enemy host inside a common battlespace, it is vital that they should adapt their plan to reflect the changed reality of the situation and act in complete concert under a single commander. This can only be Durnford, who should immediately have disengaged from the Qwabe Valley, and returned to the camp at best speed to assume overall responsibility for its defence. The only other option was for him to report to Pulleine and, by gentleman's agreement, temporarily subordinate himself to the in-place local commander. If it was necessary or desirable for the Basuto and Edendale Troops to fight a delaying action against the left horn, which it was not, then Durnford could safely have left the task to his two troop commanders, Lieutenants Henderson and Davies. The onus on Durnford personally was to extricate himself, ride back to the camp to marry up with Pulleine, to take or cede overall command, and either make, or be presented with, a combined plan of action.

Sad to say there was never any question of Durnford hurrying back to the camp, as his conduct was now being governed by the second element of his personal agenda – the inner psychological demons that demanded he fight bravely and prominently in the front line. This again is a relatively common phenomenon; it is not unknown in military history for senior officers who have never previously seen action to behave like excited subalterns when the shooting starts. Amongst the generally campaign-hardened middle ranking membership of the Victorian officer corps, nobody was more prone to this psychological phenomenon than the likes of Anthony Durnford; in a lifetime's soldiering his only combat experience amounted to a couple of minutes firing in the Bushman's River Pass. And so it was that he fell all too readily into the trap of fighting a subaltern's skirmish and not a colonel's battle. Ultimately then, there can be no doubt that the men who fought at Isandlwana were failed by the tactical level commander who quite simply neglected, either to fulfil the role, or to cede it to somebody who would.

But, whilst it is true that Durnford must take the lion's share of the blame for command failure at the tactical level, we must not forget either, that it was not Durnford who deployed the 24th Regiment's firing line. Whilst the regiment came within a hair's breadth of saving the situation with a well disciplined withdrawal, the firing line was outflanked and must by definition have been poorly sited. This surely was Henry Pulleine's fault, for it was he who sited the six companies of regulars. But then again, it is clear from the 07.30 a.m. alarm that fighting well forward of the camp was not his preferred course of action. At breakfast time he stood to in front of the tents and was not drawn out into the Isandlwana bowl. The difference between the breakfast-time alarm and the start of the battle proper, was that Durnford had disappeared a long way into the eastern plain, had got himself embroiled with the enemy left horn in the Qwabe Valley, and had left Pulleine, an honourable man, feeling that he was duty bound to act in support of a brother officer. It has always been an unwritten rule of the British officer corps that if one officer asks another to come to his assistance, then there is no option but to comply. By deploying into the bowl, Pulleine was probably seeking to establish a safe corridor along which Durnford could be protected from interception by the *amabutho* of the Zulu chest. So it was that Durnford got back safely, as far as the Nyogane Donga.*

In due course the British right was turned because of Durnford's mismanagement of his withdrawal from the donga; it was peremptory, completely unheralded to other commanders on the battlefield, and therefore panicky by definition. He himself failed to command it. Due almost certainly to misplaced, ostentatious personal bravado, he was one of the last men away from the Nyogane Donga. As a consequence

---

* It is often stated that Durnford left the Nyogane Donga at the height of the battle and came back to the camp to speak to Pulleine, but there is absolutely no source evidence to support this and, as established in *How Can Man Die Better*, Pulleine was not at the camp anyway – he was forward on the firing line as the duties of a battalion commander required.

there was no senior figure at the head of his command – nobody to
lead them to a rallying point, nobody to tell them when or where to
dismount, and nobody to direct and organise the occupation of a new
defensive position short of the saddle. The careless and panicky nature
of Durnford's withdrawal gave Lieutenant Charlie Pope (the officer
commanding G Company, 2nd/24th) absolutely no opportunity to
withdraw in conformity. Had Durnford given as little as six or seven
minutes' advanced notice of his intention to quit the Nyogane, Pulleine
and his company commanders would probably have been able to use
such a head start to fall back safely to a new defence line in front of
the tents.

But the defence of the British right is not the only key issue at the
tactical level of command. What of the enemy right horn on the
opposite side of the battlefield? There is an argument to say that had
the perimeter not collapsed when it did, then the slaughter would have
been even more comprehensive. Those fugitives who were lucky
enough to survive did so because they were able to get out along the
Manzimyama Valley before the right horn attacked via the saddle
against the British rear. Hence there is an even more fundamental issue
here – one which would tend to exonerate any officer operating at the
tactical level of any share of the blame, if not for a massacre, then at
least for a logistic disaster – the looting and wrecking of the camp and
the loss of the trek oxen. But events did not unfold merely as a logistic
disaster – there was wholesale slaughter too.

'I don't understand it,' said a despondent Lord Chelmsford later in
the day, 'I left a thousand men there.' It was closer to two thousand
actually – but was it enough? In fact the total number of defenders was
not important – it was the number of regular infantry companies
assigned to Pulleine that mattered, as crucially these were the only
assets capable of holding ground in a stand-up fight with a Zulu army.
There were only six such companies. But it was not merely a matter of
clustering all of them into a battalion 'receive cavalry' square, as has
often been mistakenly asserted. Pulleine's mission was to defend the
camp. This meant the tents, the stores, well over 2,000 oxen, almost 200
wagons and carts, and so on. The tents were spread out over a frontage
of over half a mile in length. With unit transport parks laid out behind

the tents, the unit encampments were probably at least 200 yards deep. To hold the front of the camp? A minimum of four companies. To hold the left flank, the depth, of the camp? A minimum of two companies and ideally three. Already all six companies are committed. Who is left to defend the right flank of the encampment? Who will deny Mahlabamkhosi to the enemy? Who is holding the 300-yard wide saddle between Isandlwana and Mahlabamkhosi – the rear? Nobody. The task of defending the camp at Isandlwana was one which required a minimum of ten companies. When Clery laid out the camp on Monday 20 January, he had envisaged that there would be always be twelve companies of regulars available to defend it, the combined strength of both battalions of the 24th. The decision to march out with six companies at 4.00 a.m. that morning was not discussed with Richard Glyn, Henry Degacher, Henry Pulleine, Arthur Harness or any other field officer. The only men in a position even to raise the matter of the security of the camp with his lordship, as he sat on the edge of his camp bed deciding what to do about the situation at Mangeni, were Clery and Crealock. Neither man did so. It is certain however, even if they had, that Chelmsford would have brushed their objections aside.

That precise moment, 1.30 a.m. on the morning of Wednesday 22 January, was when the Battle of Isandlwana was lost – for the immobilisation of the column and the loss of its stores must necessarily have been regarded as a defeat. But by the same token, Lord Chelmsford's decision did not, of itself, necessarily presage wholesale massacre. Chelmsford was not dummied or duped by the Zulu high command as has been suggested. When Dartnell made contact on Magogo the previous afternoon, it was with a 1,500-strong force assigned to shield the forward move to the Ngwebeni Valley. It all happened purely by chance, as the British and the Zulus were manoeuvring across the great eastern plain in opposite directions, the British to the south and the *amabutho* in the north. The fact that this was a chance encounter does not excuse Chelmsford's rash camp-bed decision. He was dividing his force in the near presence of a supremely mobile enemy, without knowing exactly where their main strength lay, and in doing so would be exposing a sprawling and badly sited encampment with no defensive fieldworks and an inadequate garrison.

Had he run into the main *impi* with his half of the column, it is certain that he would have met with a disaster in the Phindo Hills, every bit as extensive, and probably worse, than the disaster which took place at Isandlwana. Neither component of the British force was strong enough on its own to meet 25,000 warriors in open battle, without the advantage of a strongly fortified or naturally impregnable position. Chelmsford was to claim of Isandlwana that 'there never was a position where a small force could have made a better defensive stand'.* But this cannot be true. It is far better to hold a position with a 360-degree field of fire out to only intermediate ranges, than it is to have a position with unlimited fields of view over arcs of say 300 degrees. In fact, the camp was both vulnerable from the rear and completely blind across a 180-degree arc to its northern flank.

There is every reason to feel sorry for Richard Glyn. He was a sound and steady commander and knew the mettle of Southern Africa's black fighters well. His strong performance in the Ninth Cape Frontier War would tend to suggest that, if only he had been left to his own devices, then all would have been well for No. 3 Column. The next senior man to the general, he should have confronted him over the way things were going, in particular over the air of complacency emanating from the army staff. One suspects that he knew this and that his failure to grasp the nettle preyed on his mind for the rest of his life. Easier said than done though; it was not the way of the Victorian officer corps to question the wisdom of their general officers.

Back then, to Pulleine. It is indeed useful that there were two alarms at Isandlwana on 22 January. The first illustrates that given the choice Pulleine would have fought his battle close in on the camp. His share in the blame is derived from the fact that he was not hard-nosed enough to leave the reckless Durnford to his own devices (the mobility of Durnford's force would always enable him to extricate himself), or to concede parts of the sprawling camp to the enemy. These are hardly crimes; he did his best to support a brother officer and he tried faithfully to carry out the impossible defensive task with which he had been entrusted. He was not to blame for the fact that the defence of the

* Chelmsford's observations on the proceedings of the Isandlwana Board of Inquiry.

camp was under-resourced. Pulleine advanced into the plain to help Durnford. The evidence would indicate that even so he would have got his battalion back to the camp intact, if only Durnford had given him the merest hint that he was about to abandon the right. Now facing a changed situation, in which the preservation of the camp and the oxen had become subordinate to survival, there might just have been enough time to form a strong battalion square before the right horn came crashing over the saddle – and such a square would almost certainly have been able to hold its ground around the ammunition wagons. Perhaps Pulleine's only offence was that of being too acquiescent. He felt obliged to do what a marginal superior had asked him to do, even though fighting forward on the plain was against his better judgement.

Having contemplated the various arguments, we must surely, in scrutinising the issue of blame, arrive at two inescapable conclusions. First, one man alone, operating without the slightest regard for the views and opinions of his principal subordinates, set the conditions in which a massive host was able to descend upon a force too weak to hold what was essentially a substantial and strategically vital logistic installation, sited on a piece of ground with blind spots embracing arcs of not less than 240 degrees. The 2nd Baron Chelmsford assigned Brevet Lieutenant Colonel Henry Pulleine an unachievable mission (by proxy), and in the wider scheme of things undoubtedly fell into the timeless trap of badly underestimating his enemy.

There is every reason to regard Frederick Thesiger as a military incompetent. He might have been a sound enough battalion commander in his day, and his service in Abyssinia certainly showed that he was an effective organiser on the staff. But as a general officer tasked with confronting a highly capable enemy, he was entirely out of his depth. His blunders guaranteed that the camp would be overrun and hence that logistic disaster must necessarily ensue, but did not of themselves dictate that wholesale massacre was also inevitable. In January 1879 he betrayed his unsuitability as a senior field commander, but he was assuredly nobody's fool and, having been taught a bitter lesson in the art of war during the course of the Isandlwana campaign, was able to learn from his mistakes and put in a greatly improved performance over the course of the rest of the war, albeit a ponderous one based almost exclusively on a policy of safety first. Few defeated British generals have been fortunate enough to get a second bite at the apple. Those who use his second half performance to argue that he was tactically competent, miss the point entirely. General officers are required to get it right first time – it goes with the territory – it is the difference between victory and defeat.

Deciding what role subordinates are to play in a plan of campaign is as much a part of generalship as any of its more obvious dimensions; nobody compelled Chelmsford to give Durnford a combat command and it was evidently a choice that others would not have made. In South Africa there had always been a question mark over his judgement. Most notable amongst the doubters was Sir Theophilus Shepstone, who knew Durnford well, and whose son George was killed at Isandlwana:

> It is strange but true that when I heard he had been appointed to serve with Colonel Durnford, I felt as if I had heard his death warrant. I had no confidence in Durnford's prudence or capacity to suit himself to the circumstances in which he might be so suddenly placed.

Colonel Anthony Durnford's selfish personal agenda, highly questionable powers of judgement, and his inexperience, mark him out as a man temperamentally unsuited to hold an independent field command. If Lord Chelmsford set Pulleine an unachievable mission, it was Anthony Durnford whose impulsive decisions and actions contrived to bring about wholesale slaughter. The famous and protracted argument between the Durnford and Colenso families on one hand, and Lord Chelmsford and his supporters on the other, has served as a red herring for well over a century.

There were, in fact, two military incompetents in the field that day, a startlingly simple conclusion indeed. One of them of course was appointed by the other. So much for blame.

But Isandlwana was not merely a British defeat, it was also a stunning Zulu victory. Whilst its outcome was governed, in part, by the incompetence of two senior British officers, it does not necessarily follow that it was correspondingly matched by a display of military genius on the part of the Zulu commanders. Ntshingwayo and Mavumengwana did no more than choose an excellent avenue of approach, devise a sound plan of attack based on Zulu tactical norms, and then execute it to perfection. It has been argued that the Zulu co-commanders decoyed Lord Chelmsford out to Mangeni, with the specific aim of dividing the British force – not so. There is not the merest hint of any source evidence to substantiate the notion, as there otherwise must have been, no matter how passionately advocates of the theory advance their case.

The brush at Mangeni on Tuesday evening occurred purely by chance: it was a far-roaming mounted police patrol under Major John Dartnell that first made contact with the Zulus, not the other way round. If Ntshingwayo's plan had called for a deliberate attack on the camp early on Wednesday morning, rather than on Thursday, then time and space considerations would have demanded that a decoy force make contact early the previous morning, Tuesday, so as to lure the British out during the course of the day. He could not have anticipated or relied upon Chelmsford's somewhat improbable 1.30 a.m. decision to move out with a flying column as early as 4.30 a.m. on Wednesday. There could in any case be only a very low probability that the British would respond to the exposure of a small Zulu force, at some considerable distance from the camp, by dividing their force and rushing out to meet it. But the British were not even at Mangeni on Tuesday morning, in order to be decoyed, in the first place. The whole decoy story has its origins in the immediate aftermath of the battle, when senior staff officers and other apologists for the GOC were speculating wildly about Zulu strategy, in an attempt to account for so crushing and improbable a defeat.

The strongest likelihood is that the 1,500 Zulus who chased Inspector George Mansel's patrol back down the Magogo spur at last light on Tuesday had been detached by Ntshingwayo from the main *impi*'s bivouac at Siphezi Hill early on Tuesday afternoon, as a direct response to the sudden arrival of elements of the British force at Mangeni. The purpose of the deployment was to establish a flank-guard or screen to the forward move of the main body to the Ngwebeni Valley. By the time the flank-guard had fended off the inquisitive mounted police patrols, it was getting dark. The Zulus over-nighted on Magogo, their camp-fires being visible to the Dartnell/Lonsdale force encamped on the other side of the valley atop Hlazakazi.

At first light the flank-guard moved off through the dead ground to the rear of Magogo to re-join the main *impi*, by now safely ensconced in the Ngwebeni Valley. Hence, by the time Lord Chelmsford arrived at Mangeni with the lead elements of the flying column, there was not a single Zulu in sight. The British had to advance some way into the Phindo Hills before they again made contact, this time with an entirely different Zulu grouping – the 500 or so local warriors of Chief Matyana. Ntshingwayo and the other senior Zulu indunas did indeed display command skills of the very highest order, but decoys formed absolutely no part of their plan. Their great accomplishment was manoeuvring 25,000 men across relatively open terrain, without detection, to an extremely well chosen place of concealment on the British left flank. As ever their goal was to fight a battle of decision; their intent was the restoration of the territorial integrity of the kingdom. The means of achieving it was to be the annihilation of No. 3 Column, not merely of half of it. Ntshingwayo was almost certainly oblivious to the departure of Chelmsford and the flying column; attempting to keep the camp under continuous surveillance would have required an observation post on Itusi Hill or the Nyoni escarpment, ground features already occupied or observed by British vedette posts. Pushing observers forward would have run the risk of compromising the presence of the *impi* in the Ngwebeni Valley and sacrificing the all important element of surprise. For a shrewd commander like Ntshingwayo this was far too great a risk to run. Chelmsford left camp at 4.00 a.m. but the battle did not open until noon, so that there can be no question of Ntshingwayo having launched an opportunistic attack on a weakened camp.

Given the eight-hour interval, it was clearly Durnford's foray that brought the battle on some seventeen hours earlier than Ntshingwayo had intended. From that point on the success or failure of the attack rested with the ordinary fighting men of the Zulu army. Above all else, it was their extraordinary determination and formidable courage that lay at the heart of a truly remarkable victory.

Epilogue

Footnotes in History

Official British returns indicate that 76 officers and 1,007 other ranks were killed in action in the Zulu War. Some 37 officers and 206 other ranks were wounded. In addition to the battle casualties, 17 officers and 330 men died of disease, and around 100 officers and 1,300 men were invalided home sick. Overwhelmingly the fatal loss in battle fell upon the 24th Regiment of Foot. Although some of Natal's resident magistrates did their best at a local level, no authoritative return for the casualties amongst the allied native contingents was ever compiled. The Zulu fatal loss in battle was not less than 6,000 men and may have been much higher; probably several thousand more died of their wounds.

In the end a war launched without the specific sanction of the London Government cost its Exchequer well over £5 million; and this in an era when a man who cleared £300 per annum was considered more than merely well to do. War to the knife it may have been, but at least there were no significant losses amongst the civilian populations of either side.

The Defenders of Rorke's Drift

John Chard received an immediate brevet to major. He stayed on at the mission after the battle but quickly contracted a fever. He had to be sent down the line to recuperate in Ladysmith. The Natal newspapers carried reports of his death at one point, which happily proved to be much exaggerated. He made a good recovery, returned to duty with Evelyn Wood's column, and was present at the Battle of Ulundi. He was presented with his VC by Sir Garnet Wolseley in July 1879. He was soon homeward bound. In a quite extraordinary coincidence, one of the porters sent to carry his bags at Durban was the *voorlooper* lad who had stolen his horse at Rorke's Drift. Chard disembarked at Spithead in early October 1879, to be greeted in person by the Duke of Cambridge, who notified him that he was expected at Balmoral in less than a fortnight's time. Queen Victoria was rather taken with him. Chard served on in the Royal Engineers for the rest of his life but never saw action again. Eventually he rose to the rank of colonel, but whilst serving in Scotland he became terminally ill with cancer of the tongue. He went to stay with his brother at Hatch Beauchamp, Taunton, and suffered terribly before he died on 1 November 1897, just short of his fiftieth birthday. He is buried in the churchyard at Hatch Beauchamp. Chard's soldier-servant, Driver Charles Robson, was still with his master when he made his triumphal return to England in the summer of 1879. He left the army not long after the Zulu War but was recalled from the Regular Army Reserve to serve in the Sudan. He left the service finally in 1894, and became a London cabbie. He lived in relative poverty in his later years and died in the capital in July 1933. He is buried at Woolwich Cemetery.

Like John Chard, Gonny Bromhead also received an immediate brevet to major. In March he was transferred from B Company to command F Company. Wolseley presented him with his VC at Utrecht on 22 August 1879. On his return to the family home at Thurlby Hall, he was presented by the tenants with a revolver which he kept with him for the rest of his life. He was invited to Balmoral at the same time as Chard, but was fishing in Ireland when the invitation was extended. The date had already passed by the time his mail caught up with him. He wrote to the palace to explain but was never re-invited. He soldiered on into his middle years and served in Gibraltar, India and in the Burma Campaign of 1886–8. Having returned to India, he contracted enteric fever and died at Camp Dabhaura, Allahabad, on 8 February 1891. He was forty-six. He is buried in the New Cantonment Cemetery, Allahabad. He never married.

James Henry Reynolds received immediate promotion to surgeon-major and was presented with his VC by Richard Glyn at Pinetown on 26 August 1879. He married his wife Elizabeth the year after the battle and continued to serve in the medical branch of the service. He was promoted to surgeon-lieutenant colonel in 1887 and retired without further promotion in 1896. Reynolds lived into ripe old age and died in his late eighties in London on 4 March 1932. He is buried at Kensal Rise RC Cemetery, Harrow Road, London.

The Reverend George 'Ammunition' Smith was offered and accepted a commission as a regular army chaplain. Three years after Rorke's Drift he was present at the Battle of Tel-el-Kebir, where Wolseley inflicted a crushing defeat on Arabi Pasha's Egyptian army. He also served in the campaigns of the mid-1880s against the Dervishes and was present at the Battles of El Teb and Ginnis. He kept his great patriarchal beard long after the fashion for such extravagant facial hair had moved on, and in later life was known affectionately by the men as 'Daddy' Smith. Towards the end of his career he was stationed for a number of years at Fulwood Barracks, Preston. On his retirement he took a room at a local hotel where he lived out the rest of his days. He died in his early seventies, a fortnight after Armistice Day in November 1918, and is buried in Preston Cemetery.

Commissary Dalton was given six months' sick leave after Rorke's Drift, during which time the Commissariat and Transport Department lobbied for his distinguished service to be appropriately recognised. In his formal report John Chard paid a generous tribute to Dalton's role in the battle, and it was well known that his courageous conduct was widely admired amongst the enlisted men. The lobbying campaign was successful and in November 1879 Dalton received his VC from General Gifford at a parade held at Fort Napier, Pietermaritzburg. Three months later he returned to England for a spell, but it was not long before he was back in South Africa. At first he tried his hand at gold prospecting in the Transvaal, but then returned to his old stomping ground in the Eastern Cape. He died of natural causes in a Port Elizabeth hotel only eight years after Rorke's Drift, and is buried in the RC Cemetery in Russell Road, Port Elizabeth.

Commissary Walter Dunne had a most dramatic start to his military career. Having already seen extensive active service against the Xhosa and the Zulu, he was still in South Africa when the Transvaal Rebellion broke out. He was present at the siege of Potchefstroom, which alone amongst the various investments of the British garrisons was pressed hard by the rebels. Trumpeter Martin, an N Battery survivor of

Isandlwana, was also present and likewise survived the ordeal. The following year Dunne was at Tel-el-Kebir. Later he saw active service against the Dervishes. He became a lieutenant colonel in 1888, was made a Companion of the Bath in 1896, and was promoted again the following year. He died in Rome in July 1908 having seen more than his fair share of war. Sadly, whilst Dalton's name is well known amongst the army's modern-day logisticians, Dunne has been somewhat forgotten. He, too, was a fine officer and displayed formidable courage as he laboured atop the mealie-bag redoubt.

In common with most of the officers of the 2nd/24th, Wilsone Black had lost his batman at Isandlwana. He took on Harry Hook in his stead. The two of them got on well together. Hook was still at Rorke's Drift in August 1879 when Wolseley presented him with his VC. That apart, there had been little to commend life in the regular army and Hook decided to buy himself out at a cost of £18. When he got home it was only to find that his common-law wife, believing him to be dead, had sold his house in Monmouth and married somebody else. Hook went to seek a new life in London. In 1881 he was taken on as a cleaner and then a cloakroom attendant at the British Museum; Lord Chelmsford and Major Bromhead VC provided his references. In 1897 Hook found love again and married Ada Letitia Taylor with whom he had two daughters. He maintained his links with the military by serving on as a part-timer in the 1st (Volunteer) Battalion of the Royal Fusiliers, in which unit he rose to sergeant. Though he barely felt it at the time, the scalp wound he received whilst fighting in the hospital caused him a great deal of discomfort in later life. The scar is clearly visible in his photographs but is often erroneously taken for a centre parting in his hair. He retired to Gloucestershire at the end of his working life, but was carried off by tuberculosis in the spring of 1905. He was fifty-four when he died. Hook's funeral was a grand affair and attracted a big turnout; the body was carried on a Royal Artillery gun-carriage and the 24th Regiment provided the pall-bearers, amongst whom was Fred Hitch's son. Fred himself was also present as a mourner, whilst the band of the Royal Fusiliers accompanied the coffin's progress with sombre tunes. Hook is buried in the village churchyard at Churcham, mid-way between Gloucester and the Forest of Dean.

Surgeon Reynolds removed more than thirty pieces of bone from Fred Hitch's shattered shoulder. Inevitably he was invalided out of the army almost immediately. He received his Victoria Cross from the Queen Empress in person, whilst recuperating at Netley Military Hospital. In July 1880 Fred married Emma Matilda Maurice, with whom he had three sons and three daughters. At first he worked as a member of the Corps of Commissionaires at the Fine Art Society, then the Imperial Institute, and finally at the Royal United Services Institute in Whitehall, where famously his VC was stolen from his coat – after he had been taken to hospital following a fall from a ladder. The War Office approved a replacement medal in 1908, some seven years after the theft. In due course Hitch became a well-known and tremendously popular London cabbie. He died suddenly of pneumonia and heart failure on 6 January 1913, at the age of fifty-six. He was buried with full military honours at St Nicholas's Churchyard, Old Chiswick. John Williams (Fielding) VC and Frank Bourne both attended the funeral, as did over a thousand of Hitch's fellow cabbies. Legend has it that it was all but impossible to get a cab in London the day they buried Fred Hitch. In fact Fred and his colleagues were on strike at the time of his death.

Swiss-born he may have been, but Ferdnand Schiess came to be regarded as a naturalised South African and is commonly thought of as the country's first VC winner. He was presented with his medal by Wolseley in the market square, Pietermaritzburg, on 3 February 1880. After the war he was employed in the telegraph office in Durban, but for some reason lost his job and quickly fell on hard times. His desperate appeals for work in the government service went unheeded. In 1884 he was found on the streets of Cape Town in poor physical condition. The Royal Navy took him into its care and offered him free passage for England. He accepted and sailed aboard the troopship *Serapis*, but he was already ill and died not long after setting sail. His Victoria Cross was recovered from his pocket. He was buried at sea off what is now the Angolan coast. He was only twenty-eight years of age.

Corporal Allen made a good recovery from his wound and by November 1879 was back at work at the regimental depot in Brecon. The following month the Queen presented him with his VC at Windsor

Castle. Private William Roy received his DCM at the same investiture, having been discharged the service due to his failing eyesight only two days earlier. In January 1880 the mayor and corporation of Brecon presented Allen with a gold watch. In 1886 the then Sergeant Allen was posted to Monmouth as the permanent staff instructor of musketry with C Company of the 4th (Volunteer) Battalion of the South Wales Borderers. He and his wife Sara Ann, whom he had married three years before the Zulu War at the Brecon registry office, had six children in all, five of whom were alive when Allen was carried off in an influenza epidemic in February 1890. Tragically none of the children would live into their teens. Their father was buried with full military honours in Monmouth Cemetery. He was forty-six when he died.

Private Roy drifted to Australia at some point in the 1880s but soon went blind from his syphilis and fell on hard times. He was taken into the care of a charitable institution, where somebody took pity upon him. A grand military concert was held in Sydney to raise money for his care. It is not altogether clear from the sources what he did to be awarded the DCM ahead of the other 24th men in the battle.

Private John Waters was medically discharged late in 1879, after twenty-one years' service, with a small disability pension to sustain him. He was last recorded as living in Britten Street, Chelsea, where he disappears from history.

William Jones 593 was at the next royal investiture in the lobby of Windsor Castle and received his VC on 13 January 1880. Only a month later he was medically discharged as a result of worsening rheumatism. He went to live in Manchester where he took the recently widowed Elizabeth Frodsham as his second wife. Elizabeth had five children by her previous marriage and she and William had two more. He is said to have toured England with Buffalo Bill's Wild West Show in 1888, and he occasionally went on the music hall stage in Rochdale to recount his story of the battle. By 1893 he was struggling to make ends meet and felt compelled to pawn his VC for £5. Next he sold the pawn ticket. Towards the end of his life he became senile and would often become distressed by the notion that the Zulus were coming. On occasions he was so terrified that he would flee the house, sometimes with his infant grand-daughter in his arms. He disappeared completely on one occasion, but was eventually located at a local workhouse. The police had found him wandering the streets aimlessly, quite unable to remember his name. He died at his daughter's house on 15 April 1913 at the age of seventy-four, and is buried in the Philips Park Cemetery in Manchester.

Not long after the defence of Rorke's Drift, Colonel Glyn offered Colour-Sergeant Frank Bourne a commission in the regiment. In the wake of the Isandlwana disaster there was no shortage of officers' vacancies. Without private means of his own, Bourne was forced to decline and soldier on in the ranks. He served in India and Burma in the 1880s. He married Eliza Mary Fincham in Bombay in 1882; they would have five children together. Eleven years after the initial offer of a commission he was appointed honorary lieutenant and quartermaster. Towards the end of his career Bourne served as the adjutant at the school of musketry in Hythe. When the Great War broke out he volunteered for recall and was appointed honorary major and adjutant of the school of musketry in Dublin. He was promoted to honorary lieutenant colonel just in advance of his second retirement at the end of the war and was awarded an OBE for his wartime service. He made a radio broadcast about the defence of Rorke's Drift in December 1936, which sadly was subsequently destroyed by BBC archivists in a crass display of poor judgement. Eliza Bourne died in 1931 at the age of seventy-seven, but Frank lived to see his country victorious in the Second World War and died at the ripe old age of 91. He is commonly believed to have been the last of the defenders of Rorke's Drift to die. He is buried at Beckenham Cemetery, Elmers End, Kent.

Robert Jones 716 also received his Victoria Cross from Wolseley at Utrecht. For a while he served with the 2nd/24th in Gibraltar and India. He was a short service enlistment, elected not to re-engage and saw out his time at Brecon. He married Elizabeth Hopkins in 1885, with whom he had a son and four daughters. He found employment as a farm labourer with a retired officer called Major De la Hay, at Crossway House, Peterchurch, Herefordshire. He lived a happy enough life in the country, but in 1898 in only his forty-second year, he began to complain periodically of pains in his head. In August that year he suffered a convulsion at work. On the morning of 6 September 1898 his wife noticed he was behaving oddly. At work he borrowed the major's shotgun, claiming that he was going to shoot crows, but instead he wandered off into the grounds and shot himself in the mouth. The coroner's jury returned a verdict of suicide whilst of unsound mind. He was buried in the churchyard at Peterchurch.

John Williams soldiered on in the 2nd/24th for a while, went with the battalion to Gibraltar, where he was presented with his Victoria Cross by Major General Anderson in front of the entire garrison, and thence to India. He took his discharge in 1883. He obtained civilian employment, married Elizabeth Murphy and had five children. He kept up his military ties by serving as a sergeant in the 3rd (Volunteer) Battalion of the South Wales Borderers. In his fifties he re-enlisted as a recruiting sergeant for the duration of the Great War. Sadly his son Tom was killed whilst serving with the 24th on the Western Front. John retired from his work at Brecon Barracks in 1920. He outlived Elizabeth and saw out his days living amongst his family in Cwmbran. In non-military circles he was always known by his real family name, Fielding. The longest surviving Rorke's Drift VC winner, he eventually died of natural causes, in his mid-seventies, on 24 November 1932. He was buried at St Michael's Church, Llantarnam. Again, it was a big funeral.

Corporal Jack Lyons was invalided out of the service. He is believed to have become a member of the Corps of Commissionaires in London. He retired to his home town, Newport, where he died in May 1923 of pneumonia and heart failure at 22 Oxford Street. He is buried in St Woollos Cemetery. In 1936 another well known B Company man, Corporal Alfred Saxty, was buried in the same graveyard.

Sergeant George Mabin, the staff clerk, was still in South Africa when the Transvaal Rebellion broke out. At the time he was employed as chief clerk to Major General Sir George Colley. He observed the Battle of Laing's Nek, was in the engagement at Ingogo, and is said to have been close to Colley just before he was killed at Majuba. Afterwards he became known in army circles as 'the fighting clerk'. He took his retirement in South Africa and went to live in Cape Town. He was one of the longest lived of all the defenders of Rorke's Drift. He died in October 1938 at the age of ninety.

Lord Chelmsford

Lord Chelmsford returned home to a mixed reception. The events of the Isandlwana campaign were now much better understood, whilst the Ntombi River incident and the death of the Prince Imperial had done little for his faltering reputation. Many of the politicians and newspapers pilloried him, but he continued nonetheless to enjoy the support and patronage of the Queen. As far as the military establishment was concerned, however, there was a tried and tested formula for dealing with a failed general officer. It is part of the ethos of the service that a man who holds the Queen's Commission is not merely in a job. He has taken on a way of life in which extraordinary demands can be made of him; he can expect a certain amount of loyalty in return. Precisely because it is a way of life and not a job, a regular officer can only be stripped of his commission or otherwise humiliated for acts of criminal or moral misconduct. It is not simply a matter of dismissing a man from a field of work that he is not very good at. The problem with Lord Chelmsford was that he had attained a rank far in excess of his talent, a fact that, as is so often the case, was only uncovered in the cauldron of active operations against the enemy – by which time it is invariably too late. What is certain is that a failed general will not again be allowed to command troops on active service. So it was with Lord Chelmsford.

A general can be superseded in the field if there is a strong case against him on grounds of competence, and there is another general officer close at hand with which to replace him. The trouble for Horse Guards in February 1879 was that it was extremely difficult to establish the facts. News from South Africa travelled at the speed of the steamship. An average run was about three weeks. Allowing for a week's contemplation in London, it took close to two months for a despatch to travel to London and be replied to, and this to Cape Town. If the operations at issue were being conducted upcountry, then there was an additional three- or four-day run for the mail to come down from Durban, and an overland leg beyond that. The Commander-in-Chief, the Duke of Cambridge, is commonly portrayed as a royal nonentity of limited intellect who owed his position only to his birthright. He is of course the arch-reactionary of the era. Some of this is true – but not the limited intellect part. The Duke was no fool. He was not taken in by any of the self-deluding obfuscations in Chelmsford's official despatches. Rather he saw directly to the heart of the issue: for good or ill Chelmsford had been in command. Horse Guards could have its moments of cleverness and began to probe all its independent sources for alternative interpretations of events. Helped by discreet glimpses of the private correspondence of officers writing home from the front, it did not take the C-in-C's staff long to raise their doubts.

Chelmsford could not be superseded in the immediate aftermath of Isandlwana – it took weeks to establish the facts, and there was in any case no other general officer in Southern Africa to whom they could turn. This is precisely why at the outset of the war three brigade-sized columns were in the hands of the senior battalion commanders, Glyn, Wood and Pearson. Horse Guards' first reaction was to do what it had to do in any event – despatch reinforcements in large numbers and quickly. Consider the flash-to-bang factor – that Isandlwana was not known about in London until a month after the fact, and that Wolseley was on his way to the front by June, and it is clear that Horse Guards rumbled Lord Chelmsford pretty quickly. That Chelmsford himself was left in no doubt that the game was up is shown by this directed letter from the Adjutant-General, Sir Charles Ellice. It was written in August 1879, a little over a month after Ulundi:

> My Lord,
>
> The Field Marshal Commanding in Chief, having very carefully considered the evidence taken before the Court of Inquiry on the Isandlana [sic] disaster; the supplementary evidence afterwards sent home and the answers transmitted by your Lordship to certain questions I had the honour to address to you on the subject, I have it in Command to acquaint your Lordship that His Royal Highness has come to the conclusion that the primary cause of the misfortune, and that which led to all the others, was the under estimate formed of the offensive fighting power of the Zulu army.
>
> This was not unnatural. Nowhere either in Southern or Central

Africa, did such a powerfully organized, well disciplined and thoroughly trained force of courageous men exist as lay at the disposal of Ketchwayo [sic].

It would appear that your Lordship, and those with you, expected to encounter foes and a mode of warfare differing in degree indeed, but not in kind, from that of the Caffres [sic] with whom they had lately been contending in the Cape Colony.

The idea of a well disciplined native force advancing firmly on, and closing rapidly in the open with British battalions armed with the breechloader and supported by rifled guns was not duly realised.

In fact such confidence in the superiority of the breechloader in British hands was felt that your Lordship did not hesitate to base your plan of campaign upon the power of three isolated columns none of which contained a real fighting force of more than a couple of English battalions, a battery, and a small body of mounted infantry or irregular cavalry, to penetrate, unsupported, into the heart of Zululand. Such a division of force was justifiable only on the belief that each of these columns was able to support alone, the impact of the whole Zulu power.

To this belief in the crushing effect of our weapons, and the small probability of the enemy venturing upon a flank attack in the open, is evidently due the immediate causes of the defeat at Isandlana [sic] viz:

1. The advance from Rorke's Drift without any persistent effort being made to put this, the immediate base of our operations in Zululand, in a proper state of defence before it commenced.

2. The non-preparation on the 21st January, either by the formation of a laager formed out of the wagons not told off to return to Rorke's Drift for supplies on the following day, or by the construction of a small redoubt or any means of defence for the troops in Camp in case of attack.

3. Your Lordship moving out of Camp on the morning of the 22nd with a battalion of infantry, four guns, and the mounted infantry to attack the enemy some ten miles off, whilst it was in this

defenceless state, even though you had ordered up Colonel Durnford's Native Contingent to reinforce it.

4. The not thoroughly searching, with horsemen, the country to the Northeast of the Camp, when the enemy was known to be in force ten miles to the East on the Ulundi Road.

5. The evident discredit attached from the first, by those at Headquarters, to the idea of a really serious attack being made upon the Camp when thus left.

6. The dissemination, in two directions, of the one regular battalion which remained in Camp on the attack being actually delivered, when the only chance of safety consisted in the immediate construction of a small laager, or in massing the troops in square, with a supply of ammunition in the centre, ready to break through one or other of the Zulu encircling wings.

This letter marked the end of Chelmsford's active career as a fighting soldier but not of his military service. Only the last of the six points of detail relates to the conduct of the Battle of Isandlwana at the tactical level; the other five point an accusing finger directly at the operational level commander. The major fault, that of underestimating the enemy badly, or attempting to fight a new war against a new enemy in exactly the same manner as the last one, is Chelmsford's responsibility alone. Thus we would be wrong to think, as is so commonly portrayed, that Chelmsford got away with his disastrous conduct of the Isandlwana campaign. But nor was he publicly humiliated in its aftermath, for that is not the way of the military establishment. In 1882 he was confirmed as a lieutenant general (his rank in South Africa had been local not substantive), and then moved swiftly into the margins. He became Governor of the Tower of London, was able to attend the House of Lords, and became Regimental Colonel of his own 95th Regiment. Later he became the Colonel of the Life Guards, the most prestigious of all the regimental colonelcies. In April 1905 Chelmsford died suddenly whilst playing billiards at the United Services Club. He was seventy-eight. As a matter of interest, his eldest son, the third Lord Chelmsford, went on to become Viceroy of India.

If the military establishment took care not to humiliate failed military commanders, the political establishment was far less subtle. The new Gladstone government recalled Sir Bartle Frere almost immediately. He died only five years after the end of the Zulu War at the age of sixty-nine.

On to Greater Things

Sir Garnet Wolseley marched remorselessly on for the top of his profession, becoming more insufferably opinionated with each passing day. Even now one needs only to dip briefly into his diaries and correspondence to sense his egotism and arrogance. He defeated Arabi Pasha at Tel-el-Kebir in 1882, but two years later failed to get down the Nile to Khartoum in time. Gordon was killed on 25 January 1885; the British steamers sailed within sight of his smouldering palace on the 27th. It was widely held that this was the fault of Gladstone's political machinations, not of Wolseley's painstakingly methodical military plan. In 1895 Wolseley beat Roberts to Horse Guards, in the race to succeed the Duke of Cambridge. Ironically, the post of Commander-in-Chief was subjected to modernisation at precisely the time Wolseley took office, so that the arch reformer found himself all but powerless to influence military affairs in the way he had always envisaged he would. Unfortunately his mind started to wander as he marched further into his sixties, and no amount of effort on the part of his aides could conceal the fact. He retired in 1900 and died thirteen years later at the age of eighty.

Major General Sir Evelyn Wood VC returned to Natal in the later stages of the Transvaal Rebellion and graciously agreed to serve under Sir George Colley, who was his junior in the Army List. Struggling to regain credibility in the wake of his defeats at Laing's Nek and Ingogo, Colley deliberately kept Wood away from the centre of things, so that no credit for any subsequent redeeming victory could be attributed to his presence. Redemption was to prove elusive, however. It was Wood who led the peace negotiations with the Boers, following Colley's death in the Majuba fiasco. The following year Wood served under Wolseley in Egypt. Although he never held another major operational command, Wood rose to attain the highest rank in the service. He retired as a field marshal and died not long after the Great War at the age of eighty-one.

On his return to England, Colonel Richard Glyn took command of the 24th Brigade Depot at Brecon and superintended the regiment's change of title to 'The South Wales Borderers'. In 1882 he was promoted to major general and made a Knight Commander of the Bath. He was promoted to lieutenant general before he retired. In 1898 he was appointed to the regimental colonelcy. He died in November 1900, just short of his sixty-ninth birthday, and not long after seeing the 24th embark for a new South African War. He was buried in his family plot at Ewell, Surrey. Lord Chelmsford was still alive when Glyn died, and so far as is known, Glyn never committed his memories of the Isandlwana campaign to paper.

Henry Degacher also rose to be a general officer and succeeded Glyn as Colonel of the Regiment. Like Glyn and Degacher, Wilsone Black also maintained a dignified silence about the failings of his superiors and rose to be a major general. Aided in his progress, like so many other heroes of the Victorian era, by his nation's supreme award 'For Valour', Edward Browne VC also attained general officer's rank. The Queen granted Mrs Sarah Melvill a pension against the Civil List of £100 per annum. In due course both Henry Pulleine's son and Teignmouth Melvill's elder son followed their late fathers into the 24th. The younger Teignmouth Melvill became one of the most accomplished polo players in the army, transferred to the 17th Lancers for the sport, and rose to command his new regiment. His younger brother Charles commanded a brigade of 'Kiwis' in the Great War.

For the most part, the members of Lord Chelmsford's army staff went on to successful careers. Lieutenant Colonel John Crealock and Major Matthew Gosset both rose to major general. Crealock died in Rawalpindi in 1895. The naval ADC Berkeley Milne rose to admiral, was knighted, served in the Great War, and died in his eighties just before the outbreak of a new German war. Colonel Richard Glyn's principal subordinates also fared well in their later lives. His chief of staff, Major Francis Clery, played a role in deflecting underhand attempts by Chelmsford and Crealock to blame Glyn for some of the mistakes made in the Isandlwana campaign, at a time when Glyn was too stunned and despondent to defend himself. Clery went on to be a lieutenant general and returned to South Africa to command a division under Buller in the Ladysmith campaign. He died in 1926 at the age of eighty-eight. Given his dismal performance at Hlobane, it is astonishing that Local Lieutenant Colonel John Russell also rose to the rank of major general. He died in 1909, the same year as Matthew Gosset and Wilsone Black. Major John Dartnell, the commandant of the Natal Mounted Police, served with distinction in the Boer War, rose to the rank of brigadier-general and in 1902 was knighted in recognition of his long and distinguished service in South Africa. He died only two years later.

Captain Penn Symons of D Company, 2nd/24th, went on to achieve great things in India, before returning to his old African stomping grounds in time for the 1899 outbreak of hostilities with the Boers. In the interim he saw service in Burma, was commanding officer of 2nd South Wales Borderers (1891–3), and commanded brigades in Waziristan (1894–5) and in the Tochi Field Force (1897). He went on to command a division in the Tirah Expedition, was knighted in May 1898, and a year later became GOC Natal. One prominent Boer War historian recently dismissed him as an Indian Army general with no experience of Africa. In fact, he could hardly have known the ground better. He was largely instrumental in Sir George White's ill-considered decision to detach a brigade forward to the defence of Dundee. When the invasion came, the Boers seized the commanding high ground around the town and waited for a response. As soon as the sun was up Major General Sir Penn Symons attacked the enemy positions on Talana Hill. Sadly, in the course of the morning he was mortally wounded, leading his infantry from the front. He expired on 23 October 1899 and is buried in the Anglican churchyard at Dundee.

After the battles of Talana Hill and Elandslaagte, Sir George White VC then did the one thing General Sir Redvers Buller VC had ordered him not to do: he got the garrison of Natal trapped on the wrong side of the Tugela at Ladysmith. The attempts to force the river and lift the siege would end in disaster at Colenso and Spion Kop, and would cost Redvers Buller his hard-won reputation. Prior to his Boer War demise, Buller had served under Wolseley in Egypt and the Sudan. For those with the eyes to see, there were indications in the Sudan that

Buller had reached his ceiling. In fact, with the exception of Wolseley, nobody else of importance seems to have worked it out. With a second Boer War looming it became necessary to appoint a general officer to command the newly established army corps, a conceptual precursor to the BEF of 1914. Rather than see his arch-rival Roberts appointed, Wolseley pushed Buller's candidacy instead. As a direct consequence of Wolseley's jealous politicking, a good many lives would be lost unnecessarily on the road to Ladysmith. One such life was that of Lieutenant Freddie Roberts, killed at Colenso in a foolhardy attempt to save Colonel Long's stranded guns from an exposed position just south of the Tugela. The attempt was made in broad daylight at Buller's personal instigation, when he need only have waited for sunset to recover the guns in perfect safety. Instead the rescue ended in disastrous failure. Bizarrely, having got young Roberts and many other men killed unnecessarily, Buller then withdrew before nightfall, compounding his error and needlessly abandoning the guns to the enemy. It must have made for a very awkward scene when the grieving Lord Roberts arrived in South Africa to supersede him.

Maori Browne was around thirty-two years of age in 1879 and had already lived an adventurous enough life for most men, having campaigned against the Maoris, the Sioux (allegedly), and the Xhosa. After the Isandlwana campaign he was sent back to the Cape with Rupert Lonsdale to raise a corps of irregulars, but by April 1879 he was back in Natal. He was sent to bear despatches to Chelmsford during the operations to relieve Eshowe and was present in the square at Gingindlovu. After the war he continued to serve as a volunteer officer and almost immediately saw a fresh spell of active service in the Basutoland rebellion of 1880–1. His faithful Irish servant Quin had stayed on with him, but was killed at his master's side during a skirmish. Browne subsequently served as a major in Warren's Bechuanaland Expedition of 1884–5, as adjutant of the Diamond Fields Horse in Kimberley until 1891, and as a staff officer in Rhodesia during the First Matabele War of 1893. In the second war he commanded a volunteer unit called the Umtali Rifles. His adventures came to an end in Jamaica in 1916 just short of his seventieth birthday.

Like Maori Browne, most of the notable volunteer officers from the

Isandlwana campaign soldiered on to see the Zulu War through to a victorious conclusion. Charlie Raw, the NNMC officer whose troops had discovered the main *impi* in the Ngwebeni Valley, fought at Hlobane and Kambula. Offy Shepstone left the carbineers and raised a new unit of native horse which fought at Ulundi; many of his men were Isandlwana survivors. Inspector George Mansel remained deeply inimical to regular soldiers for the rest of his life, not least when the subject of Isandlwana came up. Late in 1879 he wrote to Edward Durnford to encourage him in his belief that his late brother had been made a scapegoat for the failings of others. Mansel, though, was not the most able of officers. In the early days of the Isandlwana campaign Lord Chelmsford had remarked in correspondence that, 'Mr Mansell [*sic*] does not appear capable of getting oats for his horses without Major Dartnell's assistance.'* Such views did not prevent him, in due course, succeeding John Dartnell as commandant of the Natal Mounted Police.

Twenty years after the Zulu War, having by now risen to the command of his own 99th Regiment, Henry Harford found his unit quartered at Peshawar, alongside his old friends the 1st/24th. He was invited to dinner in their officers' mess and to his delight, 'was permitted once more to handle the old Colour, now wreathed with laurels'.

'The Lucky Five'

Captain Edward Essex served on Colley's staff throughout the Transvaal Rebellion. He was amongst the staff officers who participated in the foolhardy frontal attack on Laing's Nek conducted at Colley's order by the 58th (Rutlandshire) Regiment, and the only one of them to come out of it uninjured. The remnants of the 58th were brought back down the hill by a subaltern, their senior surviving officer. Essex was also present at the Battle of Ingogo, another of Colley's ill-conceived enterprises. Fortunately he was not amongst the men taken to the summit of Majuba Hill for the final debacle. It is not entirely clear at what point the nickname came into use, but he would be known as 'Lucky' Essex for the rest of his life.

* Chelmsford to Frere 13 January 1879.

In the aftermath of Isandlwana, Captain Alan Gardner attracted considerable controversy. He did not stay on with the other survivors at Helpmekaar, but rode on to alert Evelyn Wood in the north. He made it as far as Utrecht before he was overcome by exhaustion. Somebody else carried the news the rest of the way. When rumours spread that Gardner was to be recommended for the Victoria Cross, the idea was pilloried by many of his brother officers and by the Natal press, which shamelessly suggested that his motives for riding on to the far north were more to do with self-preservation than duty. Only a few weeks after Isandlwana he had to ride for his life once more; he was with Buller on Hlobane, and was then subsequently wounded in action when the *impi* moved on to attack Wood's position at Kambula. He resigned two years after the war. He stood for Parliament in his sixties and was successfully elected in 1906. He died only a year later.

Of all the veterans of the Isandlwana campaign, Horace Lockwood Smith-Dorrien had by far the most spectacular military career. When the 'contemptible little army' sailed for France in 1914, he unexpectedly found himself in command of II Corps as a lieutenant general, following the sudden death of General Sir James Grierson. It is commonly held that, during the retreat from Mons, he saved the BEF from disaster with his famous stand at Le Cateau. The following year, during the trench warfare around Ypres, his relations with an ungrateful Sir John French went into chronic decline; famously Smith-Dorrien was notified of his dismissal from the command of Second Army by the ex-ranker General 'Wully' Robertson, allegedly with the immortal words, "Orace you're for 'ome' (also variously reported as, "Orace you're for the 'igh jump'). Subsequently Smith-Dorrien was sidelined to the East African theatre. He died in his early seventies in a car crash.

Lieutenant Henry Curling of N Battery was badly shaken up by the loss of his guns and the slaughter of his men. He was subjected to additional stress by inadvertently earning the enmity of colonial society, in much the same way that Durnford had done over the Bushman's River Pass fiasco. The cause was a private letter to his parents which they rather indiscreetly permitted to be published in *The Standard*. In discussing the Isandlwana disaster the offending missive incorporated the sentence, 'Most of those who escaped were volunteers and native contingent officers, who tell any number of lies.' Sadly for Curling this was picked up and repeated in the Natal press. He served on in South Africa and participated in the second invasion, but was not present in the square at Ulundi. He served in the closing stages of the Second Afghan War, and in Egypt, rising in due course to the rank of colonel. He retired in 1902 and died in 1910 at the age of sixty-three.

Lieutenant William Cochrane, Durnford's transport staff officer, led the Edendale Troop at Kambula. He did well enough subsequently and rose to command a brigade in the Egyptian Army. Eventually he became a provincial governor in the reconquered Sudan. He was one of the most crucial eyewitnesses to events at Isandlwana, the only survivor to have witnessed the conversations between Pulleine and Durnford. Unfortunately his testimony left as many questions unanswered as it addressed.

The Zulu Leadership

In the immediate aftermath of the war King Cetshwayo was separated from his people and detained in the old Cape Castle, which ironically only a few short years before had been home to the 1st/24th when it first came to South Africa. He was well looked after and lived in some style in a comfortable suite of rooms. He lobbied the authorities to be allowed to visit England in order to make a case for his restoration, and in due course got his way. In the meantime Wolseley had partitioned Zululand into thirteen separate chiefdoms. Cetshwayo's arrival in London in August 1882, caused a stir in the press and roused considerable public interest. The king was entertained at some of the most prestigious addresses in London. Eventually he would be invited to an audience with the Queen Empress herself. Victoria rather liked him. The London public adored him.

In 1883 Cetshwayo was allowed to return home and was conditionally restored to his throne. His second reign was extremely short-lived, however. Sadly the internal politics of Zululand had been a matter of acute disinterest to both the imperial and the colonial authorities and the country had been allowed to collapse into civil war. Ntshingwayo kaMahole, the victor of Isandlwana, was one of many veterans of the 1879 war to meet his death at the hands of his fellow countrymen. He was killed in a raid on Ulundi in July 1883. So far as is known, no European ever interviewed him about his greatest campaign. Cetshwayo himself was forced to flee his capital to seek British protection at Eshowe. He died as a powerless exile, ostensibly of natural causes, on 8 February 1884. The doctor who attended his corpse was prohibited by the king's retainers from performing an autopsy and privately harboured the suspicion that the great man had been poisoned.

In an attempt to secure his succession, Cetshwayo's son Dinuzulu foolishly enlisted the help of Boer freebooters from the Transvaal. These consummate land-grabbers were soon up to their old tricks and snatched large parts of northern Zululand. Dinuzulu appealed next to the British. In 1888 the imperial authorities reluctantly annexed Zululand to the Crown. For a while there was peace. The country was left largely untouched by the Boer War, though in one incident a raiding commando was trapped in a kraal and all but wiped out with the loss of over fifty men. In 1906 the colonial authorities instituted a poll tax on all unmarried males. A Natal chieftain from the Greytown area called Bambatha fired on colonial troops in protest and fled with his retainers to Zululand where he is known to have met with Dinuzulu. Although Dinuzulu did not directly throw in his hand with the rebels, many other Zulus did. Amongst them was Mehlokazulu kaSihayo who left such a valuable series of observations on the Battle of Isandlwana. If they stood a poor chance in most of the stand-up fights of 1879, the Zulus stood no chance at all in the skirmishes of 1906. The Martini-Henry had been replaced with magazine-fed rifles, and the hand-cranked Gatling by the belt-fed Maxim. The rebels were crushed by colonial troops without any recourse to the services of the regular army. Mehlokazulu was amongst the many Zulu dead at the Battle of Mhome Gorge. Bambatha too was killed in the fight. In all over 2,000 Zulus died in the short-lived rebellion. Only twenty colonial soldiers lost their lives. When the hubbub died down Dinuzulu was arrested and imprisoned for treason.

Prince Dabulamanzi met a particularly disgraceful end which in many ways heralded the approaching nightmare for twentieth-century South Africa. Dinuzulu's dalliances with the Boers had established their influence in northern Zululand. In September 1886, Dabulamanzi and his son Mzingeli were unjustly accused of stock-theft. They were arrested by a Boer veldcornet who ordered two of his men, Wilhelm Joubert and Paul van der Berg, to escort the prisoners into Vryheid. When the opportunity presented itself, Dabulamanzi and his son kicked up their horses and crossed the Nondweni River into British territory. Here they took refuge in a nearby kraal. The two Boers gave chase across the jurisdictional boundary, but Dabulamanzi refused to be detained again. He would only be taken before the British authorities, he insisted. A struggle ensued when van der Berg tried to tie up the prince. The two men stepped apart and according to Mzingeli, Dabulamanzi said at this juncture, 'You won't shoot me on government ground.' Ruthlessly, van der Berg then did precisely that, shooting the prince through the stomach at point-blank range. Dabulamanzi attempted to flee on foot, but in covering around 200 yards was hit twice more, once in the left hip and once in the right elbow. One of these rounds also went on to shatter his left wrist. Mzingeli was also fired on as he rode away but, although he was unhorsed and injured in the fall, he was not hit. The two Boers quickly rounded up the two riderless horses, committing thereby precisely the crime of which their two prisoners stood accused, and then went on their way. Dabulamanzi was helped by the villagers back to their kraal, but died of his wounds at dawn the next day. His body was recovered to the coast and buried on the site of his old homestead, long since razed to the ground during the war of 1879. His killing was a plain and simple case of cold-blooded murder.

A Unique Honour

On the voyage home Mrs Anne Glyn sat patiently with her sewing basket and carried out much painstaking repair work to the Queen's Colour of the 1st/24th. In due course Queen Victoria commanded that the colour be brought before her. The new commanding officer, Lieutenant Colonel J. M. G. Tongue, who had been commanding a company of the 2nd Battalion at Mangeni on the day of the battle, took a regimental colour party and paraded both colours at the Queen's residence at Osborne House on the Isle of Wight on 28 July 1880. One of the ensigns was Lieutenant Phipps, who had served as Richard Glyn's orderly officer in the second invasion and had been wounded at his side at Ulundi. When the colour was lowered in salute before her, the Queen placed a wreath of flowers over the head of the pole which she described as a 'Wreath of Immortelles' and which she said was in recognition of the sacrifice of Lieutenants Melvill and Coghill, and of the 'Noble Defence of Rorke's Drift'. Also present at Osborne House that day was Private John Power, the Isandlwana survivor who had subsequently won the DCM at Hlobane. In December of that year, the Adjutant-General, Sir Charles Ellice, directed the general officers commanding the Colchester and Secunderabad garrisons to inform the two battalions of the 24th that:

> As a lasting token of her act in placing a wreath on the Queen's Colour to commemorate the devotion displayed by Lieutenants Melvill and Coghill in their heroic endeavour to save the Colour on January 22nd, 1879, and of the noble defence of Rorke's Drift, Her Majesty has been graciously pleased to command that a silver wreath shall in future be borne round the staff of the Queen's Colour of the Twenty-Fourth Regiment.

The silver wreath remains a unique regimental distinction. So revered was the Isandlwana colour within the regiment that it was carried by the 1st Battalion, The South Wales Borderers, long after it would ordinarily have been laid up. It was not retired until 1933, when it was finally laid up in the regimental chapel at Brecon Cathedral. By then it had been embroidered with the bloodily-won battle honours of the Great War. Normally colours are allowed to dissolve gracefully to dust in the century after their retirement. Uniquely, the Isandlwana colour has now been preserved in a vacuum-sealed case so that future generations may yet gaze upon this great relic of the nation's past. Mounted on the wall just below is the length of pike-staff and the gold crown, that are all that was ever seen again of the 2nd Battalion's colours. These relics were conveyed back to the Queen on 15 March 1881 by Major C. J. Bromhead, Gonny's elder brother. Before eventually coming to the regimental chapel, they resided at the Queen's direction in a place of honour in the armoury at Windsor Castle. Also preserved in the regimental chapel at Brecon are the remnants of the Queen's original Wreath of Immortelles. Laid up on the other side of the altar is the Regimental Colour brought safely out of action after the charge at Chillianwallah. For members of the regiment the cathedral is a very special place, where still to this day hundreds of old soldiers gather annually on 22 January, to commemorate the two great fights on the Buffalo River. Perhaps uniquely amongst occasions of its kind, it is invariably the practice to pay generous tribute to the regiment's one-time mortal enemies, now close friends – the noblest of warrior races – the mighty Zulu.

Today the officers' dining room of The Royal Regiment of Wales contains many reminders of the events of 1879. The modern day Queen's Colour is still adorned with a silver Wreath of Immortelles, whilst hung in a place of honour between the two colours is to be found Nevill Coghill's sword. As a matter of tradition the sword is worn on parade by the Queen's Colour ensign. A guest dining with the battalion may well be offered a cigar from the silver cigar-box presented to Richard Glyn and his officers by Sir Bartle Frere, in gratitude for their hospitality towards him during his long stay in their mess at King William's Town, whilst the Ninth Cape Frontier War was in progress. The guest may be drinking from a silver water goblet presented to the mess on promotion by Teignmouth Melvill. In the ante-room he may have noticed a silver cigarette box, inside the lid of which is to be found a tiny Union Flag made up of fragments of the Isandlwana colour. On the coffee table he might notice a horse's hoof ash-tray, which came from Richard Glyn's horse, 'Yellow Rose'. Or perhaps his eyes will fall upon the 'Relic of Melvill', more fragments of the Isandlwana colour, this time larger and stained with blood said to be Melvill's own. Each year on Rorke's Drift Day, the subaltern officers show these items and other treasured mess property to the men of their platoons, whose annual pilgrimage to the officers' mess is always an eagerly anticipated event.

*****

Wednesday 22 January 1879 was one of those days in history that epitomise the folly of waging war except as a genuine measure of last resort. The British and the Zulus had been on generally cordial terms for more than a generation. Cetshwayo was only too keenly aware of the power of the British Empire. He neither sought nor provoked war. One senses that the primary British objective, the neutralisation of Zulu military power, could probably in the long run have been achieved by patient diplomacy and without recourse to war. Negotiated change might have taken a decade. Would Cetshwayo have attacked Natal in the interim? There are few certainties in international relations, but the maintenance of an amicable relationship with the British was probably the most important strand of the king's foreign policy. When war came it was supremely violent and extremely dramatic. The manpower losses aggregated over six months of war were grievous. Yet perhaps because admiration for a worthy opponent was deeply ingrained in both of the contending societies, post-war reconciliation was not by any means an uphill struggle. British officers and Zulu indunas swapped war stories together with Ulundi smouldering on the horizon.

Today the British and the Zulus consider themselves the best of friends and their admiration one for the other sets an example many other former enemies would do well to emulate, in bringing closure to the tragedies of their own respective pasts. Yet to many of the individuals or organisations with the wealth or influence to wield British benevolence to a greater good, the Anglo-Zulu War was a thousand years ago. To the Zulus themselves and those of us who have pitched our tents amongst them, it was the day before yesterday. Perhaps uniquely amongst all the lands annexed in the British imperial age, Zululand received none of the customary post-conflict benefits – no change for the better, no roads, no railways, no universities, no wealth creation, no employment, no opportunity, no justice. It is easy to find excuses: British pre-eminence in South Africa was so short-lived; the world wars demanded a close focus on Europe; the nationalist seizure of power in South Africa precluded a role for the former colonial power. But these dark times are now a thing of the past and there is much that can be done today by way of well targeted aid programmes, to bring at least some succour to a people greatly in need of it. Poverty, malnourishment, unemployment, social ills born of lack of opportunity, and worst of all, pandemic HIV Aids, all stalk the land.

It is not enough to brush it aside as being typical of Africa – too vast a problem to confront. Still to this day, rooted deep in our collective national consciousness, we can all instinctively sense the admiration our forefathers felt for the legendary Zulu. We in the West have to make a start somewhere in addressing the problems of Africa. Perhaps, if you have been moved by the story I have recounted in these two books, you will agree that Zululand would be a good place to begin.

*'For **Queen** and **Country** Jesu Mercy'*

Appendices

Nominal Roll of the 24th Regiment at Isandlwana

1st Battalion

Officers Killed in Action

Brevet Lieutenant Colonel Henry Burmester Pulleine

Captain William Degacher

Captain William Eccles Mostyn

Captain Reginald Younghusband

Captain George Vaughan Wardell

Lieutenant Edgar Oliphant Anstey

Lieutenant Charles John Atkinson

Lieutenant Charles Walter Cavaye

Lieutenant Nevill Josiah Aylmer Coghill (Staff)

Lieutenant James Patrick Daly

Lieutenant George Frederick Hodson

Lieutenant & Adjutant Teignmouth Melvill

Lieutenant Francis Pender Porteous

Second Lieutenant Edwards Hopton Dyson

Honorary Major Francis Freeman White (Paymaster)

Quartermaster James Pullen

Other Ranks Killed in Action

1-24/671	Sergeant Major Frederick Gapp	1-24/1881	Sergeant John Edwards
1-24/557	Quartermaster Sergeant Thomas Leitch	1-24/1849	Sergeant Thomas Fay
1-24/601	Ex-Sgt Major Wm. Seaton (Canteen)	1-24/1510	Cook Sergeant Alfred Field
1-24/1125	Colour-Sergeant James Ballard	1-24/1850	Orderly Room Clerk Sergeant Gerald Fitzgerald
1-24/1118	Colour-Sergeant Thomas Brown		
1-24/1289	Colour-Sergeant William Edwards	1-24/315	Sergeant James Fowden
1-24/1887	Colour-Sergeant William Whitfield	1-24/570	Band Sergeant David Gamble
1-24/617	Colour-Sergeant Frederick Wolfe	1-24/968	Sergeant Edward Giles
1-24/1699	Sergeant Peter Ainsworth	1-24/1754	Sergeant John Greatorex
1-24/1895	Sergeant George Bennett	1-24/400	Armourer Sergeant Henry Hayward
1-24/909	Sergeant Daniel Bradley	1-24/1806	Sergeant Christopher Heppenstall
1-24/1011	Sergeant Instructor of Musketry George Chambers	1-24/824	Sergeant Michael Hornibrook
		1-24/896	Pay Sergeant George Mead
1-24/954	Sergeant John Clarkson	1-24/581	Sergeant William Parsons
1-24/1019	Sergeant William Coholan	1-24/1045	Sergeant Alfred Piall
1-24/1313	Sergeant Thomas Cooper	1-24/1260	Sergeant John Reardon

1-24/1370 Sergeant Joseph Smith

1-24/559   Tailor Sergeant John Smedley

1-24/843   Drum Major Robert Taylor

1-24/565   Sergeant George Upton

25B/232   Lance Sergeant John Millner

25B/126   Corporal Nicholas Ball

25B/421   Corporal Peter Bell

1-24/1415 Corporal John Bellhouse

1-24/1391 Corporal Alfred C. Board

25B/75   Corporal William Burns

25B/125   Corporal Richard Simpson Davies

25B/28   Corporal Edward R. Everett

25B/23   Corporal John Franks

1-24/1886 Corporal John Knight

25B/415   Corporal James Lawler

25B/524   Corporal Patrick Markham

1-24/1616 Corporal Matthew Miller

1-24/1736 Corporal Henry Richardson

1-24/885   Corporal John Rowden

1-24/1538 Corporal John Tarbuck

25B/193   Corporal Robert Williams

1-24/2003 Drummer William H. Adams

25B/267   Drummer Charles Andrews

1-24/1786 Drummer George Dibden

25B/2   Drummer John Frederick Orlopp

1-24/1226 Drummer Charles Osmond

1-24/1   Drummer Thomas Perkins

25B/318   Drummer Timothy Reardon

25B/114   Drummer Michael Stansfield

1-24/1787 Drummer John Thomspon

1-24/1237 Drummer Daniel Trottman

1-24/2004 Drummer Alfred Wolfendale

1-24/1399 Drummer James Wolfendale

1-24/1442 Private Richard Abbott

1-24/476   Private Thomas Allingham

1-24/937   Private Edward Amos

1-24/1230 Private Alfred Atkins

25B/710   Private Joseph Bailey

1-24/1496 Private Elijah Baker

25B/466   Private John Barry

25B/727   Private John Barry

25B/300   Private Elias Barsley

1-24/1476 Private John Bartles

25B/451   Private Claude Bastard

25B/501   Private Robert Beadon

25B/349   Private John Benham

1-24/1469 Private Alfred Bennett

25B/647   Private Richard Bennett

25B/643   Private Robert Benson

1-24/1656 Private Noah Betterton

25B/635   Private Joseph Birch

25B/154   Private John Bishop

1-24/1681 Private Robert Blackhurst

1-24/1474 Private James Blower

25B/221   Private Frederick Bodman

25B/64   Private Samuel Boulton

25B/106   Private John Boylan

1-24/950   Private James Bray

25B/487   Private John Breese

25B/43   Private John Wilson Brew

25B/718   Private Jeremiah Broderick

25B/628   Private Joseph Brown

25B/320   Private William Brown

25B/452   Private Frederick Bugby

1-24/1875 Private James Bull

25B/55   Private Timothy Burke

25B/176   Private William Burke

25B/886   Private William Burke

1-24/1461 Private Thomas Busby

1-24/1908 Private William James Butler

25B/449   Private Joseph Cahill

1-24/825   Private James Camp

25B/840   Private Michael Campbell

25B/713   Private James Cantillon

25B/468   Private William Henry Carpenter

25B/337   Private Peter Carrol

25B/507	Private James Casey
25B/204	Private Edward Ceiley
1-24/406	Private William Chadwick
1-24/2001	Private William Chalmers
25B/389	Private James Chatterton
1-24/206	Private William Chepman
1-24/117	Private John Christian
25B/1545	Private Alfred Clarke
1-24/1801	Private Michael Clarke
25B/226	Private William Henry Clements
25B/724	Private William Clutterbuck
25B/334	Private Albert Cole
25B/749	Private James Coleman
25B/359	Private Daniel Collins
25B/245	Private Thomas Collins
1-24/205	Private Thomas Colston
1-24/1424	Private George Conboye
25B/722	Private Cornelius Connolly
25B/199	Private John Connolly
25B/290	Private Samuel Connors
25B/112	Private James Cook
25B/18	Private Henry Cooper
1-24/1690	Private Richard Coughlan
25B/505	Private James Cox
1-24/290	Private Thomas Cox
1-24/797	Private Martin Cullen
25B/101	Private Jeremiah Cullenan
25B/640	Private Aaron Davies
25B/1042	Private William Davies
25B/1099	Private Edward Davis
25b/184	Private Mark Diggle
25B/115	Private Thomas Diggle
25B/395	Private John Dobbin
25B/550	Private William Dobbs
1-24/1790	Private Christopher Donohoe
25B/242	Private Michael Doran
1-24/1845	Private John Dorman
25B/674	Private Patrick Dowde

25B/235	Private William Robert Dredge
25B/438	Private Thomas Duck
1-24/1677	Private George Duckworth
25B/185	Private John Duffy
1-24/1327	Private Edward Dugmore
1-24/446	Private Francis Dunn
25B/215	Private John Dyer
25B/562	Private John Edwards
124/1799	Private William J. Edwards
25B/66	Private Thomas Egan
1-24/1582	Private William Egan
25B/211	Private William Elderington
1-24/1318	Private George Elderton
25B/312	Private Owen Ellis
25B/163	Private Henry Ellison
25B/450	Private James Ellsmore
25B/566	Private David Evans
25B/109	Private John William Evans
25B/518	Private Thomas Evry
25B/21	Private John Faircloth
25B/178	Private William Farmer
25B/403	Private George Henry Fay
25B/354	Private Michael Ferris
25B/73	Private Thomas Fitzgerald
1-24/1897	Private Edward Flint
1-24/1752	Private William Flood
25B/459	Private James Fortune
1-24/862	Private William Freeman
1-24/1305	Private Thomas Gilder
25B/22	Private John Gillan
25B/830	Private Charles Gingell
25B/408	Private George Glass
1-24/1794	Private Ashley Thomas Goatham
1-24/863	Private Charles Goddard
1-24/1872	Private George Goodchild
1-24/1750	Private Thomas Goss
1-24/1854	Private William Green
1-24/1423	Private William Gregg

1-24/514	Private William Gregson
25B/535	Private George Griffiths
1-24/667	Private George Hadden
25B/153	Private Isaac Hale
25B/633	Private John Hall
25B/11	Private Jacob Hannaford
1-24/1459	Private Thomas Harkin
1-24/678	Private John Harman
25B/565	Private Daniel Harney
1-24/787	Private Denis Harrington
	Boy Thomas Harrington
25B/234	Private Thomas H. Harris
25B/392	Private William Harris
25B/400	Private William Hayden
25b/542	Private John Haynes
25B/30	Private James Hedges
25B/696	Private Charles Hemmings
1-24/7	Private John Hewitt
1-24/1295	Private James Hibbard
25B/747	Private William Henry Hicken
1-24/1856	Private Thomas Hicks
25B/720	Private Thomas Higgins
1-24/1857	Private James Hind
25B/776	Private John Hitchen
1-24/1757	Private William Holden
1-24/1780	Private John Holland
1-24/833	Private David Horgan
1-24/1673	Private John Horn
1-24/1501	Private Charles Hornbuckle
1-24/1444	Private William Hough
25B/533	Private Edwin Hughes
25B/237	Private John Hughes
25B/404	Private John Hughes
25B/324	Private Owen Hughes
25B/206	Private Thomas Hughes
1-24/1892	Private Alfred Iggulden
1-24/1822	Private Frederick George Ilsley
25B/536	Private Ernest Ivatts
1-24/1083	Private Watkin Jenkins
1-24/1767	Private William Jenkins
25B/553	Private George Johnson
1-24/1774	Private Henry Johnson
25B/287	Private Joseph Johnson
1-24/1449	Private William Johnson
1-24/1465	Private George Johnston
1-24/633	Private James Johnston
25B/381	Private John Johnston
25B/1	Private Alexander Johnstone
25B/350	Private Evan Jones
25B/360	Private John Jones
25B/428	Private John Jones
25B/259	Private Thomas Jones
25B/341	Private William Jones
1-24/1682	Private William Jones
25B/88	Private John Keane
1-24/1259	Private James Keegan
25B/432	Private Andrew Kelly
25B/645	Private Fenton Kelly
25B/520	Private James Kelly
25B/789	Private John F. Kelly
1-24/1890	Private Nelson Kempsell
1-24/883	Private John Kempster
1-24/1155	Private James Knight
25B/275	Private John Lamb
25B/707	Private Thomas Lambert
25B/1541	Private John Lawrence
25B/131	Private Robert Leach
25B/326	Private Thomas Leaver
25B/882	Private John Lee
25B/72	Private Henry Lewis
25B/478	Private Richard Lewis
1-24/1277	Private James Ling
25B/531	Private John Linnane
25B/133	Private Stephen Lippett
1-24/710	Private George Lisbeck
1-24/1862	Private George Lloyd

25B/296	Private William Lockett
25B/521	Private Charles Lovell
1-24/1649	Private Charles Samuel Lowe
1-24/1841	Private Richard Lowe
25B/268	Private James Lycett
1-24/258	Private John Lyons
25B/663	Private Miles McDonald
25B/1393	Private Matthew McFarlane
25B/330	Private John McHale
1-24/1378	Private Hugh Anthony Mack
25B/630	Private John J. Mackenzie
25B/47	Private George Richard Maer
25B/590	Private Charles Mahoney
25B/137	Private Martin Maloney
1-24/992	Private William Mann
25B/916	Private Luke Marley
1-24/1348	Private Cornelius Marney
1-24/1758	Private David Martin
25B/293	Private John H. Meredith
1-24/1509	Private Charles Millen
1-24/508	Private Patrick Miller
1-24/1398	Private Richard Moore
25B/803	Private John Morgan
25B/490	Private William Morgan
25B/610	Private George Morris
1-24/730	Private Richard Morse
25B/63	Private John Murphy
25B/862	Private Patrick Murphy
1-24/594	Private John Murray
25B/399	Private Patrick Nash
1-24/1928	Private Alfred Newberry
1-24/1906	Private Thomas Newberry
25B/648	Private Walter Nicholas
1-24/1839	Private William E. Nye
1-24/1245	Private William Oakley
25B/754	Private George Odey
1-24/1417	Private James Ogden
1-24/1478	Private James Padmore

1-24/980	Private Thomas Painter
25B/471	Private Robert Parry
25B/12	Private Henry Patterson
25B/310	Private John Peters
1-24/845	Private James Nicholas Phillips
1-24/237	Private John Phillips
25B/87	Private Jabez Reid Pickard
1-24374	Private Samuel Plant
25B/181	Private James Plunkett
1-24/1368	Private Augustus Pollen
1-24/1793	Private William Pope
25B/222	Private Uriah Pottow
25B/739	Private Henry Powell
25B/950	Private John Proctor
25B/597	Private George Prosser
25B/797	Private John Prosser
25B/182	Private Walter Pugh
25B/856	Private William Pugh
25B/513	Private James Quirk
1-24/1826	Private Edward Remington
1-24/1650	Private William H. J. Retford
1-24/840	Private George Richards
25B/265	Private (Boy?) Robert Richards
25B/871	Private Mitchell Richardson
1-24/808	Private John Rigney
1-24/504	Private John Rittman
25B/355	Private William Roberts
1-24/1866	Private Henry Rodgers
1-24/740	Private Patrick Roubrey
25B/510	Private Henry Rowman
25B/548	Private Walter Rule
25B/40	Private Frederick Russel
1-24/1452	Private Thomas Rutter
25B/909	Private James Ryan
25B/488	Private George Salter
25B/529	Private Frederick Sarney
25B/279	Private Henry Sears
1-24/1971	Private William Sellwood

25B/147	Private Frederick Sharp
25B/200	Private Robert Shaw
25B/497	Private Daniel Shea
1-24/1130	Private Henry Sheather
1-24/1396	Private John Shrimpton
25B/649	Private Robert Silcock
25B/384	Private Walter Skelton
25B/506	Private Charles Smith
1-24/1867	Private Charles Smith
25B/1047	Private Edwin Smith
25B/58	Private George Smith
1-24/1903	Private James Smith
1-24/396	Private Thomas Speed
1-24/851	Private Henry Stevens
25B/20	Private William Stevens
25B/900	Private Edward Strange
1-24/1495	Private John Sullivan
25B/888	Private Patrick Sullivan
25B/161	Private Patrick Sutton
25B/664	Private Richard Swoffer
1-24/1779	Private Reuben Tate
25B/659	Private Edward Taylor
1-24/1760	Private James Terry
1-24/1753	Private William Theobald
25B/636	Private John Thomas
25B/765	Private John B. Thomas
25B/34	Private Thomas Thornett
25B/33	Private Charles Throssell
25B/317	Private Henry Tillison
25B/383	Private Thomas Tinnery
1-24/1782	Private George Todd
25B/209	Private Joseph Townsend
25B/543	Private Edward Trowell
25B/14	Private James Tullett
25B/946	Private Edward Turner
25B/85	Private George Vines

1-24/925	Private Edward Walker
25B/444	Private Edward Walker
25B/285	Private Thomas Walsh
25B/493	Private Thomas Walsh
25B/851	Private Thomas Walsh
25B/596	Private William Walton
1-24/531	Private Joseph Warner
25B/380	Private William Henry Watkins
1-24/1152	Private John Watley
1-24/1919	Private Henry Watts
25B/697	Private Thomas Webb
1-24/489	Private Henry Wetherhead
25B/642	Private John Whelan
1-24/1184	Private Thomas Whelan
1-24/591	Private Elijah Whybrow
25B/297	Private Arthur Wilkinson
25B/134	Private Frederick Wilks
25B/455	Private Ellis Williams
25B/778	Private Evan Williams
25B/545	Private James Williams
25B/582	Private John Williams
25B/868	Private Joseph Williams
25B/288	Private Matthew Williams
25B/534	Private Thomas Williams
25B/624	Private Thomas Williams
25B/698	Private William E Williams
1-24/1267	Private John Wilson
1-24/533	Private Samuel Wilson
1-24/227	Private William Wisher
1-24/888	Private James Wood
1-24/1266	Private John Woolley
25B/589	Private Enoch Worthington
1-24/1768	Private Robert Wright
1-24/1654	Private Thomas Young

2nd Battalion

Officers Killed in Action

Lieutenant & Adjutant Henry Julian Dyer

Lieutenant Frederick Godwin-Austen

Lieutenant Charles D'Aguilar Pope

Sub-Lieutenant Thomas Llewellyn Griffith

Quartermaster Edward Bloomfield

Other Ranks Killed in Action

2-24/1689	Q'master Sergeant George H. Davis	25B/1177	Private William Bryant
2-24/1777	Bandmaster Harry T. Bullard	25B/517	Private Robert Buckley
25B/927	Sergeant Henry Carse	25B/1262	Private Thomas Bull
2-24/1416	Cook Sergeant Charles Chew	2-24/1500	Private Edward A. Byard
2-24/2227	Sergeant John Lines	25B/721	Private John Byrne
2-24/1078	Sergeant William J. G. Reeves	2-24/1671	Private John Byrne
25B/50	Sergeant John Ross	25B/1336	Private Thomas Carroll
2-24/2336	Sergeant William Shaw	25B/1510	Private William Charles
25B/899	Sergeant George Wilkins	2-24/1598	Private Fred Cherry
25B/1217	Lance Sergeant Joseph Haigh	25B/723	Private Maurice Cleary
2-24/1755	Lance Sergeant James McCaffery	25B/819	Private Thomas Cornish
2-24/1268	Corporal William Greenhill	25B/1031	Private George Davies
25B/1248	Corporal James Henshaw	25B/743	Private John James Davies
25B/657	Corporal John M. Low	25B/1414	Private David Davis
25B/725	Corporal Henry Mortlock	25B/894	Private James Davis
25B/673	Corporal George Sims	25B/121	Private John Davis
25B/1103	Corporal George Thompson	25B/1026	Private Michael Donegan
25B/929	Lance-Corporal John Elvey	25B/872	Private John Dowle
2-24/2161	Drummer John Anderson	2-24/2081	Private John Earish
2-24/2153	Drummer John Holmes	25B/1166	Private Edmund Edwards
25B/1266	Private Joseph Allen	25B/786	Private John Edwards
25B/1142	Private J. William Barton	25B/1378	Private Robert Emerson
25B/1471	Private Samuel Beavan	25B/1389	Private John Evans
25B/1413	Private Thomas Bennett	25B/1041	Private Alfred Farr
25B/1550	Private Henry Bishop	25B/1963	Private Thomas Finn
25B/854	Private Arthur Bray	2-24/2307	Private George Fitton
25B/1141	Private Francis Bridgewater	25B/1519	Private Michael Fitzpatrick
2-24/2053	Private George P. Brierly	25B/1030	Private David Flyn
25B/960	Private Michael Broderick	2-24/2222	Private Joseph Flyn

25B/738	Private Michael Fortune
25B/1162	Private Thomas Fox
2-24/2335	Private James Fry
2-24/1771	Private William Gee
25B/619	Private George Ghost
25B/1491	Boy Daniel Gordon
2-24/1056	Private William Griffiths VC
25B/1494	Private (Boy?) James Gurney
25B/1272	Private Samuel Hacker
25B/1527	Private Benjamin Hall
2-24/1636	Private Charles Hall
25B/1260	Private John Hall
25B/1297	Private William Hall
25B/618	Private Leonard Hankin
2-24/2323	Private William Hawkins
25B/1219	Private John Healey
25B/1313	Private James Edward Hill
25B/887	Private Robert Harry Hopkins
25B/866	Private George Horrocks
25B/791	Private Robert Howells
2-24/1678	Private George Hudson
25B/1024	Private Francis Hughes
2-24/1593	Private John Hunt
25B/1135	Private William Jenkins
25B/1025	Private William Johnstone
25B/1097	Private Abraham Jones
25B/983	Private Edward Jones
25B/948	Private James Jones
25B/976	Private Thomas Jones
25B/1382	Private Thomas Jones
25B/1511	Private Thomas Jones
25B/804	Private William Jones
2-24/2400	Private John Kelly
2-24/1707	Private Thomas Kennedy
2-24/1057	Private Joseph King
25B/654	Private Benjamin Latham
25B/1532	Private Edward Lewis
2-24/1957	Private James Lewis

25B/70	Private James Llewellyn
25B/762	Private Charles Long
25B/1273	Private Thomas Lynch
25B/671	Private Joseph Machin
25B/1225	Private Patrick McCaffrey
2-24/2276	Private James McCormack
2-24/1458	Private Samuel McCracken
25B/1221	Private George McDoon
25B/1387	Boy Joseph S. McEwan
25B/1388	Private James McGuire
25B/1197	Private James Mack
25B/1050	Private Edward Malley
25B/1349	Private John Marsh
2-24/2434	Private Ernest Martingale
25B/168	Private Michael Mockler
25B/1128	Private Thomas Montgomery
25B/726	Private Frederick Moore
25B/1506	Private James Morgan
25B/788	Private Alfred Morris
25B/1412	Private James Morrisey
2-24/1994	Private Patrick Mulroy
25B/1469	Private John Murphy
25B/1036	Private Timothy Neagle
2-24/1901	Private Robert Nobes
2-24/1549	Private Terence O'Keefe
25B/1134	Private Hugh Perkins
25B/1383	Private David Phillips
25B/586	Private Samuel Poole
2-24/1709	Private Samuel Popple
25B/945	Private Henry Price
25B/1098	Private John Price
2-24/1576	Private David Pritchard
25B/949	Private Thomas Quilford
2-24/1868	Private John Quinn
25B/1411	Private William Rees
25B/692	Private Walter Rice
25B/781	Private John Roche
25B/1505	Private Michael Roche

25B/850	Private Thomas Saunders	25B/653	Private Thomas Vedler
2-24/813	Private James Scott	2-24/2038	Private Samuel Walker
25B/779	Private John Sheehan	25B/1543	Private Edmund Waters
25B/1169	Private Samuel Sherwood	2-24/513	Private William Waterhouse
25B/79	Private William Shuttleworth	25B/1191	Private John Watkins
25B/895	Private Henry Slade	25B/1518	Private George Watson
2-24/1487	Private Charles M. Smith	25B/1132	Private James White
25B/1096	Private Daniel Smith	25B/794	Private Thomas White
25B/1143	Private Frank Smith	25B/1095	Private Adam Wightman
25B/907	Private Henry Smith	25B/463	Private Edward Williams
25B/1056	Private John Smith	25B/1470	Private Edward Williams
25B/912	Private Patrick Smith	25B/1023	Private Evan Williams
25B/1495	Private Robert Smith	25B/987	Private George Williams
25B/1484	Private Robert Stephens	25B/1140	Private Theophilus Williams
25B/782	Private William Terrett	2-24/2047	Private James Williamson
25B/1218	Private David Thomas		(Orderly to GOC)
2-24/1107	Private George Thompson	25B/689	Private George Wood
25B/951	Private Richard Treverton	25B/1138	Private John Wright
2-24/2358	Private Edmund Turner	25B/1093	Private Edwin Young

24th Regiment Survivors

25B/375	Corporal J. McCann (No. 1 Sqn IMI)	25B/499	Private John Power (No. 1 Sqn IMI)
1-24/1173	Private J. Bickley (Band)	25B/196	Private James Trainer (Rocket Battery)
25B/194	Private Henry Davis (No. 1 Sqn IMI)	25B/139	Private John Williams
25B/665	Private H. Grant (Rocket Battery)		(Orderly to Col Glyn)
25B/299	Private W. Johnson (Rocket Battery)	25B/13	Private E. Wilson (Band)
25B/611	Private William Parry (No. 1 Sqn IMI)		

Nominal Roll of the Defenders of Rorke's Drift

Officers

Lieutenant John Chard, Royal Engineers

Lieutenant Gonville Bromhead, 24th Regiment

Surgeon James Reynolds, Army Medical Dept

Rev George Smith (Civilian Chaplain to No. 3 Column)

Assistant Commissary Walter Dunne

Acting Assistant Commissary James Dalton (Volunteer)

Lieutenant Gert Adendorff, 2nd/3rd NNC

Acting Storekeeper Louis A. Byrne (Volunteer)

1st Battalion, 24th Regiment

25B/56	Sergeant Edward Wilson	25B/625	Private Edward Nicholas
25B/135	Private William Beckett	25B/372	Private Thomas Payton
25B/568	Private Patrick Desmond	1-24/1542	Private William Roy
1-24/1861	Private William Horrigan	25B/104	Private Henry Turner
25B/841	Private James Jenkins	1-24/447	Private John Waters
25B/259	Private David Jenkins		

2nd Battalion, 24th Regiment

2-24/2459	Colour-Sergeant Frank Bourne	25B/987	Private Robert Adams (D Coy)
25B-623	Sergeant Robert Maxfield (G Coy)	2-24/913	Private James Ashton
2-24/735	Sergeant Joseph Windridge	25B/1381	Private Thomas Barry
25B/81	Sergeant Henry Gallagher	25B/918	Private William Bennet
2-24/1387	Sergeant George Smith	2-24/2427	Private John Bly
25B/82	Lance Sergeant James Taylor (E Coy)	25B/1524	Private Joseph Bromwich
25B/1328	Lance Sergeant Thomas Williams	25B/1184	Private Thomas Buckley
2-24/1240	Corporal William Allen	25B/1220	Private Thomas Burke
2-24/2389	Corporal John Key	2-24/2350	Private James Bushe
25B/1112	Corporal John Lyons	25B/1181	Private William Camp
25B/849	Corporal Alfred Saxty	25B/1241	Private Thomas Chester
25B/1287	Lance-Corporal William Bessel	25B/1335	Private James Chick (D Coy)
25B/1282	Lance-Corporal William Halley	25B/1459	Private Robert Cole (F Coy)

25B/801   Private Thomas Cole

25B/1396   Private Thomas Collins

25B/906   Private John Connolly (G Coy)

2-24/2310   Private Anthony Connors

2-24/1323   Private Timothy Connors

2-24/2453   Private William Cooper (F Coy)

25B/470   Private George Davies

25B/1363   Private William Davis

25B/1178   Private Thomas Daw

25B/1467   Private George Deacon (alias Power)

25B/1357   Private Michael Deane

2-24/1697   Private James Dick

2-24/1634   Private William Dicks

25B/971   Private Thomas Driscoll

25B/1421   Private William Dunbar

25B/972   Private George Edwards
                (alias Orchard)

25B/969   Private John Fagan

2-24/1713   Drummer Patrick Galgey (D Coy)

2-24/2429   Private Edward Gee

25B/798   Private James Hagan

25B/1062   Private John Harris

2-24/1769   Private Garret Hayden (D Coy)

2-24/2067   Drummer Patrick Hayden

25B/1362   Private Frederick Hitch

25B/1373   Private Harry Hook

25B/1061   Private John Jobbins

25B/1428   Private Evan Jones
                (alias Pat Cosgrove)

25B/970   Private John Jones 70

25B/1179   Private John Jones 79

25B/716   Private Robert Jones

2-24/593   Private William Jones

2-24/2437   Private Peter Judge

25B/972   Private Patrick Kears

2-24/2381   Drummer James Keefe

25B/1386   Private Michael Kiley

25B/963   Private David Lewis
                (alias James Owen)

2-24/1528   Private Henry Lines

25B/1409   Private David Lloyd

25B/1176   Private Thomas Lockhart

25B/1304   Private Joshua Lodge

25B/942   Private Thomas Lynch

2-24/1441   Private John Lyons (A Coy)

2-24/1731   Private John Manley (A Coy)

25B/964   Private James Marshall

25B/756   Private Henry Martin

25B/1284   Private Charles Mason

2-24/2483   Private James Meehan

2-24/1527   Private Minehan

25B/968   Private Thomas Moffat

25/1342   Private Augustus Morris

25B/525   Private Fredrick Morris

25B/1371   Private Thomas Morrison

25B662   Private John Murphy

25B/1279   Private William Nevil

25B/1857   Private Robert Norris

25B/1480   Private William Osbourne

25B/1399   Private Samuel Parry

25B/1410   Private William Partridge

2-24/2404   Private Arthur Pears (A Coy)

25B/1186   Private Samuel Pitt

25B/1286   Private Edward Robinson

25B/1065   Private James Ruck

25B/1185   Private Edward Savage

25B/1051   Private John Scanlon (A Coy)

2-24/1618   Private George Shearman

2-24/914   Private John Shergold

2-24/1387   Private George Smith

2-24/1005   Private John Smith

25B/1777   Private Thomas Stevens

2-24/1812   Private William Tasker

25B/973   Private Frederick Taylor

25B/889   Private Thomas Taylor

25B/1280   Private John Thomas
                (alias Peter Sawyer).

25B/1394	Private John Thompson
25B/879	Private Michael Tobin
25B/641	Private Patrick Tobin
25B/281	Private William John Todd
25B/1315	Private Robert Tongue
25B/1497	Private John Wall
2-24/977	Private Alfred Whetton

25B/1187	Private William Wilcox
25B/1395	Private John Williams 95 (alias Fielding)
25B/934	Private John Williams 34 (E Coy)
25B/1398	Private Joseph Williams 98
25B/1316	Private Caleb Woods

N Battery, 5th Brigade, Royal Artillery

Bombardier T. Lewis

Wheeler John Cantwell

Gunner A. Evans

Gunner Arthur Howard

Army Hospital Corps

Corporal R. Miller

2nd Corporal Michael McMahon

Private T. Luddington

Natal Mounted Police

Trooper Robert S. Green

Trooper Sidney Hunter

Trooper Harry Lugg

3rd Regiment, Natal Native Contingent

Corporal M. Dougherty

Corporal Jesse Mayer

Corporal Carl Scammell

Corporal Ferdnand Schiess

Corporal J. Wilson

Miscellaneous

Sergeant George Mabin (Staff clerk)

Sergeant Frederick Millne (2nd/3rd Buffs)

Corporal J. Graham (90th Regt – a recovered patient)

2nd Corporal Francis Attwood (ASC)

Driver C. Robson (Chard's RE batman)

Mr Daniels (Civilian pontman)

Mr Pearce (Civilian: Dr Reynolds's servant)

Unknown isiGqoza Private (1st/3rd NNC)

Rorke's Drift Casualty Return

Killed in Action

1. Acting Storekeeper Louis Byrne (Volunteer – Attached Commissariat & Transport Department): Shot in the head whilst offering a drink to Corporal Scammell.
2. Sergeant Robert Maxfield (G Company, 2nd/24th): Non-combatant patient. Killed in the hospital.
3. Private Robert Adams (D Company, 2nd/24th): Non-combatant patient. Killed in the hospital.
4. Private James Chick (D Company, 2nd/24th): Combatant patient killed on barricades but circumstances of his death not recorded.
5. Private Thomas Cole (B Company, 2nd/24th): Shot in the head defending the retrenchment barricade.
6. Private John Fagan (B Company, 2nd/24th): Mortally wounded by a gunshot after dark. Died during the night.
7. Private Garret Hayden (D Company, 2nd/24th): Non-combatant patient. Killed in the hospital.
8. Private William Horrigan (1st/24th): Combatant patient killed fighting alongside Private Joseph Williams in defence of the western ward.
9. Private James Jenkins (1st/24th): Non-combatant patient killed in the hospital. Circumstances unclear.
10. Private Edward Nicholas (1st/24th): Combatant patient shot in the head at the front corner of the retrenchment barricade.
11. Private John Scanlon (A Company 2nd/24th): Combatant patient killed on barricades but circumstances of his death not recorded.
12. Private Joseph Williams 1398 (B Company, 2nd/24th): Killed defending the door of the western hospital ward in order to protect the men within.
13. Trooper Sidney Hunter: Non-combatant patient. Stabbed in the back during the dash from the hospital to the storehouse.

14. An unknown isiGqoza Private (1st/3rd NNC): Non-combatant patient. Killed in the hospital.
15. [Corporal William Anderson (3rd Regiment, NNC): Killed by 'early enemy fire.']*

Died of Wounds

16. Lance Sergeant Thomas Williams 1328 (B Company, 2nd/24th): Shot through the ribs defending the front corner of the retrenchment barricade.
17. Private William Beckett (1st/24th): Stabbed in the stomach whilst making a breakout from the hospital.

Severely Wounded

18. Acting Assistant Commissary James Dalton (Volunteer – Attached Commissariat & Transport Department): Shot through the shoulder and back whilst defending the north wall.
19. Corporal William Wilson Allen (B Company, 2nd/24th): Shot in the arm whilst defending the storehouse corner of the retrenchment barricade.
20. Corporal John Jeremiah Lyons (B Company, 2nd/24th): Shot in the right side of the neck whilst defending the storehouse corner of the retrenchment barricade. Round travelled on to smash two vertebrae of his spine and lodged there.
21. Corporal Carl Scammell (3rd Regiment, NNC): Shot in upper right shoulder, exiting through left shoulder.
22. Private Frederick Hitch (B Company, 2nd/24th): Shot in the shoulder joint whilst defending the front corner of the retrenchment barricade.
23. Private John Waters (1st/24th): Shot in the shoulder whilst defending the hospital compound

---

* I am of course obliged by loyalty to my regiment to sustain the 127-year-old conspiracy of silence about the fate of Corporal Anderson!

Other Wounded

24. Corporal Ferdnand Christian Schiess (3rd Regiment, NNC): Combatant patient. Shot through instep whilst fighting inside the storehouse compound.

25. Private James Bushe (B Company, 2nd/24th): Wounded in the nose whilst defending the retrenchment barricade, by a spent round that had just killed Private Tom Cole.

26. Private Patrick Desmond (1st/24th): Combatant patient. Shot through thumb. Circumstances unrecorded.

27. Private Robert Jones (B Company, 2nd/24th): Three minor assegai lacerations in the abdomen whilst defending a doorway during the evacuation of the hospital.

28. Private Alfred Henry Hook (B Company, 2nd/24th): Grazed scalp sustained in the defence of a doorway during the evacuation of the hospital.

29. Drummer James Keefe (B Company, 2nd/24th): Gunshot graze in scalp. Circumstances unrecorded.

30. Private John Smith 05 (B Company, 2nd/24th): Assegai cut in abdomen. Circumstances unrecorded.

31. Private William Tasker (B Company, 2nd/24th): Splinter of musket ball breaking skin of forehead. Circumstances unrecorded.

32. Trooper Robert Green (NMP): Non-combatant patient. Struck by a spent round whilst crawling from the hospital to the retrenchment.

Appendix 4

Honours and Awards

The Victoria Cross Roll*

Lieutenant John Rouse Merriott Chard (No. 5 Coy, Royal Engineers)

Lieutenant Gonville Bromhead (OC B Coy, 2nd Bn, 24th Regt of Foot)

Surgeon James Henry Reynolds BA MB ChB (Army Medical Department)

A/Assistant Commissary James Langley Dalton (Att. Army Commissariat & Transport Department)

Corporal Ferdnand Christian Schiess (3rd Regt, Natal Native Contingent)

Corporal William Wilson Allen (B Coy, 2nd Bn, 24th Regt of Foot)

Private Alfred Henry Hook (B Coy, 2nd Bn, 24th Regt of Foot)

Private Frederick Hitch (B Coy, 2nd Bn, 24th Regt of Foot)

Private John Williams 395 [AKA John Fielding] (B Coy, 2nd Bn, 24th Regt of Foot)

Private Robert Jones 716 (B Coy, 2nd Bn, 24th Regt of Foot)

Private William Jones 593 (B Coy, 2nd Bn, 24th Regt of Foot)

Distinguished Conduct Medal (DCM)

Colour-Sergeant Frank Bourne (B Coy, 2nd Bn, 24th Regt of Foot)

Second Corporal Francis Attwood (Army Service Corps)

Private William Roy (1st Bn, 24th Regiment of Foot)

Wheeler John Cantwell (N Bty, 5th Bde, RA)

Nominated for DCM but subsequently withdrawn for Misconduct

Second Corporal Michael McMahon (Army Hospital Corps)

---

* Private Joseph Williams 1398 (B Coy, 2nd Bn, 24th Regt of Foot) would have been recommended for the Victoria Cross 'had he lived', it not being possible in 1879 to receive the award posthumously.

Appendix 5

Lieutenant Chard's Report to the Queen

The following report was written by John Chard for Queen Victoria at her specific request. It is rather more comprehensive than his official report to the military chain of command, which was written in the immediate aftermath of the battle. This second Chard report was submitted to the Queen at Windsor Castle on 21 February 1880. The original document is archived in the Royal Collection at Windsor and is reproduced by gracious permission of Her Majesty Queen Elizabeth. Some archaic punctuation, abbreviations and spelling have been corrected to reflect modern usage and so make for a slightly easier read. None of Chard's words have been omitted or changed.

*****

Early in January 1879, shortly after the arrival of the 5th Company, Royal Engineers, at Durban, an order came from Lord Chelmsford directing that an officer and a few good men of the RE, with mining implements etc, should join the 3rd Column as soon as possible. I was consequently sent on in advance of the company, with a light mule wagon, containing the necessary tools etc, and in which the men could also ride on level ground; with a Corporal, three Sappers and one Driver, my batman, who rode one, and looked after my other horses. The wagon was driven by a Cape black man, with a Natal Kaffir lad as voorlooper. The roads were so bad, that in spite of all our exertions our progress was slow, and although we got a fresh team at Pietermaritzburg, we did not reach Rorke's Drift until the morning of the 19th January 1879. The 3rd Column was encamped on the other side (left bank) of the River Buffalo and the wagons were still crossing at the ponts. I pitched my two tents on the right (Natal) bank of the river, near the ponts, and close to the store accumulated there for keeping them in repair. On the 20th January the 3rd Column broke up its camp on the Buffalo River and marched to Isandlwana, where it encamped and the same evening, or following morning, Colonel Durnford's force arrived and took up its camp near where the 3rd Column had been. There were two large ponts at the river, only one of which was in working order and my sappers were during this time working at the other, which was nearly finished, to get it also in working order.

Late in the evening of the 21st January, I received an order from the 3rd Column to say that the men of the RE who had lately arrived, were to proceed to the camp at Isandlwana at once. I had received no orders concerning myself. I reported this to Major Spalding, who was now in command at Rorke's Drift, and also pointed out to him that the sappers leaving, there were no means at my disposal for putting the ponts in working order, or keeping them so. Major Spalding had also received no orders respecting me, except that I was to select a suitable position protecting the ponts for Captain Rainforth's Company 1/24th to entrench itself. I consequently asked, and obtained permission from Major Spalding to go the camp at Isandlwana and see the orders.

On the morning of the 22nd January, I put the corporal and 3 sappers in the empty wagon, with their field kits etc, to take them to camp of the 3rd Column, and also rode out myself. The road was very heavy in some places, and the wagon went slowly; so I rode on in advance, arrived at the Isandlwana camp, went to the Headquarters tent, and got a copy of the orders as affecting me and found that I was to keep the ponts etc in working order, and also the road between Helpmekaar and Rorke's Drift, and the orders also particularly stated that my duties lay on the right bank of the Buffalo.

An NCO of the 24th Regiment, lent me a field glass, which was a very good one, and I also looked with my own, and could see the enemy moving on the distant hills, and apparently in great force. Large numbers of them moving to my left, until the lion hill of Isandhlwana, on my left as I looked at them, hid them from my view. The idea struck me that they might be moving in the direction between the camp and Rorke's Drift, and prevent my getting back, and also that they might be going to make a dash at the ponts.

Seeing what my duties were, I left the camp, and a quarter of a mile, or less, out of it, I met Colonel Durnford RE, riding at the head of his mounted men. I told him what I had seen, and took some orders, and a message all along his line, at his request. At the foot of the hill, I met my men in the wagon and made them get out and walk up the hill with Durnford's men. I brought the wagon back with me to Rorke's Drift, where on arrival I found the following order had been issued. The copy below was given me, and preserved from the fact of its being in my pocket during the fight.

Camp Rorke's Drift
22nd Jany. 1879

Camp Morning Orders

1. The whole force under Lt Col Durnford RE, having departed, a Guard of 6 privates and 1 NCO will be furnished by the detachment 2/24th Regt. on the ponts. A Guard of 50 armed natives will likewise be furnished by Captain Stevenson's detachment at the same spot. The ponts will be invariably drawn over to the Natal side at night. This duty will cease on the arrival of Capt Rainforth's company, 1/24th Regt.

2. In accordance with Para. 19 Regulations for Field Forces in South Africa, Capt. Rainforth's Company 1/24th Regt., will entrench itself on the spot assigned to it by Column Orders.

H. Spalding,
Major
Commanding.

The Guard as detailed was over the ponts. Captain Rainforth's company had not yet arrived. I went at once to Major Spalding on arrival, told him what I had seen, and pointed out to him that in the event of an attack on the ponts, it would be impossible with 7 men, (not counting the natives), to make an effective defence. According to the orders, Captain Rainforth's company should have been already at Rorke's Drift. Major Spalding told me he was going over to Helpmekaar, and would see about getting it down at once. Just as I was about to ride away he said to me,

'Which of you is senior, you or Bromhead?'

I said, 'I don't know.'

He went back into his tent and looked at an Army list and coming back said,

'I see you are senior, so you will be in charge although of course, nothing will happen, and I shall be back again this evening early.'

I then went down to my tent at the river, had some lunch comfortably, and was writing a letter home, when my attention was called to two horsemen galloping towards us from the direction of Isandlwana. From their gesticulations, and their shouts, when they were near enough to be heard, we saw that something was the matter, and on taking them over the river, one of them, Lieutenant Adendorff of Lonsdale's Regiment, Natal Native Contingent, asking if I was an officer, jumped off his horse, took me on one side, and told me, that the camp was in the hands of the Zulus, and the army destroyed; that scarcely a man had got away to tell the tale, and that probably Lord Chelmsford and the rest of the column had shared the same fate. His companion, a Carbineer, confirmed his story. He was naturally very excited, and I am afraid I did not, at first, quite believe him, and intimated that he probably had not remained to see what did occur. I had the saddle put on my horse, and while I was talking to Lieutenant Adendorff, a messenger arrived from Lieutenant Bromhead who was with his company at his little camp near the Commissariat stores, to ask me to come up at once. I gave the order to inspan the wagon, and put all the stores, tents etc we could into it. I posted the Sergeant and six men on the high ground over the ponts, behind a natural wall of rocks, forming a strong position from which there was a good view over the river and ground in front, with orders to wait until I came or sent for them. The guard of natives had left some time before and had not been relieved. I galloped at once up to the Commissariat stores and found that a pencil note had been sent from the 3rd Column by Captain Alan Gardner to state that the enemy were advancing in force against our post.

Lieutenant Bromhead had, with the assistance of Mr Dalton, Dr Reynolds and the other officers present, commenced barricading, and loopholing the store building and the Missionary's house, which was used as a hospital, and connecting the defence of the two buildings by walls of mealie-bags, and two wagons that were on the ground. The Native Contingent, under their officer Captain Stephenson,* were working hard at this with our own men, and the walls were rapidly progressing. A letter describing what had happened had been sent by Bromhead by two men of the Mounted Infantry, who had arrived fugitives from Isandlwana, to the Officer Commanding at Helpmekaar. These two men crossed the river at Fugitives' Drift, with some others, and as they have since reported to me, came to give notice of what had happened, to us at Rorke's Drift, of their own accord, and without orders from anyone.

I held a consultation with Lieutenant Bromhead, and with Mr Dalton, whose energy, intelligence and gallantry were of the greatest service to us, and whom, as I said in my report at the time, and I am quite sure Bromhead would unite with me in saying again now, I cannot sufficiently thank for his valuable services. I went round the position with them and then rode down to the ponts where I found everything ready for a start, ponts in midstream, hawsers and cables sunk etc. It was at this time that the pontman, Daniels, and Sergeant Millne, 3rd Buffs, who had been employed for some time in getting the ponts in order and working them under Lieutenant McDowell [sic] RE, (killed at Isandlwana), offered to defend the ponts, moored in the middle of the river, from their decks, with a few men. Sergeant Williams, 24th, and his little guard were quite ready to join them. We arrived at the Commissariat stores at about 3.30 p.m.

Shortly afterwards an officer of Durnford's Horse reported his arrival from Isandlwana, and I requested him to observe the movements, and check the advance, of the enemy as much as possible until forced to fall back. I saw each man at his post, and then the work went on again. Several fugitives from the camp arrived, and tried to impress upon us the madness of an attempt to defend the place. Who they were I do not know, but it is scarcely necessary for me to say that there were no officers of HM Army among them. They stopped the work very much – it being impossible to prevent the men getting around them in little

---

* Although Chard writes of 'Stephenson', there is now reasonably general agreement that the name was spelt with a 'v' not a 'ph'.

groups to hear their story. They proved the truth of their belief in what they said, by leaving us to our fate, and in the state of mind they were in, I think our little garrison was as well without them. As far as I know, but one of the fugitives remained with us – Lieutenant Adendorff, whom I have before mentioned. He remained to assist in the defence, and from a loophole in the store building, flanking the wall and hospital, his rifle did good service.

There were several casks of rum in the store building, and I gave strict orders to Sergeant Windridge, 24th Regiment, who was in charge, (acting as issuer of Commissariat stores to the troops), that the spirit was not to be touched: the man nearest it was to be considered to be on guard over it, and after giving fair warning, was to shoot without altercation anyone who attempted to force his post, and Sergeant Windridge being there was to see this carried out. Sergeant Windridge showed great intelligence and energy in arranging the stores for the defence of the Commissariat Store, forming loopholes etc.

The Reverend George Smith, Vicar of Estcourt, Natal, and acting Army Chaplain, went for a walk, (before the news of the disaster reached us,) to the top of the Oscarberg, the hill behind Rorke's Drift. Mr Witt, the missionary, went with him, or met him there. They went to see what could be seen in the direction of the Isandlwana camp. He [Smith] saw the force of the enemy which attacked us at Rorke's Drift, cross the river in three bodies, and after snuff-taking and other ceremonies, advance in our direction. He had been watching them for some time with interest, and thought they were our own Native Contingent. There were two mounted men leading them, and he did not realise that they were the enemy until they were near enough for him to see that these two men also had black faces. He came running down the hill, and was agreeably surprised to find that we were getting ready for the enemy. Mr Witt, whose wife and family were in a lonely house not very far off, rode off, taking with him a sick officer, who was very ill in the hospital and only just able to ride. Mr Smith, however, although he might well have left, elected to remain with us, and during the attack did good service in supplying the men with ammunition.

About 4.20 p.m. the sound of firing was heard behind the Oscarberg. The officer of Durnford's returned reporting the enemy close upon us, and that his men would not obey his orders but were going off to Helpmekaar and I saw them, about 100 in number, going off in that direction. I have seen these same men behave so well since, that I have spoken with several of their conduct and they all said, as their excuse, that Durnford was killed, and it was no use. About the same time Captain Stephenson's detachment of the Natal Native Contingent left us – probably most fortunately for us. I am sorry to say that their officer, who had been doing good service in getting his men to work, also deserted us. We seemed very few, now all these people had gone, and I saw that our line of defence was too extended, and at once commenced a retrenchment of biscuit boxes, so as to get a place we could fall back upon if we could not hold the whole.

Private Hitch, 24th, was on top of the thatch roof of the Commissariat store keeping a lookout. He was severely wounded early in the evening, but notwithstanding, with Corporal Allen, 24th, who was also wounded, continued to do good service, and they both when incapacitated by their wounds from using their rifles, still continued under fire serving their comrades with ammunition.

We had not commenced a wall two boxes high when, about 4.30 p.m., Hitch cried out that the enemy was in sight, and we saw them, apparently 500 or 600 in number come around the hill to our south, (the Oscarberg), and advance at a run against our south wall. We opened fire on them, between five and six hundred yards, at first a little wild, but only for a shot or two: a chief on horseback was dropped by Private Dunbar, 24th, the men were quite steady, and the Zulus began to fall very thick. However it did not seem to stop them at all, although they took advantage of the cover and ran stooping with their faces near the ground. It seemed as if nothing would stop them, and they rushed on in spite of their heavy loss to within 50 yards of the wall, when they were taken in flank by the fire from the end wall of the store building and met with such a heavy direct fire from the mealie wall, and the hospital at the same time, that they were checked as if by magic. They occupied the cookhouse ovens, banks and other cover, but the greater number, without stopping moved to their left around the hospital, and made a rush at the end of the hospital and at our north-west line of mealie-bags. There was a short but desperate struggle during which

Mr Dalton shot a Zulu who was in the act of assegaing a corporal of the Army Hospital Corps, the muzzle of whose rifle he had seized, and with Lieutenant Bromhead and many of the men behaved with great gallantry. The Zulus forced us back from that part of the wall immediately in front of the hospital, but after suffering very severely in the struggle were driven back into the bush around our position.

The main body of the enemy were close behind the first force which appeared, and lined the ledge of rocks and caves in the Oscarberg, overlooking us, and, about three or four hundred yards to our south, from where they kept up a constant fire. Advancing somewhat more to their left than the first attack, they occupied the garden, hollow road and bush in great force. The bush grew close to our wall and we had not time to cut it down. The enemy were thus able to advance under cover close to our wall, and in this part soon held one side of the wall, while we held the other. A series of desperate assaults was made on the hospital, and extending from the hospital, as far as the bush reached; but each was most splendidly met and repulsed by our men, with the bayonet. Each time as the attack was repulsed by us, the Zulus close to us seemed to vanish in the bush, those some little distance off keeping up a fire all the time. Then as if moved by a single impulse, they rose up in the bush as thick as possible, rushing madly up to the wall, (some of them being already close to it), seizing where they could, the muzzles of our men's rifles, or their bayonets, and attempting to use their assegais, and to get over the wall. A rapid rattle of fire from our rifles, stabs with the bayonet, and in a few moments the Zulus were driven back, disappearing in the bush as before, and keeping up their fire. A brief interval and the attack would be again made, and repulsed in the same manner. Over and over again this happened, our men behaving with the greatest coolness and gallantry. It is impossible for one individual to see all, but I particularly myself noticed the behaviour of Colour-Sergeant Bourne 24th, Sergeant Williams 24th, Corporal Schiess NNC, Corporal Lyons 24th, Private McMahon AHC, Privates Roy, Deacon, Bush, Cole, Jenkins, 24th, and many others. Our fire at the time of these rushes was very rapid – Mr Dalton dropping a man each time he fired his rifle, while Bromhead and myself used our revolvers.

The fire from the rocks and caves on the hill behind us was kept up all this time and took us completely in reverse, and although very badly directed, many shots came among us and caused us some loss – and at about 6.00 p.m. the enemy extending their attack further to their left, I feared seriously would get in over our wall, behind the biscuit boxes. I ran back with 2 or 3 men to this part of the wall and was immediately joined by Bromhead with 2 or 3 more. The enemy stuck to this assault most tenaciously, and on their repulse, and retiring into the bush, I called all the men inside our retrenchment – and the enemy immediately occupied the wall we had abandoned and used it as a breastwork to fire over. Mr Byrne, acting Commissariat Officer, and who had behaved with great coolness and gallantry, was killed instantaneously shortly before this, by a bullet through the head, just after he had given a drink of water to a wounded man of the NNC.

All this time the enemy had been attempting to force the hospital and had at length set fire to its roof and got in at the far end. I had tried to impress upon the men in the hospital the necessity for making a communication right through the building: unfortunately, this was not done. Probably at the time the men could not see the necessity, and doubtless also there was no time to do it. Without in the least detracting from the gallant fellows who defended the hospital, and I hope I shall not be misunderstood in saying so, I have always regretted, as I did then, the absence of my four poor sappers, who had only left that morning for Isandlwana and arrived there just to be killed.

The garrison of the hospital defended it with the greatest gallantry, room by room, bringing out all the sick that could be moved, and breaking through some of the partitions while the Zulus were in the building with them; Privates Williams, Hook, R. Jones and W. Jones being the last to leave and holding the doorways with the bayonet, their ammunition being expended. Private Williams' bayonet was wrenched off his rifle by a Zulu, but with the other men he still managed with the muzzle of his rifle to keep the enemy at bay. Surgeon Reynolds carried his arms full of ammunition to the hospital, a bullet striking his helmet as he did so. But we were too busily engaged outside to be able to do much, and with the hospital on fire, and no free communication, nothing could have saved it. Sergeant Maxfield,

24th, might have been saved, but he was delirious with fever, refused to move, and resisted the attempts to move him. He was assegaied before our men's eyes. Seeing the hospital burning, and the attempts of the enemy to fire the roof of the store, (one man was shot, I believe by Lieutenant Adendorff, who had a light almost touching the thatch).

We converted two large heaps of mealie-bags into a sort of redoubt, which gave a second line of fire all around, and formed a strong position to hold, and rally round in case the store building had to be abandoned, or the enemy broke through elsewhere. Assistant Commissary Dunne worked hard at this; from his height, being a tall man, he was much exposed, in addition to the fact that the heaps were high above our walls, and that most of the Zulu bullets went high. Trooper Hunter, Natal Mounted Police, escaping from the hospital, stood still for a moment hesitating which way to go, dazed by the glare of the burning hospital, and the firing that was going on all around. He was assegaied before our eyes, the Zulu who killed him immediately afterwards falling.

While firing from behind the biscuit boxes, Dalton, who had been using his rifle with deadly effect, and by his quickness and coolness had been the means of saving many men's lives, was shot through the body. I was standing near him at the time, and he handed me his rifle so coolly that I had no idea until afterwards of how severely he was wounded. He waited quite patiently for me to take the cartridges he had left out of his pockets. We put him inside our mealie sack redoubt, building it up around him. About this time I noticed Private Dunbar, 24th, make some splendid shooting, seven or eight Zulus falling on the ledge of rocks on the Oscarberg, to as many consecutive shots by him.

I saw Corporal Lyons hit by a bullet which lodged in his spine, and fall between an opening we had left in the wall of biscuit boxes. I thought he was killed, but looking up he said, 'Oh, sir, you are not going to leave me lying here like a dog?' We pulled him back in and laid him down behind the boxes where he was immediately looked to by Reynolds. Corporal Scammel of the NNC, who was badly wounded through the shoulder, staggered out under fire again, from the store building where he had been put, and gave me all his cartridges, which in his wounded state he could not use.

While I was intently watching to get a fair shot at a Zulu who appeared to be firing rather well, Private Jenkins, 24th, saying 'look out, sir,' gave my head a duck down just as a bullet whizzed over it. He had noticed a Zulu who was quite near in another direction, taking a deliberate aim at me. For all the man could have known, the shot might have been directed at himself. I mention these facts to show how well the men behaved and how loyally [they] worked together.

Corporal Schiess, Natal Native Contingent, who was a patient in the hospital, with a wound in the foot which caused him great pain, behaved with the greatest coolness and gallantry throughout the attack, and at this time creeping out a short distance along the wall we had abandoned and slowly raising himself, to get a shot at some of the enemy who had been particularly annoying, his hat was blown off by a shot from a Zulu the other side of the wall. He immediately jumped up, bayoneted the Zulu and shot a second, and bayoneted a third who came to their assistance, and then returned to his place.

As darkness came on, we were completely surrounded. The Zulus wrecking the camp of the company 24th and my wagon which had been left outside in spite of the efforts of my batman Driver Robson, (the only man of the Royal Engineers with us), who had directed his particular attention to keeping the Zulus off this wagon in which were, as he described it, 'our things.' They also attacked the east end of our position, and after being several times repulsed, eventually got into the kraal, which was strongly built with high walls, and drove us to the middle wall as we abandoned it. This wall was too high for them to use it effectively to fire over, and a Zulu no sooner showed his head over it than he was dropped, being so close that it was impossible to miss him.

Shortly before this, some of the men said they saw redcoats coming on the Helpmekaar Road. The rumour passed quickly round – I could see nothing of the sort myself, but several men said they could. A cheer was raised, and the enemy seemed to pause, to know what it meant, but there was no answer to it, and darkness came on. It is very strange that this report should have arisen amongst us, for the two companies 24th from Helpmekaar, did come down to the foot of the hill but not, I believe, in sight of us. They marched back to Helpmekaar on the report of Rorke's Drift having fallen.

After the first onslaught, the most formidable of the enemy's attacks was just before we retired behind our line of biscuit boxes, and for a short time after it, when they had gained great confidence by their success on the hospital. Although they kept their positions behind the walls we had abandoned, and kept up a heavy fire from all sides until about 12 o'clock, they did not actually charge up in a body to get over our wall after about 9 or 10 o'clock. After this time it became very dark, although the hospital roof was still burning: it was impossible from below to see what was going on and Bromhead and myself getting up on the mealie sack redoubt, kept an anxious watch on all sides. The enemy were now in strong force all around us, and every now and then a confused shout of 'Usuthu!' from many voices, seemed to show that they were going to attack from one side, and immediately the same thing would happen on the other, leaving us in doubt as to where they meant to attack.

About midnight or a little after, the fire slackened, and after that, although they kept us constantly on the alert, by feigning as before, to come on at different points, the fire was of a desultory character. Our men were careful, and only fired when they could see a fair chance. The flame of the burning hospital was now getting low and as pieces of the roof fell, or hitherto unburnt parts of the thatch ignited, the flames would blaze up, illuminating our helmets and faces – a few shots from the Zulus, replied to by our men – again silence, broken only by the same thing repeatedly happening. This sort of thing went on until about 4.00 a.m. and we were anxiously waiting for daybreak and the renewal of the attack, which their comparative, and at length complete silence led us to expect. But at daybreak the enemy were out of sight, over the hill to our south-west.

One Zulu had remained in the kraal and fired a shot among us, (without doing any damage), as we stood up on the walls, and ran off in the direction of the river: although many shots were fired at him as he ran, I am glad to say the plucky fellow got off. Taking care not to be surprised by any ruse of the enemy, we patrolled the ground around the place collecting the arms and ammunition of the dead Zulus. Some of the bullet wounds were very curious. One man's head was split open, exactly as if done with an axe. Another had been hit between the eyes, the bullet carrying away the whole of the back of his head, leaving his face perfect, as though it were a mask, only disfigured by the small hole made by the bullet passing through. One of the wretches we found, one hand grasping a bench that had been dragged from the hospital, and sustained thus in the position we found him in, while in the other hand, he still clutched the knife with which he had mutilated one of our poor fellows, over whom he was still leaning.

We increased the strength of our defences as much as possible, strengthening and raising our walls, putting sacks on the biscuit boxes etc, and were removing the thatch from the roof of the Commissariat store to avoid being burnt out in case of another attack, when at about 7.00 a.m. a large body of the enemy, (I believe the same who had attacked us), appeared on the hills to the south-west. I thought at the time that they were going to attack us, but from what I now know from Zulus, and also of the number we put hors de combat, I do not think so. I think that they came up on the high ground to observe Lord Chelmsford's advance; for from there they could see the Column, long before it came in sight of us.

A frightened and fugitive Kaffir came in shortly before, and I sent for Daniels, the pontman, who could speak Zulu a little, to interview him. Daniels had armed himself with Spalding's sword, which he flourished in so wild and eccentric a manner that the poor wretch thought his last hour was come. He professed to be friendly and to have escaped from Isandlwana, and I sent him with a note to the Officer Commanding at Helpmekaar, explaining our situation, and asking for help: for now, although the men were in excellent spirits, and each man had a good supply of ammunition in his pouches or pockets, we had only about a box and a half left besides, and at this time we had no definite knowledge of what had happened, and I myself did not know that [sic – whether] the part of the column with Lord Chelmsford had taken any part in the action at Isandlwana, or whether on the camp being taken, he had fallen back on Helpmekaar.

The enemy remained on the hill, and still more of them appeared, when about 8.00 a.m. the column came in sight, and the enemy disappeared again. There were a great many of our native levies with the column, and the number of redcoats seemed so few that at first we had grave doubts that the force approaching was the enemy. We improvised a flag, and our signals were soon replied to from the column. The mounted men crossed the drift and galloped up to us, headed by Major Cecil Russell and Lieutenant Walsh, and were received by us with a hearty cheer. Lord Chelmsford, with his staff, shortly after rode up, and thanked us all with much emotion for the defence we had made. The column arrived, crossing by the ponts, and we then had a busy time in making a strong position for the night.

I was glad to seize an opportunity to wash my face in a muddy puddle, in company with Private Bushe, 24th, whose face was covered with blood from a wound in the nose caused by the bullet which had passed through and killed Private Cole, 24th. With the politeness of a soldier, he lent me his towel, or, rather a very dirty half of one, before using it himself, and I was very glad to accept it. In wrecking my stores in my wagon, the Zulus had brought to light a forgotten bottle of beer, and Bromhead and I drank it with mutual congratulations on having come safely out of so much danger. My wagon driver a Cape Coloured man, lost his courage on hearing the first firing around the hill. He let loose his mules and retreated, concealing himself in one of the caves of the Oscarberg. He saw the Zulus run by him and, to his horror, some of them entered the cave, afraid to speak or move, and our bullets came into the cave, actually killing one of the Zulus. He did not know from whom he was in the most danger – friends or foes – and came down in the morning looking more dead than alive. The mules were recovered; they were quietly grazing by the riverside.

On my journey homewards, on arriving at the railway station, Durban, I asked a porter to get me some kaffirs to carry my baggage to the Hotel. He sent several, and the first to come running up was my voorlooper boy who had taken me up to Rorke's Drift. He stopped short and looked very frightened, and I believe at first thought he saw my ghost. I seized him to prevent him running away, and when he saw that I was flesh and blood, he became reassured. He said he thought I had been killed, and upon my asking him how he thought I got away, he said, (the solution of the mystery just striking him), 'I know, you rode away on the other horse.' As far as I could learn and according to his own story, the boy had taken the horse I rode up from the river to the Commissariat stores, and, wild with terror, had ridden it to Pietermaritzburg without stopping, where he gave it over to the Transport people. But having no certificate to say who he was, they took the horse from him and would not give him any employment.

During the fight there were some very narrow escapes from the burning hospital. Private Waters, 24th Regiment, told me that he secreted himself in a cupboard, in the room he was defending, and from it shot several Zulus inside the hospital. He was wounded in the arm, and remained in the cupboard until the heat and the smoke were so great that they threatened to suffocate him. Wrapping himself in a cloak, or skirt of a dress, he found in the cupboard, he rushed out into the darkness, and made his way into the cookhouse. The Zulus were occupying this, and firing at us from the wall nearest us. It was too late to retreat, so he crept softly to the fireplace and, standing up in the chimney, blacked his face and hands with the soot. He remained there until the Zulus left. He was very nearly shot in coming out, one of our men on the wall raising his rifle to do so at the sight of his black face and strange costume – but Waters cried out just in time to save himself. He produced the bullet that wounded him, with pardonable pride, and was very amusing in his admiring description of Dr Reynolds' skill in extracting it.

Gunner Howard RA ran out of the burning hospital, through the enemy, and lay down on the upper side of the wall in front of our north parapet. The bodies of several horses that were killed early in the evening were lying here and concealed by these, by Zulu bodies and the low grass and bushes, he remained unseen with the Zulus all around him until they left in the morning.

Private Beckett, 24th Regiment, escaped from the hospital in the same direction: he was badly wounded with assegais in running though the enemy. He managed to get away and conceal himself in the ditch of the garden, where we found him next morning. The poor fellow was so weak from loss of blood that he could not walk, and he died shortly afterwards.

Our mealie-bag walls were afterwards replaced by loopholed walls of stone, the work making rapid progress upon the arrival of half the 5th Company RE with Lieutenant Porter. As soon as the sappers arrived, we put a fence around, and a rough wood cross over, the graves of our poor men who were killed. This was afterwards replaced by a neat stone monument and inscription, by the 24th, who remained to garrison the place.

I have already, in my report, said how gallantly all behaved, from Lieutenant Bromhead downwards, and I also mentioned those whom I had particularly noticed to have distinguished themselves.

On the day following, we buried 351 bodies of the enemy in graves not far from the Commissariat buildings. Many bodies were since discovered and buried, and when I was sick at Ladysmith, one of our sergeants, who came down there, invalided from Rorke's Drift, where he had been employed in the construction of Fort Melvill, told me that many Zulu bodies were found in the caves and among the rocks a long distance from the mission house, when getting stone for that fort. As, in my report, I underestimated the number we had killed – so I believe we also underestimated the number of the enemy that attacked us, and from what I have since learnt I believe the Zulus must have numbered at least 4,000. As the Reverend George Smith said in a short account he wrote to a Natal paper, 'Whatever signs of approval may be conferred upon the defenders of Rorke's Drift from high quarters, they will never cease to remember the kind and heartfelt expressions of gratitude which have fallen both from the columns of the colonial press and from so many of the Natal colonists themselves.'

And to this may I add that they will ever remember with heartfelt gratitude the signs of approval that have been conferred upon them by their Sovereign and by the people and press of England.

John R. M. Chard
Captain & Bvt Major
January 1880

Lieutenant Colonel Wilsone Black's Reports

Wilsone Black's reports on the two return visits he made to Isandlwana, a fairly brisk patrol in March, and the other spread over three days in late June, when he buried the regimental dead, are fascinating sources and hence are reproduced here in full. It is interesting to note that Black missed so much in March that he noted in June. There are three reasons for this. First, there was still a great deal of long grass on the battlefield at the time of his first visit, which must have concealed many of the bodies he and his soldiers subsequently located for burial. Second, the bodies of the slain were still in an appalling state of decomposition in March, preventing Black and his companions from approaching too close, and certainly precluding any search for personal effects which might have helped to identify individuals. By late June, the flesh and bone of March had been reduced to bone alone and a process of identification, as far as it was possible, could begin. Third and most obviously Black had much more time to look around in June, when the war was within a week of its conclusion, than in March when his party felt rather nervous in the area and was indeed fired upon.

First Report

On Friday the 14th of March, a party of volunteers, under Lieutenant Colonel Black, 2nd/24th Regiment, consisting of Captain Symons, Captain Harvey, Lieutenant Banister and Sergeant Tigar of the 2nd/24th, Commandant Cooper, and twelve officers of the Natal Native Contingent, and ten of the Natal Mounted Police, left Rorke's Drift, at 7 A.M., crossed the Buffalo on the pont, and rode through the Bashee [*sic*] Valley to make a reconnaissance of the camp at Isandwhlana [*sic*]. The scouts in advance saw fires burning in the kraals in the Bashee Valley, and disturbed three armed men with guns near the drift at the foot of Isandwhlana Hill, who ran off at the approach of the party. Arrived on the now well-known and oft-described 'ridge,'* a horrible scene of desolation was spread before them, and the still highly-tainted air filled their nostrils. After posting vedettes on all sides to guard against a surprise, they proceeded systematically to examine the whole of the battlefield. Some thirty Zulus were seen running from the kraal in front of the camp, and when out of sight they fired several shots, with the intention, no doubt, of giving the alarm, and shortly afterwards signal fires were seen burning in the hills. The Guard-tent of the 2nd/24th Regiment was first searched, in hopes of finding some trace of the two colours of the regiment, which had been left there on the morning of the 22nd of January last. The tent, colours, and belts had all been taken away. They next searched each camp in detail and afterwards rode down by the side of the 'donga' that ran in front of the camp; and then still farther afield, where the different phases and incidents of the battle were supposed to have taken place, and observed the following: the Zulu dead had all been removed. The wagons to the number of over 100 were uninjured, and stood for the most part where they were left. All the tents had been burnt, cut up and taken away, the poles only being left. Everything of value had been looted, and what had not been taken away had been stabbed with assegais. Sponges, boots, brushes of all descriptions, quantities of books, papers, photographs, gaiters, and various other articles were scattered about. Horses and mules were lying, still tied to the piquet-ropes and wagons, and a good many skeletons of oxen were scattered here and there. The bodies of our poor brave soldiers showed where the fury of the enemy had overtaken them. They were all in and about the camp, or down the path the fugitives took; not a dozen could be found in the whole surrounding of the camp, nor in the 'donga,' bearing out the testimony of survivors, who relate that while the soldiers held the donga they suffered no loss. The greatest number counted together within a very small compass was sixty-eight, and these were in the left rear of the 1st/24th, near the officers' mess-tent. The majority were 24th men but there were some of other arms as well. As regards the state of the bodies, a subject of morbid but painful interest, they were in all conditions of horrible decay. Some were prefect skeletons; others that had not been

* By which Black means the saddle.

stripped, or only partially so, were quite unapproachable, and the stench was sickening; with but few exceptions, it was impossible to recognise any one, and the only officer that was seen was discovered by his clothes. It was considered that it would be three or four weeks before the bones could be collected and buried. Were an attempt to be made to do so now, nothing could be done but to throw earth over the corpses. Close to the small heap of dead bodies before mentioned, the colour-belt of the 1st/24th Regiment was found by Corporal Groschky, Natal Mounted Police; it was the most interesting thing found, though not perhaps the most valuable, as Captain Symons found a large bundle of cheques belonging to him that had not been opened. Having thoroughly searched the camp, they proceeded to look for the two guns. One limber was found on the road leading down the valley towards the Isipezi [*sic*] Mountain about a quarter of a mile to the front of the camp.* The other limber much broken, was found lying in the ravine where Lieutenant Curling R.A., described the guns as having been upset and lost; and the team of six horses, all harnessed together, was lying by it; the ravine was so steep that one or two of the horses were suspended by the harness over the stream; both the guns and carriages had been removed. This ravine is about half a mile from 'the ridge,' and numbers of bodies were lying between the two. On the order to retire being given, the party returned by the same road, being twice fired upon, without effect, by two small parties of natives; once as they were leaving the ravine, and the second time from the 'krantzes' above the Bashee Valley.

Second Report

Rorke's Drift,
28th June, 1879.

The force under my command – thirty King's Dragoon Guards (mounted), fifty on foot, 140 2nd/24th Regiment, 360 natives, and fifty Native Horse, were working on the 20th, 23rd, and 26th inst., and have completed the burial of the remains of those who fell at the battle of Isandwhlana. Major Dartnell, with some Natal Mounted Police, and

---

* Having of course been removed from the Manzimyama valley by local Zulus at some point after the battle.

representatives from the Natal Carbineers, Buffalo Border Guard, and other volunteers, co-operated with me on the first day, and looked after the burial of their own comrades. As I reported in March last, the bodies of the slain lay thickest on the 1st/24th camp; a determined stand had evidently been made behind the officers' tents; and here an eyewitness told me that while he was escaping from the camp he saw a compact body of the 24th men fighting surrounded by the Zulus; seventy dead lay here. Lower down the hill in the same camp another clump of about sixty lay together, among them Captain Wardell, Lieutenant Dyer, and a captain and a subaltern of the 24th unrecognizable. Near at hand were found the bodies of Colonel Durnford, Lieutenant Scott, and other Carbineers, and men of the Natal Mounted Police, showing that here also our men had gathered and fought in an organized body. This was evidently a centre of resistance, as the bodies of men of all arms were found converging as it were to the spot, but stricken down ere they could join the ranks of their comrades. About sixty bodies lay on the rugged slope, under the southern precipice of Isandwhlana, among them those of Captain Younghusband, and two other officers unrecognizable; it looked as if these had held the crags, and fought together as long as ammunition lasted. The proof of hand to hand fighting was frequent; three soldiers were lying by as many dead Zulus, Zulu and white man confronting each other, as living they had stood. A 24th man was found here, face downward, with a Zulu knife up to the haft in his back, evidently killed while defending himself from a front attack; an assegai bent double lay by him and another in like state near by. It is bootless, however, to multiply such instances now. For example, lower down the field an N.M. policeman and a Zulu, the Englishman uppermost, lay still locked in each other's embrace; in another place a Zulu skull was found pierced by a bayonet, while his assegai lay rusting in the man's breast. Up among the rocks a Zulu chief, covered by his shield, lay swathed in four distinct wrappings of canvas, and as many other Zulu bodies were here. I gather that this was the last scene of resistance, and that, therefore, the Zulus had less time for carrying away their dead, which they have so completely done from the other parts of the field. A soldier of the 24th was found close under the precipice head downward, with shattered skull, showing that he had fallen or been hurled from the top; hereabouts, too, was an artillery tent mallet by the side of a soldier, who had vainly matched this feeble club against the assegai. Many dead lay on the Buffalo side of the neck, and I think it will not be out of place too if I describe how the line of retreat led here. When our two lines of infantry, one facing to the left of the camp, in the position naturally taken up after retiring before the chest or main body of the Zulu army, as it swarmed over the Ugulu [sic] hill, the other facing more towards the front and parallel to the Donga, making head with the Mounted Volunteers against the Zulu left wing – when these two separate lines of skirmishers, outflanked on both sides, ammunition well nigh expended, retired almost at the same time to rally in the camp, form square around the ammunition wagons, and there refill their pouches, some of those men present tell me that the attention of all being fixed on their own front, none had realised how it fared behind them – once they turned round and saw that all was lost, the camp was full of Zulus sweeping round the flanks of isolated lines following through the gap made in them by the retreating Natal natives. The Zulus were already masters of the place of refuge, while those who had made the front attack now stormed behind the retreating lines. The ordered battle was over – all that disciplined men can do had been done – the lines melted into groups, into files, coherence ceased, friend and foe mingled in one mass, a surging stabbing crowd – their very numbers prevented the Zulus from making an immediate end. The horsemen who escaped, the footmen who struggled through the tents the very guns moved at a walk wherever a gap opened in the mass, and slowly won their way towards the neck. Once here, once on the road the hope of escape arose only to be quenched at the next glance for circling round the Isandwhlana the right horn of the Zulu horde barred the way to Rorke's Drift; the only gap in the ring of steel was the rough ground to the south between the road and the kop that faces the fatal hill. Here, then, of necessity and not of choice, the broken ranks pushed on; the Zulus on the kop fired down. Zulus in their midst and Zulus on each flank pressed on with equal pace. The tracks became rough indeed, scored by dongas, strewn with rocks, seamed with water courses, here dry and stony, with steep sides, there wet and boggy. The horsemen moved on at foot pace, and only escaped because the horses could keep up the exertion longer than the panting foot soldiers. Here to us, was the saddest sight, the camp left, the face set toward the Buffalo, all might give hope for life; but the record of death shows heavily here, and not ignobly is it written. Here and there around a wagon, here and there around a tree, a group had formed, and stood at bay – shoulder to shoulder they fired their last cartridge, shoulder to shoulder they plied the steel – side by side their bones are lying, and tell their tale; but other evidence is forthcoming, and I have heard from those who saw and live, how dearly our country men sold their lives – how fiercely fighting they fell. 800 yards from the road the guns, long ere without gunners – they died in the camp – came upon ground that no wheels could pass, and the horses which, on my first visit I saw hanging in their harness over a ravine, now mingle with the drivers' bones.

From here the bodies are even more and more apart until, about two miles from the camp, the last one lies and marks the limit reached by white men on foot. The fatal trail begins again near the river bank, where Stewart Smith, and others rest a river's breath from Natal; across the river it runs until the graves of Melvill and Coghill nearly mark its end.

Of the greater part of those buried, all that can be known is their regiment, for weather and the operations of nature have left but little that is recognizable; where clothes remained due search was made, but in most cases the pockets had been cut out, and but little property was found by us; that recovered has been sent to the relatives of the slain.

I cannot close my report without calling attention to the hard work so cheerily undergone by the fifty dismounted King's Dragoon Guards and 140 men of the 2nd/24th, who each day trudged twenty-two miles to and fro besides their labour on the widespread field. The natives were principally employed as outposts on the hills, lest peradventure another *impi* might follow the track of its forerunner across the Nqutu range, or appear on our right from the tunnelled hills between us and the Qudeni.

I need not say that no cross or stone marks the graves of the fallen; above them the Lion Kop, the majestic monument of Isandwhlana holds guard, and for ever tells that 800 sons of England lie beneath.

Appendix 7

Visiting the Battlefields

No combination of maps, sketches or photographs can ever really bring the Isandlwana battlefield to life for it is an extremely complex piece of ground. It is also a deeply significant and moving place, and for those with an interest in British military history or the history of the Zulu nation, it cries out to be visited. A glance in the atlas might at first put off the UK-based visitor but it is perfectly possible these days to visit Isandlwana and Rorke's Drift in an extended weekend. If one has an interest in the wider Anglo-Zulu conflict or the two Boer Wars then a longer trip to the region is called for.

General Travel Information

Flights and Arrival in Johannesburg British Airways, South African Airways and Virgin all offer overnight flights from Heathrow to Johannesburg. Generally you will arrive in South Africa at around breakfast time. If you have travelled in an expensive seat and had a decent night's sleep, then it is possible to move on straightaway for Kwazulu-Natal (KZN), but this is a five-hour drive and is probably best left until the following day. Unless you know Johannesburg well, or your hotel offers organised excursions to some of the big shopping precincts, it is probably advisable to confine yourself to a comfortable airport hotel for the day, as the crime situation in Johannesburg can make it a dangerous place for the unwary.

Hire Cars and the Road Hire cars can be booked in advance through the usual array of international firms and picked up at the airport. Your travel agent or airline can arrange this for you. People drive on the left in South Africa and the conventions of the road are not dissimilar to those in the UK. The one exception is stop signs at crossroads or junctions where there are no traffic lights, or 'robots' as they are known locally. Here the convention is that traffic moves off in the order in which it arrived at the junction. It is as well to drive defensively and cautiously as there will be plenty of dangerous drivers and unroadworthy vehicles about. That said, the traffic down to KZN should not be heavy. It is advisable to establish clearly with the car hire firm what you should do in the event of a breakdown. Being stranded at the roadside is to be avoided in South Africa.

Self-Drive Route Card The best route from Johannesburg to the battle-fields is as follows:

> From the airport take the main carriageway southwards and after a few kilometres filter onto the N3 for Durban.
>
> South of Heidelberg, turn off the N3 onto the R23. Be wary of turning off too early onto the exit signed R23 Heidelberg Noord. You want the exit signed R23 Heidelburg South. At the top of the exit turn left – the sign will indicate the direction of Balfour.
>
> Follow the R23 south for 100 km until you arrive at Standerton. After passing under a railway bridge in the final approach to the town, immediately turn right at the traffic lights. On the left of the road is a Total Garage where there are two fast food outlets and a public lavatory. As you are about halfway through your journey this is a good place to stop for refreshments.
>
> As you leave the Total garage be sure to turn left. Five hundred metres down the road you will come to a set of traffic lights. Take the filter lane to the left where there is a green sign marked Vrede, Volksrust, Natal.
>
> You will now cross the Vaal river and begin going uphill. You will then come into a wide residential boulevard which you should follow out of town to the south.
>
> Continue south for a further 80 km to Volksrust.
>
> On the outskirts of Volksrust turn left at a road sign marked N11 Newcastle. At the third set of traffic lights turn right – there will be a preserved steam train in the park on your right. As you head south out of town you will be looking at Majuba Hill, scene of the British defeat of 1881 and the site of General Sir George Colley's

death. Stay on the N11 and continue over the Laing's Nek pass into Natal. There are a number of sharp bends to be wary of.

Stay on the N11 until you come to a turn onto the R621 signed for Dannhauser. Follow your nose through the hamlets of Dannhauser and Hattingspruit following signs for Dundee. At the outskirts of Dundee the R621 will come to a T-junction. Turn left into Dundee.

Drive along the wide boulevard into town until you come to a prominent traffic island. Turn left keeping the Royal Inn on your right. You are now on the main street and driving straight through the town. (Major General Sir Penn Symons is buried in the Anglican churchyard in a left turn off the main street.) Continue downhill through the town and out over Smith's Nek. The Talana Hill battlefield will be on your left as you cross the nek. This was the scene of the opening battle of the Second Boer War in which General Symons was killed. A couple of kilometres over the nek take the next prominent right turn signed for Nqutu and Isandlwana. (If you are heading for the Battlefields Country Lodge do not take the right turn but keep straight on for about another 1.5 km or so and the lodge is to be found just off the road to the left. It is well signed.)

Keep on the Nqutu road until you come to a sign indicating a right turn for Rorke's Drift. This is a dirt track. From now on drive with extra care watching out for children and cattle, ruts and potholes. Keep on the track for a few kilometres until you come to a T-junction. Turn left.

Follow this road until you come down to the area of Rorke's Drift. In the final approach to the settlement there will be a road junction signed for Isandlwana to the left. If you are heading for Isandlwana Lodge turn left here. If you are heading for Fugitives' Drift keep straight on past Rorke's Drift which will be on your left. A few kilometres down the road you will come to a signed left turn for Fugitives' Drift.

To find Isandlwana Lodge, cross the Buffalo on the concrete bridge and follow the road. Just after crossing the Batshe stream and climbing to the top of the valley you will come to a T-junction.

Turn right. Just over the hill the unmistakeable silhouette of Isandlwana will be dead ahead. Follow the road into the settlement of St Vincent's. The entrance to the battlefield will be on your right. Just past the battlefield gates, turn left, and after 70 metres turn right over the cattle grid. The visitor centre where the entrance fee to the battlefield is paid is just on the right and is part of the mission. Follow the road straight uphill for the gates of Isandlwana Lodge.

Accommodation There are many options in the area of the battlefields. I would recommend using one of the two luxury lodges that are by far and away the most popular with visitors. These are *Fugitives' Drift Lodge*, home of the Rattray family, and *Isandlwana Lodge*, where the American co-owner, Ms Pat Stubbs, is normally to be found in residence. Both are hospitable and highly efficient operations. Isandlwana Lodge commands a fantastic view over the battlefield itself and has been tastefully built into the Nyoni escarpment. Fugitives' Drift Lodge is on the other side of the Buffalo and is a little way along the road from Rorke's Drift. The princiapl guide at Fugitives' Drift following the death of the legendary David Rattray is the ebullient and hugely entertaining Rob Caskie. The resident historian at Isandlwana Lodge is Mr Rob Gerrard. In both lodges there is an additional charge for their guided battlefield tours. In both it is the norm to arrive the evening before, visit Isandlwana in the morning, take a mid-day break and a fine lunch, and then visit Rorke's Drift in the late afternoon, making a two-night stay. When guiding British Army parties on the battlefields I like to take them to Isandlwana Lodge for their first evening and Fugitives' Drift Lodge for their second, as this works well and allows one to do both battlefields the justice they deserve. It should be borne in mind that the graves of Melvill VC and Coghill VC are located on the Fugitives' Drift property. Both lodges now have mains electricity and all the facilities that one would expect of the top end of the market. The staff in both lodges are invariably helpful and charming. A long talk with my friend Lindizwe Ingobese, also known as Dalton, who works as the barman at Isandlwana Lodge when he is not cutting CDs with his group of traditional singers, is to be recommended. He can also guide you on a cultural tour of the modern Isandlwana/ Manzimyama communities. Both lodges have a shop with a range of books, CDs and other souvenirs. Dress is entirely informal during the day but long trousers are the norm for dinner. Jackets and ties are not generally worn. Contact information is as follows:

Fugitives' Drift Lodge Tel: +27 (0)34 642 1843 or 271 8051; fax: +27 (0)34 271 8053; e-mail: <info@fugitivesdrift.com>.

Isandlwana Lodge Tel: +27 (0)34 271 8301; fax: 034 271 8306; e-mail: <lodge@isandlwana.co.za>; web: <www.isandlwana.co.za>.

As an alternative to the luxury lodges a cheaper but perfectly decent standard of accommodation is to be had at the *Battlefields Country Lodge* just outside Dundee. This is owned and run by Lourens and Nanette Roos, again charming hosts. A range of accommodation is to be had from backpacker standard to a conventional hotel style standard. You can be assured of a warm welcome.

Battlefields Country Lodge Tel: +27 (0)34 218 1641; fax: +27 (0)34 212 3502; e-mail: <stay@battlefieldslodge.co.za>.

Accommodation in the Ladysmith Area If you intend to spend a significant amount of time examining the Boer War then a move down to the Ladysmith area will be necessary. The *Royal Hotel* in Murchison Street was there at the time of the siege and is quite comfortable. Unless you are an experienced South African traveller it is probably best not go out in the town after dark. *Three Tree Lodge* and *Spion Kop Lodge* are out in the country and are highly recommended.

Security It continues to be necessary to exercise prudent security precautions in RSA. Violent crime is prevalent particularly in Gauteng Province (Johannesburg and Pretoria) where car hijacking and burglary with violence are serious problems. Southern KZN (Durban area) is also dubious. It is perfectly possible to move safely around the battlefields area provided you are sensible and do not place yourself in vulnerable situations. Generally you should aim to be in a safe location such as a hotel or lodge after dark. In Zululand proper, in say the area of Isandlwana and Rorke's Drift, the preservation of the old tribal system means that there is next to no crime against European visitors.

On one occasion I know of, a tourist had some valuables stolen and within a day the local headman had recovered the property and chastised the perpetrator. I have spent much time alone amongst the Zulu and have never been made to feel uncomfortable. If however, you are an inexperienced South African traveller, the use of professional guides is recommended. Importantly a self-drive trip in a reliable vehicle direct to one of the luxury lodges at Isandlwana/Rorke's Drift is perfectly safe and will be a truly memorable experience.

Weather Remember that the southern hemisphere seasons are reversed. In the KZN summer the days can be extremely hot, so a water bottle will be essential. The winter months, whilst not generally as cold as in Europe, can still be quite chilly. There is sometimes a strong wind at Isandlwana necessitating a fleece or a top coat. Rain will normally fall in the summer months and will typically come on in late afternoon.

Environmental Hazards In the event that you come upon a snake, do not be tempted to move towards it, play with it, or otherwise provoke it. The puff adder, short, fat and brown, is best described as a lazy snake – it will not necessarily move away if it senses your approach, but will lie still, relying on its excellent natural camouflage for concealment. The danger arises from the possibility of stepping on it inadvertently. Do not be deceived by the 'adder' label; it is many times more poisonous than a British adder and to be bitten by one is a serious matter. By far the most dangerous environmental hazard, however, is posed by the black mamba, long, sleek, aggressive, black-grey and utterly deadly. Neither is a baby mamba 'sweet' to be around; it bites too. Check with your lodge or hotel what you should do in the unlikely event that you or a member of your party are bitten by a snake. You must get medical attention as rapidly as possible.

Battlefield Visits

Local Advice Excellent local advice can be obtained from David and Nikky Rattray and their staff at Fugitives' Drift Lodge. Similarly Rob Gerrard and the management will be pleased to help you at Isandlwana Lodge.

Battlefield Visitor Centres If you are operating under your own steam with this or other books under your arm, then you will need to pay a R10 entrance fee at the visitor centres at both Rorke's Drift and Isandlwana. Both have shops with books and other souvenirs. Both battlefields are open to the public until 4.00 pm, seven days a week.

Isandlwana Vantage Points On an organised tour you will see the Isandlwana bowl from the saddle but not the far-flung corners of the battlefield, unless you make special arrangements with your guide. The following additional stops are recommended:

- The forward edge of Hlazakazi for a view over the area of Lord Chelmsford's operations. This will entail driving out across the plain to the east.
- Mangeni Falls – approached by crossing the stream (which is fordable) and bearing to the right along a dirt track. Take great care at the precipitous edge.
- The edge of Mabaso Ridge for a view into the Ngwebeni Valley. This is approached along a dirt track off the metalled Nqutu Road. The approach runs through a settlement. Please take great care as you drive through as the children often become over-excited at the arrival of visitors.
- The summit of Mkwene Hill for a view of the Tahelane Ridge in one direction and the approach of the Zulu chest in the other.
- The summit of Amatutshane (only for the physically fit).
- Durnford's Donga.
- The rocky ridge.
- Walking down the Manzimyama Valley from the saddle at least part way along the Fugitive's Trail. If you intend to walk the entire trail, you will need to preposition vehicles at one end or the other. It is essential to obtain the services of a guide. It is possible for the physically fit to cross the Buffalo from rock to rock in the winter months, but it does involve a short jump which can go wrong on slippery rocks and accordingly should not be undertaken by non-swimmers, the aged or young children.

Isandlwana Monuments The largest cluster of cairns on the forward slope of the saddle marks the place where Captain George Wardell and H Company were cut down in their rallying square. The largest monument in the saddle is the 24th Monument. About seventy members of the 24th were killed at this spot. On the rocky shelf on the shoulder of the mountain is a large cairn which marks the site of Younghusband's stand and charge. The cave commonly held to be the one where the last man of the 24th was killed is located just above the cairn, at the foot of the southern crag. At the foot of Mahlabamkhosi, or Black's Koppie, is a needle raised by the Natal Carbineers; this marks the spot where Durnford and the volunteers made their last stand. Other monuments include those of the Natal Mounted Police and the Pietermaritzburg High School Old Boys. Captain George Shepstone has a named grave on the western or rear slope of Isandlwana but this can be difficult to find. The Royal Artillery monument to the N Battery dead is to be found out on the rocky ridge. It is less than knee high and can also be difficult to locate in the luxuriant summer months. It should not be regarded as definitively marking the position of the 7-pounders.

Rorke's Drift Remember that neither building is original, though both have been built pretty much on the foundations of their historic predecessors. The storehouse is now a functioning church; on a Sunday morning you may be lucky enough to hear something of the beautiful singing voices of the Zulu people. The hospital building serves as a museum and has a number of exhibits which can help to bring the events of January 1879 to life. Look out in particular for a model of the original floor plan. The lines of the barricades and the position of the redoubt are marked out with stones, though it should be noted that the size of the curving outer barricade in front of the hospital is significantly underplayed. There is a shop and a café on site where a range of books, souvenirs and snacks are on sale. There is an excellent terrain model in one corner of the shop which conveys the nature of the ground between Rorke's Drift and Isandlwana extremely well. At the rear of the buildings is the British cemetery. Here the seventeen men killed in action are buried along with a number of others who died subsequently of disease. Their names are faithfully recorded on opposite sides of Bandsman Melsop's obelisk. There are two Zulu mass graves at the front of the post. A new monument to the Zulu dead is currently out to tender and should have been erected by the time this book is published. Jim Rorke's grave is at the foot of Shiyane. It is well worth the effort to walk to the top of the hill, not only to obtain a Zulu rifleman's view of the mission, but also to look out in the direction of Isandlwana as Reynolds, Smith and Witt did. Down at the river, remember that the concrete bridge has no relevance whatsoever to the events of 1879. The drift is downstream to the right. It is possible to drive down to it from the main road along a rough track in the grass. The ponts were located on the deep-water pool upstream of the bridge. It is worth walking up to the ridge above the pool to see the jumble of boulders that is all that is left of Fort Melvill. Short stretches of wall are still standing so that it is still possible to trace the rough layout and dimensions of the post. On the far side of the river from the drift, there is a small British cemetery hidden in a grove of trees, where a number of soldiers who died later in the war are buried. It is possible to drive to this along a dirt track running to the right of the main road. There is also a small British cemetery behind the police post at Helpmekaar. On the whole, it is best not to push south of Helpmekaar on the old border road for Tugela Ferry and Greytown, for security reasons.

Other Sites of Interest The places listed below are within relatively easy striking distance of Isandlwana/Rorke's Drift. Many of them are in remote locations where the services of a guide are desirable. If you are an expert visitor and have a knowledge of the battles and the ground then all well and good. Take your maps and books with you as there will generally not be anybody to show you around. If you are visiting simply as a tourist then it will be best to stick to the locations shown as either *recommended* or *highly recommended*.

- Blood River Battlefield – *highly recommended*. The site has both Afrikaaner and Zulu visitor's centres; perhaps unsurprisingly they portray markedly different versions of events. Note that the replica wagon laager is slightly further from the river than the original. The commando sited its wagons hard up against the banks of the donga and the hippo pool. The replica wagons are cast in bronze and are sited where they are to prevent their considerable weight carrying away the edges on which they would otherwise stand.

- Kambula Battlefield – remote. Graveyard. Guide desirable unless you know the battle well.
- Intombi River – remote. Monuments and mass-grave. Guide essential.
- Ulundi Battlefield. Monument and graveyard. Best taken in on the way to the Hluhuwe-Umfolozi game reserve, but not worth the long trip in its own right unless you are a real AZW buff. Watch out for the potholes on the Babanango road; it is best not to be out on the road after dark.
- Hlobane Battlefield – professional guide essential. Increasingly difficult due to failure to maintain the rough roads to the mines.
- Site of the death of the Prince Imperial – very remote. Professional guide essential.
- Laing's Nek Battlefield. Not much to see. 58th Regt monument on the 'Table' mountain. Watch out for road safety on the road over the pass.
- Ingogo or Schuinshoogte Battlefield. Graveyards and monument.
- Mount Prospect Cemetery (graves of General Colley and others). Good view of Majuba and Laing's Nek.
- Majuba Hill Battlefield – *highly recommended* but only for the physically fit.
- Talana Hill Battlefield – *recommended*. Museum. Visitor centre.
- Elandslaagte Battlefield. No facilities but a few monuments. British cemetery.
- Colenso Battlefield and Clouston Field of Remembrance. Monuments.
- Ladysmith Siege Museum – *recommended*.
- Wagon Hill/Platrand (Siege of Ladysmith). Scene of the charge of the Devons. A number of significant monuments. Original stone sangars and gun pits.
- Tugela Heights Battlefield. Not much to see.
- Spion Kop Battlefield – *highly recommended*. Monuments. Mass

trench-graves. No facilities. The Tugela has been dammed south of the kop to make an inland lake. The south bank is a game reserve. It is possible to contemplate Redver's Buller's tactical problems whilst standing amongst kudu, giraffe and other non-predatory animals. From the top of the kop, keep an eye out for rhinos in the low ground below you.

- Site of the armoured train ambush and W. S. Churchill's capture. Not much to see. Be prepared to be disappointed; but it's nice to be able to say you've been there!
- Hluhuwe-Umfolozi Game Reserve – *highly recommended*. Overnight stay probably required.

Bibliography and Sources

Primary Sources

The following primary sources were consulted for *How Can Man Die Better* and *Like Wolves on the Fold*:

British

Sir Bartle Frere (High Commissioner)
General Sir Garnet Wolseley
Lt. Gen. Lord Chelmsford (GOC)
Col. Richard Glyn CB (24th Regt)
Col. Evelyn Wood VC (90th Regt)
Maj. Wilsone Black (24th Regt)
Maj. Francis Clery (Staff)
Maj. John Crealock (Staff)
Maj. Matthew Gosset (Staff)
B/Maj. Henry Spalding (Staff)
Comdt. Rupert Lonsdale (NNC)
Comdt. George Browne (NNC)
Capt. Edward Essex (Staff)
Capt. Alan Gardner (Staff)
Capt. Henry Hallam-Parr (Staff)
L/Capt. Henry Harford (99th Regt/NNC)
Capt. W. Penn Symons (24th Regt)
Surgeon James Henry Reynolds VC (AMD)
Surgeon Blair Brown (AMD)
Charles Norris-Newman Esq. (Correspondent)
Archibald Forbes Esq. (Correspondent)
James Brickhill Esq. (Civ)
Lt. Gonville Bromhead VC (24th Regt)
Lt. John Chard VC (RE)
Lt. William Cochrane (Staff)
Lt. Nevill Coghill (24th Regt/Staff)

Lt. Henry Curling (RA)
Lt. Harry Davies (NNMC)
Lt. Wallie Erskine (NNC)
Lt. William Heaton (24th Regt)
Lt. Alfred Henderson (NNMC)
Lt. Walter Higginson (NNC)
Lt. William Lloyd (24th Regt)
Lt. Henry Mainwaring (24th Regt)
Lt. Berkeley Milne (RN/Staff)
Lt. Charlie Pope (24th Regt)
Lt. Horace Smith-Dorrien (Staff)
Insp. George Mansel (NMP)
Comm. James Hamer (Vol)
Asst. Comm. James Dalton VC (Vol)
Asst. Comm. Walter Dunne (AC&TD)
Rev. George Smith (Civ)
Rev. Otto Witt (Civ)
CSgt. Frank Bourne DCM (24th Regt)
CSgt Gittins (24th Regt)
Sgt. George Mabin (Staff Clerk)
Sgt. Frederick Millne (3rd Regt)
Sgt. George Smith 387 (24th Regt)
Cpl. William Allen VC (24th Regt)
Cpl. John Bassage (24th Regt)
Cpl. Jack Lyons (24th Regt)
2nd Cpl. Francis Attwood DCM (ASC)
Gnr. Abraham Evans (RA)
Pte. James Bickley (24th Regt)
Pte. Hector Grant (24th Regt)
Mr. Bob Hall (Civ)

Pte. Frederick Hitch VC (24th Regt)
Pte. Henry Hook VC (24th Regt)
Gnr. Arthur Howard (RA)
Pte. John Jobbins (24th Regt)
Pte. William Johnson (24th Regt)
Tpr. Harry Lugg (NMP)
Pte. Robert Jones 716 VC (24th Regt)
Pte. William Jones 593 VC (24th Regt)

Pte. Thomas Parry (24th Regt)
Pte. William Roy DCM (24th Regt)
Tpr. Richard Stevens (NMP)
Pte. Thomas Stevens 777 (24th Regt)
Tpr. Fred Symons (NC)
Pte. James Trainer (24th Regt)
Pte. John Waters (24th Regt)
Pte. Edmund Wilson (24th Regt)

Zulu

H.M. King Cetshwayo kaMpande
(Correspondence in captivity)
Mehlokazulu kaSihayo
Mzingeli kaDabulamanzi

Uguku (Warrior umCijo Regiment)
uMhoti (Warrior umCijo Regiment)
Other anonymous accounts by
Isandlwana participants

Secondary Sources and Published Primary Sources

Adams, Jack, *The South Wales Borderers (The 24th Regiment of Foot)*,
London, 1968

Bourquin, S., 'The Zulu Military Organization and the Challenge of 1879',
South African Military History Society Journal, Vol. 4, No. 4

Castle, Ian, *British Infantryman in South Africa 1877–81*, Oxford, 2003

Child, Daphne (ed.), *The Zulu War Diary of Colonel Henry Harford*,
Pietermaritzburg, 1978

Clammer, David, *The Zulu War*, London, 1973

Cope, Richard, *The Origins of the Anglo-Zulu War of 1879*, Pietermaritzburg,
1999

Cunynghame, General Sir Arthur, *My Command in South Africa 1874–78*,
London, 1879

Droogleever, R. W. F., *The Road to Isandhlwana: Colonel Anthony Durnford
in Natal and Zululand 1873–1879*, London, 1992

Edgerton, Robert B., *Like Lions they Fought: The Last Zulu War*, New York &
London, 1988

Emery, Frank, *The Red Soldier: Letters from the Zulu War 1879*, London, 1977

Glennie, Farquhar; Paton George; and Symons, William (eds.), *Historical
Records of the 24th Regiment*, London, 1892

Gon, Philip, *The Road to Isandhlwana*, Johannesburg, 1979

Guy, Jeff, *The Destruction of the Zulu Kingdom*, Johannesburg, 1979

Hamilton-Browne, Colonel G., *With the Lost Legion in New Zealand*, London,
1911

Hamilton-Browne, Colonel G., *A Lost Legionary in South Africa*, London, 1912

HMSO, *Field Exercises and Evolutions of Infantry*, London, 1877

Holme, Norman, *The Noble 24th: Biographical Records of the 24th Regiment in the Zulu War and the South African Campaigns 1877–79*, London, 1999

Hummel, Chris (ed.), *The Frontier War Journal of Major John Crealock 1878*, Cape Town, 1988

Jackson, F. W. D., *Isandhlwana 1879: The Sources Re-examined*, 24th/RRW Museum, Brecon, 1999

Jones, Alan Baynham, and Stevenson, Lee, *Rorke's Drift By Those Who Were There*, Brighton, 2003

Knight, Ian, *Great Zulu Commanders*, London, 1999

Knight, Ian, *Brave Men's Blood; The Epic of the Zulu War, 1879*, London, 1990

Knight, Ian, *Zulu: Isandlwana and Rorke's Drift 22–23 January 1879*, London, 1992.

Knight, Ian, *The Anatomy of the Zulu Army from Shaka to Cetshwayo 1818–1879*, London, 1995.

Knight, Ian, *Isandlwana 1879: The Great Zulu Victory*, Oxford, 2002

Knight, Ian, *The Zulu War 1879*, Oxford, 2003

Knight Ian, *The National Army Museum Book of the Zulu War*, London 2003.

Laband, J. P., *Rope of Sand*, South Africa, 1995; reprinted as *The Rise and Fall of the Zulu Nation*, London, 1997.

Laband, J. P., and Thompson, P. S., *Field Guide to the War in Zululand*, Pietermaritzburg, 1979

Laband, J. P., and Thompson, P. S., *Kingdom and Colony at War*, Pietermaritzburg, 1990

Lock, Ron, and Quantrill, Peter, *The Red Book. Natal newspaper reports on the Anglo-Zulu War, 1879*, (compilation), Pinetown, KZN, 2000

Lock, Ron, and Quantrill, Peter, *Zulu Victory: The Epic of Isandlwana and the Cover-up*, London 2002

Mackinnon, J. P., and Shadbolt, Sydney, *The South African Campaign 1879*, London, 1880; reprinted London, 1995

Mitford, Bertram, *Through the Zulu Country*, London, 1883; reprinted London, 1995

Morris, Donald R., *The Washing of the Spears*, London, 1966

Myatt, Frederick, *The British Infantry 1660–1945: The Evolution of a Fighting Force*, Poole, 1983

Norris-Newman, Charles L., *In Zululand with the British throughout the War of 1879*, London, 1889; reprinted London, 1988

Rattray, David and Greaves, Adrian, *David Rattray's Guidebook to the Anglo-Zulu War Battlefields*, UK, 2003

RHQ RRW, *A Short History of the Royal Regiment of Wales (24th/41st Foot)*, Cardiff, 1993

Smith-Dorrien, Horace, *Memories of Forty-Eight Years Service*, London, 1925

Spiers, Edward M., *The Late Victorian Army 1868–1902*, Manchester, 1992

Stalker, Reverend John, *The Natal Carbineers 1855–1911*, Pietermaritzburg and Durham, 1912

Tavender I. T., *Casualty Roll for the Zulu and Basuto Wars South Africa 1877–79*, Suffolk, 1985

Thompson, P. S., *The Natal Native Contingent in the Anglo-Zulu War, 1879*, Pietermaritzburg, 1997

War Office (Compiled by J. S. Rothwell), *Narrative of Field Operations Connected with the Zulu War of 1879*, London, 1881; reprinted London, 1907 & 1989

Webb, C. de B., and Wright, J. B., *A Zulu King Speaks: Statements made by Cetshwayo kaMpande on the history and customs of his people*, Pietermaritzburg, 1978

Whybra, Julian, *England's Sons: A Casualty and Survivor's Roll of British Combatants for Isandlwana and Rorke's Drift*, UK, 2004

Wood, Evelyn, *From Midshipman to Field Marshal*, London, 1906

Yorke, Edmund, *Rorke's Drift 1879; Anatomy of a Zulu War Siege*, Stroud and Charleston SC, 2001

Young, John, *They Fell Like Stones: Battles and Casualties of the Zulu War, 1879*, London, 1991

Glossary

amaNgwane: one of the native clans of Natal which provided levies for the British force. The clan was led by the chief Zikhali, and found D and E Companies of 1st/1st NNC, and Nos. 1, 2 and 3 Troops (known collectively as Zikhali's Horse) of the NNMC.

assegai: not actually a Zulu word but now synonymous in common usage with the short stabbing spear more properly known as the *iklwa*. Also used to mean spear in the wider sense e.g. 'throwing assegai'.

BBG: Buffalo Border Guard. A small part-time unit of mounted volunteers from the remote farms along Natal's Buffalo River frontier with Zululand.

boy: rank by which those under the age of eighteen serving in the British Army as drummers or bandsmen were known. Many of them were the orphaned sons of Army families.

brevet rank: an officer's paid rank is known as his substantive rank. It was the practice in the Victorian era to grant an officer a brevet promotion to the next higher rank in recognition of distinguished service. He would wear the insignia of the higher rank and be addressed by it, but he would not be paid in that rank until he received substantive promotion into an appropriate vacancy on the establishment. Down to the modern day, a unit's establishment regulates what the taxpayer is prepared to pay for; the establishment may not be exceeded.

colour-sergeant: the equivalent in 1879 of a company sergeant major (CSM) today. He was the senior non-commissioned man in his company and was responsible to the company commander for its discipline, drill, turnout and administration.

drift: natural river crossing, ford.

GOC: General Officer Commanding. In this case GOC South Africa – the senior British officer in the colony.

horns of the buffalo: the Zulu battle formation aimed at achieving the rapid double envelopment, encirclement and consequent destruction of an enemy. In Zulu, *impondo zankomo*, or 'the beast's horns'.

ibutho (plural amabutho): a Zulu regiment formed by mustering the youths of a new generation into a formed and disciplined body of troops. Hence a Zulu army consisted of a number of *amabutho* in or approaching middle age (typically kept in reserve), *amabutho* in their early twenties (which were usually assigned to the horns), and *amabutho* in the prime of life (normally assigned to the 'chest' or centre).

IMI: Imperial Mounted Infantry. Detachments of regular infantrymen mounted on African ponies. Although such units were formed in lieu of regular cavalry, they were incapable of shock action and customarily dismounted to fight on foot.

impi: a Zulu army consisting of a number of *amabutho*.

induna (plural izinduna): a Zulu headman or officer-grade leader in an *ibutho*.

isiGqoza: a Zulu faction forced to flee to Natal after the war of succession fought to determine King Mpande's successor; they had opposed Cetshwayo and thus found themselves on the losing side. When the NNC was levied, they found Nos. 8, 9 and 10 Companies in Maori Browne's 1st/3rd NNC.

ka: used in Zulu as a prefix to mean 'son of'; hence Cetshwayo kaMpande.

knobkerrie: African hardwood club; a crude round-headed cudgel.

koppie: Afrikaans name for a low hill or ridge, typically covered in sandstone scree-boulders.

kraal: Though this is not a Zulu word, it was in common usage amongst the European population of nineteenth-century South Africa to describe an African homestead, village, or barracks. It survives in many modern place names in modern South Africa. Typically a 'kraal' consisted of a ring of beehive huts arrayed around a central stock pen or arena and inside an outer enclosure fence. Royal or military kraals could consist of hundreds of huts.

mealie: South African Dutch colloquial name for the cereal plant maize and, synonymously, its cob. For transportation as a bulk foodstuff and fodder, maize cobs were packed into hessian sacks holding around 200 lb.

NC: Natal Carbineers. Fashionable, part-time unit of mounted volunteers, recruited from the well-to-do families of Pietermaritzburg. Formed 1855.

nek: geographical term – in more common usage a saddle. The lower ground lying between two adjacent high points.

NMP: Natal Mounted Police. The professional quasi-military constabulary of Natal. Formed in 1874.

NNC: Natal Native Contingent. Temporary native infantry battalions levied from the black population of Natal. NNC battalions had European officers and NCOs recruited from the settler communities of Natal, or the Ciskei (in particular King William's Town).

NNMC: Natal Native Mounted Contingent. A regiment of irregular horse raised from the black population of Natal by Colonel Anthony Durnford RE. Five troops accompanied Durnford to Isandlwana.

picket (plural pickets): also 'picquet'. A picket is a group of soldiers thrown out at a distance to give early warning of an approaching enemy. It was the practice for a picket company to deploy its men across a wide frontage in groups of four. Pickets withdraw closer to the main position by night. Also used as a verb: e.g. 'it was decided to picket the heights'.

vedette: the cavalry equivalent of a picket – mounted soldiers thrown out even further afield than the outlying infantry pickets, in order to provide early warning.

veldkornet: A junior grade citizen-officer within the Boer military system. Such men were elected to office by their peers within the local commando.

voorlooper: literally 'one who goes ahead'. Used to mean an assistant to a wagon driver, usually a black in his employ, who walked at the head of the trek-oxen to set direction, to prevent the animals becoming entangled and to keep them on the move.

uSuthu: the name of King Cetshwayo's faction in the Zulu civil war that brought him to power; also a battle cry of the Zulu *amabutho* of 1879.

Index

The PRIME MINISTERS

REFLECTIONS ON LEADERSHIP
FROM WILSON TO MAY

'There has been no better time to absorb oneself in some modern political history, and there is no better person to guide you through it than Steve Richards. The great thing about Steve's book is that it helps us understand how our last nine prime ministers viewed things themselves and why they took the decisions they did.'
Evan Davis

'A pure pleasure to read. In Richards' bright, sharp portraits of nine prime ministers, all our modern history springs to life. An enlightening retrospective.'
Polly Toynbee

'Steve Richards' ability to get inside the heads of our modern prime ministers is extraordinary – some of them might even look at themselves with a new acuity.'
Kirsty Wark

'Steve Richards' excellent portraits of prime ministers are both penetrating and sympathetic. Written from his expert perspective as a broadcaster and political journalist, this book is deeply insightful about the people who have tried to govern us.'
Adam Boulton

'Steve Richards offers a real treat to readers. Covering no fewer than nine prime ministers, he displays his talents to the full: an unsurpassed grasp of the context of leadership, empathetic yet properly critical assessment of records, and a communication style that can reach out to anyone interested in politics and power.'
John Bercow

About the Author

Steve Richards is a political columnist, journalist, and presenter. He regularly presents *The Week in Westminster* on BBC Radio 4 and has presented BBC radio series on Tony Blair, Gordon Brown, David Cameron and Theresa May. He also presented the BBC TV programmes *Leadership Reflections: The Modern Prime Ministers*, *Turning Points* and *Reflections: The Prime Ministers We Never Had*. He has written for several national newspapers including the *Guardian*, the *Independent* and the *Financial Times*. He also presents a popular political one man show each year at the Edinburgh Festival and across the UK.

The PRIME MINISTERS

REFLECTIONS ON LEADERSHIP
FROM WILSON TO MAY

STEVE RICHARDS

Atlantic Books
London

First published in hardback in Great Britain in 2019 by Atlantic Books, an imprint of Atlantic Books Ltd.

Copyright © Steve Richards, 2019

The moral right of Steve Richards to be identified as the author of this work has been asserted by him in accordance with the Copyright, Designs and Patents Act of 1988.

10 9 8 7 6 5 4 3 2 1

A CIP catalogue record for this book is available from the British Library.

Hardback ISBN: 978 1 78649 587 7
E-book ISBN: 978 1 78649 589 1

Printed and bound in Great Britain by TJ International Ltd, Padstow, Cornwall

Atlantic Books
An imprint of Atlantic Books Ltd
Ormond House
26–27 Boswell Street
London
WC1N 3JZ

www.atlantic-books.co.uk

To Lachlan, who was born as one prime minister fell and as another hopeful figure prepared to acquire the thorny crown.

CONTENTS

—

INTRODUCTION

There are memoirs by prime ministers. There are biographies of prime ministers. This is the first book to reflect at some length on all the modern prime ministers, from Harold Wilson, who ruled first in 1964, to Theresa May, who entered Number Ten in the aftermath of the seismic 2016 referendum.

Some modern prime ministers are viewed more vividly than others. Margaret Thatcher and Tony Blair are still recalled with a multicoloured intensity. The explosive consequences of Theresa May's and David Cameron's leaderships will still be taking shape for another decade at least. Other prime ministers are ghostly, distant figures, even though there are many lessons from their leaderships that are urgently relevant.

This book is an attempt to make sense of their leaderships, to take a step back and look at the political stage as it seemed to them. The reflections aim to bring to life the complex three-dimensional human beings who made it to the very top – a triumphant ascent that became, for some, a nightmare when the peak was reached. Shakespeare is cited as much as other, more recent political observers. The lessons learned will also hopefully appeal to those in any field who are interested in the qualities required of leaders.

My definition of 'modern' prime ministers is based on two factors. The leaders from Harold Wilson to Theresa May were part of the television era, when a more direct and potentially hazardous form of communication with the electorate took hold. The later ones were also navigating the social-media revolution, one in which politics speeded up. Wilson became neurotically angry about newspapers and the BBC, as did all his successors at various points. Even so, if he was worried about a poor performance at Prime Minister's Question Time he would have nearly twenty-four hours to await the verdict of the next day's newspapers. Today, advisers to prime ministers alert them to the verdict on Twitter immediately after the event, while twenty-four-hour rolling television news is a constant, never-ending commentary. Wilson's immediate predecessors, Alec Douglas-Home and Harold Macmillan, faced no such pressures. Macmillan read Jane Austen in the afternoons quite often. Now even he, a lover of literature, would be distracted by Sky News and Twitter.

The other defining factor is that these are the prime ministers I knew directly or observed closely. What was written about them at the time, and to some extent since, did not seem to me anywhere near the full story. I never met Wilson, but I observed him at first hand. The other prime ministers I knew, with varying degrees of access. The purpose of the book is not to attack them from the left or the right. That has been done a thousand times before. I do not accept the political fashion that the divide between left and right has become irrelevant. On the role of the state, raging questions about how to deliver decent public services and how governments can mediate in a global economy, the left-versus-right divide is as relevant as ever. But to write relentlessly about recent prime ministers from one perspective would not be especially illuminating. Instead, based on a career in political journalism that has so far included many conversations and interviews with prime ministers, aspirant prime ministers and their numerous critics, this book aims to challenge prime ministerial caricatures. In doing so, I seek to reflect on the qualifications of leadership and on how perhaps no one is, or can be, fully equipped for the mighty tasks involved. Looking at each of the prime ministers again, I am constantly surprised by what I see – by their unexpected strengths and weaknesses.

I turn to them now, at a time of epic national crisis, partly because the Brexit drama in the UK was brought about, and then deepened, by failures in leadership. Conversely, the dangerous anti-politics mood – both a cause and a consequence of Brexit – is deepened by misreadings of leaders and politicians more generally. Some voters felt 'left behind' with good cause and ached to 'seize back control' as work patterns became fractured and public services were fragmented in the name of 'empowerment', only to disempower. But the leaders who were culpable for hopelessly misjudged policies did not act out of wilful malevolence or for reasons of corrupt venality. Their motives were more interesting than that. There is no evidence to suggest that modern prime ministers were criminal, corrupt or lacked integrity, as is widely assumed. Their flaws were epic, but had little to do with their perceived sleaziness. Yet most prime ministers left office tormented by perceptions of their rotten lack of integrity.

This book is by no means a defence of modern prime ministers. How could it be, when contemplating such a diverse group? The modern prime ministers faced many crises, and caused some of them. The deepest is the Brexit saga, one that was partly the consequence of panic-stricken and weak leadership. Indeed, the current leadership crisis in the UK is a result of the lack of impressive leaders of depth, fuelled by the vast numbers of self-proclaimed potential leaders who are deluded enough to assume that a nation's destiny lies in their inexperienced hands. Leadership is now an urgent theme in the UK and across much of the Western world.

———

In the autumn of 2016 I recorded six unscripted television talks for the BBC on modern prime ministers. Each talk lasted thirty minutes and was recorded in a single take. The historian A. J. P. Taylor was a model of sorts. In the 1960s and 1970s he spoke, without an autocue or any notes, on topics ranging from how wars start to how they end, and from Bismarck to Lloyd George. Taylor was mesmerizing and mischievous on many different subjects. I focused on the easier task of looking at modern prime ministers, the backdrop to a political journalist's life. I was keen to do so because politics on television can be cluttered and speedy. I am a big fan of letting topics breathe in order to give context to current events. Nothing makes sense without context. The series was called *Reflections on Leadership* and the prime ministers featured were Harold Wilson, Margaret Thatcher, John Major, Tony Blair, Gordon Brown and David Cameron. The talks have been repeated several times and are often available on BBC iPlayer. There were subsequent series on other themes, including one on *The Prime Ministers We Never Had*.

This book is based on those television talks, but differs from them in several ways. The chapters are longer than the original transcripts, and three additional prime ministers are considered: Edward Heath, James Callaghan and Theresa May. In the television talks there was no space to compare the conduct of the different prime ministers, but in these chapters all of them recur, like characters in a crowded Iris Murdoch novel. They recur for a purpose: the conduct of one shines light on the others.

I find the demands of leadership, and the characters of leaders, so endlessly fascinating. Prime ministers tend to be viewed at the time they are in power, and subsequently, as cartoon stereotypes. The newspapers in the UK are on the whole biased to the right and they still influence nervy BBC editors. But the much bigger bias is one that favours political fashion at any given time. This leads too often to what the former BBC director-general, John Birt, once brilliantly described as a 'bias against understanding'. I am biased in favour of understanding, partly because the characters of our prime ministers – as well as the demands placed upon them – thereby become more compelling, and not less.

One of the lessons of leadership is that fashionable assumptions are nearly always wrong. A prime minister can walk on water. Later the same prime minister can be mad and a criminal. A prime minister can be a 'modernizer', whatever that overused term means. Later the same prime minister can be hopelessly out of step with the times. A prime minister can be admirably dutiful, an assiduously committed public servant. The same prime minister can be a self-interested liar, no longer to be trusted. The extreme perceptions held in relation to the same individual do not add up. What if both are wrong? Whatever my views about her policies and their consequences, I am fascinated by Thatcher's skills as a leader. Although widely lauded by some journalists and writers to the point of deification, her precise qualities as a leader have in some respects been underestimated. The same applies to prime ministers who have been largely forgotten. Wilson, in particular, merits considerable rehabilitation. Conversely, the flaws associated with modern prime ministers are based on misunderstandings about the pressures on leaders, and a tendency in the anti-politics age to assume the worst.

Sometimes we choose to see what we want to see, or are told to see, rather than what is happening in front of our eyes. This is a lesson of leadership that I learned at a youthful age, and one that I have applied ever since. Do not assume that what you are told to see is what you are seeing. For me, this lesson took the form of a political rally that I attended in the 1970s, only just a teenager and yet drawn towards the theatre of politics.

During the October 1974 election I went to see the then prime minister, Harold Wilson, speak at a rally in north London. This was the distant era when security was less tight and anyone could get in to big campaigning events with ease. Wilson had been prime minister since February of that year, having won a handful more seats than the Conservatives. The mid-1970s were a sensational time to become interested in politics. There were two elections in 1974 and a referendum on Europe in 1975. Big politicians seemed to be on the campaign trail in nerve-shredding contests all the time. When there were no elections or referendums, the Labour government struggled to win key votes in the Commons. Parliament also became the location for epic dramas. It was no coincidence that James Graham's glorious play *This House* was set in late-1970s Westminster and became a hit in the twenty-first century. In the 1970s there were charismatic politicians lighting up the political stage at Westminster and out on the campaign trail. Politics was as exciting and unpredictable as football and almost as glamorous as rock music, two more familiar teenage passions.

Wilson intrigued me. I had read in the newspapers that he was exhausted, paranoid and useless. Some television interviewers appeared to be disdainful, as if they shared the assumptions of the influential newspapers they read. Yet Wilson was prime minister having performed better in the February election than most pundits had assumed. He was leading a country in turmoil and was planning a referendum on Europe. Coming to politics fresh and for the first time, I felt a bit like Hercule Poirot, who would often turn to his sidekick, Hastings, and make an observation along these lines: '*Mon ami*, something is not quite right. We jump to conclusions, but they are not necessarily the right conclusions.' From my uninformed perspective, something did not add up. How could a prime minister facing a range of nightmarish challenges be exhausted, paranoid and useless?

I wanted to make sense of Wilson by seeing him live during that dark autumnal campaign in 1974. As a teenager I went to live gigs as well as buying records. For me, David Bowie and the Sex Pistols only started to make much sense when seeing them perform. I assumed that a prime minister might acquire greater definition at a live event as well.

At the rally I attended during the October 1974 election, Wilson was the star turn at a large and packed town hall. The prime minister walked onto the stage to the sound of comically incongruous pop music. At first he looked old, grey and stooped by the burdens of leadership. He was dull, looked well beyond his fifty-eight years and repeated tediously familiar phrases like a machine: '…the social contract… price freezes… help with rents…' I was both excited to be seeing a prime minister live and wondering whether the media caricature was right. Perhaps Wilson had peaked long ago and this was a ghostly shadow, a prematurely aged and lifeless leader.

Then there was a dramatic twist. After around ten boring minutes of the speech, a protester threw an egg at Wilson. The contents trickled inelegantly down the prime minister's face and onto his crumpled suit. I looked on in horror, wondering what the tired, old and useless prime minister would do. Wilson looked up after the egg had landed and declared: 'You know, I'll tell you something very interesting. During the June 1970 election, after six years of a Labour government, somebody threw an egg at me like the man has just done, the one who's being escorted from this hall. In February 1974, during the election campaign a few months ago, nobody threw an egg at me at all. I think that the contest was an egg-free campaign. And now somebody has thrown an egg at me again.' Wilson paused. He brushed the yolk away from his ruined shirt and looked up again and said with great mischievous passion: 'Which goes to show you can only afford to throw eggs under a Labour government.'

There were spontaneous cheers in the hall, people were laughing and suddenly Wilson looked ten years younger. He had changed the political mood beyond recognition. For the rest of his speech he sprang into life, as if liberated by the egg challenge. The audience left raving about what a class act he still was. In the space of a couple of hours I had seen the Wilson of caricature and the Wilson who could think speedily and transform the political mood. So it was during his final phase in power between 1974 and 1976. He was exhausted, drank too much whisky, lacked much visionary purpose, viewed colleagues and others with suspicion and loathed most of the media. But he won two elections and a referendum on Europe and, uniquely, left Number Ten on his own terms. He continued to master complex policy detail while plotting several steps ahead of his internal and external opponents. His old friend Barbara Castle was convinced that if Wilson had stayed on, he would have beaten

Margaret Thatcher at the next general election. I am not sure about that, but I am certain that the fuller picture of Wilson is more interesting than the caricature. Instead, we chose to see what we wanted to see. In Wilson's case, we still do.

Much later, in the mid-1980s, the then Labour MP and former adviser to Wilson, Gerald Kaufman, told me that 'Wilson had learned to have a sense of humour'. The observation added to Wilson's ghostly enigma. He had been very funny that evening in 1974 and could use wit like a weapon. Apparently this was not a natural attribute, but one that he had deliberately acquired. He had the timing of a stand-up comic, without having a natural sense of humour. Unlike some of his successors, Wilson recognized that humour was a powerful force in politics.

Each modern prime minister has the equivalent of the Wilsonian rally – a sequence that does not make full sense of how they are perceived. In subsequent decades, Margaret Thatcher was sometimes portrayed as mad in her evangelical convictions. Edward Heath, Jim Callaghan and John Major were portrayed as useless. Tony Blair became a deranged war criminal. Gordon Brown was seen by some as bonkers. David Cameron was apparently a lazy dilettante. Theresa May was a dangerously self-absorbed leader who stubbornly led her party to the right after the 'modernizers' had taken it triumphantly to the 'centre ground'.

Again, we were choosing to see what we wanted to see. I feel like Hercule Poirot once more: none of this makes much sense. What if Thatcher's projection of shrill certainty was partly an act, at least until her final phase when her lofty and elevated status had blunted some or her sharper political instincts? Sometimes she was brutally unyielding in her simplistic convictions, but not by any means all of the time that she led. She could be smartly pragmatic, too.

If Heath, Callaghan and Major were useless, how did they survive at, or close to, the top for so long in often dark circumstances? If Blair was a thoughtlessly crusading warmonger, how to explain his sleepless mission to bring peace to Northern Ireland? Perhaps Blair possessed other flaws that propelled him towards Iraq. If Brown was so unreliably temperamental, how to make sense of his record-breaking tenure at the Treasury (the longest-serving Labour chancellor) and his focused response to the financial crash in 2008? If Cameron was lazy – the so-called 'essay crisis' prime minister, as he became known to some – how to explain his leadership of a coalition that introduced more radical reforms from the right at a speedier pace than any government in recent times, including Thatcher's? The 'essay crisis' epithet implied that he acted only at the last minute when a deadline loomed, opting to 'chill' the rest of the time. But no modern prime minister has time to chill for very long, not even the self-assured and occasionally over-confident Cameron. His reforms might have been misjudged, but that is a different matter. How was May's leadership, deeply flawed in so many ways, a leap to the right when she was the first Conservative leader since Heath to argue that the state could play a benevolent role in some circumstances and that markets did not always work? In some respects, under the influence of her close adviser Nick Timothy, May was to the left of her predecessor, but was seen as being to the right partly because, as the most tribal of Tories, she felt the need to appease the Brexit hard-liners in Parliament and in the party membership.

Step back a little and nothing quite adds up. Thatcher's claims to be giving power to the people were widely hailed, when all but the affluent were being disempowered. Blair and Cameron were portrayed as 'modernizers' without much scrutiny as to what the term meant. In some respects, both were fearful of moving on from the era in which Thatcher had cast her spell. Both paid homage to the recent past as much as they leapt away from it. May was praised for being dutiful and honest, when she was sometimes being self-interested and making assertions at odds with reality. How was Brown perceived as a stealthy chancellor when he became so well known for being stealthy? How was Wilson devious when he was so famous for being devious?

The characters of leaders are more interesting than they seem to be, but their conduct is also explained by the many actual or imagined external constraints. The modern prime ministers possess Shakespearean qualities and suffer dark fates brought about partly by character and partly by other factors beyond their control.

My favourite essay title when studying Shakespeare's plays was 'Character is Destiny. Discuss'. The instruction to discuss was a wonderful way of understanding politics as much as the great Shakespearean tragedies. Although Shakespeare's characters were creations of genius, three-dimensional and complex, their tragic destinies were determined by much more than who they were. Their fates were rooted in the wider context of the plays, the other characters, the situations they were in, the need to sustain a plot for a night out at the theatre. As my English teacher used to joke, Hamlet delayed murdering Claudius partly because the play would have ended very quickly if he had acted immediately. There were also many external factors that explained the delay.

In *Hamlet and His Problems* (1921), T. S. Eliot argued that the external factors in *Hamlet* did not fully justify the character's behaviour: 'Hamlet (the man) is dominated by an emotion which is inexpressible, because it is in *excess* of the facts as they appear.' I would argue that being told by your father's ghost that he was murdered by his brother, who is now king and married to your mother, was enough to justify all that Hamlet expressed. Either way, there was something rotten in the state of Denmark, and the rotten element needs analysing to make sense of Hamlet's actions. Hamlet's character alone did not make his destiny inevitable. Similarly, Othello was furious in his jealousy partly because he had good cause to be jealous. He assumed his wife had been unfaithful. Othello had the misfortune to face Iago. He might have acted differently if he had a less villainously deceptive ally, but then the play would have been different. Again, character alone did not determine destiny. I could write a whole book on Macbeth and the degree to which his character determined his destiny. I would argue it did so only to a limited extent.

The essay theme taught me how to view politics. A leader acts partly because of the appalling constraints he or she might face at any given time. The characters of the prime ministers matter hugely, but Wilson, Callaghan and Heath would have led differently if they had not faced economic turmoil, and Blair and Brown would have been unrecognizable as leaders if Labour had won elections in the 1980s rather than being slaughtered. Major might have been a genuine 'modernizer' if he had not faced the nightmare of a party divided over Europe. Heath might have been a more imposing leader if he had not been beaten by Wilson in the 1966 election, his first as leader and a calamitous debut.

To make sense of a leader's rule, an understanding of the context matters as much as the personalities of those who acquire the crown. Heath, Wilson in 1974, Callaghan, Major, Brown, Cameron and May faced daunting contexts. Thatcher, Blair and Wilson, in his first term in the 1960s, made their preliminary moves against political backgrounds that were benevolent. In spite of the benevolence, Blair and to some extent Wilson saw daunting constraints wherever they looked, some real and some imaginary. Labour prime ministers tend to regard themselves as imposters, disturbing the natural order, where England – not the rest of the UK – ensures that Conservative governments are elected. The sense that they have much to prove partly explains why Wilson was wary of tackling the vulnerable pound before devaluation was forced on him in 1967, why Blair went to war in Iraq in 2003 and why Brown wooed senior bankers. The Shakespearean irony is that in seeking desperately to prove they were part of the natural order, Labour prime ministers moved towards their doom.

Leaders become more interesting when situations are viewed from their nervy perspectives. They are obliged to appear in command, when most of the time they are not. If a prime minister confessed to an interviewer that he or she had no idea about the state of the UK economy at some future date, they would seem 'weak'. Yet the state of the global economy, over which they have little or no control, will play a major role in determining the fate of the UK's fortunes. Quite a lot of the time prime ministers have to act with their fingers crossed, needing to keep voters on board, a party together, an economy on track, public services at a high standard (although some prime ministers have not seen this as a priority) and to respond around the clock to a noisy media. From the outside, they can seem lofty and arrogant. From their point of view, the challenges of leadership can seem almost impossible to meet. Commentators and interviewers may attack leaders for acting weakly, evasively or bizarrely if they convey any hint of their sense of political incarceration. Yet even prime ministers with big majorities can feel trapped.

In spite of the presidential culture in UK politics and the obsessive focus on leaders and potential leaders, the qualities required for the titanic demands of leadership are under-explored. Partly for good reasons, a leadership contest tends to divide along ideological lines and did so even when UK politics appeared, deceptively, to be moving in a less ideological direction in the late 1990s and early twenty-first century. After the 1997 election, Conservative contests were based largely around candidates' positions on Europe. Polls suggested that Ken Clarke, a towering figure in the Conservative Party who had held numerous ministerial roles, was the most popular candidate with the wider electorate in the many contests in which he stood, and yet he never had a chance of winning because of his pro-European views. In Labour's 2010 contest, Ed Miliband won as the candidate to the left of New Labour, but not as far to the left as Diane Abbott, another candidate in that muted battle, which now seems like ancient history. In 2015 Jeremy Corbyn won because he was the change-making radical. He brought the leadership contest to life because he had convictions and was not too timid to express them. A candidate's views and convictions, where they stand on Europe and on the wider political spectrum, are pivotal in leadership contests, and so they should be.

Their qualifications for leadership are also pivotal, but are much less scrutinized. If it had not been for the Conservative Party's obsession with Europe, Clarke would have been a more popular and better-qualified leader than William Hague, Iain Duncan Smith and David Cameron. Clarke described his hobby as standing in leadership contests and losing. He stood against all those victorious candidates in various eccentric leadership contests. In some respects

Yvette Cooper was more suited to leadership than Jeremy Corbyn, who won Labour's 2015 contest. She did not stand a chance in spite of her greater experience, her capacity to master policy detail and her authoritative voice in the Commons. The rise of Corbyn highlighted an ache for a leap away from orthodoxies that had taken hold in the UK since 1979. Inevitably Corbyn lacked the leadership skills to make a success of his ascendancy. He became close to invisible for large periods of time after he won the contest, as the storms raged. Corbyn had been a backbencher since 1983, with no need to agonize over the demands of leadership. His sudden rise was the equivalent of a tennis player in a local park being asked to play on the Centre Court at Wimbledon. The demands are different.

The 2015 Labour leadership contest was important for marking a rare break with the past. The BBC and *The Times* newspaper were both demanding that candidates should apologize for the Labour government's 'profligate spending' – seen widely, and wrongly, as the cause of the financial crash. Candidates agonized over how to deal with this narrow, outdated interrogation. Up popped Corbyn and declared the Labour government should have spent more. He was ahead of the media zeitgeist. Soon the Conservative government abandoned its plans to wipe out the deficit largely by spending cuts. But Corbyn's exuberant ideological confidence, an important qualification of leadership, should not have obscured the obvious fact that he lacked other pivotal qualifications.

This makes politics an unusual vocation. When vacancies are advertised for senior posts in other fields, previous experience of running an organization is often specified as an essential qualification. Similarly, if a passer-by popped into the National Theatre and declared a wish to play Hamlet, he or she would be told that some previous experience of acting in demanding roles would be necessary. Playing the equivalent of Hamlet at the top of politics requires no previous experience, however. The opposite is the case. Perversely, not having any previous experience can be an overwhelming advantage. Donald Trump became the most powerful elected leader in the world by proclaiming his lack of experience in politics. In the UK, Tony Blair and David Cameron became prime ministers with no previous ministerial experience. In 2010 Nick Clegg became deputy prime minister in a coalition facing daunting economic turmoil. He had been an MP for only five years.

Yet it should be a statement of the obvious that having served as a Cabinet minister, observing and working closely with a prime minister, must be a significant advantage for a candidate seeking to be a leader and to rule from Number Ten. Other demands of leadership also transcend a candidate's convictions. Leaders must have the capacity to communicate and persuade, internally and with the wider electorate; they must manage unruly parties, giving the impression of unity when intense division is unavoidable; they must translate their convictions to policy detail and then ensure successful implementation of the policies. In the UK, responding to the media is another essential requirement. Even in its fragmented state, the media still mediates politics. Few people watch leaders perform unmediated; they watch or read from a media outlet of some form or another. In reflecting on modern prime ministers, here are a few of the lessons of leadership that I have learned.

The longest-serving modern prime ministers are Harold Wilson, Margaret Thatcher and Tony Blair. These election winners were different from each other in many ways, but shared a common quality. At their peak, they were all political teachers. They sought to make sense of what they were doing or of what was happening around them. This was especially the case with Thatcher and Blair. Thatcher was an instinctive teacher, making complex ideas and contentious policies become reassuringly accessible. Her ability to teach was helped by the fact that she did not delve deeply into the complexities herself. She seized on terms like 'freedom', 'the people' and 'choice' in ways that voters and activists in her party could relate to. Blair could frame an argument more effectively than any modern leader and would advance the arguments across all media outlets most days of the year. He introduced monthly press conferences in Downing Street, a highly effective innovation – at least for him. During the late phase of Blair's leadership, the media would be full of stories about his bleak vulnerability. Up he would pop for two hours at a press conference, putting the case that his expediency was a form of 'boldness' (one of his favourite terms) and answering all questions from fickle journalists who had become fleeting admirers once again. In his early phase Wilson, too, was a teacher, witty and evidently able, making his form of social democracy seem safe and yet exciting in its overdue modernity.

This trio – Wilson, Thatcher and Blair – won three elections each. Thatcher and Blair won two landslides each. There were many factors that explain their durability, but the common one was their skill as teachers. This is a form of artistry that is different from 'spin', an overused term that became derogatory. There is nothing sinister in prime ministers seeking to present what is happening in the best possible light. But the teacher prime ministers do more than that. They sense instinctively that voters will not listen to lists of aspirations or policies without having a sense of the values that underpin them. So few leaders, and aspirant leaders, recognize the need to explain, opting instead only to assert. They never explain *why* they are acting in the way they are. They only proclaim that their actions are the right ones. Thatcher was fascinated by the 'why' question and liked to answer it. One of May's failings, as she navigated the impossible waters of Brexit, was an indifference to explanation and persuasion. She possessed no language to make sense of what she was doing, or the skill to frame an argument. Even if she needed to be opaque to keep her party together, there were ways of making evasiveness seem purposeful. She opted for near-silence punctuated by speeches every six months or so, which sought to paper over the cracks, but never did so.

There is, though, an important twist that highlights the degree to which leadership is multi-dimensional. This trio of teachers does not represent the deepest thinkers in the list of modern prime ministers, although Wilson had a grasp of policy detail and a strategic wiliness that were a form of depth. When it came to policy detail, Blair and Thatcher often skated on thin ice. Curiously, the two prime ministers who thought most deeply and had the widest range of insights were not long-serving. Both also suffered traumatic leaderships. They were Edward Heath and Gordon Brown, both of whom became unfashionable even before they had left office, and even more so subsequently.

Heath arrived in Number Ten in 1970 with a highly developed sense of how he saw the UK's place in the world, unique for a modern British prime minister. Most prime ministers begin their time in Number Ten with no clear international outlook. Thatcher had campaigned in the 1975 referendum for the UK to stay in the Common Market and had even argued in the late 1970s that the UK should join the European Monetary System, the embryonic move towards a single currency. Only in government did she adopt a foreign policy that was tonally hostile to the European Union, while never advocating withdrawal, and that was intensely Atlanticist.

Blair was a supporter of the euro and yet he 'loved the pound' as he made his way to power in 1997, hoping conveniently to be a 'bridgehead' between the US and the EU – convenient in that the metaphor conveys diplomatic muscularity rather than incoherence. Wilson and Callaghan were opponents of the UK's membership of the European Community and yet were the two figures who secured the voters' consent for membership, when they were back in government. Cameron was an opponent of the UK leaving the EU and yet held a referendum that brought about its departure. In opposition he hinted at doubts about the war in Iraq, but as prime minister he authorized air strikes in Libya that led to a similar chaos that arose in post-war Iraq. May arrived pledging to unite the UK over Brexit and led the most spectacularly divided government, party and country in modern times. Heath was different. He was convinced that the UK's destiny lay in Europe and he negotiated its membership with an unqualified focus and enthusiasm. He also arrived in Number Ten with a deep knowledge of how government and the parliamentary party worked, as a former Cabinet minister and chief whip. Yet his three and a half years as prime minister were stormy as well as brief.

The other prime minister who could range widely, and who thought deeply about policy and politics, was Gordon Brown. He arrived in Number Ten as Labour's longest-serving chancellor, buttressed by a profound sense of political history in general and of the Labour Party more specifically. He could delve below the surface in analysing policies and the ideas behind them, the only senior figure from the New Labour era who dared to reflect on the relationship between markets and the state, the limits of 'choice' as a driving force in the delivery of public services, and who sought to claim Adam Smith as an economist of the centre left. He had regular conversations with the then Archbishop of Canterbury, Rowan Williams, as well as with authors, poets and historians. But Brown was equally at ease with the populist soundbite. He devised the phrase 'tough on crime, tough on the causes of crime', as well as 'prudence for a purpose'. He was obsessed with the media and with securing the support of Rupert Murdoch and his newspapers. Brown had range, a capacity for mastering detail and a hunger to project.

Yet his period as prime minister was around the same length as Heath's and in some ways more turbulent. Heath was never challenged while prime minister. There were several attempted internal coups against Brown, who also faced the nerve-shredding nightmare of the 2008 financial crash. He left office in 2010, having finally achieved his aching ambition to be prime minister in the summer of 2007. He dreaded being a 'tail-end Charlie' prime minister, and yet that is what he became.

Heath and Brown were very different in many ways, but had similar failings that overwhelmed their capacity for range, depth, curiosity and intelligence. Neither was good at handling colleagues, even if they commanded intense loyalty from those who worked closely with them. Both assumed that voters followed politics as closely as they did and would understand the nuance of what they were trying to do. Heath introduced a pay policy – a way of controlling inflation by restricting increases in wages, and prices – that had a certain logic to it, one that came in three different phases. Most voters found each phase an act of provocation, rather than a reasoned way of managing soaring incomes. Brown sought endlessly to make sense of the global economy, of the opportunities and the need for governments to do more to counter the downsides. Most voters paid no attention. Both men lacked empathy and were wooden as performers. Brown became wooden when he acquired responsibility for the economic brief after Labour's defeat in 1992. Prior to that, he was a lively and witty speaker. He faced the mighty Nigel Lawson when he was acting shadow chancellor in the late 1980s, and often got the better of him. Heath was never a great performer, but was at his worst by far as prime minister. Before he became leader, he conveyed a certain dynamic authority rooted in a partly unjustified self-confidence.

Both men faced complex political backgrounds when they became prime minister. Heath had been slaughtered in his first election as leader in 1966 and never fully recovered his authority. Many in his party thought he would lose again in 1970. Heath was conscious of having much to prove. He never looked a 'winner' – a perception that is hugely authority-enhancing – except for the briefest of honeymoons after the 1970 election victory. Brown waited a long time for Blair to leave Number Ten and, when he got in, faced the delicate task of indicating distance from Blair, but not too much, as he wanted the support of newspapers that had only been sympathetic to Labour because of Blair. Both Heath and Brown were partly destroyed by mistimed elections. Heath went early and lost. Brown very publicly contemplated an early election and then did not call one, fatally undermining his strategic and policy ideas as well as his public voice. In some respects, they were the two biggest figures in modern times and yet they struggled to stay afloat at the top.

In both cases, the Cabinets over which they ruled were relatively passive and united. Another essential requirement of leadership is the skill to manage the frontbench, the parliamentary party and the wider party. In the UK there is a presidential culture and yet the system is inescapably party-based. If a party is divided, a leader has a duty to bind it together. This is relentlessly tough. The much-derided Wilson had no choice but to be a party manager, given the scale of the divisions in the Labour Party during his leadership. He led a Cabinet that included Tony Benn and David Owen, Michael Foot and Roy Jenkins, all political giants who disagreed on the big issues. The largely forgotten James Callaghan was the most effective manager of all the modern prime ministers. He led the divided Cabinet that he inherited in 1976 from Wilson through stormy economic times. There was not a single resignation over policy throughout his three or so years at the helm. The contrast with May is revealing. She lost more ministers through resignations over policy than any modern prime minister. She had the excuse that she was dealing with Brexit, an even thornier challenge than the ones facing Callaghan. Nonetheless, his Cabinet had many bigger and more charismatic figures in it than May's and he kept them all on board, a smart act of leadership. Yet it did him no good in electoral terms. Callaghan lost the only election he fought as leader, in 1979.

Keeping a Cabinet and a party together is not enough to win an election. Winning elections is an essential quality of leadership, and Callaghan lost. Those who become prime minister without winning an election lead with far less confidence. Brown ached for his own mandate, but blew the election timing and had to carry on awkwardly until the 2008 financial crash gave him fresh purpose. He had a strategy to move on stealthily from Blairite New Labour for around a year and then call an election. Such was his early popularity, which he had not anticipated, that he got caught up in a frenzy over a much earlier election that he did not in the end call. May felt obliged to woo the hard-line Brexiteers in her party, having become prime minister without winning an election. When she sought her own mandate, she lost her party's majority and became weaker still, or at least she acted in a politically fragile context, even if she was largely unyielding in her approach to leadership.

Winning and governing successfully requires a UK leader to espouse and implement policies that bind members while appealing to a wider electorate. This is not easy. One of Thatcher's great strengths was to act with radical conviction while convincing enough of the wider electorate that she was on their side. In doing so, she changed her party rather than appeased it – epic leadership. Blair challenged his party's convictions and rarely appeased them, but while Thatcher moved to the radical right, Blair was more cautious and technocratic, arguing for 'what works'. No one supports what does not work. Wilson managed to excite his members and the wider electorate in the run-up to the 1964 election with his plan to harness the 'white hot heat of this technological revolution'. Only leaders at their peak can be change-makers in policy terms, keeping their party with them and winning the backing of most voters. Yet remove one of those three components from the sequence and leadership becomes impossible, or pointless.

Leaders must also know how much space they have in which to act, on what is always a crowded political stage. This is an overlooked qualification for leadership, but an essential one. Commentators will be urging prime ministers to do X or Y, without acknowledging that if they did X or Y, their party would fall apart. To be successful, he or she must be an astute reader of the rhythms of politics. What are the underlying trends? How long will a damaging story run? How far do they dare to go in terms of policy? For various reasons, Wilson, Major, Brown, Cameron and May led with virtually no room to move at all. After 1997, Blair had more room than he dared to realize. Until the end, Thatcher was smart in recognizing just how much room she had – cautious at first, bold after the schism in the Labour Party that led to the formation of the Social Democratic Party (SDP). Wilson was a brilliant operator, given the ridiculously cluttered political stage that he faced for much of his leadership. Cameron created space by forming a coalition, which he managed with considerable skill. May had more space than she realized when she first became prime minister, and then none at all after she called an early election in May 2017 and lost her party's majority. To his surprise, Brown had space during his early honeymoon as prime minister – space he made the most of until he became distracted by the temptation to hold an election. After that he was doomed, but his long tenure at the Treasury meant he was supremely well qualified to respond to the 2008 financial crash. An economic emergency cleared the stage for him and he could act.

———

Of the nine prime ministers in the following chapters, I got to know most of them one way or another and observed them all in the flesh. As well as seeing Wilson speak live, I went to the spectators' gallery in the Commons to see him perform at the despatch box in the mid-1970s. He was wily and in command, yet he looked knackered, as he did at the rally in the October election. I interviewed Heath several times, including on the night Thatcher fell from power, when he was on an unqualified and transparent high. I also interviewed him at his home in Salisbury a few times for GMTV's *Sunday Programme* and Heath usually invited us to stay for tea afterwards. He made the biggest impression on me when I was at university in the early 1980s. He came to give a talk on foreign policy and spoke brilliantly, without notes, for an hour and then answered questions. His command and range were scintillating, although he was no orator.

I met Thatcher for the first time when she was guest at our primary-school summer fete. The school was in her constituency. She was Education Secretary at the time and I had been assigned the task of showing her around the stalls at the fete. Thatcher had a go on the coconut shy and, at her first attempt, succeeded in throwing a ball with such determined ruthlessness that the coconut fell to the floor within a nanosecond. Here was a sign of things to come. She was competitive and knew her targets. Her visit was on an unusually hot day and, in her speech, she made a joke about how the headmaster's bald head was exposed to the sun and perhaps he should borrow her hat. The headmaster, Mr Sharpe, struggled to hide that he was a little taken aback by the reference to his baldness. Thatcher did not notice his fleeting discomfort – again a sign of things to come. I traded on this early meeting. She never forgot encounters, however trivial.

'Do you remember that time you were triumphant at the coconut shy at Queenswell School in 1969?' I asked her once.

'Of course I do,' Thatcher replied. She reminisced with a smile that suggested to me that, contrary to her reputation, she did possess a slight sense of humour, an awareness of how things could be a little ridiculous. I should add that of those people I have met who knew her far better, no one agrees with me on this.

I interviewed Callaghan several times, including for what I assume was one of his last long interviews, which I quote in the chapter on his leadership. He had a capacity for reflectiveness after his leadership that he did not always possess when he was in power. I observed Major at close quarters as a BBC political correspondent, although did not know him. As political editor of the *New Statesman* in the early New Labour era, I saw a lot of Blair and Brown and managed to remain engaged with both throughout their increasingly tense relationship. This was unusual. Most commentators were either 'Blairite' or 'Brownite' and were barred from contact with one circle or the other. I was seen as more of a Brownite because I recognized qualities in Brown, and his close allies, that most 'Blairite' commentators refused to see or disapproved of. But any journalist would have been able to recognize qualities in Blair, too. Both had failings. Quite a lot of their differences were ideological and strategic, although these were largely hidden at the time, and since. Roy Jenkins, a senior Cabinet minister, former SDP leader and author of weighty biographies, once said to me at the height of the New Labour era that it must be difficult being a commentator when there were only two interesting figures in politics, Blair and Brown. He compared it to the time of his political peak, when there were charismatic, enigmatic titans in both the main parties. In retrospect, there were other big figures around in the New Labour era, but they wielded little power, such was the control of the duo at the top.

As David Cameron sought to adopt some of New Labour's techniques from the other side of the political spectrum, he wooed non-Conservative commentators including me, at least when he was leader of the Opposition. I seemed to be the chosen columnist when he took trips to East Anglia. I travelled with him three times on day-trips to Norwich. One of them coincided with the height of the expenses scandal, and Cameron had to break off from the itinerary to sack someone or other from the frontbench. He acted with an elegant ruthlessness and then got on with the demands of his visit with a cool energy. He passed a test of leadership: to act with speedy brutality when necessary and then to compartmentalize. He returned to the task in hand as if nothing had happened. Blair was the best for compartmentalizing – almost eerily so, by the end. He could have a cup of tea and discuss market economics while a vain police inspector waited to interview him about 'cash for honours', an outrageous police inquiry that carried the possibility of jail for Blair and his senior advisers.

After trips or meetings with Blair and Brown, I returned with lots of notes and ideas. Cameron was something of a blank canvas. He asked me a lot about Blair and Brown. Perhaps that was the sole purpose of my trips with him to Norwich: to provide him with information. His small entourage was efficient, friendly and relaxed, perhaps too relaxed. I was surprised how high the stakes were for Blair and his advisers when he went on excursions, even towards the end of his leadership. I recall one visit with him to Manchester during which we visited the set of *Coronation Street*. I was in the car of his press secretary, David Hill, on the way back. Blair was in a different car and he phoned Hill several times to seek assurances that the trip had gone well – and this was after he had won three elections. Prime ministers are human. Blair had been battered by onslaughts after Iraq, but had been received enthusiastically by the cast of *Coronation Street* and by onlookers. He could not quite believe it, and needed Hill to make sense of what had happened. No wonder he was so dependent on Alastair Campbell to guide him through the torrents of media and public scrutiny. Brown was just as dependent on individuals, especially Ed Balls. Brown might have terrified some Cabinet colleagues and external opponents, but he listened to the relatively youthful Balls on policy and strategic decisions, often phoning him several times a day even when he was prime minister and Balls was running his own department as a relatively new Cabinet minister. In terms of policy-making, Balls was the third most influential figure of the New Labour era, after Blair and Brown.

I got to know May a little while presenting GMTV's *Sunday Programme*. The show was broadcast live at the ridiculously early hour of 7 a.m. In opposition, May was one of the few frontbenchers willing to come on live, getting a taxi from Maidenhead. I assumed she was merely being assiduous, but came to realize that wilful ambition played a part, too. She was impeccably polite and solicitous. The other regular live guest was Jeremy Corbyn. He lived relatively near the studio and was also willing to come on whenever we asked him, sometimes at short notice. The two occasionally appeared on the same programme and would stay for a quick cup of tea at the end. This was at the height of the New Labour era. If anyone had told me that one would be prime minister and the other leader of the Opposition, I would have assumed it to be a drug-induced fantasy, at least in the case of Corbyn, who showed no signs of being burdened by personal ambition. May gave no indication then of being the 'bloody difficult woman' that Ken Clarke identified during the short, eccentric Conservative leadership contest in 2016. Her obstinacy and insularity developed when she was a long-serving Home Secretary. She learned then the wrong lessons about how to lead, assuming that an unyielding insularity would work in Number Ten, as it had done at the Home Office.

In the following chapters I attempt to root their leaderships in context, seeking to understand how it seemed to them at the time, and the dilemmas and opportunities of power. Any further references to my conversations with the modern prime ministers and other senior politicians are in the Notes. These characters were all deeply flawed and, unsurprisingly, given that they made it to the top, they had great qualities, too. All are more complex than the caricatures that defined them. None had all the qualifications of leadership. Perhaps such candidates for power do not exist. But if the job were advertised in the way other senior positions are, here is what the advertisement would specify.

The Country is Looking to Elect a Prime Minister

He or she must have the following qualifications:

- He or she must be a political teacher with a skill for explanation and making sense of complex issues. This is an essential qualification.

- He or she must be able to manage a party that is bound to be divided, and must also lead that party with a sense of purpose and ideological verve.

- He or she must respond astutely to the demands of the media at any time of any day.

- He or she must link values to policies in ways that bind a party and appeal to the wider electorate.

- He or she must show a deep understanding of the wider currents of domestic and foreign policy and a developed sense of political history.

- He or she must read the political rhythms in order to assess correctly the space available to act as prime minister.

- Highly desirable: experience of government before seeking to lead one.

Voters are expected to take into account the constraints on a prime minister when making an appointment, but probably will not do so.

———

Harold Wilson was the first of the modern prime ministers to apply.

1

HAROLD WILSON

Harold Wilson is the most misunderstood of post-war prime ministers. He enjoyed a political honeymoon of intoxicating popularity, with high personal poll ratings and a generous media, from his election as Labour leader in 1963 until soon after his landslide election victory in 1966. Soon after Wilson's big election win, the way he was perceived changed wildly. Neither his ambitious senior colleagues nor much of an increasingly disdainful media sought to recognize the impossible context in which he made his many energy-draining, stressful and often successful moves. After he ceased to be Labour leader there was little desire to understand Wilson, either. Instead something odd happened. The leader who had dominated British politics during the heady 1960s and for a pivotal part of the dark 1970s became a ghostly figure very quickly. From being the most talked-about figure in British politics for more than a decade, Wilson was rarely referred to. By the time Labour returned to power in 1997 he had become part of 'Old' Labour. The Labour Party's complex past, and its longest-serving leader, were dismissed as being no more than part of a distant chronology that had become irrelevant at best.

Yet the present constantly redefines the past. After 2010, the era of large or landslide election wins had passed. Deeply divided parties struggled to govern and to oppose. Once again a referendum on Europe was contested amidst economic turbulence. Suddenly we were closer to the fragile parts of the Wilson era than we were to the landslide parliaments of 1997 and 2001, or to the 1980s when Margaret Thatcher won huge majorities. For the few who bothered to look, Wilson acquired a new relevance. There were lessons to learn. From being a ghost, he had now become a potential guide.

After the 1964 election Wilson became prime minister with a tiny majority of just four seats. Ten years later he became prime minister in a hung parliament, and then in one with another puny majority. In order to make sense of more recent events, there is an urgent need to understand Wilson, to return him from the shadows. For most of his leadership he led a deeply divided party. The policies that divided Labour included the UK's relationship with the EU – or the Common Market, as it was known in the Wilson era. Other divisive policy areas included state ownership and nuclear disarmament. After 2010 there were many echoes from the Wilson era.

Most specifically, the echoes relate to Wilson's final phase in power, which is much overlooked and yet highly significant and instructive. Those final years in power, from 1974 to 1976, reveal partly how leaders are perceived. We choose what we want to see, or what we are told to see, rather than what is in front of our eyes. What we chose to see was an exhausted, paranoid, devious prime minister who had lost all sense of purpose and moral mission. What was happening in front of our eyes was rather different.

The caricature was not a complete distortion. Stereotypes of leaders are always based on an essence of truth, and there was something to the narrowly defined image. Wilson was tired beyond his years. He was only in his late fifties and looked much older. He lacked any great visionary zeal. But he still had spark and the skill to transform a political mood. He could think quickly and strategically. He was artful. He could master complex policy detail.

The lesson about misleading stereotypes applies precisely to the last period of Wilson's leadership, which began in February 1974 and ended with his resignation in March 1976. These stormy, nightmarishly challenging years highlight vividly the need to go beyond stereotype. This is the period of his leadership that is largely ignored, to the point that it is rarely referred to. Even Wilson's best biographer, Ben Pimlott, rushes over the final phase of power. In order to learn the Wilsonian lessons, we must start at the end rather than the beginning.

The tired Wilson achieved a range of extraordinary feats in those final two years. Winning in February 1974 was one of them. He only just won. Edward Heath and the Conservative government in power at the time secured more votes, but Wilson's Labour Party won a handful more seats. Even so, that narrow win was a significant triumph for Wilson, for several reasons.

The February 1974 election was the most bizarre of modern times, taking place against the backdrop of a miners' strike, a three-day week under Heath's government and power cuts. Sometimes Britain was literally in the dark, although wisely Heath lifted some of the tougher restrictions during the campaign itself. Still, it was highly unusual for an election to be contested in the depths of winter, even if most of the lights were fleetingly back on.

Wilson's narrow win in February 1974 was remarkable, however puny the margin of victory. Above all, no one had expected him to return to power – including Wilson himself. The diaries of his frontbench colleagues from that era are darkly comic. Tony

Benn writes towards the end of the February campaign: 'I saw Harold probably for the last time as Labour leader. He was tired and exhausted.' Barbara Castle and Roy Jenkins make similar observations. They sensed that Wilson's career was about to end. Benn, who was often an astute reader of political rhythms, could hardly believe it when he was back in power as a Cabinet minister and wrote in his diary: 'A week ago, I thought I might be out of parliament altogether and now I'm in the cabinet as Secretary of State for Industry.'

In his own memoir – an important source for understanding the multi-layered complexities in relation to Wilson – Roy Jenkins wrote: 'My last encounter with Wilson before polling day was on the final Sunday afternoon when we spoke at a big Birmingham Town Hall meeting and talked for some time afterwards. He seemed tired, depressed and expecting defeat, keeping going with some difficulty and gallantry until by Thursday night he would have completed his final throw in politics. We are both wrong.' Jenkins returned to government as Home Secretary. He had been a historic reformer as Home Secretary in Wilson's previous government. After the February 1974 election Jenkins moved back to the Home Office, with much less enthusiasm for the task ahead. Soon he was to leave British politics for Brussels, before returning sensationally to form a new political party.

Wilson was at least as surprised as Jenkins to be in government once again. His senior adviser at the time, Bernard Donoughue, revealed subsequently that Wilson had expected to lose and did not want to give journalists the pleasure of seeing him defeated. Bizarrely, Wilson had planned to hide from the journalists in the aftermath of defeat, arranging for a discreet flight back to London from his Houghton constituency in the north-west of England, without appearing in front of the media at any stage. The deranged plan was for the pilot to land in an obscure part of Bedfordshire, and Wilson would then be driven away to a hidden venue. The idea was wild enough to suggest that, at this late stage in his career, Wilson had lost all reason in relation to his dealings with the media; but then again, parts of the media had given him cause to become irrational. In his early years as leader most newspapers, even the Conservative-supporting ones, had hailed Wilson as a 'modernizer'. By 1974 all the newspapers, including the non-Conservative ones, had become highly critical of him, to his despair. The BBC had also turned against him. In 1971 it broadcast a programme on Wilson and his shadow Cabinet with the provocative title *Yesterday's Men*. Both the title and the programme were not only biased, but wrong. Yesterday's men were back in power before very long. Wilson was justifiably furious with the BBC. He would have struggled with the later era of rolling TV news and Twitter, when no party leader could even contemplate disappearing from public view in the immediate aftermath of an election. As it turned out for Wilson, there was no need to attempt an elaborate escape. Instead he became prime minister again: quite a spectacular alternative route to determined anonymity.

The assumption that he would lose – often an assumption that feeds on itself – was not the only reason why Wilson's return from the seemingly political dead was an unusual triumph.

By February 1974 the Labour Party was divided in ways that made it almost impossible to lead. The divisions were unusually intense partly because there were titanic figures on either side of all the epic issues from that era. Leading is easier when mediocrities fall out with each other from within a party. It becomes a nightmare when political giants articulate conflicting visions. From the very top down, Labour was split over Europe, over whether more industries should be nationalized and over the degree to which public spending was the way out of the economic crisis or a contribution to it. These were divisions of unique range. From the late-Thatcher era onwards, the Conservatives were split over Europe, but broadly agreed with each other on economic policy and public-service reforms. Labour's leading figures did not agree with each other on very much at all.

All the titans around Wilson's frontbench also enjoyed deep support within the Labour Party. They were impossible to lead, and yet Wilson led them back into government. Those he appointed to his new Cabinet included Denis Healey, James Callaghan, Roy Jenkins, Tony Crosland, Shirley Williams, Tony Benn and Michael Foot. This group concurred on very little. In addition, most of them wanted to be leader and regarded Wilson with disdain. But it was Wilson who had taken them back to government. The Labour Cabinet formed in 1974 was the weightiest, most experienced and most charismatic of all the governments elected since 1945. The weight and charisma lit up the political stage and, at the same time, added to the burdens of a prime minister needing to manage big political egos.

There is a third reason why Wilson's return to power in February 1974 was extraordinary. After he was unexpectedly defeated in June 1970, when someone threw an egg at him for the first time in an election campaign (see Introduction), he almost disappeared from public view. He was deeply disappointed and shaken by defeat. Election outcomes are surprising in their capacity to surprise. Wilson had not expected to win in February 1974. He had not expected to lose in 1970. Almost as a way of coping with the trauma after the 1970 defeat, he kept a low public profile and spent a lot of time writing his memoirs. He was not seen that often in public. Parliament was not televised, so voters did not see or hear his speeches in the Commons. There were no TV news channels following leaders around at every hour of the day. It was much easier to disappear. And Wilson largely disappeared.

In the twenty-first century a leader who unexpectedly loses an election is almost always doomed. Indeed, leaders who lose when they are expected to do so also tend to resign in the immediate aftermath. Wilson discovered what Tony Blair would call a 'third way' – a political magician's third way. He disappeared from public view, but did not resign. He stayed on as leader of the Opposition and won another two elections.

The final two election victories were part of the underestimated phase of his career. He began in February 1974 as prime minister of a minority government. Wisely, he chose not to try to form a coalition; probably that option was not available to him. The outgoing prime minister, Edward Heath, had already sought a coalition with the Liberals and failed.

Wilson liked and admired the leader of the Liberals, Jeremy Thorpe, but kept astutely clear of any negotiation about a partnership in government. Instead when Heath moved out, Wilson moved in, the leader of a single-party minority government. He had become a smart reader of the rhythms of politics, a pivotal qualification for leadership. He knew when to make a move and how to do so. While Heath negotiated with Thorpe over the frenzied weekend after the election, Wilson was filmed walking with his Labrador, seemingly relaxed but ready for action. The only action he contemplated was to be prime minister of a minority Labour government.

If David Cameron had followed Wilson's precedent after the 2010 election, he might have found the space on the political stage to rule more assertively as a new prime minister and to carry his party with him more authoritatively. Wilson governed for a few months with a minority administration, held a second election – the one where another egg was thrown at him in October – and won a small overall majority. Almost certainly Cameron would have secured a majority in a second election if he had chosen this course, and probably a more substantial majority than Wilson secured. Being younger and far less experienced, Cameron was not as smart a reader of the complex political rhythms.

Wilson won a tiny overall majority of four seats in October 1974. He thought the margin would be bigger and was disappointed, the third successive election in which he was surprised by the result. But to win an overall majority of any sort in the context in which that election was contested – raging inflation, industrial unrest again, after a brief pause when Labour came to power six months earlier – was another electoral achievement. Above all, establishing Labour as a majority government was near-miraculous, because the party's divisions over Europe were intensifying.

In a way that Cameron failed to do, Wilson held a referendum on Britain's membership of the Common Market – and won. He won decisively. In navigating the victory, he made several moves that Cameron did not make when he held, and lost, the referendum on Europe in 2016. Cameron was a world expert on Tony Blair and New Labour, so much so that his leadership was partly an act of imitation. But he would have been well advised to spend more time studying the unfashionable Wilson, leading a party divided over Europe into a referendum.

Wilson's first smart move was to ensure that the political consequences of merely offering the referendum worked decisively for him. There is no point in a prime minister pledging a referendum, with all the risks involved, unless the offer in itself works for the leader.

He was a reluctant convert to the idea of a referendum on Europe. Like Cameron, he pledged to hold one not because he had discovered a passion for direct democracy, but to prevent his party from splitting fatally over the issue. Wilson made the offer well in advance of the elections in 1974 and his party calmed down a little. There was an acceptance that the referendum would settle the issue, that Cabinet ministers would publicly disagree with each other during the campaign and that the voters would decide.

The sequence before the formal referendum campaign was rather messier under Cameron. There was a fundamental difference. The Conservative prime minister had hoped to persuade all of his Cabinet to support the case for staying in the EU. Cameron felt an intense sense of betrayal when some of his Cabinet, particularly Michael Gove, came out against remaining in the EU. The stakes were high as he embarked on his renegotiation, precisely because he had hopes of convincing most, or all, of his Cabinet to back him.[7]

Wilson had no such hopes for his Cabinet. He knew, from the beginning of his renegotiation, that his ministers would be split on the issue. Ironically, the overt scale of the division in the Labour government simplified matters. Wilson had given up hoping for unity long ago. The knowledge of the split helped him, crucially, in limiting the significance of his 'renegotiation' of the UK's membership of the Common Market. But while the prospect of a referendum had cooled the political temperature in Wilson's party in some respects, Cameron's offer raised the temperature in his. Cameron was under almost unbearable pressure to deliver a 'renegotiation' that reassured the likes of Gove and Boris Johnson, who was the Mayor of London when Cameron first proposed a referendum. Wilson was under no such equivalent pressure because he knew that he could never persuade Tony Benn, Barbara Castle, Peter Shore and Michael Foot, four of the big Cabinet heavyweights who had resolved to campaign for the UK to leave Europe. The purpose of Wilson's renegotiation was therefore much more limited. It was a fig leaf to justify his support for EU membership, when he had opposed joining in the first place.

Before the February 1974 election, Wilson secured a significant electoral benefit from the referendum pledge. He successfully nudged the Conservative MP, Enoch Powell, to declare his support for Labour on the basis of the offer. Powell resigned as a Conservative MP at the start of the February campaign, an ominous opening to the election for Heath. The fleeting support for Labour of the Conservatives' intellectual populist in a closely fought election was a significant bonus for Wilson. For him and his party, the referendum was paying off even before he had held it.

Powell despised Heath, but as a politician, Wilson was as far removed from Powell as it was possible to be. Wilson was the pragmatic leader who had been on the frontbench for most of his political career. Powell was the right-wing troublemaker who was sacked from Heath's frontbench after his explosive 'Rivers of blood' speech in 1968 and would never serve in a senior capacity again. The impact of Powell's intervention is not easy to measure precisely. But his resignation as an MP, and his support for Labour, conveyed a vivid sense of a deeply troubled Conservative Party at a time of national crisis. Such an impression could only have helped Labour, a party that almost managed to hide its own deep troubles during the two elections in 1974.

Wilson went on to win the 1975 In/Out referendum on the UK's membership of the Common Market by a big margin – around

67 per cent voted to remain – a more historic victory than his two election wins the previous year. In terms of timing, he waited until he was virtually certain he would win. He found excuses to wait until one opinion poll after another pointed to a decisive victory for staying in the Common Market. For several years public opinion had been as febrile as it was in the build-up to the 2016 referendum on whether the UK should stay or leave the EU. Polls in the early 1970s suggested strong opposition to the UK's membership. It was far from clear in early 1974 that a referendum would deliver the result Wilson sought – one that backed continued membership. The anti-marketeer Tony Benn had been a passionate advocate of a referendum, partly because polls suggested that his side could win. Wilson waited until he was wholly confident of victory. When he called the referendum for June 1975, every poll pointed to a substantial win for the UK staying in the Common Market. This was not the case in the 2016 referendum, when polls suggested a much closer contest.

During the campaign Wilson was smarter still. He was more than self-aware enough to know how unpopular he was by 1975. In some ways he was too self-aware, one cause of his neurotic introspection. Still, in some respects Wilson was correct in his self-awareness. Voters were fed up with him, as they tend to be with any leader who has been on the political stage for a long time. More than two decades later an outgoing Labour prime minister, Gordon Brown, reflected that in the modern media age, public figures had around seven years on the political stage before voters tired of them. By June 1975 Wilson had been a leader of his party for around twelve wearying years. As a result, he took careful steps not to make the referendum about himself. He delegated his Foreign Secretary, James Callaghan, to renegotiate Britain's terms of membership cosmetically, announced the referendum at a point when the polls showed decisive margins in favour of staying in, and then he all but disappeared during the campaign. Wilson made two or three weighty interventions, but gave no one the chance to frame the campaign as a test of his own leadership and, therefore, an opportunity to kick him. His low profile made it difficult for the 'Out' campaign to suggest that voters could bash Wilson. Equally, Wilson's political opponents felt at ease campaigning for 'In', knowing that the prime minister would not acquire huge personal capital if the referendum backed continued membership of the Common Market. The campaign was not about him. In terms of personalities, the referendum was dominated by sparkling or weighty figures. Roy Jenkins, Shirley Williams, Jeremy Thorpe, Edward Heath and, to some extent, even Margaret Thatcher put the case for the UK's continuing membership. Tony Benn, Michael Foot, Barbara Castle and Enoch Powell were the main advocates for withdrawal. Wilson was almost nowhere to be seen.

In 2016 one of the reasons why some Labour voters struggled to back 'Remain' was their sense that they would be giving an enormous boost to Cameron and his chancellor, George Osborne, the two dominant figures in the campaign. Perhaps the duo were not self-aware enough at the start of that fateful referendum. Again, they should have studied the late-Wilson era, where there were lessons to learn.

Cameron did not seek to learn them. He fought a high-profile campaign, which was admirably energetic in some respects. But the referendum became partly about him and his political future. No one who wanted to bring down Wilson would have used the referendum to achieve their objective. He won without making the entire sequence partly about his own fate. He chose to be irrelevant.

In relation to economic policy, Wilson was also agile in this final overlooked phase of his leadership. He left much of the hard grind to his chancellor, Denis Healey, a formidably robust figure, and yet one who became ill with exhaustion by the end of his five and a half years at the Treasury. To some extent Wilson also gave a lot of space to his new Employment Secretary, Michael Foot, whom he hailed publicly as the great success of the new government. For a leader who was not especially interested in character, Wilson was unusually smart at making Cabinet appointments. Like Powell, Foot was as far removed from Wilson as it was possible to be: a left-wing rebel, a bibliophile and writer. Wilson had been an expedient and ambitious frontbencher for most of his political career, was no lover of books and was an inelegant writer. Yet Wilson recognized that Foot was moving towards a more pragmatic approach without reneging on his deeply held convictions. So he put Foot in a key post. As Employment Secretary, Foot was trusted by key union leaders, especially the mighty Jack Jones, General Secretary of the Transport and General Workers' Union.

At first, Wilson based the government's relationship with the unions around a vaguely defined social contract. The vagueness was deliberate. As Wilson recognized, precision would have been far too dangerous. Agreement between government and union leaders would have been impossible if the details were explored too fully. The idea behind the contract was that, on a voluntary basis, the government would deliver a social programme and some price controls that the unions welcomed, while the unions would act with restraint in relation to pay. Wilson had opposed Heath's formal incomes policy, in which limited pay rises were imposed by the government over three successive phases, so he had no choice but to hail a voluntary alternative. Heath had become prime minister in 1970 as an opponent of incomes policy, but like other prime ministers in the 1970s he became so panic-stricken that he turned towards one – in his case, a highly convoluted one.

The only problem with Wilson's social contract was that some union leaders, or their members, were reluctant to deliver their side of the deal. Immediately after returning to power, the government had ended the miners' strike by awarding a substantial pay rise, more or less what the National Union of Mineworkers (NUM) had been seeking. The settlement triggered a debate about whether the miners were a 'special case'. Unsurprisingly, other unions concluded that the miners were not, and also sought pay deals on a similar scale. Inflation soared further, although the trigger for the high inflation of the 1970s had nothing to do with the British government. The tripling of oil prices in 1973 was the context against which unions, most obviously the NUM, became more muscular. The market gave more power to the miners, as Enoch Powell recognized from the right.

In one of his final acts, Wilson performed with Wilsonian guile. Trapped by publicly declared opposition to an incomes policy in any form, Wilson set tough guidelines on pay. He insisted that they were voluntary, but that his government would use emergency powers to enforce them if the unions failed to adhere to them voluntarily. Wilson was an early pioneer of Tony Blair's 'third way'. He announced a voluntary pay policy that could become compulsory, just as Blair banned fox-hunting in a way that allowed fox-hunting to continue.

These were grim contortions. From the perspective of the Treasury, Denis Healey despaired of what he regarded as Wilson's weak manoeuvring. Indeed, most Cabinet ministers were scathing of Wilson at this late stage, although many were to change their minds retrospectively.[8]

Yet Wilson's contortions managed to keep the show on the road, more or less. Like Heath before him and Jim Callaghan afterwards, Wilson was gripped by the need to avoid the high unemployment levels of the 1930s, the likes of which he had seen at first hand during his political upbringing. He wanted to avoid strikes that could wreck an already fragile economy. Incomes policies had failed spectacularly under Heath. Wilson navigated his third way, but shared with Heath a determination to avoid high unemployment. In the 1970s there were Heath's incomes policy, Wilsonian guile that disguised an incomes policy, and James Callaghan's later incomes policy. An alternative approach arrived in 1979.

As well as winning elections and a referendum on Europe, keeping a divided Cabinet together and establishing an incomes policy that did not appear to be one, Wilson has one more claim to distinctiveness in that short period of his final premiership. He chose the moment of his departure, resigning in March 1976. He is the only prime minister in modern times to leave Number Ten according to a carefully planned timetable of his own choosing. How ironic that after years of feverish speculation that Wilson would be forced out by an internal coup, he chose voluntarily both the timing and the manner of his going. The contrast with Margaret Thatcher is powerful. For much of her time as prime minister – at least after the Falklands War in 1982 – there was not much speculation about her being forced out. Yet in November 1990 she was removed against her wishes in the most dramatic of circumstances. She never recovered from an intense, raging sense of betrayal. Wilson, who had spent much of his leadership looking over his shoulder and neurotically fearing a coup, left with rare dignity.

Few expected Wilson's departure. He had told a handful of close friends that he would go when he was sixty, and he did. He chose the timing, he chose the context and to some extent he chose his successor, in that he made it relatively easy for the senior colleague he wanted to succeed him, Jim Callaghan, to be the victor in the contest that followed. Consider the tortuous, agonized context of most prime ministers' departures. Wilson took a bow calmly, which was remarkable given all the speculation about possible leadership coups since around 1968. In the end, no one forced him out.

All his successors left in traumatic circumstances. Callaghan lost the election in 1979. Thatcher was forced out by Cabinet colleagues and by some in her parliamentary party. Major was slaughtered in the 1997 election. Blair was forced out by Gordon Brown and his parliamentary allies. Brown lost an election. Cameron lost a referendum. May left reluctantly and tearfully as her Cabinet and party turned against her. If a leader is defined partly by the manner and context of his or her departure, then Wilson is uniquely placed.

And yet it was this final period that diminished his already declining reputation. By 1974 Wilson had become, in the eyes of most voters and ministerial colleagues, an untrustworthy trickster, a leader who viewed politics purely in managerial terms, with no vision, and indeed no principle. Like all caricatures of leaders, there is some truth in this one; but like all leaders, Wilson was a complex, multi-dimensional human being. His overt expediency did not present the whole picture, nor was his wilful pragmatism a wholly fatal flaw.

His leadership in relation to Europe is one example of this. Towards the end of his leadership Wilson had a conversation with his friend and colleague Barbara Castle. She revealed the discussion many years later:

> He was a man of principle. Harold always wanted to go into Europe, but he didn't want to get too ahead of the party. In the early 1970s, I remember he was having a terrible time. He was making pathetic evasive speeches and some of his friends became very worried about him. I said to him, 'Harold, you've got to come out on Europe, one way or another.' He replied, 'Barbara, I regard it as my sacred duty to keep the party together. I know where I want to go on Europe, but I'm not going to do it if it wrecks the party.' And then he said to me, 'I've been doing this for eight years over Europe and it's been hell.'[9]

Wilson's side of the conversation is the pragmatists' charter.

He opposed Britain's membership when he was Opposition leader in the decisive Commons vote in advance of the UK joining in 1973. He did so not because he was a convinced opponent. He had no choice, as this was the position of most in his party. Wilson knew that if he had joined the forceful minority in favour of entry, his party would have fallen apart.

Originally Wilson was opposed to a referendum, but he changed his mind when he saw that it was the only way he could keep his frontbench and wider party together. In February 1974 he claimed that his support for membership would be dependent on a successful renegotiation, and he took the same line in October 1974. In reality, he had been a pragmatic supporter of staying in the Common Market once the UK had signed up. However, he had no choice but to twist and turn to keep his party together. Wilson is not alone in this. For UK leaders of both main parties, Europe has demanded wiliness attached, in some cases, to a principled strategic endgame. Wiliness is draining. Managing an unruly party is the least glamorous dimension to leadership, but is an essential demand. By the early 1970s Labour had become impossibly difficult to manage. But we tend to notice the leader's behaviour without always acknowledging the context. Plucked out of context, Wilson appeared pathetically expedient, a mere manager without vision or principle.

The caricature was partly true, as all caricatures of leaders tend to be. Behind the scenes, Wilson's management in his last period as prime minister was dysfunctional. His two senior advisers, Joe Haines and Bernard Donoughue, loathed Marcia Williams, Wilson's long-standing aide and friend. In their memoirs, both describe scenes of breathtaking hysteria. Haines reveals a wild plot that could easily take the form of a fictional thriller, suggesting that Wilson's personal doctor, Joe Stone, proposed killing Williams with a lethal injection.[10] The level of internal despair must have bordered on the deranged, for murder to be contemplated. At the height of the intense loathing between the courts of Blair and Brown, murder was never considered.

But both Haines and Donoughue acknowledge that while Williams' behaviour drove them – and sometimes Wilson – to the edge of despair, as she allegedly stormed out of meetings or failed to turn up at others, she had great strategic insights. To some extent Wilson obeyed her, a supposedly mighty prime minister following the whims of an erratic friend. But Wilson followed her advice partly because he admired her and rated her judgement on the basis of a long relationship.[11]

Marcia Williams was one of the many enigmatic figures from the Wilson era. She rarely gave interviews after she emerged from behind the scenes to take a seat in the Lords. She never spoke in the Lords. Yet throughout Wilson's long career she was a constant factor and a significant influence. While Haines and Donoughue came to view her with disdain, others liked and admired her. Even after Wilson turned against Tony Benn, she showed an affection for Benn's unfailing charm; and Benn, who by the early 1970s despised Wilson, approved of Williams' mischievous political energy. While she could be intolerant, she could also be kind. Williams was at Mary Wilson's side before and after Wilson's funeral on the Isles of Scilly in July 1995, the two of them walking arm-in-arm on the high street of St Mary's, where the Wilsons had purchased a modest bungalow. Wilson's funeral was both cinematic and restrained. On a hot day that made the Scillies seem like Greek islands, the small town of St Mary's was invaded by the stars of glossy New Labour and by those who had been unglamorously and unfairly defined as 'old Labour'. Tony Blair and Gordon Brown were there, alongside James Callaghan and Michael Foot. Mary Wilson and Marcia Williams were always side-by-side, in the public spaces of a town that briefly hosted a coming together of Labour's generations. In his death, Wilson fleetingly unified his party.

Between March 1974 and Wilson's departure in March 1976 there was little scope for arm-in-arm friendship of any sort. Like their leader, Wilson's advisers were exhausted and surprised to be there. They struggled to work together from hour to hour. There was hardly any room for vision or long-term strategic planning.[12]

Yet, at his best, Wilson did have some ideological verve as well as a deep pragmatism that could sometimes lapse into desperate managerial lunges. His leadership qualities and flaws were formed early in his political career. This is very common in leadership. The seeds of leaders' success and downfalls are often the same and are sown very early on. Most vividly in the cases of Margaret Thatcher and Tony Blair, their dark fates were sealed as they rose to the top.

So it was with Wilson. The factors behind his rise also explain his fall. As an Oxford student Wilson was hard-working, achieving a distinguished first in PPE, but unlike many of his Cabinet colleagues he was not gripped by party politics or the glamour of the Oxford Union. A key influence was his socialist-history tutor, G. D. H. Cole. In his memoirs, Wilson wrote a typically formal and distant tribute to Cole; he was incapable of flowery emotion: 'I had long held G. D. H. Cole in high regard and found this closer contact with him most congenial.' His endorsement was wooden, but it was with the encouragement of Cole that Wilson eventually joined the Labour Party. He continued: 'It was G. D. H. Cole as much as any man who finally pointed me in the direction of the Labour Party. His social and economic theories made it intellectually respectable.'[13]

These are the deadly dull words of a student most emphatically not roused by an ideological crusade. Even so, like many of his political contemporaries in both the main parties, high unemployment in the 1930s shaped Wilson's views and gave him a degree of conviction. Wilson twisted and turned on many issues, but not on what he regarded as the social and economic scourge of unemployment. Again he writes with the limited passion of an accountant explaining a tax return, but his conclusion on unemployment is climactic:

> My attitudes had been clarifying for some time and the catalyst was the unemployment situation. I had seen it years before in the Colne Valley, with members of my class jobless when they left school. My own father was still enduring his second painful period out of work. My religious upbringing and practical studies of economics and unemployment in which I had been engaged at Oxford combined in one single thought: unemployment was not only a severe fault of government, but it was in some way evil, and an affront to the country it afflicted.

For leaders, early impressions are defining. Being younger than Wilson and Heath, Margaret Thatcher dared to risk high unemployment in her early years as prime minister. For her, the 1930s were a more distant decade. Her approach to social and economic policy was determined more by what she saw as the weak vacillations of the Heath government in which she served as a loyal, dutiful and energetic minister. John Major was obsessed with the threat of soaring inflation, even though the risk was not especially high during his leadership. He had been brought up politically on high inflation in the 1970s, being acutely aware that it was those on lower incomes who felt most destabilized by rising prices. Tony Blair was defined by his party's four election defeats in the 1980s and early 1990s. For Wilson and his opponent, Edward Heath, and his Labour successor, Jim Callaghan, it was the unemployment of the 1930s that they were determined to avoid.

In the 1970s each of the three prime ministers could see that their corporatist policies were failing and yet they could not change them, for fear of returning to 1930s-style unemployment. Leaders are trapped by their pasts. None fully escape from them, even if the external circumstances of the present are unrecognizably different. We may choose to see what we want to see in our leaders. Leaders choose to see what happened in the past, rather than what is happening in front of their eyes in the present.

Wilson's own politics deepened when he worked with the economist William Beveridge on the early stages of what became the Beveridge Report on social security and unemployment, published in 1942, which led to the creation of the NHS and the founding of the welfare state. He began working with Beveridge in 1937, before joining the Civil Service. Beveridge was demanding, and Wilson often began his working day at seven in the morning. They worked long, earnest hours without any great personal rapport. Yet Wilson's views were beginning to form quite strongly at that point, combining a sense of fairness as a defining theme in politics with a forensic awareness of poverty and inequality, the statistics that highlighted the plight of the poor and some of the possible ways of addressing it. Sometimes Wilson described himself as a statistician, a term he regarded as high praise. He became a Labour Cabinet minister at the early age of thirty-one. Attlee made him President of the Board of Trade in 1947. At that point Wilson was more a grey technocrat than a future leader. He was assiduous, hard-working and conscientious, but not charismatic at all.

More than any other modern prime minister, Wilson changed as a public personality. The transition evolved long before he got to Number Ten, but it was quite a metamorphosis nonetheless. After the 1950 election a sequence took place that was to shape the rest of his career. The sequence had all the key ingredients to turn a technocrat into a leader, one who became an alert reader of strange political rhythms. To be an astute reader of political rhythms is a necessary qualification for leadership. Edward Heath and Theresa May were poor readers of the political rhythms. Most of the other modern prime ministers were readers by instinct. Wilson acquired the skill as a result of what happened in the early 1950s.

The prime minister, Clem Attlee, had become a considerable admirer of the future leader, Hugh Gaitskell. He made Gaitskell chancellor in his re-elected government after the 1950 election. On the whole Attlee was a thoughtful team manager, but at times he could be coldly insensitive in his handling of ministers. Although younger than Gaitskell, Wilson thought he was better qualified for the senior post. Unsurprisingly, having presided over the creation of the NHS, Aneurin Bevan also believed that he should have been promoted to the Treasury or given another top job. Attlee had given little consideration to managing their respective ambitions, fully formed in the case of Bevan and growing in the case of Wilson.

The two of them, Wilson and Bevan, displayed defiance when Gaitskell as chancellor proposed prescription charges in order to pay for growing demands on defence spending. This was in 1951, a pivotal year for Wilson and his party. Bevan and Wilson resigned from the Cabinet over the issue – an explosive move for a relatively fragile government with a tiny majority. Bevan's departure was much more noteworthy at the time, the glittering star of the Cabinet walking out over policies relating to the purity of the NHS, public spending and the importance that should be attached to defence spending. But in the longer term it was the departure of Bevan's more junior colleague that had more significant consequences.

For Wilson, the drama was one of great profundity. This was not only because he had resigned from the Cabinet, a big moment for anyone in a political career. His resignation taught him that managing the Labour Party was about a series of interrelated highly charged factors: how a leader manages colleagues, the ambitions and egos of those colleagues, the ideological divisions between right and left, and the danger to a Labour government when all of these factors coalesce over a single policy area.

The prescription-charge issue remains totemic and exposes a divide that continued in the Labour Party throughout the 1950s into the 1960s, and arguably well into the twenty-first century. The questions erupting in the aftermath of the resignations became familiar ones. What form should, or could, universal healthcare take? How should the demand for health provision be paid for? What priority should a Labour government give to defence spending? What are the overall spending levels required to provide decent public services? These are timeless and thorny questions.

Wilson concluded, more or less from 1951 onwards, that if he became leader in the future, one of his objectives would be to prevent ideological or policy divisions revolving around strong personalities turning into fatal opposition, which appeared to be Labour's fate in the 1950s. His own experience as a Cabinet minister who was provoked into resignation for reasons of ambition, positioning and conviction defined his later approach to leadership.

Arguably he made his first wily moves during those years of seemingly eternal opposition. There was an assumption in the party, and in the media, that Wilson was a Bevanite, largely because he resigned from the Cabinet with Bevan. Yet in the heated internal battles between followers of Bevan on the left and those on the right of the party, Wilson stood largely above the fray. This lofty positioning enabled him to appeal to both sides when a vacancy unexpectedly arose. This is about the only parallel between Wilson and Theresa May. As Home Secretary, May declared her support for 'Remain' in the 2016 Brexit referendum, but deliberately kept a low profile during the campaign. She was the only senior minister not clearly defined by the referendum – a key part of her armoury as she moved speedily into Number Ten in the summer of 2016. Wilson had been regarded as a 'Bevanite' and yet was never quite a 'Bevanite'. He got his chance to lead in 1963, when Gaitskell, then leader of the Labour Party, died suddenly. Here is another rather dark lesson about leadership, certainly in relation to the Labour Party.

The two most electorally successful Labour leaders both inherited the crown in unexpected contexts, when the previous leader died suddenly. Wilson became leader in 1963, very close to the next general election that was held the following year. Tony Blair became leader after John Smith's unexpected death in 1994, relatively close to the next general election, which many anticipated would be called earlier than it was. Neither Wilson nor Blair was tormented and undermined by endless speculation about their leadership-scheming ambition, because there was no obvious vacancy. Endless predictions about a particular individual becoming leader can kill off any chance of that individual rising to the top. In the case of both Wilson and Blair there had been no energy-sapping speculation, a framing that can make aspiring leaders seem unattractively self-serving. The assumption was that Gaitskell would be leader for many years to come. The same assumptions were in place when Smith died suddenly in 1994. In a party as full of tensions as the Labour Party, an unexpected vacancy seems to be the best context for a Labour leader to win a contest and move towards a general-election victory.

In striking contrast, those who become Labour leaders after an election defeat at the beginning of a parliament have gone on to lose. That was the fate of Ed Miliband, who became leader after the 2010 election and lost after five wearying years. Neil Kinnock took over after Labour's slaughter in 1983 and, for him, the long haul became a problem in itself. Kinnock was seen to be too often immersed in thorny party matters rather than acting as a determined prime minister-in-waiting. Theresa May gave Jeremy Corbyn a boost by calling an early election when he was still a fresh leader, albeit a battered one, having fought two leadership contests in the space of twelve months. But Corbyn did not win the 2017 election, even though the removal of May's majority was an electoral triumph for him. For Labour, the election winners acquired the crown halfway through the parliament when no one was preparing for a contest or even anticipating one. Almost immediately on becoming leaders, Wilson and Blair were seen as prime ministers-in-waiting, a flattering perception that feeds on itself. Kinnock and Miliband were never seen widely as prime ministers-in-waiting – also a self-feeding perception.

———

The unexpected death of Gaitskell gave Wilson his chance, and he performed with energetic, mischievous guile as leader of the Opposition. In a short period of time he managed to convey a dazzling modernity, even though he looked older than he was. Later the gap between his actual age and the way he looked was to widen considerably, but voters and the media chose to see what they wanted to. At the beginning of Wilson's leadership quite a lot of voters and much of the media saw youthful modernity, and at the end they saw an old man, when Wilson was more politically agile than he looked.

As a new leader, Wilson recognized the potency of wit, an underused weapon in leadership. Of the modern prime ministers, only Tony Blair deployed wit with the same deadly force. David Cameron was witty at times, but often in the style of Blair. Imitation is common in leadership. Wilson partly copied Harold Macmillan, his opponent for many years and a political figure who greatly influenced him. Often, in the case of leaders, their main opponent or the opponent they grew up with politically exerts a disproportionate influence over them. Blair was greatly influenced by Thatcher, and Cameron by Blair. With Wilson it was the often charmingly amusing Harold Macmillan whom he partly sought to copy.

Macmillan was witty. Wilson became wittier. In 1962, when a weakened Macmillan sacked several prominent Cabinet ministers in what became known as the 'Night of the Long Knives', Wilson popped up and said, 'I see Harold Macmillan has sacked half his Cabinet – the wrong half.' That was all he had to say. It was a perfect soundbite in the era before the term had even been invented. Political journalists and voters laughed with Wilson and they got the message behind the joke: that Macmillan had become fatally incompetent.

Like Blair, Wilson chose as his theme 'modernization', that overused, safe and evasive apolitical term. But Wilson framed an argument in a way that excited the left as well as other parts of the electorate that he sought to win over. He famously delivered a speech at his party's 1963 conference, the one before he was elected as prime minister, in which the central theme was about harnessing the 'white hot heat of this technological revolution'. The focus on technology made him sound entrepreneurial and modern in a way that appealed to businesses and the media, while the 'harnessing' theme gave the speech a statist social-democratic perspective. Both wings of his party, and many Conservative newspapers, were excited by the Wilsonian vision, a phrase that was soon to become a contradiction in terms.

In his early years as leader, Wilson enjoyed almost as positive media coverage as Tony Blair in his long honeymoon phase after becoming leader in 1994. But Wilson never fully recovered when the media turned on him. Being human, leaders never do. Also being human, Blair did not recover when the media, or parts of it, turned on him.

When Wilson won by a tiny overall majority in 1964, he showed he was genuinely serious about harnessing the technological revolution. He ambitiously set up a Department of Economic Affairs to act as a counter to the Treasury, the intimidating department of economic orthodoxy that dominates Whitehall. Other prime ministers had contemplated such a move, but had pulled back. Wilson acted. He put his old rival, George Brown, into the top post and told him to adopt a robust industrial strategy. Brown was a formidable character when sober, but too often he was drunk. The department never found its footing in the Whitehall orbit and imploded quite quickly. Nonetheless, the attempt at establishing an alternative economic department was an example of Wilson's radical ambition. In the early days he sought to be more than a party manager. Equally important, he had the space to be more than a manager, leading a party that was in awe of his skills and excited to have regained power. A useful way of making sense of a leader is to look at the space he or she has on the political stage. At the beginning Wilson had a fair amount of space. By the end he had virtually none at all.

Wilson won again in 1966, this time by a landslide. Many of his critics argued that the landslide parliament was his lost opportunity, a terrible failure of leadership. He had a near three-figure majority and failed to make radical changes. The criticism is valid. Wilson was already, at this point in his leadership, becoming obsessed with keeping the show on the road and managing what was becoming once more an unmanageable party. He failed to make the most of a landslide parliament, when a prime minister is much freer to act. But Wilson also suffered the near-fatal blow of a devaluation crisis in 1967, early in this theoretically malleable parliament. He was never the same again, irrespective of what legislation he could or could not have got through the House of Commons.

Here is another lesson in leadership. In the UK a formal

devaluation kills off political careers. Prime ministers do not fully recover from them. John Major's already limited authority and self- confidence never revived after the UK fell out of the Exchange Rate Mechanism (ERM) in September 1992. The Conservatives did not lead in the polls again until after their slaughter in the 1997 election – and for a long time after it. Major's life became a form of political hell from the day the pound left the ERM.[14] Wilson made matters worse by attempting to play down the significance of the 1967 devaluation. In a TV broadcast on 18 November he asserted, in relation to the lower pound: 'That doesn't mean, of course, that the pound here in Britain, in your pocket or purse or in your bank, has been devalued.' Like many prime ministers in a crisis, Wilson went too far in his attempt to reassure voters. His reputation for being untrustworthy, evasive and devious took rigid shape with the sterling crisis and his handling of it. He never shook it off.

Up until the devaluation crisis in 1967 Wilson had enjoyed an unusually good media, for a Labour leader. After devaluation, most of the newspapers and parts of the BBC went for him. Wilson, who was thin-skinned, could not bear the onslaughts. The attacks changed him. The sunny modernizer moved speedily towards becoming the wary old man.[15]

As he became warier, Wilson also had to deal with a range of internal feuding and scheming from big figures who were growing under his leadership. By 1969 there was so much speculation about his leadership that Wilson had to use a speech to declare wittily: 'You may have been wondering what has been going on in recent days. I'll tell you what's going on. I'm going on.'[16] Here is another lesson from his leadership that few follow. When in trouble, make a joke of it.

Much of the speculation focused on Wilson's most successful Cabinet minister, Roy Jenkins, a reforming Home Secretary of historic significance and then a steady, stabilizing chancellor. But Jenkins was not the only possible alternative. James Callaghan also had ambitions to lead. So did Denis Healey, who was then Defence Secretary. Tony Crosland, president of the Board of Trade in the late 1960s, had his devoted followers. In the end the ambitious rivals preferred Wilson to any of their competitors. In some respects it is safer for a leader to have lots of rivals rather than one, as Blair reflected privately towards the end of his period in power.[17]

From the left, Tony Benn's relationship with Wilson became dire. Yet at its lowest ebb, Benn could see no other option as leader. After being demoted from the Department of Industry to Energy Secretary after the 1975 referendum, Benn was furious, but noted in his diary on Tuesday 10 June:

> If Harold goes, I should think Denis Healey would take over as the strong man in a crisis, or perhaps Jim [Callaghan]. Roy [Jenkins] would not get it and I certainly would not because the PLP [Parliamentary Labour Party] would be too nervous I would lose them the election. I suppose I have a vague interest in Wilson going on...[18]

For all the media speculation about the fate of prime ministers, Benn's reflections are a glorious illustration as to why leaders remain in place. Even for those humiliated by a leader or in deep disagreement over policy direction, the alternatives are often worse.

Benn was reflecting in 1975. Several years earlier, following the devaluation in 1967, Wilson's authority was hugely diminished. The decline in his authority as leader was one of the reasons why he failed to implement Barbara Castle's White Paper proposals known as *In Place of Strife*, a framework within which trade unions could function with some constraints and some formalized freedoms. The proposals were published in 1969 when Wilson was still reeling from the destabilizing devaluation, speculation about whether he might, or should, be toppled, and a sense – widely shared in his Cabinet – that his leadership lacked purpose. Wilson could not persuade his Cabinet, let alone the rest of his party, to back the proposals. Several Cabinet ministers, most notably Wilson's successor, Jim Callaghan, had strong connections with the unions and were resistant to reform. Their resistance was short-sighted. The reforms that were finally implemented were Margaret Thatcher's, after the chaos of the 1970s.

Many commentators have argued since that if Wilson and Castle had prevailed with *In Place of Strife*, the 1970s would have been entirely different. There is something in the assertion. But Wilson acted weakly in relation to Castle's proposals, because he was in a weak position. A leader cannot become strong simply by declaring an unswerving determination to prevail. If Wilson had been in the honeymoon phase of his leadership, ambitious Cabinet colleagues might have been less stroppy. But his honeymoon had passed. If a leader cannot convince his most senior colleagues – in this case, Callaghan and several other major figures were ferociously against *In Place of Strife* – he or she is not going to get a policy through.

A leader cannot impose a policy and face a revolt that would destroy his or her leadership. Knowing that his space on the political stage was narrowing, Wilson did not seek a futile confrontation. *In Place of Strife* was a sensible, modest, forward-looking document. Its ministerial author, Barbara Castle, was on the left of her party. The paper never stood a chance of being implemented when most of the Cabinet was opposed. Prime ministers can only be strong when they are in a politically strong position.

Even so, the landslide government had one policy that Wilson personally instigated which highlights his instincts as a social reformer – the instincts that had taken shape in the late 1930s. The Open University (OU) was Wilson's big idea. He drove the policy through with the support of Jennie Lee, Bevan's wife. Lee was Minister for the Arts and reported directly to Wilson on the progress of the project. The institution became a creation in some ways as remarkable as the NHS, although on a much smaller scale. The OU opened up the possibility of adults becoming students, liberating some of them from unfulfilled lives. Later, Wilson described the OU as his proudest policy achievement. He did so with justification.

Perhaps Wilson would not have survived for so long as prime minister in the era of rolling news and Twitter, when fleeting rumours can become a full-blown political crisis for a leader in the space of hours. But he stayed doggedly in place for several more years after speculation about his possible demise began in 1968. He fought three more general elections and a referendum before resigning voluntarily.

His durability became a feat of leadership in itself. In the end, for all the frenzied speculation in the UK's media about the possible fall of a prime minister, they tend to be hard to budge. The reasons for Wilson's staying power apply more widely. Internal dissenters can rarely unite around a single alternative leader. Potential leaders worry that another rival might be victorious if they make a move for the crown. There is no single cause to justify making such a move.[19]

Despite the confidence-sapping devaluation of the pound, as the next election moved into view the economy had stabilized under the calm but determined Roy Jenkins, who replaced Callaghan as chancellor. With considerable optimism, Wilson called a general election in June 1970. But the unexpected happened, as is often the case in general elections. The polls got the outcome wrong and Wilson lost. Most polls had predicted a comfortable Labour majority. Wilson was more popular than the publicly awkward Ted Heath. The economy was performing relatively well. One of the great myths of UK politics is that a party wins when its leader is more popular than his or her opponent and the economy is doing well. Margaret Thatcher was less popular than Jim Callaghan in 1979. The economy was growing faster than had been anticipated in 1997 when John Major was defeated. Major won in 1992 when the economy was in the doldrums. Cameron won in 2015, even though austerity economics was scheduled to last at least another five years. For Wilson, the June 1970 defeat competed with the devaluation in 1967 as the event that most shook his confidence in a way that was transformative. For a leader, the sense of rejection that accompanies an unexpected defeat is almost unbearable. It is bad enough when leaders are ready for the humiliation because they had expected such a bleak outcome. The blow is much worse when they are unprepared. As with economic crises, they never fully recover.

When Wilson won again in February 1974 he did so cleverly, by focusing on the issues that he knew, almost by instinct, voters cared about: prices, the standard of living, getting the miners back to work. His personal campaign avoided the great ideological debates in the country, and certainly in his party, at the time. He simply ignored them. He was not overtly ideological, to the fury and disdain of both left and right. When Wilson did resign in October 1976, to the stunned amazement of most of his Cabinet, he gave one long interview to the BBC. When asked what his greatest achievement was, he replied in part that it was keeping the Labour

Party together in a challenging era. At the time, and for some years to come, that observation seemed pathetic and anticlimactic. Here was a long-serving prime minister. When he became leader, Wilson was far more experienced than Blair, Cameron or even Thatcher. As a leader he had experienced many intense political dramas. He led his party, one way or another, to four election victories in dark economic circumstances.

At the end of it all, he concluded that a great achievement was keeping his party together. The claim condemned him because, from that moment onwards, commentators and writers wrote of Wilson as the devious managerialist who was not up to the task of meeting the crises erupting around him. Indeed, as a leader, Wilson appeared to have ended in the worst of all worlds: being famous for being devious, therefore making it impossible for him to be successfully devious. Successful devious leaders are those that no one regards as being devious.

But in retrospect, Wilson's leadership of a deeply divided party seems like an immense achievement. Labour's election-losing divisions in the 1980s, and after Labour left power in 2010, show that a party that Wilson led for so long has an almost unique capacity for fracturing and losing elections. In the heat of all the battles during Wilson's leadership, Cabinet ministers loathed him. The political diaries are full of their anger. Tony Benn, who rarely expressed personal abuse towards anyone, noted at one point, 'Harold looked at me with his piggy eyes.'[20] Benn was often furious with Wilson. Roy Jenkins was equally distant. Michael Foot disapproved of him. So did Denis Healey.

But after Wilson died, Benn, Jenkins and others began to change their minds. Away from the intensity of all their internal battles, Benn made this observation during his tribute to Wilson in the

House of Commons: 'Harold Wilson recognised that for a bird to fly it needed two wings, a left wing and a right wing.'[21] Jenkins, in his memoir, was more generous in some ways about Wilson than he was about his close old friend and ally, Hugh Gaitskell. He recognized retrospectively that Wilson had given him the space to introduce the social reforms of the late 1960s, which were another historic landmark of that government.[22] Wilson was not especially concerned with the life-changing progressive reforms, but he let Jenkins get on with implementing them. The unlikely figure of Wilson created the space for Jenkins to legalize abortion, end theatre censorship and introduce other substantial socially liberal reforms.

So what seemed a puny conclusion from Wilson at the time – 'I kept my party together' – now seems like a titanic achievement. By maintaining a form of unity, he gave colleagues the room to be more creative than himself and led an unleadable party to election victories. His journey was tough and, apart from the early honeymoon phase, unglamorous. There were rarely moments of great crusading joy. By the end there was no ideological verve. But in some very fundamental ways Wilson's leadership was far more effective than historians have recognized so far. In the light of what happened to his party subsequently – and what happened to another prime minister who also held a referendum on Europe – they will come to realize the scale of his achievement in the future.

Wilson's successor as prime minister in 1970, Edward Heath, assumed that he was an unrecognizably different type of leader, more serious and less playful, with a greater sense of moral mission. Yet Heath was to suffer a similar fate to Wilson. He was also tormented by economic and industrial turmoil. Unlike Wilson, however, he was not to last very long at the top, partly because he was not playful enough.

2

EDWARD HEATH

Few leaders were better prepared for the tasks of leadership than Edward Heath by the time he became prime minister in 1970. Heath had flourished in the intense student politics of Oxford University in the 1930s. As a student he had travelled widely in Europe. While rising to the top in politics, his ministerial responsibilities included a demanding negotiation to join the Common Market under the leadership of Harold Macmillan, a test of any potential leader's stamina and durability. In addition, Heath had been an energetic and reforming Cabinet minister at a point when a tired Conservative government lacked momentum. Earlier, he had been chief whip at a highly sensitive and traumatic period, giving him a developed sense of how the parliamentary party behaved and how to make it behave. He was also the first leader of the Conservative Party to be elected by MPs, an authority-enhancing act of democratic engagement.

This was quite a CV for leadership, compared with most other modern prime ministers. Yet, as prime minister, Heath endured a traumatic, dark and brief leadership. His political career ended in terrible failure and a long sulk, as he observed his successor transform the Conservative Party and win landslide elections. How to explain the mismatch between Heath's considerable qualities and mighty qualifications for leadership with the hell that erupted around him soon after he became prime minister?

Such was the enduring sense of failure associated with Heath, his fall and his subsequent transparent grumpiness that these qualities are easily overlooked. They might even seem to relate to an entirely different figure than the one who ruled in troubled times, called an early election and lost. But before being elected leader in 1965, Heath had been an unusually self-confident Cabinet minister. Even more unusual, he left his Cabinet posts with greater self-confidence than he had when he arrived. He made a practical impact, implementing some radical changes with a wilful resolution and buttressed by a clear 'one nation' philosophy. Indeed, Heath was the last 'one nation' Conservative to lead his party. David Cameron claimed to come from the same tradition, and probably genuinely thought he was, but he was much closer to the Thatcherite model. Heath's politics lay well to the left of Cameron's. Although Heath was never as popular as Harold Macmillan, or acquired the same variety of ministerial roles as Rab Butler, who never made it to the top, his career before he became leader comes closest to offering a precise definition of what it was to be a 'one nation' Tory – another of British politics' overused and imprecise terms.

As a bonus for his party, seeking wider electoral appeal in the mid-1960s, Heath was the son of a carpenter, brought up in Broadstairs and therefore far removed from the Etonian grandeur that had become a problem for the Conservatives. Wilson had ruthlessly mocked the privileged affluence of Tory leaders. He could not do so with Heath. All these factors were in the minds of MPs who backed Heath in the first formal election of a Conservative leader.

Heath had another essential quality at the time of the leadership election. He wanted the job with a greater single-minded intensity than his rivals. His main opponent in the contest was Reginald Maudling, a former chancellor and therefore more senior than Heath. Although ambitious, Maudling was a more laid-back politician who fought a languid campaign. Heath was focused on winning. One lesson of leadership is that an aspiring leader must be willing to work around the clock to win. Heath went for it with tireless determination. As a former chief whip, he understood the parliamentary party, which had the vote for the first time. He worked the tiny electorate sleeplessly. Maudling had more charm and political agility, but as the contest intensified he could still relax and enjoy a drink or two. He relaxed too much.

Heath deserved to win. He was fully formed when he became leader of his party, having been engaged with politics in various forms for decades. He knew more or less what he stood for, by the mid-1960s. As far as Heath was concerned, government was not always the problem but could also sometimes be part of the solution, whether in framing new welfare policies or intervening in markets. No Conservative leader had a similarly benevolent view of the state until the election of Theresa May in 2016, when she occasionally put the case for government as a force for good – at least she did when Nick Timothy was her special adviser. At the same time Heath was driven by a desire to make government more efficient. Unusually, as a Cabinet minister, he became interested in how his departments were run and how to make them more effective. When he became prime minister he similarly resolved to make Whitehall and local government more efficient. Partly he was a technocrat, but not wholly. He had some sense of ideological purpose, too.

Heath was part of the glittering generation of politicians who went to Oxford in the 1930s. All of them were shaped in different ways by the decade that ended in a second world war. In Heath's case, he travelled intensively around Europe during university vacations. He was in Spain during the civil war, in Nuremberg for the Nazi rallies, in Salzburg for the annual festival of music and the arts, an event that attracted legendary conductors from that era. Heath also hitchhiked his way across France. Only Denis Healey, amongst the embryonic politicians from 1930s Oxford, travelled as widely and with the same level of intense fascination. Heath's journeys played a part in his youthful opposition to appeasement, an issue that threw up so many themes and opportunities for students with an insatiable appetite for politics.

Unlike Harold Wilson, and later Tony Blair and David Cameron, Heath adored student politics at Oxford. The raging themes combined domestic and international affairs in a way that meant even student politics could not be too insular or parochial. The future of the UK and much of the world was at stake. Heath's first major speech at the Oxford Union in 1936 outlined his opposition to appeasement. In June 1937 he was elected president of the Oxford University Conservative Association as a pro-Spanish Republic candidate. In his final year at Oxford, Heath was president of Balliol College Junior Common Room, an office held in subsequent years by his near-contemporaries Denis Healey and Roy Jenkins, and as such was invited to support the Master of Balliol, Alexander Lindsay, who stood as an anti-appeasement 'Independent Progressive' candidate against the official Conservative candidate, Quintin Hogg, in the epic 1938 Oxford by-election.

Heath described Lindsay, a socialist, as his biggest influence at university, although he stressed that the consequence of political discussions was to strengthen his 'innate Conservatism'. Heath became a forbidding and self-absorbed figure, deepening his beliefs as a result of contact with someone well to the left of him. He became president of the Oxford Union in 1939, his final year at Oxford. Part of his university experience was a potent brew of intense foreign-policy debates, engagement with socialist ideas via Lindsay, electioneering, campaigns, manoeuvring for posts in student politics and travelling. By his early twenties Heath had been the most politically active of modern prime ministers, taking formative stances that were unavoidably contentious at the time, campaigning against the foreign policies of the Conservative prime minister, Neville Chamberlain, while being a committed Conservative.

Yet, curiously, the modern prime ministers who immersed themselves in politics at university were not electorally successful. Heath went on to lose three elections. Gordon Brown was as comparably addicted, a brilliant and in some respects glamorous student at Edinburgh University, who dated a Romanian princess and became a youthful rector of the university. He lost the only election he fought as party leader and prime minister in 2010 or, more precisely, he did not win it. The election led to a hung parliament. Already politically ambitious, Theresa May was active in the Oxford Conservative Association and, according to the journalist and her contemporary, Michael Crick, was quite a good speaker at the Oxford Union. She lost her party's small majority in the 2017 election. Student politics help to form embryonic politicians, but are not adequate preparation for the hurdles of leadership or a sign as to who will flourish as leader subsequently.

And there is another curiosity. Some of Heath's contemporaries or near-contemporaries glittered more at Oxford and later in the

House of Commons. Denis Healey, Roy Jenkins, Tony Crosland, Michael Foot – all from the left – were more exuberant and charismatic than Heath. At some stage in their careers all sought to be prime minister. But it was Heath who became one. He wanted it more than they did.

The route to leadership was tough, but one that Heath travelled with deceptive ease. He deceived himself, as well as his party, that he would be similarly at ease with leadership. Heath was a subtle chief whip under Anthony Eden during the epic drama of the Suez Crisis in 1956, a traumatic episode for a restive parliamentary party. When Egypt's President Nasser nationalized the Suez Canal, Eden felt the need to prove his own and the UK's imperial swagger by launching a military response, one opposed by the US and a significant number of his MPs. It was the first post-war example of a prime minister misreading the national mood and his own party in relation to a military venture. Tony Blair was another who was to misread it, although Blair assumed that voters and the media would expect him to back the US in a military venture. In both cases, Suez and Iraq, there was a pattern. There was exuberant media support followed by disillusionment. Heath's task during the Suez Crisis was to maintain the loyalty of increasingly bewildered MPs and then be a key mediator, after Anthony Eden's resignation.

After Eden resigned in January 1958, Heath's duties included informing Rab Butler that he would not be Eden's successor, at precisely the point when the normally modest Butler assumed he would be. In conveying the message, Heath passed a key test of leadership. He could act ruthlessly. In addition to being the deadly messenger, he had told senior party figures involved in managing the succession that Conservative MPs would prefer Macmillan, with his textured flair, to the less publicly flamboyant Butler.

When Heath delivered the news in a one-to-one meeting, Butler was devastated. Uncharacteristically, Butler had gone so far as to prepare a prime ministerial address to the nation, on the assumption that he would be Eden's successor. Butler was rarely over-excited or unrealistic in his assumptions about how high he would rise, but on this occasion he had good cause to assume that he would be prime minister. By 1957 his career had been as wide-ranging as that of any incoming prime minister. Butler had guided MPs towards supporting Indian independence when he was a youthful minister in the 1930s; had been a reforming Education Secretary, a modernizing party chairman, a solid chancellor and Eden's deputy. This was not bad preparation for leadership, but Heath told Butler that he was not the chosen one. 'I had a sad mission to carry out, but there was nothing I could do to soften the blow. "I am sorry, Rab," I said, "it's Harold". He looked utterly dumbfounded.' Such exchanges, demanding unavoidable ruthlessness, are formative for aspirant leaders. They become stronger.

Heath also held two substantial departmental Cabinet posts before becoming leader. In each he was far more dynamic than most of his ministerial colleagues. As Labour Minister under Harold Macmillan, he was the model of engaged pragmatism. He maintained a largely constructive dialogue with the unions, regarding Sweden as a model of sorts. On a visit to Sweden Heath wrote that 'I was struck by how much employers and unions socialized together. The atmosphere of co-operation coupled with the high level of their social services, confirmed my belief that good industrial relations were both the product of, and essential to, a prosperous and fair society.'

Here was Heath's version of 'one nation conservatism' taking shape. As Labour Minister, Heath was a believer in selective forms of state intervention, introducing a Local Employment Act that provided incentives for industry to locate to areas of high unemployment. He rejected right-wing calls for a royal commission on trade unions – demands that aimed to curtail the rights of unions. Expediently but contentiously, he agreed a pay deal with the railways that avoided a strike. This pragmatism gave him the dangerously misplaced confidence that a balanced approach to industrial relations would serve him well as prime minister. As ever, the seeds of a leader's rise were a cause of his fall. Heath looked back to his ministerial past and complacently assumed that a similar approach would work as successfully in the storms of the early 1970s.

His next ministerial post also set the scene for his short period in Number Ten. Macmillan appointed Heath to be Lord Privy Seal at the Foreign Office. In effect he was Foreign Secretary in the Commons, with Alec Douglas-Home, the official Foreign Secretary, still in the Lords. Macmillan was the first prime minister to decide that the UK should join the Common Market, then consisting of six countries. Heath was the second, after his election victory in 1970. After Heath, no prime minister, with the partial exception of Tony Blair, conveyed any great public enthusiasm for the European project. Under Macmillan, Heath's task was to negotiate the terms of membership. The challenge was nowhere near as great as Theresa May's task of negotiating the UK's departure from the EU, but it was still mountainous. During the talks Heath made twenty-seven visits to Brussels, eleven to Paris and twenty-seven to other countries.

Macmillan and Heath faced an impossible barrier. Perhaps wisely, President de Gaulle saw only the deep ambiguities of the UK. The French president feared that the UK misunderstood the European project and might undermine the cause by a semi-detached approach, reinforced by its apparent close relationship with the US. De Gaulle's veto in 1963 meant that Macmillan's detailed planning for membership could not take effect. The rejection did not deter Heath. If anything, the blocking of his early efforts made him more determined to join later.

Heath did not like losing and he was difficult to push to one side. At the earliest opportunity he returned to the cause. His commitment to Europe was deep and unyielding. He was not interested in Europe as a political device to play dangerous games in the UK political arena, as other leaders were. He was committed to Europe as a cause. This made him unique amongst modern prime ministers.

In his final Cabinet post under Alex Douglas-Home in 1963, Heath was given the job that helped to define him as a significant reformer. In the dying days of the long-serving Conservative government, Heath was made president of the Board of Trade, the job that had also provided Harold Wilson with a platform in Attlee's government. Heath made more of it than Wilson. In a drab political context, a governing party running out of steam, Heath was energized. His abolition of Resale Price Maintenance, known as the RPM, had near-revolutionary consequences in terms of its impact on voters' lives.

The RPM had allowed manufacturers and suppliers in the UK to set the retail price of their goods. The effect was to prevent large retailers with greater buying power from undercutting the prices charged by smaller shops. Heath sided with the supermarkets, while taking on some powerful manufacturers and Tory-supporting small businesses. As he did so, the Conservatives' chief whip warned him that the policy would split the party – quite a warning as an election approached. Heath went ahead. The act marked a turning point in the growth of the major supermarket chains in the UK. As food shopping formed a prominent part of voters' lives, Heath had been a radical change-maker.

It took dogged determination and wilful political courage to implement the meaty reform during the election year of 1964. Risks over policy are rarely taken when elections loom, but Heath took a large risk. Again, the experience gave him a false sense of what could be achieved by focused determination in government, and in his own abilities as a dynamic policy-maker.

His successful ministerial career was partly shaped by his determined drive. Heath was ambitious and ferociously competitive, a qualification for leadership. He loathed losing and never contemplated giving up, in the event of defeat. The same competitive spirit propelled him to win the Sydney-to-Hobart boat race in 1969, when he was a long-serving leader of the Opposition and a relatively inexperienced sailor. There was a stubborn quality. He was hard to cast aside.

At the same time, he had deeper interests outside politics than any of the other modern prime ministers. Above all, music was a great passion. Even when facing draining challenges, he had time for music and to conduct concerts with a hint of exuberance never seen in his role as a leader and prime minister. The sailing helped to humanize him. Heath's boat, *Morning Cloud*, became as well known as any of his policies. Theresa May, the other shy prime minister, became fleetingly popular for the awkward dance that she performed with more gracious gyrators during a visit to Kenya in 2017. The media mocked her, but focus groups suggested that May's clumsy dance was one event in a stormy leadership that voters noticed and liked. Heath seemed more human when he sailed and conducted at concerts, more animated than when he was a political leader.

His drive was the constant factor in all these diverse pursuits. He wanted always to prevail, winning a music scholarship to Oxford University and becoming a decent musician; and not only taking part in sailing competitions, but winning them. Heath was as wilful as any prime minister in his determination to get to the top, and had fewer distractions in his burning ambition. This unyielding hunger marks out some of those who become prime minister, compared with those who do not.

Given the range and depth of Heath's political repertoire, why did his leadership include three election defeats and a traumatic, short-lived premiership? What went wrong, when so much had gone so smoothly up until the point when he became leader? Do intense political experience, inside and outside government, a deeply held sense of purpose and forbidding ambition not matter very much when it comes to leadership? Of course they do. Heath's leadership was bleak in spite of his qualifications for the top job. There are other reasons why it all went spectacularly wrong.

———

Heath's immediate route to Number Ten was a haphazard one. Most leaders of the Opposition who become prime ministers have, or affect, a sense of sustained momentum. Thatcher and Blair dazzled with energy and apparent purpose from the day they were elected leaders of their parties to the day they won a general election. Cameron also did so, if more erratically. Heath stumbled more awkwardly towards Number Ten.

The context was strategically challenging when he became leader in 1965. The Conservatives had been in power for thirteen years, losing to Labour narrowly in 1964. For a long-serving governing party, electoral defeat is unavoidably devastating. Leading figures tend to be exhausted after being senior ministers. They are also unused to the intense but different demands of Opposition. In this case, the Conservatives were facing a dazzling and wily Harold Wilson at his peak. Why did they lose in 1964? Was there comfort in the narrowness of their defeat, or was that a complacent interpretation of the way their party was perceived? Heath was keenly interested in the questions, as any leader would be, but he lacked the magician's art of making his answers seem big and compelling. Being leader of the Opposition is partly an art form. He or she has only words to make an impact and cannot be tested by policy implementation. Heath was not especially interested in words or projection. Although more passionate about the arts than any other modern prime minister, he was not a political artist.

In his first party conference speech as leader in October 1965, Heath did what David Cameron was to do later, in a more expansive manner. He portrayed Labour as backward-looking compared with the Conservatives:

> It is no paradox, strange though it may seem, that in a period of rapid change like this, what the nation needs is leadership from a progressive and modern Conservative Party, for it is only we Conservatives who will get moving and seize the opportunities which exist for us as a country. It is only we Conservatives who will act, and it is only we Conservatives who will remember and care, as change goes on, for the individuals – and there are always many who find it difficult and uncomfortable. Above all, it is only the Conservatives

who will have the foresight and the sense of history to keep and protect those elements which are fundamental and valuable in our society, to keep the things which make this country the place where we want to live.

Influenced by New Labour, Cameron made 'change' his defining motif when he became party leader. Heath was a more substantial figure than Cameron and yet he was not interested in framing big themes to match his assertions. To claim his party was the 'progressive' option was an act of counter-intuitive provocation that might have led him towards fertile terrain. But Heath chose not to develop the narrative. During his leadership there were not many further references in the years to come to a modern and progressive Conservative Party.

Instead, the narrative was confused and blurred. Heath was much more gripped by policy, the details of policy and determined implementation, an interest that was to his credit and a necessary qualification for muscular leadership. Yet in opposition after so long in government, any party needs a leader who can bring people together in an exercise of political renewal. The Conservatives elected a political loner, who preferred to work with a small number of trusted and largely devoted advisers. Heath was not one who could easily inspire.

When voters got a chance to give their initial verdict on the party's first elected leader, Heath was slaughtered. In 1966, the year after he won the leadership, Labour won a landslide, a nearly 100-seat majority. This was ominous for the Conservatives. Heath was the fresh leader on the scene, and yet Wilson shone more brightly. In an era when television was beginning to dominate election coverage, Heath was wooden and humourless. During an election campaign or outside one, he had no great interest in how messages were conveyed in the medium that was watched by millions of voters. During his leadership, even when prime minister, a year could pass without Heath giving a TV interview. Many modern leaders are fascinated by television and how they come across on the screen. Heath could be self-obsessed but, again like Theresa May, he gave little thought as to how he was seen or, indeed, whether he was seen. Such reticence defined the way Heath and May were perceived, unhelpfully from their points of view.

The 1966 election defeat was hugely significant for Heath's leadership. On one level, he carried on as if not much had happened. Landslide defeats would wreck the confidence of most leaders and fatally undermine a party's backing of a leader. This was not the case with Heath in 1966. He concluded, without hesitation, that he had only been elected leader a short time before the general election; he could not be held responsible for a calamitous defeat, as there had been no time for him to revive his party's fortunes. Characteristically, he did not for one nanosecond contemplate resignation. Less characteristically, his party did not consider removing him, either. Both leader and party decided that another leadership contest was out of the question. Heath was given more time to make his mark.

Yet on another level, the defeat framed Heath's leadership. He had lost, outwitted in every way by Wilson. Although he and his party carried on without contemplating a change of tack, he had less space than other Opposition leaders to impose his will. So early on he was a loser. Only perceived winners have the space on the political stage to do as they want. This unflattering context – an early calamitous election defeat – explains partly why a leader with a clear and coherent sense of ideas did not convey momentum and direction. A loser is rarely allowed the luxury of perceived clarity and dynamism.

His party had its doubts about Heath, and part of his mission was to reassure rather than inspire. After the 1966 election he became incoherent as a leader. The late 1960s represented an odd phase in political leadership. After the trauma of devaluation, industrial disputes and a failure to win Cabinet support for trade-union reform, as proposed in the White Paper *In Place of Strife*, Harold Wilson had lost his way, or was widely perceived to have done so. Yet Heath had not found his. He had been more suited to government than to the performance art of opposition.

There were few moments that attracted great game-changing attention as Heath made his publicly awkward moves towards the 1970 election. He courageously sacked Enoch Powell from his frontbench after Powell delivered his deliberately provocative and immediately notorious 'Rivers of blood' speech in 1968. Powell had a following in the Conservative Party and could hold a conference hall with mannered but intoxicating oratory. Heath's act was a commanding and, to some extent, defining act of his leadership.

Yet at the Selsdon Park Hotel gathering of the shadow Cabinet in 1970, shortly before the general election of that year, Heath appeared to move towards Powell in terms of economic policy. More precisely, he allowed Harold Wilson to frame the way he was perceived, as a result of an uneventful and shapeless meeting of his frontbench team. The meeting, soon to be mythologized, was to discuss strategy and ideas, with an election moving close into view. In reality, the event was meandering and inconclusive. The sole radical idea floated at the meeting was that the NHS should meet only 80 per cent of treatment costs, with individuals taking out insurance to meet the other 20 per cent – a form of electoral suicide that was rejected speedily by Heath's shadow chancellor, Iain Macleod. Nothing much else of any significance was agreed.

Selsdon was a talking shop for frontbenchers. Like most leaders, Heath was wary of deciding a programme with an entire shadow Cabinet. But political journalists had turned up at Selsdon Park expecting some exciting developments. Macleod, a former editor of *The Spectator*, alert to the rhythms of news, recognized the need to generate some headlines.

As a result, Macleod persuaded those present that even though they hadn't decided anything, they should at least give the impression of being decisive, so he drafted a statement that expressed general support for law and order, trade-union reform, tougher immigration controls and the free market. Since it proved to be a slack week for news, the Selsdon Park conference was widely reported and interpreted as evidence that the Conservative Party had swung to the right.

This was a view that Harold Wilson was only too willing to endorse and he coined the term 'Selsdon Man' in response, even though Heath did not regard the meeting at Selsdon as signifying the adoption of any kind of new political philosophy. On the other hand, he did little to contradict the impression, since it served his purposes at the time to be seen as offering something new to the British electorate. Distinctiveness was not what Wilson had in mind when he invented the term. Wilson meant that Heath had leapt to the right – what he assumed would be the vote-losing right.

Heath sent out conflicting messages, misunderstanding one of the fundamental requirements of his role: an Opposition leader must at least convey a sense of determined coherence even if, in reality, much is incoherent. His close allies were convinced of his moderate 'one nation' philosophy and yet Heath did little to challenge the mythology around Selsdon in the build-up to the 1970 election.

Unsurprisingly, his government became confused, following the election held in the same year. Was it going to be tough on unions, as implied by 'Selsdon Man', or closer to Heath's approach as a conciliatory Labour Minister? Was it to be a small-state, free-market government, as 'Selsdon' appeared to suggest, or take a more balanced approach, as Heath's closest allies assumed? There were gaping gaps in the programmes of Wilson, Blair and Thatcher when they were in opposition, but in their very different ways the three leaders knew where they wanted to go in government and spoke accordingly. Heath was less clear. In opposition, what is said and done has a huge influence on a leader in government. Blair's equivocation about a single currency, when in opposition, made it much harder for him to put the case to join, as prime minister. Thatcher's relative caution in the build-up to the 1979 election meant that she had no choice but to be cautious in the immediate aftermath of victory. Indifferent to framing a narrative in opposition, Heath became a prime minister who was too easily blown off-course, because he had not established his chosen course with clarity and in public.

In spite of his failings as an Opposition leader, Heath won the election in 1970 – to everyone's surprise except his own. His confidence had been mildly undermined by defeat in 1966, but he had plenty in reserve to sustain him. He did not rate, respect or like Wilson, and assumed voters would take a similar view, even though opinion polls suggested that Labour was on-course for victory. In this assessment Heath was correct. By 1970 the Labour government had been thrown off-course following the trauma of devaluation, industrial unrest and internal tensions as senior figures contemplated their chances of becoming Labour prime minister. Wilson in particular had lost authority and his own self-confidence.

Heath was the only alternative and he won. The victory was a triumph of endurance: five years as an Opposition leader, which included a big election defeat. With one exception, the night of the victory was the best in Heath's career. The exception was the celebratory mood on 1 January 1973 when the UK joined the Common Market.

Heath had been a relatively weak leader of the Opposition, never fully recovering from being defeated in 1966. The weakness led him to convey unclear messages as to what his governing philosophy would be. But that did not mean Heath arrived in Number Ten without a clear sense of his own ideological purpose. William Waldegrave, a close ally, elegantly defined what that was. Waldegrave understood Heath better than most and was also a stylish writer. Like Wilson, Heath was a wooden writer of prose. His writing did not save him from the unflattering stereotypes that formed during and after his prime ministerial trauma. Waldegrave came to the rescue in explaining Heath's governing ideas much more powerfully than Heath himself ever did.

The economy rationally managed; Europe as the modernising catalyst (the Treaty of Rome embodying as it did commitment to free enterprise); British industry revitalised by European competition and Europe (with Britain) returned to the centre of the world stage as equal partners with the US; a rational reform of trades union law; huge capital investment in new projects like the Channel Tunnel; a fair solution to the problems of Northern Ireland; class barriers and prejudice swept away. All this and more was to be done, and quickly (as well as dealing with the usual menu of unforeseen crises). The model was how Heath had swept away Resale Price Maintenance in the dying days of Douglas-Home's government, confounding reactionaries and lobby groups.[8]

This was a vision as dynamic as any of those espoused by other prime ministers as they walked into Number Ten after an election victory; indeed, more galvanizing than some who lasted a lot longer in power. Heath lasted for slightly more than three and a half years. Very quickly his government struggled amidst industrial and economic chaos. The ambiguity of Heath's approach in opposition was only a small part of the explanation for his inability to communicate his ideas effectively. There were several other factors.

———

Partly, Heath was an unlucky prime minister. Only Gordon Brown could compete in terms of misfortune, soon after he moved into Number Ten. There is a cliché that leaders create their own luck. That is true to a limited extent, but leaders need luck that extends well beyond their own orbit of control. Heath had none.

His first misfortune was also a tragedy, and happened almost immediately after the 1970 election. Heath's chancellor, Iain Macleod, died of a heart attack in July. Prime ministers' choice of chancellor is nearly always central to their fate. Even though Geoffrey Howe came to annoy Margaret Thatcher intensely, he was an indispensable architect of Thatcherism, arguably more so in terms of policy detail than the lady herself. If Howe had disappeared in the summer of 1979, with his early budgets already written and his dogged capacity to turn her instinct for slogans into substantial economic policy, she would have wobbled even more than she did in her early years. Without Gordon Brown, Tony Blair would have had no economic policy; there was no one sitting around his Cabinet table qualified to replace Brown in 1997. David Cameron would have been lost without George Osborne, who arguably had even more space than Brown to shape policy and strategy.

Macleod had the potential to be as significant for Heath as those chancellors were for Thatcher, Blair and Cameron. He was a stylish counterpart to the awkward new prime minister, with an interest in communication and language that Heath lacked. Macleod had been editor of *The Spectator* and could sparkle when making speeches. He was loyal to Heath and shared a similar 'one nation' outlook, in a party already starting to show embryonic signs of the divide that Thatcher was to describe at the end of the 1970s as 'wets' v. 'dries'. From Thatcher's perspective, the 'wets' were the villains, opposing her monetarist policies and her opposition to intervening very much as unemployment soared. The 'dries' were her supporters. Heath and Macleod were embryonic 'wets'. Macleod had an economic programme of sorts, even if the perceptive and constantly curious Roy Jenkins sensed that Heath and Macleod were too alike, both unable for virtuous reasons to contemplate higher unemployment, while being confused in their attitudes towards the role of the state as an intervening force.

But for a prime minister to have a sophisticated, loyal chancellor with similar views and a greater capacity to communicate than him, there were only upsides. These were never realized. After Macleod's death, Heath replaced him with a middle-ranking mediocrity. Anthony Barber was propelled into the Treasury suddenly, without a thought-through set of economic ideas and policies. From the beginning he lacked weight, authority and a clear sense of purpose – unsurprising as Barber had no idea he was going to be chancellor in a new government, a role that demands years of preparation, until he became one. In effect Heath became his own chancellor, determining the oscillating economic policies. For leaders, such autonomy never works. When Thatcher sought to give her adviser Alan Walters too much influence over economic policy, she began to sow further seeds of her demise. Her second chancellor, Nigel Lawson, resigned at the attempted dominance. By instinct a control freak, Heath had even greater control freakery thrust upon him with the death of his key Cabinet colleague. It was a personal tragedy beyond Heath's control that began the dark sequence of events.

Other forms of misfortune partly determined Heath's fate. There was little he could do to stop war erupting between Israel and a number of states in the Middle East in October 1973. In response to the conflict, the Arab members of the Organization of the Petroleum Exporting Countries (OPEC) implemented an oil embargo for some countries and a quadrupling of oil prices for others. For Heath, the timing was a nightmare. The National Union of Mineworkers imposed an overtime ban in November 1973, with the aim of securing pay increases well above the limits of Heath's incomes policy. Heath might have been able to cope with the miners' strike, but faced also with reduced oil imports and higher energy prices, he had no choice but to introduce a state of emergency in December.

He was also unlucky in his main internal opponent. Leadership is partly about managing dissenters, but Enoch Powell was impossible to manage. Heath was a hopeless manager of people, but even a tactile charmer would have struggled with Powell.

Enoch Powell was not especially ambitious in career terms, or tribal in his attachment to the Conservative Party. He was at least as content on the backbenches as he was on the frontbench. Powell was largely untroubled when he left the Conservative Party in 1974. His lack of ambition and tribalism made him a much bigger threat than any internal dissenters, who would not consider leaving their parties and hoped to be a leader of that party. Powell was immune to the patronage that empowers most leaders, and would happily sacrifice party loyalty to maintain his principles. At the same time, Powell had doting admirers in the Conservative Party and could cast a spell over them whenever he spoke. He was an academic with a highly developed populist streak, happily appealing to those voters who feared or loathed immigrants, while espousing a nationalism that became a form of defiant patriotism. He was a powerful orator, the best speaker in the Conservative Party, and flourished in front of a big audience, while being a shy bibliophile away from the political stage.

Powell left the Conservative Party and became a Unionist MP in October 1974. He was a unionist, a passionate anti-European and was opposed to Heath's many attempts to support troubled industries. Powell was most emphatically in the 'dry' camp on economic issues, although that led him to some surprising and counter-intuitive conclusions at times. He supported the miners' pay demands in the autumn of 1973 because the quadrupling of oil prices had increased their worth in the marketplace. He challenged Heath on most policy issues, from the 1970 general election until he announced that he was not standing as a Conservative candidate in the February 1974 election. Major, Cameron and May were tormented by dissenters. None of their tormentors were in the same league as Powell.

But bad luck and his erratic performance as leader of the Opposition cannot, and does not, solve the mystery of the contrast between Heath's relatively smooth path to the leadership and the wild oscillations when he became prime minister. Heath was thrown further off-course almost immediately, facing industrial unrest that was far more determinedly intense and widespread than when he was Minister for Labour in Macmillan's government. The scale threw him. Heath looked back to his ministerial past for guidance, but there were no equivalents of scale when he had engaged successfully with union leaders in a distant context.

Strikes by the dockers and the power workers forced him to introduce two states of emergency within the first six months of winning power. The need to ration heating and lighting in December 1970 led to a rush on candles. Rooms lit by candles became one of several primitive symbols that marked Heath's rule. He was supposed to be a modern leader, fascinated by how government could be organized more effectively and updated to meet the demands of the modern era. Yet voters needed candles to light up their homes within a few months of his premiership.

For Heath, what became a familiar sequence unfolded early in his rule. Lord Wilberforce, who was appointed to arbitrate on the destabilizing early disputes, awarded the power workers a pay increase of 15 per cent, a rise that implied the striking workers had a stronger case than ministers had acknowledged. At the same time, the ruling triggered higher pay demands from other unions. Heath often seemed to be on the wrong side of pay disputes. A union would make a claim and he would resist, but then an independent body appointed by his government would more or less back the union.

In spite of the early strikes, or perhaps because of them, Heath pressed on with his own plans to place the unions in a new legislative framework. His Industrial Relations Bill in 1971 was tougher than Harold Wilson and Barbara Castle's *In Place of Strife* proposals, but less severe than some of the later reforms implemented by Margaret Thatcher. Heath's plans were less subtle than either Wilson's or Thatcher's, and badly timed. Thatcher was much smarter when it came to the important matter of timing. She introduced incremental reforms rather than a single Industrial Relations Act. Accumulatively her changes were far more stifling than Heath's, but she chose her moments to act. Wilson dropped his *In Place of Strife* proposals at the early whiff of trouble from his own Cabinet and subsequently adopted the vague social contract and other wheezes. At the worst possible time, as industrial relations soured and the unions became more muscular, Heath proposed legislation that sought to define 'unfair industrial practices', the introduction of secret ballots and a 'cooling-off' period before strike action could take place. The Act eventually came into force in March 1972, but never took practical form. The unions resisted.

This is another element of the mystery in relation to Heath's rule. He sought constructive relations with the unions and yet proved to be less politically sophisticated than Thatcher, who challenged the unions only when she was confident of winning, deploying blunter instruments than Heath would have contemplated. Under Heath, many unions adopted the simple but effective tactic of failing to register with his new Industrial Relations Court, established to regulate labour laws. Within six months the government had effectively abandoned its own Act.

Unlike his career as a Cabinet minister, but with echoes of his leadership in opposition, Heath was all over the place. He wanted to tame the unions, but was not aggressively anti-union as Thatcher was. He met with them just as assiduously as Labour prime ministers did, whereas Thatcher had nothing to do with them. Heath occasionally spoke the language of embryonic Thatcherism, but when there was a steady rise in unemployment in 1971 – and despite his vaguely declared policy not to help 'lame ducks' – he authorized the rescue of Rolls-Royce in January, and

Upper Clyde Shipbuilders in June of the same year, interventions more in tune with his wider philosophy.

At the beginning of 1972, when unemployment went over the one-million mark and miners began a strike, Heath opted to intervene further, not out of weakness, but out of a long-held belief in intervention. An Industry Bill empowered his government to assist individual companies, resulting in increased state investment in British Steel and in the coal industry.

The plan was in line with Heath's moderately interventionist instincts. He had pursued similar policies when he was Labour Minister under Macmillan. Now his moves appeared to be a panic-stricken response to fast-moving events, partly because they were. He managed to make what he believed in, as a matter of conviction, be perceived as weak-kneed 'U-turns'. This was the opposite of Thatcher's leadership. Even when she was being weak, she gave the impression of being strong and consistent. Heath became trapped because he had spoken loftily of a new approach to economic policy in his final years as Opposition leader, without fleshing out fully what he really meant.

Heath's character is also part of the solution to the mystery: why was he such a troubled leader, even though he arrived in Number Ten with such weighty qualifications? As with Shakespeare's tragic heroes, character alone cannot explain destiny, but in Heath's case it played a significant role. He could be transparently self-absorbed, grumpy and rude. He did not have a devious bone in his body, but the lack of deviousness meant that he could not hide how he felt. The only child of a relatively poor family in Kent, Heath went on to be the only unmarried prime minister of modern times. He was publicly shy and awkward, while being unable (or disinclined) to disguise these qualities. If he disapproved of someone, he showed it, too. After he was succeeded by Margaret Thatcher, Heath was open about his disdain for her and the transparency of his contempt sealed his reputation as a grump. In a column for the *Daily Telegraph* in 2008 the author, Craig Brown, wrote about Heath's rudeness. It triggered so many responses from victims of Heath's insensitivities that he wrote a follow-up with examples. Here are two of them:

> My favourite Heath story is when he was on the campaign bus with a bunch of apparatchiks and journos. The bus was involved in a minor crash. No one was hurt, but one middle-aged lady was thrown to the floor and was obviously shocked. Heath immediately called for brandy, impressing the rest of the bus with his decisiveness and compassion. When the brandy arrived, he drank it himself.

The second relates to an exchange with a single journalist, as recalled by Brown:

> In his wonderful memoir, *Cold Cream*, Ferdinand Mount describes Heath as the holder of the UK Allcomers' Record for Incivility. Heath concluded an interview with the young, tipsy Mount by saying, 'I didn't realise this was going to be such a superficial interview', while fixing him with a glare of 'loathing and contempt'.[9]

Here is a key lesson: self-absorption and rudeness are disqualifications for leadership. And they are central to the failures of Heath. When he needed colleagues and others to work with him, and to want him to flourish, quite a lot struggled to find much goodwill towards him.

Like Theresa May, Heath was a poor communicator. He was almost casual in his ambiguity in opposition, and that left him in some ways unprepared for the epic demands of prime ministerial power, in particular for explaining what he was trying to do. He was even worse in government, not trying very hard, or in ways that were accessible, to make sense of what he was seeking to do.

Heath had assumed, like Gordon Brown, that leading a government was a small leap from being a successful Cabinet minister. The gulf between the two is gaping. His lofty manner – partly, in itself, a failure to focus on communication – alienated some unions, even though union leaders who negotiated with Heath in fraught circumstances came to respect him. They recognized his integrity and grounded decency in relation to issues and policy, even if he had no capacity for interpersonal relations.

When a prime minister appears to lose grip, the chaos feeds on itself. The hunger for agreement with the unions, and his desperate desire for order as his government lost control, propelled Heath to dump his previous opposition to an incomes policy. The same dark sequence happened to Wilson and Callaghan. The three prime ministers from the 1970s could all see the dangers of rigid incomes policies, and yet all three were drawn towards them as they appeared to offer some shape amidst the fearful shapelessness. At least they were a way of controlling wage inflation when inflation was starting to soar, or appeared to be a means of doing so.

Modern British prime ministers from Wilson to May all discovered that they were not as strong as they thought they were, or as weak as they had feared. In the 1970s, incomes policies and referendums were dark attractions, as an apparent response to prime ministerial powerlessness. The prime ministers thought they were an escape from political hell, but in most cases they propelled them towards their bleak fates.

Heath's incomes policy was characteristically complex. Like Brown, Heath could delve deep as he reflected on policy. Unlike

Brown at his peak, Heath misread the political rhythms that often determined the fate of policies. His incomes policy was to be introduced in three phases, a theoretically sensible attempt to impose restraint incrementally. But the policy inevitably triggered rebellions at each stage. After striving in vain throughout the autumn of 1972 to reach a voluntary agreement with the unions, Heath felt compelled to introduce a ninety-day statutory freeze on salaries. This was followed in April 1973 by Stage Two, under which pay rises were limited to £1 a week plus 4 per cent. Stage Three, unveiled in October 1973, limited pay rises to £2.25 or 7 per cent per week, up to a maximum of £350 per year.

The logic was one of phased generosity. Heath had thought through the substance of each phase with characteristic care, but failed to see the fatal dangers. Each phase was a cause for further strikes. More fundamentally, the phases were not generous enough. The miners' strike followed the introduction of Stage Three. Heath responded to the growing crisis with drastic measures, announcing a three-day week and a wider range of power constraints. TV stations closed at 10 p.m. in the evenings. Football matches started earlier in the day to avoid the use of floodlights. Like May, Heath was not a theatrical prime minister. Like May, he presided over epic, nerve-shredding political theatre.

During a cold winter, the UK was in a crisis of primitive and yet epic proportions, a darkness that Heath made no attempt to hide. In a TV broadcast at the end of 1973 he acknowledged that this would be a 'harder Christmas than we have known since the war'. This was the background to his decision to call an election in February 1974, posing the question 'Who governs Britain?' The voters replied, in effect, 'not you' and delivered a hung parliament and a few more seats for Labour than for Heath's Conservatives.

The framing of the election was typical of Heath. His question had a superficial appeal to a prime minister calling an election. Heath assumed most voters would give backing to the democratically elected government rather than to non-elected trade-union leaders. But leaders who are political artists would recognize the dangers of framing an election in this way. They would note in their multi-layered calculations that the need to ask the question would reflect badly on a government struggling to govern. Heath was not a political artist. He assumed, with his rigid stubbornness and lack of empathic artistry, that his question would produce one answer: we want *you* to govern.

———

There are in this sequence several lessons of leadership. Again, like Gordon Brown, Heath could become almost indiscriminately immersed in policy detail, assuming that if the multifaceted complexities made sense to him, they would make sense to his party and the wider electorate. Unlike Heath, Brown was gripped obsessively by the need for a strategic course, even if he lost his skills as a navigator when he became prime minister, and in his final years as chancellor. Heath never had the skills, or sought them. He acted as if what he said and did were explanation enough and that his chosen course was the one that would prevail. Heath thought his own conversion to legalized wages and price constraints made sense. At a time of rising inflation and industrial unrest, a staged incomes policy of increasing generosity and yet firm rigidity was the only available course. But he never effectively explained this, and he lacked the guile and charm to stick to the course, or to persuade others to do so.

Some trade-union leaders respected his integrity. The president of the NUM, Joe Gormley, preferred negotiating with Heath than with Wilson, whom Gormley did not trust. But Gormley still led the miners' strike that forced Heath to announce the three-day week. Thatcher had more expedient guile. She chose to take on the miners ruthlessly only when stocks of coal were high. Heath challenged them when oil prices had soared and he desperately needed the coal. He was being defiant when he had no levers to support him, and when those he was confronting had acquired incomparably greater strength in the marketplace.

Heath's misreading of the rhythms of politics brought about his downfall. He fought a mistimed election on the wrong issue. Prime ministers often get the timing of elections badly wrong, or struggle to deal with the issue of timing. In some senses the Fixed-term Parliaments Act of 2011, rushed through for shallow and immediately self-interested reasons by the coalition government after the 2010 election, liberated prime ministers from making the choice. The liberation was limited, though. Theresa May showed how easy it was to subvert the Act when she called an early election in 2017. In the light of the 2017 result, May should have studied – before she went to the country earlier than she needed to – what happened to Heath when he called one early in February 1974.

In theory, Heath could have stayed on as prime minister for nearly eighteen months longer before holding an election. He went early for the substantial reason that he could find no way through in his dealings with the NUM and other unions. He had negotiated sleeplessly with the NUM, taking over responsibility for industrial policy, just as he had done with most aspects of detailed economic policy.

In UK politics, certainly before the Fixed-term Parliaments Act and to some extent afterwards, speculation about the need for an election was often feverish. Would, or should, John Major call an election after the first Gulf War in 1990? Would, or should, Gordon Brown call an early election in 2007? Would the Brexit crisis from 2016 trigger an election? The speculation in itself can be deeply destabilizing for a prime minister. Heath was resistant to an early election over Christmas and New Year, in spite of some senior colleagues urging him to call one. He succumbed only when he could see no alternative way through.

There were other reasons he called an early election. Like May in 2017, Heath went early because he assumed he would win. No prime minister volunteers an early election on the assumption they will lose. The Conservatives were ahead in the polls, Labour was deeply divided on several policy areas, Harold Wilson was seen as tired, politically lonely and paranoid.

But Heath's framing of the campaign (the government versus the striking miners) was too crude and the timing turned out to be ill-judged. Having warned voters a few weeks earlier that they were about to endure their hardest Christmas since the war, Heath sought to win an election. There was some sympathy with the miners, not least when, during the campaign, an independent report suggested they deserved a more substantial pay rise than Heath was proposing. It was on 21 February, in the middle of the campaign, that the Pay Board released a report on miners' pay, which unexpectedly revealed that they were paid less in comparison with other manufacturing workers, contrary to the claims of the National Coal Board. Four days later there was further bad news for Heath, with the latest trade figures showing that the current-account deficit for the previous month had been £383 million, the worst in recorded history. Heath claimed that the figures confirmed 'the gravity of the situation' and the need for a new mandate, prompting Labour's Roy Jenkins to respond, 'He presumably thinks a still worse result would have given him a still stronger claim.'

Although Jenkins thought Heath was heading for victory, he highlighted the flaw of the outgoing prime minister's pitch. In effect, Heath's contorted argument to the voters could be summarized as 'Things are going so badly that I deserve to win.'

He did not do so, and Heath's attempt to cling on to power was as doomed as Brown's attempt in 2010. But the context was worse for Heath. Before the 2010 election, political commentators had thought the Conservatives under David Cameron would win the election with a substantial majority, assuming that their own hopes and partisan judgements were shared by the wider electorate. When voters elected a hung parliament, it was Cameron who was disappointed and Brown who was buoyed by a result that was better than expected.

With Heath, the opposite applied. The media and most politicians had assumed he would win with relative ease, and therefore his attempts to cling on in a hung parliament seemed more stubbornly unrealistic. He explored the possibility of a coalition with Jeremy Thorpe's Liberals, but the talks were fleeting and Heath had left office, never to return to government, by the Monday after the election. He had called an election to resolve an industrial crisis. Instead the crisis was to deepen.

Heath's meeting with Thorpe over the weekend after the February election has a novelistic quality. The two leaders – soon to be consigned to different forms of powerless hell – fleetingly wondered whether both could be part of a mighty new governing partnership. The duo could not have been more different: the shy and introverted Heath meeting up with the exuberant Thorpe.

Jeremy Thorpe's tragic fall was part of the whacky turbulence that swept the UK in the 1970s. He had been the vivacious star of the February election campaign, more energetic and mischievously charismatic than either Heath or Wilson. Largely as a result of Thorpe's leadership, the Liberals won more than six million votes, but only fourteen seats. In spite of the relatively small number of seats, Thorpe was still in a strong position to negotiate terms for a coalition, or at least he was in theory.

A hung parliament is the dream for the UK's third national political party, giving them considerable bargaining power in the formation of a government. Oddly, the first two post-war hung parliaments have turned into a nightmare for the Liberals. In 2010 they formed a coalition with the Conservatives, a partnership that nearly destroyed them at the 2015 election. Soon after February 1974, Thorpe became a huge problem for his party rather than an asset. He was forced to resign the leadership in 1976, and in May 1979 Thorpe lost his seat in North Devon as he waited to face trial for alleged conspiracy to murder. Minutes after losing his seat he was asked by the BBC's Robin Day, live on TV: 'Do you think that the fact that you are facing a trial for conspiracy to murder contributed to your defeat?' With characteristic quick-witted charm, Thorpe replied: 'Put it this way, Robin, I don't think it helped.'

Thorpe was a gracious showman who was also curious enough to be a good political listener; he was fascinated by debate and the arguments advanced by political opponents. He was also gay and a promiscuous risk-taker, in an era when it was not possible for a leader to be open about homosexuality in politics. Heath had tentatively offered Thorpe the post of Home Secretary in a coalition government. Given the scandal soon to erupt around him, Thorpe would have been a former Home Secretary before very long.

While it lasted, a Heath/Thorpe coalition would have been well to the left of the Con/Lib coalition that was eventually formed many decades later, after Margaret Thatcher had transformed British politics, propelling the prevailing consensus well to the right. When Heath negotiated fleetingly with Thorpe, the Thatcher era had not happened and was not even taking embryonic shape.

The arrangement was not attempted. No agreement was reached between Heath and Thorpe over the Liberals' support for a change in the voting system. Thorpe must have had personal doubts and did not try hard to persuade his sceptical party about the merits of a partnership with the Conservatives. Having lost his party's majority, Heath might not have had the authority to lead a partnership with the Liberals. He was finished as a prime minister, with no time to pursue developing ideas about new structures for Northern Ireland, public-service reforms, the role of the state and, above all, the UK's new role as a member of what was then known as the Common Market.

Heath left office in the bleakest possible circumstances and yet, after fewer than four years as prime minister, he was guaranteed to become a historic leader. With typical dogged focus, he was the prime minister who took the UK into Europe. In doing so, he showed the energy, resourcefulness and mastery of detail that he had deployed as Macmillan's Minister for Europe. It remains doubtful whether anyone else could have negotiated the deal, if only because no alternative leader from that era cared as much.

Given the UK's stormy relationship with the rest of Europe, Heath was attacked unfairly at the time, and subsequently, for taking an elitist approach to his mission and for not being truthful about the loss of sovereignty. A significant section of his parliamentary party was opposed to membership, with Enoch Powell being the most articulate internal adversary once more. Heath won the vote in the Commons only by offering a free vote on the issue, enabling Labour rebels led by Roy Jenkins to back him. Heath agreed to a free vote only at the last moment. The device saved him, and his dream of joining the Common Market. His reluctance to deploy the device was another illustration of how poor a reader he was of the rhythms of politics. Like Theresa May later, Heath's instinct was to opt for the attempted imposition of unyielding parliamentary discipline. As a former chief whip, he loathed the idea of free votes. Yet it was a free vote that saved his dream, enabling him to secure parliamentary backing for membership of the Common Market.

The accusations of lofty elitism and deceit about the loss of sovereignty have no basis in reality. Heath was not a natural teacher on any front, including Europe. This was a fatal flaw in relation to many policy areas. He failed to explain accessibly and coherently what he was trying to do in relation to economic and industrial policy. The same applied to Europe. He negotiated with other European leaders and put the case to the UK Parliament, where a majority of MPs was supportive even if the Labour leadership was opposed, or at least affected opposition while being privately more ambiguous.

As a result of Heath's indifference to communication, and Labour's equivocations, the UK made a historic leap without great public engagement at first. Heath was a leader who did what he believed to be for the best, but he did not have the language or the inclination to be a campaigning persuader. The likes of Thatcher and Blair never stopped campaigning. Heath never really began, when he was prime minister.

Yet he did so afterwards, and with compelling authority. When Wilson put the UK's continued membership of the Common

Market to a referendum in 1975, Heath rose to the challenge and was one of the leading campaigners, being far more high-profile than Thatcher, who was by then leader of the Opposition. Questions about sovereignty were explored and debated in much greater depth in 1975 than they were during the 2016 referendum. Heath explained well his understanding of what it meant to be a sovereign country in a wider world.

In the 1970s the BBC and ITV broadcast political programmes at peak times, and with a greater willingness to allow discussions to breathe. To take one example of many, ITV broadcast a debate between Heath and the then Employment Secretary and anti-marketeer, Michael Foot. The title was *A Question of Sovereignty*. The two of them debated for an hour. Foot put the case that the likes of Boris Johnson and Michael Gove occasionally argued in the 2016 referendum, but at greater length.

Foot insisted that the Common Market was not democratic and that it represented a transfer of power to non-democratic institutions. With an echo of Jeremy Corbyn's concerns about the European Union, Foot expressed worries that a radical Labour government would be blocked from implementing some policies, especially in relation to state ownership.

Heath responded at length. The exchanges became bad-tempered at times. Foot preferred to debate with witty adversaries. Heath never used wit, a big flaw in his political personality. But he made clear that he regarded sovereignty as the 'power of a nation to look after its citizens... sovereignty is to be used and not hoarded'. He pointed out that the Council of Ministers was accountable to the parliaments and electorates, and that the European Commission could not act without the permission of the Council of Ministers. He argued that, as with NATO, the UK 'contributed its sovereignty' for a wider purpose.[10] There was no mendacity or deliberate distortion. Heath and other prominent supporters of membership took a different view of how sovereignty worked in an increasingly interdependent world, and expressed it openly. They did not downplay the issue.

Heath and Roy Jenkins, who was back as Home Secretary, led the 'In' campaign. They would both have been dismissed as part of an 'out-of-touch elite' in 2016, but they were commanding then. Heath had lost an election less than eighteen months earlier, but he was back as a key campaigner and was respected, too, as the prime minister who took the UK into Europe, putting the case powerfully in a campaign. Heath had a much higher profile than the prime minister, Harold Wilson. Heath's authoritative prominence in the 1975 referendum was in itself a sign that the UK had not then been infected deeply by the anti-politics bug. A year before, Heath had lost two elections. In the 2016 referendums, former prime ministers were hidden away by the 'Remain' campaign, out of fear that in advocating 'Remain' they would trigger support for Brexit. In 2016 Heath would have been nowhere to be seen. In 1975 he was allowed to be ubiquitous.

Heath's role in the referendum was a triumph, but his post-prime ministerial career was not smooth. He loathed Margaret Thatcher, partly because he would have disliked whoever had removed him from the leadership against his wishes. He was a bad loser. One of the many reasons he fumed against Harold Wilson was that the Labour leader beat him in three elections and outwitted him several times in between. Heath's unyielding determination to prevail could be both a strength and a terrible weakness. But his torment over Thatcher was also to do with her policies, many of which he genuinely opposed. If Heath had been more effective at explaining what he was for, and why her policies outraged him, he would have seemed less self-serving. Instead he appeared to be succumbing gracelessly to the biggest sulk in British politics. The intensity of his transparent disdain for Thatcher was only purged when she fell from power in November 1990.

On the day Thatcher resigned as prime minister, Heath was a panellist on BBC1's *Question Time*. Before the programme was broadcast, a BBC political correspondent interviewed him in the programme's green room to get his reaction to her fall. Heath was too shy to look directly at the interviewer or anyone else in the green room, but he was openly jubilant: 'I hear you want to get my reaction to her removal from power... I think that will be possible.' He paused and laughed joyfully, the famous shoulders heaving up and down with unqualified pleasure. In the interview Heath argued that the fall of Thatcher was good news for the country and for the Conservative Party. He did not utter a single word to soften his message or even express sympathy for her, on what would have been a deeply traumatic day.

He had been waiting a long time for this moment – since February 1975, to be precise – when she had replaced him as Conservative leader. Heath had never been an actor. He could not hide his fuming frustration during the many years that followed his enforced resignation. Now he could not disguise his joy. He was like a spoilt child who had finally got the gift he yearned for.[11]

Heath had always possessed the intellectual gifts to forensically demolish a lot of Thatcher's simplistic populism, but managed to suggest most of the time that he was motivated solely by personal jealousy. On the night of her fall, he reinforced the sense that his feud with her was beyond reason. That was partly because it was. He loathed her with a burning intensity. As Thatcher cast her spell in the 1980s, some Conservative MPs expressed bewilderment as to how their party had elected Heath as their leader and then stuck with him for nearly ten years. They saw him as a failed leader and then a disloyal former prime minister, a combination so unattractive that Heath's rise to the top was a mystery to star-struck Thatcherites.

Some leaders empathize as a matter of instinct, knowing what needs to be done in order to appear gracious and dignified. Heath did not give grace and dignity much thought. He was the victim of his own thoughtlessness. Yet, like perceptions of Wilson being old and paranoid, the image of a joyful Heath on the night that Thatcher fell is only one part of a much bigger story. Heath was the awkward, lonely leader who still commanded intense loyalty from those who worked for him, much like Gordon Brown, who could be even more explosively temperamental at times. But above all, Heath was so much bigger than his inability to act with endearing elegance on the public stage. The depths of this most complex of political figures gradually became hidden, but they were on view in the early phase of his career.

What has happened since Heath died would have troubled him far more than the torment he endured as the despised Thatcher won her landslide election victories. A police investigation into allegations that Heath had been guilty of sexual abuse was carried out, with the highest media profile, including one police press conference outside Heath's home in Salisbury. The subsequent investigation came to the convoluted conclusion that Heath would have been questioned over sex-abuse claims if he was alive, but that 'no inference of guilt' should be made from the fact that he would have faced questioning.

Some of those who worked closely with him observed that they saw no evidence that Heath was gay, and even if he had sought to abuse teenage boys, there would have been no chance.[12] There were protection officers with him at all times. Heath reflected on this constraint in one of his final TV interviews with Nanette Newman, before the allegations against him were made: 'I've had protection officers since 1965 when I became leader of the Opposition. You get used to them being around.'[13]

Heath might have coped with the trauma of a clumsy, defensively naive police investigation, but he would have been horrified by the referendum on Brexit in 2016, a shallow act of direct democracy that threatened to undo his historic act as prime minister, the moment the referendum was called. Heath endured many of his political assumptions being challenged by Thatcher, but even she never contemplated leaving the EU when she was prime minister. The publicly displayed agonies of Heath's old pro-European colleagues who lived through the 2016 referendum – Michael Heseltine and Ken Clarke – are ones that Heath would have felt with even greater intensity. He would have found Brexit unbearable.

Instead, while he was alive, he witnessed the Labour Party moving from being an anti-European party to one that was for a time strongly pro-European. The role of Wilson and Callaghan, who both voted against entry in 1973, was to cement the UK's position as a member. For Callaghan, who became prime minister in 1976, his relations with European leaders were an upside to his leadership. There were few other upsides for him. Callaghan's leadership was just as nightmarish as Heath's, and for precisely the same reasons.

3

JAMES CALLAGHAN

Take a look at any footage of Jim Callaghan and he comes across as a calm and steady political figure. In some respects, this impression is accurate. Callaghan was a relatively stable, rooted politician and was not especially flamboyant or temperamental. There seemed to be no mystery about him. He was never accused of being an enigma. Although sometimes irascible, he always looked solid, the hair neatly greased back, slightly receding but not at an unmanageable pace, with the large glasses that framed a mischievously cheerful face. He usually wore a smart suit, a crisp white shirt and, quite often, a neat red tie. Unlike Wilson, Callaghan did not age noticeably as a public figure. When Callaghan left Number Ten in 1979 he did not look greatly different from when he became a relatively youthful chancellor in 1964. Over the years he was always prominent, ebullient, assertive, irritable, decent and, at times, bewildered by events.

Yet there is a strange twist to the career of sustained prominence. Callaghan's career was wildly oscillating and the patterns were not reliable. He was the committed trade unionist who was tormented by the trade unions when he was prime minister. He was an old-fashioned Eurosceptic who cemented the UK's membership of the European Union. He was the brilliant manager of a divided Cabinet, but left behind a Labour Party suffering more internal strife than at any point in its history. His leadership was a triumph of Cabinet government and also signalled its demise.

Callaghan was a short-serving prime minister, in office for just over three years. Many lessons of leadership arise from his brief tenure; few were learned. In the introduction to this book, the skills of Hercule Poirot were cited as ones that might help to make sense of the modern prime ministers. This applies in particular to Callaghan. In the first half of our investigation of Callaghan the mysteries are laid out: the apparent contradictions, the fractured patterns that shaped the career of a seemingly solid, old-fashioned politician. In the second half the mysteries are solved, or at least the attempt at a solution is made. As Poirot might have noted, 'In the case of Monsieur Callaghan, nothing was quite as it seemed.'

Like John Major later, Callaghan was a prime minister who had not been to university; and again like Major, he was deeply insecure about his limited education. Both prime ministers were surrounded by Cabinet ministers from Oxbridge. Both were too aware of the difference between their backgrounds and those of the ministers over whom they presided. Callaghan came from too poor a background to be able to afford the costs of university, an enduring regret. Yet his career was extraordinary. He was the only modern prime minister to have held the three senior Cabinet posts: before moving to Number Ten, Callaghan had been chancellor, Home Secretary and Foreign Secretary in that order, a chronology that in itself was curious. The move to the Home Office in 1967 was a demotion from the Treasury, a sign that his career was heading downwards. Unusually for a demoted Cabinet minister, he moved upwards again several years later, triumphantly defying the normal laws of political gravity to become Foreign Secretary in 1974. Having been around for a long time, he made the final leap to Number Ten in 1976.

As Labour's first prime minister for thirteen years in 1964, Harold Wilson in effect made Callaghan the second most powerful figure in his administration. The two were not especially close and already Wilson was wary of rivals. But Wilson gave Callaghan the central task of running the economy, even if he created a rival Department of Economic Affairs under the erratically charismatic George Brown. Callaghan and Brown had been rivals for several years. Both had stood in the 1963 leadership contest, losing to Wilson. Brown was more exuberant and, when he was sober, was one of the more formidable Labour politicians of the 1960s. Quite often he was drunk or had drunk too much and could not hide his consumption in public. Callaghan was much the steadier of the two, but from the beginning he struggled at the Treasury. He inherited a negligently managed economy from a tired, long-serving Conservative government. Indeed, the outgoing chancellor, Reginald Maudling, left Callaghan a note in which he declared, only half-jokingly: 'Good luck, old cock… Sorry to leave it in such a mess.' Outgoing Treasury ministers should never leave notes for their successors, even for a laugh. The Labour Treasury minister, Liam Byrne, wrote a note as he left in 2010, stating, 'There's no money left.' Incoming ministers quoted the words for years to come.

In Callaghan's case, the inherited mess as described by Maudling included a balance-of-payments deficit of £800 million. Labour chancellors face tougher hurdles than Conservative ones. The markets are warier and the media is less supportive. They feel a greater need to reassure. Callaghan had not expected the deficit to be so steep and felt compelled to introduce an emergency budget, which included public-spending cuts and a hike in interest rates to stem a panic selling of sterling. Even after he had acted, the markets looked on at the conduct of a Labour chancellor with hawkish disdain.

The greater the disdain, the more reluctant Wilson and Callaghan were to act against an overvalued currency. The desire to challenge perceptions fuelled by a hostile media is the curse of Labour governments. In seeking to appear strong in areas where they are perceived to be weak, Labour governments become weaker still. Tony Blair's various military interventions were partly explained by his fear of being seen as 'soft on defence', and Labour's reputation in the 1980s as being 'anti-American'. In seeking to prove that he could be tough in relation to 'defence', Blair moved towards the nightmare of Iraq. Although winning a landslide in 1966, Wilson and Callaghan were determined not to feed the perception that Labour could not be 'trusted' with the economy. In their reluctance to act of their own volition in relation to sterling, they were forced to devalue in 1967, a traumatic humiliation for the chancellor in particular, even though the devaluation started to revive the economy.

Chancellors who suffer an economic trauma under their watch rarely recover. Callaghan offered to resign and Wilson moved him to the Home Office, swapping him with Roy Jenkins, who quickly acquired a reputation for economic competence at the Treasury, one that Callaghan never secured.

Fast forward to 5 April 1976 when the once humiliated chancellor became prime minister. Not only had Callaghan managed to recover from his bleak phase as chancellor, but he had become much more authoritative. He inherited an economic nightmare that was far worse than that in 1964 when Maudling left his 'good luck' note behind. Neither Heath nor Wilson had managed to find a way to deal with the increasingly muscular unions. Inflation was raging. The government was running out of money and lacked any obvious means of raising more. Callaghan had the tiniest of majorities in the Commons at the beginning and, with a relatively elderly parliamentary party, was soon to be leading a minority government. Yet the former chancellor was not impeded by his past. Instead he proved to be a guide through the economic storms – not always a reliable one, but steady enough to retain high personal ratings in raw polls. Even Callaghan's opponents struggled to portray him as a leader out of his depth in terms of the tottering economy, even if at times he was.

The final dramatic event under Harold Wilson's leadership had set the scene for Callaghan. Days before Wilson left Number Ten, the government had lost a vote in the Commons on its public-spending White Paper. The proposals for spending cuts in the defeated White Paper were relatively modest compared with those that his chancellor, Denis Healey, was to advocate soon after Callaghan became prime minister, but enough Labour MPs rebelled to block the plans.

That was the immediate context when Callaghan moved into Number Ten. Very quickly the nightmare got much worse. Once again the markets moved in for the kill, as they had done when Callaghan was chancellor. Sterling came under intense pressure during the long, hot summer of 1976. As Healey noted in his memoir:

> By this time the Conservative press was screaming for public spending cuts; its frenzy was not discouraged by the Treasury's own misleading statement that public spending was taking 60 per cent

of GDP and by the official Treasury forecasts which overestimated that year's PSBR [public-sector borrowing requirement] by over £2 billion... it was all I had to go on and it was worrying the markets...[1]

Frenzied and irrational debate shaped government policies in the UK long before the era of so-called 'Fake news'. In some respects, the fakery was more dangerous in the 1970s, as the reporting of economic policy came from seemingly respectable sources – national newspapers and broadcasters.

Attempting to appease the combination of the UK media and the markets, Healey proposed £1 billion of spending cuts in July 1976. This was largely an act of appeasement, and not rational policy-making. As ever, such forces are never appeased when they sense blood. Sterling was under pressure again in September. Healey described the next four months as 'the worst of my life'. He famously turned back, on his way to catch a flight to Hong Kong where he was due to attend a meeting of Commonwealth finance ministers. Instead Healey stayed in London to intensify his negotiation for a loan with the International Monetary Fund (IMF). In return for the loan, the IMF demanded further severe spending cuts. Almost on the spur of the moment, Healey decided courageously to head for Labour's conference in Blackpool and spoke from the floor, with a supportive Callaghan looking down from the platform above.[2]

Healey talked for a few minutes, provoking loud boos and cheers as he spoke of coming from the 'battlefront' to explain to the conference why the austere course was necessary and unavoidable. The images remain extraordinary: a chancellor speaking from the conference floor, with a red light indicating that his time was up, as those attending showed their passions live on TV. The watching prime minister – the most observed of the observers – knew what the sequence portended: the political nightmare of getting agreement for more drastic spending cuts without a majority in the Commons, and with an assertive party in revolt.

On the whole, Callaghan and Healey got their way. They negotiated a loan with the IMF in the autumn of 1976 and introduced spending cuts, after many Cabinet meetings, sessions of the party's National Executive and parliamentary battles. There were numerous storms to come. The IMF loan and the spending cuts marked a historic outbreak of turbulence in themselves. Yet here is the first example of the fractured pattern: Callaghan, the failed chancellor, having the authority to be the prime minister to prevail, in a much deeper crisis nine years later.

Europe is the second example. Here again, there was no pattern. Callaghan started out as something of an old-fashioned British nationalist, more strongly opposed to the UK's membership of the Common Market than Wilson. In speeches he made bad jokes about the French. Opposed to the UK's membership in 1971, he declared in a speech of tabloid crudity, 'If we have to prove our Europeanism by accepting that French is the dominant language in the Community, then my answer is quite clear, and I will say it in French in order to prevent any misunderstanding: *Non, merci beaucoup.*' This was silly on many levels, but reflected Callaghan's fairly simplistic wariness of the Common Market.

Yet as Foreign Secretary from 1974, Callaghan conducted the renegotiation of the UK's EU membership in order to win a referendum on continued membership. Wilson delegated much of the responsibility to the more energetic Callaghan. Like Wilson, Callaghan had voted against the UK joining the Common Market in the parliamentary vote under Heath. Like Wilson, he played a key role in ensuring that the UK would remain a member of the Common

Market or European Union, well beyond their own political careers. As prime minister, Callaghan formed a close relationship with the German chancellor, Helmut Schmidt, and at no point expressed any doubt about the UK's membership. In joint interviews the two of them pulled off a neat informality. 'I agree with Helmut…' / 'Jim and I always agree…' Callaghan was nowhere near as committed as Heath, but he became more or less at ease with Europe.

As prime minister, Callaghan had more harmonious relationships with European leaders than he did with trade-union leaders in the UK. Yet he was the most committed trade unionist to have become prime minister. After the economy and Europe, Callaghan's relationship with the unions was the third example of the oscillating rhythms and disruptive patterns of his career.

Indeed, Callaghan's relations with the trade unions generated the most Shakespearean twists. He chose to be shaped by his genuine rapport with the unions, and most union leaders respected him, at least until he became prime minister. More than any other modern Labour prime minister, Callaghan was steeped in trade unionism. At the age of seventeen, he worked as a clerk for the Inland Revenue at Maidstone in Kent. While working as a tax inspector, Callaghan joined the Maidstone branch of the Labour Party and the Association of the Officers of Taxes (AOT), a trade union for those in his profession. Within a year of joining he became the office secretary of the union. In 1932 he passed a Civil Service exam that enabled him to become a senior tax inspector. The same year he became the Kent branch secretary of the AOT. The following year he was elected to the AOT's national executive council. In 1934 he was transferred to Inland Revenue offices in London.

Following a merger of unions in 1936, Callaghan was appointed a full-time union official and to the post of Assistant Secretary of the Inland Revenue Staff Federation (IRSF). He resigned from his Civil Service duties in order to become a senior figure in a trade union. His union position at the IRSF brought Callaghan into contact with Harold Laski, the chairman of the Labour Party's National Executive Committee and an academic at the London School of Economics. Laski encouraged Callaghan to stand for Parliament. His commitment to the vocation of a trade unionist led to a political career. Wilson learned to be close to the unions, while Tony Blair and Gordon Brown felt the need to convey distance from the unions. After being elected an MP, Callaghan retained close links with the unions, out of instinct, conviction and ambition. The links endured through all the political dramas until the tragic final scenes, when some of those to whom Callaghan had felt close contributed to his fall.

On the eve of Callaghan's victory in the 1976 leadership contest, the *Guardian's* columnist Peter Jenkins noted that 'By a process of elimination the mantle has fallen upon the Keeper of the Cloth Cap',[3] a patronizing evocation of the old-fashioned trade unionist rising to the top, but also a reflection on Callaghan's enduring association with the unions. At times the unions formed the buttress of his support in the Labour Party. He reciprocated by representing their points of view often in Cabinet and beyond – most famously in 1968 when the Cabinet minister Barbara Castle presented her proposals for a modest legislative framework for trade unions, *In Place of Strife*, and Callaghan opposed them without qualification. If he had supported them, they might have stood a chance of being implemented. The unions were opposed and, without delving too deeply, Callaghan opposed them, too. Yet when he became prime minister, he found himself battling it out with some union leaders in conflicts of historic significance.

Images of the so-called 'winter of discontent' in the early months of 1979 were centre-stage in Conservative broadcasts up until the 1992 election, such was their potency. There were plenty of disturbing images for the Tories to deploy: the consequences of lorry and train drivers, ambulance drivers, gravediggers and refuse collectors taking industrial action. The Callaghan years, as much as the Heath era, were seen as ones in which the government lost control over the unions. At times Callaghan did not know what to do with them. Like Heath and Wilson, he changed tack several times, opposing and then adopting an incomes policy. Nothing seemed to work for him, in terms of resolving the tensions. The strikes were a result of Callaghan's attempt to control inflation by a forced departure from the government's supposedly voluntary social contract with the unions, by imposing rules on the public sector that kept pay rises below 5 per cent. The imposition was meant to be an example to the private sector. However, some unions conducted their negotiations with employers within mutually agreed limits above this limit. While the strikes were largely over by February 1979, the government's inability to contain the strikes earlier helped to propel Callaghan towards his doom. He no longer knew what his relationship with the unions was – a bewildering position that challenged his political identity and purpose.

Callaghan faced his changing relationship with the unions as prime minister of a deeply divided Cabinet in a hung parliament. As with Wilson, there were mighty ministers in Callaghan's Cabinet with competing views on economic policy, the economy being the key test of a government at any time. On the whole, Callaghan got his way in policy terms without provoking a single Cabinet resignation during his time as prime minister. Given the composition of the Cabinet, this was almost an act of genius.

Sometimes Callaghan's judgements in terms of policy were wrong, but in relation to managing his Cabinet he was always smart. His astute handling of deep division is the fourth example of a wild pattern. Callaghan was a master at achieving unity, and yet he left behind a party that was impossibly divided.

During his first nerve-shredding summer as prime minister, Denis Healey noted that at first only Roy Jenkins[4] and Edmund Dell[5] were prepared to accept any spending cuts at all. Tony Benn was developing his alternative economic strategy, a programme that included import controls and extensive state ownership. The newly elevated Foreign Secretary, Tony Crosland, argued – correctly, as it turned out – that the situation was already under control and there was no need for further spending cuts. At the time, the IMF demanded the cuts and the UK Treasury had calculated that they were necessary. Healey wrote later:

> The consummate skill with which Callaghan handled the cabinet was an object lesson for all prime ministers. His technique was to allow his colleagues to talk themselves to a standstill in a long series of meetings… as they did so they came to recognise that their proposals would involve as many cuts as the IMF route.[6]

Roy Hattersley, an ally of Crosland's in these seemingly eternal Cabinet meetings, agreed: 'We met day after day. There was the Chancellor's view. Tony Benn's view. Tony Crosland's view. Each was fundamentally different… and yet we came to an agreed position.'[7]

From his very different ideological perspective, Benn concurred: 'Jim used to say when we disagreed subsequently, "But your point was put at length in the cabinet" and that legitimised the policy… I was very fond of Jim.' Benn added that when he clashed with

Callaghan, as he often did, they would have a conversation along these lines: 'Jim would say to me, "I'm not as nice as I look" and I said to him, "Neither am I…" On that basis we got on very well.'[8]

This was partly retrospective papering over wide cracks. Benn's diaries are crammed with a fuming sense that the Callaghan government was betraying the Labour movement, while Callaghan could hardly hide his despair at what he regarded as Benn's reckless disloyalty.

Yet there was an essence of truth in Benn's recollection of Callaghan's leadership. By the late 1970s, Benn was the most talked-about politician in the UK, feared and loathed by some, yet idolized by a significant section of the Labour Party. He was a mesmerizing speaker of unbounded energy and determination. Even so, he never resigned from Callaghan's Cabinet and accepted that he had lost arguments over economic policy, having been given the space to make his case. As Hattersley observed, Callaghan held as many Cabinet meetings as was necessary until a consensus emerged that the prime minister had sought from the beginning. Nearly always Callaghan backed Healey. The beleaguered chancellor, who was not quite as robust as he appeared to be, was hugely grateful to Callaghan for his reliable supportiveness.[9] Callaghan held together a Cabinet that included Benn, Michael Foot and three of those who went on to form the SDP: David Owen, William Rodgers and Shirley Williams. Compare Callaghan's record as a manager of Cabinet with Theresa May, leading in a similarly nightmarish context: she lost two Brexit Secretaries and a Foreign Secretary in the space of a few months in 2018, along with a record-breaking number of other Cabinet ministers and junior ministers.

The management of his Cabinet was Callaghan's greatest triumph as prime minister, a triumph of leadership. He had the confidence to let dissenting ministers put their case forward, before asserting his own position and nearly always prevailing – the dream model, as far as prime ministers are concerned. In another curious irony, his subtle management of the most divided government in modern times triggered the end of Cabinet government.[10] Callaghan's collegiate approach was a vindication of Cabinet government and yet his mastery of a warring Cabinet became the death-knell for collective rule. The concept of senior ministers debating policy candidly in some detail, before a prime minister was in a position to implement his or her programme, went out of fashion, simplistically dismissed as 'weak' leadership.[11] The main figure claiming weakness was the leader of the Opposition, Margaret Thatcher. She made the claim with good cause. She appeared 'strong' in comparison. But even then, in her early years, Thatcher had a genius for turning a self-interested assertion into a widely held point of view, the new consensus. Cabinet government became a sign of 'weak leadership', so much so that Tony Blair later followed the Thatcher style partly in order to be 'strong'. Callaghan's astute management of his Cabinet went out of fashion even before he left office, as Thatcher made her moves.

———

As ever with Callaghan, there was another twist. Civil war within the Labour Party followed his astute enforcement of Cabinet collective responsibility up until 1979. After election defeat, Callaghan stayed on as leader. Benn decided not to serve in the shadow Cabinet and instead toured the country rousing party activists with his brilliant oratory, accusing the Labour government of betraying party members and demanding new forms of accountability within the party, as well as for the economy more widely. With verve and wit, Benn was reflecting and articulating the anger of many activists. At the 1979 party conference, delegates turned on Callaghan, accusing him of betraying members in opting for a cautiously expedient manifesto rather than choosing a more radical programme. The angry election post-mortems at the conference were broadcast live on BBC2 as part of the BBC's conference coverage. As TV theatre, the debates were electrifying. But for Labour, the open warfare was calamitous. Callaghan was both the leader who brilliantly maintained Cabinet unity and the leader who was pathetically impotent as civil war erupted.

There was yet another seemingly conflicting sequence during Callaghan's leadership. He was a tribal Labour leader who would never have contemplated leaving his party. When Tony Blair and Gordon Brown proclaimed a divide between new and old Labour in 1994, Callaghan suggested in a rare intervention that he was 'original Labour'.[12] This was authentically mischievous without being overtly disloyal to Blair, at a point when he was on the eve of becoming prime minister. Callaghan was indeed original Labour, a trade unionist who climbed the ranks of the parliamentary party, despairing at times of what Labour had become during his period at or close to the top, but never being anything other than Labour.

In spite of his tribalism, it was Callaghan who agreed the Lib/Lab pact in 1977 when he was prime minister and went on to form a close relationship with the Liberal leader, David Steel. The Lib/Lab pact was far less rigid than a formal coalition, but is the only example of two parties working together in the Westminster Parliament before David Cameron and Nick Clegg joined hands in 2010. By the late 1970s, Callaghan was a wily operator. As a leader who had kept his Cabinet together during the IMF crisis, he knew how to manipulate Steel, a new leader of a much smaller party. But Steel was smart, too. Both derived quite a lot from the strange arrangement. Callaghan secured what was, for him, the equivalent of gold dust: a degree of parliamentary stability. He did so without having to agree a formal coalition with the Liberals, a move that would have torn his Cabinet and his party apart. Instead he agreed vaguely to a consultative committee with leading Liberals, and the space for Liberal spokespeople to 'shadow' their equivalent Cabinet ministers. When the chancellor, Denis Healey, was asked what influence his Liberal shadow, John Pardoe, would have on policy, he replied, 'None whatsoever.'[13]

But Steel, a greatly underestimated leader and a figure of some historic importance, also got something out of the arrangement. After the trauma of Jeremy Thorpe's resignation as Liberal leader, amidst allegations that he was involved in a conspiracy to murder a former male lover, Steel's party needed a renewed sense of purpose and seriousness. Being close to government, or appearing to be so, gave the third party some momentum.

Steel ended the loose arrangement with the Labour government after fifteen months, but he remained close to Callaghan. Indeed, Callaghan would sometimes treat Steel as a confidant. Although there was no formal pact, the two of them continued to discuss policy and strategy. As an example, Callaghan had a conversation with Steel over whether he should call an election in the autumn of 1978. Steel urged him to do so, predicting another hung parliament. He pledged to form a post-election coalition with Labour, one that would have been very different from the Thatcher government that was formed in 1979.

Callaghan did not take Steel's advice. But although Callaghan was tribally Labour, circumstances forced him to discover that he could form a rapport of sorts with a leader of another party. It helped that Steel was a figure firmly rooted on the centre left, and in some respects to the left of Callaghan.

Callaghan had other ways of demonstrating a flexibility in his politics that was at odds with his seemingly rigid and unchanging personality. He came from the party's right, and yet he had a rapport of sorts with his deputy, Michael Foot, who was of the left and a political romantic far removed from Callaghan. Indeed, it was Callaghan who chose to make Foot his formal deputy. He did so for pragmatic reasons, but the relationship deepened once he had taken the decision to formalize Foot's role. Callaghan had been an expedient senior frontbencher for decades. Foot had only become a minister after the February 1974 election, preferring before then to be a writer and journalist of elegant and committed prose, a brilliant left-wing orator whose political hero was Nye Bevan. In spite of their striking differences, Callaghan managed Foot smartly, and Foot took his role seriously. He was the mediator in the divided Cabinet, holding endless meetings with Tony Benn, Peter Shore and others who were closer to his political outlook. Callaghan also made Foot Leader of the House, the ideal post for a parliamentarian with a feel for the Commons at a time of theatrical fragility.

By the mid-1970s Foot was close to Neil Kinnock, a newish Labour MP on the left who had voted several times against the government in Wilson's final phase. As a former rebel, Foot knew well those Labour MPs, including Kinnock, who were inclined to vote against the government. He worked assiduously to minimize the destabilizing revolts. Parts of the left were wary of Foot's loyalty to Callaghan, but Foot, who would one day be leader, was convinced that a struggling Labour government was incomparably better than a Conservative one. Late in his career, Foot became expedient, without losing his socialist convictions. Callaghan gave him the space to develop his expediency. It is telling that Foot was far less enthusiastic about Wilson, even though Wilson brought him into the Cabinet.[14] From Benn to Foot and on to Steel, the leader of another party, Callaghan was a skilful manager of colleagues. He needed them all on board for the rocky ride. The ride would not have been possible if some of them had stormed out. There he was, the self-proclaimed 'original Labour' leader, working with the leader of another party and wooing assiduously the stars of other wings of his party. He was the non-tribal tribalist.

More widely in the Callaghan era, there was a strange disjunction between the conservatively cautious personality and the times in which he ruled, as there was with Theresa May after she became prime minister in 2016. Callaghan was a seemingly uncomplicated prime minister who led at a time of dark political drama and parliamentary theatre. As Home Secretary in the 1960s, he would never have contemplated the social reforms implemented with historic verve by his predecessor at the Home Office, Roy Jenkins. Indeed, Jenkins and Callaghan were worlds apart. Jenkins was the daring reformer, the author of dazzling political books, the lover of good wine, illustrious social gatherings and a Lothario. Callaghan was the modest family man who relaxed on his farm. In political outlook, Jenkins was a liberal progressive. Callaghan was a solid labourist, with a sense that his fellow trade unionists valued law and order, family life and reliably rising living standards. Blair turned to Jenkins for inspiration, but when the Labour leader from 1994 sought to woo Conservative newspapers such as the *Daily Mail* and its Middle England readers, he had a streak of Callaghan's politics.

Yet in spite of the conservatism and relative caution during Callaghan's leadership, there were knife-edge votes in the Commons so nerve-shredding and bizarre that the scenes of mayhem became the plot of a brilliant play in the twenty-first century. *This House* by James Graham evocatively portrayed the parliamentary mayhem of the late 1970s. The largely unshowy Callaghan led a government that provided the backdrop for a West End hit. Those great political actors Margaret Thatcher, Tony Blair and David Cameron got no West End drama in which their government was the dramatic context, even though each of them has been the source for various films and novels. It was Callaghan and his precarious government that formed the backdrop to a timeless production about high-stakes parliamentary theatre.

Although Callaghan was not an actor in the league of Wilson, Thatcher, Blair and Cameron, he did like the performance of politics. He was the only prime minister to sing songs with a joyful exuberance when delivering a speech at a conference or at a political gathering such as the Durham Miners' Gala. He did not have the wit or cunning of Wilson, but he was playful. Unlike the shy and self-conscious May – the first prime minister to dance onto the stage, at the start of her speech to a Conservative conference – Callaghan could be an authentic performer. His background was far removed from the Oxbridge political games that excited Edward Heath as well as many of his Labour rivals. Yet he could play the games of politics and could occasionally enjoy the fun.

The contrasts, fractured patterns, contradictions and dramatic ironies were already striking when Callaghan finally secured the crown at the age of sixty-four. He was older than the departing Harold Wilson, who made great play of his long-planned intention to retire at sixty. After Wilson announced his resignation in March 1976, Callaghan won the leadership against the most formidable set of candidates who had stood in a contest for any party since

1945. While his rivals had been students and stars at Oxford before lighting up the political stage, Callaghan had not been to university and had a less-glittering public personality, in spite of the tendency towards mischievous playfulness. He won the contest with ease against his ambitious colleagues and was in one key respect by far the best qualified of the candidates, having served at the top of the Cabinet longer than any of the other leadership contenders.

Callaghan's slow rise to the very top is an example of his almost unprecedented wilful staying power. Only Gordon Brown displayed the same resolute determination to move from 'leader-in-waiting' to leader. Most perceived leaders-in-waiting never become leaders, partly because of the pressures that arise from the perception.

The candidates who stood in the 1976 leadership contest after Wilson's resignation were all 'leaders-in-waiting' at one time or another, in contrast to the barren New Labour era, when Brown was the only one. One of the other candidates in the 1976 contest, Michael Foot, was to become a leader. The others who stood were Tony Benn, Anthony Crosland, Denis Healey and Roy Jenkins. Although a good speaker and a lively interviewee on TV and radio, Callaghan was the least sparky of a competitive field. All the candidates had depth and political vivacity. The others were scintillating writers, orators of varying brilliance, gripped by ideas and history. In contrast, Callaghan chose not to shine at times, at least in his victorious leadership contest. Sensing that his greatest strength was to be seen as being above the fray, Callaghan played little part in the 1976 Labour battle. This was an era when it paid to be laid-back. Wilson had kept a low profile in the 1975 referendum and won. Callaghan was rarely heard or seen during the 1976 leadership contest and he won, too. Labour MPs alone selected the leader, and in this case the new prime minister. On the basis of his longevity and his combative authority, a large majority of MPs chose Callaghan. Michael Foot came second. In a sign of what was to follow, Foot topped the poll in the first ballot, but Callaghan came through to win by a big margin in the second.[15] As the former Labour MP, Giles Radice, pointed out in an illuminating book, it might have been possible for one of Healey, Jenkins and Crosland to be leader. Labour's glittering social democrats chose to be rivals rather than to coalesce around one of the three, a move that would have involved the other two casting aside their leadership ambition. Few in politics are ready to make such a sacrifice.[16]

Although there appeared to be no mysteries in relation to the enigma-free Callaghan as he rose erratically to the top, there were plenty of riddles and conundrums. How did he flourish later in his career, having been a failure as a chancellor, not least becoming the sensible 'sunny Jim' leading a country in dark economic times? How did he become a pro-European, having been at times a crude anti-marketeer? Why was an ardent trade unionist incapable of forming a constructive relationship with the trade unions as he moved towards his fall? How to explain his role as an astute unifier when prime minister, and yet the leader who left behind a party tearing itself towards seemingly eternal Opposition? How was a prime minister who made Cabinet government work effectively also the figure who brought about the demise of Cabinet government? Why did high-stakes parliamentary theatre form the backdrop to the leadership of a figure who was less actorly than several prime ministers? This is where Hercule Poirot's skills as an investigator must be applied. Here are the answers to the riddles and conundrums, and with them come several lessons of leadership.

Callaghan's staying power was both a personal triumph and the consequence of a less hysterical age. Politics became even more unforgiving after Callaghan had left the fray. We should not exaggerate the scale of the difference. With good cause, Callaghan – and Wilson even more so – felt besieged in the build-up to devaluation in 1967 and beyond. The media could torment and destroy politicians then, too. Even so, there was more space in the mid- to late 1960s for political recovery. The media's coverage of politics, although ragingly intense and partisan enough to make leaders paranoid and insecure, was less screeching than it subsequently became. In the 1960s there were no political programmes on a Sunday, no rolling TV news; newspapers gave more space to parliamentary debates and less to the soap opera of politics; and, of course, there was no social media. Callaghan could move to the Home Office from the Treasury and get on with the job, his authority within the Labour Party not greatly undermined by the around-the-clock scrutiny that was to follow a few decades later.

But even then, in the 1960s, TV had become a dominant medium. Callaghan's career was boosted considerably because he was a brilliant television interviewee, another key to his durability. Being an effective interviewee is an important part of a leader's or aspiring leader's ammunition. Of modern prime ministers, only Tony Blair beats Callaghan as an intoxicating interviewee. Callaghan was engaged, calm, witty and authoritative. He managed to perform well even when he was struggling at the Treasury. These are important attributes when political authority is being challenged. He was a prime minister, and aspiring prime minister, in an era when TV interviews were broadcast regularly at peak time and at length, often with a panel of distinguished and weighty columnists. There were far fewer political interviews, but their rarity meant they had much more impact. Callaghan had the knack of appearing and, to some extent, being candid, while also managing to be discreet. Again, only the very different personality of Blair had a similar skill as an interviewee.

There were only a handful of political writers for newspapers in Callaghan's era, and their output created far greater waves than political writers do today in the age of social media. Callaghan took on the commentators with verve when he faced them in a TV studio. He enjoyed the format. There are several full-length interviews on YouTube from the time when Callaghan was prime minister navigating his way through the economic fog. No viewer could discern how dark it all appeared to be, from Callaghan's demeanour in a studio. He was relaxed and engaged, unless an interviewer irritated him, in which case he made his irritability part of his engaging repertoire. He would often retort along these lines: 'I know what you'll do with my answer. You will put the answer to another of my colleagues, hoping that he or she will disagree. So I'm not going to answer… Come on, Robin [Day], you've had several attempts but you're not going to get anywhere.' The viewer could not help but empathize with the evasive politician. Callaghan became unfashionable as a leader very quickly, but any aspiring leader could do worse than take note of his skills as an interviewee. They assisted him greatly when he was down, as he was quite often in his oscillating career. His capacity as a performer explains partly how Callaghan kept going when others would have fallen.

His position within the Labour Party was also a pivotal buttress after his short-lived tenure at the Treasury. In the UK there is a presidential culture, but a party-based system. The relationship between aspirant leader and party is therefore pivotal. By the time he became chancellor, Callaghan was already a formidable figure within his party and beyond. He had become an MP after Labour's

1945 landslide and had held several portfolios in the parliamentary party by the time he became chancellor nearly twenty years later. He was close to being fully formed by the time economic storms overwhelmed him in the 1960s, and had a developed sense of who he was as a public figure by the time he became prime minister. Compared with the mere eleven years they spent in Parliament, before Blair became prime minister and Brown took over as chancellor, Callaghan had been around for a long time and was harder to remove from the political stage as a result, even if he made mistakes.

The Labour Party, or enough of its influential components, was supportive of him for other reasons. Football supporters like to cheer players who are local, chanting that they are 'one of our own'. Callaghan was one of Labour's own. This was another reason for his durability. His father, who had been a chief petty officer in the Royal Navy, died suddenly when Callaghan was nine, leaving his mother to struggle on without the aid of a pension. His education was patchy, a part of his past that he would often highlight. He made the right to a decent education one of his great political passions. As prime minister, his first significant speech was on the importance of a decent education for all. He had neither the time nor the political space to develop his ideas in this area, but the intent was genuine and intensely felt.

The appearance of authority when he became prime minister was partly a facade. For effective leaders, the facade is not an act of duplicity. Quite often leaders need to appear calm when they are not, funny when they are fuming, determined and focused when they are lost.

In public, Callaghan became calmer and more self-confident than he was. There were times as prime minister when he despaired.

Unlike Theresa May, he could hide his nervy anxiety when the cameras rolled. Behind the scenes, he would occasionally display red-faced indignation and doubt about policy direction, which is unsurprising given the external circumstances. At one never-ending meeting of Labour's ruling National Executive Committee in the late 1970s, Callaghan looked up at one point and declaimed: 'Why don't we throw away the keys and stay here for the rest of our lives?'[17] He was prime minister at the time. In spontaneously exploding at his incarceration at Labour's HQ, he exposed as ridiculous the pompous declaration of some in the media that it is their duty to 'hold the powerful to account'. A lot of the time even prime ministers are powerless and are accountable, in a thousand different ways, every minute of the day. Non-elected figures are often far more powerful, wealthier and largely unscrutinized.

But under scrutiny, Callaghan conveyed calm in public, even when he was privately alarmed. At times, and in private, the impossible scale of the task came close to overwhelming him, but the avuncular, authoritative public face was nearly always in place. MPs and party members make their judgements based partly on the public personalities of senior politicians in their party.

Callaghan kept going when flimsier politicians would have fallen. His senior adviser in Number Ten, Bernard Donoughue, noted that 'Although apparently an agnostic, his Baptist upbringing showed through when, especially during a crisis, he would suddenly burst out singing hymns. Before he left his Commons room for the big debate on our pay sanctions policy he sang to us one of his favourites, "We'll meet again with the Lord".'[18] There were many crises from 1976 till his fall in 1979. Callaghan must have sung a lot of tunes. But his personality, his position within the Labour Party and the quieter volume at which politics was reported at the time all contributed to making Callaghan a symbol of solidity when he was prime minister, even when the economy was tottering chaotically.

There was another reason why Callaghan as prime minister seemed to epitomize calm in the midst of a bleak tempest. He was so evidently keeping the creaking show on the road in a way that nobody else in his party could. Most obviously, he had won a leadership contest and, unlike Theresa May, did not undermine the authority-enhancing benefits of winning by calling an early general election. May never recovered from losing her party's majority in the 2017 election. In spite of all the crises that erupted around Callaghan and the intense divisions, there was no serious speculation about a leadership challenge while he was prime minister. Partly because of his reasonably secure position internally, he was able to manage an unruly Cabinet. As a prime minister he appeared to be strong in part because he was. No one threatened to challenge him.

The next riddle is connected with calculated, cunning politics. The explanation as to why a successful period of Cabinet government led to the demise of this form of rule comes in the form of the then leader of the Opposition, Margaret Thatcher. Given the wider turmoil, she saw by instinct an opportunity to present herself as the model of 'strong leadership' compared with the 'weak' Callaghan, who was forever chairing crisis Cabinet meetings. She derided such teamwork, insisting that she would lead from the front and would have little time for internal discussion. This, too, was partly an act, but a highly effective one nonetheless.[19]

Subsequently Cabinet ministers, including those who were highly critical of her leadership, insisted that to some extent Thatcher did allow and encourage Cabinet discussion as prime minister, even if she became irritable when probed intelligently for too long. But Thatcher had smartly framed an argument around 'strong leadership' in order to make Callaghan's collegiate style seem weak. The bigger leap came with the leadership of Tony Blair, who dismissed his party's past as 'old Labour' and took as his guiding philosophy the idea that 'new Labour' must be entirely different from all that was associated with the 1970s – including Cabinet ministers speaking their minds.

As fashions change, Blair, who was widely praised initially for showing 'strong' leadership, was then heavily criticized for turning away from Cabinet government, most specifically in relation to the war in Iraq. This was unfair on Blair's leadership. There was nothing to stop Blair's Cabinet acting as Callaghan's ministers had done. On the whole, Blair's Cabinets chose to be pathetically subservient and unquestioning, with the exception of Blair's chancellor, Gordon Brown, who managed to pressurize Blair with almost the same intensity of all of Callaghan's ministers put together. Callaghan had to manage his Cabinet because his ministers chose to be assertive. Blair's ministers were grateful to be in power and saw Blair as the leader who had taken them there.

Callaghan also proved to be a wider team player as prime minister. He had no choice but to be. That is the key. The tribal leader had to look beyond his tribe and found the experience a congenial one. For much of his time as prime minister, Callaghan had no Commons majority and a substantial number of Labour MPs inclined to vote against their frail government. Prime ministers in hung parliaments have to work with what they have got. Callaghan had David Steel. He was lucky to have a thoughtful leader of the Liberals. He knew how to get the best out of potentially awkward people partly, again, because he had to. Without forming an internal alliance with Michael Foot, his government might well have collapsed.

Callaghan was a pragmatist, working with whoever he needed to and often changing with the flow of the tides. He was against the Common Market until the UK joined, after which he recognized that departure would be counter-productive. He was against incomes policies until he feared that no other option was available to him, at which point he favoured incomes policies. He was an ardent trade unionist out of conviction and self-interested calculation. When self-interest and conviction demanded a different response, he became less ardent. Callaghan was a poor reader of long-term political and economic trends, but he was flexibly astute at responding to the more immediate rhythms. He could be stubborn until he sensed a need to change, and then he could swiftly pull a reverse gear.

Given these agile attributes, at odds with his apparent rigid old-fashioned politics, here is another riddle: why did Callaghan quickly become an unfashionable prime minister, referred to dismissively (if at all) in the decades that followed? This is a leader whom Denis Healey, a figure who was not easily impressed, placed second only to Attlee in the pantheon of Labour leaders.[20] Shelves creak with books on Attlee. There are few on Callaghan.

Part of the answer is obvious. Prime ministers who serve briefly at the end of an era, and without winning an election with their own distinctive agenda, are easily dismissed. Roy Jenkins, who had more curiosity about leaders and leadership than any of his colleagues, dismissed Callaghan as a 'tail-end Charlie', a quote that tormented Gordon Brown as he agonized over how to win an election in his own right after Blair's long reign. Callaghan ruled only from April 1976 until the election that was forced on him in May 1979. This election campaign triggered the Thatcher revolution that made Callaghan seem like ancient history very speedily.

———

The end of Callaghan's reign was also traumatic and bleak, arguably bleaker than the fall of any other prime minister in the modern era, including even that of Theresa May. The darkness took many forms. Like Brown, Callaghan clumsily mishandled the timing of the election. He had dropped a few hints that he might call an election in the autumn of 1978, when some polls suggested that Labour had a chance of winning, or at least being the largest party in a hung parliament. David Steel was by no means alone in advising Callaghan to call the election. His deputy, Michael Foot, urged him to go to the country earlier. Healey, too, was of the same opinion. So were senior trade-union leaders. In July 1978 Callaghan was interviewed on peak-time TV by a panel of journalists. He was asked about the possibility of an early election and replied truthfully that he would have a summer holiday and decide after that. His words merely fuelled speculation, as he had not ruled out the idea. Like Gordon Brown, he was too transparently keeping all options open.[21]

Over the summer holiday he concluded that he would lose an autumn election. Subsequently, in a dramatic television broadcast in September 1978, Callaghan announced that he would not be calling one: 'The government must and will continue to carry out policies that are consistent, determined, that don't chop or change and that brought about the present recovery in our fortunes.'[22]

Prime ministers always hope that something might turn up, if they stay on. Hope is a huge driving force for leaders. To outsiders it might appear that a prime ministerial cause is without hope, but prime ministers rarely reach the same conclusion. Even in the depths of despair, they wonder if there is a way through. In addition, Callaghan was not in despair. For all the intense pressures on him, he was enjoying the job that he had waited so long to get. He did not want to give it up.

Sometimes he even appeared to be enjoying himself too much, a bizarre problem for a prime minister who is deeply aware of the political and economic turmoil. Only a fool would not be aware.

Famously, in the depths of his final winter as prime minister, Callaghan had been photographed at a sunny international conference in Guadeloupe. The gathering took place just a few months after his decision not to call an election. He returned with a suntan to a freezing UK that was enduring the chaotic consequences of various industrial disputes, declaring at the airport: 'I don't think other people in the world would share the view [that] there is mounting chaos in this country.' The headline in the *Sun* newspaper the following day was: 'Crisis? What Crisis?'[23] Here is another vivid reminder that so-called 'Fake news' existed long before the eruption of social media. The headline was an exaggerated summary of Callaghan's comments, but it cemented an impression of a prime minister who was 'out of touch' – a cliché that makes little sense when applied to any politician dependent on winning elections. His actual words were complacently phrased, but Callaghan was far from out of touch. Governing had become close to impossible, and no prime minister becomes detached in such circumstances. Yet Callaghan's strength as a communicator became his weakness. His calm authority misleadingly conveyed an indifference to the chaos.

The 'Crisis? What Crisis?' saga was just one of many that erupted around Callaghan, as if he was being punished for dragging out an unruly parliament beyond its natural life. Prime ministers such as May and Heath were torn apart for calling early elections. The political gods turned on Callaghan for seeking to avoid an election until the last possible moment.

The so-called 'winter of discontent' was at its worst as he returned from sunny Guadeloupe in January 1979. This doomed Callaghan to defeat. The strikes and the failure of the government to impose its own pay policy without triggering industrial unrest combined to make Labour's electoral task far more mountainous after he had lost the election.

The election defeat in 1979 was preceded by the government losing a vote of no confidence in the Commons. Callaghan was only the third prime minister in the twentieth century to lose a vote of no confidence.[24] Such a parliamentary defeat is a humiliating way to open an election campaign. Until the Fixed-term Parliaments Act, rushed through for superficial reasons by the 2010 Con/Liberal Democrat coalition, a prime minister had a degree of freedom about when to call an election, a freedom that often tormented the individual who had to make the decision. Callaghan had been forced into an election, placing him on the defensive and making the Opposition leader, Margaret Thatcher, seem already a powerful player before she had acquired power. She had won the decisive vote that triggered an election. The dynamic was flattering for Thatcher and made Callaghan appear even weaker.

The build-up to the no-confidence vote was theatrical in its stressful unpredictability. This was another twist of the Callaghan era. Curiously, interest in the Callaghan era has faded, yet the real-life drama was epic and edgy. Ian Aitken was the *Guardian*'s political editor in the late 1970s, reporting on every twist and turn. On Aitken's death, another journalist, David McKie, evoked vividly what it was like being a reporter at Westminster during Callaghan's premiership:

For much of the day he [Aitken] would operate not in the members' lobby of the House of Commons, to which senior political correspondents enjoyed privileged access, but much more in the corridors and the bars. Of these, the greatest, at any rate in the 1970s and 80s, was Annie's Bar, a particularly important information exchange when the life of James Callaghan's government was imperilled almost nightly, as it was from 1976 to 1979... At some time between 7 p.m. and 8 p.m., Ian would move to the telephone, assemble his notes, some of which had been made on torn-up cigarette packets, and dictate a story that was a model of its kind.[25]

It is the phrase 'imperilled almost nightly' that conjures up the challenges of leadership in a hung parliament with a restive, rebellious governing parliamentary party. The government was finally killed off in the no-confidence vote, after a day of frantic negotiations with minority parties, whips on both sides summoning a few dangerously ill MPs on stretchers, and some epic speeches in the Commons as the deadline for the 10 p.m. vote drew closer. The final full speech of the parliament was made, appropriately enough, by the great parliamentarian Michael Foot, as Leader of the House. He was funny, gracious and passionate in his defence of the tottering government. After the wit and passion of Foot's words, MPs headed for the lobbies. Callaghan lost the vote of no confidence by a single vote, 311–310. Afterwards, amidst much frenzy, he stood up at the despatch box and declared that he would now 'Take our case to the country' – the final affirmation of a Labour prime minister in the Commons for eighteen years. The defeat added to the sense of chaos that marked Callaghan's leadership. Yet in some respects this particular compelling and nerve-shredding parliamentary drama was irrelevant. Callaghan would have had to call an election later that year, even if he had won the no-confidence vote. There is no reason to assume the election outcome would have been different in the autumn. There were deep currents driving the tides.

During the 1979 campaign Callaghan turned to his senior adviser, Bernard Donoughue, and observed: 'You know there are times, perhaps once every thirty years, when there is a sea change in politics. It then does not matter what you say or what you do. There is a shift in what the public wants and what it approves of. I suspect there is now such a sea change and it is for Mrs Thatcher.'[26]

Callaghan's observation appears prophetic, in the light of what followed. Yet for a smart reader of the political rhythms, he was late to recognize the tidal wave that propelled Margaret Thatcher towards power. His insight also provided him with a convenient get-out clause, implying there was nothing he could do to reverse that tidal wave.

Elections elsewhere suggest this was not the case. France elected a socialist president in 1981 at about the point at which Thatcher's popularity was so low that *The Times* ran an opinion poll under the headline 'The Most Unpopular Prime Minister This Century'. The tidal change was a limited one. The waves did not engulf West Germany, an economically more vibrant country, which often elected social-democratic chancellors as part of a coalition. Northern European countries, all with economies performing better than the UK's, were often governed by social-democratic parties.

Callaghan explained what he meant by his tidal metaphor in a candid interview many years later. In December 1996, months before the New Labour landslide, he reflected on the historical forces that shaped the assumptions of his leadership and, by implication, those of the other prime ministers who ruled in the 1970s before Thatcher:

A new generation was growing up in the 1970s and had reached the stage where their ideas were becoming popular – and we failed to adjust to that. To understand the reason one has to go right back to the war and before. In the thirties, what we now call the market economy failed. There was the 'Great Depression' with millions unemployed. As soon as the war came that disappeared. We had a centralised economy which provided work for everyone. So when my generation came into the public eye we said there was no going back to the twenties and thirties and we said 'Look what happened during the war – a centralised economy has shown that we can plan for success...'

But by the 1970s a new generation had grown up that did not have our wartime experiences and didn't think it was relevant. So I think we failed to recognise the new expectations of the younger generation. The think tanks of the right – we failed to pay any attention to them.[27]

Callaghan was intelligently insightful, admirably reflective and yet too defensive. He was speaking when Tony Blair was walking on water, heading towards a big victory in the 1997 election, while Callaghan had lost his. Leaders who only fight and lose an election are tormented by their failure and usually agonize for the rest of their lives about what they did wrong. Gordon Brown adopted a self-deprecating approach in the years that followed his defeat in 2010. 'Don't take my advice. I lost an election,' he would say in his rare public appearances, normally at book festivals.

Although, in the same interview, Callaghan was subtly critical of Blair at times, he was also coming to terms with New Labour's overwhelming popularity as it turned its back on the centralized state and hailed markets and the private sector as agents of delivery. If Callaghan had been interviewed after the 2008 financial crash, he might have taken a different line. But he was also onto something. For noble reasons, those leaders shaped by the 1930s – Heath, Wilson and Callaghan – feared, with good cause, the social and economic consequences of unemployment. As erratic defenders of the corporatist state, Wilson, Heath and Callaghan had several objectives, but above all they intervened to protect jobs. For them, there could be no return to the 1930s. But as they agonized over what to do about pay, prices and jobs, they almost failed to notice the rise of an alternative set of beliefs and assumptions, personified partly by the leadership of Thatcher. They were defined by orthodoxies that no longer applied, in the same way that later disciples of Thatcher could not see that the ideas behind Thatcherism were partly the cause of the 2008 financial crash, and not the solution to the dark consequences.

Having a vision, some ideological momentum and policies that make tangible sense of that vision is essential for a leader to endure and develop. This is not easy, and the combination is rare. Some leaders have visionary ideas or phrases, but lack the policies. Others have policies in which they believe, but do not have the ideological verve to bring them together into a coherent whole. Callaghan was not a visionary, and would probably have taken it as an insult if he had been described as such. But he was opposed by Margaret Thatcher, an ideological populist with a simple but clear sense of what had gone wrong and of what was required to put it right. Callaghan had none of the skills required to counter with a populism from the left. His appeal depended on a projection of solid competence. That only works if an economy, and much else, is running smoothly. No one could claim this was the case in the late 1970s.

Wilson had, in part, acquired an unfairly negative reputation for wiliness and a lack of vision long before he retired from the leadership. Callaghan was regarded by colleagues, and even by the anti-Labour newspapers, as more solid. Yet he lacked clarity of purpose, too. For partly understandable reasons, he changed tack almost as often as Wilson.

Nowhere was the clarity less clear than in Callaghan's relationship with the trade unions. He ensured that the *In Place of Strife* proposals never had a chance of implementation and then, with a Shakespearean twist, became arguably the biggest political victim of the weak legislative framework that he had helped to bring about. Some of the unions turned on him, or his attempts to impose pay restraints, and Callaghan was at a loss to know what to do about it. A large part of him still regarded himself as a trade unionist, and yet some trade unions were making his life hellish. Bernard Donoughue reports a despairing Callaghan asking in January 1979, 'How do you announce the government's pay policy has collapsed?'[28]

That is quite a question for a prime minister to ask, even in private. Yet pay policy had indeed collapsed spectacularly. In the autumn of 1978 Callaghan had attempted to impose a 5 per cent ceiling on pay rises. Within weeks of his announcement, workers at some companies (including Ford, then a big employer in the UK) were demanding 15 per cent. Public-sector unions sought higher increases. In December legislation required to enforce the pay policy was defeated in the Commons. In February 1979 the 5 per cent ceiling was raised to 10 per cent. The pressures on Callaghan over this period – partly self-induced – were as intense as those on Theresa May as she sought to navigate Brexit in a hung parliament.

They were self-induced in the sense that Callaghan, like Heath and Wilson, failed to understand what was happening and what needed to happen. Thatcherism did not have to be the answer to the chaos of the 1970s, but it became the only answer for a time, or at least the only answer that commanded enough support for a government to govern.

For all his ebullient authority, Callaghan was all over the place in terms of policy coherence when he was prime minister. His first speech to his party conference as prime minister, delivered in September 1976, is widely cited as the first move towards Thatcherite monetarism. Thatcher saw monetarism – governments controlling the supply of money circulating in the economy – as the solution to high inflation and the generator of sustained economic growth. In a script written partly by the economist and Callaghan's son-in-law, Peter Jay, the newish prime minister told his party:

> We used to think that you could spend your way out of a recession, and increase employment by cutting taxes and boosting Government spending. I tell you in all candour that that option no longer exists, and that in so far as it ever did exist, it only worked on each occasion since the war by injecting a bigger dose of inflation into the economy, followed by a higher level of unemployment as the next step. Higher inflation followed by higher unemployment. We have just escaped from the highest rate of inflation this country has known; we have not yet escaped from the consequences: high unemployment.

But this was not an endorsement of monetarism in the way that Thatcher was to espouse it in the early phase of her premiership. In the same speech, which was confused and contradictory, there was also a strong defence of public spending in many areas of government. Callaghan was also addressing an immediate crisis: the demand from the IMF for further sweeping spending cuts. Yet as Healey was later to reflect: 'The whole affair was unnecessary. The Treasury had grossly overestimated the PSBR.'[29]

Callaghan was not to know this at the time, and after his traumas as chancellor he had become fixated with the need to reassure the markets. He needed to put the case to his party, and be seen doing so. In some ways he was being politically courageous. Yet his attempts to sway his party and reassure the IMF and the markets left him lacking an argument, or the space to frame one against Thatcher. In the end, he could only argue that Labour would not cut public spending as brutally as she would. In doing so, he had handed her victory in the ideological battle, almost before it had begun. Those like Crosland and Benn, from very different perspectives, who had opposed the spending cuts were not the reckless extremists they were portrayed as being.[30] In some respects, their analysis was more closely related to the economic realities and, unlike Callaghan, they came equipped with ideological armoury, a narrative to challenge Thatcher's instinctive and, in some respects, simplistic anti-state populism.

The oscillating relationship with the trade unions was mirrored in Callaghan's erratic approach to incomes policies. Like Heath and Wilson, Callaghan often opposed incomes policies, only to turn to them. For these three prime ministers, incomes policies were like a 'femme fatale' in film-noir thrillers. Legal constraints on pay attracted them, even though they knew deep down that in adopting them, they were walking towards their doom. Incomes policy brought about the fall of Heath. Wilson got into a contorted nightmare seeking to impose a pay policy without calling it a pay policy. Callaghan noted the agonies of his predecessors and opposed pay policy, before fatally adopting one.

In spite of strong international relationships, Callaghan was not a visionary in foreign affairs, either. He failed to articulate powerfully what he was up to. This was in contrast to most of his colleagues, a number of whom wrote entire books articulating their visionary politics. Crosland was Labour's great philosopher in the 1950s. Benn's books included *Arguments for Socialism* and *Arguments for Democracy*. Healey and Jenkins had written many articles and books that gave a clear guide to their ideological journeys. There are none from Callaghan. He was a social conservative, committed to family, law and order, the value of a good education and improving the lives of the poor. His opening broadcast as a new prime minister focused almost entirely on his old-fashioned values, as well as the need for tough decisions on easing government debt. Later, Callaghan was to look back and recognize his lightly-worn ideological baggage as a flaw rather than a strength:

> 'You see I never had a really developed theory of Socialism. People like John Strachey or Denis Healey or Barbara Castle or all those lucky people that went to university.'
> 'Do you feel that you missed something by not going?'
> 'I feel I missed a great deal. I gained things that they never had through having a practical life but I missed the discipline of thought and the opportunity to exchange ideas with other people who were thinking in the same way. I think that I would have enjoyed going if I'd had the opportunity.'[31]

Callaghan had been surrounded by Oxbridge titans. As he hinted, his strength was a practical focus on the matters in hand, but the most formidable leaders need a weighty sense of thought-through purpose. When Callaghan observed the 'sea change' during the 1979 election, he was partly seeking to make sense of the rise of a radical Conservative leader with an ideological mission. In contrast to Thatcher, he was openly uncertain about how to deal with the mountainous challenges and had no guiding ideology to lead him. These are problems for a leader, even one who was sometimes celebrated for his hard-headed, well-intentioned pragmatism.

There is another reason why Callaghan's reputation sank rapidly or was viewed with indifference. He mishandled his approach to leadership after the election defeat in 1979. Some prime ministers are casually negligent about their post-prime ministerial careers, in a way that changes how their entire leaderships are perceived. Thatcher and Blair were viewed differently, and more critically, by some partly because of their conduct after they left Downing Street. Major's reputation grew on the basis of his behaviour post-Downing Street. Callaghan's reputation fell for very different reasons than Thatcher's or Blair's, but is also partly explained by what happened after he lost power in 1979.

Callaghan decided to stay on as Labour leader. He thought he could calm down a deeply divided party after the trauma of power, creating a path for Denis Healey to succeed him. He calculated that Healey was such a contentious figure, after more than five years as Labour's chancellor, that a period of solid leadership from a leader with no further ambition was required before Healey could win.

Instead, the divisions deepened and there was no stability whatsoever. Callaghan had little authority to impose his will, as both sides of the divide knew that he would be going fairly soon. Under Callaghan's fading leadership, internal rule changes were made that began to give new powers to party members.

Labour's party conferences in 1979 and 1980 – Callaghan's final annual gatherings as leader – were febrile, the fieriest in the party's history. Furious speakers talked of the betrayal of the Labour government, with Callaghan looking down once more from the platform. The 1980 conference was especially dramatic. From the podium, Tony Benn pledged that the next Labour government would nationalize the banks, abolish the House of Lords and leave the Common Market within days. At a fringe meeting, Shirley Williams, soon to leave the Labour Party, spoke of a 'fascism of the left'. Callaghan looked weak and impotent. Indeed, during the

1980 conference his sudden resignation was clumsily leaked to the media. It was a dark ending to a long career at the top of British politics. Callaghan wanted Healey to be his successor, but Michael Foot was chosen by Labour MPs instead. Ever since, Callaghan's reputation has been poor, defined by images of the 'winter of discontent', his inability to keep the left of the party in line and the dominance of Margaret Thatcher, who swept him aside.

He was more or less airbrushed from history soon after he stepped down from the leadership in the autumn of 1980. Unlike Wilson, Callaghan continued to be physically and mentally alert for decades to come and yet, after he retired as an MP in 1987, he was largely forgotten or ignored by his party.

Labour's successive leaders wanted nothing to do with him, for different reasons. Although they had worked well together in government, Michael Foot – Callaghan's immediate successor – wanted to pursue a policy programme well to the left of the former prime minister's beliefs. Most specifically, Foot was a committed believer in unilateral nuclear disarmament and Callaghan was a passionate opponent, even speaking out publicly and angrily against Labour's defence policies in the years to come. When Neil Kinnock followed Foot, after Labour's 1983 electoral slaughter, the new leader was desperate to be seen moving on from the nightmare of the late 1970s. He sought no public association with Callaghan. More woundingly for Callaghan, Tony Blair, after becoming leader in 1994, turned to Roy Jenkins for guidance, as an experienced former Labour Cabinet minister and SDP leader. He made no attempt to seek advice from the last Labour figure to have occupied Number Ten.[32]

Callaghan lacked the vision to be a great prime minister, and the circumstances would have made greatness impossible: a hung parliament, raging inflation and a divided party. But the agile manner in which he prevailed over dissenting ministers of intimidating weightiness, and navigated his way through the nightmarish terrain of the UK economy – while explaining to the country via authoritative TV interviews what he was seeking to do – were historically significant achievements. Callaghan looked at Thatcher and Blair with envy as they led with landslide majorities. But his envy was misplaced. Probably he would not have been a very different prime minister if he had faced a more malleable Commons, given that he got his way more often than not as prime minister. His way was erratically resolute and conservative, amidst an epic sea change that he recognized only when it was too late to make an ideological case for an alternative route. He left the stage clear for Margaret Thatcher.

4

MARGARET THATCHER

Margaret Thatcher is the great change-maker of modern prime ministers. The sweeping alterations to Britain during her premiership took a distinct form. By the end of her leadership, she had transformed her country beyond recognition – a remarkable feat for a leader – and the 1970s seemed like a distant land. After thirteen years of her rule, parts of the UK flourished, as an entrepreneurial spirit was unleashed. She won three elections in a row. Yet as a result of her dominance, parts of her country no longer knew where to turn for accountable leadership. She was the hyperactive leader who did not believe in an active state; she was the strong leader who left the UK with weak forms of democratic leadership. This was one of the most significant consequences of her time in power. By the time she left office, local government had either been abolished or reduced to cranky irrelevance. Even a city as big as London had no body to represent it. If the Tube trains did not turn up or buses did not arrive, travellers had nowhere to turn to make their protests. In other parts of the country, jobs that had once been for life were not available for even a small part of a life. While parts of the economy boomed spectacularly, some voters lost control of their previously orderly lives, and others felt as if they had been left behind. Margaret Thatcher was a control freak who was not specially interested in how others sought some sense of control over fractured public services. Instead she was a believer in the concept of 'freedom' almost unmediated. She deployed the term 'freedom' like a weapon, refusing to acknowledge that the concept is complex or nuanced. She sought to set the people free. Which voter would opt for incarceration?

Part of Thatcher's genius, and a reason for her historic endurance, was a capacity to make sense of the vibrant or impoverishing chaos that she unleashed. Instinctively she could articulate what she genuinely believed. She made her sometimes shallow radicalism seem like sound common sense. Thatcher was freeing people from the manacles of the state and, on the whole, quite a lot of people were grateful. Some were making money and could do more with their lives than they had been able to during the shabby, nerve-shredding 1970s. Thatcher was strong, and her ghostly predecessors had been weak. In her strength, she made the state – in most of its various manifestations – weaker.

Margaret Thatcher is the most analysed of modern prime ministers. Unsurprisingly, there have been many books about her; only Winston Churchill has inspired more. As a modern prime minister, she has the field of largely flattering biographies almost to herself. The reasons for the enduring interest are obvious. She was a determined, wilful reformer, transforming not only her country, but her party, too. In terms of domestic policy and her later approach to Europe, Thatcher's influence lasted much longer than Churchill's, extending well beyond the end of her career and, indeed, her death.

Seeking to fully explain Thatcher's addictive love of politics from an early age is almost impossible, the equivalent of solving the mystery of the Beatles' masterful musicianship. Her father, Alderman Roberts, the assiduous owner of a grocer's shop in Grantham, was the key early influence, in the same way that Paul McCartney's father was a factor behind his love of music. Neither fully makes sense of what followed. Thatcher cited her father often. He believed in concepts that were to shape her outlook: 'individual responsibility' and 'sound finance'. The latter formed the basis of her future economic policies. Although her brilliant biographer, Charles Moore, reveals that she had boyfriends and set aside time in her pursuit of them, her immersion in politics was total, and unusual in an era when politics was largely a male vocation. From early in her life she became intoxicated by politics and by the Conservative Party, the ideas, the performance, the battles. After she had left Number Ten she continued to intoxicate many of those in her party.

One of the questions posed during the 2016 Brexit referendum was: 'How would Thatcher have voted?' The question continued to be asked for a long time after the result. Following the 2008 financial crash, the Conservatives' youthful leaders, David Cameron and George Osborne, turned to the 1980s for guidance on how they should respond. Their economic policies were recognizably Thatcherite. A more sensitive figure than his reputation suggested, Osborne was in tears during Thatcher's funeral. Thatcher's ideas shaped and defined him, and Cameron, probably more than they dared to realize. She had cast a spell long ago and, remarkably in the fast-moving world of British politics, her capacity to intoxicate a new generation of Tories had not diminished. In their different ways, Labour leaders also paid homage to the potency of her leadership, until the election of Jeremy Corbyn in 2015. Even Corbyn's supporters referenced Thatcher. Some suggested that he was the left's answer to her. This represents the dominance of a rare political force.

Yet for all the worship and scrutiny, Thatcher possessed two qualities as a leader that remain under-explored. The first was those instinctive skills as a political teacher. All leaders announce policies and take strategic positions. Many do so most days of the week. Surprisingly few explain *why* they are doing so. They make announcements as if the declarations need no explanation. The most effective leaders explain as well as announce. Thatcher was explaining what she was up to most of the time, in a populist language that voters could easily relate to.

The second overlooked quality was her unerring ability to read the unpredictable political rhythms and apply them to her advantage, while also acting with conviction, or at least appearing to do so. With good cause she is seen as a 'conviction politician'. But she was wily, too. The fact that most voters regarded Harold Wilson as devious exposed the limits of his wiliness. Thatcher was seen as deeply principled and courageous, showing that she was smartly devious enough to keep her political calculations well hidden. Perhaps sometimes she hid them from herself. But until close to the end, they were there.

Most leaders fail to read properly what is happening on the crowded political stage, let alone respond in ways that enhance their position. But Thatcher possessed a rare ability to recognize the space she had on the political stage to act either radically or cautiously. She was a restless, impatient leader and yet she took the time at each phase of her career, again almost instinctively, to judge how far she could go in sating her hunger for radical change. Thatcher was both impulsive and cautious. She usually knew which of the two characteristics should prevail at any given time. Until the dramatic final phase of her leadership, she was able to control her own impulsiveness.

Before exploring both qualities and an under-examined, but deep flaw, there is a wider lesson from Thatcher's leadership, one that is a common theme with all our leaders and prime ministers. In a way that is Shakespearean in its epic theatricality, the origins of a leader's rise to the top are often the cause of their downfall. They do not see that they are moving towards their fall by acting in ways that earlier had propelled them to the top. Harold Wilson's career is an earlier example and Tony Blair's is a later one.[1] To some extent, the same dark sequence applies to the other modern prime ministers.

This was precisely the case with Margaret Thatcher. Oddly, given the vivid drama of Thatcher's leadership, her rise and fall are connected to the dry theme of local government, and how to raise finance for councils. Her remarkable ascent to the top of the Conservative Party happened, at least in its breathlessly fast-moving final phase, because of the last two portfolios she was given by the then leader of the Conservative Party, Edward Heath. The first of these portfolios made her responsible for the Conservatives' approach to local government and housing. The second pitched her into battles over economic policy. The first was at least as important as the second.

After the Conservatives' defeat in the February 1974 election, Heath appointed Thatcher, previously his assiduous and loyal Education Secretary, to the seemingly humdrum post of shadow Environment Secretary. She irritated him, but no more than that, at this particular point in what had always been a cold relationship. Thatcher had acquired what appeared to be a dull remit, in the aftermath of one of the great dramatic elections of recent times. But it was this supposedly humdrum brief that gave her the opportunity to become the headline-grabbing populist Tory politician during turbulent times.

When she became shadow Environment Secretary she started working on a policy that she privately had some doubts about: the abolition of the rates system, the local property tax from which councils raised some of their revenue. Like most taxes, rates were unpopular and she began working on ways to abolish them, putting in characteristically long hours in order to come up with a striking proposal.

In August 1974, when most Conservative politicians were exhausted and on holiday after their traumatic period in power and the lost election in February, Thatcher held a press conference. Again, characteristically, she was not on holiday, preferring to focus on property taxes rather than lie on a beach. She now proposed that the next Conservative government would abolish rates. In the August news vacuum, she commanded the front pages with her plan. She attacked the likely rate increases and promised that, in the short term, a Conservative government would reduce them by spending more from the centre, while imposing 'efficiencies' on councils. With a flourish not altogether backed up by substance, Thatcher pledged to remove the property tax over time and replace it with one that reflected the ability to pay. This was a safely vague alternative, although it proved a convoluted proposition. She partly sought to address her wariness of central-government spending with a pledge to increase it, in order to keep local taxation under control. Her lengthy assertions in the summer of 1974 are worth reading in full, as they suggest that she could be a confused thinker at times:

The capacity of governments to spend has gone beyond the capacity of ratepayers to pay. The first essential therefore is to limit total public expenditure. This means looking at existing expenditure in terms of value for money and scrutinising any proposed increases. Stories of large staffs, high expenses payments to councillors and needless subsidies to those who can afford to pay for things themselves cause alarm and anger among ratepayers and taxpayers alike. In this situation some reassurance about next year's rate burden is needed… I believe that the least we can do for next year is to transfer to the exchequer the cost of teachers' salaries… Other expenditure such as that on the police or fire services could rank for increased grants in the same way as the last Conservative Government decided to put 90% of the cost of student grants on to the exchequer. It would be a condition of any such transfer that local authorities would not spend more in other directions. Otherwise the citizen as both taxpayer and ratepayer would be worse off than before the changes. In the long-term the system of local government finance must be changed so that it reflects the ability of people to pay.[2]

The contradictory messages – higher public spending while reining in public spending, insisting on the freedom of councils to make decisions while imposing new constraints – did her no harm at all. They were to do her much more harm when she returned to this theme towards the end of her career. In August 1974 she lit up the political sky, as far as bewildered Conservatives were concerned. Their internal polling suggested that most property owners welcomed help with their rates bills and paid little attention to the detail.

During August 1974, Thatcher was also the star of a party election broadcast, an important outlet when a second general election was moving into view. In the broadcast she hailed a property-owning democracy, including an expensive plan to subsidize mortgages. She also vaguely reiterated her plans to abolish the unpopular property tax. Then, during the October election, Thatcher was the star of another Conservative Party broadcast. The dry remit of shadow Environment Secretary was giving her the kind of peak-time TV exposure that her colleagues would have died for. She had not sought the glamorous slots, but even then she was a performer and discovered that she enjoyed performing.

At this early phase she was contemplating a replacement to the rates based on the ability to pay. When she revisited the policy in her 1987 manifesto, she was no longer bothered by the ability-to-pay principle, with fatal consequences. Soon after that triumphant 1987 election campaign her new plan to abolish the rates by replacing it with the poll tax would propel her towards her doom. But in the summer of 1974 Thatcher was heading for the top of her party, although she did not realize it at the time.

She was fortunate not to know. Potential leaders are placed at a considerable advantage when they do not recognize how close they are to the crown. Recognition leads to nervy, self-conscious ambition and a giddy excitement, a near-fatal combination. As we have seen, one of the persistent lessons of leadership is that most leaders-in-waiting do not become leaders. In the summer of 1974 neither Thatcher nor anyone else realized that she was in such an elevated position. She became a leader without being a leader-in-waiting, a major factor in her ascendancy.

A few weeks after Thatcher's hyperactive summer, Harold Wilson, once again prime minister, called a second election. It was to be held in October. Thatcher was the Conservative star of the contest. In another dark campaign, where politicians were battling it out over who could be least unpopular, there she was, self-confidently saying in effect, 'I can do something that a lot of you would like.' She had been a severe Education Secretary, famous for ending free school milk, but in this subdued autumnal election she had changed into an early Santa Claus, promising help with mortgages and the end of rates. Polls suggested her policies were popular. Desperate to win the election, or not lose it too heavily, Conservative strategists deployed Thatcher regularly on TV throughout the campaign. In her star appearance during the party election broadcast, she explained in safely broad terms her approach, and highlighted how she would help those facing big mortgage repayments – another set of proposals that she privately had doubts about. But she conveyed no doubts whatsoever in public. During this period of her career she learned the art of unswerving advocacy, whatever her private doubts. Suddenly the former Education Secretary of limited prominence became one of the great Tory media stars.

The timing of her rise was accidental, but a form of political perfection for a potential leader. Other factors outside her own direct control also played into her hands. After the October election and another defeat for the Conservatives, Heath unintentionally delivered for her again, by putting Thatcher in his shadow Treasury team. Growing in confidence as a public performer, she more than held her own in the House of Commons, even against the formidable Labour chancellor, Denis Healey. Conservative MPs took note. Thatcher was seen to be flourishing in the key area of economic policy-making, just as a significant number of Conservative MPs were beginning to decide they had endured Heath's leadership long enough. By then he had lost two elections in a year. In retrospect, the level of support for Heath was remarkable, given his record of election defeats, even if he was taken aback by the disloyalty of those who turned against him.

Heath, more than anyone else, gave Thatcher the chance to become leader of her party, by making her shadow Environment

Secretary first, and then giving her an economic brief. He never forgave her for succeeding him, but she was his inadvertent creation.

After the October 1974 election defeat, some Conservative MPs wondered whether the right-wing candidate in any leadership contest should be Sir Keith Joseph. Thatcher and Joseph were close ideologically, while being incomparably different political personalities. Joseph agonized almost visibly as he moved from being a hyperactive Housing Minister under Harold Macmillan, and a relatively high-spending Social Services Secretary in Heath's Cabinet, to becoming an advocate of free-market conservatism and monetarism after the party's election defeat in February 1974. Thatcher endured no equivalent ideological stress. Joseph was a deeper thinker, but a much poorer communicator and without a populist bone in his political body. Thatcher adored him and assumed that he would stand in a leadership contest, if one were held. This genuine assumption helped her enormously. While few perceived her as a leader-in-waiting, she was content to focus on Joseph as leader of the Tory right. She was not in agony about her own ambitions to be leader, which helped her a great deal.

However, during the latter part of 1974 Joseph lost credibility as a potential leader, with a series of controversial speeches that highlighted his distinct unsuitability for leadership. In one speech he suggested that poor people should stop having so many children, an argument that at the very least conveyed a lack of sensitivity when framing a case. Joseph had poor judgement. He had a thousand ideas before breakfast, but in expressing them he alarmed significant sections of the electorate and the media. He was a deep-thinking intellectual, but a political innocent. In contrast, Thatcher was highly political and not as deep-thinking – a more convenient combination for modern leadership. Already she was learning to frame radical policies in ways that had a populist appeal. She was as ideological as Joseph, but the difference was that she was a natural communicator and most of the time knew how far she could go in her public declarations. Joseph was an awkward conveyer of ideas, and possessed no safety valve to prevent avoidable controversy. Neither Joseph nor Thatcher had a great interest in the media at this point, but Thatcher had an instinctive sense of how to use newspapers and broadcasters. There were occasions when Joseph gave interviews to broadcasters when he had no idea whether they were live or recorded, or quite what the distinction might imply.

Painfully self-aware, Joseph did not try very hard to build support for a challenge to the leadership. He knew his cause was doomed. Thatcher was the obvious alternative candidate on the right. Her prominence just when a leadership contest seemed inevitable was an early example of her luck as a potential leader. She was to become a lucky leader, too.

She was fortunate in that the leadership contest was perfectly timed for her and she didn't look self-serving. She had been carrying out her duties as a middle-ranking shadow Cabinet member rather than scheming for the top job. Thatcher had nothing to be transparent about; she was not calculating her moves towards the leadership until close to her battle with Heath in early 1975. By then a lot of Tory MPs ached for a contest. Thatcher would be the right-wing candidate, even though she hadn't displayed a great deal of ideological verve, or a sense of intense personal ambition. She had been solidly loyal to Heath as he battled with the unions and conducted various policy U-turns. She had got on with her job at Education without ranging very much further, publicly or privately. To Heath's fuming surprise, she challenged him early in 1975.

A combination of her starring role from February 1974, including her headline-grabbing policy to abolish the rates – a proposition that she never forgot – and the implosion of Joseph's leadership bid meant that she became a candidate in the contest held in February 1975. The contest was both intimidating and relatively undemanding. For her, the context was close to political bliss. Heath had lost three elections and was a curmudgeonly and awkward campaigner, unable to hide his dismay at being challenged by this annoying woman with strident right-wing views, whom he had tolerated on his frontbench.

But on another level, Thatcher was taking on the party's establishment, and with little time to prepare for the psychological challenge of a contest. Most of the Tory heavyweights backed Heath in the contest. They included those figures perceived to have wider appeal in the country, such as the popular and emollient Willie Whitelaw, who had been under pressure to stand himself, but was too loyal to Heath to contemplate such an act of insurrection.[3] Others who backed Heath were his shadow chancellor, Robert Carr; Lord Carrington, who was to become Thatcher's Foreign Secretary; and James Prior, Thatcher's first Employment Secretary. Their support for Heath showed the degree to which she was the insurrectionary candidate, and her willingness, once leader, to work with them.

'One nation' Tories, those regarded as moderate pragmatists, gathered around Heath not only out of loyalty, but because they were part of an ideological battle, even if the divisions were only vaguely defined. Thatcher was campaigning from the right, but largely with a series of clichés about rewarding hard work. She was filmed for ITV's *World in Action* washing up at home, before dashing off for a meeting – a woman of action. In other interviews she conveyed a restless energy, but was smart enough not to be too clearly defined. After Thatcher won the contest, the *Guardian*'s columnist Peter Jenkins suggested that we knew little about the Conservatives' new leader, despite the fact that she had dominated the media. It had been 'Thatcherated', as he wrote the day after she was elected. He added that in spite of Thatcher's ubiquity, little was known about the direction in which she would lead the party.[4]

Heath knew more than Jenkins seemed to do. After he was defeated in the first ballot of the contest he looked up at his adviser, William Waldegrave, and declared, 'It has all gone wrong then.' In his memoir, Waldegrave suggests that the outgoing leader was referring to the end of 'one nation' conservatism as well as his own career. If Heath was indeed looking beyond the death of his career, he was prophetic. 'He realised that his defeat meant that a sea change was coming over the British right.'[5]

Whitelaw entered the second round of the contest, but by then Thatcher had momentum, benefiting with good cause from launching a challenge in the first place. In this contest, and for many years to come, Thatcher was smart at making the most of perceived momentum. She often appeared as if she was being thrust forward unstoppably by a gust of wind, almost as if resistance was pointless.

Even so, in the immediate aftermath of her leadership victory, she did not stride on indiscriminately. Instead she displayed one of her more overlooked qualities as a leader. In the early years of her leadership Thatcher recognized that the amount of space available to her on the political stage was extremely limited. She might have appeared strident, but in policy terms and in her use of patronage as party leader, she moved cautiously, knowing she had no choice but to do so.

Her genius was to know when she had more space to act. She was politically agile. This was her wiliness, an essential part of leadership. At the beginning she wisely appointed most of Heath's allies to senior posts. She knew this was not the time to make ideological appointments. Thatcher might have won the contest, but her relative inexperience and the range of internal doubters made her fragile, and she knew it. She was disinclined to spend time on introspective reflection, a major flaw, and yet she sensed how far she could go without needing to calculate for too long.

Thatcher made Willie Whitewall her deputy. Whitelaw proved to be loyal, but occasionally candid. Arguably he was too loyal at times, wary of challenging her unless he had no choice but to do so. She was not to know this when she appointed him to the second most senior post in the party. With his authority and experience, Whitelaw might have made life difficult for her.

Those she later dismissed as 'wets' – Jim Prior, Peter Walker and Ian Gilmour – were also appointed to senior positions in her shadow Cabinet and first government. Norman St John-Stevas, a mischievous observer of Thatcher's rise, was also given a post, even though Thatcher had no time for mischief or humour. This was not because she had no sense of fun. Contrary to the mythology, she could sometimes fleetingly see the funny side of situations, but she had no tolerance of humour deployed against her and no understanding of topical comedy references. Indeed, her populism did not extend to an affected attachment to popular TV culture or sport, a big difference with some of her successors and predecessors.

―――――

Even if she did not pretend to follow sport or fashionable TV, beyond the glorious satire *Yes Minister*, Thatcher was one of the great political actors and relished politics as performance, in contrast to the UK's second female prime minister, Theresa May. Thatcher also gave the impression of unyielding purpose. From February 1975 to the election in May 1979, her leadership was a model of how to move a party towards a more radical position without fatally alienating its more cautious wing. Her dance with colleagues in the early years was a delicate one, compared with the more punk routine a few years later, when she knew she had the space to let her hair down.

Part of the fascination is that Thatcher kept her internal critics more or less at bay without being tonally emollient, or especially cautious, in the expression of her ideological verve. Her correspondence with colleagues in the late 1970s, chronicled illuminatingly on the Thatcher Foundation website, is full of exclamation marks and written shrieks of assertive disapproval. One such document on the website is the draft 1979 manifesto, with Thatcher's scribbled handwriting on every paragraph proposing, from her perspective, smart revisions. There are exclamation marks and question marks as paragraphs are underlined by her. She was a natural sub-editor. Her proposed revisions made the final version in 1979 far more accessible.

In interviews she made clear that she would not have time for long Cabinet discussions on policy if she won the election. She gave a long interview to the *Observer*'s Kenneth Harris a few months before the 1979 election, in which she conveyed unqualified intolerance towards internal dissent: 'As Prime Minister I couldn't waste time having any internal arguments. My Cabinet would have to be a conviction government.'[6]

Indeed, after her election as leader in 1975 she had an insatiable appetite for discussing why she had reached her unyielding convictions – a hunger that was novel in British politics. Most leaders of the Opposition, especially those with limited experience, avoid reflecting on their ideological beliefs, if they happen to have any. They prefer to deploy banal terms such as 'modernization' and the 'radical centre' in their search for wide electoral support. As part of their cautious strategy they avoid challenging interviews. In striking contrast, Thatcher sought to meet her hunger for debating ideas almost immediately after becoming leader of the Opposition.

From the time when she became leader of the Conservative Party in 1975 to her election as prime minister in 1979, Thatcher never shied away from formidable TV interrogators, both in the UK and the US. One of her favourite US programmes was *Firing Line*, an hour-long interview with the right-wing radical William Buckley. She appeared on his show on several occasions as leader of the Opposition. Buckley shared many of her convictions, but that made him in some respects a tougher interviewer. He was steeped in the work of F. A. Hayek and many other philosophers that the Republican right was turning towards. He could be scathing to interviewees on the right. But Thatcher could not get enough of his programme, even though her appearances, broadcast only in the US, were of limited value to a domestic audience in an era when they would not be seen on YouTube or highlighted by fans or critics on Twitter. She appeared on his shows because she relished the discussions. In her first appearance on *Firing Line* she framed arguments around opportunity: 'I regard opportunity as the chance to be unequal as well as the chance to be equal.'[7] Later in the same interview she declared sweepingly, 'Property is freedom.'[8]

Such assertions raise a multitude of questions. What is the role of the state in addressing inequality for those who have limited opportunities? What does Thatcher mean by 'opportunity', given that inequality of opportunity is deeply entrenched? Does she accept that she had more 'opportunities', as the wife of a millionaire? Why is property necessarily an agent of freedom? What precisely does she mean by 'freedom'?

And on we could go. But the assertions, when repeated to UK audiences on TV and other platforms, had a wide and accessible appeal. It is not easy to argue that voters should not own properties or should not be 'free'. In 1979 Labour tried to challenge some of her ideas by opposing the sale of council homes. It lost the election. Who can be against 'opportunity' and yet win the argument? The challenge for Thatcher's opponents was to frame the debate in a different way, showing how the state can be an agent of freedom and opportunity. They failed to do so confidently and effectively, although Labour's deputy leader after 1983, Roy Hattersley, made the best attempt. His book outlining Labour's ideas and values was called *Choose Freedom*, a title that purloined from Thatcher two of her favourite words. But Hattersley made little impact when his book was published in the late 1980s. He was too late. By the late 1970s Thatcher was framing arguments that moved the tides rightwards. The policies would follow, but first she made the arguments. Labour had given her the space to do so, by failing to come up with a coherent and accessible left-of-centre alternative. There was a powerful left-of-centre critique to be made that might have challenged

Thatcherism in the late 1970s and beyond, but the left split in many different ways, whereas over time much of the Conservative Party coalesced around Thatcher.

As Opposition leader, Thatcher was also fearless in facing interrogations in the UK. In July 1977 she appeared on BBC1's *Panorama*, then a more nuanced and weighty programme. For nearly an hour Thatcher was interviewed by the broadcaster David Dimbleby and three of the more formidable columnists from that era, Peter Jenkins, Anthony Shrimsley and Mary Goldring. This was in the era when there were only a handful of political columnists, each of them influential. Thatcher more than held her own, although the BBC helped by giving the programme the flattering title of *The Alternative Prime Minister*. Once again she was blunt in her ideological arguments, unswervingly self-confident, but again less specific in terms of policy. At one point she was asked, 'Are you a pragmatist?' She replied astutely and revealingly: 'I'm a pragmatist in the true sense of the word… putting your principles into practice.'

In seeking definition, another of the interviewers asked her, 'Are you right-wing?' Without hesitating, Thatcher made the term one that could have wide electoral appeal: 'Define what you mean by right-wing… you can't look after hard-working people unless you create enough wealth to do so… My views don't differ very much from Iain Macleod [Heath's short-serving chancellor, who died of a heart attack and was widely seen as having been much closer to Heath's politics than to Thatcher's] … If you want lower taxes it's called right-wing… If you support the police it's called right-wing… If you want to sell council homes it's called right-wing… If you want to uphold standards in education it's called right-wing… If you call that right-wing, I'm right-wing.'

She went on to argue that the 'whole philosophy of the Conservative Party revolves around the freedom of the individual… a belief in the sanctity of the individual'.

Any individual voter watching the interview might well like the idea of being sanctified, but in order for a country to be governed effectively there needs to be powerful and efficient mediating agencies. Thatcher was less interested in the binding forces and much more enthused about 'liberating' individuals from what she, and quite a lot of voters, regarded as the stifling state. Her focus was potent. For voters, it is more flattering to hear that the alternative prime minister valued them, above all, as individuals. The state would get off their backs and allow them to flourish. At this stage, because Thatcher framed arguments that were accompanied by relatively vague policies, Peter Jenkins asked her whether her heart was on the right, but her head was on the centre. Her response was unequivocal: 'I'm in politics to say and do what I believe… I do believe in things passionately [and] I have to compromise… but I'm not an eternal compromiser.'[9]

Many years later, some of Ed Miliband's closest advisers suggested that he 'do a Thatcher' and take part in a series of tough interviews in which he posed radical arguments. Miliband liked to think of himself as Labour's Margaret Thatcher. But he was too fearful of the intimidating TV interview, and too constrained by his New Labour upbringing, to be her equivalent from the left. Her equivalent from the left was Tony Benn in the 1970s and 1980s and, to some extent, Jeremy Corbyn when he succeeded Miliband in 2015. But unlike Thatcher, Corbyn was wary of the long interview with sceptical interviewers. He hardly ever took part in interviews. Thatcher relished them.

But in one important respect she was playing safe in her radical assertiveness. Once again, almost instinctively, she could sense what would work for her electorally. The wider political context of the late 1970s was the key to making electoral sense of her early ideological declarations and her assertive leadership style.

As prime minister, Jim Callaghan chaired seemingly never-ending Cabinet meetings before heading off to struggle through equally interminable gatherings of Labour's National Executive Committee, so Thatcher's insistence that she would not tolerate much Cabinet dissent seemed compelling, in contrast to the seemingly weak prime minister. Part of Thatcher's risky ideological relish was therefore utterly expedient; there were immediate advantages for her in claiming to be ideologically self-confident when her main opponent appeared to be bewildered by seismic events. In effect, she was implying 'I am strong. Callaghan is weak' – not a vote-losing pitch in British politics.

She was also championing the individual, when corporatism was in obvious and vivid crisis. It was not especially daring to talk about the need to set individuals free when the state was failing so vividly. She had both eyes on the wider political situation, even though she seemed to be gripped by ideological verve. Crucially, she knew this verve placed her in a flattering light compared with her troubled, traumatized political opponent, a prime minister facing economic crises and industrial unrest in a hung parliament and with a divided Cabinet. Here was an early example of Thatcher sensing how much space she had on the political stage and using it to teach a political lesson, in the coming together of her two distinct skills. She could perform with a degree of crusading zeal partly because she was a performer with convictions, but also because the troubles of Callaghan meant that it was in her interests to convey 'strong leadership'.

In the early years there was a constant interplay between her two leadership skills. She was a teacher, making accessible sense of what she was up to. Often she appeared politically daring, when she had calculated instinctively that what she was saying would win or sustain support. She knew how to win elections.

Her manifesto in 1979 reflected her distinct convictions and her capacity for expediency. Her personal introduction displayed her populism and her essential vision: that the state stifled the freedom of the 'people'. One of her favourite words was 'people':

> For me, the heart of politics is not political theory, it is people and how they want to live their lives. No one who has lived in this country during the last five years can fail to be aware of how the balance of our society has been increasingly tilted in favour of the State at the expense of individual freedom... The State takes too much of the nation's income; its share must be steadily reduced. When it spends and borrows too much, taxes, interest rates, prices and unemployment rise so that in the long run there is less wealth with which to improve our standard of living and our social services.[10]

Her introduction to the 1979 manifesto showed how effectively Thatcher could frame an argument, even a highly contentious one. Most 'people' like the idea of deciding how they want to live their own lives, even if the aspiration is ridiculously simplistic. A left-of-centre politician might have replied that it is only through the state that 'people' can fulfil their potential. This was part of Roy Hattersley's case, as he sought to make an ideological narrative to counter hers, but his arguments got lost in Labour's internal battles.

The Labour leader, Neil Kinnock, also got close to challenging Thatcher's small-state populism when he spoke of the case for an 'enabling state' in his party conference speech in 1985. This was an attempt to show what the state could do, in contrast to Thatcher's caricature of 'the state versus the people'. But this was the speech during which Kinnock launched his famous onslaught against Militant Tendency, the left-wing group described widely and vaguely as 'Trotskyist', which had infiltrated parts of the Labour Party. Kinnock singled out the Militant Tendency leadership of Liverpool council, accusing them of hiring taxis to hand out redundancy notices. The highly theatrical confrontation of Militant Tendency was a pivotal moment in Kinnock's leadership and was widely regarded as one of the great speeches in British politics from the second half of the twentieth century. But as a result of his challenge to Militant Tendency, few noticed his well-argued case for the state as an enabler – an alternative route to Thatcherism. From the late 1970s until the end of her leadership, Thatcher had the space for her ideological populism. She used it ceaselessly. Her ideas and her skill to communicate them were her main political weapons.

Her words in the 1979 manifesto formed the essence of early Thatcherism: let the people be free from the burdens of the state. She pledged to 'restore the balance of power in favour of the people'. Which 'people' would be opposed to giving them 'power' – a conveniently ill-defined term from the great political teacher? In contrast to her desire to liberate the 'people', Labour would 'enlarge the role of the state and diminish the role of the individual'. Again, which individual seeks to be diminished? But Thatcher chose not to recognize that the state could enhance the lives of individuals. Such recognition would challenge her entire crusade.

In terms of policy, the 1979 manifesto was more cautious. The teacher carefully selected policies to illustrate her anti-state lessons. There would be a switch – 'to some extent' – from taxes on earnings to taxes on spending. Despite her exhalations about the virtues of low taxation, there was little detail on this. There needed to be 'responsible pay bargaining' – evasive words partly applied to bind together her shadow Cabinet, which had split over the need for incomes policies. The promise to allow tenants to buy their council homes was the most radical policy, but in setting some tenants 'free', there was no reflection as to what impact it would have on affordable housing in the UK.

Privately Thatcher was opposed to incomes policies, but she equivocated over her attitude in public and at the election. She was a firm opponent of devolution, but her 1979 manifesto promised to review the options. When she won in 1979, she clearly wanted to take her country to the right and she hoped to take on the miners at some point, partly in order to purge memories of the nightmares of the Heath government. She wanted to clamp down on public-sector pay as part of a wider attempt to cut public spending, or to cut the rate of growth in public spending.

But after 1979, with many senior colleagues viewing her warily in spite of her authority-enhancing election victory, she recognized that she had limited space to follow some of her radical instincts. She was not strong enough in the Conservative Party, and, arguably, was not strong enough in the country, to push the boundaries too far. Once again, she knew instinctively how far she could go.

When the miners flexed their muscles early in her first term in power, when she was already deeply unpopular in the polls, Thatcher gave in. She did not believe she was strong enough to win. Similarly, she was cautious on public-sector pay. She tended to give the pay awards that were due without any challenge, even though she wanted to constrain public spending.

But when she sensed space on the political stage was finally opening up for her, she moved at the speed of light. There is a much-repeated myth that after the victory in the Falklands in 1982, Thatcher became almost invincible. Contrary to this widely held view, the Falklands War was not what gave her political space on the stage. Her military victory undoubtedly changed her as a public performer: she became more regal, self-confident and assertively strident. She started to refer more often to Churchill as 'Winston', implying that the two of them were the great war leaders of our times. She saw herself, as much of the media did, as a formidable, courageous leader in the light of the war. But the war was not what propelled her to a landslide victory at the following election.

The key development that guaranteed her future election victories had already taken place by the time of the Falklands. In relation to that easily mythologized conflict, there is a misleading tendency to view her actions through the distorting prism of 'courage' or its opposite lens, 'weakness'.

In reality, Thatcher had no choice but to go to war. Her decision to do so was not 'strong' or 'weak'. The only alternative to a military response would have been her resignation as prime minister. In the immediate aftermath of the invasion by forces of the Argentinian junta in April 1982, the House of Commons met, unusually, the following Saturday. During that extraordinary historic gathering, even the Labour leader, Michael Foot – a unilateralist who sought the removal of nuclear weapons in the UK – demanded a robust military response. Foot's speech was widely praised by Conservative MPs. One of the MPs Thatcher admired most, Enoch Powell, who was by then representing the Unionist Party, implied that she would have to resign if there was no military response. He ended his speech with a challenge in relation to the pride she took in being known as the 'Iron Lady':

The Prime Minister, shortly after she came into office, received a soubriquet as the 'Iron Lady'. It arose in the context of remarks which she made about defence against the Soviet Union and its allies; but there was no reason to suppose that the right hon. Lady did not welcome and, indeed, take pride in that description. In the next week or two this House, the nation and the right hon. Lady herself will learn of what metal she is made.[11]

Whether right or wrong from Thatcher's perspective, the politically brave decision would have been to let Argentina keep the Falklands. Margaret Thatcher's decision to take on the junta and go to war was not an act of bravery. No leader is ever fully prepared for taking a country into war, and to do so demands steeliness, but for Thatcher going to war was the politically safe option. As an Iron Lady, she had to show her mettle if she wished to survive.

There were many consequences arising from her victory. The subsequent inquiry into the war, the Franks Report of 1983, was highly critical of government policy towards the Falklands in the months preceding the Argentinian invasion. But few voters noticed. Thatcher had won. That was all that mattered, as far as they were concerned. Shortly after the Falklands War, a young Tony Blair was the Labour candidate in a by-election for the safe Conservative seat of Beaconsfield. Blair noted how commanding Thatcher had become, in the eyes of voters, as a result of the war, and that victory wiped out any questions about her culpability in advance of the war. Later, when Blair made his moves towards Iraq, his former Foreign Secretary, Robin Cook, an opponent of the Iraq War, was convinced that Blair's first electoral test in the immediate aftermath of the Falklands conflict played its part in his mindset. Thatcher's Falklands victory seemed to suggest that, in the UK, wars were popular and enhanced the authority of a prime minister. What was said and done before the war was soon forgotten, if a tyrant was toppled. One of Blair's many calculations as he moved towards Iraq was that a similar sequence might apply. There was much talk after 1982 of the 'Falklands Factor'. After the fall of Saddam Hussein, Blair's Downing Street spoke with naive optimism about a 'Baghdad Bounce' – a deliberate echo.

But the Falklands War was not what gave Thatcher wider political space to move her government and the country rightwards. This was due to the split in the Labour Party. The formal schism in the Labour Party, which began to take shape in 1980 when Michael Foot was elected leader, and was formalized in 1981 with the creation of the SDP, meant there was one near-certainty in the wildly unpredictable world of politics: only the Conservative Party could win the next election. If the left-wing alternative was split in two, the non-Conservative parties would inevitably cancel each other out. There was a brief phase during the SDP's honeymoon when it looked as if the new party might sweep the country, such was the excitement generated by charismatic former Labour figures leading a new party. But the SDP was never going to defeat Labour in parts of Scotland and the north of England. Conversely, Labour was more threatened by the SDP than the Conservatives were. The SDP had been formed against Labour, and largely defined itself against Labour as a centrist party. The historic schism, rare in British politics, meant that Margaret Thatcher had the good fortune to face a split Opposition. The formation of the SDP was another example of her luck as a leader. In terms of securing her future as prime minister, it was far more significant than the Falklands.

When the schism within Labour was formalized, Thatcher started to make her more radical moves. In September 1981 she purged her Cabinet of her despised 'wets', sacking some of them and moving Jim Prior to Northern Ireland, which was in some ways a more severe punishment. She brought in Norman Tebbit to become her new Employment Secretary, replacing Prior, and a few other like-minded allies and started to become more daring, because she knew she could win the next election when facing a divided Opposition. The key reshuffle took place six months before the Falklands War.

Similarly, in the second term, having won a landslide in 1983, she became more willing to take risks because she saw that she had even more political space. For a radical prime minister, landslides are liberating. There was no internal opposition by then. She had purged her Cabinet of severe critics. The new Labour leader, Neil Kinnock, was inexperienced and faced mountainous internal challenges, while the formidable David Owen, as leader of the SDP, was more anti-Labour than anti-Thatcher at this stage in his topsy-turvy political career.[12] Seeing that her opponents were still fatally split, Thatcher knew she could make her next moves. With detailed policies relating to privatization, income-tax cuts for high earners, light regulation for the financial sector, and the defeat of the miners, Thatcherism took shape when she sensed – rightly – that she could take the risks. In policy terms, her programme from 1983 was closer to what she meant when talking about setting the people 'free' in the mid- to late 1970s.

———

In the UK, political leaders and journalists were to become overly obsessed with the benefits of 'spin' and the need for 'spin doctors', or media advisers, to guide leaders through the wild storms. But effective leaders need no guidance. Thatcher was her own spin doctor.

She was an instinctive communicator. You could agree or disagree with what she was saying, and many of her messages were banal or economically nonsensical, but they made sense of complicated, dry economic policies. She gave a running commentary on monetarism and other policies, without an Alastair Campbell figure or a Peter Mandelson to spin it for her. She had media instructors to tell her how to speak on TV, but she did not need them. Indeed, she seemed over-rehearsed after sessions with them, sometimes absurdly so. To take one example, in the late 1970s Thatcher hired a voice-coach and, following the sessions, her voice became noticeably low. Thatcher was a good political actress, but the change was too noticeable and clunky. The clunkiness was equally evident when she read out jokes written by someone else, attempts at wit that she did not fully understand. She was most effective as a performer when following her own instincts.

Her press secretary, Bernard Ingham, was devoted to Thatcher and dealt with the media. But Ingham was a civil servant and not as overtly committed as some of his successors. Of course she benefited from a largely doting set of newspapers, another significant weapon in her political armoury. Nonetheless, she spoke about politics with a partisan accessibility. During the late 1970s, in trying to explain her growing support for monetarism, she told voters that her father, who had owned a grocer's shop in Grantham, never spent more than he earned. She argued that, like her father, a country should never spend more than it earned. She was being simplistic to the point of economic illiteracy – the state is starkly different from a grocer's shop – but the lessons from her youth were powerful ways of conveying what she was trying to do, and her opponents never discovered an alternative language. Her messages were easy to understand and they appeared to make sense of what might have been more widely perceived as draconian, radical economic policies.

While she was making sense of highly complex and contentious economic policies Thatcher was building up an important and, at that point, constructive relationship with her shadow chancellor, Geoffrey Howe. In some respects Howe was as pivotal to the economic revolution as she was, and arguably even more so. That was certainly Howe's own view, even though much of the time he was a decent, modest and tolerant political figure. Thatcher found him deeply irritating, partly because of his reticent qualities, but she could not have done without him.

Howe had written his first budget before he arrived at the Treasury in 1979 and already had a good idea what his second budget would be. As Howe's colleague and ideological critic, Ian Gilmour, was to argue brilliantly in his book *Dancing with Dogma*, written after he was sacked as a Cabinet minister, some of the government's early economic policies had catastrophic consequences and were wholly counter-productive, making worse the matters they were seeking to address. To take one example, some of the early policies fuelled inflation, when Thatcher and Howe regarded inflation as one of their overwhelming challenges. But in terms of leadership, Thatcher and Howe were a model. She was the wilful communicator and he was the dutiful policy-maker. When Gordon Brown and Ed Balls planned their move to the Treasury in 1997, their model in terms of readiness for power was Howe. Brown had almost written his first budget in advance and was ready with his plan to make the Bank of England independent.[13]

Long after Thatcher had watered down her own and Howe's monetarist policies – while insisting the lady was not for turning – she continued to be a political teacher. 'We're giving industries to the people' was her explanation for privatization.[14] She was always trying to make sense of what she was doing. Tony Benn, who was in this respect her equivalent in the Labour Party, noted regularly in his diaries that Thatcher was a teacher. Although they disagreed with each other profoundly, he saw this as one of her great strengths. Benn was one of the few senior Labour politicians who recognized from the beginning that Thatcher would be formidable. Towards the end of her career, Thatcher became in turn an admirer of Benn's, turning up in the Commons to listen to his speeches on Europe and nodding passionately. Benn was a political teacher, too.[15]

The two lessons of Thatcher's leadership place her in a formidable light. She was the teacher who made sense of contentious policies, and a smart reader of the rhythms of politics, knowing when, as a leader with radical ambitions, she could act and when she needed to be more restrained. Both explain her longevity.

The third overlooked lesson about Margaret Thatcher's leadership is based partly on retrospective criticisms. These come as much from her former colleagues in their memoirs as from her opponents. The critics extend well beyond Gilmour, in some respects. As she pursued radical policies, sometimes with apparent success, she was often indifferent to addressing the consequences of the changes, the hardest element of policy-making. There is the glamour of introducing a policy and being hailed as a change-maker. Then there is the hard grind of making sure there are no unintended consequences. For a workaholic, Thatcher was uninterested in the hard grind of following up policies, or perhaps she was too impatient to reflect on the follow-ups that would be required. Her lack of forensic curiosity was part of Gilmour's much wider critique, but it is also a failing that was noted by other former colleagues who were less critical.

The sale of council houses, a policy from Thatcher's 1979 manifesto, was an early example of the radical dash towards implementation followed by a restless moving on. Here was an innovation that transformed not only housing in Britain, but electoral politics in general. Suddenly some tenants became house owners and they moved into the market at a point when property was booming in parts of the UK. Tenants who took the opportunity to sell in a booming private market became quite well off as a result. Some of them sold their council houses and voted for Thatcher gratefully. The prime minister was famously photographed visiting appreciative tenants who were now owners, and having cups of tea with them. She enjoyed the cups of tea and the potent symbolism of gatherings with traditional Labour voters. After the visits she showed little further interest. She overlooked what should follow on from such a dramatic reform.

After the council houses were sold off, her governments made no attempt to rebuild affordable housing on the scale required. As a result there has been a housing crisis ever since, a chronic shortage of affordable rented accommodation in particular. The shortage had several consequences, from rising homelessness to soaring housing benefit bills, as the state paid for those who could not find rented accommodation in the public sector to stay in expensive private accommodation.

Thatcher's sale of council properties – the policy that Labour later supported and accepted it was wrong to oppose in the first place – had no follow-through. Instead, she and her favourite Cabinet ministers became obsessed with new forms of ownership. After the 1987 election her Environment Secretary and close ally, Nicholas Ridley, announced a 'housing revolution'. His proposals included new quangos known as Housing Action Trusts, taking over rundown estates; and, separately, private landlords acquiring new rights to buy and rent council homes. It was a housing revolution without any new houses. The left had been gripped by the ideology of ownership in the 1970s and early 1980s, favouring more public ownership. Thatcher and Ridley, whom she greatly admired, were equally ideological from the right, in some ways even more fascinated by questions of ownership. For them, private ownership was the solution. They were not especially interested in constructing new affordable homes, how they should be built and by whom. These were tough and demanding questions. Thatcher did not even ask them, let alone answer them. She did not think policies through beyond their immediate impact. By the late 1980s young people were struggling to rent or buy, especially in cities where property prices were soaring.

The same sequence applied to the defeat of the miners in 1985, a victory for Thatcher that marked the end of the era that had partly defined her. She had been brought up politically with muscular unions wreaking havoc under Heath, Wilson and Callaghan in the 1970s. With a landslide parliament, stockpiles of coal and the NUM leader, Arthur Scargill, lacking the guile to compromise, Thatcher secured a different answer from Heath, who had posed the question 'Who governs Britain?' in the February 1974 election. Heath lost. Thatcher governed, and defeated the miners with a brutal ruthlessness.

Scargill might have lacked guile – to the fury of the tormented Labour leader, Neil Kinnock – but the cause of the conflict was, and remains, nuanced.[16] The government argued that 'uneconomic pits' should close. Scargill refused to accept that the pits were uneconomic. He had a stronger case than he managed to make with his inflammatory, confrontational style. He was a fierce and angry orator but, unlike Thatcher, he was not an effective political teacher, even when he had a strong case. Declaiming with little tonal variation, Scargill argued that the price of imported energy was bound to fluctuate and, because of this, there were huge risks in closing pits that could still produce home-grown energy. But Thatcher, the political teacher, won wider electoral support with her portrayal of striking miners acting recklessly and unpatriotically. At one point, with a reference to the Falklands War, she provocatively described the miners who had been on strike as 'the enemy within'.

As several members of her Cabinet have written since, her government made little attempt to rebuild the communities that had been dependent on mining. Cash-strapped local authorities were in no position to do very much, either. As a result, once-vibrant communities became hollowed out. There should have been a follow-through, when all those jobs were lost and there was very little to replace them. But once again Thatcher had lost interest and moved on to other areas.

Norman Tebbit was one of her colleagues who made this point in his memoirs, going beyond his caricature, as he sometimes did, to argue that her government should have intervened more to revive suddenly desolate towns and villages.[17] Tebbit was seen widely as a political thug. Michael Foot once described him as a 'semi house-trained polecat'. But he could be more thoughtful and friendly to political opponents than Thatcher was. Thatcher's more unyielding ideology precluded an interventionist approach. Her limited attention span was a factor, too.

In his memoir, Geoffrey Howe was especially critical of Thatcher's decision to abolish the Greater London Council (GLC) and the other big metropolitan authorities in England, without replacing them. Thatcher's argument was that there were too many tiers of government in England. Instead of deciding what the appropriate tiers might be, she rushed to abolish the metropolitan authorities, all of which happened to be Labour-led. She felt especially provoked by the GLC, which was headed in its final phase by Ken Livingstone, at his peak a much smarter left-wing leader than Arthur Scargill. Polls suggested that Livingstone was popular in London, in spite of the usual indiscriminate media-bashing that he received. Unusually for Thatcher, instead of attempting to beat him in an ideological battle, she abolished him, or at least his power base. But as usual there was no follow-through. In effect, she nationalized parts of London's services previously run by the GLC. Vaguely accountable quangos became responsible for running an increasingly dysfunctional transport system. The capital had no leadership and no one accountable for what was happening. The political teacher, who talked about the stifling state and giving power to the people, gave more power to the state by scrapping metropolitan councils, and left people in the big cities utterly powerless in the face of declining public services. She never understood that democratically accountable mediating agencies can empower users of public services. She had got rid of a tier of government and then largely lost interest in the consequences. Always in a hurry, she moved on yet again.

So it was with her radical economic policies. Many of them were regarded as successful. The Big Bang in 1986 – the new, light regulatory touch in relation to the City – generated great wealth for individuals and much additional revenue for the government, as London became a global financial centre. But sweeping deregulation also created an environment in which there was little control. Governments ceased to seek greater regulation, or didn't dare make the case for it. In the 1980s the seeds were sown for the financial crash that followed in 2008.

For someone who could immerse herself in policy detail if she wanted to, Thatcher could become quickly indifferent. Strong leaders must address the consequence of their reforms or the chickens will come home to roost. Some of Thatcher's roosting chickens included an acute shortage of affordable housing; widening inequality, with some communities being more or less wiped out while those in the financial sector earned a fortune; and poorly led cities with haphazard and badly run services. These were avoidable consequences of significant reforms. They were not inevitable. If she had paid more attention as to what happened next in relation to her restless radicalism, the consequences would have been nowhere near as significant.

In 2018 Michael Heseltine neatly summarized Thatcher's contradictory nature, as the shallow thinker who was capable of deeper analysis:

If you went to cabinet with a paper that was your responsibility before you got three sentences out she would be haranguing you and yet deep down she hated people who gave in to her. She had a respect for those that did not give in. So you would wait until she drew breath and start again. You would say 'I've heard what you said but this was the point… if I may continue…' There were two Margaret Thatchers. There was the Margaret Thatcher with lots of shallow instincts and personal experiences… She would talk about a policy or idea based on a farmer she met or what tenants she met did with their council house… and this wasn't intellectually appealing… There was another Margaret Thatcher where you would seek to change a discussion from her gut instincts to more of an intellectual dialogue… then you could persuade her.[18]

Towards the end of her leadership, Europe came to dominate, with Heseltine hovering on the backbenches as a passionate pro-

European. Thatcher was the first Conservative prime minister partly to fall over Europe, but she was by no means the last. Her three immediate successors as Conservative prime minister, John Major, David Cameron and Theresa May, also fell as a result of Europe. The third successor, Theresa May, led a government in which the issue of Europe overwhelmed all others.

Over Europe and much more, Thatcher had transformed her party into one with a much more radical cutting edge. The dance between leader and party can be tense and jagged. The one between Thatcher and her party was neat and symmetrical. The Conservative Party became much more Thatcherite. She personified the changes in her own party. As part of the change, she moved the Conservatives towards a more Eurosceptic position and became, in the end, the first prime ministerial victim of that move.

In tone she was increasingly hostile to Europe, although rarely in practice. She was, after all, a great advocate of the 1986 Single European Act and of the single market that was its consequence. It was she who signed the UK up to every single treaty during her period as prime minister. But she viewed with alarm the moves towards the integrationist Maastricht Treaty. She had left power by the time her successor, John Major, signed the Treaty with several big opt-outs for the UK, but her influence lingered: she actively encouraged backbenchers to vote against Maastricht, in spite of Major's significant efforts to extract substantial concessions in difficult negotiations.

Yet to her credit, while prime minister, Thatcher was happy enough to appoint senior Cabinet ministers who took a very different position from her in what became a highly charged and emotive policy area for the Conservative Party. Her senior ministers tended to be pro-Europeans: Ken Clarke, Douglas Hurd, Geoffrey

Howe, Michael Heseltine. Her political generosity contributed to her fall. These Cabinet ministers, or former Cabinet ministers, were growing increasingly alarmed by Thatcher's tendency to be shrill at European Union gatherings and to display hostility towards the EU in the House of Commons. Days before Sir Geoffrey Howe made his famous resignation speech in the autumn of 1990, she screamed, 'No, no, no' in relation to various integrationist propositions that had emerged from an EU summit in Rome.

The removal of Margaret Thatcher marked one of the final assertive acts from senior Conservatives in favour of the European Union. This act of regicide, however, weakened their position in a party that had become ideologically wary of Europe. But Europe alone did not bring Thatcher down. The policy that made her in the first place was the one that led to her fall. Always at the back of her mind, she remembered that election in October 1974 when she became a TV star by pledging to scrap the local property tax.

In a partial repeat of her rise to the leadership, she went into the 1987 election pledging to abolish rates. In marked and fatal contrast to the mid-1970s, she had a precise alternative, the Community Charge, which soon became known, disastrously, as the poll tax. Focusing more on the abolition of the rates than on its alternative, she assumed the proposal would be as popular as it had been in October 1974. She referred to the Community Charge as the 'flagship' reform of her third term. Crucially, Thatcher made the mistake of proposing an alternative flat-rate tax. This was the policy that ultimately brought her down. In the mid-1970s her vague alternative property tax had been based on the 'ability to pay'.

The poll tax became unpopular in Scotland to the point that the Conservatives were virtually wiped out as a political force. Thatcher introduced it there first, a year early, which was seen by many Scottish voters as an unforgivable act of provocation from the Conservative government at Westminster. Arguably the rise of the Scottish National Party (SNP) began with the poll tax. The policy certainly explains the decline of the Conservative Party in Scotland up until the election of Ruth Davidson as party leader in Scotland. But when she introduced the same policy in England it proved to be equally unpopular, not only in Labour areas, but in Conservative ones, too. In particular, Conservative leaders at local government conferences were up in arms, which was wholly out of character. By instinct they were usually loyal to the national leadership. This was an early sign of the way the Conservative Party was changing. Support for the national leadership from senior activists was no longer automatic. This became a much bigger theme from the fall of Thatcher onwards. In the late 1980s the emollient Local Government Minister, David Hunt, would say to journalists as he headed towards the podium to make a speech to councillors who were previously Tory loyalists, 'Into the lions' den once more.' The lions tore him apart at every available opportunity.[19]

Chris Patten was Environment Secretary at the time and he used to take the projected poll-tax bills to Margaret Thatcher. In some cases they showed huge increases. As Patten told journalists privately, 'I show Margaret Hilda these poll-tax projected levels and she looks up to me and says, "Chris, I don't believe you."'[20] She was so convinced that the policy would be popular, and that it was necessary as a means of holding councils to account while making them more efficient, that she would not listen.[21]

But by the end Thatcher did listen. She was still alert to danger, even though she was by then losing her unusually sharp political antennae. She had lost her great skill of recognizing the space available to her on the political stage. In a frantic last-minute bid to hold on to power, she offered a whole series of revisions to the poll tax, exempting large numbers of voters and imposing caps on the amount that local authorities could charge, in a way that undermined the principle of the proposal in the first place. She showed, as she often had in the past, that in the end she was willing to compromise to hold on to power. But it was too late.

She was making increasingly frantic moves when the parliamentary party alone determined who would be leader. In effect, Conservative MPs removed her in the most dramatic internal act of political execution in modern times. They did so because enough of them feared they would lose their seats under her leadership. Having been a sharp reader of her own political strength at any given time, Thatcher strongly underestimated her vulnerability by the autumn of 1990.

This is not wholly unsurprising. She had won a landslide election victory in 1987, three years earlier. Landslide winners are usually secure. But she misread the wider political picture, particularly the degree to which the poll tax had alienated party activists (many of whom worked in local government as councillors), the despair of some Cabinet ministers and the availability of big figures to challenge her.

Often, for modern political parties, leadership crises arise because they have no obvious leaders. Towards the end of Thatcher's leadership, the Conservative Party had plenty of potential successors, all with weighty ministerial experience after a long period of Conservative rule. Above all, Michael Heseltine was waiting to pounce from the backbenches, where he had been since January 1986 after his resignation from the Cabinet.

Geoffrey Howe's resignation speech delivered in the Commons in November 1990 was the trigger. The manner of his departure provides another lesson of leadership. Leaders should treat senior colleagues thoughtfully and with sensitivity. Their seniority in government gives them authority. Howe irritated Thatcher and she could not disguise her irritability, treating him with growing disdain. Whereas she exuded restless energy around the clock, Howe was assiduously modest, mild-mannered and yet dogged. He worked as hard as her, but less ostentatiously. He had convictions as deep as hers, but did not display them with such theatrical exuberance. Howe detonated a political bomb that brought her down. His speech was vivid, full of colourful sporting metaphors, and yet delivered in his usual subdued style. The combination was political theatre at its most compelling. The modest Howe had become an actor, too. MPs listened in disbelief. Thatcher did too, taking in what she regarded as an act of treachery without quite realizing that Howe's deadly words would seal her fate.

Much has been made of Thatcher's useless campaign manager in the subsequent leadership contest. She was not a good judge of people, and her choice of Peter Morrison – heavy-drinking, lazy, secretly and promiscuously gay – to lead her campaign was another sign that she could no longer read political situations. She had become complacent. After three election victories, success had gone to her head, made her more imperious and less aware of her fragilities. To some extent such a course is unavoidable for a leader. As a new leader, Thatcher was surrounded by colleagues more experienced than her. By the end she was the mightily experienced one, working with presidents across the globe. She had become politically careless. To some extent, the same happened to Tony Blair. Even if Thatcher had appointed a political titan to run her leadership campaign, she was doomed. No leader could survive for long with Howe's words to torment her. Her former chancellor,

Nigel Lawson, had also been scathing when he had resigned a few months earlier. Backbench MPs were getting restless and fearful of losing their seats at the next election.

After her dramatic departure, Thatcher never got over what happened, most specifically the lack of loyalty from her own Cabinet colleagues, who one by one told her in November 1990 that she had to go, even after she won by a relatively small margin in the first ballot of the leadership contest.

Her fall traumatized the Conservative Party for decades to follow – a final lesson on leadership from Margaret Thatcher's long reign. There are times when parties become trapped. They need to remove a leader to have any hope of winning an election, but in doing so they are inevitably deeply troubled for a long time to come. The key figures in the removal of Margaret Thatcher were never fully trusted again by the party membership. Heseltine stood in the subsequent leadership contest of MPs and did not win. That was partly because members were telling MPs they should not support the one who wielded the knife.

But much more than that, the Conservative Party lost some sense of what it stood for. Had they turned against Thatcher because they were no longer Thatcherite? Had they turned against her because they were Thatcherite, but thought she had lost the ability to lead? Had they turned against her because they thought that not only were they no longer Thatcherite and she had lost the ability to lead, but they wanted to move towards a new position on the so-called centre ground? Even to attempt to answer the questions would have torn the Conservatives apart. Yet failure to provide a definitive answer made the party extremely vulnerable. The ambiguity of the regicide, the unanswered questions, meant that whoever succeeded her was going to find the inheritance a nightmare.

Thatcher's legacy for the country was also highly controversial. Public services were on their knees, even if some voters were incomparably better off. Communities dependent on industries that she deemed to be unproductive, or inefficient, struggled for decades to come. In different ways, both increasingly affluent voters and poorer ones became disconnected from the state in all its various manifestations. In terms of winning the battle of ideas there was no ambiguity. She was the triumphant winner. Thatcherism continued to define UK politics for decades to come, a remarkable achievement.

Although always possessing a brittle self-confidence, she was tormented in the early years of her leadership by her predecessor, Ted Heath, who behaved gracelessly towards her. Heath never got over the fact that Thatcher replaced him, and he disagreed fundamentally with a lot of the policies that she implemented. More to the point, he made it absolutely clear how he felt. She did the same with the leader who replaced her. John Major won the leadership contest in November 1990 and was her chosen successor. Yet very soon after his accession, Thatcher began to orchestrate revolts against his leadership and to give interviews suggesting he was not up to the job. It was another sign that she had lost that early ability to know when the political stage is crowding in on you, and when you need to be very careful what you say and do. A former prime minister has virtually no space on the political stage. Indeed a former prime minister has no defined role at all.

When a leader loses the crown, the best course is to say, 'Thank you very much', write your memoirs and keep out of what follows next in your party. Thatcher could not do that, which was probably a sign that those ministers and MPs who wielded the knives were right to do so. Their long-serving leader – winner of three elections and many more ideological victories – had lost her judgement as to how far she could tug at the boundaries of acceptable behaviour. For a long time Thatcher was an astute reader of politics, aware of how far she could go and adept at explaining to the voters why she was acting in the way she was. These skills enabled her to be the biggest change-maker as prime minister since Clement Attlee in 1945. When the skills faded, she was gone.

5

JOHN MAJOR

John Major became prime minister in November 1990 in arguably the most politically traumatic circumstances of any modern prime minister, with the exception of Theresa May. Jim Callaghan, another contender for this title, had faced an economic nightmare, but his transition to leadership was smooth. Major's was far from smooth, even if it seemed so at the time.

Major became prime minister after the act of regicide by Conservative MPs, when ministers and backbenchers contrived the sensational removal of Margaret Thatcher, the three-times election winner, against her will. It was an insurrectionary move that many MPs could hardly believe they had carried out.

As part of the challenging context, Major was not well prepared. Like Theresa May, he was ambitious. He had wanted the top job, but had not expected a vacancy to appear so suddenly in the autumn of 1990, just as Theresa May had not anticipated it in the summer of 2016. No one knew that the act of regicide was going to happen until it did. A few weeks earlier the Conservative party conference had been singing 'Happy Birthday' to Thatcher, and she had responded with exuberant waves from the conference platform. Major was her chancellor at the time, having been a short-serving

Foreign Secretary. He had held the two top jobs in the Cabinet, but only very briefly.

Less experienced than the candidates he defeated in the 1990 leadership contest, Major faced some titanic challenges as a new prime minister. The Conservatives had been well behind in the opinion polls and had lost a by-election in the theoretically safe seat of Eastbourne a short time before his victory. This was one of the reasons why Tory MPs turned against Margaret Thatcher. They feared they would lose their seats. The government of which Major had been a part had introduced its flagship policy, the poll tax. Major also faced a negotiation with the rest of the European Union over the forthcoming Maastricht Treaty. Some of his MPs opposed Maastricht, as did Margaret Thatcher herself. And the economy was sluggish.

His own position as a new prime minister was also deeply ambiguous. Ambiguity can help propel an ambitious figure into leadership, but can also bring him or her down. Major was Thatcher's choice as a successor. Most of her admirers voted for him in what was the last Conservative leadership contest dominated by 'one nation' Conservatives. Major beat Michael Heseltine and Douglas Hurd to secure the thorny crown. All three were well to the left of the leaders elected after Major. To varying degrees they were all pro-Europeans, with Major being the most sceptical. No one in the Conservative Party complained at the time about the narrow choice, a sign that even after Thatcher's long reign, the party's journey rightwards still had a long way to go. It became even more Thatcherite after Thatcher had fallen.

Major was not a Thatcherite, yet there was just enough in his political repertoire to convince her that he was 'one of us'. He was more of a Eurosceptic than the other candidates, although he was a believer in the UK's membership of the EU. In terms of the economy, he was obsessed by the dangers of inflation, and that gave the impression that he was economically 'dry', a supporter of Thatcherite economic policies. He was to some extent, but with significant qualifications. During the leadership contest he kept all options open in relation to the poll tax, a policy to which Thatcher was still emotionally attached. Privately he knew the tax had to be scrapped. Only Heseltine was committed to the policy, and at this stage it was Heseltine who was the subject of the Thatcherites' fury, because he was the one who had betrayed her. But where did that leave Major as a new prime minister? Was he there as a calmer Thatcherite, or as a leader to move his party in a different direction? He never fully answered the question, even though retrospectively he was emphatic that he was part of the 'one nation' tradition of the party, pointing out accurately that he was well to the left of David Cameron, and half-jokingly suggesting that he was to the left of Tony Blair.[1]

He came closest to answering the question during the first phase of his leadership. Obscured by subsequent traumatic events, Major's leadership between November 1990 and the election in April 1992 was a triumph. Against many odds, he won the 1992 election, the Conservatives' fourth successive victory. With more than fourteen million voters backing his party, Major secured a higher vote share than Margaret Thatcher in her three election victories, even if he won only a small overall majority of twenty-three. He did this by giving the impression that there had been a change of government when he took over, without a general election. Major's style was dramatically different from what had gone before, and to a limited extent so was his policy focus. It was almost as if the Conservative Party under Major in his early phase had moved from being a party of Thatcherite crusading zeal to one closer to the Christian Democrats in Germany.

Major managed to convey a sense of change in a number of ways. Partly it was that his own personality, almost to the point of naivety, was incomparably different from Thatcher's. He was not grand, lofty or screeching in his assertiveness. While she was a strident performer, he gave the impression of being modestly self-effacing, which to some extent he was.

He loved nothing more than stopping off at a motorway café to have coffee and a fried breakfast. Although this was inevitably contrived, as every public move by a prime minister is, there was an authenticity to it as well. For a political scene so used to Thatcher, his personality was in itself refreshing and calming.

He also acted smartly to convey that he was a different leader. During an early Prime Minister's Questions, a Conservative MP asked Major a question that was critical of the BBC, assuming the new prime minister would approve of his onslaught. Major chose quite deliberately to praise the BBC. He changed his mind about the Corporation quite often in the years to come, but he started off by distancing himself from the attacks on the broadcaster by those Conservative MPs who were convinced, wrongly, that the BBC was left-wing. He also announced in an early Prime Minister's Questions some small amount of additional money for the National Health Service. The announcement symbolized at least a recognition that public services had declined in recent years and that public spending was not always a 'waste'.

Major also made a series of important appointments that indicated significant change, a softening from the Thatcher era. The key one was the promotion of Chris Patten to become chairman of the Conservative Party. It was the combination of Major and

Patten that made it look as if there had almost been a change of government. Patten was a pro-European and from the left of the party. His politics were far removed in many respects from Margaret Thatcher's. As Major and Patten set about their course with evident rapport, Major's predecessor became increasingly alarmed. This was in itself a tribute to the way Major was adapting his party to the demands of changing times.

Fleetingly, a tortured political party seemed more at ease with itself. Major appeared relaxed and looked as if he was enjoying his new job. Most Cabinet ministers felt relieved to be working with him rather than her. At first he had the authority of winning a leadership contest convincingly. There was no talk of ministerial insurrection during Major's early phase. Most MPs were loyal to him, even those who took their lead from an increasingly restive Thatcher.

As Major moved towards the 1992 election he dealt skilfully with two seemingly impossible obstacles. The first was the poll tax. During the leadership contest he was smart enough not to be entirely clear about what he was going to do with the tax. He knew that Margaret Thatcher and others supported him and the policy, so he promised no more than a 'review'. But the moment he got into Number Ten he knew exactly what he had to do. To win an election he needed to abolish what Thatcher regarded as her flagship policy. He gave the task to Michael Heseltine, the figure who had wielded the knife against her in the early stages of the leadership contest.

This was an astute appointment. Heseltine had been against the poll tax from the beginning, opposing the policy passionately and forensically when he was on the backbenches. Now he had the challenge of coming up with an alternative, a challenge that proved to be quite stressful for him. He took a long time over it. There were feverish leaks over what he might do, and other leaks over what he might not do. It was a huge issue in British politics at the time. In the end, Heseltine came up with the Council Tax, which was pretty similar to the previous property tax, the rates. Within a single parliament, a governing party had introduced a major new tax, scrapped it and announced a replacement that was close to the local tax that had been expensively abolished. Such a governing party deserved to be punished at an election, but voters were relieved that the government had abolished the poll tax. They were almost grateful. Heseltine was responsible for selling the policy to the party, which he did rather well. He did not admit at the time that he had more or less resurrected the rates, although he did so later when it was safe to reflect from a distance on what had happened.

Major's government had removed one of the great vote-losing policies that Labour had hoped would propel them to power in an election. His next challenge was Europe, the eternal issue for Conservative prime ministers.

By the autumn of 1991, the Maastricht negotiations were looming. In the proposed treaty there were two policy areas that a lot of Conservative MPs found unacceptable: the introduction of the single currency and the Social Chapter, the section of the treaty aimed at improving working conditions and employees' rights.[2] How was Major going to square the circle of signing up to a treaty while addressing those two issues? He negotiated with considerable skill. When a prime minister is confident about the mood of his parliamentary party, he or she can perform more effectively in relation to Europe. Major had grounds to be very confident – after all, only Conservative MPs had voted in the leadership contest that gave him his victory. Having removed Thatcher, they were not going to turn on him. Major used the authority of a newly elected leader to sign the Maastricht Treaty, but he got two vital opt-outs from the single currency and the Social Chapter – significant concessions that proved the European Union was far from indifferent to British demands. One of the ironies about the Conservative Party's anguish over the UK's membership of the EU was that the UK usually got its way. In this case, Major got his opt-outs. At the end of the summit in December 1991, with the next election moving into view, he declared, comically prematurely as it turned out, 'Game, set and match to the UK.'

Major's leadership eventually became hellish because of his party's response to the Maastricht Treaty, but in the build-up to the 1992 election he had manoeuvred neatly. The opt-outs just about kept his parliamentary party happy, and yet he had signed up to the treaty. He gave a number of speeches, co-written with Chris Patten, in which he talked about wanting Britain to be 'at the heart of the European Union'. The words were punctuated with much Euroscepticism. Major was not as pro-European as Patten, but the tone was markedly different from Margaret Thatcher's. The speeches also helped to establish relatively constructive relations with key EU leaders.[3]

Major made one other significant change during the 1990–92 period. The initiative was much mocked, but it was a clever idea, based partly on models from other EU countries that had established more user-friendly public services. Major announced a Citizen's Charter, in which those who used public services would be more empowered to demand better value. Given that citizens had become virtually powerless in the face of dire public services with bewildering layers of accountability, this was a big leap, at least in theory. Voters would be able to get some of their money back, if trains failed to arrive within a certain time. There was even a cones hotline, for motorists stuck in traffic jams for hours with little evidence of work being carried out on closed motorway lanes. For some reason this became the biggest joke of all, and yet the hotline addressed a sense of impotence, as drivers were left in never-ending queues without knowing how to protest or to whom. Margaret Thatcher had declared that she would give 'power to the people' and yet had left most people powerless in the face of poor public services. As a Tory leader from a working-class background in Brixton and a former councillor who had struggled assiduously with questions over how to improve local provision, Major recognized the urgent need to improve public services and make them more accountable.

The Citizen's Charter became a joke partly because there was little practical impact. Public services were poor, and Major was not inclined to greatly increase public spending. On the whole, voters did not notice improvements. The failure highlights a contradiction in Major's approach: a leader who recognized the need for better public services, without being willing to find the resources required.

Instead he had a different economic objective. Major was gripped by the need to curb inflation. Here is another example of a prime minister defined by his political upbringing. Wilson, Callaghan and Heath were determined to avoid the social and economic upheavals of the 1930s, most specifically high unemployment. Thatcher was resolved not to make the mistake of those 1970s governments. Major noted that high inflation impacted most severely on the poor and was alert to any danger that it might rise again. He was too alert. There were few inflationary seeds when he was prime minister and yet he sought ways of bearing down on public spending, while sensing that public spending on some services needed to rise. This preoccupation led him to support the privatization of the railways, a policy error more calamitous than the poll tax in terms of its disruptive impact on people's lives, but less politically potent. Although on most matters Major was to the left of Thatcher, this was a privatization she wisely did not dare to implement. Soon after the privatization, polls suggested that most voters supported re-nationalization. But this policy was implemented after the 1992 election, when Major was already doomed. The privatization of the railways, his stingy approach to public spending, and some of his approaches to the EU after the 1992 election meant that he never fully answered the question about whether he saw his task as to move his party on from Thatcherism. Later he was clear. He felt he never had the chance to do so fully because he was trapped by the party's civil war over Europe and by the small majority after 1992.[4]

Before the 1992 election, Major's symbolic focus on public services through the Citizen's Charter felt like another leap away from harsh Thatcherism, even if the change was more tonal than real.

In a very short period of time between 1990 and the 1992 election, Major had abolished the poll tax; repaired, to some extent, relations with EU leaders while securing opt-outs on the euro and the Social Chapter; and conveyed a concern for public services that was partly matched by policy initiatives. Indeed, it is arguable that between November 1990 and the 1992 election, Major, Patten and Heseltine were the 'modernizers' of their party – to apply that overused, vague, evasive but ubiquitous term. They were more 'modern' than the Cameron and Osborne leadership, in that they moved their party on from crude Thatcherism. Cameron and Osborne chose to define 'modernization' as being socially liberal. Major took a more challenging and substantial path. If modernization means moving on from a party's immediate past, then Major was the modernizer of the post-Thatcher Tory Party, if only until the 1992 election.

———

Major won in 1992 even though the economy was in the doldrums, with many economists predicting that worse was to come. There was a widely held assumption that Major won because of a great cliché: the voters held on to Nurse, for fear of something worse. But there was more to his victory than this cliché. It was the combination of changes that had been brought about subtly, in the period after November 1990.

Curiously, the Conservative Party learned none of the lessons from Major's victory. He won by moving to the left of Thatcher, tonally and to some extent in terms of policy. Every subsequent leader, with the partial exception of Theresa May, moved to the right and either failed to win a majority or, in David Cameron's case in 2015, won very narrowly. The combination of Major and Patten, with Heseltine, Clarke and Hurd playing prominent supporting roles, gave the Conservatives a share of the vote that their successors could only dream of.

But Major's leadership, more than that of any other prime minister, is one of two halves. If his early period is too easily overlooked, the hell that followed is almost underestimated, too. Oddly for such an undemonstrative figure, a leader who lacked language and was no performer, Major's leadership was a compelling theatrical drama of two utterly different acts. The sequence is counter-intuitive. Normally a historic election victory enhances a prime minister's authority, rather than ushering in a form of political hell. But, as ever, the seeds of Major's tragedy were sown in the very moment of triumph.

Major misread the reasons for his victory. He concluded, with uncharacteristic immodesty, that his own personal performance in the 1992 campaign was an important factor. His personality might have made a contribution to the victory, but his performance in the campaign emphatically did not. In the course of a very odd election, contested on some unusually cold days in March and early April, Major fought an embarrassingly naff campaign. On several occasions he went out on a soapbox with a megaphone, shouting at shoppers in town centres. He assumed that this kind of folksy campaigning was highly successful, that his soapbox and megaphone made a direct connection with the voters. Take a look at the footage on YouTube. The images seemed dated at the time and are absurd now, like a *Monty Python* sketch.[5]

That is not why Major won. But he thought it was one of the reasons, and he kept on repeating the same technique during the traumatic phase of his leadership after the election. His contortions looked even more ridiculous, as he was making them without much authority and with his party in revolt. In politics, we choose to see what we want to see, and not what is necessarily in front of our eyes. During the 1992 election Major was still on his honeymoon as a newish prime minister who was less lofty than Thatcher at her most imperious. When he was on his silly soapbox he got away with it, even though he looked ridiculous. Some voters saw 'a man of the people' rather than someone being silly. After the election win, during his dark period, the media and most voters saw him as weak and incompetent. When he got his soapbox out, as he occasionally did in the years that followed the 1992 election, or was door-stepped on a visit to a muddy school playing field – as he often was – he was no longer hailed for his rooted values. Now, some voters chose to see him as silly and beleaguered.[6]

Although Major won the 1992 election, his most important ally, Chris Patten, lost his seat in Bath. The loss partly explains Major's curiously downbeat response to his triumph. Indeed, on the Friday after the election, Major told Patten prophetically, 'We've pushed what should happen in electoral politics beyond its normal boundaries, and it will be almost impossible to do so again.' By this he meant that the Conservatives had won for a fourth time in a row and would struggle to win a fifth election. At his moment of triumph, he foresaw his terrible electoral fate.

He was an insecure figure in many ways, and was dependent on people he liked and could trust. He missed Patten intensely in the tragic drama that unfolded.[7]

Major's sense of doom on the day of his victory was encapsulated by Patten's defeat. The same night, Margaret Thatcher and other like-minded Tories had been at an election party hosted by the former Treasurer, Lord McAlpine. When Patten lost his seat, some of the guests raised their glasses and cheered. They were celebrating the defeat of Major's chosen party chairman and political soulmate – a vivid symbol of a deeply troubled party. The euphoria of McAlpine's guests was a sign that Major had only papered over the cracks between November 1990 and the 1992 election. This was still a party that had only recently removed its election-winning leader, was not quite sure what the removal implied and, in some respects, regretted what it had done. A section of the party represented extensively at McAlpine's gathering was becoming increasingly hostile to the European Union. It was thrilled by the defeat of the pro-European Patten.

A troubled party becomes much less troubling for a prime minister if he or she commands a large majority in the Commons.

But the other dark twist of the 1992 election was that although Major secured a historic share of the vote, he won only a small majority of seats. He had twenty-three seats more than the other parties combined. With legislation on the Maastricht Treaty looming, this was a fragile parliamentary base. Few realized the scale of that fragility in the immediate aftermath of the election. Even if Major was not exuberant after his win, he did not anticipate how quickly and deeply the turmoil would take shape.

It is widely assumed that Major's nightmare – exceeding even his well-developed sense of foreboding – was triggered by the trauma of Britain leaving the Exchange Rate Mechanism in September 1992, just a few months after the election. But by then there had already been a significant development, one that was wholly beyond Major's control.

In May 1992 – before there was a hint of the ERM drama to come, and just a few weeks after Major's election victory – Denmark voted against the Maastricht Treaty in a referendum. David Cameron was only the second prime minister to be thrown by a referendum on Europe. Major was the first, although (unlike Cameron) he had no cause to resign, as the referendum in Denmark was nothing to do with him.

At the point when Danish voters rejected Maastricht, there had been no parliamentary legislation in the UK that was required to ratify the treaty. The parliamentary sequence was still to come. When the Danes voted against Maastricht – an act of defiance from a supposedly pro-European nation – Eurosceptic Tory MPs in the UK became much bolder. They had concrete proof from another country that voters regarded Maastricht as an integrationist leap too far. Major had secured his substantial opt-outs from the treaty, but some of his MPs were still opposed to what they regarded as the fundamental purpose of Maastricht: political and economic union.

Coincidentally, two BBC political correspondents had booked to have a lunch with John Redwood, one of Major's Eurosceptic ministers, on the day after the result of the Danish referendum.[8] The lunch was in an arty basement of a Westminster restaurant. Redwood, who was not instinctively exuberant, leapt down the stairs of the restaurant joyfully. He sat at the table, looked up and said to us: 'Here's to Denmark!' He was thrilled at the outcome of the Danish referendum, and at what it might portend. But this wasn't the UK government's position. The government supported the Maastricht Treaty, with the UK opt-outs. Redwood, however, spoke of little other than the opportunities opened up via the Denmark vote, and of the need to reconsider the UK's entire relationship with the EU. It was that referendum in Denmark that emboldened Tory MPs to seek to wreck the Maastricht Treaty when Major presented the legislation in Parliament.[9]

Inevitably, when the UK tumbled out of the Exchange Rate Mechanism in September 1992, the Eurosceptics were further strengthened. For them, the humiliating collapse of the pound and the hysterical rises in interest rates, in a failed bid to prop up the currency, were vivid confirmation of their fundamental view. EU-related constraints were against the national interest.

More significantly, Major became a much weaker and less confident figure after the ERM crisis. One of the lessons of leadership is that leaders do not recover from a traumatic devaluation of the currency. In terms of self-confidence and the way he was perceived by the media, Harold Wilson never soared again after the devaluation in 1967. Major's trauma was more dramatic than Wilson's. During 'Black Wednesday' on 16 September 1992, as the UK headed towards the ERM exit, Major put up interest rates again and again until they reached ridiculous levels of 15 per cent. Then he had to give up. His top team of ministers gathered around him as he made his increasingly desperate moves.

Yet the senior ministers who were supporting Major during that traumatic day were also part of his forthcoming political nightmare. They held conflicting views on the EU in general, and on this drama in particular. The chancellor, Norman Lamont, let it be known that he was singing in the bath, after the pound left the ERM. In contrast, Michael Heseltine and Ken Clarke, supporters of a single currency, continued to defend the decision to join the ERM in the first place. On a calamitous day for British politics and economics, Major's senior ministers could not agree whether they felt relieved or downcast at the end.

From the day of the ERM saga until the 1997 election, Major and his party were never again ahead in the opinion polls, having won a decisive election victory just a few months before. At this point the crisis fed on itself, as often happens in politics; disconnected events and developments become conflated, to give the impression of a prime minister out of control. It happened to Gordon Brown after he built up speculation about an early election, but did not call one; and it happened to Major after the ERM crisis.

Away from the energy-sapping ERM saga, Major lost another close ally just a few months after Patten had lost his seat. In the same month, September 1992, David Mellor was forced to resign from a newly created Cabinet post in the clumsily named Department of National Heritage. Major and Mellor were both supporters of Chelsea FC, their political outlook was fairly similar and Major liked and trusted Mellor. But Mellor was forced out because he was having an affair. As the revelations reached fever-pitch, the woman involved claimed that Mellor liked to have his flings wearing a

Chelsea football shirt. This was a lie, made up on the advice of the public-relations guru Max Clifford, who later died in jail – the end of another dark sequence.

Major had created the new culture-focused department specifically for Mellor, who would have flourished in the role. He would have been one of the few Culture Secretaries with a real passion for culture. Within months he was gone. Major had tried desperately to keep hold of Mellor, but in the end had to give in. This was another big blow to Major's confidence, in some ways as deep as the one arising from the ERM, although much less significant. As a prime minister who had recently won an election, he had assumed at first that he would have the authority to protect Mellor. He did not regard the affair as a resignation matter. But much of the media was in uproar. They wanted Mellor's scalp, partly because he had taken a robust approach to newspaper regulation, which was part of his new remit. He had warned that some newspapers were 'drinking in the last-chance saloon'. Sections of the media sought revenge. They won, and Major lost. When a politician becomes a prime minister there is a part of them that assumes they possess unique gifts and unusual powers, sometimes with justification. Failure brings them down to earth. They are humanized to the point of feeling extremely vulnerable, rather than special.[10] When Major lost his battle with the media over Mellor's fate, he knew that the newspapers and some broadcasters would come for him again, and they did.

September 1992 was a month that demonstrated the power of the newspapers in the UK. Major was terrified of their response to the ERM sequence. At the end of that nightmarish 'Black Wednesday', he spoke to several newspaper editors, hoping that direct contact would bring about more sympathetic treatment. But he did not even get sympathy in the phone calls. The editor of the *Sun*, Kelvin MacKenzie, told Major: 'Well, John, let me put it this way. I've got a large bucket of shit lying on my desk and tomorrow morning I'm going to pour it all over your head.'[11] He did so the next day – and for a long time to come. The *Sun* had been a vibrant supporter of the Conservatives during the Thatcher era and into the 1992 election. Equally significantly, it portrayed the Labour leader, Neil Kinnock, as a dangerous fool, the Welsh windbag who would wreck the UK. Now the paper turned on Major, a significant factor in making his leadership more nightmarish.

Shortly after the ERM fiasco another crisis flared up, when the government became embroiled in a draining battle over pit closures. It was wholly unprepared for what happened and deeply troubled by the conflict. As president of the Board of Trade, Michael Heseltine announced that the government planned to close one-third of the UK's deep coal mines, with the loss of 31,000 jobs. Heseltine had spent many hours negotiating a compensation package with a reluctant Treasury, and finally extracted £1 billion to pay the cost of redundancies and assist mining communities. He assumed that the arguments that had prevailed during the miners' strike in the mid-1980s would receive even more widespread support this time, that the pits were uneconomic and there were cheaper, more efficient options. Similarly, he assumed that the compensation package would be contrasted with Thatcher's mean-spirited approach to mining communities after the pit closures that followed the miners' strike. Major made the same assumption, as far as he paid any attention to what Heseltine was planning – the ERM crisis and its aftermath were sucking up virtually all of his attention and energy.

Their assumptions were spectacularly wrong. All hell broke loose. This was partly because miners who had defied the strike in the mid-1980s were losing their jobs under Heseltine's proposals. Job losses were also threatened in some Conservative-held seats and, with a small majority, the government faced a serious backbench revolt. Above all, the mood of the media had changed. Thatcher-supporting newspapers, such as the *Sun* and the *Daily Mail*, had already turned on Major, partly because he was not Thatcher. The ERM crisis had been the trigger for the intensification of their onslaught, but these powerful newspapers had already decided Major was weak and had started to bash him around. Such newspapers set the agenda for the BBC. Based on the newspapers' hostile tone, parts of the BBC followed suit, reflecting and sometimes heightening the new, wildly critical mood.

Sensing more blood, and having already secured the departure of Mellor, the *Sun* and the *Mail* sympathetically reported big demonstrations against the proposed closures. Around 200,000 people attended one protest. Polls suggested that even Conservative voters were on the miners' side. Major and Heseltine panicked. Heseltine found the whole process nerve-shredding and draining. Political journalists who met him in the middle of the saga were struck by how he was simultaneously absorbed with, and shaken by, the crisis. At one lunch with two political correspondents, Heseltine used the entire dining table and all the implements on it to demonstrate what he was trying to do. The salt and pepper became one pit. A wine glass became another community. He was wholly wrapped up in the crisis and could reflect on nothing else.[12] Arguably the most formidable and thoughtful Conservative politician of his generation, Heseltine – the Cabinet minister under Thatcher who dared to focus on the revival of some inner cities, who later put the case forcefully for a more active state when he worked for Cameron and Osborne, and who played a big part in the fall of Thatcher and then scrapped the poll tax while devising an alternative – was fleetingly reduced to becoming a nervous wreck over the pit closures.

Major was on edge, too. The prime minister who had conveyed an almost innocent calm at the beginning of his leadership was now becoming unrecognizable as the one facing the storms. He could not bear being tormented by the media, and he was not alone in this. No prime minister copes well with the screaming front pages of disdain. Wilson was driven to exhausted paranoia. Blair made his final speech as prime minister attacking the 'feral' media. Brown awoke early each morning and read the newspapers, which meant that he was often in fuming despair before breakfast. Thatcher is the only modern prime minister not to have been tormented by the media, and that was largely because, with a few exceptions, the newspapers doted on her. Theresa May was also relatively untroubled, but that was because she took the extreme step of not reading them.

From September 1992 the media decided, almost collectively, that Major was a weak prime minister behaving weakly. The collective decision inevitably became self-fulfilling. Reading the critical newspapers, Conservative MPs became more strident in their onslaught. When weakness is perceived, a prime minister becomes weaker still.

This was the context in which Major presented the Maastricht Treaty to the UK Parliament. He had to pull every lever to get the legislation on the statute books. His struggle was an early sign of what was to come – a major staging post on the road towards the Brexit referendum in 2016.

———

Most fundamentally, Major discovered that the Conservative Party had become unleadable on Europe. The party conference in 1992, held a few weeks after Britain had fallen out of the ERM, was the first indication of the new febrile mood in the party. The gathering was an event of historic significance, in retrospect a key episode early on in the Brexit saga and in the related transformation of the Conservative Party.

On the whole, Conservative party conferences had been loyal rallies. Party activists attended to pay homage to the Cabinet and the prime minister. The 1992 conference was much closer to the Labour Party gatherings of the late 1970s and 1980s. Speakers attacked Major and his government for what had happened in relation to the ERM. Dissenters included the former party chairman, Norman Tebbit, who was cheered to the rafters. Packed fringe meetings on Europe were marked by intense clashes. Tory conferences were usually dull, polite affairs. This one was angry.

Tebbit's speech in the conference hall had provocative echoes of Mark Antony's at Julius Caesar's funeral. Mark Antony's address appeared to praise Brutus, while damning him. Mischievously, Tebbit claimed to be supportive of Major while inserting a very large blade into the back of the suddenly fragile prime minister. Tebbit began by expressing the hope that the prime minister would resist calls for the dumping of Norman Lamont, the Chancellor of the Exchequer, because Mr Lamont had not taken sterling into the European ERM in 1990. It was Major who had been chancellor at the time. He added: 'The cost in lost jobs in bankrupt firms, repossessed homes, in the terrible wounds inflicted on industry, has been savage… But we have established our credentials as good Europeans.'

Tebbit went on to prompt pantomime-style responses from his audience, asking them whether they wanted a single currency, and Brussels meddling in immigration controls, foreign affairs, industrial policy, education and defence. Each question was greeted with a chorus of 'No'. 'Do you want to be citizens of a European union?' he asked, to a final roar of opposition. 'Now is the time to negotiate anew. Kohl and Mitterrand no longer speak for Europe. John Major should raise the flag of patriots of all the states of Europe... Let's launch the drive for Maastricht Two; a treaty with no mention of more power to Brussels, no mention of economic and monetary and political union. It's a task in which I stand ready to join John Major whenever he is ready to begin.' Tebbit might as well have declared – as Mark Antony did of Brutus – 'And John Major is an honourable man.'

Major was sitting on the podium as Tebbit played to the crowd, looking pale while trying to convey a mild-mannered calm. He knew he was in the midst of an unprecedented drama, with many more acts to come.

The Conservative Party has never been the same since. Most obviously, the split over Europe deepened, but the conference marked a more profound and wider change in the character of the party. For years to come, party conferences had more ideological verve than Labour's equivalent events. Under Blair, Brown and the more left-wing Ed Miliband, Labour's annual gatherings were heavily controlled by the leadership, partly as a reaction against the vote-losing 1980s, when divisions were displayed vividly and in public.

Like partners in a curious dance, the Conservative conferences became wild while Labour's became controlled and dull. The Conservatives began to stage fringe meetings where insurrectionary charismatic or eccentric figures were hero-worshipped. In the mid-1990s Michael Portillo was idolized with almost the same intensity as Tony Benn had been at Labour conferences. At one Conservative conference in Blackpool, Portillo packed an entire cinema with devotees. Later Boris Johnson and Jacob Rees-Mogg became heroes of some activists. In ways that were partly admirable, Conservatives discovered the thrill of public debate, just as Labour became terrified of exploring ideas in the open. As well as Europe, other contentious themes included the role of the financial markets, the degree to which social liberalism marked a modernizing leap, the relationship between state and users, or providers, of public services. A party that had been pragmatic as a matter of conviction now became gripped by ideas. Above all, it became obsessed by Europe.

Major could not fully control the party conferences or his MPs in Parliament, some of whom voted repeatedly against the legislation required to implement the Maastricht Treaty. During the summer of 1993 he was forced to hold a vote of confidence in order to secure parliamentary assent. If he had lost, he would have had no choice but to call a general election, at a point when the Conservatives were well behind in the polls. Such a threat meant he won the vote of confidence, but the fact that he had to call it, because of the behaviour of his own MPs, was extraordinary and, again, a sign of what was to come. Cameron and May were to feel similarly tormented by their own MPs and found leadership as problematic as Major did.

In the immediate aftermath of winning the vote of confidence, Major gave an interview to ITN. At the end, assuming the tape had stopped running, he referred to the 'bastards' in his Cabinet. The words were recorded and broadcast.

Major's bastards were Eurosceptics, even though Major was himself fairly sceptical. The bastards clashed in particular with the chancellor, Ken Clarke, who opposed the idea of a referendum on the single currency.[13] The question of whether or not to hold a referendum on the euro was raging at this time. In the end, both Major and Tony Blair entered the 1997 election proposing to hold a referendum, although one was never held. This is another lesson of leadership in British politics. Referendums can be the source of intense splits and infighting. Often referendums are not held. The only UK-wide referendums have been on Europe in 1975 and 2016 and on electoral reform in 2012. Yet the rows over what question might be asked in a potential referendum, and whether a referendum should be held, come close to breaking parties at times. Mistakenly, leaders turn to referendums, or the offer of a referendum, on the assumption this will ease their burdens. The opposite happens nearly every time. The burdens only intensify. Later, Michael Heseltine described his reluctant decision to support a referendum on the euro, in advance of the 1997 election, as the biggest mistake in his career.[14]

Major had to manage a divided party and a split Cabinet. There are often intense personal rivalries and loathings, in politics as in other vocations, but a division over policy is much more serious. Major's Cabinet was unusual in that quite a lot of its members were old friends from Cambridge University. For the most part they remained friends, but they fell out over one policy: Europe. Once again, the falling-out over policy was an early sign as to what would happen with Cameron and Europe. Cameron did not learn the lesson. Friendships do not provide a protective shield in relation to the Conservative Party and Europe. The fact that Michael Gove and his wife joined the Camerons at Chequers for some festive fun on Boxing Day was not enough to sway Gove in the Brexit referendum. Gove chose to follow conviction rather than friendship.

In Major's Cabinet, friends were fighting their corner and then meeting for a drink to reflect happily on old or new times. Over the issue of Europe they followed their convictions, irrespective of friendship. Most specifically Ken Clarke, Norman Lamont and Michael Howard had been good friends at Cambridge. Yet they spanned the divide over Europe: Lamont was a critic from outside the Cabinet after he was sacked as chancellor;[15] Howard was a polite critic from within the Cabinet; and Clarke was the passionate pro-European. A leader can manage personal tensions in a government, but only the very best can manage a split over policy.

Major's attempt at managing his government and his party took a sensational turn. In July 1995 he announced that he was resigning as Conservative leader. He was still prime minister, but he intended to trigger a contest almost against himself, in order to get MPs to back him. Here, long before Brexit, was a vivid sign that the Conservative Party was suffering an existential crisis over Europe. To Major's surprise, one of his ministers, John Redwood – the one who was so excited after the Danish referendum result – stood against him. In a whacky campaign, Redwood was defeated, but Major did not win by a hugely commanding majority.[16]

Still, his victory was enough to give him the space to carry on. He carried on in a dark gloom that had not become brighter as a result of the bizarre contest.

Europe remained the cause of his gloom, the backdrop to every crisis. Even when, prior to the 1995 leadership contest, Major tried to move away from Europe in an attempt to focus on domestic policies, there was no escape from it. He lacked the capacity to excite. His language was also wooden. Unlike Thatcher, he was not a political teacher. At his party conference in 1993 he proclaimed that his government was going 'back to basics'. The slogan was almost wilfully uninspiring, as if Europe had sucked up too much passion. What he meant by 'back to basics' was a renewed focus on education, crime and housing. But one of his spin doctors said mistakenly, in a pre-speech briefing to journalists, that Major's chosen theme was also an attack on the 'permissive society'.

In more reasoned times, a misinterpretation could easily be addressed and batted away. In what were the early stirrings of a long era of hysterical unreason, one crisis after another erupted. Conservative MPs who were not in conventional heterosexual marriages, or who were having affairs, were in danger of looking like total hypocrites as they supposedly espoused a government agenda that challenged permissiveness, even though that was not the idea behind the agenda. There was one front-page story after another revealing ministerial affairs or the bizarre private lives of Tory MPs. The stories were aimed at destabilizing Major and they succeeded in doing so. Instead of escaping from the hell of Europe, Major found that when he tried to move away, matters got darker still.[17]

Even during the 1997 election campaign, when he faced Tony Blair at his most formidable, Major was still pleading with his party. He declared at one point, during one of the daily election press conferences that parties still held, with a naive hope of good publicity: 'Please don't bind my hands before I go to Amsterdam for the next EU treaty.' This was an extraordinary message from a prime minister supposedly addressing a wider electorate. Usually even desperate leaders find election campaigns liberating, as they no longer have to deal with internal party matters. To take one example, the Labour leader, Michael Foot, enjoyed the 1983 campaign, as it was a break from managing his unmanageable party. Foot did not enjoy the result, as Labour was slaughtered, but the campaign was a form of liberation. Such were the tensions in the Conservative Party that Major had to address them in the midst of an election.[18]

By then he was doomed. This was in part because Tony Blair walked on water, in the eyes of the electorate and much of the media at this point, but also because of everything that had preceded in this five-year period. The Tory Party had become unelectable. Although Major led subtly between 1990 and 1992, he was not equipped for the intense stress that followed. Arguably no one would have been, and Major certainly was not.

Ironically his brave work in initiating the peace process in Northern Ireland was a form of political escapism for him. There are several heroes in the peace process, and Major was one of them. At least negotiating with Gerry Adams, Martin McGuinness and leading unionists was a break from seeking to appease his Eurosceptics, and a much more constructive use of time. One of the lessons of Major's leadership was that the Eurosceptics could not be appeased. Neither Cameron nor May learned this lesson, with calamitous consequences for them, their party and the UK. In contrast, following secret talks with the British and Irish governments, the IRA announced a ceasefire in the summer of 1994. Adams looked to a political solution, and Major helped to give him, and others, the space to start exploring what form that might take. But by 1997 even this striking initiative was being undermined by some Conservative MPs, ardent unionists who were worried that Major had gone too far. The peace process was in danger of imploding – another victim of internal Tory divisions.

As the divisions deepened, Major got much of the blame in the media for being 'weak', as if 'strength' could magically bind a party together. He became even more sensitive about newspaper coverage, and at least as worked up as Harold Wilson. His Foreign Secretary, Douglas Hurd, later reported that allies used to hide the newspapers from Major. Having requested the first editions the night before, he would not be able to sleep, fuming at what he regarded as unfair coverage. His advisers had to hide the *Evening Standard* when the first edition arrived in the early afternoon, because he would get too worked up. His chancellor, Ken Clarke, revealed that he used to get phone calls from John Major on Boxing Day, saying, 'Have you seen page eight of the *Daily Express*?' – a page that few voters would have read on Boxing Day, or any other day.

Like other prime ministers, much of Major's despair with the media was justified. As well as being vilified for 'back to basics', his whole government was seen through the prism of sleaze, a term that became briefly ubiquitous but, as is usually the case with repeated words or phrases in British politics, hopelessly ill-defined.[19] There is no doubt that a few ministers and MPs in Major's party were 'sleazy'. Jonathan Aitken ended up in jail, and other Tory MPs were forced to stand down from various senior positions. But Major himself – for all his substantial faults and his flaws – was not remotely corrupt. He was a decent figure, trying his best in very difficult circumstances. Yet opinion polls published at the time suggested that sleaze was one of the issues that most concerned voters about his leadership. Voters' misperceptions of the innocent Major showed the distorting impact of a feeding frenzy, and were another reminder that we choose what we want to see, rather than what lies in front of our eyes.

Here is one of the lessons of leadership. When a government totters, for whatever complex reasons, the media and voters see a prime minister in an entirely different light. At which point

Harold Wilson outside the Palace of Westminster awaiting the result of the Labour Party leadership election, 7 February 1963.

The leaders of the three main political parties side by side: Jeremy Thorpe (left), Harold Wilson (centre) and Edward Heath (right) at a ceremony in Westminster, 25 November 1970.

Margaret Thatcher, the first woman to be elected prime minister, waves to well-wishers outside 10 Downing Street on the day of her election victory, 4 May 1979.

Thatcher shares a moment of levity with US president Ronald Reagan at a meeting to mark the UN's 40th anniversary, October 1985.

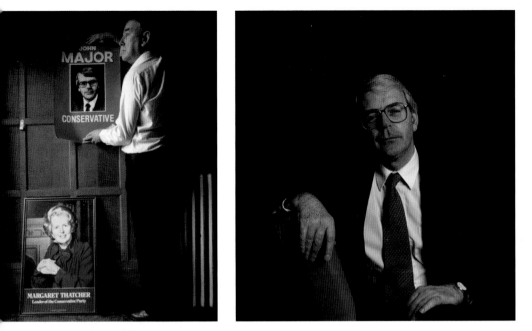

Above left: A poster of the new prime minister, John Major, replaces a poster of Margaret Thatcher on the day of her resignation after eleven years in power, 28 November 1990.

Above right: Prime Minister John Major, 1995.

Queen Elizabeth II inside 10 Downing Street during her Golden Jubilee year with Prime Minister Tony Blair (far left) and former prime ministers Margaret Thatcher, Edward Heath, James Callaghan and John Major.

Above left: Tony Blair and his wife Cherie inside 10 Downing Street after New Labour's landslide election victory, May 1997.

Above right: Blair and Brown during the first New Labour government, 27 September 1999.

Above: Blair and Brown at the Labour Party Autumn Conference – Blair's last as prime minister and party leader – 25 September 2006.

Right: Blair addresses soldiers on duty in Basra during the Iraq War before stepping down as prime minister, 19 May 2007.

Above left: Prime Minister Gordon Brown with Margaret Thatcher outside 10 Downing Street, 13 September 2007.

Above right: David Cameron, the so-called 'heir to Blair', talks to the press after winning the Conservative Party leadership election, 6 December 2005.

Below: Leader of the Opposition David Cameron listens to US Democratic presidential candidate Barack Obama during a tour of Parliament, 26 July 2008.

Prime Minister Cameron and Home Secretary Theresa May arrive for a ceremony at Horse Guards Parade in London, 21 October 2014.

Above left: Prime Minister Theresa May with European Commission President Jean-Claude Juncker, shortly after May triggered Article 50, 26 April 2017.

Above right: May announces her resignation outside 10 Downing Street, 7 June 2019.

the supposedly mighty leader is powerless to change perceptions. Indeed, attempts to do so tend to reinforce the dark prism. In this case a prime minister who was not corrupt, or 'in it for himself', was perceived in such a light because everything else was going wrong.

With hindsight, we can see another important twist. Major claimed credit for the state of the economy when he left office in 1997, but although he was unfairly tormented over 'sleaze', he has been too generously treated for the legacy he left to the incoming Labour government.

While Major could point to falling unemployment, steady growth and stable finances, he failed lamentably to address the shoddy state of public services. Any government can balance the books by not investing very much. By 1997 the NHS was in such a wretched state that hospitals were being compared unfavourably with those in Eastern Europe. In London, theatres issued warnings to audiences, urging them to leave much more time than they might anticipate to get to the venue, because public transport had become so unreliable. Across the country newly privatized trains were even more unreliable than the Tubes and buses in the capital. The infrastructure of the UK was creaking. Business leaders were crying out for more investment in capital projects. Outside London, public transport was even more unreliable. Bus services that had been privatized under Margaret Thatcher were expensive and some routes that were not profitable ceased to run. Voters who could not afford cars were left behind. The incoming Labour government was to inherit a situation where voters were aching for improved public services, without necessarily being willing to pay higher taxes. Contrary to a simplistic mythology that suggests Labour took over a booming economy, this was a challenging inheritance for Blair and Brown.

The dire state of public services was also an underestimated factor in the demise of the Conservative government, though without doubt impossible divisions over Europe, as well as the related issues of 'sleaze', were the main causes of the slaughter. Yet one of the ironies is that during the 1997 election campaign, when his party was defeated by a bigger margin in terms of seats than Michael Foot's in 1983, some of Major's messages were smart and prophetic.

He campaigned forcefully against Labour's devolution plans and on the last day he was prime minister, during the final twenty-four hours of that election campaign, he flew to different parts of the UK, warning that devolution could lead to the break-up of the UK. At the time his tour seemed rather pathetic and outdated, part of his outmoded 1950s traditionalism. As Blair walked on water, Labour's devolution plans seemed sensible, modest and very much with the times. But in retrospect, Major had a strong case. Instead of ending the momentum towards nationalism, the devolution settlement triggered a renewal. Two decades later, the UK seemed far more fragile than in 1997. Brexit was the main cause, but Labour's devolved power in Scotland provided the wider backdrop, with the SNP looking to hold a second referendum on Scottish independence. Major had appeared desperate when he was being prescient.

But his messages were not heard in 1997. When an unpopular prime minister, or former prime minister, makes a powerful case, voters turn away. Blair discovered the same as he framed potent arguments against Brexit before and after the 2016 referendum. In the 1997 election campaign Major was heading for a bleak defeat and was aware of his fate.

When he lost, he went to the Oval to watch some cricket on the Friday after the election. He looked relieved, and has looked relieved ever since. Subsequently Major became much calmer, more relaxed and, indeed, authoritative when he gave interviews. He was often witty. Voters started to listen again. He is the only modern prime minister to have looked liberated after he was brutally forced out of Number Ten. His relief suggests that, for all his early overlooked success, he was the wrong person for that particular job at that particular time.

But was there a right person available? Once again, the wider context is a reliable guide. The issue of Europe and the Conservative Party would have challenged the most titanic of prime ministers in the 1990s. Modest and insecure about his limitations, John Major would not have claimed to be a titanic prime minister.

In contrast, Tony Blair appeared to have mesmeric qualities when he became Labour leader in 1994. While no one listened to Major, Blair could utter banalities in his early years as Labour leader and they would be hailed as statements of historic significance. As Major left to watch the cricket, much of the country held euphoric celebrations to greet the arrival of the youngest of modern prime ministers. Major resented the way he was dismissed by much of his party, the media and the electorate, in contrast with the adulation around Blair. But for Blair, the euphoria became a curse.

6

TONY BLAIR

The arc of Tony Blair's leadership is the most extraordinary and Shakespearean of all modern prime ministers. After he became leader of the Labour Party in the sunny summer of 1994, Blair resolved to be trusted, respected and widely popular, not just as a newly elected leader, but as a prime minister. He assiduously wooed the newspapers and the BBC in the hope of fair coverage. He enjoyed a soaring honeymoon with voters and the media, which lasted far longer than that of any other modern prime minister. Everything he said and did in the early years was aimed at forming a new bond of trust with the electorate. There were annual reports to show that the government had delivered what it promised. There were pledges that ministers in a Labour government would be purer than pure, and would be seen as such. If there were protests, Blair sent a minister to join the demonstration, as a symbol of empathy. Poor Michael Meacher, an old ally of Tony Benn and an unlikely Environment Minister in the first Blair government, was told to join the march of the Countryside Alliance, even though it was a protest against government policies.[1] Blair ached to be a leader who was trusted in the most fundamental sense, as a prime minister of integrity.

Yet after Blair left office in 2007, he spent large amounts of time abroad, partly to keep out of a country where he provoked intense loathing from some. He could not even attend the launch of his memoirs, because of the security risks. Everywhere he went in the UK he was accompanied by bodyguards, a fate of all prime ministers, but far more necessary for Blair than for any other. When he first became leader of the Labour Party, he could utter any banality and much of the media would hail the words as an insight of profound depth and significance. A thousand columns would analyse his words and conclude, appreciatively, that the UK had a radical leader of unusual depth. After Blair left office, quite a lot of the UK turned away, even when he was speaking deeply.

To take one example: in his early years Blair would argue that Labour stood for social justice and economic competence. No party claims that it stands for economic incompetence and social injustice. Yet Blair's analysis was widely treated as if he had uncovered a magical insight of unfathomable depth. After the Brexit referendum in 2016, Blair's interventions were of the highest quality, elegant, crisp, accessible and forensic. Few appeared to take much notice.

What happened? How to make sense of his transition from a leader who walked on water and sought to navigate a 'third way' in policy-making, to a former prime minister viewed with fuming disdain. Blair's third way was similar to Harold Macmillan's middle way, even if Blair claimed for his ideas a profound distinctiveness. His third way was neither left nor right, but a route that in theory at least would keep Middle England on board, without alienating fully either the left or the right. In theory, his approach was a route towards eternal popularity. Instead, his limited philosophy propelled him towards intense unpopularity. Margaret Thatcher's career at least had a visible pattern. She emerged surprisingly and controversially. She departed suddenly, surprisingly and with breathtaking controversy. The end and the beginning make sense. Blair's end seems so different from his beginning.

———

Tony Blair was aged forty-one when he became leader of the Labour Party in the summer of 1994, the youngest leader in the party's history. The moment he became leader – indeed, even during the leadership contest that preceded his landslide victory – Blair was widely seen as the UK's next prime minister.

The authority-enhancing perception of Blair obscured almost entirely his youthful inexperience. He had not been a Cabinet minister, or a minister of any sort. He had never seen a prime minister working at close hand, from the perspective of being in a Cabinet. Instead, during arduous years in opposition, he had become the world's expert on Labour in the 1980s, and that expertise formed the basis of his calculations throughout his period as prime minister and as leader of his party. From the start of his leadership he had the forbidding, enigmatic aura of a winner, and yet electoral defeat had framed his political outlook.

Blair became an MP in 1983, the year that Labour was slaughtered in the general election. He was elected in the safe seat of Sedgefield, in the first of the Thatcher landslides – a big three-figure victory for the Conservatives, with a second to come four years later. Blair arrived at Westminster in 1983 at the same time as Gordon Brown. Their first direct experience of being candidates in general elections was of constant defeat for their party. Although they won their safe seats, Labour lost in 1987 and again in 1992.

During the 1992 election many, though not Blair, expected Labour to form the government. Under John Major, the Conservatives won for the fourth time in a row.

Blair's boundary-breaking leadership of his party is largely explained by the defeats Labour suffered in the 1980s. But there were other factors. His background played a part. Blair was educated at Fettes, a private school in Edinburgh, the son of a committed Conservative supporter who had contemplated standing for Parliament. Such a context can stir rebellious instincts and did so with Blair, but only to a limited extent. At Oxford, Blair joined a rock band and was dismissive of snooty orthodoxy. He performed in various comedy revues and plays. As a student, lawyer and politician, he was a performer fascinated by the art of performance. He was a prime minister who could perform so compellingly that he came to believe passionately in what he was arguing for, even when the ammunition was limited. As a Christian at Oxford, Blair was greatly influenced by Peter Thomson, an Australian Anglican priest, a committed Christian socialist who, when he died, was described as the 'irreverent reverend'.[2] Blair too had an irreverent streak, a sense of the absurd. He is one the few modern leaders to deploy humour and wit potently – those important political weapons. His calm and decent demeanour, combined with humour, ensured that colleagues who worked with him in Number Ten felt an intense personal loyalty, even if many of them were politically to the left of him. Blair was fascinated by charisma and was drawn to charismatic figures, irrespective of their politics; Thomson was also often described as 'charismatic'. Blair was as content socializing with the eccentric Italian prime minister Silvio Berlusconi or watching a film in the White House with President Bush as he was having a drink with President Clinton – in some respects more of a soulmate.

But contrary to the mythology, Blair's faith played little or no part in his approach to leadership. His politics were wholly secular, shaped by his sense of how to win elections, stay in power and make power as worthwhile as possible. In a political context, he was more likely to consult the *Sun* newspaper than the Bible. His commitment to the Labour Party came after Oxford, when he met his wife, Cherie, a fellow lawyer and an active Labour supporter. She was his route to the party. Roy Hattersley, who worked with Blair when he was the party's deputy leader up until the 1992 election, noted that while the rising star showed forensic brilliance and energy, he had no interest in the party's philosopher-kings. Hattersley once cited R. H. Tawney to Blair and noted that he might as well have been speaking Latin.[3]

The personal past of a leader is significant in a political career, but not decisive. A more important factor in shaping Blair's leadership was his lack of ministerial experience. He arrived in Number Ten as a youthful prime minister, fully formed as a party leader, but with no direct sense of the challenges of government in its many forms. While much of the media focused wrongly on the supposed arrogance and 'control freakery' of the New Labour leadership, there was a far more illuminating story to be told: the daunting challenge of assuming power after eighteen years of rule from a Conservative government of the radical right. Most of the senior ministers and advisers had no experience of government from the time when Labour was last in power in 1979. John Smith, the Labour leader whom Blair replaced in 1994, had been a Cabinet minister in the Callaghan government. Had he lived, he would have entered Number Ten with the kind of confidence that arises from knowing directly what government is like. Smith was cautious in many respects too, but government was not a mystery to him. New

Labour was accused of arrogance, but it was not arrogant enough – being terrified by opinion polls, focus groups and the latest verdicts in the media. Above all, its leaders had no sense of what government was like until they won stunningly in 1997.

What if Blair had been a junior Foreign Office minister, or Foreign Secretary, before becoming prime minister? At least he would have seen, and interpreted, intelligence – an explosively contentious issue in the run-up to the war in Iraq. He would have had a stronger feel for the reliability of intelligence, or the wisdom of citing it as definitive when it is inevitably tentative and often incorrect. Perhaps he would have seen at close hand Britain's so-called 'special relationship' waver, on good grounds. What if he had been Education Secretary or Health Secretary? His public-service reforms, well-intentioned though they were, might have been subtler and more finessed, in recognition of the complexities of delivering public services free at the point of need or use. Instead he was a leader with very limited experience, and that experience was largely confined to navigating the nightmarish internal politics of the Labour Party.

By 1994 when he became leader, Blair possessed a clear, well-developed and yet narrow sense of what Labour needed to do to win, following seemingly never-ending election defeats. He, Gordon Brown, Peter Mandelson and others had spent a huge amount of time together analysing what was going wrong and what was necessary, in their view, to put it right. Curiously he was the best-prepared leader of the Opposition in Labour's history, even though he had no idea that a vacancy would arise when it did. No one knew there would be a sudden leadership contest, and yet when the unexpected moment came, Blair was more than ready for the epic demands of being leader of the Opposition. This is not to suggest that he was well prepared for government. He was not. But in knowing what he wanted to do as Opposition leader, he was ruthlessly focused from the beginning. His project to win power was as tight and thought-through as Thatcher's, although very different.

Like Harold Wilson in 1963, Blair became leader after the sudden death of the current occupant. In Blair's case, John Smith died after suffering a heart attack. Smith had been a robust leader, travelling back and forth to Scotland as well as leading a party that makes impossible demands on its leaders. At weekends, he climbed the Munro mountains in Scotland in order to keep fit.

The suddenness of Smith's death was both a tragedy and part of what appears to be a dark pattern of Labour leaders winning elections. It seems that these terrible and unexpected personal tragedies pave a primrose path to elusive power for whoever takes over. Wilson acquired the crown when Hugh Gaitskell died unexpectedly. Blair is the only other leader to have done so in a dark funereal context. Both Wilson and Blair went on to win the next election. In contrast, Labour leaders who acquire the crown at the beginning of parliaments, perhaps five years before the next election toil, struggle and then lose.[4] The journey is too long.

Leadership is never easy; it is often close to impossible. Nonetheless, the context in which Blair acquired the crown was close to a dream one. The governing Conservatives were tearing themselves apart over Europe. John Major had little authority over his parliamentary party in the still-mighty media. In contrast, when Tony Blair arrived on the scene as Labour's leader there was excitement in the media about his rise, even among the Conservative-supporting newspapers. From the beginning, Blair generated a high voltage of political energy, but he did so in propitious circumstances. He looked a winner partly because he was bound to win.

Significantly, this was not Blair's own view. As he put it, with focused discipline, he was constantly fighting a 'war on complacency'. He fought the war to the point that he underestimated the potency of his appeal as the 1997 election approached. He became too disciplined. Blair genuinely assumed that a small Labour majority or a hung parliament were likely results, even up to election day in 1997, when the polls pointed to a big Labour win. The assumption determined a lot of his moves as he headed towards power.

Blair's leadership in opposition offers many lessons. Because of all those election defeats, he had a strong sense of what a party – any party – needed to say and do in order to win an election, or at least not to lose one. His heightened sense was accompanied by ideological timidity, although he argued, and believed, that he represented the 'radical centre', another imprecise term.

The concept may have lacked precision, but Blair's focus on policy detail was forensic at this stage. He was the most high-profile Opposition leader of modern times, rarely off the TV, although every now and again he would take a few days away from the Westminster frenzy on his own to analyse every proposition that was part of Labour's programme. This was to ensure, as he put it, that the policies were 'bombproof' in the context of a general election. Based on his background as a lawyer, and as an observer of Labour leaders being ill-prepared during elections, he would ask of himself the questions that he knew the media would pose in the forthcoming campaign. If he had any problems answering them, he would change the policy.

To take one highly charged example, during one of the intensive bombproofing exercises Blair hit upon a potentially explosive inconsistency in Labour's programme. He noted that Labour was proposing a referendum on whether the UK should join the eurozone, on constitutional grounds. He and Gordon Brown had justified their sudden support for a referendum on the euro on the basis that entry would mark a profound constitutional change. As ever in relation to leaders justifying a referendum, they were being disingenuous. They offered a referendum because John Major had done so, and because they were fearful of alienating Rupert Murdoch's newspapers if they did not.

Nonetheless, their public position was an apparently noble one. Voters must be consulted on a matter of such constitutional significance. Blair then noted that Labour was not offering a referendum on Scottish devolution, a policy with profound constitutional consequences, even if he did not realize quite how seismic they would prove to be at the time. Blair returned from the 'bombproofing' session and, to the astonished fury of the Scottish Labour Party, announced a referendum on the party's long-established proposal to introduce a Scottish Parliament in Edinburgh.[5] This was a brave leap. The revision meant that the election of a Labour government would not guarantee a Scottish Parliament. A referendum would follow. But Blair was not willing to be exposed on any policy during the intense scrutiny of an election.

Every policy in Labour's 1997 manifesto was bombproofed in a similar fashion. As a result, the media – albeit a sympathetic media – never caught Blair out in the absurd rituals of a UK election campaign. There were no 'cock-ups' or 'policy disarrays' that tend to mark elections in the UK. Labour leaders in particular had been destroyed during campaigns for some apparent policy cock-up or another. Blair was prepared and avoided any traps.

It might be assumed that bombproofing election manifestos is an obvious duty of leadership – in which case, many leaders are not dutiful. As an example, Theresa May got caught out in the 2017 election campaign, having not fully thought through the electoral consequences of her elderly-care proposals. In her manifesto May proposed that elderly care for affluent pensioners should be paid for partly by extracting equity from the value of their homes, a so-called 'dementia tax'. The panic in the middle of the Conservatives' campaign, when the policy was changed, was a failure of leadership. But May's inability to anticipate what might happen during the scrutiny of an election campaign was a minor lapse, compared to what had happened to Labour's leaders in the three elections during Blair's time as an MP. In the middle of elections, Labour's policies on tax and defence appeared almost to fall apart. This happened under the relentless gaze of a hostile and biased media. Even so, rows or damaging confusion about future income-tax levels, and how Labour would defend the UK, suggested that in spite of working around the clock, Blair's recent predecessors lacked the knack of bombproofing an election manifesto, a necessary part of leadership.[6]

The second skill Blair applied as leader of the Opposition was a form of genius, even if it contributed to his ultimate doom. Political leadership is an art form, and the artistry is not an added bonus; it's a precondition to success on other fronts. At all times a successful leader must give the impression of decisive purpose and momentum. Blair did so, even if the reality was much more complex.

Blair, Brown and the few other senior figures who mattered were indecisive and, indeed, divided on several key themes in the build-up to the 1997 election. They were not clear about whether they wanted to be in or outside the single currency, which was a huge issue in British politics at the time. Blair and Brown could not even agree at first on whether to offer a referendum on the issue. They prevaricated for some time after John Major had pledged to hold one. Ironically, it was Brown who was reluctant, seeking the option of joining the euro without the barrier of a referendum. Later in government, it was Blair who was keener on moving towards the euro and Brown who was passionately opposed.

Electoral reform was another significant issue in the run-up to the 1997 election, because Blair was forming a close relationship with the Liberal Democrats' Paddy Ashdown. Blair was keen on close ties with Ashdown and his party, knew that electoral reform was the policy that made a relationship possible, and yet viewed the actual policy warily. Before and immediately after the 1997 election, Blair was far from sure whether or not he wanted to introduce electoral reform. Personally, he was not keen on it, but as a leader of the Labour Party wanting to work with the Liberal Democrats, and assuming he might have to work with them in a coalition, he conveyed guarded enthusiasm.[7]

With a similar evasiveness Blair spoke of 'modernizing' welfare policies, without any clear sense of what that might mean. At the same time he and Brown were not at all sure how their rigid pledges to stick to the Conservatives' spending plans for two years, and not raise income tax for the lifetime of the next parliament, would still give them room to greatly improve public services, as they wanted to do. Indeed, Blair had proclaimed his three priorities as being 'Education, Education, Education'. But there were also similar, and equally vague, commitments to 'save' the NHS.

Under a less agile and forensically prepared leader, such evasiveness could have been disastrous. Do you support membership of the euro? Do you support electoral reform? How will you find the money to invest in public services when you won't raise income tax? What precisely will you do to reform welfare? The true answers to these questions were: 'I don't have much of a clue.'

But because of Blair's artistry as a leader, none of this mattered, at least in the build-up to overwhelming electoral victory. He gave the impression of complete confidence, direction and momentum. He managed to mock Major for the divisions in his government over the single currency, without revealing the fact that his side was just as bewildered and divided. Indeed, the number of referendums Blair offered in the 1997 campaign was a sign of how unsure he was on several pivotal issues. There were proposed referendums on electoral reform, the euro, the introduction of mayors, a Scottish Parliament and a Welsh Assembly. Blair did not hold as many as he offered, but the pledges were significant in themselves – an indication that he did not have the confidence to make the election a vehicle for profound change in relation to highly charged issues. If he wanted those issues resolved, he would win power first and then address thorny issues in referendums.

Few noticed. Much of the media, and most voters, saw only dynamism, excitement, novelty, strong leadership and a sense of purpose. If leaders look like winners, they have the space to cast spells. Even when Blair described his proposals as being 'on the radical centre' – a phrase that was both reassuring and inspiring – few noted any contradiction. In some respects, Blair made 'change' his theme, but in an unusual way. He had changed the Labour Party by promising not to do too much to change the country after eighteen years of Conservative rule. In essence, his message was that the UK had become a rundown, almost derelict mansion. He pledged to change the ashtrays. Quite a lot of voters looked forward to a renovation of the entire mansion.

Blair's genius at making the incremental seem so exciting and radical became part of his problem as prime minister. He won a landslide of huge proportions, a bigger majority than either of Margaret Thatcher's two landslides.[8] Partly because there had been a change of governing party for the first time in eighteen years, there was a sense of huge excitement. The colossal landslide triggered a further frenzy, even if the scale of the victory obscured the incremental manifesto on which it was based. The result was historic. The excitement was almost physically tangible in the immediate aftermath. There were street parties in parts of the UK. The newspapers could not contain their excitement, even those that had previously endorsed the Conservatives. And yet Blair had been elected on one of the most cautious manifestos of recent times.

The ambiguity was there from the beginning. On the night of the election, Labour politicians held a party at the Royal Festival Hall. Blair arrived in the early hours to declare, with a metaphorical flourish, 'A new day has dawned, has it not?' On one level, a new day had dawned. Here was a youthful incoming Labour prime minister after the long rule of Margaret Thatcher and John Major. At the same time, Blair was a resolutely expedient politician, wary at all times of alienating the Middle England voters and the newspapers they read. His own views were both complex and simplistic. As a matter of genuine conviction, he accepted that on some pivotal issues the Conservative rulers had been right and Labour had been wrong. Yet the sincere conviction was also a convenient one, in that it meant Blair did not have to confront some of the right-wing orthodoxies that were deeply held by powerful figures in the media and in business.[9]

As with President Obama in the United States, disillusionment with Blair was bound to come. Once again, voters saw in a prime minister what they wanted to see. At first some of them chose to see a radical change-maker. In contrast, some Tory voters saw a Labour leader who, to their delight, would not worry them, because he would not change very much. Blair hailed the 'big tent' of support for Labour, but the bulging canvas was bound to burst at some point. Here is part of the answer to the conundrum about Blair's arc as a leader: from being the country's saviour to being forced into near-exile. Expectations were high in 1997, because he was an exciting political personality and he symbolized change after eighteen years of rule from a right-wing Conservative Party. And yet, simultaneously, part of Blair's appeal was to those who had voted Conservative. He was doomed to disappoint.

Although the two perceptions of a change-maker and a leader who would not change very much are contradictory, both were true, at least in the early phase of Blair's leadership. After the election in 1997 there was a partly paralysing caution. The new government stuck to the Conservatives' spending plans, feared holding some of the promised referendums, hailed even the obviously flawed privatizations of the Thatcher/Major era and sought to help the City of London and the banks benefit from a lighter regulatory touch. Complex decisions were often kicked into the long grass. As one minister observed to a political commentator at the time, 'We've hit the ground reviewing.'[10] The observation neatly captured the tangible sense of energy in the early New Labour era, and a partial sense that the hyperactivity was not leading to deep change.

Yet at the same time the new Labour government was a change-maker. It introduced the minimum wage, the Scottish Parliament and the Welsh Assembly. The introduction of a London mayor was as significant as any reform aimed at liberating the City during the 1980s, in terms of reviving the capital, and one with no destabilizing consequences.[11] There was also the pledge, implemented belatedly in the second term, to increase investment in the NHS to the EU average – a policy that hugely improved healthcare and saved many lives. The introduction of Sure Start children's centres integrated previously fragmented services aimed at helping poorer families. New tax credits helped to make low earners better off, even if many of the voters who benefited had no idea that the extra cash came from a government policy. Blair and Brown's fear of a Middle England revolt against 'redistribution' meant that they never used that term or made much of what they – mainly Brown – were doing in relation to tax credits. The Foreign Secretary at the time, Robin Cook, noted that his constituents in Scotland assumed the extra money in their wages arose from a technical adjustment by the Inland Revenue. He urged Blair and Brown to be less stealthy and to proclaim what they were doing.[12]

Alongside all this, the Good Friday Agreement for Northern Ireland, reached in 1998, was a titanic achievement, involving courageous and tireless work from many, including Blair's predecessor, John Major. But Blair was pivotal in his willingness to keep going through long nights until the deal was signed.[13] The agreement negotiated with some previously unyielding opponents in Northern Ireland, and with the agile cooperation of the Irish government, was almost a work of art. Blair and all the other senior figures involved had to find a way through two seemingly unbridgeable perspectives: the unionists' resolute commitment that Northern Ireland must remain part of the UK – the essence of their political being – and, in impossible contrast, the nationalists' yearning for a united Ireland. Yet somehow the Good Friday Agreement formed the bridge. There would be a more clearly defined, soft border between Northern Ireland and Ireland, making the two countries far more tangibly connected than they were previously; a Northern Ireland Assembly, as part of the wider UK devolution settlement, to give a voice and potential power to all sides; as well as continued elections to the UK Parliament. A thousand other ideas and compromises helped to secure an agreement that remained fragile, but more or less in place, at least in the aftermath. Relatively minor outbreaks of terrorism in Northern Ireland did not undermine the Good Friday Agreement. The outcome of the Brexit referendum in 2016 posed a much more substantial threat.

The whole draining and lifesaving sequence played to Blair's strengths. He took risks when there was little danger of the outcome triggering the hostility of some newspapers and their Middle England readers. If there were such risks in any policy area, he became extremely cautious. On one level, he had nothing to lose politically by immersing himself in the peace process. Failure would be tragic, and yet without significant political consequence for a UK prime minister – the *Sun* would not have condemned heroic failure. There would be no obvious benefit to the main Opposition. The Conservatives had been as committed as Blair, in that John Major had instigated the peace process. Now they were under the leadership of the young and inexperienced William Hague, who would be given no political space if Blair failed. The project itself involved no ideological premise rooted on left or right. Blair's technocratic assertion 'What works is what matters' applied to the peace process in a way it did not apply to economic policy or the delivery of public services. The nightmare of the troubles in Northern Ireland liberated him from the constraining prism through which he viewed the battle with the Conservatives and the media. Even so, Blair must have been tempted to turn away from the negotiations at times, as he dealt endlessly with leaders from Northern Ireland who were capable of twisting and turning unpredictably. He lasted the course heroically.

Elsewhere, the new government introduced many smaller innovations, from free entry to museums, to the 'right to roam', which enhanced the quality of many lives. Blair and Brown were too scared to frame their policies in terms of a more active and benevolent state. They assumed that any reference to the state being active might alienate some voters and newspapers. But the government intervened selectively, and often with beneficial consequences. There was the introduction of civil partnerships, a leap as big at the time as the jump when David Cameron legislated for gay marriage. Blair's government introduced a smoking ban in public places, an innovation as important as the spending increase on the NHS. As prime minister, Blair managed to implement significant change while winning elections with big majorities – an unusual combination for a Labour prime minister.

———

Blair also changed the style of politics. He was in a constant dialogue with the voters. Thatcher was a political teacher, but she did not engage directly with the electorate very often. She hardly ever gave interviews on the *Today* programme and few TV interviews between elections. But Blair gave long interviews, press conferences and took part in a range of public events on a regular basis. He was a brilliant communicator, tonally light and flexible, framing arguments with clarity, modesty and wit. Cameron tried to copy him, but was not in the same league, as impersonators never can be. Some Conservatives referred to Blair as 'the master'. This was a doubled-edged sword for Blair, not least because the Conservatives were sincere in their endorsement.

His skills as a communicator became, over time, part of the media's obsession with 'spin'. Admittedly he was over-dependent on his main media adviser, Alastair Campbell. Both conceded that in the early years of government they continued as if they were in opposition, when successful presentation was of overwhelming significance. An Opposition leader cannot be tested by policy implementation. In government, Blair and Campbell had a tendency to mistake a presentational success for implementing policy. But the whole issue of 'spin' became overblown. Campbell's transparent duty was to place Blair and the government in the best possible light. Given the anti-Labour bias in the newspapers, and the newspapers' influence at that time, Campbell's ability to read the rhythms of news, to project positive stories and deflect negative ones, was a key part of Labour's electoral success. Gordon Brown pleaded with Campbell to work full-time for him when he was prime minister, and Tory leaders have sought an equivalent figure. The demands of the UK media are such that any leader would become reliant on a figure who understands how to address them.

The incoming Labour government also had a worked-through economic policy, although this had little to do with Blair. Gordon Brown and his senior adviser, Ed Balls, worked sleeplessly before the 1997 election to frame an economic policy that won the trust of voters, the media, the markets and business – an almost impossible challenge. Their aim was to create space to implement policies that would improve public services and address, to some extent, widening inequality, without all hell breaking loose in the markets and the media. Brown was as well prepared as Geoffrey Howe when he became chancellor in 1979. Blair was equally well prepared in some other policy areas, but gave little thought to economic policy. This became clear later when he gave his name to 'Blairism'. This school of thought found prominent advocates in the parliamentary Labour Party and the media long after Blair had stood down, yet it was an 'ism' without an economic policy.

Indeed, unlike Thatcherism, Blairism lacked a clearly defined ideology. Blair was defined by his revealing opening statement outside Number Ten, when he moved in to become prime minister in May 1997. He uttered words that were more remarkable and bizarre than they seemed at first. Amidst euphoric cheers – Downing Street was crammed with supporters, in a meticulously choreographed manner – Blair declared: 'We ran for office as New Labour, we will govern as New Labour. This is not a mandate for dogma or for doctrine, or a return to the past.'

What was so unusual about the assertion is that the core of most opening prime ministerial statements – albeit in banal or bland ways – is about the country. Blair's statement was partly about the country, but above all his message was rooted in his view of the Labour Party. He wanted to make clear from the beginning that this was not a return to 'old Labour', a conveniently vague term that created a chronological divide rather than an explicitly ideological one. From the beginning, Blair's governing philosophy was not to be Old Labour. His priority was to reassure sceptical voters that he genuinely was 'new Labour', particularly former Tory voters in Middle England, who read newspapers that were also opposed to Old Labour. If this can be called an ideology or political philosophy, it is a very narrow one. At least Thatcher had her philosophical heroes, F. A. Hayek and Milton Friedman, as guides, even if she was an erratic follower. Blair's ideological timidity was partly defined by context. He led a party that tended to lose elections. Thatcher led one that tended to win them, even though her party had been on a pretty bad run when she became its leader in 1975.

In his first term, Blair was also defined by the policies he had already inherited. When he became leader, the Labour Party had been out of power for so long it had accumulated a mountain of policies, many of which Blair had no choice but to accept. When David Cameron sought to 'do a Blair' with the Conservative Party after he became leader in 2005, he overlooked a key difference. Neil Kinnock and John Smith had done a considerable amount of detailed heavy lifting, in terms of policy and internal reform, before Blair became leader. Yet Cameron, who was not greatly interested in policy detail, inherited an empty canvas. There had been no equivalent of Smith and Kinnock, although Michael Howard, Cameron's predecessor, is underestimated in the way he kept the show on the road towards the 2010 general election, and in the selflessly smart way in which he cleared the path for his successor.

Blair used to describe New Labour's early policy programme dismissively, and yet revealingly, as 'low-hanging fruit'. Some of the early reforms were complex – Blair meant they tended to be changes that pleased his party. Perhaps he also meant that the reforms had not originated from him. He became more excited in the second term, when he felt a little freer and could move the policy agenda to the right, closer to his comfort zone and away from his party's. That is when he began to pursue his erratic public-service reform agenda, changes to the NHS and education reforms. These often stretched the boundaries of support within his party, so much so in certain cases that David Cameron is reported to have described himself as the 'heir to Blair'. Cameron made the assertion with sincerity, and without feeling much need for painful contortion in terms of the Conservative Party's policy programme. Yet in Blair's first term the combination of detailed work carried out by predecessors, as well as the nervily forensic revisions from Blair and Brown after 1994, led to a series of formidable reforms.

Blair probably regarded his announcement that the government would increase spending on the NHS to EU average levels as 'low-hanging fruit', but it was a pledge of great significance, even if it was made in chaotic circumstances. He transformed the spending projections for the NHS on the sofa of a BBC studio one Sunday in January 2000. Crucially, even newspapers like the *Daily Mail* were demanding more spending and higher pay for nurses at around this time. In an interview earlier that month for the *New Statesman* the TV presenter and Labour peer, Robert Winston, suggested that, on the basis of his mother's recent experience, hospitals offered better health provision in Eastern Europe:

> She spent 13 hours in a casualty department before being placed in a mixed-sex ward – an environment Labour has pledged to abolish. Drugs were not dispensed on time. She missed meals, and was found lying on the floor one morning after having fallen out of bed during the night… she caught an infection and came out of hospital with a leg ulcer. It is normal. The terrifying thing is that we accept it.[14]

The *Daily Mail* and other newspapers put the Winston interview on their front pages. The BBC followed up the front pages, as it usually did.

When reflecting on leadership, Blair hailed the virtue of strategy over tactics, but at times he moved with panic-stricken and tactical haste. He often argued in private that he was strategic while Brown was tactical, but this was an example of one leader viewing subjectively his own approach over a rival's.[15] Blair often acted as a short-term tactician, from pledging suddenly to abolish child poverty, to making un-costed spending pledges. The one for the NHS was the biggest of these and Blair was wholly right to make this long-overdue spending commitment, but the announcement had not been discussed with his chancellor, Gordon Brown, let alone any of the Cabinet. The commitment to a massive spending increase was made without any sense of how it would be met. Neurotically alert to the priorities of the *Daily Mail* and the *Sun*, Blair was responding to a media campaign while coming to recognize that far more investment was required, and knowing that if he had raised the issue with Brown in advance, he would have been stopped from speaking out on the BBC sofa. So Blair chose to speak first.

He was demonstrating speedy flexibility, an important leadership skill at times, but was also revealing a wilful capacity to convince himself that his moves were the 'right thing to do', even if his latest position in relation to 'tax and spend' contradicted an earlier one. In most respects, Blair was steady in his 'third way' approach, sometimes too steady. But on 'tax and spend' he waxed and waned. Blair moved into Number Ten convinced that the priority for Labour was to show it could be ruthlessly prudent in relation to public spending. If anything, his priority was to cut taxes. He told the *Independent* before the party's conference in 1998 that lower taxes 'were the way the world was moving'.[16] Indeed, one of the reasons Brown, as chancellor, got so furious with Blair was over his contradictory instincts. After one stormy conversation with Blair, Brown returned to his advisers, Ed Balls and Ed Miliband, and declared, 'You'll never guess what he now wants from me. He wants me to increase public spending and cut taxes... without explaining how.'[17]

There was a small part of Blair that recognized his limitations in relation to economic policy-making, though this was a subject rarely discussed with his advisers in Number Ten unless they were complaining about Brown. More widely, no other Cabinet minister reflected in any depth on economic policy during the Blair era. The lack of an internal debate on the economy was in marked contrast with the Labour government of the mid-1970s, when senior ministers debated economic policy endlessly, with at least three different approaches being espoused by various ministerial heavyweights.[18]

Blair's partial recognition of his own limitations in this most fundamental area partly explains his ambiguity towards Brown.[19] After the first few years in government, quite a big part of Blair wanted to sack Brown or at least move him to the Foreign Office,[20] but he never did so. By the beginning of the second term, Brown was demanding on a regular basis that Blair depart. Typically, their first discussion after the 2001 election, when they met back in Downing Street, included a demand from Brown that Blair plan for his own departure. Unsurprisingly, Blair was far from thrilled by this. But there was still a bit of Blair that knew Brown was the only substantial economic policy-maker in his government. Every now and again Blair would thrill his closest advisers by declaring that he would sack Brown, but he never did. There was no one else in the Cabinet remotely qualified to take command of economic policy. It is to Blair's credit as leader that, reluctantly and erratically, he realized this was the case, although he also believed that Brown would be impossibly dangerous on the backbenches. He was right about that, too.

After much agonizing, Brown raised the additional money from a tax rise directly linked to the NHS, almost a form of hypothecation or earmarked taxation. He did so having moved carefully and with considerable political skill, commissioning a seemingly independent report from a senior banker at a time when bankers' views on the best way to fund healthcare demands were still respected. The senior banker recommended a rise in National Insurance – in effect, a substantial tax rise. This was a huge moment in the history of New Labour, a political project that had defined itself partly against the 'tax and spend' caricature of the past.[21] Nervily and warily, Blair endorsed the tax rise, which was formally announced in the 2002 budget. He had no choice but to do so, given that he had made the spending pledge without knowing how it would be met. Some of his senior advisers in Number Ten were so anxious about the initiative that they feared it would lose them the next election. This was soon after Labour had won a second landslide and faced the weak Iain Duncan Smith as leader of the Opposition. New Labour was always fearful and nervy about disturbing the natural order of things in the UK, and this was understandable given voters' habit of electing Conservative governments, if given half an excuse to do so. Some feared that a tax rise would fatally disrupt the natural order.

The fear was reflected in what followed. Blair was anxious to prove that every penny of the money was being well spent and was accompanied by 'efficiencies'. His chosen method was what he presented as 'reform' of the NHS. At the beginning of the second term he had appointed Alan Milburn as Health Secretary, a figure who was big on vision and flaky on policy detail. Like some of Blair's other favourite ministers, Milburn had engaging charm and fleeting political energy, but no staying power. For a time, both he and Blair enthused about 'empowering patients', 'patient choice' and creating foundation hospitals that would be largely self-governing. More widely, they sought to attract the private sector to play a larger role, partly by offering some generous conditions to lure companies into new arrangements.

Blair insisted that anyone who opposed his ideas was 'anti-reform', as if only one version of change was possible. Neither Blair nor Milburn had given much thought to how their goals would be achieved. What would happen if a hospital was forced to close, on the grounds that it had run out of money? How could patients 'choose' their hospital, without hospitals being run with lots of empty beds and spare staff, a system that would create surplus capacity? How could a market work effectively in a service where patients paid nothing directly for the service they required? In an attempt to answer these questions, vast numbers of mediating agencies were required, but that raised further issues about blurred accountability and responsibility.

In his deceptively emollient memoir, Brown's close adviser from this period, Ed Balls, made an important observation. For a moment his buoyant tone became more candid:

> New Labour was never ever about trying to turn our state schools and hospitals into a marketplace where competition and profit should be drivers of excellence; and yet people like Alan Milburn defined it in that way... We won the definitive argument on a tax rise in the 2002 budget and won it comprehensively. But instead of taking that success and applying it to other public services in need of modernisation and proper funding we just invented a new argument on health and turned in on ourselves... That as much as Iraq was the New Labour tragedy.[22]

Choosing to see what they wanted to see, reviewers overlooked the one provocative paragraph. But the words were of historic significance, and Balls was right to compare the sequence with the calamity of the war in Iraq. Instead of focusing on how effectively to spend every penny of the additional NHS cash, and showing to voters that the money was spent well, the project got lost in a huge internal row about the structure of the NHS, the degree to which internal competition was desirable or feasible, and how much the private sector could get involved. Meanwhile, Blair hailed 'patient choice' when to some extent, even with the additional resources, choice was bound to be restricted. At the same time Brown feared that if Milburn's plans went ahead, hospitals could go bankrupt, as Labour was supposed to be proclaiming its unprecedented commitment to the NHS. A messy compromise between Blair and Brown was finally agreed, but as Balls noted, the spending increase on the NHS – an epic moment for a centre-left party in government – was partly lost in internal rows and clumsy reforms.

Even so, the increased investment and some of the reforms were substantial enough to briefly transform the quality of health provision in the UK. For a short time investment was indeed as high as the EU average, but soon after the 2008 crash it started to fall again, while the chaotic structures in the NHS remained in place and were fragmented further under David Cameron's leadership.

From 2001 onwards, some of Blair's allies briefed to the chorus of supportive commentators that Brown was 'anti-reform'. Subsequently the simplistic 'reform versus anti-reform' became an enduring and wholly misleading juxtaposition in British politics. Cameron adopted the same juxtaposition when his government generated more complex structures and mediating agencies, as he 'reformed' the NHS.

———

After winning a second landslide in 2001, Blair felt freer to pursue his own agenda. As is often the case with prime ministers, this is a dangerous liberation. In Blair's case, he chose to move towards his dark end at a point when he had maximum space on the political stage. This became apparent during the first few weeks of his second term when he had a revealing conversation with the former Cabinet minister Chris Smith, who had been Culture Secretary for the entire first term. Blair did not reappoint Smith for the second term, but, as a leader, Blair was smart about being convivial to ministers he had sacked. He invited Smith for a cup of tea in Number Ten. According to Smith, Blair told him he had three objectives for the second term. These were joining the euro, reforming public services and proving that a Labour prime minister could work closely with a Republican president, at a point when senior Conservatives were parading their Republican credentials. The third objective, pursued resolutely, led towards the war in Iraq or, more precisely, the UK backing the US.[23]

George Bush had begun his first term as president of the United States in January 2001, succeeding Blair's good friend and political soulmate, Bill Clinton. Neurotically alert to whatever the Conservative Party was up to, Blair noted soon after his cup of tea with Smith that the new Conservative leader, Iain Duncan Smith, was making overtures to the Bush administration. He sensed political danger. Blair wanted to give no space to Duncan Smith, fearing that post-Clinton it might be the new Conservative leadership that claimed a greater rapport with the new Washington administration. As he had told Smith, Blair was absolutely committed to showing that he could work as closely with the Bush administration as he had done with the Clinton administration.

This was one of the key strategic calculations as he made his moves towards Iraq. That is not to say there weren't others. No doubt Blair felt there was a robust case for removing Saddam Hussein, but if the case for war had been made by someone on the

Moon or the leader of North Korea, he would not have backed the invasion. It was the fact that a US president was making the case that propelled Blair towards supporting the war in Iraq. This was partly a strategic calculation about what he saw as the need for a Labour prime minister to be seen to be close to a US president, but also one of substance. Blair knew the Bush administration would act unilaterally in Iraq, if need be. He wanted to keep them engaged with allies like the UK.

As ever with Blair, he tried to navigate a third way in relation to Iraq. Quite a lot of commentators described his approach to Iraq as a terrible lapse of judgement, a big leap that was wholly out of character. On this reading, he metamorphosed from the cautious centrist to an unyielding evangelist. This is a misinterpretation of what happened. Every step Blair took in the build-up to war was wholly in character. He did not simply back President Bush as a crusading advocate of military intervention. Blair became evangelical, but only after seeking an expedient way through the path to war.

Here were Blair's multi-layered calculations. After Bush made his speech in January 2002 about the 'axis of evil' – a sweeping term that linked the Saddam regime to the terror attacks on the US on 11 September 2001 – Blair knew for sure that the US administration was planning to remove the dictator by force. With a convenient naivety, Blair saw the case in favour of war partly on the basis of his experience in Kosovo, where liberated families gratefully named their babies after him, an intoxicating tribute. Without exploring deeply what was happening in Iraq and beyond, he assumed that an Iraq liberated from Saddam would be similarly grateful. He also became convinced that he could influence the Bush administration by supporting it, and that after the 9/11 attacks on the US he had a duty to remain a loyal ally. Soon he was to discover, as other prime ministers had, the extreme limits of UK influence. But these related assumptions were by no means his sole or overwhelming calculation. There were many others.

Blair knew little about Iraq or the surrounding region, but he was a world expert on the Labour Party and how it lost elections before he became leader. He assumed that, as a Labour prime minister, his Middle England supporters (and the newspapers they read) would expect him to support a US president when that president was challenging a brutal dictator. Previous Labour leaders had been seen as 'weak' in relation to defence policy. Blair would never be perceived in such a light. He was also aware that Rupert Murdoch would be watching him closely, and Murdoch was a strong supporter of removing Saddam by force.[24]

Blair also planned at some point to hold a referendum and to campaign for the UK to join the euro. He was normally worried by newspaper onslaughts on him, but he was entirely relaxed when the Labour-supporting *Daily Mirror* newspaper accused him of being 'Bush's poodle'. He sensed that some voters would prefer a Labour prime minister to be working closely with a Republican president and he assumed that, after such attacks, no newspaper could criticize him for being indifferent to the US and 'soft' on Europe when he led the euro referendum campaign. But the referendum on the euro never happened, even though Blair saw such a campaign as part of his historic destiny.[25] After backing the US in Iraq, he hoped to complete his global 'third way' by putting the case for the UK joining the euro.

There was one final calculation. Every leader must seek to assess where their moves will leave them politically. There is nothing wrong with this. Margaret Thatcher knew she would have to resign if she did not fight the Falklands War, so unsurprisingly she went to war. Blair assumed that backing Bush would be, at worst, the least unpopular course to take. But he had some hope, when Saddam fell, that the war would be popular.[26] The former Foreign Secretary, Robin Cook, who resigned from the Cabinet in advance of the war, recalled that the first by-election after the Falklands War in 1982 was fought in Beaconsfield. Blair was the Labour candidate and, when Cook went to campaign for Blair, he told Cook how voters were in awe of Thatcher after the Falklands. She had acquired a new aura. Cook became convinced that Thatcher and the Falklands Factor were on Blair's mind as he moved towards Iraq. He assumed that, in the UK, war leaders became popular.

Blair was also leader of a party that was bound to be divided in relation to war. Labour had a strong Atlanticist wing that would be inclined to support Bush. At the same time, Cook's wing of the party loathed Bush and parts of his administration, and was committed to the UN as a means of resolving issues. Meanwhile, on the other side of the multi-layered equation, senior figures in the Bush administration had no faith in the UN and were impatient to invade Iraq, unilaterally if necessary. This was a daunting political and international context for a Labour prime minister.

Faced with a plethora of complex calculations, Blair navigated his latest third way. The question he had to answer was not the one that is often applied to him. It was not: 'Do I want to invade Iraq?' The question he had to answer was a more difficult one: 'Do I want to back the US president, who plans to invade Iraq in order to remove Saddam?' Blair had been the United States' close ally after 11 September 2001. President Clinton had come to his aid in the Balkans, intervening decisively in a military campaign that was originally of uncertain outcome. For Blair, the question was a genuinely thorny one. A bigger, more experienced figure would still have turned away. But even a titan would have struggled with the dilemmas, which looked far more forbidding in advance of the war than they did afterwards, when Blair was lazily dismissed as a crazed war criminal.

Prematurely and with timid naivety, Blair told Bush that the UK government would support the US mission, come what may. 'I will be with you whatever' were the words of a note from Blair to Bush written in July 2002 and highlighted in the Chilcot Inquiry into the war, whose report was published in July 2016.

But Blair made that commitment as part of a negotiation in which he persuaded Bush to seek the support of the UN in enforcing resolutions that demanded the removal of Saddam's 'weapons of mass destruction' (WMD). The UN would not sanction the removal of Saddam through force in a resolution. But as Saddam had defied various UN resolutions in relation to his alleged WMD, Blair thought he had hit upon a feasible route. The focus on WMD arose from Blair's need to navigate the UN route – one that would command much wider support in his party and the wider electorate. Blair also placed polite pressure on Bush to revive the peace process between Israel and Palestine. This was his 'third way', part of a pattern in his leadership and not an aberration: seek UN backing rather than act unilaterally, and make progress in the Middle East. In order to encourage the US president, Blair assured him that even if both these routes failed, he would back military action.

There was a contrast between Blair's approach and that of his main opponent, who also supported military action. The Conservative leader, Iain Duncan Smith, was insisting that his party would support Bush, whether or not he sought UN backing.

Blair's position was distinct, but in a limited way. Without UN backing, he would be in the same place as Duncan Smith.

Very quickly, Blair became trapped. Prime ministers are often incarcerated politically, but can never admit to being so. In Blair's case, he was not used to being quite so constrained. Normally he found a way through thorny policy areas. This time there was no escape, although he did not realize this as he made his way towards his form of political hell.

From the summer of 2002 onwards, Blair spent much of his time putting forward his case for what he was doing. This happened to be dangerously ambiguous. He argued in interviews, speeches and seemingly never-ending press conferences that Saddam must remove his weapons. He did not, and could not, suggest that he or, more precisely, the US administration wanted to remove Saddam. The UN would regard such a military intervention as being against international law, and the Labour Party would become even more restive.

In September 2002 Blair published UK intelligence in a document that aimed to show the extent of Saddam's WMD. At the time he saw the document as part of his case, like a lawyer presenting evidence that would help him win an argument. Later, the dossier on Saddam's WMD was to be plucked out of context and assessed as if it were supposed to be an entirely neutral piece of work. When it was published, the document on Saddam's WMD was evidently part of a wider set of propositions that Blair was making, with increasingly desperate urgency.

By early 2003 there was still not a single senior figure in the UN who thought Blair had a hope of speedily securing a UN resolution to sanction war in Iraq. Blair had no choice but to cling to the hope of meeting this impossible objective. When he failed to agree a resolution of any significance, he blamed President Chirac, who had given a very reasonable interview insisting that, for the time being, France would oppose military intervention. Suddenly Blair was even more trapped, having assured Bush that he would be with him, whatever happened at the UN.

Blair was constrained in many other respects, too. He was not in charge of the timetable for war. While he spoke of standing 'shoulder to shoulder' with the US, he was following the US schedule. Occasionally he was assertive, but in a limited context, persuading Bush to give him time to seek, fruitlessly, a UN resolution that would give him the cover he required. Blair also succeeded in persuading Bush to make a vague pledge to renew the Middle East peace process. Bush made a brief statement in which, without any great assertive enthusiasm, he pledged to renew the focus on some form of two-state solution to the Israel/Palestine question. Blair was fleetingly upbeat as he watched Bush deliver his largely empty words on the Middle East, failing to notice the limits of his influence, or not daring to do so.

In reality the US administration was getting impatient. Why did Blair not give the weapons' inspectors more time to search for WMD? The question is meaningless and unfair. The timing was not up to him. The US wanted to act speedily not least because the temperatures in Iraq would soar if they waited much longer. Why did Blair not pull out of the conflict after he failed to secure a meaningful UN resolution authorizing force? There was not the remotest possibility that Blair would turn away and become the Labour prime minister who was not 'strong' or 'courageous' on the eve of war. Part of the purpose of his leadership had been to show that a Labour prime minister could be 'strong'. Why did Blair not retreat when up to a million people took part in demonstrations against the war in the UK on a freezing-cold Saturday in February 2003, shortly before the conflict began? By then the course was set. Blair was surprised by the scale of the demonstrations, and by the range of those taking part. Some of the marchers were 'his' constituency – those who had turned against Labour in the 1980s, but had voted New Labour in 1997 and were smart enough to recognize the recklessness of this particular war. For Blair, it was far too late to pursue a different course.

If Blair had pulled back in the face of one march, he would have been without a voice in the future. Many newspapers were praising his 'courage'. The former Conservative minister Michael Portillo wrote in *The Sunday Times* that he had not realized until now 'the degree to which Blair is a principled and brave leader'.[27] Only the *Daily Mirror* and the *Independent* unequivocally opposed the war. The Conservative leader, Iain Duncan Smith, continued to side with Blair rather than with the protesters, some of whom were Conservative supporters. The least unsafe route for Blair was to carry on and claim that he was acting because it was 'the right thing to do' – one of his many conveniently technocratic and apolitical phrases that punctuated the New Labour era.

What followed was an epic tragedy. Above all, the tragedy lay in the number of deaths that arose as a result of the invasion. The estimates of the numbers who died vary and are the subject of ongoing debate, but few deny that hundreds of thousands were killed as a direct or indirect result of the war. A rare piece of accurate intelligence warned in advance that the war would heighten the risk of terrorism. Blair ignored this unwelcome pre-war information. Subsequently, Iraq became a terrorists' playground while a civil war erupted between different factions that had been held in check by a tyrant's rule.

For Blair, the war had Shakespearean consequences. At the beginning of his leadership he sought to show that he could be trusted. In the 1980s Labour leaders were not trusted on matters of defence or much else. John Major was slaughtered in 1997 partly because of sleaze and a sense that the Tories could not be trusted. Blair would be different. Blair would be 'new'. But after Iraq, he was accused of lying in order to win support for the war, and of wilfully misleading voters over the existence of Saddam's weapons of mass destruction in order to implement his crusading vision. Some voters became convinced that Blair was a war criminal who should be tried in The Hague. A few years later, when no longer prime minister, Blair confided to Alastair Campbell that he preferred being in other countries rather than his own, because of the anger that he provoked.[28]

In some respects, the anger directed at Blair was overwrought, part of the exaggerated response he generated from the beginning. The early opinion of Blair as a great radical leader who would heroically transform Britain was at odds with the cautious, defensive 1997 manifesto composed by a leader with no experience of power. The later perception of Blair as a mendacious messianic murderer is also contradicted by the evidence.

One clue as to how easily Blair is misread relates to perceptions of how he managed the Cabinet both during the build-up to war and throughout the rest of his leadership. The Chilcot Inquiry into the war was typical in suggesting that ministers were prevented from expressing their views or from scrutinizing what was happening. Chilcot concluded that there should have been 'wider discussions by a cabinet committee or small group of ministers', and that the Cabinet should 'have been made aware of the legal uncertainties' surrounding the war.[29] Yet with the exception of Robin Cook, and to some extent Clare Short,[30] who resigned after the war, the Cabinet chose not to probe. Cabinet ministers did not live in an alternative universe. They were aware of the raging debate about Iraq, the risks and the questions about its legality. Blair had won two election landslides and he had given them Cabinet posts. They were grateful and keen to deliver what he wanted. Crucially, most of them were not fully formed politicians and did not seek to be. They sought to please Blair. The very big exception to this docility was usually Gordon Brown, but on Iraq, Brown agreed with Blair. If he had disagreed, he would have attempted to block what Blair was doing, as he often did in domestic policy areas. Brown raged against tuition fees and elements of the NHS reforms, both of which were being considered at around the same time as the war in Iraq, but he did not rage against Iraq.

Blair's perceived attempts to bypass or deceive his Cabinet were part of a wider disproportianate focus on his integrity. There were many other questions that could have been raised after a deadly, calamitous war. Why did he not reflect on the internal tensions in Iraq before going ahead? Later Blair expressed surprise at the near civil war that erupted in Iraq. He need not have been taken aback if he had probed more. There were also questions, still not fully answered, about why the intelligence – even with all the qualifications – was so wrong. Blair was shallow in his reading of the Middle East and then took on the role of the persuasive lawyer as he deployed intelligence to further his case. These are serious enough allegations, but they aren't the same as suggesting that Blair 'lied' to go to war, an assertion as simplistic as some of Blair's own judgements about what would happen in Iraq once it had been 'liberated'.

But even these judgements were not made in isolation. Blair had to decide whether or not he was going to support Bush. The US would have gone to war either way. Indeed, in recognition of the multiple pressures piling in on Blair in the UK, Bush suggested that the UK could step aside – definitive evidence that the US was content to invade Iraq more or less on its own. Blair refused to accept the offer because to have done so would have wrecked his entire multi-layered strategy. He also genuinely wanted the US to be part of the international community and not to act with unilateral recklessness. For Blair, the decision to go to war was about the US and his view of the Labour Party's past as well as what was happening in Iraq.

His use of intelligence was not an act of mendacity or criminality, but he was using the hopelessly speculative material to further his cause, and he knew little about how to actually read intelligence. This is no surprise, given that his first post in government was as prime minister. He had never dealt with intelligence in a previous role.

None of these issues were explored widely after the war – Blair's misreading of Iraq and the wider region, his inexperience as a youthful prime minister, the immense domestic calculations made by any prime minister when deciding whether to take military action. Instead, Blair became a messianic figure who illegally took the UK to war and was wilfully indifferent to the deadly consequences. The long hours he worked on the Northern Ireland peace process are a challenge to a bloody caricature that was too easily formed.

———

Blair's end was as multifaceted and complex as the origins of the UK's involvement in the Iraq War. Indeed, part of the complexity was to do with how the seemingly defining conflict played only an indirect role in his fall.

After the war it might have been logical for Blair to have less confidence in his leadership. Iraq had been largely a Blair solo project, from a UK perspective, and it had quickly proven to be a catastrophe on many different fronts. Because he is a human being, the entire sequence was a draining and traumatic experience for him, and it ended with questions about his integrity, deaths and a destabilized Middle East.[31] Yet perversely Blair became more confident and determined as he moved towards the end of his time in power.

His response to Iraq was a steely determination to show that his leadership was about much more than a war. He became obsessively focused on his narrow interpretation of what constituted public-service reform and made another attempt to explore the possibility of joining the euro. There were no substantial grounds for his renewed interest in the euro at that particular time, beyond a desire to go down in history as the prime minister who was as much a pro-European as one who stood by the US when its president went to war.[32] Blair's confidence and sense of resolution were also strengthened by another election victory in 2005, a dark campaign when questions about his integrity featured heavily, and during which he and Brown had to pretend they were working well together when they were not.[33] Yet with the help of Brown and his entourage, Blair did win the 2005 election after the war in Iraq. Bush won a second election in the US, and the Australian prime minister, John Howard – a supporter of the war – also won again. The invasion of Iraq came to torment the war leaders who took part, defining them darkly, yet they remained election winners.

Blair's increasingly fractious relationship with Brown partly determined his approach in the final phase. He rationalized that with Brown challenging key policies, he had a duty to stay on in order to ensure that 'New Labour' ideas continued to prevail, compared with Brown's more social-democratic version of their project. He was sincere in his mission, but the cause was a convenient one often adopted by prime ministers. For the sake of his country and his party, Blair concluded that he had a duty to remain in power.

In doing so, he depoliticized politics during his curious, intense and yet ragged final phase. The depoliticization had explosive consequences, as voters turned away from a technocratic insistence that 'what works is what matters' – as if any leader would argue for what does not work. But Blair had to deny the salience of left-wing arguments in order to make sense of the support he attracted from sections of the Conservative Party and Conservative-supporting commentators, especially after David Cameron became Conservative leader in 2005. Indeed, the once publicly self-effacing Blair loftily detected a global phenomenon from his own freakish political journey.

He regularly declared that there was no longer a left/right divide in politics, but only one between 'open' and 'closed': advocates of free trade and internationalism against protectionists and insular interventionists. But the 'open v. closed' divide was not remotely new. Indeed, the internal splits in the Conservative Party over the Corn Laws in the mid-nineteenth century represented a split between 'open v. closed'.

Blair had concluded that the left/right divide was over, when this particular ideological chasm was deepening over the role of the state, the virtues or drawbacks of public spending, the limits of markets and the role of governments in mediating a globalized market, among other issues. Debates were erupting in new ways, not least after the financial crash in 2008. They were all themes that triggered conflicting responses from both right and left. Blair was at odds with history when he felt that his 'what works' philosophy was moving with the tides.

Fragile and yet more assertive now than when he was politically strong, in the summer of 2006 Blair flew over to Rupert Murdoch's annual conference in the United States. In his address he hailed the era of political 'cross-dressing' in which opposing parties tried out each other's clothes. The metaphor worked for Blair, but he extrapolated far too widely. His ubiquitous juxtapositions were ideologically rootless: 'boldness v. caution', 'reform v. anti-reform', 'economic competence versus economic incompetence'. Years later, Blair despaired of Labour's embrace of Jeremy Corbyn, but Blair was the leader who moved outside party boundaries and turned his political travels into a creed. His third way had become 'the right thing to do'. Such technocratic banalities were a factor in the rise of the ideologically committed Corbyn, who became an MP in 1983, like Blair. Unlike Blair, he never served on the frontbench until he became a leader with deep but untested ideological convictions. Corbyn had no leaderly experience, but he was rooted in part of a political spectrum that had never become wholly irrelevant in the way that Blair and his followers suggested.

Blair's crazy dance with Brown over his departure date was the immediate cause of his increasing assertiveness. Brown behaved with insensitive and frustrated rudeness towards Blair and his senior advisers in Number Ten, but he had a reason to feel defensive. He dreaded a legacy in which he would be paralysed as an incoming prime minister. In his final days, Blair set a series of tests for Brown, with the support of the newspapers that Brown was desperate to have on his side, too. Would he be a 'reformer', as defined by

Blair, with the support of Cameron and Osborne? Would he be as resolute in foreign affairs? Was his view of New Labour the same as Blair's? At times, Blair told Brown that he would go, then he stayed on. Brown continued to press for him to go. As Brown did so, Blair became more resilient and more determined to stay on. The dance became more crazed until Blair was finally forced to indicate publicly that he would go by the summer of 2007, ten years after becoming prime minister.

Blair had a great gift for compartmentalizing. He could focus on one issue, even if mad storms were erupting around him. In this relatively stressful period, which included an absurd and disgraceful police investigation into whether Blair and his close advisers had broken the law in seeking 'cash for honours', the fallout from Iraq and the constant battering from Brown, there were some sunny days. Blair played a major role in securing the Olympics for London. When the sporting event came to London several years later, the capital, in its buoyant exuberant metropolitan liberalism, reflected Blair's vision and virtues as a leader. He was a social progressive. Securing the Olympics was another gloriously apolitical triumph that was indicative of Blair's ideal terrain. And there were further positive developments in Northern Ireland, which made the always-fragile peace agreement more secure.

Some of the public-service reforms were also delivering positive results. As part of his productive focus on public services, Blair established a Delivery Unit that held policies and policy-makers to account. He was uneasy about hailing the state as an instrument of delivery, but his own Delivery Unit was a model of how to get a grip and make government work more effectively as a whole, even if some of the specific reforms led to costly fragmentation rather than new forms of efficiency.

Inadvertently, Blair hit upon another highly effective model of delivery and, somewhat warily at first, introduced an elected Mayor of London. The wariness was partly to do with the successful candidacy of Ken Livingstone, a figure of the left who terrified the pioneers of New Labour. Livingstone was forced to stand as an independent in the first mayoral election and won easily. He proved to be such a successful reformer that Blair endorsed him, and the mayoral model, with genuine enthusiasm when he felt it was safe to do so. Livingstone appointed travel experts from the US to improve London's dire public transport. Under the body Transport for London, the best professionals were free to innovate, while the high-profile mayor was accountable to the electorate. With the introduction of the Congestion Charge to pay for more buses, and the Oyster card, London suddenly enjoyed improved public transport. Blair was more interested in his interpretation of 'reform' as defined by his changes to the NHS, but he created an alternative model for running public services, almost by chance. Transport for London, under an accountable high-profile mayor, was a structure that greatly improved bus and train services in the capital. This is the public-service reform that was an unequivocal success.

Unsurprisingly, given the ambiguity of his leadership, Blair was forced out without being forced out. He hit upon his final third way: leaving without leaving. By September 2006 some Labour MPs started to call for Blair to go, and this time it was clear Gordon Brown was ready to strike. Blair was made to issue a statement after a fraught, animated and angry conversation with his old friend. In the statement Blair said he would leave, but only after another year or so in power.

But in another lesson of leadership, Blair's authority had already started to drain away. Even before his 2005 election win, Blair had announced that he was only planning to serve one more full term and would not contest a fourth general election. He had pre-announced his departure even before he declared in September 2006 that he would be going in about a year's time.

From that first contorted announcement in 2003, the power oozed away. Some Cabinet ministers who had been Blairite became Brownite. When Blair announced an initiative – and he announced many during his final phase – colleagues, opponents, the media, and probably the wider electorate, recognized it as time-limited. Before long, a successor would be wielding power.

Blair had made a mistake. Cameron committed the same error – following Blair, as he often did – shortly before the 2015 election, declaring in an interview that he would serve a full term, but would not fight the election after that one. He had not intended to make such a foolish declaration, but Blair was often on his mind, just as Thatcher was on Blair's.

Blair resigned as an MP after he left Number Ten. His final appearance at Prime Minister's Questions was also his last contribution in the Commons. MPs on both sides stood and cheered him as he left, departing both as a prime minister and as an MP. This was highly unusual. Most former prime ministers stay on as an MP, quite often for at least one more parliament. Cameron took the same approach as Blair, by leaving Parliament speedily.

Blair's speedy exit was part of a pattern. A lot of Blair's closest ministerial allies left politics before him or soon afterwards. His ministerial allies – figures who were supposed to be great reforming figures, like Alan Milburn, Stephen Byers, John Reid and Patricia Hewitt – did not hang around to fight for their cause, partly because Blairite ideological verve was more about him than about a deeply embedded governing philosophy. When Blair went, Blairism went, too. In marked contrast, Thatcherism continued to cast a spell long after her departure. But Blair's legacy for the Labour Party and the leaders that have followed him is as complex and daunting as the one Margaret Thatcher left for the Conservative Party. Did he win because he was not really Labour at all? Is that the only way Labour can win? Was he right at the time, but the times have changed, making him wrong now? Was he wrong from the beginning, and by the mid-1990s voters were ready to elect a leader to the left of him? The future of the Labour Party will be defined partly by what Tony Blair did, and did not, do as its leader and as winner of three elections in a row. In this sense, he continues to follow Thatcher as she leaves the equivalent questions facing the Conservatives.

Here is a curious lesson of leadership. The great election winners tend to leave their parties bewildered when they depart, or almost depart, from the political stage. Most immediately, Blair left his successor, Gordon Brown, with a dilemma that Brown never resolved. How could he show that he was different from Blair, while retaining the support of the newspapers and voters who backed Labour solely because of Blair? Brown had agonized about that question in advance, and was to do so again when he finally became prime minister.

7

GORDON BROWN

There are many ways of judging the effectiveness of prime ministers. How many elections did they win? What impact did their policies have on the country? How did they manage their parties and Parliament? These are three obvious criteria: the first a matter of objective record; the second always deeply subjective; and the third a combination of the two. But there is a fourth, more illuminating method of measuring leadership.

When making judgements about leaders, we must look at the context in which they led. Some leaders are lucky. Harold Wilson took to the helm when the Conservatives were perceived as exhausted and outdated after a long period of rule. A decade later, Margaret Thatcher was in some respects more fortunate. She became leader at a time when a divided Labour government was struggling to retain its tiny majority amidst economic turmoil. Tony Blair was luckier still. By 1994 the Conservatives had been in power even longer than when Wilson led Labour towards modest victory in 1964. They were furiously divided over Europe. Some Tory MPs cared more about this issue than about winning yet another election – a gift for the leader of the Opposition. The three lucky leaders made the most of the benevolent political background by striding towards historic election victories with actual – or smartly affected – momentum.

At the other end of the scale, Gordon Brown was deeply unlucky in terms of the background against which he made his moves. Indeed, he faced profoundly challenging dilemmas throughout his career. There was no junction where he, or an objective observer, could look up at the wider political scenery and fully enjoy the view. Instead the view tended to be dark, with immense, complex political or economic challenges, even when he inherited a partially benevolent economy as chancellor in 1997. Part of the darkness was formed by Brown's internal critics, who tended to ignore the challenging background in which he made his cautious, calculating and sometimes daring moves. His angry Labour opponents often surfaced to comment anonymously on how useless Brown was, without suggesting how they would apply their apparently masterful skills to the intimidating tasks at hand. This pattern applied when Brown was shadow chancellor, chancellor and then prime minister.

The fate of leaders is determined partly by how they rose to the top: Wilson bringing together a Labour Party deeply divided in the vote-losing 1950s; Heath's successful ministerial career giving him a misplaced confidence; Callaghan's close relationship with the trade unions; Thatcher's speedy ascent as she pledged to abolish the local property tax; Major's equivocal positioning in the Conservative Party; Blair's conviction that Labour wins only by being 'new'. Both Blair and Brown were defined by their early years as MPs in the party's vote-losing years of the 1980s and early 1990s. All leaders are also shaped by their less overtly political early years, from Thatcher's upbringing in Grantham, to Major's in Brixton. Of all the modern prime ministers, Brown surfaced from his early years most fully formed, with his qualities and deep flaws. His father was a minister in the Church of Scotland, a figure that Brown cited as often as Thatcher referred to Alderman Roberts. Brown suggested that his father gave him his moral compass. His father sought to do good in the Church. Brown saw politics as the vocation in which he could make a difference to people's lives. At the same time, he became a youthful star in the Scottish Labour Party, once described by another sparkling figure from Scotland, Robin Cook, as a 'nest of vipers'. Cook, who became Foreign Secretary in the New Labour era, was one of several figures Brown fell out with. Brown learned that politics could be brutal, and sometimes should be brutal. For Brown, the ends justified the means, whether the end was his own ascent to the top of the Labour Party or prevailing with colleagues in order to pursue causes related to his interpretation of social justice.

He was a student at Edinburgh University by the age of sixteen, a youthful rector of the university, a writer of books and pamphlets, a reader of many books, a campaigner for Labour and, by 1983, an MP. He had been briefly a BBC producer, giving him some sense of how the media worked, in a parliamentary party incapable of conveying any message effectively to a wider audience. Brown was also intensely competitive. Some of the hunger to win was purged by taking part in various sports. Most modern prime ministers felt the need to affect an interest in football. Brown was genuinely passionate. While a student, he lost the sight in one eye playing rugby. He continued to play tennis and some other sports, but after that terrible injury much of Brown's competitive energy was focused on politics. He ached to win, for his party to win, for himself to win – and for his policies to be the ones that triumphed in internal battles.

In opposition and in government, Brown was responsible for Labour's economic policy for fifteen years. Few of his colleagues, including Tony Blair, gave much detailed thought to economic policy. This is partly because Brown would fume ferociously if anyone ventured onto his terrain. He was the most controlling of control freaks. At the top of the Labour Party, it was only Brown and his closest advisers who thought deeply about economic policy for more than a decade. From the left, John McDonnell reflected from the safety of the backbenches on economic policy, and these reflections gave him authentic authority when he became Jeremy Corbyn's shadow chancellor in 2015. None of Blair's frontbenchers dared to show any interest, in the face of the intimidating Brown. This was in marked contrast to the 1970s, when most Labour Cabinet ministers thought of little else other than economic policy, whatever their theoretical department briefs.

The background to Brown's thorny ascent merits a quick view. The circumstances at the start of his phase as a pivotal Labour figure partly explain the dramas that followed, and are as important in terms of making sense of his tempestuous career as his complex personality.

After the party's fourth defeat in 1992, the new Labour leader, John Smith, made Brown shadow chancellor. This is one of the toughest jobs in British politics at the best of times. But for a Labour politician of insatiable ambition, this was the very worst of times. The outcome of the 1992 election had been the most painful of the party's four successive losses. The party leadership had hopes they might win, even if Blair and Brown never thought they would, and most commentators predicted a Labour victory with Neil Kinnock as prime minister. The distinguished political columnist Peter Jenkins headed for Lancashire during the campaign, an area with several marginal seats, and concluded in his *Independent* column that Labour would win.[1] Most polls pointed to a Labour victory or a hung parliament. Yet Labour lost again, triggering much speculation – not least in Labour's ranks – that the party might never win. The conditions had seemed favourable: since the previous election in 1987, Kinnock had seen off the threat from the SDP, the Conservative government had introduced the deeply unpopular poll tax, the economy was in serious trouble and John Major was, in some ways, an awkward public performer. But Labour lost, a defeat that suggested seemingly never-ending opposition.

At Labour's National Executive post-election meeting the party's polling and focus-group guru, Philip Gould, was blunt. He told the shell-shocked and funereal gathering that Labour had lost again because it was not trusted with the voters' money. Specifically, voters did not trust Labour to 'tax and spend' – the narrow and distorting prism through which UK elections are largely fought. Labour's outgoing leader, Neil Kinnock, had tried hard to appear more like a technocratic bank manager, in an attempt to reassure voters. Kinnock tried so hard to become what he was not that he lost the exuberant qualities that had propelled him to the leadership in the first place. Yet he had reformed his party and modified its policies over nine draining years. His shadow chancellor, John Smith, had introduced carefully costed proposals, every halfpenny accounted for, even if he had mistakenly unveiled a 'shadow budget', which the Conservatives leapt upon gratefully.

Smith looked, and sounded, even more like a reassuring bank manager. Kinnock had wanted to propose an earmarked tax to pay for much-needed NHS improvements as part of the party's manifesto in 1992. With good cause, he wanted to add some verve to the party's pitch. Smith vetoed the idea. In spite of the carefully calibrated and fearful caution, the party was still regarded as a reckless spender by a significant section of the electorate and a hostile media. The projection of a leader and shadow chancellor as two bank managers, when the banks were still trusted, did not remotely purge the party's reputation for profligacy.[2]

So this was Brown's joyless inheritance as shadow chancellor. Labour was not trusted to run the economy, and the mistrust was shaped by a distorted but potent 'tax and spend' debate that his party always seemed to lose.

For Brown, the challenge was even more daunting. Labour was not trusted to raise money, but money was obviously needed. By 1992 public services in the UK were in deep decline. NHS waiting times were dangerously long, and the quality of health provision lagged behind equivalent countries, as did investment levels. Public transport creaked along unreliably and would get even worse with the ill-thought-through privatization of the railways. In schools there was much talk of teacher shortages, rundown buildings and the use of battered old textbooks. Everywhere there were vivid images that suggested public spending needed to rise. So how would Brown, as shadow chancellor, square the circle? Labour was not trusted to tax and spend, and yet money was urgently required for public services.

In a way that was too easily overlooked when Brown went out of fashion, he managed it. By Labour's second term, the government was investing in services, sometimes by huge amounts, without becoming unpopular or losing credibility with the markets. Even much of the media remained onside – a miraculous development, as most newspapers had worked on the assumption that services could be improved without spending any additional money.

At the beginning, as the new shadow chancellor, Brown condemned every tax rise introduced by the Conservative government, describing them repeatedly as 'Tory Tax Rises'. In his ubiquitous condemnations he sought to change the perception that Labour put up taxes while Conservatives cut them. There were obvious risks in his relentless attacks. Brown allowed little space for a left-of-centre narrative in which tax ceased to be a 'burden'. But after the election defeat in 1992 there was no such space for Labour. The party could not risk fighting another orthodox 'tax and spend' election, when it had so much evidence this led to electoral slaughter. Instead on Brown went, like a 'Speak your weight' machine: 'Tory tax rises…! Tory tax rises…' The New Labour era can only be understood in the context of the 1992 election and the gloomy lessons to which it pointed.

Brown was equally rigid in relation to Labour's spending plans. To their frustration, and sometimes fury, he would not allow shadow Cabinet colleagues to utter a word that implied an increase in expenditure. Brown eventually recognized that he must address the decay in public services and welfare provision, but at first he saw the necessity of winning over the trust of the media – however right-wing – business leaders and the wider electorate. In contrast to the profligate Conservatives, he would be Mr Prudence, and his frontbenchers would not be allowed to announce policies that implied any additional spending. The discipline and focus that Brown showed are qualifications of leadership. The message was painful for many in his party, but he needed to find a way of moving on from four election defeats. He imposed the pain like a brilliant surgeon who lacked a patient-friendly manner.

Brown's wooden and over-rehearsed declarations were formed partly because he was carrying the heavy weight of economic policy-making. He knew that one word out of place could bring the whole edifice down. Previous shadow chancellors had got into difficulties by going beyond a contrived phrase. He would not do so. As a former TV producer, he also assumed – wrongly – that the soundbite on a TV news bulletin was virtually all that mattered as a form of communication. He would reach that audience whenever he could, happily missing the second half of a live or televised rugby match on a Saturday afternoon to deliver twenty seconds on a TV news bulletin. This was a major sacrifice, as he was one of the few aspiring leaders, or actual leaders, who genuinely adored sport.

The repetitive messaging was only Act One of what Brown assumed would be a long drama, during which he would move on to expand on the purpose behind the prudence. He did not plan to spend the rest of his career railing against tax rises and banning hints of more investment. But as Act One was reaching a prudent climax, there was a dramatic twist in the plot when John Smith died suddenly in the summer of 1994.

Brown had ached to be leader of his party, so much so that he almost assumed he would be. He never recovered from the shock that Tony Blair had not only decided to stand in the 1994 leadership contest but, from the evidence, would probably beat him. There was a part of Brown that sensed, with little evidence to back him up, that he could have fought Blair from the left and won. But Brown did not contemplate doing so for long. Such positioning would have undone all his work as shadow chancellor, in which he had sought to reassure the mighty right-wing newspapers, even though beneath the deceptive surface he was, indeed, to the left of Blair. Instead, a traumatized Brown announced that he would not be standing for the leadership and, although in torment, wrote some of Blair's campaign speeches, and even parts of his victory speech. This is one of many ambiguously vivid images of the New Labour era: the anguished figure who thought he deserved the crown writing key speeches for the close ally who had become leader in his place.[3]

Brown's agonies over the leadership are a running theme for the rest of his political career. The path by which he became leader has its origins in the torment from 1994. He was a figure of unyielding ambition in every field. Like Edward Heath, he needed to prevail in all circumstances. He wanted to be leader more than Blair did. Indeed, when Roy Hattersley urged Blair to stand in 1994, Blair replied, 'But Gordon wants it more than me.'[4]

In many respects, by 1994 Brown deserved it more. He had been the senior partner in his relationship with Blair, teaching Blair the art of speech-writing to the point where Blair became much the better speech-maker. In relation to policy, Brown had been deeply involved in the pivotal area of economics, much the most demanding and complex of policy remits. As for the media, Brown began as the more obsessed and fascinated, although Blair caught up fast. It was Brown who composed Blair's most famous soundbite, when he was shadow Home Secretary. Blair declared that 'Labour would be tough on crime and tough on the causes of crime' – an early example of a clever soundbite that invited a big, bulging tent of support, but the line was Brown's.

In their cramped Westminster office, they watched TV reports of Neil Kinnock's initiatives, and Brown would instinctively offer a running commentary of what worked and what did not, in terms of presentation. He was, for a time, closer than Blair to Peter Mandelson, the party's presentational guru. Brown also arrived at Westminster with a deep sense of Labour's history, having written several books and pamphlets before becoming an MP, and being an avid bibliophile. With all these qualifications, Brown almost assumed that Blair would be his brilliant deputy, the modernizing English counter to his Scottish voice.

There was much talk in the early 1990s, and afterwards, about how close they were as friends. Younger allies of both were later bewildered by this, given the extent of the falling-out and their differing personalities. The explanation is partly that Brown did not, or could not, view politics in terms of friendships. He regarded the vocation as much bigger than that. Colleagues were friends if they served a purpose in the great political venture; they were often enemies if they did not. From 1983, when they both became MPs, Brown recognized Blair's great strengths. To some extent they viewed the political challenges in precisely the same way. They agreed on the need for Labour to change beyond recognition or face eternal opposition; on the centrality of reaching out beyond core support, in terms of messaging and the policies that made sense of the messages; on the sense that England in particular was a conservative country and would not turn to Labour until the leadership could reassure as well as inspire. These common assumptions bound them together as they worked relentlessly in their shared office. They also shared a sense of the ridiculous and laughed together quite a lot before the summer of 1994, as they were struck by the many absurdities in politics. There was little laughter after that summer.

Brown viewed the friendship in political terms. Here was an ally who could help in a joint project to revive Labour, and then become an even more important colleague when Brown went for the leadership. When this did not happen, the limited basis of the friendship more or less collapsed. In the summer of 1994 Brown could not see, or chose not to see, that all the momentum was with Blair. MPs across the party were urging Blair to stand. Influential columnists and newspaper editorials went for Blair. Polls suggested that Labour would soar if Blair became leader. Normally Brown was the most astute reader of the wider context, but this particular background was too bleak for him to contemplate.

His response to the loss of leadership was multi-layered. Above all, it made Brown even more determined to be the next Labour leader. He succeeded against the odds, a rare case of a leader-in-waiting becoming leader. Partly his response was to display aggressive rudeness to allies of Blair, and quite often to Blair himself. He rarely spoke to Mandelson or Blair's chief of staff, Jonathan Powell. Others in Blair's Number Ten, with political views closer in some respect to Brown's, were alienated by what they regarded as a thuggish approach that shocked and alarmed them. Brown's transparent anger was largely counter-productive. His fuming disappointment was too transparent. But it was partly the anger that drove him on. Most of Blair's close ministerial allies from the New Labour era were nowhere near as driven. As a result, they did not last very long, their shaky grasp of policies and the values that underpinned them combining with a lack of determined resolve to stay the course. Alan Milburn left the furnace twice, to spend more time with his family. Steve Byers was forced to resign and did not return. Patricia Hewitt left the fray soon after Blair stood down. John Reid moved from Cabinet post to post with such speed that he was never fully tested and headed off to be chair of Celtic Football Club soon after Blair stood down. They all had their qualities, but staying power was not one of them. Like the equally stubborn Edward Heath, Brown had no intention of moving to one side. He had a pretty clear idea of the course he wanted to take.

Those who seek to be a leader must make many calculations and face a multitude of dilemmas. The TV series *House of Cards* would not have been a hit if leadership and ambition were straightforward. Of all the modern prime ministers, Brown faced the most complex and multifaceted of dilemmas. The problems started to take shape when he knew that he could only challenge Blair from the left in the summer of 1994. After that, they grew into a conundrum that could only be addressed by increasingly painful contortions.

Brown calculated that he would be destroyed if either the media or the wider electorate learned that he was to the left of Blair, even if he was more relaxed about his party recognizing the difference between the two of them. There were genuine ideological and strategic differences over the role of the state and markets in the provision of public services, tax and spend, welfare reform, the euro and how best to present the way the Labour Party had changed.[5] These ideological tensions became more marked over time, but they placed Brown in a straitjacket. He concluded – probably correctly, given the way New Labour had chosen to project itself – that if he were seen as being a millimetre to the left of Blair, he was doomed. As Blair moved further to the right, Brown's anguish intensified. He opposed quite a lot of what Blair was doing and saying, but could not articulate in full the nature of his opposition without alienating what he regarded as the mighty newspapers. He was especially preoccupied by the *Sun* and *The Times*. Like Blair, he developed politically in the 1980s, a time when the newspapers contributed to the destruction of Labour leaders. He worked on the assumption that if the *Sun* turned against him, he would not have the space to succeed in British politics. Ironically, the *Sun* still turned, although by then Brown was prime minister and was probably going to lose anyway. This dilemma lingered, even when he became prime minister, as he ached for the endorsement of the newspapers in an election, while seeking to mark the distance from Blair.

The dance between the two New Labour figures was more or less the sole focus of the media for thirteen years.[6] The soap opera of conflicting ambitions was usually the focus. But the New Labour era was always more subtle and interesting than it seemed. From the summer of 1994, Brown was by no means only in torment about the leadership. For big political figures, many emotions can run in parallel. Brown was also partly excited by his new freedom under Blair's leadership. He had been close to Blair's predecessor, John Smith, but their views on economic policy, and the strategy that arose from it, did not always coincide.

Under Blair's leadership, Brown had much more space, at least in the early years. He famously insisted on a huge degree of control when he agreed not to contest the 1994 leadership contest. Whatever else happened when Blair and Brown met at Granita, the restaurant in Islington where they made their pact in the summer of 1994, both agreed that Brown had demanded control over key policy areas. Such was the unprecedented degree of autonomy he had secured that when the *Guardian*'s political columnist, Hugo Young, went to see Brown for a cup of tea, after it was clear Blair would be the new leader, he discovered Brown on something of a high. 'I'll be able to do a lot more now,' he said. Young saw Brown at his Westminster office on 24 May 1994 and noted: 'GB seemed oddly liberated. No sign of the uptight neurotic fellow I've seen before. Perhaps not a man desperately worried about the leadership?'

Brown was unquestionably worried about the leadership, but as ever in the New Labour era, there was another dimension. Young went on to observe: 'As with Margaret Beckett [Labour's then acting leader] death seems to have released confidence. Not that they are not more reckless with their words: they just seem less defensive.'[7]

Brown made the most of the space, once Blair was leader, and worked intensively with his young special adviser, Ed Balls. Theirs is an under-explored relationship, partly because the two of them are wary of exploration. Indeed, one of the challenges to understanding the New Labour era is the one-sided nature of the memoirs published so far. Blair and his allies have published detailed onslaughts against Brown, as part of their vivid and surprisingly well-written reflections on their time at the top. There are fewer books from the alternative perspective, partly because the key figures are unsure how to make sense of what happened, and why.

The Brown/Balls partnership was as important as any other relationship in the New Labour era, and more significant in policy terms than the relationship between Blair and Alastair Campbell. Working intensively in opposition, as well as in government, the duo sought a new economic framework that would help to resolve the impossible conundrum of how Labour was not trusted to spend money and yet public services needed investment. Balls was the economist and Brown the obsessive strategist. Their objective was to establish a reputation for prudence that ultimately gave the government space to increase public spending. Brown espoused 'prudence for a purpose', another smart soundbite aimed at the big tent of support. The right-wing newspapers hailed the prudence, but the purpose was focused on higher pay for low earners and more cash for public services, previously dismissed by the media as reckless profligacy. Brown and Balls planned for Bank of England independence, a policy implemented immediately after the 1997 election. Shortly before the general election in 1997, Brown announced that there would be no increases in income tax for an entire parliament. He would stick to government spending plans, which the outgoing chancellor, Ken Clarke, had regarded as 'eye-wateringly tight'. In government, Brown kept to those targets, which Clarke had every intention of breaking if he had been returned to the Treasury.

———

Brown was too prudent after Labour won a landslide in 1997. The need to secure 'trust' trumped the demands of public services. Hospitals, schools and public transport continued to totter in the early years of the Labour government. But over time, Brown secured the space to increase spending in ways that made Labour electorally popular, rather than fatally mistrusted. Crucially, he kept the markets from panicking. He found other ways of raising money without putting up totemic taxes in ways that drove the newspapers into a frenzy. Some of the revenue-raising policies got him into deep trouble retrospectively. He sold gold when prices were low. He launched costly and convoluted Private Finance Initiatives in order to raise cash for hospitals. These short-term emergency measures were a consequence of a political and media culture that assumed public services could be improved without raising taxes. That had been Blair and Brown's experience of fighting elections in the 1980s and in 1992. Until Labour's second term, Brown worked on the assumption that no Labour chancellor could overtly raise taxes on income.

His alternative searches for much-needed revenue were unavoidable. He needed the money. But over time they had an impact on his reputation. Brown became famous for raising taxes stealthily – a comical contradiction in terms. His reputation as the stealth chancellor suggested he was not being anywhere near stealthy enough, or else he would not have been well known for raising hidden taxes. The same contradiction applied to Harold Wilson, who became famous for being devious. If Wilson had been devious, he would not have been known for this characteristic. The successfully devious prime ministers act in ways that make the trickery almost impossible to recognize. Wilson did not acquire this reputation until he had been prime minister for several years. Brown became well known for his stealthiness long before he was prime minister. He arrived in Number Ten with a well-developed reputation. Here is another lesson: leadership is more straightforward in its early phase if leaders have more of a blurred image. The fuzziness gives them space to develop their public persona.

In his early years as chancellor, Brown managed to combine prudence with purpose. He was one of the few chancellors to direct the Treasury rather than be directed by it. The already mighty department became mightier still, with an expanded remit to consider the needs of public services and to narrow inequality. Brown began to invest in tax credits for the lower-paid and raised a one-off tax on privatized utilities. This was cleverly chosen as a popular tax, another contradiction in terms. The money funded a largely effective welfare-to-work programme, branded as a 'new deal'. In his first term, when Brown did find extra money for public services, he diverted the cash to poorer areas. The prudence – or the appearance of prudence – kept the Tory newspapers and their readers on board. After the 1999 budget the *Daily Telegraph*'s front page declared: 'Brown's Budget for Middle England'. In reality, quite a lot of Middle England was being asked to pay more in order to finance projects for those on low incomes and benefits. Over time, there was a downside for Labour, and for Brown, in the messaging. Those on lower incomes did not always make the connection between their higher pay and the government policies that brought about the increases.

To the surprise of Blair and the relief of Brown, the big tent of support survived an overt tax rise to pay for a substantial increase in NHS spending in 2003. Brown's route towards the announcement of a big tax rise for most earners proves that he could be an epic strategist, and also shows how quickly political orthodoxies can change. The saga is worth a book in itself, and is like going back to ancient history.

Brown sought respectability by being associated with revered senior bankers. This was another strategic move. How could he be perceived as to the left of Blair when being seen with Alan Greenspan, the chair of the Federal Reserve in the US; or when playing a prominent role in the opening of the Lehman Brothers' bank in London? Brown assumed in that distant era that being seen with bankers helped his political project, rather than the opposite. He was right to do so. The bankers were the trusty wealth-creators, the innovators making the global economy spin. In order to acquire a protective shield for the planned tax rise to pay for NHS funding, he asked Derek Wanless, the former chairman of NatWest Bank, to conduct a review of how the increase could be paid for.

Wanless soon concluded what Brown had indicated he wanted as a conclusion: a substantial increase in National Insurance payments was needed. When Brown made the announcement in his 2002 budget, he made sure that Wanless was cited repeatedly: 'Wanless says the only feasible way is through an increase in National Insurance contributions…' Wanless got the citations, Brown got the credit. Voters gave his 2002 budget the thumbs up, with polls indicating that a large majority of voters supported the tax rise enthusiastically. One of Brown's other senior advisers, Ed Miliband, noted in the immediate aftermath that Brown showed his authentic voice in the 2002 budget. Yet his voice was smothered again, as internal battles erupted over what reforms should accompany the additional cash.[8]

Eventually Brown became the longest-serving Labour chancellor. This was too long, as far as he was concerned. Still, to be a Labour chancellor for ten years is a momentous achievement, not least because the media and markets are more wary of Labour chancellors. The scrutiny is much greater. Denis Healey, a robust political figure, was chancellor for five years and was physically ill by the end. Healey was responsible for the economy in tumultuous times, but Brown's task was mountainous, too. He became chancellor following four election defeats and lasted a decade at the Treasury, having already been responsible for economic policy in opposition from 1992. Although the economy he inherited was far more stable than the one Healey took over in 1974, public services were in decay. He also faced epic decisions over whether the UK should join the single currency, an issue that Blair, as prime minister, saw as his historic role. If nothing else, Brown's tenure was a feat of endurance and ruthlessness.

In standing his ground with admirable powers of endurance, he also went way over the top, alienating some potential allies. In the Blair court that Brown loathed, there were advisers who were in some respects closer to Brown's politics than they were to Blair's. Peter Hyman, in his book *1 Out of 10*, about his time as an aide to Blair, noted that the prime minister did not see the need for higher public spending beyond existing commitments, after the 2001 election. Hyman could see that more increases were evidently required. In some ways, Hyman was closer to Brown politically, but he was utterly loyal to Blair and disdainful of Brown, partly because of the chancellor's behaviour. Alastair Campbell's *Diaries* are punctuated with tense exchanges with Brown, even as Brown points out that Campbell is politically closer to him than he is to Blair. Part of the fascination with Campbell as a chronicler is that he does not disclose whether or not he agrees with Brown. In the later volumes, as important and revelatory as the earlier ones, he reports on a whole range of people who were critical of Blair's reforms, from his GP and psychiatrist, to his partner, Fiona Millar, but does not expand on where he stands in terms of policy. His loyalty to Blair is unyielding and his despair of Brown is intense. If Brown had managed some of Blair's allies less brutally, they would have become stauncher allies. His angry frustration drove him on to the top, but it was also a cause of his downfall. When he finally got to the top, there were a lot of influential Labour figures who wanted him to fall.

Brown's anger was not only about unfulfilled ambition. The division became more starkly ideological and strategic over time. Along with Alastair Campbell's GP, Brown had genuine concerns about Blair's public-service reforms. One instance of this emerged in 2003, when Brown laid out in a speech why the markets do not always work when services are financed centrally and delivered free at the point of use. He focused mainly on the NHS.[9]

In his relentless critical scrutiny of Blair's reforms, Brown saw that 'patient choice' would only become a reality if hospitals were half-empty. If they were full, the choice became non-existent. Yet if hospitals were half-empty, there would be fury about the waste and inefficiency. Similarly, if there was a particularly good local school, not all nearby children would be able to attend or it would become packed and would then cease to be as appealing. The good schools tended to find ways of picking the pupils, and not the other way round. Brown delivered the speech to the Social Market Foundation in February 2003 and tried to outline where the markets worked and did not work – a key area for any government, but a theme rarely explored. What is striking retrospectively is how characteristically cautious Brown was in exposing the limits of the markets. At the time the Blairite wing regarded the speech as an act of provocative treachery.

Brown hailed the markets in most areas and was careful to distance himself from some on the left. Once again, he wanted to make a case from the left, but did not want to be seen as to the left of Blair. He put the case for a different kind of 'third way':

> The argument that is often put as public versus private, or markets versus state, does not reflect the complexity of the challenges we face: that markets are part of advancing the public interest and the left are wrong to say they are not; but also that markets are not always in the public interest and the right is wrong to automatically equate the imposition of markets with the public interest. The challenge for New Labour is, while remaining true to our values and goals, to have the courage to affirm that markets are a means of advancing the public interest; to strengthen markets where they work and to tackle market failures to enable markets to work better. And instead of the left's old, often knee-jerk, anti-market sentiment, to assert with confidence that promoting the market economy helps us achieve our goals of a stronger economy and a fairer society.

Having cautiously set out the general terrain, Brown focused on the NHS:

> In healthcare we know that the consumer is not sovereign: use of healthcare is unpredictable and can never be planned by the

consumer in the way that, for example, weekly food consumption can. So we know that: the ordinary market simply cannot function...[10]

The speech was a subtle way of engaging with the internal battle over NHS reform but, weeks away as it was from the Iraq War, it got little attention. As far as the commentariat noticed, Brown's carefully chosen words were regarded as a leadership bid, an attempt to please 'old Labour'. While the leadership was always on Brown's mind, his motives were more multi-layered, as was the speech. Brown knew why he opposed some of Blair's reforms, and it was not just about winning support for a leadership bid.

Brown was the only figure in the New Labour era capable of stepping back and reflecting more deeply. The other modern prime minister who had a similar capacity was Edward Heath. As both Brown and Heath endured traumatic times in Number Ten, perhaps one lesson of leadership is that a capacity to delve beyond the surface is no requirement for lengthy leadership.

Still, leadership was always on his mind. If Brown had been told, when he delivered the speech on the markets and public services, that he would have to wait more than four years before he became prime minister, he would have been horrified. The haul was a long one. By the time Brown acquired the crown he was exhausted. He had been at the centre of the political stage, as shadow chancellor or chancellor, for thirteen years. He had calculated that a modern prominent politician had a shelf life of seven or eight years, given the level of round-the-clock scrutiny. On that basis, Brown had gone well beyond his shelf life even before he became prime minister.

The seemingly calm and yet deranged circumstances in which he finally acquired the crown were part of a pattern of ambiguously Shakespearean sequences. Blair was typical of prime ministers. From the outside, the stresses of leadership in his final phase seemed nightmarish, with Iraq, a police investigation into allegations of 'cash for honours' and the polls suggesting that, for the first time since he became leader, the Conservatives were well ahead. But Blair was reluctant to let go. From within Number Ten, cosily cocooned at times, power retains its attractions. Later the same applied to Theresa May. Governing was a form of hell, but she wanted more of it. Being prime minister can be like the Woody Allen joke: 'The food in this restaurant is awful... and the portions are so small.'

Blair rationalized that he was staying on to ensure Brown had no choice but to follow his version of New Labour. The trap for Brown was that Blair's version of New Labour was different from his in some respects, and yet he did not want to define himself too clearly, fearing he would be seen as moving to the 'vote-losing left'. The dynamic produced one of the whackier dances between the duo, in a highly competitive field of awkward choreography. Eventually, under pressure from Brown and his supporters, Blair announced in 2006 that he would serve for one more year. True to form, Blair had hit upon a third way in resignations, and his announcement triggered a mountain of tributes. After he made the farewell announcement he returned to work as prime minister. For the next year – more so than ever before – Brown was on formal trial as the prime minister-in-waiting. Every word he uttered, and every policy announced, was made with this in mind. Unsurprisingly, the pressure was too much, even for a figure who had been a leader-in-waiting since 1994. Brown began to make big mistakes. In his final budget, assuming that he was sowing the seeds of a prime ministerial triumph, he contributed to his traumatic downfall. This took the form of an income-tax cut to come into effect later in the parliament, by which time he would be in Number Ten. The cut would be paid for by cuts in tax credits, a policy to which he had been passionately committed. As a result, there was another political crisis when Brown became Prime Minister as low earners faced a drop in their income.

Brown was neurotically determined that he should face no other candidate when Blair stood down. This desire has generated several myths. Above all, his many internal critics complained of the thuggishness of his operation. They complained that if an embryonic leadership candidate seemed to be emerging, he or she would be pushed aside by Brown's entourage in vicious briefings to the media. In fact they were being far too precious, and were treated too generously by those parts of the media that loathed Brown. If any of Brown's internal opponents had been fully formed politically, they would have stood their ground. Instead they ran away and told political journalists what a bully Brown was, not exactly a substantial manifesto for leadership from his critics. The political temperature was much lower than in the 1970s, when major figures, from Tony Benn to Roy Jenkins, were fighting for causes and their own ambitions. They kept going in spite of the intense heat of the political battle. Brown's opponents did not. The New Labour era was so dominated by two individuals, and their advisers, that no one else grew into a big political figure. The reason Brown faced no formidable rival was that there were no formidable rivals.[11]

Curiously, the other myth from this time contradicts the first one – namely, that Brown was so fearful of confrontation that he could not contemplate a challenge. This was not the case. In 2007 Brown would have beaten David Miliband, David Blunkett, Alan Johnson or any other candidate who might have stood. The reason he wanted to avoid a contest was that persistent fear of having to define his position. He would have to publicly compete against a so-called Blairite opponent from the left, when he wanted to be seen as the prime ministerial 'father of the nation'. Brown and his advisers described the contest without an opponent as a 'smooth transition'. In retrospect, this is a laughable description, but at the time it was partially accurate. When Brown became prime minister, support for Labour soared in the opinion polls.

Ironically, Brown's honeymoon was another cause of his fall. He had not expected to be popular quickly. Blair had set him several tests of leadership, as had the newspapers, and Brown assumed he would have to prove himself as prime minister before voters would give him their backing. He ached to win an election on his own terms, but had calculated that he would need a year in Number Ten before he would be in a position to do so. The reality was that voters immediately approved of Brown's 'father of the nation' act. He worked around the clock to show he was up to the job, breaking off his holiday in the late summer of 2007 to respond to a foot-and-mouth outbreak, visiting President Bush and subtly conveying a degree of distance and yet continued support, announcing cautiously constitutional reforms that sought to symbolize a rebuilding of trust between government and voters. In September 2007 the Northern Rock bank nearly went bankrupt, a preview of the drama that was to erupt the following year. As account holders queued outside branches to withdraw their cash, Brown feared his honeymoon was ending. Instead, his support went up. It was at this point that he contemplated for the first time calling an early election. If the near-collapse of a bank made him more popular, perhaps he could realize his dream of winning an election in order to get his own mandate.

As he wondered, he made a spectacular – and in many respects fatal – miscalculation. Without deciding whether to call an election, he assumed the speculation about one would destabilize the Conservatives under their newish leader, David Cameron. Brown encouraged his allies to fuel the speculation in interviews. Predictably, Cameron stayed calm, while the feverish media focus on the possibility of an early election intensified to the point where momentum alone almost demanded that one was held. Labour's conference in September 2007 was dominated by this one issue. Cabinet ministers close to Brown asked journalists a single question: should we call the election? As they were asking the question, Brown was receiving private opinion polls suggesting that marginal seats were swinging towards the Conservatives, even though they also indicated that Labour would win by a smaller majority. The polls triggered a second question that Cabinet ministers close to Brown began to agonize over: if they won with a smaller majority than the one secured in 2005, would this be regarded as a form of defeat rather than an authority-enhancing victory? Brown was used to being in various forms of torment, but this decision became a unique form of agony. After thirteen years he had finally become prime minister, yet he was faced with the possibility of throwing it away after a few months by losing an election. But what would happen if he did not call an election, having stirred up speculation? Over this hung the possibility that if he called the election, and won, Brown would escape the ghost of Blairite New Labour.

Here is another lesson of leadership. Early elections are dangerous, whether or not they are held. Edward Heath lost when he called one in February 1974, and Theresa May lost her majority in 2017. By not holding an early election, having so publicly contemplated going ahead, Brown lost his political voice, his credibility and his momentum. He never recovered.

An over-rehearsed and inauthentic public voice will be exposed if a leader stays on the political stage for a long time. Brown was not in reality a 'father of the nation' apolitical figure – the image that he sought to project in his early months as prime minister. On the contrary, he hoped to slaughter the Conservatives in an election and press ahead, after an authority-enhancing victory, with an agenda that was to the left of Blair's, but nowhere near as left-wing as the programme Labour was to adopt a decade later.

In the first few months Brown moved incrementally, but each tiny move symbolized greater ambition. This had been New Labour's tactical approach in the early years: the party's pledge card in the 1997 election included relatively puny offers, but offered hopes of a leap towards new priorities for government. Initially Brown hinted at a new constitutional settlement, a different debate about how most effectively to reform hospitals and schools, and a less hawkish approach to the UK's continuing role in Iraq and Afghanistan. But after deciding against the early election in October 2007, Brown was doomed to carry on until close to the end of the parliament in 2010. He could hardly generate speculation about another early election, having failed to call one. Suddenly his small incremental changes made no sense any more. They were not designed for a parliament that would last until 2010, and yet he had no authority to develop his personal agenda without winning an election.

As he struggled to work out what he stood for, and what he could do without holding an election until 2010, Brown foolishly denied that the opinion polls were a factor in his decision not to call one in the autumn of 2007. At the Prime Minister's Questions held a few days after Brown had announced there would be no early election, David Cameron wittily declared that his suddenly bewildered opponent 'was the only Prime Minister in history not to call an election because the polls suggested he was going to win'.

Brown arrived at that parliamentary session looking as pale as a ghost, and left looking even ghostlier. For an obsessively calculating leader, he was oddly readable, unable to disguise gloom or haunted ambition when Blair was prime minister and long afterwards. He had realized he could no longer pretend to be the impartial 'father of the nation' when he had been caught plotting an early election. Subsequently he needed to find another public voice, and yet he never managed to do so. Brown failed to do what Blair did almost effortlessly – Blair's public voice was close to his private one. Privately, Brown was capable of being funny. He had a sense of humour and could laugh with a guttural spontaneity. Humour and his love of football could have been points of connection with some voters. But he could not make them so. Instead there were darkly comical attempts to connect, from contorted claims about listening to the Arctic Monkeys at breakfast, to awkward appearances on YouTube in which he sought to speak unmediated to the electorate.

There was a third consequence to the non-early election, to do with Brown's allies. At the best of times, prime ministers need a team of trusted advisers; they become insecure and exposed without them. Theresa May's senior advisers, Nick Timothy and Fiona Hill, might have been the cause of some of her problems, but she was dependent on them. Timothy, in particular, gave her ideas and a sense of purpose. Without them May became less sure of who she was, when demands on her became immense. In the fallout of the non-election fiasco, Brown's close allies for many years viewed each other with fuming suspicion, and relations between them never recovered.

The disagreements were based on traumatic misunderstandings, but that only goes to show how fragile relations were in the first place. Some allies blamed Ed Balls for briefing against them in the immediate aftermath of the election saga. Balls emphatically denied doing so, but they did not believe him. Probably what happened was that Balls told journalists, truthfully, that he favoured the early election while others advising Brown did not. The differing newspaper accounts of what had happened triggered deep divisions within the Brown camp. The close-knit inner sanctum that had gathered many times over the previous years rarely did so again. When it did, it was in an atmosphere of mistrust. As a result, Brown was isolated when he needed reliable advice.[12]

Yet he still sought the advice. Even though Balls was now a Cabinet minister with his own distinct responsibilities, Brown would phone him at all times, seeking his views on issues well beyond his departmental brief. At one point Brown asked Balls to move back into Number Ten, to work more closely with him. Brown told Alistair Darling, the newly appointed chancellor, that at some point he wanted Balls to replace him at the Treasury, though it never happened. This is one example of many showing that Brown got his way less often after he became prime minister. He was not strong enough to move Alistair Darling; their old friendship never recovered. Brown is the only modern prime minister to have pulled more levers *before* he moved into Number Ten.

An example of his relative powerlessness arose before the early election-that-never-was. Trying to be too clever by half, Brown revived Blair's attempt to increase the time that suspects could be detained without charge. Playing a similar political game, Blair had sought a ninety-day period, but lost the vote in the Commons. Brown opted for a forty-five-day period, a move that reflected his weakness and made him weaker still. He had intended to show that he could be 'trusted' on security and achieve an extension at least to forty-five days, thereby guaranteeing glowing editorials in the *Sun* and the *Daily Mail* while exposing David Cameron, who was affecting to espouse civil liberties as part of his 'modernization' agenda. But Brown should have relaxed a little and not tried to reassure the doubters that he was 'strong' in ways that made him appear weak. Quickly it became clear that Brown's proposal would not secure support in Parliament, either. At one internal meeting, Labour's chief whip in the Lords warned Brown that he would lose the vote in the second chamber by more than 200. Brown's response was characteristic. He asked the chief whip, 'Who should I phone?', as if hundreds of prime ministerial calls could sway the dissenters. In the Commons, the situation was just as bad. Brown's loyal ally, Ed Miliband, now a minister, was asked to appear on BBC1's *Question Time*. He was keen for exposure on the programme, but turned down the invitation because he could not defend the forty-five-day extension. Here is yet another lesson of leadership. When prime ministers try too hard to please, and are so transparent in their desire to do so, they will end up pleasing no one. The proposal was eventually dropped when few people would notice, as the banks headed towards bankruptcy.

———

Bizarrely, the global financial crash of 2008 initially saved Brown, and then became the main cause of his fall. The crash was arguably the biggest test of leadership for a British prime minister since 1945, at least until Theresa May faced delivering Brexit. In the wake of the global economic downturn, several British banks hurtled towards the verge of bankruptcy. Brown and his chancellor, Alistair Darling, had to respond speedily to an emergency of seismic proportions.

Quickly and weightily, Brown delved below the surface panic, recognizing that governments around the world were facing what he called the first crisis of the globalized economy. A tremor in the US lending markets triggered mayhem across the world. Having lost a public voice and all sense of direction, Brown now had purpose thrust upon him.

The UK government spent an estimated £500 billion keeping the banks afloat, acting sometimes with hours to spare before they would have gone out of business. Alistair Darling noted with retrospective levity that before the crash he and Brown used to agonize over whether to allocate an additional few million here and there. Suddenly they were spending hundreds of billions. For Brown, the scale of intervention represented on one level a revolutionary leap, which he struggled with initially. The struggle was not because of his convictions, but out of fear over how he would be perceived – the stifling theme of his career.

When Northern Rock had collapsed the previous year, publications ranging from *The Economist* and the *Financial Times*, to respected political figures such as the Liberal Democrats' Vince Cable, were advocating nationalization. Brown resisted at first, fearing headlines about a return to the 1970s. When he eventually made the inevitable move, he could only describe the new policy as 'temporary ownership', such was his reluctance to use the word 'nationalization'. Sensing an opportunity, David Cameron and his shadow chancellor, George Osborne, held a rare joint press conference, making the precise claim that Brown feared. This was old Labour, a return to the failed past.

Fortunately for Brown, their claims had no impact and the nationalization proved to be popular in the polls. For different reasons, Brown, Cameron and Osborne could not make sense of the implosion of the lightly regulated order that had begun in the 1980s with the Reagan/Thatcher partnership. Brown could not see it at first because he was brought up politically in the 1970s and 1980s, when Labour lost the battle of ideas to Thatcher. Cameron and Osborne were blind partly for the same reason in reverse. The Conservatives won elections in the 1980s when Thatcher was privatizing rather than nationalizing.

Leaders look back to the past for warnings or guidance because they rarely have any idea what might happen next. At least the past has happened, though it is a treacherous guide.

Still, Brown was well suited to respond, once he fully understood that Northern Rock was a tiny hors d'oeuvre compared with what followed. He was the only elected world leader who had been responsible for economic policy for a decade. His contacts book was unrivalled, and he was on the phone relentlessly to key figures around the world, all of whom he had worked with. Brown was at his most authentic when he was gripped by the need to act. In emergencies he had no time to brood and scheme, instead channelling all his furious energy into achieving outcomes.

In response to the crash, Brown led a coordinated response from G20 world leaders, persuading even the most fiscally conservative to inject cash into the global economy. The recently elected President Obama, still mesmeric and glittering, also played a key role. But with London chairing a G20 conference in the aftermath of the crash, Brown became leaderly without, for once, worrying about how he might appear to sceptical voters and the media. At one point the Nobel Prize-winning *New York Times* columnist Paul Krugman wrote that Brown had saved the world. Brown accidentally quoted the words during Prime Minister's Questions, inadvertently revealing that he had not only read the complimentary column, but had clung on to it as rare praise. He was much mocked for this, but leaders are human beings. Each morning during the earlier days of his premiership he woke early and read the UK newspapers, encountering story after story that said he was both mad and useless. Suddenly a weighty columnist from the US credited him with saving the planet. Which leader would not retain such praise in the forefront of his or her troubled mind?

As far as Brown's leadership was concerned, the crisis gave him momentum, although his formidable response did not provide him with vote-winning arguments. Instead, David Cameron and George Osborne reframed the entire debate in the UK, with the willing or gullible support of most newspapers and parts of the BBC. This is how it happened. The government's pre-crash growth projections for the UK economy were way off the mark. Spending plans had been determined on what proved to be wildly optimistic assumptions about economic growth. After the crash, the economy went into recession. Meanwhile the government was spending huge sums to prop up the banks, while injecting cash into the economy, in place of consumers and the private sector. As a result, the UK accumulated a gaping deficit.

The financial crash was the cause of the deficit, but the Conservative leadership argued that Labour's profligate spending had caused the crash. A banking crisis became one about public spending. In the build-up to the 2010 election, Osborne devised clever soundbites warning that voters should never give the keys back to those who crashed the car. Instead of receiving sustained credit for his response to the crash, Brown was blamed for its origins. The build-up to the next general election – the only one contested by Brown as leader of his party – was framed in precisely the way he had spent his career seeking to avoid: Labour's reckless spending of the past versus Conservatives' sensible cuts in the future.

The situation was made worse by deep internal divisions within Brown's government. Darling, once a good friend of Brown, took a different strategic view. He argued, publicly and privately, that the deficit was so large that deep spending cuts were required, though not on the scale advocated by Osborne and Cameron. Brown saw the terrible danger of such a 'dividing line', a device he had used to considerable effect, especially in the 1997 and 2001 elections, and which was now being used against him. He told Balls that Labour was doomed if the dividing line at the election was between Labour's 'good cuts' versus the Conservatives' 'bad cuts'. Rightly, he could see the strategic dangers of moving onto the Conservatives' terrain by accepting their framing of the financial crash.

But he was trapped. Inadvertently, the supposedly impartial BBC came to regard the Osborne framing as a form of impartiality. In interviews, every senior Cabinet minister was asked relentlessly what they were going to do about the deficit, and to specify the cuts they would make. Long before the election, Osborne had won the argument, even though the evidence suggested that the Keynesian approach – the fiscal stimulus that required governments to spend more – worked in the immediate aftermath of the crash. Brown could not find the equivalent to Osborne's car-crash metaphors, which made sense of what seemed nonsensical: in order to address a deficit, governments sometimes needed to spend more.

There was little in the 2010 election about the role of bankers in recklessly triggering the crisis to the point, in some cases, of criminality. The central question was what to cut, by how much and why did Labour spend so recklessly in the first place? The orthodoxies of the time extended well beyond the Conservatives.

From outside Parliament, Blair confided to Alastair Campbell, 'We were against borrowing... now we're in favour... voters won't understand this Keynesianism', an observation that showed Blair tended to follow the surface game more than the substance of policy. He did not say whether he agreed with the Keynesian policy – only how it would be perceived.[13]

The more fundamental problem for Brown was that he had been chancellor for ten years. His adviser, Ed Miliband, was excited by the political implications of the crash and had good cause for his excitement. Miliband liked to give the example of hearing a guest pleading for the government to intervene in the financial markets, on the BBC's *Today* programme. He assumed the voice was from a left-wing think tank, only to discover at the end that the interviewee was a senior figure from Lehman Brothers in the UK. Here was a banker panicked into making the case for the kind of government intervention that Blair and Brown had been too scared to make. In the fallout from the crash, Miliband saw the opportunity at last for Brown to show he was a left-of-centre figure who believed in the benevolent power of the state. But Miliband overlooked one key point. Brown would get a lot of the blame for the crash. Voters and newspapers were asking: Why had he not regulated the financial sector more effectively? Why did he allegedly let spending get too high? The crash was thought to have happened 'on his watch'.

Here was the tragic New Labour irony. Brown had sought to be trusted in relation to the economy, as Blair had done in foreign policy. In trying so hard to please, they both ended up deeply mistrusted. In Brown's case, having connections with bankers was suddenly the least politically helpful association in the world. From the autumn of 2008 onwards, no politician wanted to be seen near a senior banker.

Although Brown's history as a long-serving chancellor became a problem for him in terms of perceived culpability, he was evidently well qualified to respond to the crash. Such was Labour's internal angst at the time that few of his critics noticed that Brown was responding effectively to an epic challenge. Alastair Campbell's brilliantly illuminating diaries from this period make virtually no reference to the financial crash, whereas criticisms of Brown dominate. There were more plots aimed at removing Brown than any previous prime minister had faced. All of them were absurd – another symptom of the Labour Party becoming almost as whackily dysfunctional as the Conservatives were to become.

The fact is there was no alternative figure capable of becoming prime minister in the aftermath of the crash. None of the potential candidates would have known what to do, or how to do it. No other Cabinet ministers, with the exception of Ed Balls, Ed Miliband and Alistair Darling, had given any deep thinking to economic policy, let alone how to navigate away from the cliff-edge a fragile economy dependent on a vibrant financial sector. But still dissenting MPs planned various coups, to no avail. This was an early sign that many Labour MPs brought up under the Blair/Brown duopoly were half-formed politicians lacking basic political skills. The attempted coups were laughably amateurish. One began just before a Prime Minister's Questions session in the Commons and had petered out late the same afternoon.[14] But the attempted coups reflected badly on Brown and his casual mishandling of egos. The former Cabinet minister Charles Clarke was one of the most active in seeking the removal of Brown, and Brown's handling of Clarke is telling. When he became prime minister, Brown tried to appease Clarke by suggesting that he become a special envoy in Iraq. Clarke noted that the life-threatening post was one way of dealing with an internal critic. Clarke stayed in the UK and became a deeper critic. Brown did not understand how best to deal with colleagues, especially dissenting ones – an essential qualification of leadership.

The wider issue of 'trust' tormented Brown, as it had Blair and Major. In opposition, Blair had played on the mistrust of John Major, only to leave office with questions raging about his own integrity. Before he became prime minister, Brown was fairly discreet when reflecting on Blair to journalists, although his sense of fuming frustration was conveyed more candidly by senior allies. But after the 2005 election Brown said to some journalists, 'Tony isn't trusted. We have this huge "trust" problem that can only be addressed when Tony goes.'[15] Instead of addressing the issue, Brown himself was brought down at a point where mistrust between voters and elected politicians ran deep.

On this, too, he was unlucky. The saga over MPs' expenses could have erupted at any time, but it did so while he was prime minister. For quite some time certain MPs had been maximizing their allowances, on the assumption that no one would know what they were claiming. This was widely seen as an alternative to higher salaries, which it was politically impossible to implement. When exposed under the Freedom of Information Act in 2009, the expense claims looked absurd or grotesque, and sometimes both. The sequence fuelled the already intense mistrust that voters felt towards those they elected. Historically the mistrust was often irrational, voters' anger and disdain being a substitute for engagement with politics and current affairs. But here was a scandal that looked terrible, and a few MPs went to prison. It was not lost on Brown that he had become prime minister hoping to restore trust, but by the time he left some MPs were facing criminal trials, while bankers were being exposed as reckless, self-seeking and greedy. In some cases, they too faced the possibility of criminal charges.

For leaders, 'trust' is too vaguely defined. They are unwise to proclaim a restoration of 'trust' as an objective – it rebounds on them every time. Politics is too stormy a vocation, defined by subjective judgements. Blair regretted slaughtering John Major with allegations of 'sleaze' in the build-up to the 1997 election, not least because he became mistrusted, too. Brown soon discovered that attempts to restore trust were overwhelmed by events, and by behaviour that fuelled further mistrust.

Perhaps if Brown had been a more effective political teacher, he could have made greater sense of what he was trying to do, both in his first phase as prime minister and then in his response to the crash. In his memoirs, Brown argued that he was not as interested in modern ways of communicating as he should have been. That is not the case. He was obsessed with the media in all its manifestations – a big difference from Edward Heath, who was another prime minister of depth, but one who was genuinely not that concerned about how to communicate in the media. Brown became friends with Paul Dacre, the editor of the *Daily Mail*, predominantly because he hoped that the newspaper might endorse him at the 2010 election. Similarly, Rebekah Brooks was wooed assiduously as she acquired ever greater influence over the Murdoch empire, especially the *Sun* newspaper. Both the *Mail* and the *Sun* endorsed the Conservatives in 2010. Elsewhere, Brown was interested in the potency of social media, but never mastered it. He assumed he understood how to project in the media because he recognized Labour's presentational failings in the 1980s and he had briefly been a BBC producer. But he never did fully understand.

However, at times his carefully calibrated messages resonated. Brown's genius as Labour's main economic policy-maker for so long was to convey messages that reassured, while giving him space to be radical. Sometimes the messaging worked and at other times it did not. Never has a modern leader enjoyed such an oscillating relationship with voters and the media – take a deep breath and come for the ride. In the late 1980s Brown was so popular that he was spoken of as a future Labour leader and made shadow chancellor after the party's 1992 election defeat. By 1994 he was so unpopular that the party turned to Blair after John Smith died. After the 1997 election Brown became a commanding chancellor, widely perceived as being the chief executive of the government. Following the 2001 election there was much talk of Brown being peripheral, as Blair commanded the world stage after the terrorist attacks on 11 September. After the Iraq War, Blair sensed that Brown was unpopular enough to marginalize his role in planning for the next election, yet Brown proved to be so popular that Blair then had to plead with him to play a central part in the election. By 2006 Brown was so unpopular there was talk of David Miliband standing in a leadership contest against him. After he became prime minister in 2007, he was so popular he was tempted to hold an early election. When he did not, he became the least-popular prime minister since polling began.

Partly Brown's wild ride reflects febrile times. Leaders can be hailed and despised in the space of the same week, let alone during many years at the top. The varying reactions also reflect the ambiguity of Brown as a political figure. Some of those who worked with him were devoted, in spite of the tantrums and the ongoing volatility. When he moved from the Treasury to Number Ten, a lot of those who had worked in his private office wanted to move with him. Balls and Miliband were devoted in their different ways, recognizing Brown's strengths and only later appreciating the flaws. Yet the devotees were joined by those within the government who loathed Brown. Some of the loathing was calculating and self-interested. After all, being friendly to Blair was much more useful to ambitious ministers with limited political talent. As chancellor, Brown had little patronage, whereas Blair had many posts to offer. Still, Brown's mishandling of people certainly played its part in his limited range of political allies.

Aspirant leaders must be ruthless but polite in their calculated brutality; the brittle egos of colleagues often cannot cope with rudeness. Brown could be rude, without thinking about what he was doing. For him, brought up in the bear pit of Scottish Labour Party politics, the means justified the ends. His close allies noted the noble worthiness of the ends and were sometimes impressed with his command of the means to bring them about. But his enemies noted only the apparent thuggishness. Sometimes voters thought he was on their side, sometimes they did not. The ambiguities were deep, complex and revealing of the oscillations in his reputation.

Latterly the 2010 election campaign proved to be appropriately ambiguous, too, a defeat that was not as bad as expected. On the whole, the campaign had been traumatic for Brown. The defining moment came during his nightmarish confrontation with a voter in Rochdale called Gillian Duffy. Brown had been on a walkabout, a form of contact with voters that he had never mastered. Indeed, he failed to fully master any forms of contact with voters. On this occasion, after they were introduced, Duffy started berating him about immigrants. Brown eventually escaped reasonably unscathed, but in the car afterwards, unaware that he still had a microphone on, he described Duffy as a 'bigoted woman'. Within minutes the words were broadcast across the news channels and Brown was devastated. Voters are allowed to attack leaders, but leaders are never allowed to criticize voters. Brown had been caught doing this at precisely the point when he most needed the support of voters. It was the voters who held the upper hand, as they often do. Brown assumed the sequence would destroy him and propel the Conservatives to power.

But this isn't quite what happened. In the end there was a hung parliament, a rare outcome in the UK. The last one had been in February 1974. Brown, the great survivor, wondered whether he could hang on. This time, however, he could not. The leader of the Liberal Democrats, Nick Clegg, chose to form a coalition with the Conservatives, after days of frantic negotiations.

Like Heath and Callaghan, Brown left office as a short-serving prime minister. He had dreaded being what Roy Jenkins described as a 'tail-end Charlie' and yet that became his fate. But like Heath, his prime ministerial role became renowned. In Brown's case, the financial crash – a tumultuous event that he never foresaw in all his neurotic planning – and his response were as historic as the acts of much longer-serving prime ministers. Taken with his reforms as chancellor, implemented when bankers were still revered and government activity of any kind was viewed with wariness by a still-mighty right-wing media, Brown goes down as one of the most significant figures in the history of the Labour Party.

He left Number Ten on the Tuesday after the 2010 election with his wife and two children. This was a rare sighting of his family together, and an image that humanized Brown when it was far too late. A short time later, David Cameron stood outside Number Ten as prime minister of a peacetime coalition in the midst of an ongoing economic crisis. Cameron could not have been more different from Brown in terms of personality, ideology and political experience, as an incoming prime minister. He not only had to face the consequences of the financial crash, but also had to manage the Conservative Party and a unique relationship with the Liberal Democrats.

While the Labour Party had been showing signs of an existential crisis, with its coup attempts against Brown, Blair's ambiguous legacy and Brown's awkward and complex efforts to move on from his predecessor, Cameron was to discover that the Conservatives had become at least as problematic to lead as Labour, and in some ways much more so.

8

DAVID CAMERON

David Cameron will be recalled as the prime minister that took the UK out of the EU, against his own wishes. Cameron possessed a sunnier personality than most leaders and yet his ending was uniquely dark. All the modern prime ministers left office with much to be gloomy about, and in some cases they despaired for the remainder of their lives. But the chaos unleashed on so many fronts by Cameron's decision to hold a referendum, and then lose it, was a uniquely bleak legacy. The nightmare of Iraq would still have happened if Blair had boldly opposed the war, because the US administration was determined to invade. Thatcher's poll tax was addressed by abolition. But Brexit became never-ending, sucking up all political energy for years to come. As with all modern prime ministers, the seeds were sown at the beginning. Cameron's referendum was not an aberration, but part of a pattern. Even as he fought what seemed like a distinctively refreshing leadership campaign in 2005, he was moving towards his fall.

David Cameron was only thirty-nine when he became leader of the Conservative Party in December 2005, younger even than the youthful Tony Blair had been when he became Labour leader. Significantly, Cameron had far less experience of formative political battles within his party and beyond. As a result, he became a leader without quite knowing who he was as a public figure, or what he was for. His polished poise, demeanour and apparent sense of political purpose obscured his deep inexperience for a time. He rose too speedily and was neither ready nor ideologically suited to lead the UK after the many traumas of the 2008 financial crash.

Early internal and external battles matter for aspirant leaders. They test recently elected politicians in many different ways. Are they resilient? Do they possess guile? What are their convictions and values? Can they express them effectively? Blair was Cameron's model as a leader, but the Labour leader had been an MP for eleven years by the time he acquired the crown, and had been heavily involved in several intense internal debates over the future of Labour's policy and strategy. Being a prominent participant in the battles over a party's future is one way that aspirant leaders acquire some shape and definition.

While neither Blair nor Cameron had been a minister before becoming leader, Cameron had been engaged in far fewer internal struggles about the future of his party. He had only been an MP for four and a half years when he became leader. His most senior post had been as a short-serving shadow Education Secretary, the same remit held by Neil Kinnock before he became Labour leader. The difference was that Kinnock had been prominent for many years in Labour's intense civil wars in the late 1970s and early 1980s. By the time he became leader in 1983, he was battle-scarred, with plenty more scars to come. Like Blair, Kinnock had been an MP for more than a decade when he became Labour leader. We will never know, but perhaps if Cameron had been similarly engaged, battling it out with sweaty intensity on one side or another in the Conservative Party, he would have been big and strong enough to have addressed the issue of Europe when he became leader. All we do know is that he made no such attempt.

Cameron had played a few roles with elegant agility, but they were ones that had kept him a safe distance from the political furnace. He had been Norman Lamont's adviser at the Treasury during the Exchange Rate Mechanism crisis in September 1992 – a good seat from which to witness ministers responding to a national emergency, but Cameron was an observer and not a central participant. He also had the task of advising John Major on how to handle Prime Minister's Questions, and subsequently gave similar advice to Michael Howard when the Conservatives were in opposition. Major rated Cameron highly. Howard's admiration was such that he wanted Cameron to be his successor and discreetly played a part in helping to bring about his meteoric rise. Such demands test the wit and intelligence of an aspirant leader – anyone who gave poor advice about how to handle Prime Minister's Questions would be dumped very quickly. Still, advising a prime minister is a minor qualification for becoming a prime minister.

Cameron's political activities were early signs that he was a talented politician – and that talent was acknowledged widely. One of Cameron's PPE tutors at Oxford, Vernon Bogdanor, described him as 'one of my ablest students', although he added the qualification, 'I am not responsible for his views.'[1] Such endorsements and experience suggested that Cameron had considerable potential. Again, though, these were puny qualifications for immediately assuming responsibility for the titanic demands of leadership in December 2005.

Before entering politics, Cameron had been Director of Communications at Carlton TV, a decent enough job, but not one that is normally regarded as adequate preparation for becoming prime minister. His media background triggered one early slight misperception: that he was obsessed, as a politician, with 'spin' – the message and not the substance.

While it is the case that Cameron was not always gripped by policy detail, it is wrong to assume that a spell at Carlton TV made him especially preoccupied with the media. It was his fascination with Tony Blair and New Labour that led him to woo the media, but in ways that were slightly less sophisticated and clunkier than the methods applied in the not-always-subtle Blair/Brown era. Largely for images in the media as a new leader of the Opposition, Cameron visited council estates in the hope of conveying a new, compassionate Conservatism, and dashed to the Arctic Circle to 'hug a husky', in order to develop his green credentials. The detailed policies were not in place to make sense of the images, but Cameron assumed that the images themselves would be potent.

To some extent, he was right. Non-Conservative newspapers, including the *Guardian* and the *Independent*, gave him an easy time. *The Times* was a cheerleader. Greatly influenced by *The Times*, parts of the BBC portrayed him as a 'modernizing centrist'. But without policies that reinforced the images, and with some policies that contradicted the 'spin', Cameron's media strategy lacked the force of Blair's at his peak. As a symbolic contrast, Blair hired as his media adviser Alastair Campbell, a tabloid Labour supporter, who read the rhythms of the news in a way that a masterful conductor reads music. Campbell was intensely tribal and passionately loyal. Ultimately, after a long period in which Cameron ran an endearingly tiny media operation, he hired Andy Coulson, hoping to have acquired a Campbell equivalent. Coulson made a positive difference to the media coverage, but he was not in Campbell's league and, as a former editor of *News of the World*, he ended up in jail as part of the phone-hacking scandal.

The Conservative leadership contest that Cameron won in 2005 was held after the party's third successive election defeat. There had already been several odd contests since the Conservatives had been slaughtered in 1997, including the eccentric 'dream ticket' of Ken Clarke and John Redwood the same year – the party's most passionate pro-European making an absurdly desperate pitch with its most ardent Eurosceptic, a *Monty Python* double act that did not last very long. Then there was Michael Portillo's strange candidacy in 2001; the once transparently ambitious politician had become a reluctant leadership contender. Bizarrely, the candidates who fared poorly in opinion polls of the wider electorate won with ease in the leadership contests. They did so because they took a tough line on Europe. The contests, their frequency and nature, were symptoms and causes of a party in crisis.

The 2005 campaign was particularly odd because it was defined by a *Britain's Got Talent*-style session during the Conservative party conference in Blackpool. Each candidate was given a short slot to make their case in front of the audience. The favourite, David Davis, blew it with a leaden and reactionary speech, although the address was not as bad as it was immediately perceived to be. Conversely, Cameron's speech was not as good as it was immediately judged to be, but the format lent itself to instant verdicts, first by journalists and then by those attending the conference.

Cameron delivered his speech well. There were good jokes. The theme was 'change' – not a bad one, after three election defeats. He said: 'We can change this party and we can change this country… a modern, compassionate conservative is right for our times.' But the performance and message were almost consciously Blair-like.

Formidable leaders tend to be authentically distinct and original in their pitch, rather than actively imitate a recent leader. There had been no leaders like Wilson, Thatcher and Blair, in style and demeanour, before they arrived on the political stage. Cameron was like Blair. Even so, he won the contest by a big margin. This was a significant achievement for a figure who was not widely known before he became a candidate, and who could not fully know who he was as a public figure.

One of his strengths was that he was wholly at ease with himself as a human being, but that is different from being fully developed as a potential prime minister. Still, the ease was impressive. To take a minor example: Cameron and his entourage would often take a political columnist with them for day-trips out of London. On one occasion, a columnist travelled with them to Norwich. On the train back, Cameron fell asleep opposite the columnist and at one point fleetingly and inadvertently put his legs on the columnist's lap. This shows how laid-back and comfortable he was. Most leaders never switch off when there are journalists accompanying them.[2]

Although the responsibilities were huge for such an inexperienced leader, the context when Cameron became leader was fairly benevolent. The Labour government was in the final throes of the Blair/Brown duel, still bewildered and demoralized by the war in Iraq and what the ongoing bloody conflict implied for an administration that had taken the decision to go to war. Yet the Conservatives had lost three successive elections. Their purpose was unclear and they were still split over Europe. In this respect, the Conservative Party was closer to Labour in 1983, with all its internal tensions and lack of clarity about what it stood for. Cameron mistakenly worked on the assumption that his party was more or less in the same position as Labour in 1994, when Blair became leader. This was his early and most fundamental misjudgement. Blair took over a party that had already been reformed beyond recognition, since its slaughter in 1983. Cameron acquired a party that was still largely the same as it had been after its slaughter in 1997, with Europe still the overwhelmingly debilitating fault line.

As leader, Cameron continued to be the 'modernizing' candidate. At times his projection became even more of a conscious act of imitation of Blair than it was during the leadership contest. Still prime minister during Cameron's early phase as leader, Blair noted privately, 'He's being me… it's an impersonation of me.'[3] Cameron adopted the same conversational approach in interviews and wore Blair-like casual clothes at weekends and on holidays. He was reported to have told newspaper executives at a dinner during the leadership contest in 2005 that he was the 'heir to Blair'.[4] His closest allies described a book written by Blair's close adviser, Philip Gould, as their 'bible'.[5]

Cameron and his allies set out to be New Labour from the other side of the political spectrum, at least during the early phase of his leadership. In policy terms, this meant they sought to address what were seen as fatal Conservative positions in the same way Blair and Brown had done with Labour's. They noted admiringly that in the 1980s and early 1990s Labour was not trusted to tax and spend, so Blair and Brown pledged to be overtly tough on both. Although the admiration was sincere, the emulation was limited.

As they lost elections from 1997 onwards, the Conservatives were seen as 'the nasty party'.[6] This was shorthand for saying they were more bothered about tax cuts for the wealthy than about public services, illiberal in social outlook and represented largely by elderly men. Under Cameron, the Conservatives would stick to Labour's spending plans, become 'green', commit to spending on Third World countries and encourage more gays, women and ethnic minorities to stand as candidates. They would be nice rather than nasty, and modern rather than backward-looking.

To some extent, Cameron's early project was indeed New Labour in reverse, but there were several big differences. Above all, his modernizing message did not address the fundamental problem of his party: division over Europe. Cameron's only early message on Europe was that his party should stop 'banging on' about it quite so much.[7] This would be the equivalent of Blair and Brown telling their party to stop banging on about tax rises, and then retaining the same tax-and-spend policies that had contributed to their defeat in 1992. Instead Blair and Brown delivered some tough messages to their party in areas where Labour had adopted vote-losing policies. Cameron avoided the issue of Europe when he was strongest to address it, at the beginning of his leadership. Leaders always have space to act at the beginning. Some of them do not have the confidence, or the inclination, to do so.

Cameron's reticence was also because he did not know decisively what he himself thought about Europe. His first move as a leadership candidate during the 2005 contest was to support the policy of Conservative MEPs (Members of the European Parliament) withdrawing from the formal centre-right grouping in the European Parliament. Cameron's press spokesman at the time, George Eustice, who became a Brexit-supporting minister, is convinced that Cameron believed in the policy as a matter of conviction. Cameron told Eustice that he was wary of the European People's Party (EPP) centre-right grouping and thought it best that Conservative MEPs broke away. Conversely Ken Clarke, who went on to serve in Cameron's Cabinet, is equally certain that Cameron acted solely to woo Eurosceptic MPs during the leadership contest.[8]

Perhaps both interpretations are true. Cameron convinced himself that the move was the 'right thing to do' – one of his favourite phrases lifted from Blair – while assuming the policy would help him win the leadership. He almost certainly would have won without the commitment.

Ironically his main opponent in the contest, David Davis, was opposed to leaving the EPP, bravely arguing that such a move would be counter-productive. Davis went on to support Brexit, becoming the first Brexit Secretary, his only Cabinet post. But in the context of 2005, when UK withdrawal was not on the agenda, he was opposed to Conservatives leaving the EPP and said so during the contest. Cameron did not take his party on over Europe – the most calamitous example of his weak-kneed inexperience and hazy ideological grip.

In failing to do so, he became the latest leader to sow the seeds of his downfall, in a bid to seize the crown. The German chancellor, Angela Merkel, never fully forgave Cameron for the EPP breakaway, one that weakened the centre right in the European Parliament and gave a degree of comfort to the far right. Cameron naively assumed that his Blair-like charm would be enough to woo Merkel when he needed her. He liked the idea of being a prime minister being shown on TV screens in convivial conversations with other powerful leaders in Europe, mistaking his ease in dealing with individuals as a deeper rapport. But Merkel focused more on policy positions when judging other leaders, and Cameron's first policy with EPP got him off to a bad start. In some respects, Merkel preferred dealing with Theresa May – a public figure, like her, who was less interested in politics as theatre – even though the context of their meetings was always ridiculously fraught because of Brexit.

Cameron's assumption that he could be the heir to Blair is also revealing. He might have had a similar approach to the election-winning Labour leader, but he was not leading in the same context. By the time Blair became leader, his two predecessors had done a significant amount of heavy lifting. Between them, Neil Kinnock and John Smith had transformed Labour, in terms of its policy and internal organization. This touched everything, from the methods by which the party chose its leader, to a detailed policy programme that was unrecognizable from the one the party proposed in 1983 when Margaret Thatcher won her first landslide.

In contrast, Cameron's predecessors had done little to address the reasons why the Conservatives had lost three times in a row. That is why Cameron's inheritance was closer to Neil Kinnock's in 1983. Both Kinnock and Cameron led parties that needed to be challenged in policy terms. Crucially, Kinnock had to challenge himself as well as his party. He was a unilateralist who turned his party towards multilateralism – a momentous shift for him, as well as Labour, in the 1980s. Cameron was fascinated by how a vote-losing party could win again, but he never challenged his own assumptions in quite the same way, except in the area of social liberalism. This was never quite as painful as it seemed, though, even when he became an advocate of gay marriage, a policy that triggered a substantial revolt in Parliament and amongst party members. The anger was fleeting. In the broad sweep, gay marriage was something of a red herring for both party and leader, creating the impression amongst some commentators and broadcasters that Cameron was a 'centrist' – that ill-defined term that distorts many perceptions in politics. He had become a social liberal, but on economic policy and public-service reform he struggled to move on from his Thatcherite upbringing. He became politically engaged when Thatcher was at her peak.

Indeed, his wider upbringing was not one made for a natural 'modernizer' or, to be more precise, a leader who would move his party away from the Thatcherite right. It is not Cameron's fault that he had a privileged start; that his father was an affluent stockbroker; that he himself went to Eton, Oxford and enjoyed the champagne-swilling Bullingdon Club while a student. Cameron did not disown his gilded past, but sought to play down elements of it. A photograph of Cameron and other Bullingdon Club members, including Boris Johnson, disappeared from public circulation. Cameron rarely referred to his time at Eton, whereas Johnson looked back at his school days with uninhibited affection.[9] But Cameron's upbringing was not one that led him to challenge many Thatcherite assumptions. Only the relentless election defeats of his party during the New Labour era belatedly led him to question previous orthodoxies, and in a fairly limited way.

———

Cameron's victory speech in December 2005, when he was elected leader of his party, highlighted an ambiguity that extended well beyond his partly contradictory views about Europe. He had won the leadership election with a simple message, essentially about being nicer, showing that the party cared about poor people, the NHS and the environment. After winning, he declared in his victory speech: 'There is such a thing as society… it's not the same as the state.' These are the most illuminating words Cameron uttered, although not for the reasons he intended. They tell us just as much about him as the phrase 'What works is what matters' gives insights into Blair, and 'prudence for a purpose' reveals much about Brown.

Cameron's construction was as clever as those phrases from the New Labour era. The words seem to reject Margaret Thatcher's view that there was no such thing as society, while – on closer inspection – echoing Thatcher's famous assertion. He appeared to be moving on from Thatcherism while marching at one with her own simplistic assumptions. Cameron was unsure how to handle Thatcher's legacy. A friend of his recalls that in his early phase as leader, Cameron feared that his party could not move on until the death of Thatcher, such was her potency in the party. He was not being morbid, but making a political point about her spellbinding capacities, now that she had become a living legend. Yet Cameron was one of those in Thatcher's thrall, in policy terms, and most significantly on how he saw the role of the state.[10]

Thatcher argued in an interview in the autumn of 1987 that the state could not be, or should not be, a binding agency – one that people always turned to for their problems to be addressed.[11] She had been making the same argument since the mid-1970s. There were other institutions that could perform the tasks of the state, such as charities, churches and businesses. As Cameron was arguing that the state was not the binding agency, he was essentially agreeing with Thatcher. The difference was tonal. She was happy to declare, unsubtly, that there was no such thing as society. He was happy to assert, by implication, that society could and should thrive with a smaller state – a more diplomatic argument for advancing her convictions.

Here was a fundamental difference with the leader he imitated. Tony Blair came to believe passionately in the version of New Labour he advocated, and in his rejection of old Labour, a force from the past that he understood with only limited knowledge. For good and bad, at different points in his leadership, Blair sought constant definition against his party's past. Cameron did not do so in relation to his own party. He knew his party had to change, or be seen to be changing. He planted trees, toured council estates, turned up at hospital wards and appeared to distance himself from his party's support for the war in Iraq. But in policy terms, he could not bring himself to make the leaps that Kinnock and Smith had made with their party, let alone Blair. This is not necessarily a flaw. Cameron was a figure of the right, leading a party on the right. It became a flaw because Cameron claimed that his party was moving to the centre and breaking away from its past, the definition of a 'modernizer' – that overused term in British politics.

Cameron's galvanizing idea was the 'Big Society', an objective that reinforced and deepened the ambiguity of his leadership. In opposition, the 'Big Society' was explored as an idea in seminars organized mainly by Cameron's friend and senior adviser, Steve Hilton. The MP Oliver Letwin, a former shadow chancellor, was the other key organizer. Hilton appeared to personify Cameron's modernizing project. Usually he wore a T-shirt and jeans or shorts. Quite often he was barefoot at these seminars, and later in Downing Street. He was engaging and unstuffy, without any pomposity. He was also right-wing, a reminder that fun-loving libertarians are usually closer to the right than the left. In Hilton's case, he was wary of the state as a provider of services. He had some interesting ideas about the state as a regulator, intervening to challenge the excesses of big corporate companies, which he viewed with an illuminating disdain. Mostly he disapproved of the state. In his early years as leader, Cameron regarded Hilton as a close friend and the originator of big new ideas. Hilton did not last very long in Number Ten, and the two of them fell out permanently when Hilton campaigned for Brexit from the safe distance of Silicon Valley in California where, amongst other ventures, he hosted a series for Fox News, President Trump's favourite channel. This shocked some UK commentators, not least because Hilton showed support for some of Trump's more outrageous comments. But really he had not changed at all.

Letwin was charming, thoughtful and a committed Thatcherite, who had to be hidden away in an earlier election campaign for speaking too candidly about the Conservatives' planned spending cuts. He had not changed his views significantly on any element of policy, but as he was genuinely decent, thoughtful and close to Cameron, the media changed its view of him, hailing Letwin as a key modernizer in Cameron's team. Letwin worked closely with Cameron for the rest of his leadership, a behind-the-scenes fixer and generator of ideas. Quite often his ideological instincts clashed with his role as the fixer. It was Letwin who gave the go-ahead for the coalition's early calamitous health reforms, not because he was careless, but because he agreed with them. Cameron had asked his friend to check out the planned changes. Letwin gave them the thumbs up, at least initially.

The early Big Society seminars were private events, but some commentators were invited to attend. On one level the seminars were hugely impressive: here was an opposition party with energy and ideological verve. They were also a warning of what was to follow. At these events senior shadow Cabinet members expressed their determination to devolve power away from Whitehall departments. By way of example, the shadow Health Secretary, Andrew Lansley, argued that when there were crises in parts of the Health Service, he should not be on the *Today* programme to take responsibility. In 'empowering patients', NHS providers lower down the system would be in control and accountable. Other shadow Cabinet members argued along similar lines in relation to their policy briefs.

As a new model of public-service delivery, Hilton spoke enthusiastically of a large vegetable cooperative he had seen in Brooklyn; it was innovative, dynamic and owned and run by its workers. He argued that this was a model for public services, especially housing estates, where tenants could – and should – take responsibility.

At one point the Big Society had a clumsy subtitle, the 'Post-Bureaucratic Age'. This is how Cameron explained his vision while leader of the Opposition:

This is what we mean by the Post-Bureaucratic Age. The information revolution meets the progressive Conservative philosophy: sceptical about big state power; committed to social responsibility and non-state collective action. The effects of this redistribution of power will be felt throughout our politics, with people in control of the things that matter to them, a country where the political system is open and trustworthy, and power redistributed from the political elite to the man and woman in the street.[12]

But the seminars that explored the Big Society and the Post-Bureaucratic Age inadvertently exposed some of the problems. Who decides how much government money is devolved to various local initiatives? How is the money accounted for? Which agency is responsible for ensuring that high standards are maintained? Who or which agency represents taxpayers contributing the money to cooperatives and other self-run bodies, in order to ensure that the money is spent efficiently? By the end of the session, thousands of additional bureaucrats had been deemed necessary to administer the Post-Bureaucratic Age.

The same problems applied to ministerial responsibility. Was a Health Secretary not going to be held to account for the NHS, when the taxpayer was funding the service so that patients could be treated free at the point of use? How were patients being empowered, as more agencies became involved in the provision of services? At one point Letwin declared that he had an answer to issues relating to 'accountability'. He suggested that accountability was a lesser issue compared with the principle of giving away power.[13] This was only a limited answer.

Cameron played a curious role at the seminars. He was an assiduous attender, sitting in one of the rows, taking notes modestly. At the end he would often close the sessions of meandering and inconclusive discussions with a declaration that a 'redistribution of power' was the Conservatives' big idea. Again, the meaning was partly vague. Where was the power going to lie, and in what form? In a speech given to the World Economic Forum in Davos in 2006 he suggested that 'exhortation' from government was the way in which the state should play its role. He cited the TV chef Jamie Oliver as having more impact than regulation or changes to the law. But Oliver's campaigns were always aimed at changing laws and regulations; they were never limited to exhortation. Cameron did not seem especially interested in detailed answers. He was animated by the way these sessions were changing how the party was perceived, and seemed less bothered by the complexities. But one complexity soon surfaced. At first, charities applauded the Big Society and charity leaders flocked to the seminars, conferences and talks held by Cameron. That was until they learned that the Conservative leadership proposed significant cuts to grants for charities.

To his credit, at least Cameron surrounded himself with lively and radical thinkers. The only other leader of the Opposition to have done so was Margaret Thatcher in the late 1970s. But Thatcher tended to lead the ideological debates. Cameron was more passive, giving space to the likes of Hilton and Letwin. Hilton played a major part in composing Cameron's early speeches. Cameron appeared much more conventional than Hilton, but the new Conservative leader liked the company of right-wing radicals, partly because he was more radical than he appeared to be. His radicalism was largely rooted on the right. His genuinely charming demeanour fooled some in the media that he was more expedient than he was.

Before securing power in 2010, Cameron succeeded in his goal of changing perceptions of his party. Non-Conservative newspapers were beguiled for a time. In the build-up to the 2010 election there were rumours that the left-leaning *Guardian* might endorse the Conservatives under Cameron, a move that would have been as dramatic as the *Sun* backing Labour in 1997. It did not happen, but its deputy editor at the time, Ian Katz, became a fan of Cameron's when the Conservative leader was the new fashion. Katz would note approvingly, 'Cameron's the future... he's the real deal.'[14] The *Independent* also presented approvingly the new leader as green, progressive, sceptical of the war in Iraq and a true modernizer. Labour went into the 2010 election with only the clear support of the *Daily Mirror*.

If the Big Society was the galvanizing idea, then the political framework of Cameron's pitch was lifted transparently from the New Labour rulebook on how to win elections. Before the 1997 election, Blair and Brown announced they would stick with the Conservative government's spending levels for two years and would not raise income-tax levels for an entire parliament. Cameron and George Osborne announced, at the beginning of what was almost a joint leadership team, that they would stick to Labour's spending levels and that tax cuts were not a priority for them.

Later the message became that the 'proceeds of growth' would focus on public services and some tax cuts. Cameron's plan was spelt out vaguely in an 'Aims and Values' document sent to party members for ratification, in another imitation of Blair. As with all Cameron's policy gestures, the superficial appearance implied a change of approach, but the substance much less so. The document put the case for tax cuts along with some spending rises – the familiar message from Conservative leaders in their vote-losing era from 1997, and indeed from long before that:

> We will put economic stability and fiscal responsibility first. They must come before tax cuts. Over time, we will share the proceeds of growth between public services and lower taxes – instead of letting government spend an ever-increasing share of national income.[15]

At the 2006 party conference, Osborne warned that tax cuts could not be a priority. Facing the possibility of an early election a year later, he made a tax cut the centrepiece of his speech, with Cameron's enthusiastic support, pledging the near-abolition of inheritance tax. The move was politically smart and unnerved an increasingly nervy Gordon Brown, but the new policy contradicted the central theme when Cameron/Osborne were playing at being New Labour in reverse. Tax cuts were not supposed to be a priority. Cameron and Osborne were agile tacticians, but wobbly modernizers.

During the 2005 party conference, when he was still a leadership candidate but clear favourite to win, Cameron had told journalists that recent party leaders had pledged to take a different approach to 'tax and spend', then quickly reverted to the familiar Tory approach. He insisted that he would never change direction and was strong enough to resist pressure from within his party and the powerful Conservative-supporting newspapers.

But unlike Kinnock, who had to change his own views as well as his party's, Cameron's heart was never fully in it. He knew that he had to reposition his party, so at the 2006 conference the Conservative Party had posters attacking Brown for not spending enough on the NHS, with the implication that Cameron planned to spend much more. Similarly the slogan 'Vote blue, go green' was devised when the party's pollsters pointed out that a Conservative majority could be secured partly by wooing Liberal Democrat voters. Cameron had no previous record of passionate environmental activity. At a special green fringe meeting during the 2006 conference he told the *Independent*'s deputy editor, Ian Birrell, that Margaret Thatcher had inspired his green convictions – a revealing insight in so far as Thatcher only discovered a passing interest in environmental matters after the 1988 European elections in the UK, when the Green Party performed unexpectedly well. Her interest did not last. For a time, Cameron appeared to be passionate and was hailed as a radical environmentalist by some extremely generous newspapers.

But the financial crash of 2008 revealed Cameron's truer political self. Here was an epoch-changing event that raised deep questions about the UK's light regulatory rules and its dependence on the financial sector. If Cameron had been serious about changing his party's approach to the economy, he would have cited historic chaos and suddenly dwindling living standards as vivid examples of the failings of the Thatcher/Reagan era. If he had been following the admittedly crude New Labour model for winning elections with conviction, he would have argued that 'old' Conservatism had been right for the 1980s, but that it had gone too far and the appropriate response was a leap towards modern 'one nation' Conservatism.

Instead, Cameron's response to the crash out-Thatchered Thatcherism. Cameron and Osborne were the only mainstream leaders in the Western world to argue for real-term spending cuts. Even President Bush in the US supported an emergency fiscal stimulus. The supposedly modernizing Conservative duo chose to blame government profligacy for the crash. None of Cameron's ideological advisers were thrown by the shift after the crash. They were enthused by the leap rightwards. Steve Hilton noted in the autumn of 2008 that Cameron's calls for spending cuts would boost the Big Society rather than hinder it. The smaller state was the essential backdrop to Hilton's vision.[16]

Cameron carried on wooing non-Conservative commentators who, in most cases, continued to fall for the charm and genuine decency of the political personality. When Cameron insisted that his main priority could be summed up in three letters – 'NHS' – he was widely praised as a new type of Conservative leader, even though his then shadow Health Secretary, Andrew Lansley, was devising a reform to the NHS that would challenge the basic premises of the institution. Although he later denied it, Cameron knew what Lansley was up to. Indeed, Lansley was being guided partly by the principle that Cameron's historic objective was the 'redistribution of power'. In the case of the NHS, this meant the government accepting no further formal responsibility for the delivery of healthcare. Cameron presented the vaguely explored proposition as giving greater power to patients, and his plans received little scrutiny up to and during the 2010 election.

Occasionally, though, his mask slipped. In his 2009 party conference speech Cameron attacked the state, in the manner of a right-wing tabloid columnist, less subtle than Thatcher at her most strident:

Why is our society broken? Because government got too big, did too much and undermined responsibility. Why are our politics broken? Because government got too big, promised too much and pretended it had all the answers... This idea that for every problem there's a government solution, for every issue an initiative, for every situation a czar... It ends with them making you register with the government to help out your child's football team. With police officers punished for babysitting each other's children. With laws so bureaucratic and complicated even their own Attorney General can't obey them. Do you know the worst thing about their big government? It's not the cost, though that's bad enough. It is the steady erosion of responsibility. Our task is to lead Britain in a completely different direction. So no, we are not going to solve our problems with bigger government. We are going to solve our problems with a stronger society. Stronger families. Stronger communities. A stronger country. All by rebuilding responsibility.

'For every situation a czar?' Only the *Daily Mail*'s most polemical columnists would try that one out. This was meant to be a modernizing, centrist leader in his final conference before the next election. But Cameron's theme was clear: the state was the problem. He was equally blunt a few weeks later, in front of most of the *Guardian*'s staff, when he delivered the annual Hugo Young Lecture at Kings Place, the paper's HQ: 'The recent growth of the state has promoted not social solidarity, but selfishness and individualism.'[17]

Cameron's pitch as a centrist leader was partly because he focused smartly on what are often seen as left-wing themes. His Hugo Young Lecture was partly about tackling poverty. His arguments might have been made from the right, but he appeared to be a compassionate Conservative, in that he gave the impression that he sought progressive objectives. Indeed, he deployed the term 'progressive' often.

Cameron was also close to some who were more 'centrist' in outlook. *The Times*' columnist Daniel Finkelstein and his own internal pollster, Andrew Cooper, both of whom originated from the SDP, were allies and friends. His head of office, Ed Llewellyn, had worked for the former Liberal Democrats' leader, Paddy Ashdown, in Bosnia. They were nuanced and thoughtful. But rather than achieving a unique synthesis of radical right and SDP-style moderation, the combination made Cameron a confused leader.

The synthesis was problematic, but the strategic objective was clear. Cameron ached to be seen as being on the 'centre ground'. During the 2006 party conference, Osborne reflected with journalists on a chart that traced where voters saw politicians across the political spectrum. Osborne pointed to the middle point of the chart: 'That's where voters see Tony Blair… bang in the centre. That's where we need to be.' Within two years Osborne was to announce economic policies that were to the right of Margaret Thatcher's, in response to the 2008 crash, proposing those real-term spending cuts. Cameron and Osborne mistook a desire to be on the centre ground with being *on* the centre ground.

Yet away from economic policy and public-service reform, they made some headway. They genuinely changed the look of their party. Within a few years those attending Conservative conferences were much younger and more diverse. There were many more women. Debates were livelier and sharper than at Labour conferences, where deadening control freakery reduced fringe meetings to exchanges of cautious banalities – a stifling political atmosphere that partly enabled the rise of Jeremy Corbyn, a figure not known for his expedient caution. By copying Blair in terms of leadership style, Cameron personified the change in the Conservative Party. He was energetic and witty, and he conveyed a sense of dynamic purpose, even if that purpose was more muddled than it seemed, in terms of policy and party.

———

The muddle played a part in the 2010 election result. Cameron failed to win an overall majority, in fairly propitious circumstances: it was the aftermath of the crash, living standards were falling, the long-serving Labour government had lost most of the media, and the prime minister was unpopular. Even though the Conservatives won more seats than Labour by a considerable margin, they did not secure an overall majority. Steve Hilton's 'Big Society' theme took centre-stage at the Conservatives' epic manifesto launch, held at Battersea Power Station. In effect, the voters were asked to do more for their country as the state got smaller. This request was billed as 'an invitation to join the government of Great Britain'. Not enough voters accepted the invitation for Cameron to win outright.

The outcome was a hung parliament – the first since February 1974. This was both a symptom and a warning. Voters were breaking away from familiar patterns. In this case, they were unable to elect a government with a decisive majority. Cameron had campaigned as a dynamic and youthful leader who was accessible, charming and articulate. Yet he was privileged – the Old Etonian and a child of Thatcherism. He did not quite come together as a convincing political figure, as his role model Blair had done in 1997. Some voters detected, perhaps, the internal confusion behind the confident exterior. Cameron arrived in Number Ten unsure, deep down, about what he wanted to do. The confusion was never fully resolved.

But in order to get to Number Ten he acted with leader-like brilliance in the immediate aftermath of the election. The outcome, while disappointing for him, played to his strengths. He was fascinated by the choreography of politics – how to win, how to secure power, how to outmanoeuvre opponents. In the days after the vote, he made a dramatic and 'comprehensive' offer to the Liberal Democrats to form a coalition, offering Nick Clegg the post of deputy prime minister. A key figure in this course of action was Oliver Letwin, who had done something highly unusual in British politics. He had read the speeches of his opponents and had noted that Clegg's various addresses had chimed with the ideas of the Conservative leadership. Letwin had observed what voters had failed to do. Most voters backed the Liberal Democrats in 2010 on the assumption they were to the left of New Labour. After all, the Liberal Democrats were opponents of the Iraq War, pledged to abolish tuition fees and advocated a fiscal stimulus, rather than Osborne economics. But Clegg's speeches in the years leading up to the 2010 election had been scathing of Labour's record, and not necessarily from a left-wing perspective. He argued that social democracy had failed and that the state was too often seen as part of the solution, when it should not be. He was an economic liberal of a purer form than his recent predecessors. Ming Campbell, Charles Kennedy and David Steel were all social democrats, openly on the left of centre. By closely reading Clegg's speeches, Letwin identified his ideological essence and its uses to the Conservative Party. Still, the parliamentary arithmetic was key: a Con/Lib coalition had a safe majority. A partnership with Labour would not have been secure, in terms of numbers in the Commons. Within days, Clegg had accepted Cameron's offer. Cameron had achieved his ambition. With Liberal Democrat support, he was prime minister.

Cameron's response to the 2010 election showed great agility – an important qualification for leadership. He had little space on the political stage, as a leader who had not won in the way many of his admirers assumed he would. But within hours of the result he had created acres of political space, a route to Number Ten and an arrangement that allowed him and Osborne to pursue most of their radical objectives in policy terms. No other potential Conservative leader from that era could have pulled off such a feat in such difficult circumstances. Cameron accomplished it with energetic aplomb. The energy he displayed during the tortuous coalition negotiations was miraculous, particularly given how tiring the election campaign was. But the prospect of power can light up ambitious politicians as if it were the equivalent of a high-voltage charge from the National Grid. Cameron was lit up, even agreeing to Clegg's demand for a referendum on electoral reform. In his creation of the coalition and its subsequent management, Cameron passed a key test of leadership. He was an astute manager of people and could lead effectively in a hung parliament. He would have been much more effective at working with other parties over Brexit than Theresa May, who was incapable of reaching out in any meaningful way.

What followed the formation of the coalition was extraordinary. The Con/Lib government implemented radical policies at the political equivalent of the speed of light. In pursuit of its ideological goals, Cameron's government was far bolder than New Labour in 1997, yet New Labour had won a landslide majority, while Cameron had not even secured a majority of one. The dazzling speed of implementation suited Cameron's lack of interest in complex policy detail. This is not to suggest that he was lazy or too relaxed, another inaccurate caricature of modern prime ministers.

He worked long hours, as any prime minister must. But he was not excited by policy detail. Strategy and projection animated him more.

Within a year his government had pledged to wipe out the UK's huge deficit by the end of the parliament through the introduction of real-term spending cuts; announced sweeping reforms of the NHS; pledged referendums on all future EU treaties; implemented a Fixed-term Parliaments Act; imposed new rules on schools, while further fragmenting the structures governing education; and, in effect, almost privatized universities by announcing a trebling of tuition fees, while beginning a massive overhaul of welfare provision and holding a referendum on electoral reform.

Each radical reform had historic or chaotic consequences – and quite often both. Policy implementation is the best guide to a prime minister's character, and whether he or she is up to the job. On this basis, Cameron was not a laid-back Etonian, but a restless reformer. This is also the context for his decision to hold the Brexit referendum. He sought to clear the ground in order to embark on more reforms in his second term. But there was no ground-clearing with Brexit.

The economic policy of unyielding ambition failed, on its own terms. The deficit had not by any means been wiped out by the end of the parliament. With the self-confident chutzpah that defined the coalition, both governing parties went into the next election pledging to wipe out the deficit in the following parliament, and mocking Labour for failing to make the same pledge. Eventually the pledge was dropped in 2016. Apart from other considerations, the policy was threatening to wreck the Conservatives' electoral chances. The framing of the policy had been smart politics for a time, but it sowed the seeds for later political trouble, not least the

Brexit referendum and the 2017 election in which Conservative MPs warned that the cuts were biting too hard, even in affluent constituencies. When senior Conservative ministers declared that wiping out the deficit was no longer an immediate objective, the media no longer focused on the issue, having previously been obsessed by it.

Austerity's role in the Brexit referendum was significant. 'Leave' voters were rebelling partly against the impact of the cuts. They felt 'left behind' and sought 'control', because outside London and a few of the more affluent cities, the state had left them to cope with the consequences of globalization. In her party conference speech in October 2018 Theresa May announced the 'end of austerity' with the deficit still far from wiped out, but with some public services, welfare reform and local government in a state of crisis. Significantly, quite a few Conservative MPs were highlighting the crises.

The coalition's new NHS reforms were as chaotic as they were ambitious. Cameron's Health Secretary, Andrew Lansley, unveiled a White Paper almost as large as the one that introduced the NHS in the first place. Although Clegg was enthusiastic at first, naively seeing the plan as a celebratory conflation of the Liberal Democrats' support for localism and the Conservatives' attachment to markets, his party was alarmed.[18]

Cameron had been supportive of Lansley, partly because he was excited by the political implications of Lansley's proposal. He assumed the changes would have the support of Tony Blair and the vocal Blairites in the parliamentary Labour Party, thereby fuelling tensions in the post-Blair Labour Party. Cameron was alarmed when Blairites, including the former Health Secretary Alan Milburn, expressed their opposition. Lansley's reforms, as originally envisaged and as largely implemented, formed the most extensive reorganization of the NHS in its history. Wholly in line with the 'Post-Bureaucratic Age' seminars that Cameron held while in opposition, Lansley proposed removing formal responsibility for health provision from the Secretary of State for Health. The aim was to make local providers more accountable and, by increasing competition, to deliver better outcomes for patients. As ever with the 'Post-Bureaucratic Age', the outcome was many additional mediating agencies often competing with each other, and none of them taking responsibility as the lines of accountability became blurred.

Cameron dodged responsibility for the proposed reforms by coming up with a curious excuse. He claimed that he had not known what Lansley was up to, and announced 'a pause' – a rare example of the coalition catching a breath rather than accelerating further. The breath was limited. Under the changes after the 'pause', the NHS was further fragmented and more agencies were involved in the delivery of healthcare, in what had already become a complicated flowchart of lines of responsibility and accountability. The fragmentation began at the top, where it was never clear whether a supposedly mighty quango, NHS England, pulled the strings or whether this was still the responsibility and prerogative of the Health Secretary. Cameron was one of those who became confused.

Fearing a winter flu crisis before the looming 2015 general election, Cameron asked his Health Secretary, Jeremy Hunt, to phone the managers of hospitals individually and demand that preparatory actions be taken. Hunt pointed out to Cameron that the government had given away the powers to act in such a way. In fairness to Cameron, he smiled at the ironic impotence.[19] The effects were already being felt and, when a series of scandals surfaced in relation to Mid Staffs hospital in 2013, the government decided to make a parliamentary statement. Cameron made the statement himself, pledging to take personal responsibility to ensure the hospital improved and the lessons were learned. But the spirit of the NHS reforms contradicted this act of prime ministerial muscularity. Again Cameron had not determined clearly in his own mind what he believed, or what the implications of whatever beliefs he possessed would be, when they were put into action.

His former head of policy, Camilla Cavendish, concluded in a smart article from 2018 that fragmentation had failed:

> I have observed the NHS for more than 10 years: as a journalist, as a non-executive director of the NHS regulator Care Quality Commission, as a patient and relative, and as head of David Cameron's policy unit in No. 10. Unlike many patients, I have a map. Yet like many patients, I can still feel lost. There are more job titles in the NHS than in many multinational corporations – some of them jobs that exist simply to tie together the disparate pieces.

What if we really had one truly unified national medical system?[20]

The same question could have been asked in terms of the costs of paying all the mediating agencies required to regulate and supervise them.

Moving so fast in eye-catching policy areas, such as the economy and the NHS, Cameron's constitutional reforms did not receive the scrutiny they required. After losing the referendum on Brexit in 2016, Cameron was widely accused of being too casual and complacent in his approach. The signs were there much earlier, when he had legislated to hold referendums on all future EU treaties. This meant that if Cameron had not held his later

In/Out plebiscite, the UK would probably have left the EU anyway. A referendum on an EU treaty would almost certainly not have been winnable – harder to win, in some ways, than a binary choice of such vastness as the one he posed to voters in 2016. If the UK could not have signed a treaty, it would have been on its way out of the EU.

The Fixed-term Parliaments Act had more precise consequences, which have been felt ever since it was passed. The reform was rushed through in 2011 largely for short-term considerations. In a hung parliament, Cameron wanted to be prime minister for a full term, and Osborne was similarly enthused about being chancellor for a long time. The Act essentially facilitated this, making an early election much less possible. But the policy had a perverse consequence.

If a prime minister is popular there is usually no need for an election. Popularity suggests a degree of stability. Yet it is only when a prime minister is well ahead in the polls that an early election becomes possible, under the Act. The MPs from the governing party will only vote for an election if they are confident they will win. In effect, under the Act, MPs from the governing party must support an early election. Conversely, when a government is in trouble and Parliament is close to paralysis, an election is almost impossible. MPs from a governing party are unlikely to back a dissolution that will lead to their political demise. These consequences were tested in dramatic circumstances when Theresa May called an early election in 2017, at a time when she was twenty points ahead in the polls. As her subsequent minority government struggled to stay afloat in a near-paralysed hung parliament, she and her senior colleagues showed no similar hunger for an election. This was the consequence of the Fixed-term Parliaments Act. Yes, the coalition served a full term, but the UK was left with a situation in which when there might be a need for an election, there would never be one. When there was no need for an election, a popular prime minister might be tempted to hold one. The 2017 Conservative manifesto pledged to scrap the Fixed-term Parliaments Act, one of several sensible proposals that were not implemented when Theresa May lost her party's majority.

Elsewhere in Cameron's raft of rushed-through policies, the decision in the summer of 2010 to triple university tuition fees had echoes of the NHS reforms that were unveiled that autumn. He assumed that Blairite Labour MPs would be sympathetic to the rise in fees for students. Blair and his adviser in Number Ten, Andrew Adonis, had introduced tuition fees during Labour's second term. But so-called Blairites were alarmed at the leap, regarding the increases as far too steep. Adonis was a passionate opponent. There were many consequences. Disillusioned students faced significant debts. Universities started to pretend they were in a marketplace when they were not, paying out vast incomes to vice-chancellors and other senior staff for doing very little – the corruption of a pretend market. The Open University was a sad victim, unable to attract as many students, with the higher fees.

The rapid decline of the Liberal Democrats from strong third force to a puny parliamentary party of near-irrelevance can be traced to this single policy. Clegg's party had pledged to scrap tuition fees, but within months of the election it supported the increase. Indeed, as is often the case with newly elected British governments, the seeds of the coalition's fall were being sown during its honeymoon. As political commentators praised the coalition for showing how two parties could work together to 'save' the UK – wondering all the while whether a new permanent realignment of British politics was taking place – policies were being implemented that made the chance of a second coalition impossible. The Liberal Democrats were heading for an electoral meltdown in 2015, to the benefit of Cameron, who went on to win a small overall majority.

In the summer of 2010 Cameron wondered too about whether he had been an agent of a permanent realignment on the centre right between his party and the Liberal Democrats.[21] By 2018 the agents of the realignment, Cameron and Clegg, were out of Parliament; and Cameron's successor, Theresa May, had announced a review of tuition fees, with some of her senior advisers convinced they had to reduce the costs to students if they were ever to win another election. Under Jeremy Corbyn, Labour had pledged in the 2017 election to abolish tuition fees. The coalition's 300 per cent increase in student fees was radical and yet fragile.

Cameron's economic policies and public-service reforms were often an outdated cheer for Thatcherism. Because they came so late in the long era in which Thatcher cast her spell, they showed few signs of enduring. The Fixed-term Parliaments Act would have been scrapped, had May won a majority. Subsequent Health Secretaries concluded, like Camilla Cavendish, that the NHS needed greater centralization rather than fragmentation. Elsewhere, May announced the 'end of austerity' in her 2018 party conference speech, and the UK had voted to leave the EU before a new treaty could be tested in a referendum. Never had a newly elected government moved so quickly and with such ambitious range, yet most of the reforms did not last long.

The one that will endure is the legalization of gay marriage, a socially liberal reform that enhanced the lives of many, but served to confuse the way Cameron was perceived. Cameron had moved on from possessing a Bullingdon Club lofty machismo to being a sincere social liberal. At his final Prime Minister's Questions in the summer of 2016, he cited gay marriage as the change that had given him most satisfaction. He and Osborne clung to the reform as proof that they were 'centrists', and quite a few commentators bought into the idea. But the conflation of social and economic liberalism is deceptive. Thatcher was an economic liberal and was defiantly assertive about not being on the centre ground, warning that people get run over if they walk in the middle of the road. Cameron and Osborne were also economic liberals, like her. They were, on economic matters at least, to the right of Theresa May. On social matters they were more 'liberal' and metropolitan than her, but that did not alter their position on economic policy and the role of the state. Yet several commentators reported, as objective fact, that the Conservatives had moved to the right under May. This was misleading.

Perhaps because Cameron won the referendum on electoral reform with ease, he became complacent about the anomalies and risks of direct democracy. His leadership is defined by referendums, which is odd for a British prime minister. There was a time when the UK hardly ever held referendums – for instance, under Margaret Thatcher and John Major. In the 1997 election, Tony Blair offered many, but didn't hold them all, once in power. Like the fragile Labour government in the 1970s, Cameron offered one to Scotland, this time on independence rather than devolution; and then the referendum on Europe that brought him down. In the 1970s Callaghan's referendum on devolution led to his fall, but earlier in that decade Wilson had won the plebiscite on Europe. In Cameron's case, the reverse happened. He moved on from the Scottish referendum and then lost the Brexit referendum.

The campaign on electoral reform was not exactly preparation for the referendum storms that were to follow. In the run-up to the vote, Cameron constantly outmanoeuvred Clegg, with charm and a far greater fascination with the game of politics than the politically naive Lib Dem leader. Cameron's offer of a referendum had clinched the deal during the coalition negotiations, but there was one crucial condition that Clegg meekly accepted. The referendum would be on the Alternative Vote (AV) – a different option from First Past the Post – which was not proportional and had not been previously advocated by the Liberal Democrats. In an act of comically brutal ruthlessness, the campaign against AV, authorized by Cameron, argued that voters could not trust Clegg on the basis of the way he had betrayed them in the coalition. Cameron won the referendum with ease. The Labour leadership was theoretically supportive of AV but, in reality, was indifferent at best. It would not campaign with Clegg, partly because he had opted for a coalition of the radical right, but also because the Labour leadership had its private doubts about electoral reform. Few voters showed much interest, either. The turnout was low.

As such, the referendum campaign on electoral reform was highly deceptive, dull and soporific, resulting in the status quo. But on other fronts, voters were starting to stir. The 2010 election result was a better guide to what was to come: the unusual irresolution of a hung parliament. Cameron became casual with referendums, after winning his first one with such ease. He called two when he did not necessarily have to hold either. The first destabilized British politics and yet inadvertently helped Cameron win a tiny overall majority in 2015. The second led to his dramatic fall.

After the leader of the SNP, Alex Salmond, won a majority in the Scottish Parliament in 2011, the issue of independence for Scotland soared up the agenda. At least it did for Cameron. Salmond, a leader of smart, agile cunning, spoke often about a referendum, but had no intention of calling for one with a precise date until the polls suggested he would win. In spite of his historic triumph in elections for the Scottish Parliament, there was still no definitive evidence in the polling that he would win a referendum. He twisted and turned, when asked about when he would expect the vote to be held.

In contrast, Cameron went for it, displaying the usual impatient flair that defined his speedy, risky radicalism. He did so on the assumption that he would win. No prime minister calls a referendum on the assumption he or she will lose. A prime ministerial passion for direct democracy is kindled only when victory is on the cards. Cameron named the date for the referendum on independence and rolled up his sleeves. It was only towards the very end of the campaign that he feared he might lose. He was brilliant at staying calm – perhaps too brilliant – but when a poll suggested that a majority of voters would back independence, even he was alarmed. The poll was either wrong or the mood changed in the final days. In light of the result of the Brexit referendum, the modest victory for the union of 55–45 per cent was a triumph, but the campaign in Scotland unleashed passions that fed on themselves. Although the status quo prevailed, the referendum transformed British politics and did not resolve the issue of independence.

Early the next morning Cameron stood outside Number Ten and declared that he would introduce 'English votes for English laws' in the Westminster Parliament, to appease some of his MPs who feared that too much had been given away to the Scottish executive in order to win the referendum. Cameron was the latest of a long line of Conservative leaders who felt obliged to appease his right-wing MPs, only to land in more trouble as a result of the appeasement.

In Scotland, Cameron's early-morning announcement was widely seen as further evidence of betrayal from London, a prime minister acting differently once the votes had been cast. Support for the SNP soared the weekend after the referendum, partly as a consequence of Cameron's conduct. Salmond departed, to be replaced by the equally smart Nicola Sturgeon, who instantly became commanding. The observant Labour politician Barbara Castle once said of Margaret Thatcher that 'power made her beautiful'. Castle meant that leadership suited Thatcher and gave her space to fulfil her potential. The same applied to Sturgeon. She had been nervous and gauche in her early days as Salmond's deputy. But when she took over, she was ready: a clear-sighted and articulate social democrat. Labour had ruled Scotland like a fiefdom. Under Sturgeon, the SNP became an even more dominant force.

Cameron had not planned the rise of the SNP and its destabilizing impact on the UK, but the subsequent near wipe-out of Labour in Scotland in the 2015 general election enabled him to win his overall majority. Labour's leader, Ed Miliband, had been nervily fearful of much that could go wrong under his fragile regime, but never anticipated Labour being destroyed in Scotland. Miliband was reduced to tears in the immediate aftermath of the 2015 general election, when reflecting on what happened in Scotland. After all, he would have been prime minister if Labour had performed even reasonably well there. But for Cameron, the wipe-out of Labour was an accidental consequence of his referendum. His objective had been to resolve the independence question for a generation, but his referendum failed to do so. Indeed, it heightened the intensity of the question.

There was, however, a case for Cameron's decision to hold the Scottish referendum when he did. In leadership, decisions are nearly always nightmarish, and more nuanced than the media allow. Blair once characterized most decisions that he had to take as 'Do you want to cut your wrist or slit your throat?'[22] There were no easy routes. If Cameron had not offered the referendum in Scotland, Salmond would have played games, teasing the British government and making the Westminster politicians seem defensive and uncooperative. There was a case for Cameron taking the initiative, especially when there had not been a single opinion poll suggesting that he would lose. But equally, Cameron could have called Salmond's bluff, put forward the case for the union and got on with the rest of his crammed agenda. This is what Theresa May did, when Sturgeon called vaguely for a second referendum in Scotland after the Brexit referendum. May said 'No' and Sturgeon's calls became vaguer. In a few respects May was more leaderly than Cameron, arriving in Number Ten more fully formed. But she faced Cameron's thorny legacy, and her fatal flaws soon doomed her, too.

———

His legacy took the form of Brexit. All the themes of Cameron's leadership came together in the Brexit saga. Far from being the laid-back Etonian prime minister, he was taking yet another big risk. Of all the modern prime ministers, Cameron was the greatest risk taker. He was over-confident in his ability to win the referendum, and yet lacking in confidence in his sense that he needed to make such an offer in order to survive in office. His renegotiation with the rest of the EU was rushed and ill-thought-through, and yet it might have been the basis for a long-term settlement if Cameron had not proved yet again that he was an unreliable vote-winner, this time in the referendum.

When Cameron offered the In/Out referendum during a speech in 2013, the EU was low down the list of voters' concerns, according to opinion polls. He made the offer against the advice of Osborne and his then close friend Michael Gove, because he feared more defections from his parliamentary party and voters turning to the UK Independence Party (UKIP), a party campaigning for a referendum on whether to leave the EU. Cameron calculated that a referendum would blunt the appeal of UKIP and be a winning card in a general election. Again, his calculations were understandable. UKIP's leader, Nigel Farage, claimed that he was speaking to several Conservative MPs who planned to defect. Cameron's press secretary, Sir Craig Oliver, revealed subsequently that Number Ten worried that up to twenty Conservative MPs could defect.[23]

There is nothing more terrifying for party leaders than defections to another party, and nothing more gratifying than travel in the opposite direction. Defections are evidence of momentum to one side rather than another, and of fatal disunity. They are a more reliable guide to the wider mood than opinion polls. The defections from the Conservative Party to Labour in the New Labour era were regarded as hugely significant at the time, confirming and reinforcing Labour's soaring rise and the Conservatives' fall. When the likes of Alan Howarth, Sean Woodward and Quentin Davies changed sides, they were not household names, but made huge waves because of the symbolism.

In the early 1980s the defections from Labour to the SDP were also a sign that Labour was heading for electoral catastrophe. Cameron and Osborne ached for defectors to join them in their early phase, wooing in particular the Liberal Democrat MP David Laws, who supported much of their economic policy. Their failure to attract defections reflected the fragility of their project. Defectors are attracted to a project that appears to have depth and durability. They are making a big leap. Cameron was acutely aware that if several Tory MPs switched to UKIP, the latter would be greatly strengthened and he would be conversely weakened. The right would be split at a general election, in the way the left had been in the 1980s. The Independent Group, formed in 2019 from defecting Labour and Conservative MPs, outlined the vaguest of programmes on the basis of a banal set of values, but the leaderships of the other parties feared more defections and to some extent changed their tunes accordingly. Leaders loathe defections or the prospect of them.

But while anxiety was a natural response to the stirrings of UKIP, Cameron moved too speedily towards the seemingly magical solution of the referendum. He made the pledge to hold an In/Out plebiscite before the trauma of the Scottish referendum, but after the easy ride of the vote on electoral reform. Again he acted because he assumed he would win. Partly he was paying the price of failing to challenge his party over the issue of Europe when he was strong in the early days of his leadership, preferring to take the easier path of visiting council estates as a symbol of a new compassionate conservatism or visiting Greenland to highlight concern for global warming. On Europe he had chosen appeasement when he was strong, the same mistake that May made when she was on an authority-enhancing honeymoon. Having supported his party leaving the European People's Party during his leadership contest, Cameron sought to act tough with Europe as prime minister, wielding his veto ostentatiously at key moments, while seeking and failing to block the appointment of a new EU president. By 2013 he was relatively weak. He was behind in the polls, the leader of a coalition rather than a Conservative government, and the self-confident swagger was replaced with some degree of panic.

Cameron found the art of politics compelling and yet he was not always an astute reader of its complex rhythms. His tendency to copy Blair meant that he read the rhythms as if they arose from the mid- to late 1990s, an altogether different era. Cameron was navigating his way through the aftermath of the 2008 financial crash while leading a party as riven over Europe as it was when his role model, Blair, slaughtered it in 1997.

UKIP was never as strong as it seemed, or at least as it seemed to Cameron. The party attracted two defectors during the coalition era, the ineffectual Mark Reckless and the ideologically eccentric Douglas Carswell. Both had left UKIP by 2018 and were out of the UK Parliament. Other Tory hard-liners showed little inclination to join them in defecting. They were as tribal as any other part of the Conservative Party.[24]

Support for UKIP peaked in the European elections in 2014 after Cameron had made the referendum pledge, suggesting that the offer was not a decisive factor for voters. UKIP topped the poll in terms of votes cast – a staggering achievement and a warning about what might happen in a referendum on EU membership. The result was simultaneously a warning and a red herring. Voters were stirring in unprecedented numbers, making any referendums extremely dangerous. Yet their chosen vehicle, UKIP, was weak and fragile. Its leader, Nigel Farage, was a laddishly appealing performer, who managed to keep the show on the road. Below him were a bunch of weird amateurs espousing incoherent views. When Farage resigned after the 2016 referendum, UKIP had a series of bizarre leaders who were elected during even odder leadership contests. UKIP was not the formidable force it appeared to be. By 2019 Farage had formed The Brexit Party – even he had had enough of UKIP.

After his unexpected victory in 2015, Cameron announced, with characteristically impatient speed, that the Brexit referendum would be held in the summer of the following year. There is a common myth that he offered the referendum on the assumption that he would never have to hold it – calculating that there would be a second coalition and the Liberal Democrats would veto the referendum. This is not the case. Cameron knew when he made the offer of a referendum, largely to his party, that he would have to deliver, whether leading a coalition or a single-party government. He had been unequivocal. He made the offer of the referendum because he thought he would win, not because he hoped he would never have to hold the vote.[25]

Cameron might well have won the referendum if it had not been for a series of miscalculations. The first was to overestimate his own persuasive powers, both in his negotiations with the EU and in his pitch to UK voters. He made the mistake of assuming that a few charming bilateral meetings with individual EU leaders would deliver a substantial renegotiation of the UK's already generous membership arrangements.

As usual, the EU acted as a coherent whole, and Cameron's sleepless visits to Berlin and other capitals produced only limited results. Meanwhile, in parts of the UK where his turbo-charged Thatcherite economic policies had hit hard, voters were not inclined to give him their backing in a referendum. Cameron should have taken more notice of Harold Wilson's approach to the 1975 referendum on UK membership. More than aware of his unpopularity, Wilson kept a low profile, timed the referendum when polls pointed to a huge victory, and used his 'renegotiation' to achieve some easy accessible gains, mostly relating to the price of New Zealand butter.

The context of Cameron's renegotiation was determined by his other major miscalculation. Wilson knew that his Cabinet and party were split and that his 'renegotiation' had no hope of uniting the two sides of the divide. His cosmetic deal was merely a peg to justify Wilson supporting membership, having opposed it when the UK joined under Edward Heath.

In contrast, Cameron hoped to keep his Cabinet on board and united behind his 'renegotiation'. He was also fairly optimistic of wooing the then highly popular Conservative MP Boris Johnson. The stakes in relation to his renegotiation were impossibly high, and only late in the day did he accept with great reluctance that collective responsibility had to be dropped. This was when his deal with the EU failed to satisfy several Eurosceptics in his Cabinet, including his friend Michael Gove. According to Sir Craig Oliver, Cameron knew Johnson was unreliable, but was devastated by what he saw as Gove's betrayal.[26] Cameron was fairly unflappable, but Oliver recalls how Cameron had his head in his hands in fuming despair as he heard that Gove, campaigning for 'Leave', had co-written an article with Johnson suggesting that his old prime ministerial friend could not be trusted with some of his claims in relation to Europe. Cameron was naive to expect friendship to trump conviction on an issue as emotive as Europe. In some respects, he was a leader with strong views weakly held, as the historian A. J. P. Taylor once described himself. Gove had strong views, held with a determination that would end a friendship.[27]

Probably the 'Remain' campaign was doomed from the beginning. Across the democratic world voters were giving perceived 'elites' a kicking. Looking back to 1975, although the elite (in the form of current and former prime ministers, most MPs and business leaders) campaigned for the UK to remain in Europe, their advocacy was not seen as counter-productive. In 2016 the support of a charismatic US president, as well as all current and former living prime ministers, turned out to be deeply unhelpful.

But Cameron did not perform with the agility required to give him any chance of avoiding the torrents that were sweeping perceived elites from power. Indeed, the fragile career of the onetime self-confident Etonian highlights the wild politics that carried him away. He became the prime minister of a rare peacetime coalition and never served with a hefty Commons majority. In a country that rarely held referendums, Cameron implemented three of historic significance. If prime ministers hold referendums, they must win them. Cameron lost one and, barely a year after winning an overall majority in the 2015 general election, he was gone. It was an unprecedented fall, from major triumph to fatal humiliation in just twelve months.

For a youthful prime minister, Cameron proved masterly in creating and managing a coalition. Both were epic achievements – managing people and parties is a major part of leadership. Cameron had to manage his party and its relationship with another in government. Against the expectations of many, the coalition lasted the full five years and this was largely down to his skilful dealings with colleagues. He also led the Cabinet with aplomb, avoiding too many reshuffles and keeping on board throughout the coalition years social democrats such as Vince Cable and Tory radicals like Iain Duncan Smith. IDS resigned in the build-up to the referendum, when the Conservatives had an overall majority. He stayed put during the coalition, working well with the Liberal Democrats' Steve Webb. Cameron had created the space for unlikely partnerships to form and flourish.

Fatally, though, Cameron did not know who he was as a political figure, arriving as prime minister more underdeveloped than any post-war leader. His early passion for the 'Big Society' was dropped soon after he became prime minister. He was reported as describing the Liberal Democrats' concerns for the environment as 'green crap' towards the end of his leadership, having affected a commitment to green issues early in his leadership.

Ultimately Cameron had wanted to be a different type of Conservative leader, and yet he shared many of the views espoused by recent Tory predecessors. Tony Blair was his model, but while Blair believed – rightly or wrongly – that his party should change beyond recognition, Cameron was less sure whether he could, or should, challenge the Conservatives to the same extent. He was reluctant on some policy areas to challenge himself in the way that a figure like Neil Kinnock had done. But unlike Kinnock, he won an election and was prime minister for six years. He could have ruled considerably longer, if his inexperienced ambiguity and shallow tactical instincts had not led him to fight and lose a referendum on the UK's membership of the EU. He had been too quick to assume he could convince the electorate that the EU was close to a form of paradise, despite having been largely Eurosceptic for most of his leadership. The other related trauma for Cameron was how the referendum outcome suggested that he had not understood the country he had led for six years, assuming it was close to the one that elected New Labour in 1997. But the country had changed in ways that he and his media supporters had not seen.

While Cameron had insisted in public that he would remain prime minister if he lost the referendum, privately he had told his closest advisers he would go.[28] One of those who believed his public statement was his then Home Secretary, Theresa May. She had kept a low profile during the referendum, on the assumption that a vacancy would arise at some point during the parliament. After all, Cameron had pledged, unwisely, not to seek a third term; May thought he would probably win the referendum or stay on in defeat. Wholly unexpectedly for her, he lost the vote and then stepped down. Within days she was prime minister, thrown to the top of the pile in a context, and at a time, that she had not anticipated. Cameron's sudden departure was as premature as his speedy rise. Theresa May arrived in Number Ten less prepared for the burdens of leadership than any other prime minister in modern times.

9

THERESA MAY

Theresa May's nerve-shredding, energy-sapping and joyless prime ministerial career serves as a warning to current and aspiring leaders: expect a hellish time, unless you have certain essential qualifications. May had a story to tell about Brexit and the rest of her agenda, but she was not a political teacher. She not only failed to tell her story, but did not even make an attempt. This was her fatal flaw – not only a failure to communicate, but an indifference to the art.

She also lacked a second qualification of leadership. She was not a smart reader of the political rhythms. She did at times have space on the political stage, but failed to see when she had the room to be bold and when she did not. In relation to Brexit she acted weakly when she was politically strong, and finally told her party of the need for compromise when she was hopelessly weak. Fatally she got the sequence the wrong way round.

She became weak after calling the early election in 2017, just a year into her premiership, and losing her party's overall majority. Many lessons of leadership arise from the collapse of her authority. Most fundamentally that early elections are dangerous – either contemplating them or holding them.

As May made her moves, she worked assiduously, and at times wilfully, to deliver her view of the form that Brexit should take. Soon the volcanic explosions began. Ministers resigned. Her Brexit deal was defeated in the Commons three times. There was a vote of confidence amongst Conservative MPs, in an attempt to remove her. The Brexit deadline was extended from March 2019, in spite of endless prime ministerial proclamations that the UK would be out of the EU by then. May was at the centre of it all and yet determinedly separate from the drama – a form of political isolation that was both a protective shield and a further source of her fragility.

Most incoming prime ministers have had some time to prepare for the tasks ahead. May had none. With dizzying speed, the UK had a new leader in the aftermath of the 2016 referendum, one who had never had cause to think deeply about Brexit. Her direct ministerial experience of the European Union was acquired in the Home Office. She had not been a leader of the Opposition, where it is necessary to frame arguments and reflect more widely on the UK's relationship with Europe. She had no ministerial perspective from the Treasury or the Foreign Office. Her experience of the EU as a minister had been in the more straightforward, though highly charged and important area of security. On the whole, members of the EU agree that security concerns require coordination and the sharing of information. The UK was respected for its willingness to share and coordinate. As Home Secretary, if May wanted to opt out of some EU agreements and opt into others, she prevailed with ease. The Home Office tests many qualities in a politician, but it is not the best preparation for becoming an authoritative expert on all aspects of the European Union.

Theresa May also had no idea in advance that the Conservatives' whacky leadership battle of July 2016 was going to end almost before it had begun. She assumed that she would face a second round of party members and would have until September to finalize her thoughts around Brexit, before entering Number Ten – if, indeed, she won. The immediate context of her rise is pivotal. As the contest got under way she was not to know that there would be no second round. Her thoughts about Brexit were on a single question: how to win a Conservative leadership contest when a majority of members were strongly pro-Brexit?

Her early post-referendum discussions, which were confined to her two special advisers of the time, Nick Timothy and Fiona Hill, focused largely on this narrow question: 'How can we convince the party that we are deadly serious about Brexit?' In reflecting on that question, May began to frame answers that led towards her fall. As is often the case with prime ministers, the seeds of her fragility were sown in the period in which she rose triumphantly to the top. She had no time to think for very long about what Brexit meant. She had no time to learn how the EU operates at the highest level.

Other prime ministers sought to find words to make sense of a chaotic situation, or tried to change the situation. May did neither. She was widely seen as dutiful, as she twisted and turned to stay on her chosen path – a triumph of deviousness. But her indifference to words and persuasion, essential arts of leadership, became the main cause of her undoing. Long-serving prime ministers are the ones who seek constantly to engage with MPs, voters and the media, telling stories that appear to make sense of what is happening. Margaret Thatcher was an instinctive teacher, reducing the complexities of monetarism to homilies about how her father never spent more than he earned. As she made her moves, Thatcher proclaimed that her aim was to set people free. And who is opposed to freedom? Wilson and Blair deployed the evasive term 'modernization' to explain their early initiatives. Some of the shorter-serving prime ministers were more effective than May. Edward Heath was an adequate communicator in the 1975 Common Market referendum after he had ceased to be prime minister, explaining better than most why pooled sovereignty was not a threat to democracy. Gordon Brown sparkled as a speaker before he became shadow chancellor and even, at times, after he acquired the stifling, dehumanizing economic brief. He framed some of the enduring soundbites of the New Labour era, from 'Tough on crime, tough on the causes of crime' to 'prudence for a purpose'. Nick Timothy devised May's best lines and, after he left, there were no memorable lines at all. May was not a 'teacher' prime minister, with the language and performance skills to make sense of what – in the case of Brexit – could often be nonsensical.

There were times when May needed to be opaque in order to keep her government together, but a smart political teacher can be evasive while appearing to be clear. When Thatcher declared famously in October 1980 that the 'lady's not for turning', she was, in reality, overseeing a U-turn in her economic policy. The lady *was* for turning from pure monetarism, but her skill as a teacher disguised the haphazard route she was taking. When Blair tormented John Major by asserting, 'I lead my party, you follow yours', he was referring to Major's equivocations over the single currency. Blair was equivocating in precisely the same way, but he was a communicator who could deploy words to convey resolute leadership, when he was keeping options open. Words are a political weapon. May did not have the necessary ammunition.

At the beginning of her premiership in the summer of 2016, with Brexit looming large, she said there would be no 'running commentary' on the process. In the many months that followed, both within government and outside it, May was the only person who followed this laughably unrealistic instruction. Standing apart from the political noise, there was no focus from May on strategy as the storms erupted. Instead, an unruly pattern emerged: as the latest crisis erupted, May kept going till the following day, when she inevitably became politically trapped again, wriggled awkwardly, spoke evasively and created a little more space until the next incarceration. She proved to be a durable political contortionist, but did not seek to explain what her latest painful position might be.

This determinedly insular pattern formed during the gradual phase of May's ascent. As with other modern prime ministers, the pattern of the early years recurred after May acquired the crown, and therefore merit further scrutiny. When an ambitious politician becomes prime minister, he or she often assumes that past patterns are a guide to future successful rule. But quite often they are a warning of how *not* to rule, when leading in the very different context of Number Ten. Most fundamentally, May assumed that the way she had operated as Home Secretary, and as a senior Opposition frontbencher, could be applied in Number Ten. In those previous roles she had kept public and media appearances to a minimum, decided on policies with a few trusted advisers and then made sure she prevailed, if colleagues sought to prevent her policies from being implemented.

May was not interested in engaging with journalists, either as an ambitious potential leader or as prime minister. She met them because her advisers told her to do so. No journalist can recall a noteworthy exchange. She was bewildered and disapproving of her colleagues who spoke endlessly to those in the media, assuming – often correctly – that they saw politics merely as a game. When she was Home Secretary in the coalition, and as prime minister, some of her colleagues did become far too intoxicated with the fleeting thrill of engaging with political journalists, both in private and in the broadcasting studio. The exchanges were an affirmation of their significance and, they often assumed, a further boost to their ambitions to become more significant still. Quite often the sole consequences were to provide lines for journalists – lines that came and went in the daily hurly-burly of politics.

Even so, an indifference to the art of being a political teacher is a form of neglect, and it is the media that mediates between leader and the electorate. May did not try to be a guide through the storms. If she had been an effective teacher, she would have had more followers, because there would have been a more clearly defined path for them to follow.

Instead, she saw her political past as a form of vindication. She had got to the top by focusing on policy implementation, while largely hiding away from the media and the public. This was how she had succeeded where others had failed. In her previous job she was used to making policy without great public scrutiny. She had often turned down interviews on the *Today* programme and BBC1's *Andrew Marr Show* as she navigated her course. On being made prime minister, May assumed that she could still get away with this evasiveness, even in relation to the most significant change in UK policy since 1945.

There is an important qualification to May's determination to lie low. Every now and again throughout her career she would surface dramatically, before hiding away again. For much of the time May made little public impact during her years on her party's frontbench, toiling away behind the scenes without feeling the need to explain very often what she was doing, or why. But, every now and again, she uttered words that would make waves. She was the equivalent of the plodding tennis player who occasionally had a tantrum and played spectacularly.

May had wanted to be prime minister for much of her adult life, being ambitious for the top job for longer than Thatcher or Blair. She was brought up as an only child in Oxfordshire. Her father was a vicar and her mother was an active Conservative Party member. Like Thatcher, May was hooked on politics from her teenage years, becoming a member of the Conservative Party and active at Oxford. She met her future husband, Philip, at a Conservative social evening at the university. Even as prime minister, she liked nothing more than canvassing in Maidenhead, her constituency, and taking part in local political meetings. She seemed most at ease politically when canvassing at home. Coincidentally, the UK had both a prime minister and a leader of the Opposition, Jeremy Corbyn, who flourished in their constituencies, while being much less at ease responding to national and international historic events. As Brexit raged on, both liked nothing more than to return to their home patch. May became an MP in 1997 – Tony Blair's first landslide victory – and slowly rose through the ranks as a solid, determined MP who had more time on her hands than most of her colleagues. Like Edward Heath, she had no children and few other interests to distract her from politics. Unlike Heath, she had a partner, in Philip, who shared her passion for Conservative politics. They were in it together. Heath was alone.

At the Conservative conference in 2002 May made her mark as the newish party chairwoman. Here was an early example of her making waves, before returning to semi-darkness away from the intense media glare. For a politician who rarely delivered memorable speeches, her words at that conference were never forgotten and were often quoted in the years to follow. In some respects, they defined her in the most flattering light possible – as a figure brave enough to tell her party hard truths. She was speaking early on in Labour's second term, after the Conservatives had been slaughtered in both the 1997 and 2001 elections:

> Yes, we've made progress, but let's not kid ourselves. There's a way to go before we can return to government. There's a lot we need to do in this party of ours. Our base is too narrow and so, occasionally, are our sympathies. You know what some people call us: the nasty party.

She was not posturing. She meant it. May was a politician who tended to say what she believed. Quite often her beliefs were pragmatic and uninteresting, but her speech stood out at the time, along with her daring leopard-skin shoes – exuberantly ostentatious footwear at odds with her reticent personality, as if she assumed that the wearing of attention-grabbing shoes would help her to acquire a public personality. In a way they did. The shoes were almost an act of disguise.

On the whole, May plodded on without becoming a big crusader for internal reform, after her 'nasty party' speech. As would later prove to be the case with the Brexit saga, she had uttered some words of apparent significance and then carried on, almost as if the words had not been said. Her chance for greater prominence came when she moved to the Home Office as part of the coalition in 2010. She remained Home Secretary until she became prime minister in 2016. To have survived as Home Secretary for six years was in itself a qualification for leadership. The Home Office is a tough testing ground, to the extent that few Home Secretaries become leaders. Only James Callaghan, among modern prime ministers, had served at the Home Office. In the final phase of the New Labour era Home Secretaries came and went on a regular basis. May lasted the course – a genuine triumph.

Perhaps there is a reason why this senior post is not a natural part of the path towards Number Ten. The Home Office is, in some respects, atypical. The demands are nightmarishly intense and unpredictable. A terrorist threat can disturb a Home Secretary at any time. A prison escape can trigger demands for the resignation of a Home Secretary. Immigration is an emotive issue, as well as one that is politically and practically complex. But the Home Secretary is to some extent cocooned from the rest of the government, working tirelessly, with little time to reflect on economic policy and foreign affairs or wider public-service reforms. May worked with the smallest possible team, relying mainly on her two advisers, Nick Timothy and Fiona Hill. They were utterly loyal to her and she was dependent on them, regarding them almost as oracles who were guiding her to the top. But May also worked well with senior Home Office officials, which is not always the case with Home Secretaries. Her civil servants respected her and broadly agreed with her own assessment, which was formed quietly, modestly and determinedly, that she was a potential prime minister.[1]

At the Home Office she kept a relatively low profile, compared with the more theatrical members of the coalition – the ones May regarded partly as players of politics as a game, rather than as a wholly serious vocation. Lunches with journalists or colleagues were awkward and unrewarding occasions. Shortly before the start of the 2016 referendum campaign David Cameron's director of communications, Sir Craig Oliver, took May out to lunch. He noted later, 'I tried every example of small talk I could think of in an attempt to get a conversation started. After around twenty minutes I started to feel physically sick.'[2]

Yet periodically, when she was largely hidden away as Home Secretary, May delivered a sensational speech, as she had done in opposition, lighting up the political stage in ways that made her more ostentatious colleagues seem shy and retiring. In May 2014 she addressed the Police Federation's annual conference and went for them. Referring to various topical and highly charged controversies involving police misconduct and racist attitudes, she declared:

> If there is anybody in this hall who doubts that our model of policing is at risk, if there is anybody who underestimates the damage recent events and revelations have done to the relationship between the public and the police, if anybody here questions the need for the police to change, I am here to tell you that it's time to face up to reality… It is an attitude that betrays contempt for the public these officers are supposed to serve – and every police officer in the land, every single police leader, and everybody in the Police Federation should confront it and expunge it from the ranks… It is not enough to mouth platitudes about a few bad apples. The problem might lie with a minority of officers, but it is still a significant problem, and a problem that needs to be addressed… Polls show two-thirds of the public trust the police… We should never accept a situation in which a third of people do not trust police officers to tell the truth.

The speech was one of the most powerful to be delivered by a Cabinet minister during the coalition era – courageous, principled and, to deploy Cameron's favourite political term, 'modern'. Leading members of the Police Federation were taken aback, but their response was a tribute to the force of the speech. Once she had delivered her brutal message, May disappeared again from public view.

_____

So it was with Brexit. May made a set-piece speech every few months and acted as if no more needed to be said for some time. With Brexit, much needed to be said – nearly every hour of every day. Ironically, May did have a strategy of sorts for Brexit, and a premise to justify her plan. The strategy, premise and plan were contentious and inelegant, but they were not as calamitous as her growing number of detractors were to claim. There was a case, but she never found a way of putting it: memorable phrases, the framing of an argument, a compelling narrative. Here was May's thinking on Brexit and how it evolved.

At the beginning she decided that she had a democratic duty to deliver the referendum. As far as she was concerned, the referendum was her mandate. Parliament had played its role by voting for the referendum to be held after the 2015 election. Now it was her duty to deliver and, in her view, Parliament's role would be peripheral. She did not want Parliament to have a vote on the triggering of Article 50, the move that formally began the Brexit process. MPs demanded a 'meaningful vote' on her deal. She did not want to grant them such a potent weapon. After she had negotiated her Brexit deal, she sought to bludgeon Parliament into submission with threats of far worse alternatives. As far as she was concerned, she was responding to the referendum result and, in doing so, saving the UK from a crisis of trust, if a 'Remain'-dominated Parliament took control.

In terms of the deal she sought, May had a point in claiming that Brexiteers won the referendum because of voters' opposition to free movement. Her final deal ended free movement and potentially allowed the UK to trade with other countries. As her negotiations intensified, May became more aware that the soft border in Ireland was threatened by the UK's departure from the customs union.

Acutely aware that the soft border was central to the peace process in Northern Ireland, she agreed a backstop compromise, whereby the UK remained in the customs union until alternative arrangements were agreed. Her position was not too distant from that of the Labour leadership, which sought membership of a customs union.

The flaws in May's strategy and assumptions were deep, and should have been more obvious to her. Parliament would not allow her to treat it with disdain. Her Brexit deal was a convoluted set of compromises. But given that there had been a majority in the referendum for 'Leave', and she had a plan for leaving, she did not necessarily have to endure the various forms of Brexit hell that followed. Her failure to make accessible sense of what she was doing was the main reason she struggled to prevail and her government fell apart. There were more ministerial resignations and sackings under May than any other modern prime minister, by a huge margin.

Unlike Margaret Thatcher, May was also a poor reader of the political stage. Thatcher perceived clearly when she had space to be bold and when she had no room for manoeuvre. Instead, as the Brexit prime minister, May made the right moves at the wrong times. Had she been assertive when she was politically strong, she might have suffered a slightly less draining nightmare in Number Ten. Instead, she endured a period of rule that made even James Callaghan's tempestuous leadership in the late 1970s, or Gordon Brown's after the 2008 crash, seem like a model of calm.

At the beginning of her leadership, in the summer of 2016, May was in a formidably strong and authoritative position. This was partly for the simple reason that there was not going to be another leadership contest in the months that followed her speedy victory. If she had announced that she was planning to fly to the moon, there would have been no challenge. The party had just held a traumatic contest and was hardly going to trigger another. May was walking on water, according to the opinion polls, with soaring personal ratings. Popularity is authority-enhancing for a prime minister – if polls suggest a prime minister could win an election, then he or she becomes almost as commanding as when they do hold and win a general election. As a result of winning a leadership contest with ease, May's popularity among voters rose; thanks to her steely and distant manner, Cabinet ministers were in submissive awe of her. Even in private, few said a word against her. Instead they cited May as if she was the oracle. Ministers repeated her words to journalists as if they came from a political titan. With some justification at the time, ministers – and much of the media – assumed that May would be prime minister for a long time, another assumption that often feeds on itself.

But in relation to Brexit, May did not recognize her strength when she became prime minister. As a Remainer, she felt the insecure need to reassure her party that she would deliver on the referendum. Her senior adviser, Nick Timothy, invented the phrase 'Brexit means Brexit' – words that she repeated like a machine for the first six months of her leadership. She made the phrase seem like a defiant act, but Timothy meant the words to be soothingly reassuring for Brexiteers, a promise that she would deliver on the referendum.

May was too aware of her awkward position, as the Remainer who had leapt into Number Ten on the back of a Brexit victory in the referendum. Her acute awareness became a trap. Subsequently she felt a need to please hard-line Brexiteers far more than she did the smaller number on the other side of her party who had backed Remain. In doing so, she chose to be incarcerated, in relation to Brexit, at an early phase in her leadership when she had no need to be. With reckless defiance she proclaimed her Brexit 'red lines': no customs union, no single market, no jurisdiction from the European Court of Justice (ECJ), no freedom of movement. In response, hard-liners in her party purred during those early months. Like John Major and David Cameron, Theresa May tried hard from the beginning to please her potential tormentors but, in doing so (as with Major and Cameron), she was sealing her fate.

By the beginning of October 2016 she had declared that the UK would leave the single market and the customs union and would no longer be under the jurisdiction of the ECJ. She had promised to trigger Article 50 by March of the following year. At the same time she envisaged retaining the benefits that were conferred on the UK on the basis of its membership of the EU. At no point in this early phase – her period of greatest untouchable authority – did May explain to her party that Brexit would involve some very tough choices. She could have done so in the opening months of her leadership. Some in her party would not have liked being told candid truths, but would have had no choice but to listen. She could have cleared some of the ground that became impossibly cluttered when she started to make the awkward choices that she had pretended were not there.

Instead, in the early months, May was having her cake and eating it. Later, when ministers were being publicly critical of her (in some cases defying the whip in Brexit votes) and MPs were calling on her to go, she had no choice but to be assertive, lecturing her stroppy party about the importance of maintaining the soft border in Ireland, and on the need for the UK to consider being part of a customs union until the issue of the Irish border and the backstop was answered. But at that point she was telling hard truths when few would listen.

Leaders often get the sequence wrong. Tony Blair and Gordon Brown were politically untouchable in 1997 and yet acted cautiously. When voters turned hard against Blair, he had no choice but to be strong in defending the calamity of Iraq. He became a crusading evangelical as voters were becoming restive. When he had much less to say, voters paid homage to him. Harold Wilson had more space than he dared to realize after winning a landslide in 1966. The example of May is more vivid. As prime ministers often do at the beginning of a reign, she made a series of rushed decisions when she was mighty. These decisions were the product of insecurity, but were hailed in the Eurosceptic newspapers as acts of Thatcher-like strength.

Yet prime ministers are complex human beings. May was both insecure about her relationship with the party in relation to Brexit, and over-confident on other matters. These are the kinds of contradictory forces that shape many early prime ministerial careers. Early over-confidence arises from the fact that prime ministers have reached the pinnacle that so many dream of attaining. They dare to wonder whether they are special. At the summit, the few who make it inhale a whiff of intoxicating power. During the coalition years, May must have heard much speculation that George Osborne might well be Cameron's successor, or maybe Michael Gove; or, days before she acquired the crown, she would have noted that Boris Johnson was the favourite to lead. Yet she was the one who got there. The victory gave her a partial sense of imperious triumph – as misjudged as her early insecurity about being a prime minister who voted 'Remain'.

With a ruthless swagger, she triggered a purge of Cameron's allies across Number Ten, the Treasury and the wider government. George Osborne was one of those who was brutally sacked – told to go off and learn more about the Conservative Party, an early sign that sensitivity with colleagues was not May's greatest asset. The purge had many consequences. From day one, she acquired enemies who would never forgive her brutality, when it should have been obvious to her that she would need all the goodwill she could get in order to deal with Brexit.

A more serious and overlooked consequence of the purge was a sudden loss of collective memory in relation to the European Union. The mistakes David Cameron made in his renegotiation with the EU, and the lessons learned from that flawed negotiation, would have been invaluable to a novice prime minister suddenly exposed to the task of Brexit. To have had some ministers involved in the torrid twists and turns of the late-Cameron era in the room with May and her advisers, when they were having dangerously naive conversations about Brexit, might have made her approach more agile. Instead, those who had learned lessons from Cameron's renegotiation were largely in exile. May had felt confident enough to sack them.

The early over-confidence took a deeper form, which impaired her political vision. She hoped to lead a government that instigated many historic domestic reforms. She did not realize, or accept, that Brexit would overwhelm all other ambition. This was part of her early misreading of the overcrowded political stage. Some of the early ideas were substantial and marked a genuine leap from the Conservatives' recent past, but they did not have a hope of taking shape, with the Brexit mountain to climb. The early hopes for radical domestic reform took an ideological form, influenced greatly by Nick Timothy. As an adviser, Timothy had ideas that were a distinctive and interesting blend, combining a hint of Enoch Powell's Midlands nationalism and Ed Miliband's faith in the state. He was a genuine radical and innovative thinker, who was also a committed Brexiteer. There is speculation as to whether May was a mere vessel for Timothy's bold ideas or whether she shared his distinct values. It does not matter greatly – she chose to share them, albeit erratically.

———

Like most prime ministers, May was not a good judge of colleagues or how best to deal with them. Leaders, often more insecure than they seem, self-absorbed and with no choice but to become wholly immersed in the frenzied rush of each day, have little time or inclination to reflect on the characters around them. Most value loyalty as a winning characteristic. They are often poor at evaluating who will be an effective administrator or reformer, and rarely value those who challenge and question what is happening.

Some said of Margaret Thatcher that she liked nothing more than to be challenged by other ministers. There is little evidence of this. Her test, when making appointments, was the question 'Is he one of us?' – a theme so defining that an early biography by the columnist Hugo Young took the question as its title.[3] Her chancellors shared Thatcher's economic approach and, when they ceased to do so, they were gone. Those she promoted tended to be doting admirers. Those who questioned her did not last very long. Tony Blair sought to promote 'Blairites', colleagues who had decided to agree with him in the internal battles with Gordon Brown. Cameron assumed that he had loyal colleagues until he called the referendum and discovered, in some cases – namely, Boris Johnson and Michael Gove – that their convictions or ambition trumped their loyalty to him. Wilson and Callaghan had to balance their Cabinets politically. The art of managing fascinated both of them in different ways, but like other prime ministers they were not especially curious about what made their colleagues tick. Blair was a poor judge of who would flourish in government. At the beginning he was very keen on appointing as ministers those with experience of business. Few survived in the more brutal world of politics for very long.

Immediately after becoming prime minister, May appointed three controversial Brexit supporters to key Cabinet posts. Two of them were gone within days of May finally putting a Brexit deal to the Cabinet in the summer of 2018. At the beginning, Boris Johnson was made Foreign Secretary, David Davis was Brexit Secretary in a new department, and Liam Fox was given responsibility to pursue embryonic trade deals that would be ready when the UK left the EU. Nick Timothy outlined the thinking behind the appointments:

> I can remember when we were planning the reshuffle and we went through all the different options and the way she described what she wanted to do, I remember sort of summarising it as Brexit abroad, social reform at home. And that was actually really the intent of that reshuffle. So there were leading Brexit supporters who were given the foreign-facing department, so Boris went to the Foreign Office, David Davis was in the Brexit department, Liam went to trade, Priti Patel went to International Development and then people like Amber Rudd went to the Home Office and Damian Green to DWP [Department for Work and Pensions]. And that was the logic and it was partly because I think Theresa felt that it was important that the people responsible for developing the Brexit policy should be people who really get it and really mean it. And to be honest, there probably was a calculation too that compromise would need to happen at some point and that it would be important that the leading Brexiteers were party to those compromises and that they'd helped to make the decisions.[4]

Timothy's assessment is illuminating. Here is further confirmation of May's early underestimation of the Brexit task. She assumed that Cabinet ministers in non-Brexit departments would have the space to embark on historic reforms. They never got the chance. Brexit swallowed up all political energy.

Davis had qualities as a campaigning and rebellious backbencher, but had shown limited interest in governing. Yet May gave him the brief of setting up a new government department, while negotiating Brexit with the rest of the EU and being the main navigator in a tricky UK Parliament. This was a gargantuan set of tasks. Davis was ill-equipped to accomplish them. They demanded patience, a mastery of detail, a form of administrative genius to make the new department work, a deep understanding of how the EU functioned and a capacity to work with a wilfully insular prime minister. Davis did not possess the range, experience or interests to meet any of these tasks, and his appointment reflected May's poor judgement of people.

Crucially, May did not go out of her way to engage with the new Brexit department. She reconfigured Whitehall and then proceeded to take decisions with her small group in Number Ten, as she had done at the Home Office. One of the few friends of David Cameron to be offered a post in May's first government, George Bridges, was the Brexit Minister in the House of Lords:

> I found at times I was learning more from the *Financial Times*, in terms of its reporting of what was going on in Brexit, than I was from internal papers I was being shown. And I found at times I was being asked questions in the House of Lords, very searching questions, which, given a Member of the House of Lords could think that this is an important issue, we as government should have been able to answer. And the fact that I didn't – I was often skating on very thin

ice, or even trying to walk on water – I felt deeply troubled. Number
Ten felt very, very closed. Should I have banged on the door more
often? Every so often I did raise a flag saying: what is going on?
But it felt very closed and I have to say that was one of the major
frustrations that led me to resign.[5]

Bridges resigned after the 2017 election, one of many Brexit
ministers who walked away during the years of May's rule.

May was taking the decisions in Number Ten, becoming trapped
in stages. Having declared that the end of free movement was a
'red line', and having appointed senior Cabinet ministers with the
obvious potential to make her life hellish, the next key step towards
her incarceration was a special speech that she delivered on Brexit
at the start of the Conservative party conference in October 2016.
It was during the address that she pledged to trigger Article 50 by
the end of the following March. She made the pledge not because
she had a clear idea of the route ahead, once the Article had been
triggered – she was in the dark about that. Like so many previous
prime ministers in relation to Europe, May acted for reasons of
party management. Unlike previous prime ministers, she was
triggering a timetable from which there was no escape. Once Article
50 was triggered, the UK was scheduled to leave two years later.

Throughout the summer before the conference, Conservative
MPs had been popping up, asking why she had not already triggered
Article 50. They did so politely but firmly. In response to their
demands, May thought she had hit upon a balanced approach – a
third way. She rationalized to herself that she had not triggered
Article 50 immediately when she became prime minister, as some
of her MPs had wanted, but at the same time she was assuring
impatient backbenchers and the newspapers that they did not have
to wait beyond 31 March 2017 for Article 50 to be triggered.

Her third way was widely hailed again as a Thatcher-like act of assertion, by the Eurosceptic newspapers, but the opposite was closer to the truth. She could have waited longer and a delay would have been a display of courageous strength – a leader defying the foolish impatience of hard-liners in her party. Well ahead in the polls, May was in a strong enough position to resolve at least some of the internal differences within her Cabinet before starting the clock. An attempt at resolution would have been tough for her, but she could have prevailed at this early stage, the phase when she assumed she would be prime minister for a decade at least. Instead, the Article 50 clock was ticking, without May having any clear sense of how she would bring about her objectives of leaving the EU while retaining the benefits of the EU and keeping her Cabinet united.

As a nervy communicator, May's preferred form of address was the occasional set-piece speech on Brexit. There is much to be said for the long prime ministerial address, forcing a leader and advisers to put a case at length for what they are seeking to do. But speeches twice a year were not enough to persuade voters and MPs of May's chosen course. A Brexit prime minister needed to be communicating constantly and accessibly.

When she made her first big speech on Britain exiting the EU, at Lancaster House in January 2017, May was not clear what precise course she would take. Once again she outlined her 'red lines', to the delight of Brexiteers – no single market or customs union, and no ECJ rule – but even at her most defiant, there was ambiguity running through her careful words, in a speech that was still being written and rewritten the day before it was delivered. May spoke about the possibility of 'associate membership' of the customs union. The imprecise term papered over the cracks. She was smart enough to realize the potentially dark consequences of a complete break with the customs union and yet she needed to declare, and genuinely wanted to assert, that the UK would negotiate its own deals. Liam Fox and others had convinced her that countries were queuing up to sign new deals. Although May spoke vaguely about future customs relations, Nick Timothy insists that if there was ambiguity, it was tactical. As far as he was concerned, there would be no customs union of any form under May's leadership – and he helped to write the speech. His exchange, in a BBC interview, highlights the multi-layered calculations:

> It definitely wasn't the case that she was wrestling with the possibility of staying in the customs union. Theresa has an instinctive dislike of policy options being reduced to binary outcomes and so that was her way, I think, of trying to leave open the possibility of reducing the friction in trade between the UK and EU whilst still retaining the ability to pursue an independent trade policy.
>
> **When you say she has a reluctance of binary choice, is that another way of saying perhaps she has to be, or chooses to be, quite opaque at times in this Brexit journey?**
>
> Yeah, I think a bit of both. I mean I think it's partly she has had to deal in ambiguity because that's the reality of negotiating sometimes. It's also the reality of trying to hold together complicated coalitions of factions. So I think it's probably partly that, but it does genuinely also reflect a way of thinking, which is to not leap to a particular position because it appears like you have a choice between a and b policy options.[6]

Around the time May delivered her Lancaster House speech, many within her party, including David Davis, were advising her to call an early election. The reasons for this were twofold. Most obviously, the bigger majority that Davis and others assumed the Conservatives would secure would make the Brexit legislative path much more straightforward. Of equal importance, as far as Davis was concerned, was that an election in 2017 meant there would be no need for another one in the immediate aftermath of Brexit. Instead, the government could breathe freely until 2022.

May listened to Davis and gave no indication of what she herself was thinking. She was an enigma to her Cabinet ministers, but also quite possibly to herself. She had publicly declared there would be no early election and, if she had kept to that position, she would have been much stronger. Before the 2017 election, May was one of the more commanding prime ministers of recent times.

At least she was in every respect apart from one. She had secured no mandate of her own, and yet she was openly pursuing an agenda that was different from David Cameron's. She wanted to leave the Cameron era behind. She faced the same problem Gordon Brown had faced in 2007, but with one key difference: Brown wanted to move on from Blairism without losing the support of the pro-Blair newspapers; May felt no need to worship at the altar of Cameron's leadership or to be seen doing so.

The early election of 2017 had a Shakespearean quality. For several reasons, it was the most significant since 1979, and arguably had more historic consequences than Margaret Thatcher's first victory. Unusually, the two main parties campaigned on manifestos that celebrated the potential of the state, which had the possibility of making the management of Brexit even more of a nightmare.

May is not to be compared with King Lear or Macbeth in terms of character, but there are parallels with Shakespeare's tragic heroes. Shakespeare had a theory, widely held at the time he was writing, that if leaders break with the natural order, they unleash forces that turn on them. Macbeth killed Duncan to seize the crown and began a sequence that destroyed him. Lear broke up his estate and became homeless. May called an early election in order to win big, and almost lost everything. She had declared several times that she would not call an early election, and she meant it. A cautious leader in some respects, she was partly at ease with the natural order: she was a commanding figure, with several years before the next election was due. But in the end she succumbed and called an election. Expecting a sizeable majority to reinforce her dominance, she unleashed forces that turned upon her. The early election transformed the politics of Brexit under May, as she failed to secure the mandate she needed in order to deliver her version of Britain's withdrawal.

Voters in the UK tend to elect prime ministers who are partly actors, and although they (and much of the media) claim not to like the artifice of politics, they need the artistry. Margaret Thatcher was an actress. She was nowhere near as self-confident as her public stridency suggested. Tony Blair could have acted Macbeth and Hamlet simultaneously. David Cameron was an imitator of Blair – almost consciously an imitator, in the style of Rory Bremner. These prime ministers were all fascinated by their place on the political stage and how they appeared at any given time. May was not interested in politics as a performance. Her shyness and awkwardness were, in some respects, endearing qualities. Although self-absorbed, she was not mesmerized by the glamour and glitter of politics. But in spite of her reticence, her hired strategists made the election about her. When she was the star guest on BBC1's *The One Show*, in arguably the softest interview ever given, the toughest question to be asked of her and her husband was 'Who puts out the bins at night?' May looked fleetingly horrified at this question, as if she had been asked to reveal her whole hand in the Brexit negotiation. She was shy and uneasy throughout the contest and, in a twist of historic significance, lost her majority.

Her manifesto was crammed with radical ideas, including a strong defence of the state, and it dared to put forward a policy to raise much-needed money for elderly care. Yet at no point in the campaign did May expand on the radical spirit in her programme. Instead she repeated, in a machine-like manner, that her new government would be 'strong and stable', as if the daring manifesto had no connection with her robotic pitch. The specific policy for elderly care was misjudged and mistimed. Those who needed care would have to pay substantially more from the value of their property. The policy became known as the 'dementia tax' because, unlike patients in the tax-funded NHS, the sufferer would meet the costs. The details were flawed, but it was the manner of the announcement that was so bizarre. In the New Labour era – albeit in ways that were too cautious – Blair and Brown spent months, and sometimes years, clearing the ground before announcing a specific fund-raising policy. May introduced hers in the middle of an election campaign, without the capacity to explain. Instead, the Conservatives were forced to revise the policy in a panic, only for May to declare that 'nothing had changed'. This was an early example of her tendency to make statements at odds with what was happening around her. She lacked the language to manage and explain the eruption of wild events about her. There was no greater misreading than the introduction of a deeply contentious measure during a campaign.

After the election, May faced Brexit with no overall majority. Her fragility was unique. Normally when prime ministers lose their majorities, they cease to be prime minister. Ted Heath is one of the other prime ministers who called an early election, only to find forces turning on him. In February 1974 he lost his overall majority, tried to stay on, but was gone by the Monday. Although Harold Wilson then took over as a minority prime minister, he was seen to have won. In this case, May, despite having won almost as many votes as Margaret Thatcher at her peak, was seen to have lost. It was in this context that she navigated Brexit. Yet her Cabinet stuck by her. In the months that followed, she endured more resignations than any modern prime minister, although none immediately after the election. She was no longer strong enough to act with ruthlessness, in terms of purging another batch of perceived enemies. In a Shakespearean contrast, having sacked Osborne and Gove as she acquired the crown, May was now forced to remove her two close advisers, Nick Timothy and Fiona Hill. She was almost alone, comforted only by the presence of Damian Green as her unofficial deputy prime minister. Then she had to sack him, when he faced allegations of sexual harassment.

May was often described as 'weak'. The term is close to useless in casting light on a leader, but as far as it means anything, it points us in the wrong direction here. Politically she was in a much weaker position, but as a personality she remained the most stubborn prime minister to occupy Number Ten for many decades – arguably more so than Margaret Thatcher. Often Thatcher was more expedient than she seemed. May was a wilful leader in a weak position: an explosive combination.

She mistook being stubborn for integrity. If she committed publicly to an absurd immigration target, she felt she had to stick to it. If she said that the UK must leave the single market and, ultimately, the customs union, then the UK would have to depart at the assigned date. She was not a leader of guile. May's aims in relation to Brexit were more or less constant and publicly expressed.

Yet she could not escape her early 'red lines'. The hard-liners clung to them with exuberant hope, even when May came to realize that she could not wholly deliver the contradictory objectives. The post-election sequence – 'red lines' becoming blurred, a divided party and a hung parliament – was something of a roller-coaster ride. May was one of the least ostentatious prime ministers in modern history and yet, without a great ego or a hint of narcissism, her ride was spectacular.

Leadership is partly a conjuring trick. Leaders can get away with a huge amount, if they are popular and able to win elections. For most of the time they are in power, colleagues judge them largely on this limited basis. Jack Straw once sought to explain the lack of intense Cabinet scrutiny of Blair's conduct in the build-up to Iraq by pointing out that he had made a lot of correct calls. He had won a landslide for a second time. Thatcher won elections, so the Cabinet went along with her, even when some ministers had doubts about what she was doing.

While personally stubborn after the early election, May was in a weak position because she could perform no tricks. She had been seen to be useless during an election. She would not be allowed to contest another, and therefore the art of appearing to rule into the long-distant future had gone. Instead of being the new political fashion, May became immediately the frail leader. When she proclaimed her thoughts on Brexit, the ministerial and media instinct was to question what she was saying, rather than to pay homage. If she had returned from Brussels with her Brexit deal after a landslide election win, much of her party and the media would have hailed a negotiating triumph. We choose to see what we want to see. After the 2017 election, it was the default position of Conservative MPs and May's opponents to declare her efforts to have been a disaster.

May's moves towards her Brexit deal were made even more complex by her own growing insights into what Brexit meant for Ireland and the peace process. Soon after the election, she came to realize that her early Brexit assumptions had been too simplistic. In January 2017 the UK's EU ambassador, Sir Ivan Rogers, resigned, complaining in his resignation letter of 'muddled thinking' and 'ill-founded arguments'. He went on to give a series of illuminating talks on the muddle, touching on the fundamental misunderstanding of how the EU worked, the false hope of playing some members off against others, and the unjustified swagger. He left while May still assumed that the UK could have its cake and eat it. Rogers' concerns were unwelcome to her. At that point she did not want to hear that Brexit would be more complicated than she wanted it to be. By the early autumn of the same year May came to realize that some of what Rogers had been warning her about was urgently pertinent, and that the simplistic assertions of her Brexit Secretary, David Davis, were unreliable at best. In September 2017 the senior official at the Brexit Department, Olly Robbins, moved into Number Ten. This was a symbolic and practical move of great importance. Number Ten was taking control because Davis had failed to do so at his new department. After his resignation in the summer of 2018, Davis told journalists that a key moment for him was when May changed her approach to Brexit from his fantasy version. As ever with May, she said nothing to indicate any fresh thinking. That is partly because she was incapable of articulating what she was doing.

Even if May had won a landslide, she would still have faced mountainous problems in delivering an impossible 'have your cake and eat it' strategy. She would still have found the negotiations almost impossible, and she would still have had to make her speech in Florence at the end of September 2017 on the eve of the party-conference season. Her Florence speech was intended to secure a breakthrough with the EU, as she started to appreciate that the early flourishes of UK machismo were wholly unrealizable. Tonally, the speech was conciliatory and internationalist. May agreed that the UK would pay a Brexit bill – the sum conveniently unspecified. In interviews surrounding the speech she made clear what was implicit in it: she ached for a deal. The UK machismo around 'no deal' had gone. There was no reference to 'no deal' in the speech, only a warning about what such an outcome would mean.

The Florence speech was elegantly constructed. Reading it retrospectively makes sense of all that followed: May's determination to avoid no deal, a recognition that the Irish Question must be answered, and her intention to regain a degree of democratic control, as she saw it. For her, above all that meant ending free movement, the element of Brexit that she believed in with unyielding conviction.

It was only in December 2017, when she signed up to phase one of the Brexit deal, that her willingness to compromise became more tangible. Both the UK and the EU agreed that there must be no hard border separating Northern Ireland from the rest of Ireland. Barring a technological breakthrough that no one could confidently envisage in the short term at least, that meant the UK remaining in a customs union or Northern Ireland being treated differently from the rest of the UK. When this issue surfaced the following year, it seemed to come as a surprise to some hard-line Brexiteers, but although May remained evasive and vague, the words were there for them to read in the December document. Her hard-liners were not assiduous at reading them, or chose not to reflect on what the words implied. May did not encourage any such reflections. Instead she did what she always did and kept going, hoping the dissenters would be won round at the final moment.

May might have told Osborne to get to know the Conservative Party better, but she displayed a lack of understanding herself –

namely, the degree to which the parliamentary party had changed from being largely pragmatic and expedient to becoming an ideological crusade, one in which a purist view of accountability and sovereignty meant far more to them than loyalty to a national leadership.

———

In the summer of 2018 May outlined her proposed Brexit deal. Although based on the Florence speech and the December agreement, the proposals came as a shock to her Cabinet and a lot of her MPs. But the alarm that greeted what became known as her 'Chequers plan' was also a reflection of her closed, insular style of leadership. May did not explain her thinking in the months leading up to Chequers. There was no attempt to prepare the ground. With good cause, she knew she had to sideline David Davis, but she lacked the skills to make her hard-liners feel fragile and insecure. On the contrary, she returned them to their comfort zone. They flourished as evangelical dissenters and martyrs to their imprecise cause.

The contrast between May's approach and Tony Blair's, in relation to Iraq, is striking. Blair gave a constant running commentary as he sought to persuade his party, the media and the wider electorate to support his timid decision to back the Bush administration. He spoke at regular press conferences, gave many interviews and delivered a vast number of speeches. His call to back Bush was weak and misjudged, but he showed how a leader can persuade by the power of argument. He framed arguments about the weapons of mass destruction, and about his conviction that Iraqis would hail the imposition of democracy. In some respects May had a better case than Blair's shaky one, as she sought to deliver Brexit while protecting the Irish soft border and the supply chains for the manufacturing sector. Her Chequers plan, though deeply flawed, had points in its favour. But she never made the case for it, neither before nor after it was published. By the time MPs came to vote on whether or not to support Blair in relation to Iraq, he had succeeded in the art of persuasion, admittedly helped by the willingness of most Conservative MPs to back him before he had uttered a word. He knew little about Iraq or the wider region, but could deploy words to make a case. On Brexit, May could not – and did not – deploy words artfully.

She put her Brexit deal to the Cabinet at Chequers in July 2018. Ministers were told that if any of them resigned, they would lose their cars and would have to book a taxi home. Their mobile phones were confiscated. At the end of a long, hot summer's day, May issued a statement asserting that her proposals had the backing of her Cabinet. This was the beginning of another pattern. The vicar's daughter with a sense of moral duty uttered words that were true at the time, but were to prove to be untrue very quickly. The Chequers gathering was on the Friday. Davis and Johnson resigned the following Monday, and May responded as she always did: she replaced the two outgoing ministers and carried on as if nothing had happened.

En route to the torrid summer of 2018, May had largely stopped reading the newspapers, relying on a daily digest from media advisers. She was cocooned in Number Ten, dealing only with colleagues who served her. Prime ministers tend to enjoy elements of the role, even when they appear to be under impossible pressure. With the exception of Wilson, none have left voluntarily. May flourished when faced with long hours of work. She had got to the top, when so many others had not. She looked better than when she was twenty years younger – slimmer and more coiffured. This is all part of a pattern of leadership: prime ministers tend to look good until they leave, and then they very quickly show signs of decline. In power, the adrenaline fires them up. A diabetic who had to inject insulin, May was not short of energy-enhancing adrenaline, but she was attempting the impossible.

On one level, her Chequers plan was a work of art in its attempt to bind together conflicting and contradictory forces. But May had done nowhere near enough between September 2017 and July 2018 to clear the ground. Perhaps there could be no clearing of the ground, given the circumstances, and her dogged, insular focus was the only option available. We will never know. What we do know is that May began to lose control – or even more control – after her day-long Cabinet meeting at Chequers in July 2018.

The final deal that May and her senior negotiators secured with the EU was partly based on Chequers, but inevitably some of her more contorted proposals were dropped. Instead of guaranteeing a soft border in Ireland, through impossibly complex trading arrangements, there would be a so-called 'backstop', to come into effect if no other solution was found during the transition. The UK would remain in a customs union until such a solution was found. There could be no unilateral withdrawal from this arrangement, or else it would not be a backstop. Again the proposition arose directly from the phase-one agreement the previous December, when both sides were committed to the soft border. As long as May secured an end to free movement, she was ready to accept other compromises. Again the compromises came as an apparent shock to her Cabinet and MPs, when she unveiled the deal in November 2018.

The dramas that erupted after May had published her deal highlighted once again her inability to persuade, her failure to read the political stage and her unique detached wilfulness. Through the months that followed she was both the most fragile of modern prime ministers and yet the most pivotal. She continued to make the key decisions, often without much consultation, that would shape her country's history. Yet she could have fallen at any point, and at one stage in the spring of 2019 offered to resign under certain circumstances. In true May tradition, she made the offer and then carried on as if nothing had happened.

The immediate aftermath of the Cabinet meeting that discussed her Brexit deal for the first time in November 2018 was typical. May gave a statement declaring that the Cabinet had supported the deal. The words were true at the time, but as she must have known as she delivered them, they would not be true for more than a few hours. The following morning the Brexit Minister, Dominic Raab, resigned, along with several other ministers. May had become even more of an unreliable narrator. Shortly after Raab's resignation, she gave a statement to the Commons on her deal. For an hour not a single MP had a good word to say about it. May might have thought, at the end of such a draining session, one that followed ministerial resignations, that her deal was doomed. Wilson, Blair, Brown and Cameron would have been in a state of neurotic hyperactivity after such a sequence, working out what the hell to do next, contemplating a thousand different ploys that might change the situation.

May was quite different. Instead, she acted as she always did – as if the volcanic eruptions were separate from her, and from what she was doing. She appointed a new Brexit Secretary and made other replacements. Then she conducted a bizarre nationwide tour to put the case for her deal, as if she were fighting a general election. Those warning May that her deal would be defeated in the Commons included the chair of the 1922 Committee, Sir Graham Brady. He was one of the few politicians May listened to and liked. It was his job to convey the views of backbenchers. On the several occasions when Brady warned her about a terrible defeat over her deal, May gave nothing away. She looked at him and then moved on to other issues.[7]

May was a sheltered prime minister, hearing only what she wanted to hear. In discussions with a small number of advisers, she calculated that her threat of no Brexit, or no deal, would bludgeon MPs into backing her deal. She devised no memorable phrases to make her deal accessibly appealing. Indeed, her deal was spoken of as if it were an abstract art form, rather than a dense, detailed document. Yet in spite of the density of the Withdrawal Agreement itself, it proved to be another evasive exercise in kicking the can down the road. The Irish Question was still to be resolved. The much thornier issue of the UK's future relationship with the EU was not addressed. May was asking MPs to take the historic decision to leave the EU without having a clue as to what would happen next.

Inevitably, she pulled the vote on her deal the day it was due to be held in December. When the vote eventually did take place the following month, her deal was defeated by a historic majority of 230 votes. Her senior advisers looked on in alarm when the vote was declared in the Commons. The margin of defeat was higher than any of them had anticipated. May returned to Number Ten and carried on as if nothing much had happened, once again behaving as though she was separate from such seismic events.

After the vote, May said she would reach out in order to get parliamentary approval. She did not mean it. Her sole focus was to persuade her Brexit hard-liners and the Democratic Unionist Party (DUP) to back her. She hoped also to secure the support of some Labour MPs, but she was not going to pivot significantly. She had never done so in her career, and she did not consider doing so now. During the leadership contest back in 2016 the former chancellor, Ken Clarke, had been recorded, when he was off air, describing May as a 'bloody difficult woman'. He meant that she was obstinate to the point of destructiveness at times. She clung to her deal, whatever the external circumstances.

In two more votes she failed to win the support of the DUP or a sufficient number of her hard-liners. Only a few Labour MPs were gullible enough to back her, not least after a televised statement in which May placed herself on the side of 'the people' against Parliament. The misjudged TV statement, delivered in March 2019 on the eve of another vote on her deal, was the most vivid example of her inability to read the rhythms of politics. She needed to woo MPs and she attacked them live on TV.

To be defeated three times, on the most significant proposition since the Second World War, normally would – and should – trigger a prime ministerial resignation. But May led in a weak parliament of largely half-formed politicians. Her internal opponents enjoyed the limelight, appearing on the media so often they appeared to be numerically stronger than they were. But they were hopeless strategists, not having had to think strategically very often in the past, and unable to do so when their moment came. Crucially, her critics mistimed their vote of confidence on May, holding it in December when her deal had not been put to the vote, and when she was evidently regarded as the least-bad option to most Conservative MPs. May won the vote of confidence – another event that would have traumatized most prime ministers, but one she characteristically treated as if it was just another drama that had little to do with her. In theory, Conservative MPs had no formal means of removing her for another twelve months – she was, briefly, the least secure and most secure prime minister of modern times.

Like all prime ministers, May clung to power for much longer than the surrounding political and media frenzy suggested was possible, but her approach to survival was unique. Most prime ministers who know they are in deep trouble become obsessed by the political noise erupting around them. They scheme and then watch obsessively the consequences of their manoeuvrings. In contrast, May stood apart from the noise as if she was separate from it. The detachment was breathtaking, because her fate was to become the Brexit prime minister, the most darkly demanding destiny of any post-war prime minister.

To take one emblematic example, during Prime Minister's Questions on the day her MPs held a confidence vote on her leadership in December 2018, the Liberal Democrat leader, Vince Cable, asked her a mischievous question. Cable wondered whether she preferred her own MPs condemning her or the entire House of Commons doing so, in a vote of confidence in her government. Characteristically, May did not recognize mischief, and neither could she respond to provocative questions with wit. She responded to Cable by pointing out, in a matter-of-fact way, that there was a vote of confidence in her leadership taking place amongst Conservative MPs that day. It was as if she was talking about items on a shopping list – somebody else's shopping list. She then sat down and awaited the next question on another issue. For May, detachment of this kind was constant, to such an extent that the disconnect between her public words and what was happening around her became stark.

Context partly determines the fate of leaders, and May faced the toughest set of tasks of any modern prime minister. Yet her approach to leadership made the demands more mountainous. Tellingly, she became the third modern prime minister, following Blair and Cameron, to announce her departure from Number Ten in advance – the most humiliating of pledges. The announcement is a symptom of disorder and fuels the sense of crisis, rather than alleviating it. Immediately after May told MPs she would resign if they backed her Withdrawal Agreement in March 2019, potential successors of unproven mettle made their moves. None of them were remotely qualified. Sajid Javid had been Home Secretary for a few months. Jeremy Hunt was a similarly short-serving Foreign Secretary. Boris Johnson had his chance at the Foreign Office and blew it. Others were measured by their views on Brexit, as if the fact that Penny Mordaunt had been equivocal about May's Brexit deal meant she was ready for the epic demands of leadership. Thatcher had big figures breathing down her neck, ready to lead. Blair had one big figure breathing down his. May had none.

Looking back, as a Labour politician responsible for his party's economic policy from 1992, Gordon Brown faced the most persistent set of external challenges. The markets and the media in the UK set a much higher bar for Labour, in relation to the economy. Edward Heath had to deal with the consequences of the quadrupling of oil prices, a seismic event over which he had no control. In 1974 Harold Wilson inherited raging inflation and industrial chaos. James Callaghan took over in 1976 with none of those challenges remotely resolved. Yet, by some distance, May faced the biggest mountain of the lot. Brexit would have challenged a leader of titanic qualities. When she first became prime minister she inherited a tiny majority of fifteen, nowhere near big enough to avoid parliamentary trouble. After her 2017 election she had no majority at all, although that was her fault for the way she had conducted the campaign.

There are some myths about May's misjudgements. From her exhausted chief whip, Julian Smith, to many Labour MPs, she was unfairly accused of failing to reach out to other parties after the general election. Smith told the BBC that a softer Brexit was inevitable after the election.[8] Many others have observed it was obvious, after the election, that May's approach to Brexit was doomed in a hung parliament, and as a result she should have engaged formally with Labour in the summer of 2017, as she finally did in April 2019 when, in theory, the UK was about to leave the EU.

The accusation of self-interested tribalism fits the stereotype that May could only think of her party and never beyond its fractious boundaries. In truth, she was trapped after the election. If she had opened talks with Jeremy Corbyn in the aftermath of what, for her, had been a terrible campaign – one in which Corbyn had fared better than most assumed – and she had performed much worse, she would have been removed.

Her internal Cabinet critics were strategically inept and, for all their macho posturing, dreaded taking responsibility for Brexit. Even so, they would not have allowed May to give Corbyn even more credibility than he had already acquired after the election, by being consulted over Brexit. That option was not available to her. The likes of Johnson, Davis and others, who had contemplated telling May that she had to resign on the night of the election, would have acted to remove her.

Instead of leading with Labour in the new hung parliament, she behaved with a degree of political courage by sidelining Davis in his Brexit department, fantasizing about a deal that the EU would never have agreed to. In private meetings she also dared to challenge the likes of Jacob Rees-Mogg on the seriousness of the Irish Question. Indeed, it is hard to sustain the common thesis that May put her party before the national interest, when much of her party was incandescent with rage over her Withdrawal Agreement. If May had the wit of Wilson or Blair, she would have made a virtue of the internal defiance by joking that if she had put her party first, it did not seem to be working. But May never joked, at least not spontaneously. Wit is an important weapon for leaders. May did not, or could not, deploy humour.

Looking back, that first Cabinet points to the tragedy of May's premiership. Nick Timothy's explanation of the appointments highlights an early reforming zeal that was never to be realized. May hoped that the likes of Amber Rudd, Damian Green and Greg Clark might assist her and her senior advisers to move the party on from Thatcherism. Indeed, nothing irritates Timothy more than reading commentators or hearing broadcasters observe, as if a matter of fact, that May's leadership marked a move to the right after Cameron and Osborne. Timothy had planned for a domestic agenda that was to the left of what had preceded it. Without Brexit, May might have been a genuine modernizer, the first 'one nation' Tory leader since Heath. Instead, she was doomed to become the Brexit prime minister. By the time the UK was supposed to have left the EU in March 2019, voters were more divided than when the referendum was held, and her party was in turmoil. Brexit in a hung parliament demanded a leader of imagination, empathy, tenacity, guile and mesmeric persuasive gifts. Instead it was Theresa May, emerging from the relative shelter of the Home Office: shy, stubborn, detached and inflexibly wilful.

In some respects, May was the dullest of modern prime ministers, and yet her premiership was by some margin the closest to an impossibly gripping thriller. During her misjudged early election, May told an interviewer that her most daring venture had been to run through a wheat field. Yet as prime minister, she played the starring role in the political equivalent to a James Bond film, confronting many villains (mainly in her own Cabinet and parliamentary party), racing around European capitals, sometimes flying out suddenly in the middle of the night. All the while, no one knew how the drama would end – May became utterly compelling, in spite of herself.

Finally, May ran out of road. She tried to revive her deal a fourth time, presenting a Withdrawal Bill aimed at wooing Labour MPs with various imprecise concessions that may or may not have taken effect if her bill was passed. Her MPs were alarmed at the concessions, while Labour MPs were unimpressed by the tentative nature of her offer to them. The bill was doomed and so was she. May announced her resignation tearfully on Friday 24 May 2019, stressing the need for compromise and a parliamentary solution to Brexit. If those themes had been her focus when she was politically strong, she might have been Prime Minister for longer. Instead, at the beginning, she had sought to please her hardliners. Three years later she was making her resignation statement from more or less the same spot outside Number Ten where Cameron had announced his departure. Within a day or so, more than ten Conservatives had expressed a passionate interest in replacing her. So many ached still to wear the thorny crown.

CONCLUSION

There is a leadership crisis in the UK. Leaders, or potential leaders, seek to rule in an era when right-wing populists are flourishing, globalization generates deep insecurities and Brexit presents a seemingly never-ending set of explosive demands. Yet none appear to possess the communication skills, the depth, guile, ability to manage parties and the capacity to espouse credible policies that chime with values or deeply held convictions. Most of those contemplating putting themselves forward show a shortage of qualifications, though no lack of self-confidence. A successful TV interview, well received on Twitter, is enough to get some politicians wondering whether they can be the next prime minister. The demands of leadership are high. The bar is set low.

The decline in the quality of potential leaders can be traced in the leadership contests of the modern era. In 1975 the former Cabinet minister Margaret Thatcher took on the former prime minister, Edward Heath. Willie Whitelaw, another weighty former Cabinet minister, was seen as a possible leader at the time and entered the contest in a later round. The following year, when Harold Wilson resigned, the candidates in the leadership contest included James Callaghan, Michael Foot, Roy Jenkins, Anthony Crosland, Denis Healey and Tony Benn, all mighty figures in their different ways. Fast-forward to the summer of 2019 and those contemplating becoming a candidate to be the next prime minister included Esther McVey, Andrea Leadsom, Sajid Javid, Jeremy Hunt, Boris Johnson and Dominic Raab. Whatever the qualities of these individuals, even their most ardent admirers would not claim that they possessed the depth, conviction and experience of those engaged in Tory and Labour battles during 1975 and 1976.

Recent Labour contests also descended to levels of banality that would have horrified the Labour candidates in 1976. In 2015, after Labour's defeat at the general election, vacuous phrases such as 'We turned the page back… now it's time to turn the page forward' were prominent – an attempt to disguise ideological confusion and insecurity. As candidates agonized over whether to accept media claims that over-spending by the last Labour government had been a cause of the financial crash of 2008, Jeremy Corbyn entered the fray and declared, without qualification, that the Labour government had not spent enough. He won a landslide.

Corbyn did more to change politics than any leader of the Opposition in modern times. He created a mass-membership party, at a time when membership of parties is in alarming decline. He moved his party to the left and, in doing so, widened the scope of the national political debate. Before Corbyn became Labour leader, *Newsnight* would often invite onto the programme a panel of commentators, all agreeing that Labour was doomed until it broadly endorsed George Osborne's economic policies. After the rise of Corbyn, a range of voices from the left became part of the national debate. In depriving Theresa May of her majority in the 2017 election, Corbyn also transformed the dynamics of Brexit and challenged assumptions, in parts of his party and the media, that if Labour moved to the left it would be slaughtered.

These were significant achievements. Even so, Corbyn never wanted to be leader during his decades as a backbench MP, and it showed when he soared to the top. Of all the eruptions in British politics – Brexit, the dominance of the SNP in Scotland, a rare peacetime coalition – Corbyn's rise from backbench MP to leader is the most remarkable. He had few qualifications for leadership. Although he could command huge, doting audiences, he was not a political teacher, rarely explaining why he espoused various policy positions. He was not greatly interested in policy detail, or in how to translate policies into accessible messages. He was more pragmatic than caricatures of him allowed, especially in relation to Brexit, and yet he contrived to make expediency seem like a weak and pathetic 'fudge'. He was not interested in managing colleagues, or in spending every waking hour facing the ceaseless demands of leadership. Often Corbyn opted for invisibility or silence as issues erupted around him. He was only regularly seen on national TV leaving his house, looking furious at the number of journalists and cameras gathered outside. The fury was understandable and was not typical of his emollient personality. But the art of leadership is to hide one's annoyance in such weird situations. The most effective leaders are partly artists.

Oddly, as the quality of leaders and potential leaders declined, the focus on them intensified. The door-stepping of Corbyn on a regular basis was one example of the new intensity. British politics has a presidential culture, without a president. The disjunction adds to the pressures on party leaders. Unlike presidents, or potential presidents, they have to lead and manage their parties. Their power is dependent on their parties and, if they become prime minister, they are accountable to Parliament, too. Since Thatcher – the era of the Iron Lady who was not for turning –

there is a huge pressure on prime ministers to appear presidential, in command of all situations, when the constraints are such that they cannot be.

Indeed, what is most striking about modern prime ministers is not how strong they are, but how weak. Or at least most of them felt weak and tormented a lot of the time. With the partial exception of Margaret Thatcher, they agonized over the limits of their power. 'What do we do now?', 'How do we get out of this?', 'How can the BBC be leading with that story?', 'We're screwed' – these are the panic-stricken questions and proclamations that punctuate prime ministerial lives.

There is a dangerous, darkly comical mismatch between widely held perceptions of mightily arrogant prime ministers, loftily indifferent to voters' lives, and the sense of toiling fragility at the summit of supposed power. The near-impotent toil is a gift for political outsiders. The likes of Nigel Farage can cry, 'Betrayal' from the safety of the campaign trail. Yet, to follow the Farage example, it was not that Theresa May sought to let down his ardent Brexit-supporting followers; indeed, she worked sleeplessly to deliver for them. There were many other reasons why Brexit did not take the shape that Farage claimed to seek.

This prevailing mood of fearful paralysis was unavoidable for the modern prime ministers who led in hung parliaments or with tiny majorities. From 1974 to 1979 Harold Wilson and Jim Callaghan manoeuvred endlessly to keep their fragile administrations in place, losing key votes, viewing colleagues with justified wariness. John Major lost his small majority by the end of his rule, twisting and turning to secure parliamentary support for the Maastricht Treaty and other policies – a prime ministerial trauma that was a mere walk in the park, compared with the Brexit saga that was to follow.

When Theresa May called an early election and lost her majority, she faced a period of near-impotence.

Even those prime ministers with big majorities are alert to the precariousness of their position. Soon after winning a landslide in 1966, Harold Wilson saw enemies all around him. The seemingly self-confident Margaret Thatcher did not always feel secure. In his brilliant memoir *Cold Cream*, Thatcher's former adviser Ferdinand Mount chronicles her fears about calling an election in June 1983. Nervily she put the case for a postponement to her advisers. She did not want to face the risk of an election. She panicked again in 1987, falling out with the likes of her close ally Norman Tebbit in her alarm at the way the campaign was going. Tony Blair, with his landslide majorities, had been so used to losing elections in the 1980s that he had a similar fear of losing. 'The Tories are only sleeping… they'll be back,' he warned in his conference speech in 1998, when Labour was even further ahead in the polls than Thatcher was in 1983 and 1987. But Blair always worried that it would take very little for Middle England to return to the Conservatives. That fear weighed heavily on one of his prime ministerial shoulders; the intense pressure from Gordon Brown weighed on the other.

Thatcher's faith in the poll tax was partly driven by a fear of the impact of big rises in local rates, the system in place before the poll tax. Properties were being re-valued at the time and, in many Conservative-held seats, values had soared. Thatcher's solution was to scrap the property-based tax, assuming that the measure would be popular. Blair's support for the war in Iraq was based partly on a sense that his coalition of support would collapse if he did not support the United States. David Cameron's pledge to hold a referendum on the UK's membership of the EU stemmed from a fear of defections from his party to UKIP; the referendum was not a pledge made with an Etonian swagger. Fear, rather than arrogance, forms the backdrop to much policy-making. Prime ministers might affect crusading evangelism, but quite often this is an attempt to disguise timid insecurity.

In all cases, democracy constrains. Arguably it constrains too much, inadvertently giving vast amounts of space to the posturing 'strong leader' from the outside. The impact of local elections, by-elections, the prospect of a looming general election and the composition of the Commons all play their part in what a prime minister feels he or she can do. In some cases a single by-election can trigger a fall. The Conservatives' defeat in the Eastbourne by-election in October 1990 played a significant part in the quickly forming avalanche that propelled Thatcher from power a month later. Modern prime ministers also led in an era of never-ending opinion polls and the rise of the focus group. They might have been seen as out of touch but, if anything, they were too in touch with the public mood. They could be in touch to the point of paralysis.

Many in the media would argue that it is their job to hold power to account. They are less effective at highlighting the limits of power, and are also fickle in their levels of scrutiny. Read most columnists on Theresa May before the early election in 2017 and, when she was riding high in the polls, there was much talk of the 'May era' and even 'May-ism'. When she leapt out of fashion after the election, she became a disaster area. In the early years of the Lib-Con coalition much of the media hailed two parties working together to 'save the country'. In reality, decisions were being taken that were virtually to kill off the Liberal Democrats and make Cameron a fatal advocate when he called the 2016 Brexit referendum.

There are several reasons why the weightiness of actual or potential leaders has declined, at least in the UK Parliament.

Scotland has produced some formidable leaders, including Nicola Sturgeon and, although untested by power, Ruth Davidson, the leader of the Scottish Conservatives. The fashion when selecting candidates for the Westminster Parliament is on 'localism'. Candidates are more likely to be selected if they are from the constituency. For some trade unionists or councillors, becoming a Labour candidate is sometimes a reward for long service. There are equivalent rewards for local Conservatives. Any attempt to 'impose' a candidate is frowned upon, to the point where it is almost impossible for figures without credible local connections to become candidates in safe seats. The fashion might be admirable in some respects, but local parties are selecting candidates who might become ministers or even prime ministers. The ability to lead, or to represent their party at a national level, is rarely a criterion.

Probably some big figures are also deterred by the level of scrutiny in modern politics, preferring better-paid jobs in the City, the legal profession or the media. From Edward Heath to Roy Jenkins, Denis Healey and Tony Benn, the wartime generation ached to go into politics and to stay in politics, even when they were no longer in government.

Perhaps some are also deterred by the constraints of power. An owner of a big business will have more power than some ministers. Prime ministers can wield considerable power, but they must keep a party on board; win elections with majorities, or face a nightmare in a hung parliament; respond to a relentless around-the-clock media and social media; and, accept that some powers are now devolved to other elected bodies or quangos. They do not even have the power to set interest rates any more, although they are probably relieved that those decisions lie with the Bank of England. Everywhere there are obstacles – perhaps constraints that are necessary, but often frustrating for leaders wanting to lead.

No prime minister can ever relax on the domestic front, and most of the time prime ministers are miserable. Trips abroad are different. This is when power can become a pleasure – in locations where there is uncritical recognition of a prime minister's apparent greatness. The consequences of the red-carpet treatment can be dangerous. Only Heath and, to some extent, Wilson turned away from the intoxicating draw of a visit to a president in the US. Margaret Thatcher's genuinely warm and close relationship with President Reagan was a boost to her image in the UK and beyond. There she was a powerful world leader, with the US president hailing her with gushing sincerity. Her rapport with a US president had a big impact on the youthful Blair, observing vote-losing Labour leaders being given short shrift in the US. But even with Thatcher, the 'special relationship' was limited. At the start of the Falklands War, Reagan was ambiguous, not rushing to support his close ally, on whom he doted. Reagan was also friendly with the Argentinian junta that had become Thatcher's enemy. When the US attacked Grenada in October 1983 – more than a year after the two leaders' tensions over the Falklands – Reagan did not inform Thatcher in advance. She needed him much more than he needed her.

Blair's determination to show that he could work as closely with a Republican president as he had with President Clinton was the starting point for his moves towards the darkness of Iraq. Brown ached to be seen with Obama, whenever the opportunity arose, and yet there was little evidence that Obama yearned to spend too much time with Brown. Cameron was similarly smitten, regarding Obama's speech in London against Brexit, in the build-up to the 2016 referendum, as a great coup at the time. The evidence suggests that Obama's intervention boosted the Brexit campaign. Yet still the modern prime ministers could not resist the lure. May wooed President Trump, even though he was publicly dismissive of her Brexit negotiations and praised her more exuberant rival, Boris Johnson. Modern prime ministers liked to be seen as standing 'shoulder-to-shoulder' with US presidents. The glittering vindication of their place in the world compensated for the frenetic grind of making sense of their troubled leaderships in the UK. Their search for the glamour of power distorted UK foreign policy, often for the worse.

———

Vanity and ego play their part in the characters of modern prime ministers. This is unsurprising. Who could not be flattered by the attention and constant sense of historic significance that applies to their roles? In all cases there was also a sense of public duty and conviction. The essence of democracy is to fume about, or support, the consequences of prime ministerial conduct, but whatever our views on the individuals, modern prime ministers were motivated by a desire to make changes for the better.

In Wilson's much-derided final phase of leadership he won a referendum on Europe and introduced two substantial measures, the Sex Discrimination Act of 1975 and the Race Relations Act of 1976, enhancing work opportunities for women and ethnic minorities. Heath guided the UK into Europe in the first place, and displayed a dogged integrity in his tortuous negotiations with the trade unions. Callaghan left office with even greater levels of economic turmoil than Heath and Wilson, but he had to some extent controlled raging inflation. He had hopes of doing much more, but had no political space in which to act. Thatcher was the great game-changer, putting her radical instincts into effect, finding language to make them accessible and appealing. The UK in 1990 was unrecognizably different from the country in 1979 when she became prime minister – no wonder being forced out was such a blow for her, from which she did not recover. John Major was being sincere when he declared that he wanted to lead a country more at ease with itself. Subsequently he accepted that he failed in his mission, but the purpose was there. Blair and Brown introduced a mountain of life-enhancing changes, even if they sought to be far less radical from the left than Thatcher had been from the right. Cameron assumed, sincerely, that he was coming to the UK's rescue in forming a coalition in 2010. Although his government reformed speedily, May had more radical ambition than Cameron to make a leap away from Thatcherism, even if the precariously held convictions were acquired from her senior advisers. She was stifled by Brexit, but even she rationalized a historic purpose in her attempts to deliver the outcome of the 2016 referendum. I make this point not to imply preposterously that modern prime ministers were all saintly figures. The consequences of some of their policies and political outlooks were dire. There will always be intense disagreement about which were especially calamitous and which were beneficial, a timeless debate that is the essence of politics. I highlight the common desire to do good amongst this diverse group of flawed, often beleaguered prime ministers because the anti-politics mood is dangerously intense, fuelled by the lazy assumption that elected prime ministers were wilfully malevolent and indifferent to voters' concerns.

A colleague suggested that I compile a league table of modern prime ministers and put the unexpected at the top, in order to whip up a controversy or two. I could easily have done so, and with a hint of conviction. For their depth, range and seriousness of purpose, I could have put Edward Heath and Gordon Brown at the top. As reinforcement against the deliberately provoked mockery that would have followed, I would have cited Heath's epic moves to secure the UK's place in what was then the Common Market, and Brown's formidable response to the financial crash in 2008.

Such an act of provocation highlights the absurdity of the prime ministerial league table. There is a strong case for that unlikely duo, but they evidently lacked several of the qualifications for the impossible task of leadership and were prime ministers only fleetingly. The truth is that the modern prime ministers were all so different that it is, in some senses, remarkable they ended up in the same job.

They all passionately wanted to end up there. Modern prime ministers have one common quality: a ruthless hunger for the top job. They acquire the focused determination to become leader at different points in their careers, but at one stage or another they cast aside much else in life to win the leadership. For Wilson, Heath, Callaghan, Brown and May, ambition came early. Thatcher wanted to become leader only a few months before she actually did so, but once she had decided, she acted with hyper-energetic courage, challenging her old boss, Heath. John Major knew he was one of Thatcher's favourites and yet he was to the left of her. When she fell, he was ruthlessly ready to pitch for support across the broad church of his party. Blair knew that Brown wanted to be leader more than him and yet, when the opportunity arose, Blair took it with resolute focus. Brown also got there in the end because he wanted it far more than his weak-kneed colleagues of fleeting shallow ambition. Cameron was more or less ready when the time came, self-confident in his steely exuberance. May had done the hard grind of endless constituency visits while keeping a low profile on Brexit. When Cameron fell, she had done the work to win a leadership contest.

Perhaps the 2017 election will prove to be a turning point for future prime ministers. For the first time, once-powerful newspapers raged against a Labour leader and seemed to have no impact. After the election, Jeremy Corbyn was able to joke that he hoped the *Daily Mail* would attack him even more next time. Labour had performed far better than the commentariat had assumed or predicted. In that election, both Corbyn and May focused partly on the role of the state – the great taboo after Thatcher waved her wand and virtually silenced the pivotal debate. The Conservative manifesto was tonally contradictory, hailing backward-looking fox-hunting in one section and then, in a modernizing leap, articulating the 'good the state can do' in another. It advocated an industrial strategy and interventions in some markets. Labour's manifesto was closer to the programmes of social democrats in northern Europe, implying that the state could be a benevolent force, with its proposed national education service and incremental nationalizations.

In the outcome of the 2017 election it felt as if the rules that had governed British politics for decades were changing once again. Voters were stirring, and had been since the 2008 crash. And then in the elections for the European Parliament in May 2019 voters punished both the Conservative and Labour parties in relation to Brexit. The Brexit Party soared. The Liberal Democrats returned to the fray. The Green Party made waves. The SNP topped the poll in Scotland. The 2017 general election was an affirmation of the two-party system. By 2019, the two bigger UK parties were in Brexit-related crisis. There were no patterns in unruly times. There had been plenty of signs: the inconclusive 2010 election, the rare peacetime coalition, the stormy referendum in Scotland

and, of course, the Brexit referendum. There were more signs to come, with new parties being formed and – in the case of the Brexit Party – becoming popular immediately in the summer of 2019. Leaders are slow to respond to changing times, instinctively using the past as their guide, even when all the evidence suggests that the assumptions of the past no longer apply. Most of them come up against mountainous obstacles. Rising to the very top, they feel special. They are part of a small group that has realized their ambition to lead. Then the Shakespearean themes take hold, and the prime ministers struggle with what they soon discover to be the wretched powerlessness of power.

—

NOTES

1 Harold Wilson

1   Ben Pimlott, *Harold Wilson*, HarperCollins, 1993

2   Labour won 301 seats, four more than the Conservatives. The Conservatives won 37.9 per cent of the vote compared to Labour's 37.2 per cent.

3   Tony Benn, *Against the Tide: Diaries, 1973–77*, Hutchinson, 1989, p.114

4   Roy Jenkins, *A Life at the Centre*, Macmillan, 1991, p.365

5   Bernard Donoughue, *The Heat of the Kitchen*, Politico's Publishing, 2003

6   See the following chapter on Edward Heath.

7   See the David Cameron chapter. This was a highly significant difference with Wilson. Cameron hoped to avoid an internal split, but that put much greater weight on his 'renegotiation' with the EU.

8   Healey never did change his mind and remained a critic of Wilson for the rest of his life. He much preferred working with Jim Callaghan, Wilson's successor. Michael Foot was similar, being curiously scathing for a writer and politician capable of insightful and counter-intuitive empathy. Other Cabinet ministers came to realize Wilson's formidable achievements in what was often a dark context.

9   Barbara Castle, interview with the author, *New Statesman*, February 2000; available online. By then Castle was almost blind

and yet was exuberant in her energetic and politically engaged mischievousness. Wilson liked and admired her. He also managed her smartly. I interviewed Castle during New Labour's first term, when Tony Blair was walking on water. She was also perceptive about the limitations of Blair's political project.

10 The story is related in Joe Haines' compelling memoir, *Glimmers of Twilight*, Politico's, 2003. The recollections of Haines and Donoughue in their various books and diaries are vivid, brilliantly written and almost Shakespearean in their tragicomic evocations.

11 Haines writes that Marcia Williams claimed to have had a brief affair with Wilson in the 1950s. She denied the affair and remained friends with Wilson's wife, Mary, after Wilson died.

12 Bernard Donoughue writes in *The Heat of the Kitchen* that Marcia Williams was another who told him on the eve of the February 1974 election that she did not expect, or want, Wilson to win. She wanted him away from the stressful exhaustion of the political stage. For her, Wilson was a human being as well as an aspirant prime minister. She had seen a human being at the end of his tether.

13 Harold Wilson, *Memoirs: The Making of a Prime Minister*, Michael Joseph, 1986, p.34

14 A fear of devaluation partly explained Gordon Brown's tentative support for the single currency when he was shadow chancellor up until the 1997 election. Independence of the Bank of England, implemented in the immediate aftermath of the 1997 election, addressed his fear and, under the influence of his senior adviser, Ed Balls, Brown became an opponent of the UK joining the euro.

15 The Conservative-supporting newspapers reverted to type, but arguably more shocking was the way in which the BBC joined in the bullying of Wilson – an early example of the BBC feeling compelled to join the political fashions of the time, as defined by the newspapers. This was not bias of a partisan nature, but bias in favour of what was fashionable. The documentary *Yesterday's Men*, broadcast soon after the 1970 election, is the most vivid example. It portrayed Wilson and much of his frontbench team as a bunch

of losers who were out of touch with the times. This was the team planning to fight the next election. Wilson was justifiably furious.

16 Speech at a May Day rally in London, 4 May 1969

17 He did so with the author in 2006 at a hotel in Nottingham during a prime ministerial trip to the city. I listed the large number of aspirant leaders in Wilson's Cabinets, compared to the one who had wanted Blair's job from the beginning. For understandable reasons, he agreed with me that there were advantages in having six or seven rivals, all formidable in their different ways and yet all of them cancelling each other out. Brown was more determinedly wilful than Wilson's ambitious Cabinet ministers.

18 Tony Benn, *Against the Tide: Diaries*, p.397

19 Giles Radice's book *Friends and Rivals* (Little, Brown, 2002) brilliantly shows how Roy Jenkins, Denis Healey and Tony Crosland, and their respective supporters, could not agree on which of the trio should become the candidate for Labour's social-democratic wing. In the 1976 leadership contest they all stood, and all almost certainly would have done if Wilson had left earlier.

20 Tony Benn, *Against the Tide*, p.394

21 Hansard, 24 May 1995

22 Roy Jenkins' *A Life at the Centre* has several unexpectedly flattering references to Wilson's leadership, as well as quite a few critical ones. Away from the intensity of the internal party battles, Jenkins saw how impossible it all must have been for a leader. Perhaps his own fraught leadership of the SDP lent additional personal perspective.

2 Edward Heath

1 Edward Heath, *The Course of My Life*, Hodder & Stoughton, 1998, p.31

2 Ibid., p.179

3 Ibid., p.194

4 In a powerful speech in November 2018 Gordon Brown compared Macmillan's extensive preparations for membership of the Common Market to the shallow approach of Cameron and May, the two prime ministers who moved the UK towards leaving, without much detailed thinking in advance.

5 Edward Heath, *The Course of My Life*, p.260

6 This applied to all aspects of Heath's life. When Heath invited Roy Jenkins to his house in Salisbury, his guest noted politely, 'This must have one of the best views in England.' Heath replied, 'What do you mean "one of the best views"?' Heath had to have the best views. Similarly, he had to be a leader and prime minister.

7 Obituary in the *Daily Telegraph*, 18 July 2005

8 William Waldegrave reviewing Philip Ziegler's biography of Heath, *Edward Heath*, in *The Spectator*, 16 June 2010.

9 *Daily Telegraph*, 7 June 2008

10 *A Question of Sovereignty* was broadcast on ITV on 13 May 1975 during the referendum campaign. The theme was also explored in depth when Roy Jenkins and Tony Benn debated UK membership on BBC1's *Panorama*, two Labour Cabinet ministers taking opposing views on peak-time television. Both programmes are available on YouTube and show that TV was capable of greater depth then, and that the potential loss of sovereignty was explored in more detail in 1975 than in 2016, when it was claimed by some Brexiteers that the UK had been duped into supporting membership. Michael Foot later became a strong supporter of the UK's membership. Benn remained an opponent.

11 I was that BBC political correspondent, dreading the task in case the moody Heath resented being interrupted while preparing for *Question Time*. He was on such a high that he would have given an interview to a chimpanzee.

12 In John Campbell's excellent unauthorized *Edward Heath: A Biography* (Jonathan Cape, 1993) he wonders about a possible gay affair in the army, but uncovered none of the scandalous allegations that were made after Heath's death. Campbell's insightful and fair account was published while Heath was still alive. The biography was too fair for Heath, who could cope with little less than unqualified praise.

13 Edward Heath, interview with Nanette Newman, 2000 (no date specified). The interview was carried out at his home in Salisbury and is available on YouTube. Heath is at his most relaxed, but even

in this exchange he does not look at the sympathetic interviewer. He was a shy performer.

3 James Callaghan

1   Denis Healey, *The Time of My Life*, Michael Joseph, 1989, p.427

2   Callaghan was a good actor, but there were limits. His chancellor being booed on live television as he spoke from the floor, within strict constraints, stretched those limits. Initially Callaghan advised Healey not to attend the conference, but then recognized that the situation was so grave he changed his mind.

3   Peter Jenkins, *Guardian*, 31 March 1976

4   Roy Jenkins was now Home Secretary for a second time, aching to escape from British politics for a bit, which he soon did. Jenkins became the UK's first president of the European Commission in Brussels, before returning to lead the SDP.

5   Edmund Dell was Trade Secretary during the IMF drama.

6   Denis Healey, *The Time of My Life*, p.431

7   GMTV's *Sunday Programme*, 4 March 2007. In the same programme Hattersley was joined by Tony Benn and David Owen for a discussion about the 1970s Labour governments and what followed. It was the first time the three of them had been in a studio together. I chaired the discussion, which was surprisingly convivial, given the epic scale of the falling-out. The programme is still available on YouTube.

8   This comes from the same ITV programme, available on YouTube. Benn deployed a genuine politeness and wit in order to defuse tense situations with his leaders. Callaghan was often furious with Benn for voting against government policy on the NEC, even though he was in the Cabinet. But in face-to-face meetings Benn was so friendly and engaged that Callaghan's fury melted fleetingly. Politeness is an underused political weapon. Others who have deployed it effectively include Michael Gove and Jacob Rees-Mogg. Coincidentally, both are partial Bennites in relation to the issue of parliamentary sovereignty and Europe.

9   In his autobiography and in subsequent interviews, Healey spoke of often being ill as a result of the pressures of being chancellor.

10 John Major's government was split over Europe, as was Theresa May's. Callaghan's government was divided several ways over economic policy, state ownership, relations with the trade unions and, of course, Europe, although this division had been fleetingly muted by the 1975 referendum.

11 The terms 'strong' and 'weak' in relation to leadership are two of the most misleading ones in British politics. Nearly always when the Greek chorus hails a prime minister for being strong, he or she is acting weakly. The same applies the other way round. There are countless examples of Margaret Thatcher being celebrated as the lady who was not for turning, at a point when she was revising her economic policies, to Tony Blair in the build-up to Iraq. See the chapters on Thatcher and Blair for more detail.

12 Jim Callaghan, interview with the author, *New Statesman*, December 1996

13 *Panorama*, BBC1, November 1977

14 I attended a dinner at Foot's house in 1998. Foot and his wife, Jill, sang Callaghan's praises as a leader, but were utterly and unfairly dismissive of Wilson. They both hailed Callaghan's trustworthiness and modesty while insisting that Wilson was mendacious and immodest.

15 Michael Foot won the next Labour leadership contest in 1980, the last in which Labour MPs alone elected the party's leader.

16 Giles Radice, *Friends and Rivals*, Little, Brown, 2002

17 Tony Benn, *Against the Tide*, p.653

18 Bernard Donoughue, *The Heat of the Kitchen*, p.234

19 The chapter on Margaret Thatcher shows that she was a good actress, not quite as polished as some of the actors, lacking tonal variety, but highly effective nonetheless.

20 *Guardian*, Monday 28 March 2005

21 *This Week*, ITV, 28 July 1978. The programme is available on YouTube and is an example of Callaghan as an authoritative and yet relaxed prime ministerial interviewee. He was a natural. No spin doctor advised him on the arts of broadcasting. He was wholly at ease with the medium. In contrast, Margaret Thatcher

was a shrill interviewee at times, although – as we shall see in the next chapter – a courageous one.

22 Prime ministerial broadcast, 7 September 1978

23 *Sun*, 10 January 1979

24 The others were Stanley Baldwin and Ramsay MacDonald.

25 *Guardian*, 22 February 2018

26 Bernard Donoughue, *The Heat of the Kitchen*, p.277

27 Jim Callaghan, interview with the author, *New Statesman*, 21 December 1996

28 Bernard Donoughue, *The Heat of the Kitchen*, p.268

29 Denis Healey, *The Time of My Life*, p.432

30 Benn, at least, was seen by Callaghan as a wrecker. He had more time for Crosland.

31 TUC History Online, March 1999: http://www.unionhistory. info/; Callaghan interview available as a PDF.

32 When I interviewed Callaghan for the *New Statesman* in December 1996, he could not hide his disappointment that Blair had not consulted him more, as Labour's last prime minister.

4 Margaret Thatcher

1 As discussed in a previous chapter, Wilson learned the importance of party management and the advantages of evasive political positioning as he rose to the leadership. By the time of his resignation in 1976 he was tormented by accusations that he regarded deviousness and party management as an end in itself. The reality is that the most devious leaders are too smart to acquire a reputation for being so tricksy. The common factor in Tony Blair's rise and fall is explored in a later chapter.

2 Thatcher Foundation speech, 10 August 1974. The Thatcher Foundation is a wonderful online resource, crammed with original documents from the archives. Her rise and fall can be traced vividly by a tour of the Foundation: https://www.margaretthatcher. org/

3 Whitelaw did stand, once Heath withdrew, but by then it was too late. Thatcher beat him with ease, securing 146 votes to Whitelaw's

79. Several other candidates also threw their hats belatedly into the ring and did even worse than Whitelaw.

4 *Guardian*, 12 February 1975

5 William Waldegrave, *A Different Kind of Weather: A Memoir*, Constable, 2015, pp.141–3

6 *Observer*, 18 February 1979

7 *Firing Line* with William Buckley, 9 September 1975, available on YouTube. There are many Thatcher interviews on YouTube from her phase as leader of the Opposition. In most of them she is formidable. There is also an interview between Buckley and Tony Benn, recorded in the summer of 1981 at the height of Benn's powers as a communicator and framer of arguments. Benn also more than holds his own from the left. He was the left's counter to Thatcher, although he never became leader of his party, let alone prime minister.

8 Ibid. Thatcher had been leader for only a few months, since February 1975, yet in her ideological populism she was already firing on all cylinders.

9 *Panorama*, BBC1, 11 July 1977

10 Conservative Party manifesto for May 1979

11 Hansard, 3 April 1982

12 David Owen was a much-misunderstood politician. Later he was to become a donor to Ed Miliband's Labour Party and, more surprisingly, made a smaller donation to Jeremy Corbyn's Labour Party. Towards the end of the New Labour era he despaired that inequality was not higher up the agenda of his old party's leadership. But in the mid-1980s there was part of Owen that admired Thatcher and viewed Labour with almost as much disdain as he regarded the Liberals, his partners in a fragile alliance.

13 Gilmour's book, *Dancing with Dogma* (Simon & Schuster, 1992), published shortly after Thatcher left office, should be compulsory reading for all those who believe that she presided over something close to an economic miracle. Tony Blair was too generous in his assessment of the 1980s. David Cameron even more so. Gilmour used to dine regularly with Michael Foot, John Cole (the BBC's political editor for much of the 1980s) and the *Observer's*

wonderful columnist William Keegan, at the Gay Hussar in Soho. Keegan's own book, written several years earlier, *Mrs Thatcher's Economic Experiment* (Allen Lane, 1984), is equally illuminating and should also be compulsory reading if only because, in a variation of Churchill's phrase, history has been too kind to Thatcher, partly because many of her admirers have written it. Cole was on the left, but managed to be scrupulously impartial as BBC political editor. I am told that his impartiality slipped during these lunches with friends, who were all well to the left of the political consensus that Thatcher managed to shape long after she left power.

14 One of Thatcher's most famous speeches came at the October 1980 Conservative party conference, when she delivered the famous phrase 'You may turn if you want to. The lady's not for turning.' She performed the lines with gusto, but by the time of the autumn conference, Thatcher and Howe had softened their attachment to rigid monetarism. The lady had turned a little.

15 On 4 February 1975, the day of Thatcher's election as Conservative leader, Benn recorded in his diary: 'I think we will be foolish to suppose that Mrs Thatcher won't be a formidable leader... I think the quality of the debate will be raised because the Tory Party will be driven to the right and there will then be a real choice being offered to the electorate.' *Against the Tide*, p.311. Benn made constant references to Thatcher's powers of persuasion as some of his colleagues derided her, viewing her as their best chance of electoral victory.

16 Decades later Neil Kinnock would spit out the name 'Scargill', blaming him for letting down the miners and wrecking the early phase of his leadership. Kinnock once told me, with a degree of melancholy: 'I was one of the few leaders who never had a political honeymoon.' 'Why?' I asked. 'Scargill,' Kinnock replied. After the long haul of impossible leadership, Kinnock recovered his magnetic, witty exuberance, but still had the capacity for intense anger. The other figure from the 1980s who continued to provoke fury in him was Margaret Thatcher.

17 In Norman Tebbit's autobiography, *Upwardly Mobile* (Weidenfeld
    & Nicolson, 1988), he makes several criticisms of Thatcher, while
    less surprisingly hailing her as a great prime minister. The need
    for greater intervention, after the strike was defeated, was also
    acknowledged by Sir Geoffrey Howe and Michael Heseltine in
    their weighty and significant memoirs.

18 Michael Heseltine, interview with Matt Forde, *The Political Party*
    podcast, 27 September 2017

19 I was the BBC's local government correspondent at the time.
    Neither Hunt nor the Environment Secretary, Chris Patten,
    supported the policy they were compelled to implement. There
    were echoes of Brexit after 2016, as Theresa May made her moves
    towards leaving the EU even though she did not support what she
    was doing.

20 Chris Patten often referred to his leader in private as 'Margaret
    Hilda', implying that she was an eccentric aunt. He was in the odd
    position of knowing the poll tax was a calamity, but having the
    task of implementation, similar to some ministers after the 2016
    Brexit referendum who believed that leaving the EU would have
    bleak consequences for the UK.

21 The smart editor of BBC's *Today* programme suggested that we did
    our own survey of projected bills. I appeared on the programme
    virtually every day for a few months with the latest projections.
    Patten or Hunt would often be in the studio to respond. They tried
    to put the case, but their heart was never in it. They knew the poll
    tax was going to be calamitous.

5 John Major

1   John Major, interview with Elinor Goodman at the London
    School of Economics, 24 April 2007

2   On the Social Chapter, Labour was unequivocally enthusiastic and
    adopted it after the 1997 election. On the single currency, Labour
    was much more equivocal, like John Major.

3   The most important of the speeches was delivered in Bonn on
    29 March 1991. The build-up to the speech and its contents
    reflected Major's ambiguity in relation to the EU and also those

of his prime ministerial successors. A great deal of effort was
made in preparing the speech, with the objective partly of wooing
Chancellor Helmut Kohl in Germany, but also of reassuring his
Eurosceptics that Major would not go too far. While expressing
the desire to be 'at the very heart of Europe', he also stressed that
the UK would be bringing its own proposals on the single currency
and political union. He would 'relish the debate' with other EU
leaders. The balance was not greatly different from Thatcher's
Bruges Speech of September 1988 and yet, following the final
phase of her leadership, it marked a genuine attempt to establish
warmer relations. Patten played a part in preparing the ground for
the speech. One of his advisers, Sarah Hogg, helped to write it.
Hogg was a supporter of the single currency as a way of bringing
down inflation. As ever with UK prime ministers and Europe, the
calculations were multi-layered.

4   John Major, interview with Ian Birrell at the Politics Festival, Kings
Place, London, 22 June 2018

5   There are several examples on YouTube.

6   During the 1992 election campaign there were often panic-
stricken meetings about what was going wrong, as polls suggested
the Conservatives might lose. After the victory the director of
communications, Shaun Woodward, toured the US giving lectures
about how to win a campaign.

7   Major made Patten the final UK governor of Hong Kong, a
historic posting. The appointment meant Patten was out of the UK
during the many traumas that erupted around Major. The Major/
Patten friendship was in some respects an unlikely one. Patten was
the Oxford graduate who relished being part of the establishment.
He became chair of the BBC and chancellor of Oxford University.
Major did not go to university and although he made a lot of
money in his post-prime ministerial career, he never sought or
acquired similar posts. On the whole they were bound by a similar
political outlook. They were both 'one nation' Tories when their
party was leaving behind such an approach to politics. Neither was
moneyed. Both had their doubts about Thatcher and Thatcherism,

although Major was smart enough not to reveal his doubts until he had been elected party leader.

8   I was one of the correspondents. The other was John Pienaar.

9   Although Redwood was scathing of the Maastricht Treaty, he did not mention leaving the EU as an option. At this point the Eurosceptics were not Brexiteers, but the logic of their position led to where they ended up. If the UK had not signed the Maastricht Treaty, it was not clear what would have happened next, but withdrawal would have soared up the agenda. As it was, in the end the UK Parliament voted for the Maastricht legislation.

10   Mellor told the Leveson Inquiry in June 2012 that he thought Major was determined to keep him because the prime minister feared that his own affair with Edwina Currie would be reported. The affair was not in fact revealed until after Major left Number Ten.

11   Kelvin MacKenzie confirmed this much-reported threat during the Leveson Inquiry in 2012, although John Major told the same inquiry that he could not recall this part of their exchange.

12   I was one of the journalists at the dining table. Once again, John Pienaar was the other. Heseltine had a conscience and was partly seeking to convince himself that the government had acted fairly. He appeared to be as drained as Major was after the ERM crisis. This was a government losing its nerve within months of winning an election.

13   In the end, and with great reluctance, Clarke supported a referendum, a decision of historic significance. After Major announced that his government would hold a referendum before joining the euro, Tony Blair felt obliged to make the same pledge. In effect, the two declarations meant that the UK was not going to join the euro, as no prime minister would have been remotely sure of winning a referendum. Blair saw joining the euro as his historic mission, and yet knew deep down that he could not win a referendum on the subject.

14   Michael Heseltine interview, Politics Festival, Edinburgh, 11 October 2018

15 Major offered Lamont the post of Environment Secretary, a significant demotion. Wisely, Lamont did not accept and never served in government again.

16 Major had both an outright majority and the necessary 15 per cent margin, but had received only three more votes than his private minimum target of 215. His allies organized a smart 'spin' operation, rushing to the TV studios to declare the result a prime ministerial triumph. The media became obsessed with 'spin' under New Labour, but this was an example of presenting a result one way when in reality, if a few more votes had gone against him, Major would have resigned. His contortion had not really worked – his authority as leader was as fragile after the contest as it had been before. Yet it offered clarity in one respect. Major would have the misfortune to lead his party in the forthcoming election. There would be no further leadership contests after this one until after the election.

17 Politics moves so fast that what seems overwhelmingly significant is soon largely forgotten. The 'back to basics' saga terrified some Conservative MPs. I was a BBC political correspondent at the time and I recall interviewing a married MP about another matter. Before recording, I asked him what he did for his holidays, in order to test the level of his voice. The MP replied, 'I stayed at a lovely hotel in Greece…' He paused and looked horrified, before quickly adding, 'with my wife'. One Conservative MP had been discovered in bed with another man in a hotel, in bizarre circumstances. During 'back to basics' an assertion of heterosexuality in an orthodox marriage became necessary at all times.

18 Leaders tend to view elections as a form of relief. Michael Foot found the chaotic 1983 campaign more fun than the hell of leadership, as most of the time he was out addressing adoring crowds rather than seeking to bind a divided party, even if some of the strife continued until polling day, when Labour was slaughtered.

19 Tony Blair later admitted that he regretted deploying the term 'sleaze' as a powerful political weapon. The weapon was turned upon him, once his prime ministerial honeymoon was over. From

the safety of opposition, Blair claimed that his ministers would have to be 'purer than pure' and that even a perception of sleaze would force a minister to resign. If applied to him, Blair would have had to resign. Sensibly, a perception of wrongdoing was not quite enough in itself to wreck political careers in the New Labour era, although preposterously in some cases it almost was.

6 Tony Blair

1 Michael Meacher was the only member of Blair's shadow Cabinet not to be made a Cabinet minister. He was a decent radical, but with both a naive and a vain streak. Meacher would have been excited by the rise of Jeremy Corbyn.

2 *Independent*, 15 February 2010

3 Hattersley told the author about Blair's indifference to ideas and the past in 2001, after he had become deeply disillusioned. When John Smith died suddenly in 1994, Hattersley was one of several senior party figures who told Blair he must stand.

4 However, this sequence would almost certainly not have applied to Smith, who was also elected at the beginning of a parliament. In his nearly two years as leader he had established a strong lead in the polls, and the Conservative government was imploding over Europe. Smith had a natural self-confidence, fuelled by the fact that, unusually for Labour by the early 1990s, he had been a Cabinet minister. Government was not a daunting mystery for Smith as it was for Neil Kinnock and Tony Blair, when they were leaders of the Opposition. Smith had been there, albeit briefly, in the Callaghan government. Significantly, in terms of their mindsets, Blair and close allies like Peter Mandelson and Labour strategist Philip Gould disagreed with this analysis. They assumed that Smith would lose the election.

5 He also offered a referendum in Wales on the proposal to establish a Welsh Assembly.

6 In his witty memoir *Who Goes Home?* (Little, Brown, 1995), Roy Hattersley recalls a rally that he spoke at in Cambridge as the party's deputy leader. The rally during the 1987 election was regarded as highly significant, targeting disaffected SDP voters

under the banner 'Come Home to Labour'. At the end of the rally Hattersley appeared live on the peak-time Saturday-night BBC bulletin, eagerly anticipating the chance to convey a sense that Labour was back in the game. The presenter asked him whether it was Labour's policy to increase income tax for those earning more than £22,000 a year. Hattersley dismissed the proposition haughtily. He did so as the party's shadow chancellor. The presenter replied: 'But that was what your leader, Neil Kinnock, said this afternoon.' Hattersley writes that he could tell he was suddenly part of a calamity for Labour, live on air, and adopted the only option available to him: 'I attacked the interviewer.' His memoir is hilarious. Anyone who believes, wrongly, that politics is boring should read it.

7   In July 1996 Blair gave a long interview to the *New Statesman*. At one point he was asked whether he, personally, was in favour of electoral reform. Highly uncharacteristically, he was caught off-guard and replied, 'No.' It took many phone calls to Paddy Ashdown to repair the damage, but the answer was an early sign of what was to follow. Blair never called the referendum on electoral reform.

8   Labour won a staggering 419 seats and a majority of 179.

9   I was at the Royal Festival Hall event and at one point found myself dancing next to David Miliband. He said to me revealingly, 'I'm sure we'll wake up in a few hours' time and find the Tories have won again.' Miliband spoke for much of the new administration, working on the assumption that they were imposters disturbing the natural order in which the Conservatives ruled.

10   I was the commentator. The minister was David Blunkett, the newly installed Education Secretary. He meant it partly as a joke and semi-approvingly, but the joke captures brilliantly the mood of exuberant caution.

11   The reform created a new model of accountability. After Margaret Thatcher abolished the GLC, ineffective, unaccountable quangos were responsible for running large swathes of the capital. As a result, public transport in particular was a shambles, with long

delays and even longer queues to buy tickets. The high-profile
mayor became accountable for transport and had no choice
but to make improvements in order to get re-elected. Transport
for London even includes some figures who know a lot about
transport. Because the grim culture in England determines that
subsidies are a waste and do not contribute to the overall public
good, fares in London are some of the highest in the world, but
the services have improved beyond recognition. The model works,
even if it had a haphazard beginning: Blair refused to endorse
the left-wing Ken Livingstone as Labour's candidate. Livingstone
won easily as an independent, an early sign that figures to the
left of New Labour could perform well at elections, contrary to
mythology. Livingstone was an innovative mayor, introducing the
Congestion Charge for cars, a source of income that led to a huge
improvement in bus services. Later Blair admitted publicly that he
had made a mistake in not endorsing Livingstone.

12 Robin Cook, interview with the author, fringe meeting at the
Labour party conference, September 2000

13 Blair's senior adviser, Jonathan Powell, was also central from within
the UK government, having a forensic understanding of what
was required and an instinctive ability to recognize how to deal
with those whom British governments had theoretically refused to
negotiate with, even if informal talks were frequent throughout the
decades of violence.

14 *New Statesman*, 11 January 2000

15 The *Alastair Campbell Diaries* (Biteback), especially Vols 6 (2017)
and 7 (2018), include many references to his discussions with
Blair about Brown being tactical compared with his more strategic
approach.

16 Tony Blair, interview with Andrew Grice and Don Macintyre,
Independent, 28 September 1999

17 Brown's anger about Blair's conflicting demands was relayed to
me separately by both Balls and Miliband early in the second
term. Their views are corroborated by memoirs from Blair's closest
allies, who suggest that after 2001 Blair had concluded there
was no need for further spending increases, and tax cuts must

be a priority. Peter Hyman's book, *1 out of 10* (Vintage, 2005) – largely supportive of Blair and despairing of Brown – is especially illuminating about Blair's views after the 2001 election and how, even in Number Ten, close advisers worried that he was moving too far to the right.

18 See the chapter on James Callaghan. In 1976 Callaghan and Denis Healey, prime minister and chancellor, were proposing substantial spending cuts, Anthony Crosland was calling for selective cuts and some increases to generate growth, and Tony Benn was developing his Alternative Economic Strategy, which included import controls and wider state ownership amongst its proposals. Such internal differences caused huge problems, not least for Callaghan keeping them all together, but at least they were all thinking about economic policy, the most challenging issue of them all. In the New Labour era there was no such thinking, apart from by Gordon Brown and his senior advisers in the Treasury.

19 From 1994, when Blair became leader, at least until the end of the first term he acknowledged his dependency on Brown in relation to economic policy, although he became intensely frustrated at Brown's preoccupation with spending money on tax credits rather than public services. The dependency continued, but the acknowledgement of it waned.

20 This would have been the equivalent of a sacking, as Brown would not have accepted the post.

21 There is more detail on this in the chapter on Gordon Brown.

22 Ed Balls, *Speaking Out*, Hutchinson, 2016, pp.107–8

23 Smith told me of the meeting days later. It is similar to a conversation I had with Blair shortly after the 2001 election. Blair did not meet his first objective and struggled with the second. He met the third and faced dark consequences well beyond his long leadership of the Labour Party. Around about the same time, Brown outlined to me privately his objectives in policy terms for the second term. They included ensuring that the UK would not join the euro over the next few years, and raising the money to meet the NHS spending pledge. I was struck that Brown, as chancellor, met his objectives while Blair struggled to meet his.

24 After the war, in the 2005 election Rupert Murdoch's *Sun* newspaper endorsed Labour, but did so on the basis of Blair's foreign policies alone. In particular the newspaper praised his 'courage' in supporting the US in Iraq.

25 In a conversation with the author in July 2003, Blair made precisely this point: 'At least I won't be accused of being anti-American in the euro referendum.'

26 One of the most forgotten phrases in modern British politics is the 'Baghdad Bounce'. This was the phrase used in Number Ten in the immediate aftermath of Saddam's fall, as it anticipated a rise in support in the polls, similar to the 'Falklands Factor'. Blair misunderstood much about Iraq and the wider region, but his electoral calculations proved to be largely correct. He went on to win the 2005 election, even if Baghdad provided no Bounce.

27 *The Sunday Times*, 18 February 2003

28 Alastair Campbell, *Alastair Campbell Diaries*, Vol. 7

29 Chilcot Inquiry, July 2015

30 Clare Short was International Development Secretary at the time and claims Blair had assured her that a post-war plan had been worked through in considerable detail. She resigned when she realized there had been no such detailed plan. For her resignation to be regarded as weighty and significant, Short should have resigned with Cook before the war, but she had made some substantial and daring interventions in advance of the conflict. In September 2002 Short returned from Afghanistan and warned publicly, in an interview broadcast on ITV, that al-Qaeda would regroup around Kabul if US and UK forces were diverted to prepare for war in Iraq. Her warnings provoked angry disdain amongst Blair's advisers in Number Ten, but proved to be accurate.

31 I do not believe that Blair was untroubled by Iraq on the basis that the war had been 'the right thing to do'. At the end of one long conversation I had with him about a range of issues, he sighed spontaneously and exclaimed 'Iraq'. It was a despairing exclamation, and not a resolute one. On another occasion he paused as another topic was being discussed and declared to me, 'I could not have stopped America from invading Iraq.' No doubt

he has partly convinced himself that he followed the only course available to him, but he has reflected more than that. He can never express any doubt in public, because British soldiers died in the war. He cannot ever imply that they died in a war that proved to be not the right thing to do.

32 During his first term Blair declared that it was his 'historic objective to end Britain's ambiguous relationship with Europe'. He meant he wanted the UK to sign up to the euro. After the war in Iraq he renewed his mission. During one meeting Gordon Brown's senior adviser, Ed Balls, told Blair that he was jeopardizing the economy and the future of the government in his pursuit. Blair and Balls never spoke again until after the government had fallen, when they formed a convivial relationship bound by their opposition to the leadership of Jeremy Corbyn.

33 During the 2005 election Blair and Brown were seen together eating ice cream and took part in an awkward party election broadcast in which neither could disguise his unease.

7 Gordon Brown

1 *Independent*, 2 April 1992

2 When John McDonnell became Labour's most left-wing shadow chancellor in 2015 he often cited the 1992 election to justify his caution in opposing tax cuts introduced by the Conservative government. McDonnell had fought and lost a marginal seat in 1992. Even the poorest voters in the seat expressed concerns about 'Labour's tax bombshells', he told *Newsnight* in an interview broadcast on 5 November 2018.

3 Philip Gould, *The Unfinished Revolution*, Little, Brown, 1998

4 Roy Hattersley was to regret his endorsement of Tony Blair in 1994 and became a supporter of Gordon Brown from New Labour's second term, stating openly and often that Brown should replace Blair.

5 Tony Blair explores the ideological differences in his memoir *A Journey* (Hutchinson, 2010). Gordon Brown and Ed Balls are less expansive in their memoirs, but there are hints for the assiduous reader.

6   Roy Jenkins observed to the author in the autumn of 2001, over a glass or two of red wine, 'Political columnists in the past had so many big figures to write about. You only have Blair and Brown.'

7   Hugo Young, *The Hugo Young Papers*, Allen Lane, 2008, p.417

8   Ed Miliband made the observation to the author the week after the budget. Miliband was on a high, regarding the budget as an important moment of vindication for his toil in Brown's team. He went on to say that he and Brown would spend hours late at night discussing how to address inequality, the shared political mission of Miliband and Brown. Miliband doubted whether Blair ever reflected on the challenge. Looking back at his political career, Ed Balls also told the author that the tax rise to pay for NHS investment was his proudest achievement. Balls had become a famous *Strictly Come Dancing* performer by then, but still became animated when the topic switched from celebrity fame to politics. See the previous chapter for more detail on the NHS battle between Blair and Brown. There is also a fuller account of a key episode in the New Labour era in the author's book: Steve Richards, *Whatever It Takes: The Real Story of Gordon Brown and New Labour*, Vintage, 2010.

9   Although this was regarded as Brown's most publicly left-wing intervention, Ed Miliband told the author subsequently that as far as he was concerned, the speech was nowhere near as critical of the markets as it should have been. As a leader, Miliband failed to frame arguments effectively or in a way that he was comfortable with, but in the New Labour court he was ahead of the times, or a sharper reader of where the times were heading. After the financial crash of 2008, thoughtful figures across the political spectrum were less in awe of the markets.

10 Speech by Gordon Brown to the Social Market Foundation at the Cass Business School, 3 February 2003

11 Brown was challenged in 2007 by the then left-wing backbencher, John McDonnell. Brown was more than happy with this contender, as he could challenge him from the right. They held one public debate, chaired by the author. At the time McDonnell seemed a convenient irrelevance as Brown marched towards

Number Ten. Yet McDonnell's arguments for a more radical approach to policy-making were central to the rise of Jeremy Corbyn in 2015. McDonnell did not secure enough support from MPs to enter the final round of the contest, which Brown fought alone. McDonnell became shadow chancellor in 2015 and proved to be much the most formidable figure in Corbyn's Labour Party.

12 On BBC Radio 4's *The Brown Years*, broadcast in October 2010, written and presented by the author, several of Brown's allies blamed Balls for the newspaper reports. When the allegation was put to Balls, he denied it emphatically.

13 Alastair Campbell, *Alastair Campbell Diaries*, Vol. 7

14 This was in January 2010, months before the general election. Far from undermining Brown, the failure of the coup guaranteed that he would lead Labour at the election. There was no space for another coup.

15 At least he did to me and my editor at the time, the *Independent*'s Simon Kelner.

8 David Cameron

1 *Guardian*, 17 February 2009

2 The author was that columnist. I seemed to be on a grid where I was invited to accompany Cameron when he went to Norwich. I went with him three times to Norwich and back. He only fell asleep once.

3 Tony Blair made this observation to the author in February 2006, very early in Cameron's leadership.

4 The remarks were supposedly made at a dinner during the Tory conference in October 2005. The words ring true.

5 Oliver Letwin was especially keen, carrying Gould's book *The Unfinished Revolution* with him when he met journalists for dinners during the early Cameron era.

6 Theresa May famously coined the term at the Conservative conference in 2002. See the next chapter.

7 Cameron used the words, uttered very speedily, in his party conference speech in October 2006.

8   Ken Clarke, interviews with the author for BBC Radio 4's *The Cameron Years*, first broadcast in January 2018

9   The author interviewed Johnson for a Channel 4 series, *School Days*. The interview is available on YouTube.

10 Cameron's friend told the author about their conversation on Thatcher's continuing influence.

11 Margaret Thatcher, interview with *Woman's Own*, October 1987

12 David Cameron, *Guardian*, 25 May 2009

13 Oliver Letwin, interview with the author, the *Independent* fringe meeting at the Conservative party conference, October 2007

14 That is what Katz noted to the author in November 2007 at a dinner gathering that would make an excellent play. Other guests included left-of-centre commentators, all hailing Cameron and Steve Hilton as the great progressive thinkers with innovative ideas for a fairer society. As David Miliband noted to the author at around this time, 'Cameron is playing the *Guardian* like a cello.'

15 The Conservative Party's 'Aims and Values' document, February 2006

16 Steve Hilton, conversation with the author, January 2009

17 Hugo Young Lecture, November 2009

18 The author met Clegg for a coffee on the day of the White Paper's publication. He enthused, without qualification.

19 The author had a conversation with Cameron about the NHS reforms and the unplanned consequences. Like Blair, Cameron could see the absurd side to governing.

20 *The Sunday Times*, 7 January 2018

21 In the heady summer of 2010, as the coalition was getting into its radical stride, Cameron joked with the author that there had been thousands of articles about a realignment on the centre left in the mid-1990s, and it had happened overnight on the centre right. Letwin, too, enthused about the ideological overlap between Clegg and the Conservative leadership.

22 Conversation between Blair and author in 1998, when New Labour was enjoying a sunny honeymoon, but decisions were still nightmarish on many fronts.

23 Craig Oliver, interview with the author, BBC Radio 4, *The Cameron Years*, January 2018

24 In *The Cameron Years* the Brexiteer Jacob Rees-Mogg said he genuinely knew of no other Tory MPs planning to defect. He confirmed that he would not have switched to UKIP if there had been no referendum, but stressed that he would have campaigned hard for one, from within the Conservative Party.

25 If there had been a second coalition, Nick Clegg would not have vetoed the referendum. He had espoused referendums related to EU membership on several occasions during his leadership. Cameron would have made support for a referendum a condition of the coalition, and Clegg would have agreed, again on the assumption that his case would win. If there had been a coalition after the 2015 election, with both the Tory PM and the Lib Dem deputy PM arguing for 'Remain' – and losing – the coalition would have collapsed.

26 Craig Oliver, interview with the author, BBC Radio 4, *The Cameron Years*, January 2018

27 Gove's wife, Sarah Vine, told the author that the referendum ended several of their friendships. Brexit had many consequences, and one of them was the ending of friendships.

28 His long-serving adviser Gabby Bertin confirmed this in an interview for BBC Radio 4, *The Cameron Years*, January 2018.

9 Theresa May

1 Senior Home Office officials are quite often pleased to see the back of Home Secretaries. I spoke to two who rated May very highly towards the end of her time there. Both thought she deserved to be the next prime minister.

2 Sir Craig Oliver, interview for BBC Radio 4, *Theresa May – The Brexit Prime Minister*, March 2019

3 Hugo Young, *One of Us*, Macmillan, 1989

4 Nick Timothy, interview with the author, BBC Radio 4, *Theresa May – The Brexit Prime Minister*, March 2019

5 George Bridges, interview with the author, BBC Radio 4, *Theresa May – The Brexit Prime Minister*, March 2019

6   Nick Timothy, interview with the author, BBC Radio 4, *Theresa May – The Brexit Prime Minister*, March 2019

7   Sir Graham Brady, interview with the author, BBC Radio 4, *Theresa May – The Brexit Prime Minister*, March 2019

8   Julian Smith, interview with Laura Kuenssberg, BBC1, March 2019

ILLUSTRATION CREDITS

Portrait of Harold Wilson (Bob Haswell/Stringer/Hulton Archive)

Jeremy Thorpe, Harold Wilson and Edward Heath (Central Press/ Stringer/Hulton Archive)

Edward Heath becomes prime minister (Rolls Press/Popperfoto)

Margaret Thatcher speaks on Europe (Central Press/Stringer/ Hulton Archive)

Portrait of James Callaghan (Central Press/Stringer/Hulton Archive)

Tony Benn and James Callaghan (Gary Weaser/Stringer/Hulton Archive)

Newly elected Prime Minister Margaret Thatcher (Tim Graham/ Hulton Archive)

President Reagan with Prime Minister Thatcher (Diana Walker/ The LIFE Images Collection)

John Major succeeds Margaret Thatcher (Bryn Colton/Hulton Archive)

Portrait of John Major (Gemma Levine/Premium Archive)

The Queen and the prime ministers (Terry O'Neill/Iconic Images)

Portrait of Tony and Cherie Blair (Tom Stoddart Archive/Premium Archive)

Blair and Brown at Labour conference 1999 (Steve Eason/Stringer/ Hulton Archive)

Blair and Brown at Labour conference 2006 (Scott Barbour/Getty Images News)

Tony Blair on Middle East trip (Christopher Furlong/Getty Images News)

Margaret Thatcher and Gordon Brown (Bloomberg)

David Cameron wins Conservative Party leadership contest (Bruno Vincent/Getty Images News)

David Cameron and Barack Obama (Charlie Ommanney/Getty Images News)

David Cameron and Theresa May (WRA Pool/Getty Images News)

Prime Minister May greets European Commission President Jean-Claude Juncker (Carl Court/Getty Images News)

Theresa May announces her resignation (Peter Summers/Getty Images News)

—

ACKNOWLEDGEMENTS

Huge thanks to the brilliant team at Atlantic – James Pulford, Mike Harpley and Mandy Greenfield; to Peter Knowles and Daniel Brittain-Catlin for commissioning and producing the unscripted BBC TV talks on modern prime ministers and to Leala Padmanabhan the producer of *The Cameron Years* and *The Brexit Prime Minister* on BBC Radio 4. The various BBC programmes gave me the idea for the book, but the words and judgements here are mine alone… And an equally big thanks to my agent, Andrew Gordon, at David Higham Associates.

INDEX